British Columbia, The Pacific Province: Geographical Essays

BRITISH COLUMBIA, THE PACIFIC PROVINCE: GEOGRAPHICAL ESSAYS

edited by

Colin J.B. Wood

Canadian Western Geographical Series
Volume 36

Copyright 2001

Western Geographical Press

DEPARTMENT OF GEOGRAPHY, UNIVERSITY OF VICTORIA
P.O. BOX 3050, VICTORIA, BC, CANADA V8W 3P5
PHONE: (250)721-7331   FAX: (250)721-6216
EMAIL: HFOSTER@OFFICE.GEOG.UVIC.CA

Canadian Western Geographical Series

editorial address

Harold D. Foster, Ph.D.
Department of Geography
University of Victoria
Victoria, British Columbia
Canada

Since publication began in 1970 the Western Geographical Series (now the Canadian and the International Western Geographical Series) has been generously supported by the Leon and Thea Koerner Foundation, the Social Science Federation of Canada, the National Centre for Atmospheric Research, the International Geographical Union Congress, the University of Victoria, the Natural Sciences Engineering Research Council of Canada, the Institute of the North American West, the University of Regina, the Potash and Phosphate Institute of Canada, and the Saskatchewan Agriculture and Food Department.

BRITISH COLUMBIA, THE PACIFIC PROVINCE:
GEOGRAPHICAL ESSAYS

(Canadian western geographical series; 1203-1178; 36)
ISBN 0-919838-26-X

1. British Columbia. 2. British Columbia–Geography. I. Wood, Colin J. B., 1941- II. Series.

FC3811.B776 2001   971.1   C2001-911411-7
F1087.B74 2001

Copyright 2001 Western Geographical Press

ALL RIGHTS RESERVED

This book is protected by copyright.
No part of it may be duplicated or reproduced
in any manner without written permission.

Printed in Canada

Series Editor's Acknowledgements

Several members of the Department of Geography, University of Victoria cooperated to ensure the successful publication of this volume of the Canadian Western Geographical Series. Special thanks are due to the Technical Services Division. Diane Braithwaite undertook the very demanding tasks of typesetting and layout, while cartography was in the expert hands of Ken Josephson and Ole Heggen. Their dedication and hard work is greatly appreciated.

Harold D. Foster
Series Editor

Editor's Acknowledgements

This book would not have been possible without the assistance of many individuals, government agencies, and organizations. Permission from the Queen's Printer to reproduce maps and charts from editions of the Financial and Economic Review is acknowledged with thanks; to reproduce a portion of (MAP)TRIM 92B.063, from Geographic Data BC; to BC Ministry of Forests for data on the Okanagan Timber Supply area; BC Stats for the provision of data on several variables; also acknowledged are Tourism BC; Ministry of Agriculture; thanks to Pat Bluemel and staff. The Province of British Columbia is the owner of the copyright to the above acknowledged information. Data from Stats Canada and the Census is acknowledged with thanks.

Thanks are also extended to the many individuals too numerous to mention in provincial and local government agencies who gave helpful insights into a range of topics: John Bones (LUCO) and George McKay (ski industry) are thanked in particular. The CRD, Vancouver City, and Vancouver and Victoria airports are thanked for their assistance. Several individuals gave helpful information or comments, especially R.M. (Mike) Verdiel and Frances Vyse.

Several people at the University of Victoria in addition to those acknowledged above by the Series editor were involved in the publication of this book. The staff of the library's Reference Division, especially Lori Sugden, Map Curator, are thanked for their assistance in tracking references and information. The office staff of the Department of Geography, notably Kathy Merriam and Jill Jahansoozi, gave assistance in word processing manuscripts. Cimarron Corpé gave invaluable support as the research assistant; he also co-authored two chapters. Thanks are also extended to my former geography students who commented on topics covered in many chapters and provided a great source of inspiration.

Finally, I extend a warm thank you to my wife Maggie who encouraged and supported me throughout.

Colin J.B. Wood
Editor

Plate 1 Vancouver: jewel of the Pacific ▶

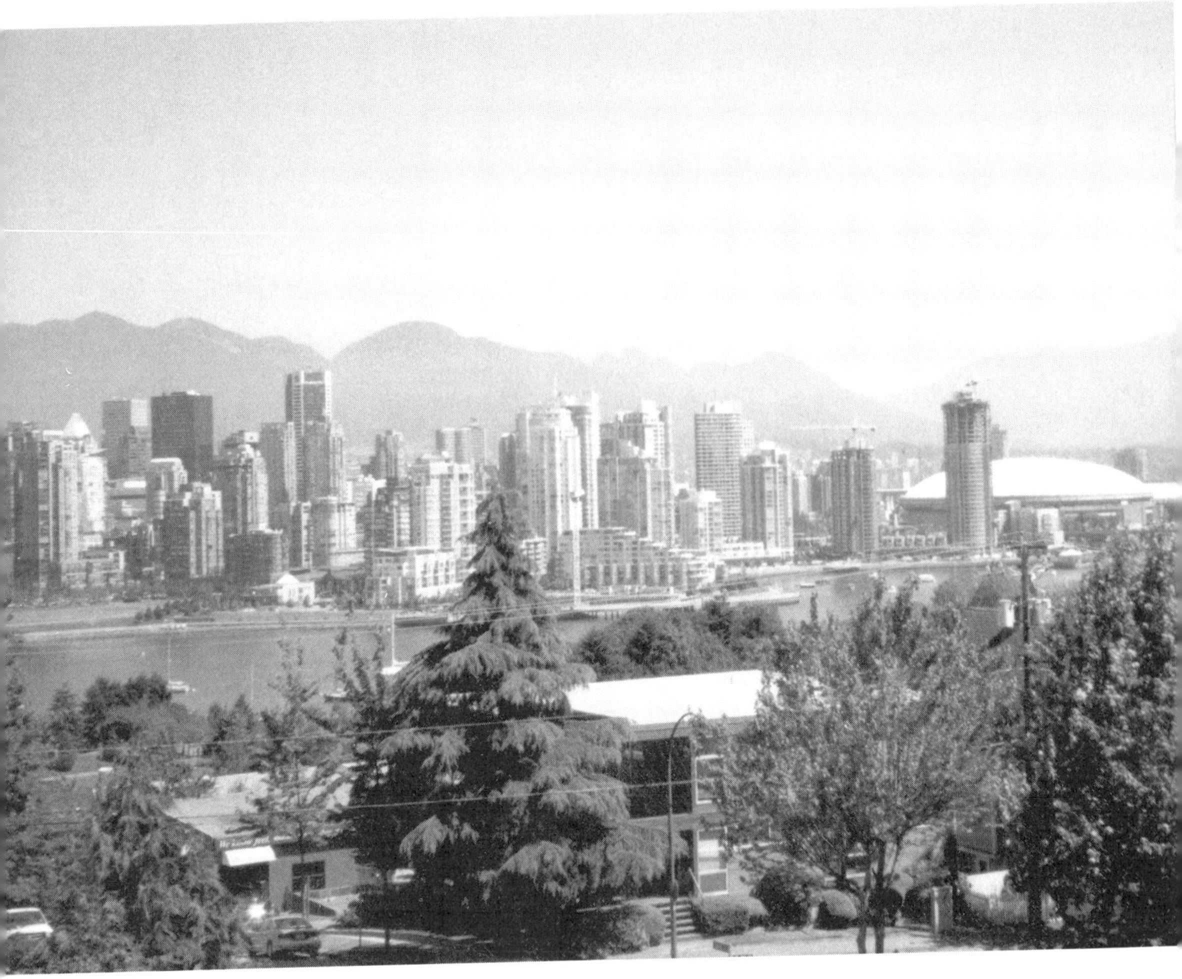

Contents

List of Figures xiii

List of Tables xv

List of Plates xvii

1   Introduction 1
      Colin J.B. Wood

Introduction 1
The Environmental Setting 1
The People 3
Major Geographic Regions 6
Demographic Characteristics 8
Perspectives 10
Main Cultural and Historical Sources 11
References 11
Endnotes 12

2   Mapping the Province: Past and Present 13
      C. Peter Keller

Introduction 13
Early Mapping 13
Recent Mapping Initiatives 15
Present and Future Challenges 23
References 25

3   Landforms and Natural Hazards 27
      Harold D. Foster

Landforms 27
Natural Hazards 29
Seismic Safety Network 37
Conclusions 42
References 43
Endnotes 44

4 Climate 45
Stanton Tuller

Introduction 45
Variation and Change Over Time 45
Solar and Net All-Wave Radiation 47
Air Temperature 50
Air Pressure 51
Wind 51
Humidity 54
Precipitation 55
May-September Climatic Water Balance 58
Temperature-Precipitation Regions 59
Conclusions 61
References 61
Endnotes 63

5 Water Resources 65
Sandra Smith

Introduction 65
BC's Water Wealth 65
Water Uses 70
Emerging Problems and Issues 71
The Institutional Framework 73
The Challenges Ahead 79
References 81

6 Vegetation 83
Michael C.R. Edgell

Introduction 83
Floristic Patterns 84
Vegetation Patterns 86
Mesothermal Forests 90
Microthermal Forests 91
Alpine Tundra 94
Conclusions 94
References 95
Endnote 95

7 Geopolitical Development: An Overview 97
Paul F. Thomas

Introduction 97
Antecedent Geopolitical Actors and
  Interests in the Pacific Northwest 97
The Clash of British and American
  Interests in the Pacific Northwest 102
Geopolitical Actors and BC's Precursor Territories
  Prior to Confederation with Canada 106
Union with Canada 112
Post-Confederation Geopolitical Highlights 117
Terms of Union 117
First Nations 118
The Geopolitics of Hydroelectric Power 119
Summary and Reflections 127
References 129
Endnotes 130

8 Geography and Treaty Negotiations 133
Frank Duerden

Introduction 133
The Legal and Historical Contexts 133
The Geography of Land Claim Settlements 137
Conclusions 144
References 145
Endnotes 145

9 Chinese: The Changing Geography of the Largest Visible Minority 147
David Chuenyan Lai

Early Immigrants and Discrimination, 1788-1884 147
The Periods of Restriction and Exclusion, 1885-1946 153
Post-War Immigrants and Integration, 1947-1999 162
Epilogue 170
References 173
Endnotes 174

10 Spatial Economy 175
Colin J. B. Wood

Introduction 175
The Growth of the Economy 175
General Features of the Economy 179
Economic Geography 184
Transportation 186
Transition 192
Conclusions 193
References 194
Endnotes 196

11 Land Recreation 197
Bruce Downie

Introduction 197
An Outdoor Recreation Activity Framework For BC 197
An Outdoor Recreation Administrative Framework For BC 203
Trends In Outdoor Recreation 208
Conclusions 211
References 211
Endnotes 213

12 Tourism 215
Rick Rollins

Introduction 215
The Significance of Tourism 216
Tourism BC: The Role of the Provincial Government 218
Tourism Markets and Marketing Strategies 218
Tourism Products 220
Toward a Sustainable Tourism Industry 223
Summary and Conclusions 226
References 227
Endnotes 228

13 Land Use Planning 229
Colin J.B. Wood, Cimarron Corpé, and Laurie Jackson

Introduction 229
Land Use Planning 229
Evolution of Land Use Planning in BC 232

Land Use Planning in Urban Areas in BC 242
Planning in BC at the Millennium 252
Conclusions 253
References 257
Endnotes 259

14 MINERAL DEVELOPMENT 261
Jo Harris

Introduction 261
The Physical Setting 263
The Mining Industry in Perspective 266
Patterns of Mineral Development 267
Conclusions 273
References 275
Endnotes 275

15 ENERGY 277
John Newcomb

Introduction 277
The Present Energy Situation in BC 277
Geography of Supply and Demand 281
Forecasting Future Energy Demands for BC 282
Demand Side Management: A New Tool for Energy Conservation 283
A Geographic Perspective on Emerging Energy Issues of BC 285
First Nations Peoples of BC and Energy Resources 286
Integrating Into Continental Energy Markets for Natural Gas and Electricity ... 286
Conclusions: The Future of Energy in BC 287
References 287

16 FORESTRY 289
Alan Vyse

Introduction 289
The Forests of BC 290
Early Exploration and Management: Green Gold is Discovered 292
The Modern Period: Forests Turned to Gold 294
Contemporary Issues: Who Owns The Green Gold? 297
Planning Future Forest Use 305
Conclusions: Forest Management for a New Millennium 306
References 308
Endnotes 309

17 Agriculture in Perspective 311
Colin J.B. Wood

Introduction 311
The Resource Base 311
Evolution 312
Recent Trends (1980s to 1990s) 315
Institutional Arrangements 315
Regional Variation and Specialties 317
Conclusions 323
References 327
Endnotes 327

18 Fisheries 329
Colin Wood and Cimarron Corpé

Introduction 329
Fisheries 331
Policies 339
Aquaculture 341
Conclusions 342
References 343
Endnotes 344

19 Marine Conservation 345
Philip Dearden

Introduction 345
Marine Protected Areas 346
Current Initiatives 348
Marine Wildlife 351
Discussion 355
Conclusions 356
References 356
Endnotes 358

Table of Contents

LIST OF FIGURES

1.1	Physiographic regions and synoptic influences	2
1.2	Human settlements	4
1.3	Major regions	7
2.1	Early representation	16
2.2	Example of 1:20,000 TRIM sheet	19
3.1	Landforms	28
3.2	Hazard response system	30
4.1	Mean monthly solar (black) and net all-wave (grey) radiation at selected stations	48
4.2	July mean daily maximum air temperature (1961-1990 normal)	52
4.3	January mean daily air temperature (1961-1990 normal)	53
4.4	Annual precipitation (1961-1990 normal) and monthly distribution at selected stations	56
4.5	Temperature-precipitation regions	57
5.1	Major rivers and lakes	67
5.2	The hydrologic cycle in BC	68
5.3	Hydrographs of selected rivers	69
6.1	Selected examples of the floristic elements	85
6.2	Treeline and altitudinal variation of selected forest zones	88
6.3	The generalized pattern of biogeoclimatic zones	89
7.1	European exploration in northwest North America	99
7.2	American and British claims in the northwest region of North America	104
7.3	The evolution of BC's position in the global transportation and trading systems	109
7.4	Trading posts and early trails in the Interior	111
7.5	The power systems of the Columbia and Peace rivers	120
8.1	Examples of tribal land claims in BC. Note their total extent and the boundary overlap issue (n.b. this is not an exhaustive list)	135
8.2a	The Nisga'a settlement	141
8.2b	The Sechelt's traditional territory	142
9.1	Distribution of Chinese, 1881	152
9.2	Distribution of Chinese, 1911	156
9.3	Distribution of Chinese, 1941	160
9.4	Distribution of Chinese, 1996	164
9.5	Distribution of Chinese population in Richmond	166
9.6	Asian-themed malls, Richmond, BC	168

9.7	Asian-themed malls in the Greater Vancouver Region	170
10.1	The main elements of BC's economy as shown by export categories and trading partners	176
10.2	A cartogram showing the main components of the BC economy	180
10.3	Employment by sector, late 1990s	183
10.4	The core area of Greater Vancouver	186
10.5	The main urban centres and transport linkages	187
11.1	Ski facilities and national/provincial parks	200
12.1	Geographic patterns of tourism	219
12.2	Cruise ship data	221
13.1	The alternative ideological polarity of Canadian sub-national governments and their landscape impacts	233
13.2	The planning continuum as applied to BC	240
13.3	The Gulf of Georgia Region showing main urban nodes and transportation linkages	245
13.4	Planning for Vancouver's CBD	247
13.5	Planning for green/blue space protection in the CRD region	250
14.1	Types and share of mineral production by value, late 1990s	263
14.2	Mines and products	264
14.3	Geologic regions	265
14.4	Sedimentary basins, hydrocarbon production, and transportation	271
14.5	Petroleum and natural gas selected statistics	272
14.6	The environmental assessment review process	273
15.1	Major coal deposits and hydroelectric dams	278
15.2	Production, consumption, and type of use of energy in BC, 1997	279
16.1	The forests of BC; harvest and pulp/paper mills	291
16.2	The forest resource system and its major components	299
16.3	Projected changes in the age class distribution for the Okanagan TSA over time	302
16.4	General parameters associated with harvesting	303
17.1	Agricultural land and factors affecting production	313
17.2	Main components of the BC agricultural production system	318
17.3	The Canadian and BC agricultural systems showing output by subsectors	324
18.1	Systems analysis of marine fisheries	330
18.2	Main marine fishing areas by type of operation and main spawning rivers	333
18.3	Salmon species showing average weight at maturity and percentage of wild salmon harvest	335
19.1	Proposed marine conservation regions and existing protected areas/reserves	352

LIST OF TABLES

1.1	Main demographic components	8
1.2	Population of BC by region, 1998	9
4.1	Mean vapour pressure at selected stations	49
4.2	May-September climatic water balance at selected stations	59
4.3	Mean data for temperature-precipitation regions	60
5.1	Length of major rivers	66
5.2	Drainage area and mean annual flow of major rivers	66
5.3	Surface water intake in Canada, 1991	70
5.4	Annual BC water withdrawals for all purposes by region	71
5.5	Federal government administrative agencies and legislation concerned with water in BC	75
5.6	BC government administrative agencies and legislation concerned with water in BC	77
5.7	Adoption of themes of Canadian water management in BC	80
6.1	Simplified classification and selected climatic characteristics of biogeoclimatic units	87
9.1	Ethnic composition of population in BC, 1881	150
9.2	Ethnic composition of population in BC, 1911	157
9.3	Number of Chinese in BC and in Canada from 1881 to 1996	158
9.4	Ethnic composition of population in BC, 1941	159
9.5	Chinese population growth in BC, 1881-1996	162
9.6	Major ethnic groups in BC, 1996	163
9.7	Major ethnic groups in Richmond, 1996	165
9.8	Elected politicians of Chinese ethnic origin in BC, 1957-2000	172
10.1	BC government accounts, 1998/99	181
10.2	Manufacturing activity in BC by shipment values and categories, 1991 and 1998	182
10.3	Household incomes in Canada and BC and expenditures in BC, 1997	184
10.4	Average population and rank of cities by periods and 1996	189
10.5	BC ferry fleet (1999)	190
10.6	Traffic growth at Vancouver and Victoria airports	191
10.7	Indicators of transition in the BC and Vancouver spatial economies	192
10.8	High tech employment	193
11.1	Recreation activities framework	199
11.2	Recreation activity and/or facility providers	204

12.1	Tourism GDP in BC: 1987 to 1999	216
12.2	Overnight visitor volumes and revenues by market areas in BC, 2000	217
12.3	Tourism-related employment in BC, 1997	217
12.4	Room revenues by region	217
13.1	Urban nuclei of the south west region of BC	243
13.2	Issues facing society in BC and some possible policy and planning responses	253
14.1	Value of mineral output, 1970-2000	262
15.1	Petroleum and natural gas industry production in BC	280
15.2	DSM load reduction, costs and impacts	285
16.1	Ownership of commercial forest land base in five temperate latitude countries which produce coniferous forest products	290
16.2	Area and potential productivity of forested ecological zones in BC	292
16.3	Forest tenures in BC	295
16.4	Canadian forestry production by leading provinces in the late	297
17.1	Classification of soils with capability for agriculture	312
17.2	Agricultural groups/institutions	316
17.3	Farm activity region	317
17.4	Livestock numbers in BC and percentage of Canadian total	319
17.5	Grain area by type 1979-1996 and tame hay/forage	321
17.6	Agricultural characteristics by province	326
18.1	BC seafood production, 1993-1997	332
18.2	Aquaculture production, 1995-1997	342
19.1	Federal and provincial statutory powers for protecting marine areas	349

List of Plates

1	Vancouver: jewel of the Pacific	vi
2	The rugged west coast of Vancouver Island is typical of Canada's Pacific shores	xviii
3	Summer rock slides in the Coast Range	26
4	BC has a large number of wild streams and rivers: Nairn Falls	64
5	Summer vegetation patterns in the southern Interior near Penticton	82
6	Murals depicting significant local historical events can be seen in many communities	96
7	A totem display in Stanley Park, Vancouver shows the variation in tribal carving styles	132
8	Dragon boat racing in Victoria's Inner Harbour	146
9.1	"An unconfirmed report that four Chinese were...thrown into the icy waters of Coal Harbour"	154
9.2	Aberdeen Centre at Hazelbridge Way, Richmond, BC	167
9.3	The Crystal at 4500 Kingsway, Burnaby, BC	169
9.4	Henderson Place at Pipeline Road, Coquitlam, BC	169
9.5	Chinatown Plaza at Keefer Street, Vancouver, BC	171
9.6	David Chuenyan Lai, C.M., a Chinese Canadian appointed as a Canadian Citizenship Ceremony Presiding Officer	171
10	Alpine centres such as Whistler have evolved into year round resorts	214
11	Mining activities contribute significantly to the BC economy	260
12	The Jordan River hydroelectric dam near Victoria	276

Photos are by H.D. Foster, D.C. Lai, J. Newcomb, and Colin J.B. Wood

Plate 2 The rugged west coast of Vancouver Island is typical of Canada's Pacific shores ▶

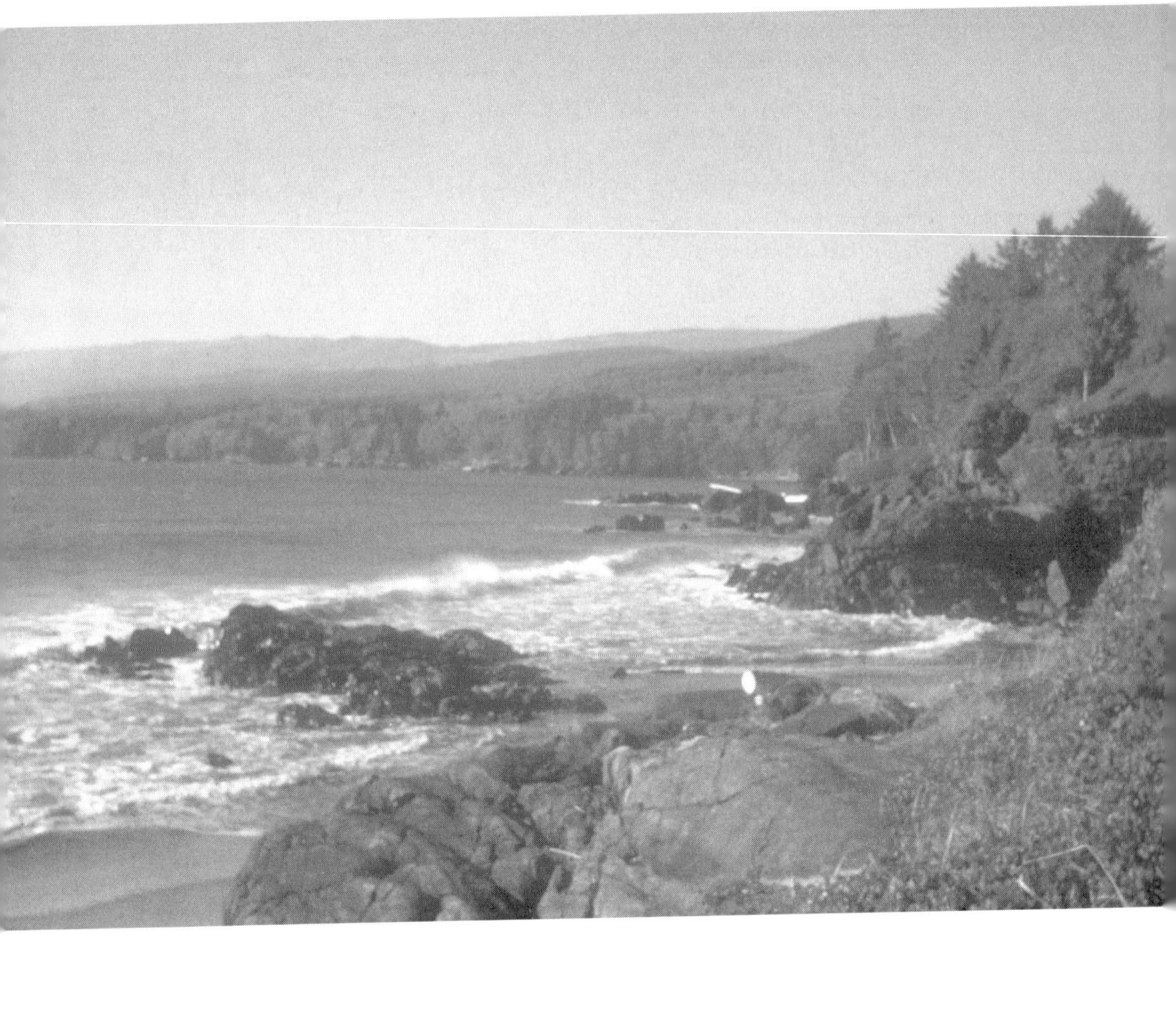

Introduction

Colin J.B. Wood
Department of Geography, University of Victoria

INTRODUCTION

British Columbia (BC) is the third largest province in Canada at close to one million square kilometres (km^2)—the size of France, Italy, Belgium, and the Netherlands combined. Situated on the Pacific coast of Canada between latitudes 48° and 60° North, and between longitudes 114° and 136° West, it is a vast region of great beauty, physical diversity, and human variety. From the ocean-washed islands and deep fiord inlets to the coastal mountains, interior plateaux, and snowcapped summits of the Rocky Mountains, it presents a spectacular succession of panoramas (Cannings and Cannings, 1996). The complex mountain and valley physiography (a product of eons of geological processes with variegated surfaces), complex drainage systems, and coastal zones more recently reworked by the last Ice Age create many diverse environments for life forms to flourish, resulting in a wealth of varied ecological systems.

The north-south barrier of the Rocky Mountains, whose summits form the eastern boundary, dramatically define BC as a separate and distinctive region of Canada (Forward, 1987; Robinson and Hardwick, 1973; Robinson, 1989). This is reinforced by the corresponding dominance of physical and human influences from the Pacific region. Paradoxically, the southern boundary, the 49th parallel of latitude, is a product of British and American territorial claims and treaty settlements in the 19th century. It runs straight east-west, arrogantly defying the north to south grain of mountains and valleys, and in its implementation it also ignored the territorial integrity of the First Nation Salish people who now straddle the boundary.

This chapter briefly sketches the environmental setting and human dimensions of the province, delineating the rich tapestry of land and nature together with the diversity of human adjustments in their variety of regional settings. In the following chapters, each author explores in greater detail fascinating, and at times controversial aspects of BC's physical and human geography. For an appreciation of the remarkable historical changes that have occurred in the province, the reader should also consult the list of major historical sources noted at the end of this chapter.[1]

THE ENVIRONMENTAL SETTING

The powerful forces at work at the boundary zone of the Pacific and North American tectonic plates have created a rugged and diverse physiography with a predominance of mountainous terrain and a north to south grain of landforms. About three-quarters of the land mass of BC is above 1,000 metres (m) in elevation. The outcome is spectacular scenery, but at times a difficult and demanding environment, prone to hazards. This massive physiography was extensively reworked by the last Ice Age and now has many deep valleys filled with long, narrow lakes (Figure 1.1). The huge ice sheet—approximately 2,500 m thick—also depressed the coastal areas, so that a significant post-glacial rebound occurred. The result is a deeply indented and fractured coastline with a multitude of islands, channels, and fiord inlets that inhibited north-south movement by land and stimulated travel by water along the coasts of Vancouver Island and the mainland (Harris, 1997).

The prevailing movement of air masses in temperate latitudes is from west to east; in BC moisture-laden air from the Pacific Ocean flows

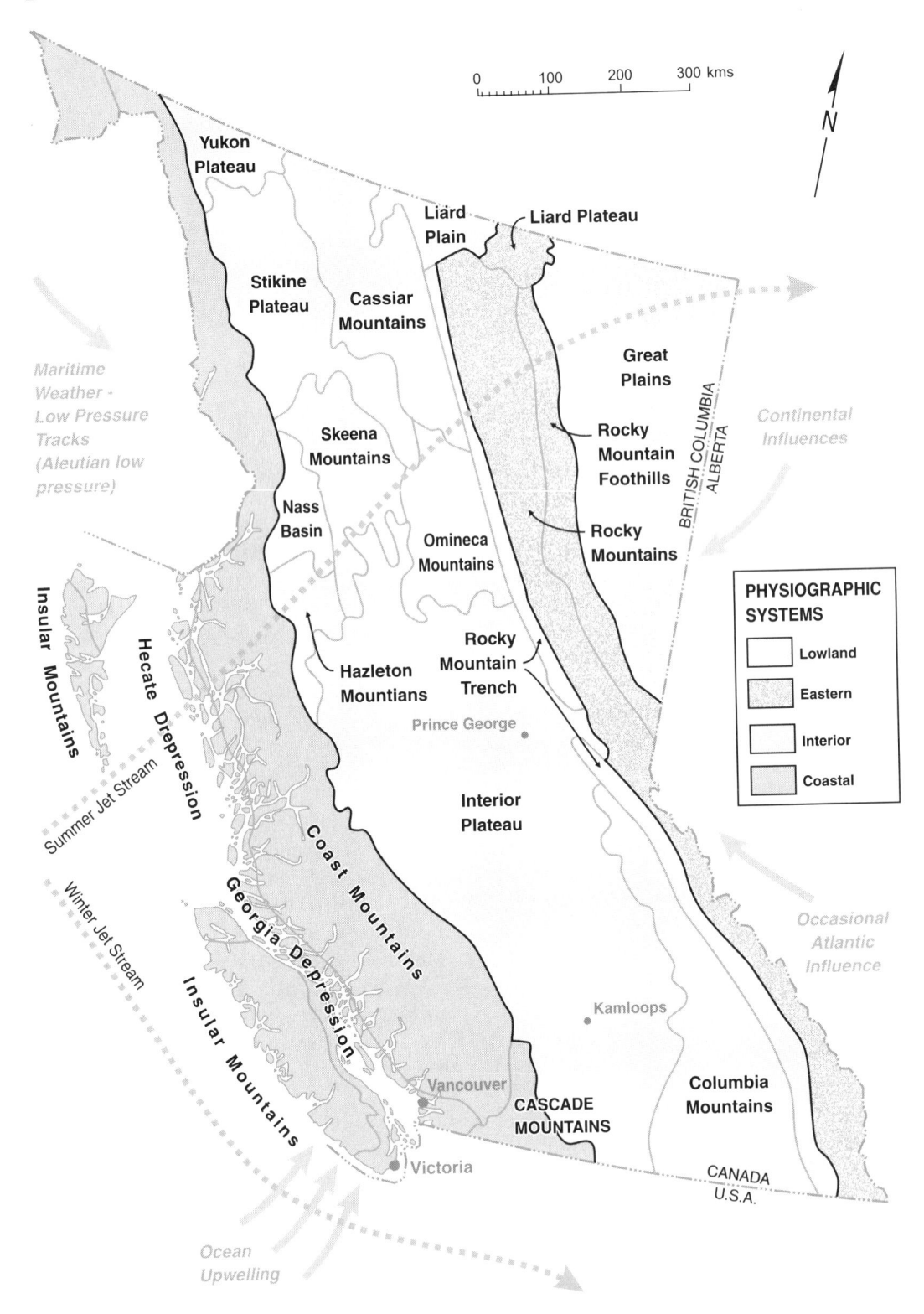

Figure 1.1 Physiographic regions and synoptic influences

onto the continental land mass. The north to south mountain ranges induce orographic conditions with heavy precipitation on the western slopes and rain shadow conditions on the eastern sides. Prince Rupert on the north coast, for example, receives an average of 2,523 millimetres (mm) per year, while Penticton in the south central Interior gets a meagre 250 mm. The coastal region, which experiences the modifying influences of the ocean, is generally humid, mild, and low in temperature variation. In contrast, the Interior experiences continental conditions with greater temperature variation in winter and summer. Thus, Victoria at the tip of southern Vancouver Island has an annual average temperature of 10°C, while Prince George in the central Interior has an annual average temperature of 3.3°C. The large and elevated landforms and long coastline, together with the humidity of the air masses, ensure that precipitation rates are high during the winter months; consequently, BC is generally well endowed with water resources, with the exception of the south central Interior and the Gulf Islands. The mountainous terrain results in much precipitation occurring as snow, high runoff rates, and freshets during the spring melt period. The diverse topography and north/south grain of landforms create seven major river basins whose rivers' combined discharge drain at the enormous rate of 12,000 cubic metres (m^3) per second and form the basis of the large hydroelectric power resources of the province.

The fabric of the landforms and drainage basins make possible the designation of 11 broad ecosystem-based regions. Within each region, localized variations at the next level of the hierarchy occur, reflecting finer textures and gradations in bedrock, soil, microclimate, drainage, and post-glacial flora recolonization (Meidinger and Pojar, 1991).[2] Furthermore, the considerable variety of terrestrial and marine environments present suitable niches for a rich diversity of plants and fauna: there are over 3,000 different plant forms with an abundance of coniferous and alpine types; it is the last great concentration of large mammals and avian raptors in North America; the shallow estuarine and coastal waters, with upwelling currents,[3] swarm with a wealth of marine life, and contain a far greater number of marine species than the Atlantic coast (Thomson, 1981); and it is an essential feeding and resting environment for migratory birds, mammals, and cetaceans along the Pacific zone of North America. With this abundance and variety of resources, it is self evident why humans have chosen to live here—and have flourished (Fitzharris, 1986).

THE PEOPLE

The nature of the prehistoric peopling of the North American continent is currently a topic of great debate. Nonetheless, it is apparent that at least one stream of migrants did come from Asia via the Siberia/Alaska land bridge when sea levels were considerably lower than they are today (Carlson, 1996; Harris, 1997; Muckle, 1998). Millennia later, during the historic era, came Chinese and European mariners: people searching for new sources of raw materials and opportunities for trade. At the time of direct European contact in the late 18th century, the Native inhabitants, who probably numbered between 100,000 and 300,000, had evolved a rich, oral culture and animist belief system with spatially distinguishable tribal groupings and their territories (Figure 1.2). There are seven main linguistic groups, with various regional subgroupings present, to give a total of about "54 mutually unintelligible languages" (Carlson, 1996, p. 32).

Technologically a stone-age society, Native life revolved around the village longhouses located along the coast and on river banks, and around the seasonal rhythms of fishing, hunting, collecting, and ceremony. The *Potlatch* was an important ceremony in which goods were distributed as gifts representing recognition and reaffirmation of status in the social and political context of the family, clan, and tribe. Occasional disruptions to this rhythm of life came with warfare and slave raiding between tribes. Catastrophic changes came with the arrival of the Europeans.

Figure 1.2 Human settlements: First Nations traditional tribal areas and present day urban centres

BC was one of the last regions in the world to be colonized by Europeans as the British North American trading companies gained ascendency over Russian and fledgling American interests that were penetrating the region in the late 18th to early 19th centuries. Small in numbers, which were then further reduced by diseases introduced by the Europeans, and fractured by geographic isolation and intertribal differences, the Native people were no match for the colonial machine and the accompanying waves of traders, miners, settlers, and religious orders pouring into the region. The colonizers established a *title* to the land and resources thereby denying Native claims, and sought to control the Native body and mind (Harris, 1997). From 1876 onward, the Native people became, in effect, wards of the Dominion (federal) government. The Native people seemed to be on an unstoppable downward trajectory toward extinction, reaching a low point in 1929 with an estimated population of only 29,000. Few treaties were signed aside from the Vancouver Island Treaty (Douglas Treaties, 1850-1854) and one in the North East (Treaty Number 8, 1900) (Muckle, 1998). Residential schools were established to "civilize" the younger generation, but gradually became viewed by Native activists and others as purveyors of cultural genocide, even though the intentions of the founders were well meant. Increasing opposition led to their closure, with the last being shut down as recently as 1984. Part of the legacy and trauma of this era has been the subsequent disclosures of abuse and mistreatment meted out in the residential schools. From the late 1930s the Native population began to increase so that the cynical expectation by some that the "problem" would solve itself through extinction failed to materialize. Instead, the relationship between the majority and the First Nations minority has re-emerged as a dominant and ongoing socio-political issue of the 21st century. Only in the last decade, through the prodding of Supreme Court of Canada judgements and enlightened provincial NDP and federal Liberal governments, which set about negotiating treaties, has a significant measure of progress occurred. This activity signals the end of over a century of opposition by conservative coalitions.[4]

Political Economy, Spatial Configuration and Social Class

The British imposed a colonial government with its associated institutions, laws, religious denominations, social order, rules of behaviour, and capitalist system. The Native traditions of custom and cooperation were replaced with the market place, individual striving, and monetary relationships. The new society sought and attracted settlers, entrepreneurs, capital, and labour—and exported staples. While English replaced the Native voice as the official language many Native place names were retained. The three colonies of Vancouver Island, New Caledonia (British Columbia mainland), and the Queen Charlotte Islands were united in 1866 to form British Columbia, with the focus of activity in the Strait of Georgia area. A decade later, the colonial legislature voted to join Canada on the condition that BC be connected to the rest of the nation by the proposed transcontinental railway (1871). The Canadian Pacific Railway (CPR) (1884) effectively drew the new Province of British Columbia into the Canadian system, while the Panama canal (1914) brought it into American industrial hegemony and nascent global capitalism. To offset the costs of construction, the CPR was allocated large sections of land along the proposed rail route in southeastern BC and on eastern Vancouver Island. In a manner similar to the American railroad oligarchy in California, the CPR grew to play a very influential role in the growth of BC, and Vancouver in particular (Wynn, 1992; Seager, 1996).

A resources-based export economy evolved with company-dominated settlements exploiting minerals, fisheries, and forests, fed by the relatively small areas of farm and ranch lands. Having only a small agricultural land base meant that, unlike most other regions of North America, geographic nucleation and the form of social order evolved around the company run mining, logging, and fishing centres. Company operations gradually evolved into large, capital intensive, corporate entities that often became foreign owned or controlled. Only in the Fraser Valley, East Vancouver Island, the Okanagan, central Interior, and later the Peace River region did a form of agricultural society evolve. Trading posts, coastal canneries, small settlements at river crossings, rail termini, and lake and coastal ports also provided foci for incipient urban growth (Galois, 1990). Mining towns that also possessed a locational advantage such as Nanaimo expanded, whereas isolated mining communities expired once the ore was exhausted. Many single enterprise resource towns in BC have undergone rapid cycles of birth, boom, decline, death—with Ocean Falls and Gold River being examples of recent corporate euthanasia.

The distribution of political and economic power was also accompanied by an evolving pattern of social and class relations. For BC, the particular form of political milieu derived from the capitalist versus worker relations of the resource industries together with the additional dimension of ethnic differentiation based on racial status (Warburton and Coburn, 1988). For example, in the struggles between corporate capitalists, managerial *bourgeoisie* conservatives, and militant British and Scandinavian workers one can identify: the roots of BC's polarized political party affiliations; the unusual and sometimes vitriolic political discord; and the loose coalitions between factions at provincial and municipal elections to exclude certain groups and the wide swings in government from left to right and *vice versa*. This regional variation in the form of Canadian society emerging in the 20th century was also set against a particular form of gender relations which were themselves evolving as women acquired voting and property rights.

In addition to the dominant British presence, Americans, Scandinavians, Russians (Doukhobors), Germans, Dutch, and Jewish people have all left an imprint in different regions of the province (Wood, 1987). Though small in numbers, African Americans and Polynesians also contributed to the social mix. Initially immigrating as cheap labour, Chinese, East Indians, and Japanese have all made important contributions to BC. Despite the strictures of exclusion and racism that continued well into the late decades of the 20th century, minorities advanced socially, economically, and politically, to the extent that the (now ex) Lieutenant Governor of the Province, His Excellency David Lam, is a Chinese Canadian, and ex-Premier of the Province, Ujjal Dosanjh, was Canada's first Indo-Canadian Provincial Premier.

Having sketched the main ingredients of BC's physical and human geography, we can now outline the major regions and then conclude with an overview of the current, basic demography of the province.

MAJOR GEOGRAPHIC REGIONS

Given the immense size of BC and its great diversity, it is often necessary to subdivide it into regions that correspond to variation in human activities. There is general agreement among geographers and regional economists that the province can be dichotomized into a distinct *core* and *periphery* (Robinson and Hardwick, 1973; Forward, 1987; Hutton, 1998) (Figure 1.3).

- *core* — the area of southwest BC including the Vancouver–Nanaimo–Victoria triangle; it contains three-quarters of the population, settlement, economic activity, urbanization, and most of the political power.

- *periphery* — the remainder of the province, including: the North, which has a very low population; the central Interior, with a focus on Prince George; the south central Interior, which has many small resource processing centres and transportation junctions, with a second-tier urban nucleation in the central Okanagan region.

It is common vernacular practice to distinguish the "Coast," the "Lower Mainland," and the northern and southern "Interior" regions. The coastal region was identified as part of Garreau's (1981) "Ecotopia" and the remainder as part of the "Empty Quarter." More recently, the realization of the ecological wholeness and the economic integration of the greater transboundary region in the southwest has resulted in the designation of "Cascadia," with a link at

Introduction

NORTHWEST (Nechako)
1.2% of population; rugged isolated region; some mineral development, two mines operating.

NORTHEAST

NORTHEAST & PEACE
1.7% of population; large plains area, mountains; grain farming, forestry, coal mining, oil, gas, hydro

PEACE

PRINCE GEORGE

NORTH COAST

PRINCE GEORGE & CARIBOO
4.5% of population; plateau region; ranching, forestry

NORTH & CENTRAL COAST
2% of population; rugged coast, mountains; forestry, mining, aluminum smelting at Kitimat

CARIBOO

CENTRAL COAST

THOMPSON

KOOTENAY
7% of population; extensive rugged mountain topography; high precipitation; skiing and forestry

VANCOUVER ISLAND & GULF ISLANDS
16% of population; diverse coastal environment; mild climate; government, toursim, forestry, fishing

LOWER MAINLAND

OKANAGAN

LOWER MAINLAND
56% of population; rich agriculture of Fraser Valley; urban focus, gateway function, tourism base, high tech and film industry

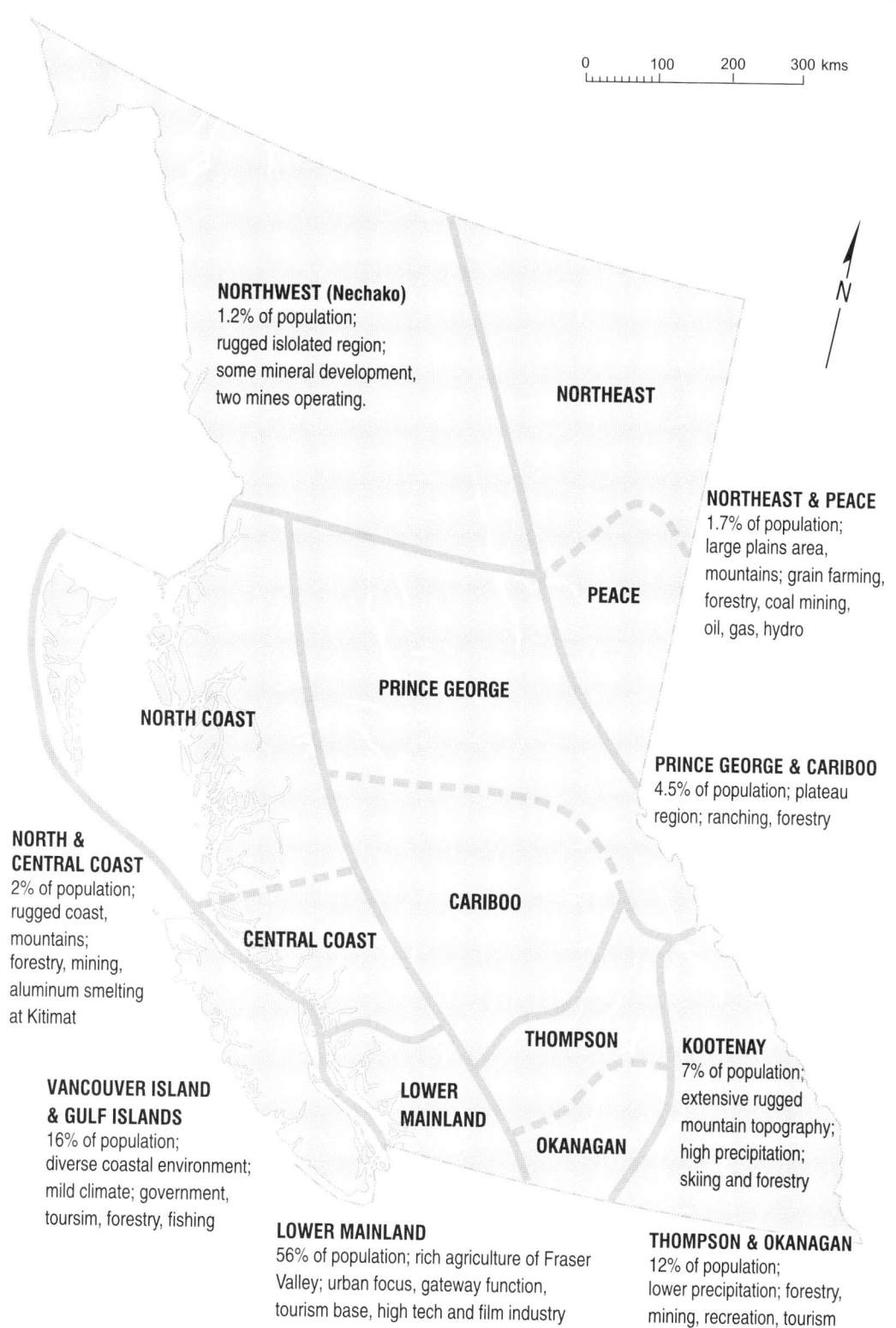

THOMPSON & OKANAGAN
12% of population; lower precipitation; forestry, mining, recreation, tourism

Figure 1.3   Major regions

the provincial and state level between BC, Washington, and Oregon, for purposes of discussion and cooperation on issues of mutual concern (Schell and Hamer, 1993). A positive step from this association is the initiative to deal with common environmental management problems in the Georgia Basin ecosystem in a cooperative manner between all levels of Canadian and US governments (BC Round Table, 1993; Environment Canada, 1999).

In the First Edition of this volume (1987), C.N. Forward divided BC into 11 major regions based on a combination of large landform regions and the associated cultural evolution of those areas. The BC government generally distinguishes eight major regions, which are similar to those of Forward and other authors, with some of the smaller adjacent sub-regions joined together. The major regions and some of their distinguishing characteristics are shown in Figure 1.3. For details of their geographical and historical evolution the reader should consult the first edition (Forward, 1987; McGillivray, 2000).

DEMOGRAPHIC CHARACTERISTICS

The population of BC in 2000 stood at approximately 4 million, an increase of 13% over 1991 figures, realizing an average annual growth rate of 2.6% during the 1990s. The province has the third largest provincial population in Canada, being 13.3% of the Canadian total, and is the only one to have increased continuously since Confederation. Indeed, no other province has matched BC's growth rate in recent years. The main demographic components during the 1990s are seen in Table 1.1.

BC's live birth rate has dropped from 23.8 per 1,000 population in 1950 to 12.4 per 1,000 in the late 1990s, a decrease of more than 45% (Danderfer, 1998). Furthermore, natural increase (1987-1997) accounts for approximately 25% of growth; the remainder is from migration (36%) and immigration (39%). The downward trend in fertility and hence birth rates over the last 25 years reflects significant socio-economic changes, new forms of social behaviour and gender relations, so that, for example, the average age of marriage has risen markedly (Table 1.1). An indication of the quality of life enjoyed in BC is that it now has one of the lowest infant mortality rates in the world at 4.9 deaths per 1,000 live births (Hu, 1999). Another feature is the increase in single parent families from approximately 10% of families in the 1970s to 14% today. Therefore, even though the natural increase in population is relatively slow and birth rates continue to dip, the demand for housing units continues to increase. The growth is pushed by the high immigration, in-migration rates and the larger number of single parent families.

Table 1.1 Main demographic components

	1971	Rate '000	2000	Rate '000
Births	34,852	16.0	41,500	10.1
Infant mortality		18.2		4.9 (1996)
Deaths	17,783	8.1	27,700	6.8
Natural increase	17,069	0.7	13,800	0.33
Percent married (25-29 years)				
Female	87		50	
Male	75		33	
Total population	2,184,621		4,099,000 (2000, estimated)	

Source: BC Vital Statistics.

Like the rest of Canada and indeed the developed world, BC has an aging population. This trend has significant implications for taxation, revenues, expenditures on social services, and the health care system. The attractions of retiring to the coastal regions and the Okanagan also mean that in some municipalities every third person is retired (BC Stats, 1997). The strong migration and immigration streams represent the "pull" of security, a vigorous economy—until the recent Asian melt-down—and an attractive environment. The "push" comes from the obverse—economic and political uncertainty in Hong Kong and other regions of Asia and Latin America. Recent decades saw a swing in immigrant origin from Europe to Asia, with metropolitan Vancouver being a major destination for the new arrivals. The result is that BC has a higher proportion of immigrants (18%) than the national average (13%). The Chinese are now the largest visible minority in the province with 313,000 (34% of the Canadian total)—7.8% of the BC population. They are mainly concentrated in Vancouver, especially in the suburb of Richmond. Illegal immigrants mainly *en route* to the US, pseudo refugee claimants, and a confused federal immigration policy have complicated relations between cultural groups and have set back the significant improvements that had been made in recent years. There appear to be several consequences to these trends:

- a shift in population composition and an increase in the dependency ratio;
- a shift in linguistic make-up and pressure on the school system;
- continued pressure on job availability;
- continued pressure on the housing market in Greater Vancouver;
- Chinese now the largest visible minority in the province;
- Greater Vancouver becoming more cosmopolitan—bilingual English-Chinese (voluntary) signage in retail areas;
- some resentment on the part of Vancouverites to the waves of immigrants (for example over the construction of 'monster homes');[5]

- emergence of certain myths and meanings to immigration and the metropolis (Ley, 1999);
- considerable variation in the response to the challenges of multiculturalism by each of the 22 local municipalities that comprise the Greater Vancouver region (Edgington, 2000);
- out migration of older families from metro areas—"downsizing";
- a new generation of hard working, ambitious young immigrants.

The variation in the regional population growth rates is illustrated in Table 1.2. Clearly, the leaders are the lower Mainland and the Thompson/Okanagan regions. The periphery lags behind considerably with a more modest growth rate.

Table 1.2 Population of BC by region, 1998 (thousands)

Region	Population by region	Growth % 1987-1997	Growth % 1992-97
Vancouver Island/Coast	716	12.2	10.9
Lower Mainland	2,154	15.2	14.3
Thompson Okanagan	474	15.1	15.4
Kootenay	153	6.5	8.9
Cariboo	174	6.0	11.9
North Coast	73	4.6	5.1
Nechako	46	5.2	9.3
North East	64	5.5	8.6
BC	3,860	13.2	13.1

Source: BC Stats, Demographic Statistics, 1999.

Population Projections

There is every evidence that BC's population is continuing to increase, mainly through immigration, and as mentioned earlier, it is also aging. Projections based on extrapolation of current conditions suggest a population of approximately 6 million by 2021, with a median age of 41.4 years compared with a median of 36 years in the late 1990s (BC Stats, 1997). There are costs and benefits to these changes. An aging population will mean greater pressure on the health care system but, at the same time, possibly a decrease in crime rates. There is, however, no clear sense of what constitutes the *optimum* population for the province for, even though the provincial government has formulated a "growth strategy," it has not come to terms with the basic cause of growth —more people.[6] The accepted premise that North America should continue to take a high level of immigrants is itself being questioned (Borjas, 1999). BC can absorb more people in the immediate future, but will they be mainly crammed into apartments and condominiums or sprawling suburbs in the southwest corner of the province? Most of the area available for development is in the central Interior and northeast BC where the climate is more extreme and economic opportunities are limited. Despite BC's immense size, the effective land for settlement is estimated to be about 10 to 15% of the total area, suggesting there are limits to future population growth if the same quality of the environment is to be maintained (BC Round Table, 1994).

PERSPECTIVES

BC has a beautiful and generally high quality environment, varied resources, and attractive towns and cities that have not lost their identity through being "malled" to death. Furthermore, despite the sometimes shrill political rhetoric, its people possess a well developed sense of orderly government and problem solving. Many long-standing equity issues are being positively addressed. This is not to deny that some pressing social and environmental issues persist. Nevertheless, the quality of life is one of the highest in the world. The people of BC are therefore in the fortunate position of having alternative directions for the future.

One important choice concerns the quality of the environment in the new Millennium, and how it may be maintained, for despite the decades of government regulation, public education, and pressures from environmental activists, a resource frontier mentality linked with a "growth at all costs" attitude for corporate or personal enrichment at the expense of the common good is a pervasive presence. This issue is not unique to BC, of course, being endemic to western consumerism. At the end of the 20th century, substantial advances were made in BC through incorporating strategies of sustainability, stewardship, comprehensive planning, and environmental accountability in public activities and private lifestyles. The Georgia Basin Ecosystem Initiatives (1999), Blue Box recycling programs, and ecological certification of forest products are good examples of these positive trends. It is important that this momentum be maintained.

Despite advances in transportation connections which have "shrunk Canada," media links, and commercial pressures to conform to some type of mediocre, amorphous, placeless, North American mass culture, in BC there is still a sense of being separate and distinct from the rest of the country and indeed from North America as a whole. Feelings of independence, superiority, and being a citizen of ecotopia often prevail (Lees, 1999). These attitudes sometimes make for difficult relationships with the federal government in Ottawa, and indeed lead to an electorate that tends to vote against it as a form of ritual, regional protest. It also shows up in the support for, strength, and commitment of environmental groups.

In the following chapters, contributing authors explore in greater detail important elements of BC's physical and human geography. On this foundation it is hoped that the reader will develop an understanding of the physical environment, aspects of BC society, and the ways in which the natural environment is being used, conserved, and might be managed for the future.

MAIN CULTURAL AND HISTORICAL SOURCES

Drucker, P. (1965). *Cultures of the North Pacific Coast*. San Francisco: Chandler Publishing.

Galois, R. (1990). BC resource development: Resource communities in BC. In D. Kerr and D.W. Holdsworth (Eds.), *Historical atlas of Canada*. Vol. III. Toronto: University of Toronto Press

Harris, R.C. (Ed.) (1987). *Historical atlas of Canada*. Vol. I. Toronto: University of Toronto Press.

Johnston, H. (Ed.) (1996). *The Pacific province: A history of BC*. Vancouver: Douglas & McIntyre.

McDonald, H.L. (1966). *British Columbia: Challenge in abundance*. Vancouver, BC: Canadian Confederation Centennial Committee of British Columbia.

Muckle, R.J. (1998). *The First Nations of BC*. Vancouver: UBC Press.

Ormsby, M. A. (1958). *British Columbia: A history*. Toronto: MacMillan of Canada.

Stouck, D., and Wilkinson, M. (Eds.) (2000). *Genius of place*. Vancouver: Polestar.

REFERENCES

BC Round Table (1993). *Georgia Basin Initiative: Creating a sustainable future*. Victoria: Government of BC.

BC Round Table on the Environment (1994). *State of sustainability: Urban sustainability and containment*. Victoria: Crown Publications.

BC Stats (1997). Fast facts. Focus on families: Marital status (1996 Census). Victoria: Government of BC.

Borjas, G.J. (1999). *Heaven's door: Immigration policy and the American economy*. Princeton, NJ: Princeton University Press.

Cannings, R., and Cannings, S. (1996). *British Columbia: A natural history*. Vancouver: Douglas & McIntyre.

Carlson, R.L. (1996). Prehistory. In H. Johnston (Ed.), *The Pacific province: A history of BC* (pp. 12-46). Vancouver: Douglas & McIntyre.

Danderfer, R.J. (Ed.) (1998). *Selected vital statistics and health status indicators*. 126th Annual Report. Victoria: BC Vital Statistics Agency.

Edgington, D.W. (2000). Multiculturalism and local policy in Metropolitan Vancouver, Canadian Association of Geographers (Western Division), Annual General Meeting, University College of the Fraser Valley, Abbotsford, BC.

Environment Canada (1999). Georgia Basin Ecosystem Initiative. Ottawa: Environment Canada; and Victoria: Government of BC, Ministry of Environment, Lands and Parks.

Fitzharris, T. (1986). *British Columbia wild: A natural history*. Vancouver: Terrapin Press.

Forward, C.N. (1987). *British Columbia: Its resources and people*. Victoria, BC: University of Victoria, Department of Geography, Western Geographical Series, Vol. 22.

Garreau, J. (1981). *The nine nations of North America*. Boston: Houghton Mifflin Co.

Harris, C. (1997). *The resettlement of British Columbia*. Vancouver: UBC Press.

Hu, W. (1999). Etiological and ecological perspectives on geographic variations in infant mortality in BC, PhD thesis, Department of Geography, University of Victoria, BC.

Hutton, T.A. (1998). *The transformation of Canada's Pacific metropolis: A study of Vancouver*. Montreal: Institute for Research in Public Policy.

Lees, L. (1999). The Pacific Northwest: Rural backwater to urban ecotopia. In F.W. Boal and S.A. Royle (Eds.), *North America: A geographical mosaic* (pp. 239-248). London: Arnold.

Ley, D. (1999). Myths and meanings of immigration and the metropolis: 1998. *Canadian Geographer*, 43(1), 2-18.

McGillivray, B. (2000). *Geography of British Columbia*. Vancouver: UBC Press.

Meidinger, D., and Pojar, J. (Eds.) (1991). *Ecosystems of BC*. Victoria: BC Ministry of Forests. Special Report Series No. 6.

Muckle, R.J. (1998). *The First Nations of British Columbia*. Vancouver: UBC Press.

Robinson, J.L., and Hardwick, W.G. (1973). *British Columbia: One hundred years of geographical change*. Vancouver: Talon Books.

Robinson, J.L. (1989). *Concepts and themes in the regional geography of Canada*. Vancouver: Talon Books.

Schell, P., and Hamer, J. (1993). *What is the future of Cascadia?* Seattle: Discovery Institute.

Seager, A. (1996). The resource economy, 1871-1921. In H. Johnston (Ed.), *The Pacific province: A history of BC* (pp. 205-252). Vancouver: Douglas & McIntyre.

Thomson, R.E. (1981). *Oceanography of the British Columbia coast*. Canadian Special Publications, Fisheries and Aquatic Sciences, #56. Ottawa: Department of Fisheries and Oceans.

Warburton, R., and Coburn, D. (Eds.) (1988). *Workers, capital and the state in British Columbia*. Vancouver: UBC Press.

Wood, C.J.B. (1987). Population and ethnic groups. In C.N. Forward (Ed.), *British Columbia: Its people and resources* (pp. 309-329). Victoria, BC: University of Victoria, Department of Geography, Western Geographical Series, Vol. 22.

Wynn, G. (1992). The rise of Vancouver. In G. Wynn and T. Oke (Eds.), *Vancouver and its region* (pp. 69-145). Vancouver: UBC Press.

ENDNOTES

1. Major sources of historical information on BC can be found in the Provincial Archives located in Victoria. The scholarly journal *BC Studies* is also a rich source of information on historical and contemporary topics concerning the province.

2. A more detailed specification of ecosystem hierarchy arrangements is: *Ecosystems of British Columbia*. 1993 (3rd Ed). Ministry of Environment, Lands and Parks.

3. The nature of the upwelling zone is related to wind direction, strength, and persistence. Due to changes in these conditions, recent years have seen a shift in location of the nutrient-rich upwelling zone and a change in shallow ocean temperatures.

4. The political scene in BC is complicated by the differences between the federal and provincial political parties of the same label. The basic dichotomy is between a labour-based New Democratic Party and various business-based, conservative coalitions. The BC Liberal Party is currently challenging Treaty Negotiations and settlements. The federal Liberal Party is generally in favour of the process. The most pro BC and proto nationalistic groups have been the WAC Bennett Socreds (see **Chapter 7**) and NDP. There is no BC independence party of any significance.

5. A survey conducted in July 1999 indicated that Vancouver residents were the "coolest" to immigrants. Approximately 47% believed too many immigrants come to Canada, mainly because it is felt that the economy and social infrastructure cannot handle the numbers (Citizenship and Immigration Canada, internal report 1999, R. Ouston, *Vancouver Sun*, Oct. 12, 1999, pp. 1-2).

6. Neither is there agreement on what constitutes an optimum population for Canada. With a declining birth rate there is good rationale for a steady immigration rate if the national population is to sustain slight growth. Canada is criticized for "creaming off" Third World professionals and the younger, better educated. Most environmentalists favour *zero population growth*.

Mapping the Province: Past and Present

C. Peter Keller
Department of Geography, University of Victoria

INTRODUCTION

Access to maps and associated geographic information is fundamental to understanding the province and to managing human activities. We use maps to: keep a record of what is where, navigate, plan and administer natural resources and infrastructure, solve legal disputes, monitor change, and conduct land-related planning and research. Of course, we also use maps to "armchair travel." So, if you are interested in British Columbia, you will most likely want to look at maps in order to visualize and understand the province and you will want to know where to find all sorts of other sources of geographic information to satisfy your curiosity.

Beginning with a brief historical overview of how BC was first put on the map, this chapter then moves on to discuss the province's present mapping efforts. A brief section outlining contemporary provincial mapping challenges is followed by an introduction to key provincial topographic and related mapping initiatives. It concludes with a section highlighting unresolved present and future mapping challenges.

EARLY MAPPING

The coastline and interior lands of BC were one of the last regions of the world to be recorded on maps by western civilization. This should not come as a surprise. Being remote from early pockets of western and oriental civilizations, the Pacific Northwest was isolated. A great mountain barrier posed an obstacle to travellers from eastern North America. Prevailing westerly winds and ocean currents from the north discouraged exploration along the coast from Mexico and California. The coastline of the Pacific Northwest and the interior territories west of the Rocky Mountains, therefore, remained unexplored by those roaming the world until the late 18th century, appearing for a long time on maps as *Terra Incognita*. Today we know that First Nations peoples occupied these lands for quite some time before explorers and European settlers arrived, but the First Nations had their own way of memorizing and recording the geography of their territories. Travel and relationship with the land appear not to have required the detailed recording of land for navigation, ownership, or resource inventories. The First Nations of BC, therefore, did not develop mapping traditions that are associated with early western or oriental civilizations.

When and how did the coast of BC first appear on maps? Europeans first navigated to this part of the world in the late 18th century. Spanish expeditions by Lieutenants Juan Perez (1774) and Bruno Hezeta (1775), venturing north along the Pacific coast from Spanish America, led to the first known chart of the coastline, the *Carta Reducida* of 1775, drawn by Bodega y Quadra, one of Hezeta's officers. Thereafter, BC's coastline began to take shape in more detail through the sea voyages of Captain James Cook (1778 and 1780), Commanders Dionisio Aleala Galiano and Coyetana Valdes, and Captain George Vancouver (1792-1794). A close examination of names along the coast of BC reveals these explorers' influence on the early mapping of the province.

In 1798, a folio atlas of the Pacific coast from 30°N to 60°N was published by the British Admiralty. The survey work for this atlas was undertaken under the leadership of Captain George Vancouver. This atlas remained the authority on coastal features until a more detailed coastal survey by George Henry Richards was commissioned by the British Admiralty in 1857. Richard's survey work from 1857 to 1863 was published in two volumes as the *Vancouver Island Pilot*.

When the province joined Confederation in 1871, coastal charting became the responsibility of the Government of Canada's Hydrographic Service. The Canadian Hydrographic Service continues this duty today, with a regional office responsible for the Pacific coast located in Sidney on Vancouver Island. The entire coastline has been surveyed, with some parts in more detail than others. Present efforts are dedicated to updating old surveys as demand dictates and to supplying nautical data in digital format to companies packaging this information for access by digital navigation software.

So much for the coast. What about the mapping history of the Interior? An important part of Canadian history was the continual push west in search of rich fur trading areas, and the quest to find a viable land route to the Pacific. Alexander Mackenzie is credited with being the first white man to have reached the Pacific coast of Canada walking west, arriving near the site of the present community of Bella Coola in July of 1793. Imagine, he arrived on the coast only about a month after Captain George Vancouver had anchored nearby. One of the earliest maps of the Interior, based in part on Mackenzie's voyage, is that published by Aaron Arrowsmith in 1802 as his map of North America. The map shows little more in the northwest than two mountain ranges and an east-west pass. It is interesting to note that, while Vancouver's early records of the coast contained little, if any, reference to First Nations' activities, Arrowsmith's map contains numerous references to "Indian territories" and settlements.

Mackenzie's journey west was the first of many treks by explorers and surveyors during the early and middle 19th century. The vital role of fur trading companies, notably the North West Company and Hudson's Bay Company, in these journeys west is well documented in Canadian history. Important contributors to early geographic information about the Interior include Simon Fraser, David Thompson, David Stuart, John McLeaod, Robert Campbell, Samuel Black, and Archibald McDonald among many others. The Arrowsmith family remained the preeminent publishers of maps of the Interior during the days of fur trading, and by the mid-1850s the major topographic and hydrographic features of the southern half of BC had been superficially mapped.

In 1846, with the establishment of the 49°N latitude as the international boundary between Canada and the contiguous United States, the Hudson's Bay Company moved its headquarters from the Oregon Territories to Victoria on Vancouver Island. Soon after, the Company was granted Vancouver Island for the purpose of establishing a Crown Colony. Colonization invariably implies the need for topographic, cadastral, and other types of administrative mapping. Making Vancouver Island a Crown Colony, therefore, started BC's formal cadastral surveys and topographic mapping. Surveys worked outwards from southern Vancouver Island, with Joseph Pemberton, one of the more prominent early survey engineers, being appointed the first Surveyor General of the Colony in 1860.

The middle of the 19th century also witnessed the discovery of mineral wealth. Coal deposits were found on Vancouver Island, and gold was discovered in the gravel of the Fraser and Thompson rivers in 1858. The gold rush that followed had a profound impact on the opening up of the Interior. James Douglas, Governor of the Colony at the time, had to request assistance from London to keep control of the tens of thousands of prospectors, settlers, and associated services that flooded into the gold regions. Maps were needed to:

- manage mineral claims and land ownership;
- map transportation routes and administrative functions; and
- select settlement sites and plan the layout of communities.

A group of Royal Engineers dispatched from England produced, in a remarkably short time, large scale cadastral surveys and town plans, smaller scale route maps, and other regional maps. This group is credited with setting the standard for future cadastral and topographic mapping for the province (Gilmartin, 1987). Initial mapping efforts focused on Vancouver Island, the lower mainland, the gold rush regions, and major transportation routes.

British Columbia became a province of the Dominion of Canada in 1871. The knowledge of its terrain during that period is summarized in the first official general map of the province produced under the direction of the Surveyor General of British Columbia, J.W. Trutch, and drafted by J.B. Launders. This map was published at a scale of 25 miles to the inch, and is entitled *Map of British Columbia to the 56th Parallel, North Latitude* (Figure 2.1).

Upon entering Confederation, some of the mapping responsibilities of the province came under the aegis of the Government of Canada, while others remained under provincial jurisdiction. One of the conditions of entry into Confederation was that the federal government would construct a railway across the new province. The survey work required to select a route for the railway tracks eventually involved 75,800 km of route exploration and 19,400 km of actual route surveys by the federal government. Other federal government mapping initiatives included studies by the Geological Survey of Canada, not only into geology and minerals, but also vegetation, soils, topography, and hydrology. The federal government also contributed financially to other provincial mapping initiatives, laying the foundations for many of the mapping programs that survive to the present day.

The rapid exploration and settlement of BC's Interior in the 19th century led to demands for cadastral surveys and maps beyond what could be delivered, and there was a period when a pre-emption system had to be instituted. This system allowed settlers to claim and occupy land before it was officially surveyed. Once the land was surveyed, ownership could be granted for 10 shillings an acre.

In today's world of technology and information, it is possible to see even remote parts of the world in satellite images, and reach most places by helicopter with little effort and in a short time. It is also possible to access and query detailed maps and satellite images of BC via computer. All this technology makes it difficult to appreciate fully the incredible pioneering efforts that were required to put this province on the map in a relatively short time period. Aaron Arrowsmith's famous 1802 map of North America showed only two crude mountain ranges and one cross-country route in the northwest. Seventy years later, when BC joined Canada, most of the major features of the province were known and at least approximately mapped. Efforts were under way to:

- produce a cadastral and topographic coverage of the province;
- produce a complete set of detailed charts; and
- conduct thematic mapping of the province's diverse resources.

Accumulating and recording all of this geographic knowledge in such a short period of time was a remarkable achievement given the few people who settled or travelled in this part of the world in this 70 year period relative to BC's huge geographic area (948,600 km^2).

Fortunately, the history of the mapping of the province has been recorded and narrated in detail by: Andrews (1954), Farley (1960), Spittle (1973, 1988), Pearson (1974), Lamb (1978, 1988), and Sandilands (1988); as well as Don Thompson's three volumes of *Men and Meridians* (1966, 1967, 1969); and the more recent *Mapping a Northern Land* by Gerald McGrath and Louis Sebert (1999). The reader is referred to this literature to learn more detail about the exciting history of exploring, surveying, and mapping in BC.

RECENT MAPPING INITIATIVES

Canada's initial systematic topographic mapping was the responsibility of the federal government. BC was an exception. The province developed an early tradition of topographic

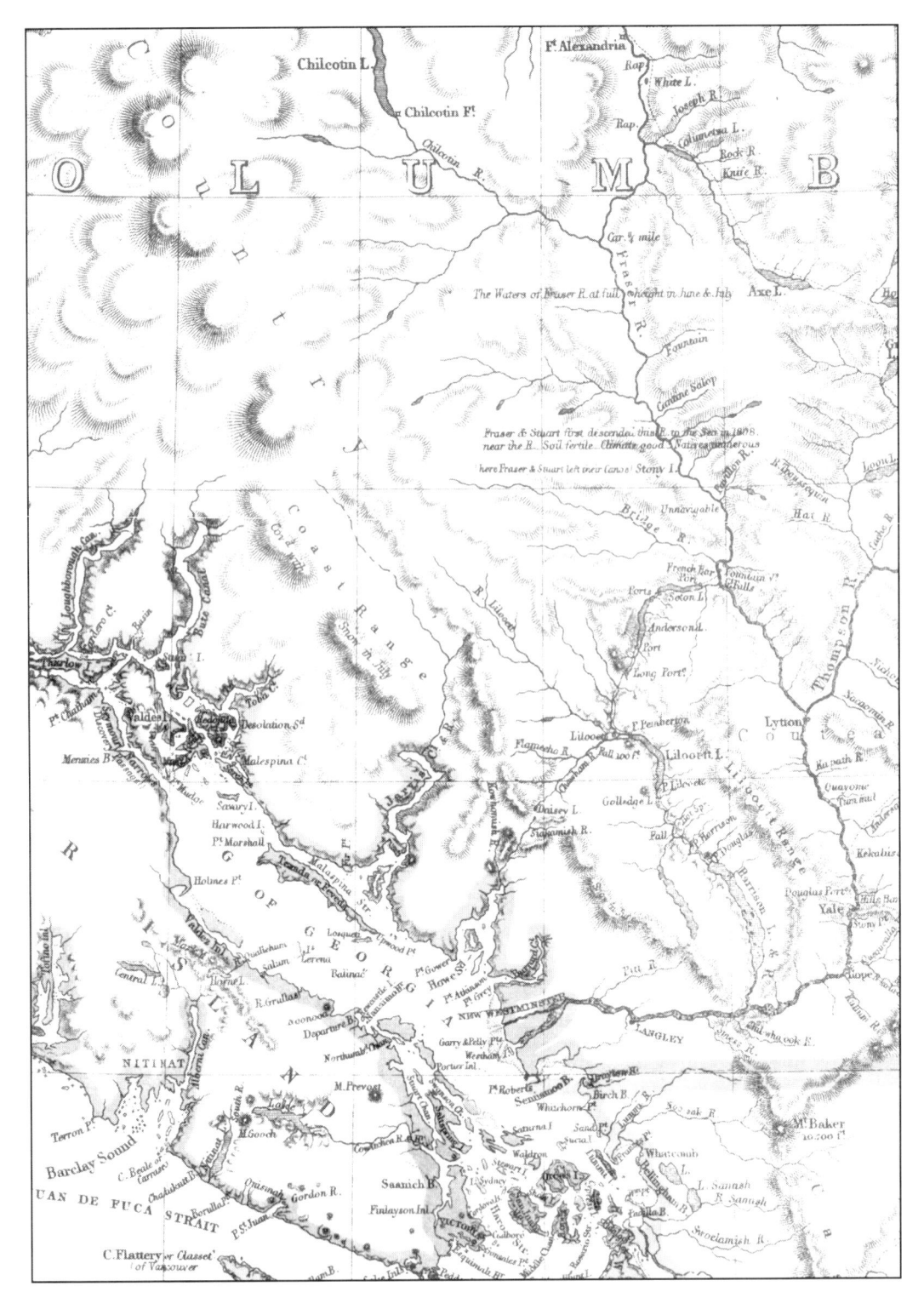

Figure 2.1 Early representation

mapping to supplement its planimetric mapping base, primarily to take into account the unique rugged and mountainous physical environment of the province. Between 1938 and 1968, BC's provincial mapping agency therefore cooperated with the federal government to deliver the One-Inch to the Mile and 1:50,000 sheets. During this time period, the province developed a reputation within Canada for its beautifully contoured maps, especially the old Two-Mile Series later published as the 1:250,000 and 1:100,000 sheets (Sebert, 1999).

By the early 1970s, BC had in place a complete topographic coverage of the province at various scales, including 1:250,000 and 1:50,000 coverages. There were also reasonable hydrographic charts for navigating the shores, ocean, and rivers supplied by the federal government, a thematic atlas of the province (BC Natural Resources Conference, 1959; Farley, 1979), and a number of resource inventories including geological coverage and all the information collected by the Canada Land Inventory. From a geographic information perspective, things were in good shape. However, mapping and the collection of associated geographic information are never static. The world's surface is forever changing, as are societal values and expectations of maps. In addition, the technologies involved in the collection, production, analysis, and distribution of maps and associated geographic information went through a major revolution between the 1970s and 2000, creating mapping opportunities never before imagined.

The digital revolution of the last 30 years includes the popularization of satellite remote-sensed data, the advent of computer mapping, computer assisted drafting (CAD), geographic information systems (GIS), global positioning systems (GPS), and the Internet. Given all of these digital revolutions and the associated fascination with technology and information, the consequence is that maps and other geographic information collected in the early and mid-20th century, stored on paper, no longer satisfy the needs of today's society. It wants access to up-to-date digital geographic data via the Internet, with the capability of analysing the data digitally, and producing customized maps for visualization purposes. The beginning of the new millennium therefore finds us in turmoil.

We find ourselves living in a period in which anything to do with information and associated information technology has little permanence. Never in the history of civilization have we had more information available to us than today. However, finding the *right* information, understanding the technology that surrounds it, and securing access to it can be challenging.

During the 1970s, 1980s, and 1990s, BC positioned itself in a global leadership role with respect to the integration of digital high technology into mapping. This should not come as a surprise in light of the province's huge geographic territory relative to a very small population base and the reliance of the provincial economy on its natural resource base. BC's government, industry, and academia thus worked in unison to champion a number of highly innovative, technological solutions to meet today's and tomorrow's mapping needs. This chapter is not the place to recognize and tell in detail the story of these diverse digital mapping efforts and of the personalities that made them happen. That can be found in McGrath and Sebert (1999). It is more important here to identify the general areas of innovation, and provincial mapping initiatives that benefited from the high technology mapping agenda.

While grappling with the challenge of how to record land cover and land use for about 950,000 km^2 of land and keep natural resource inventories up to date, BC helped to pioneer the collection, manipulation, and interpretation of digital remote-sensed data from satellites for mapping purposes. Working with the federal government, industry, and academia, the province has come a long way in developing customizable remote sensing technologies, learning how to interpret signals collected to help keep resource inventories current, and monitoring for change and environmental impacts. Of course, there is always more to learn and the research agenda is ongoing.

Collecting and interpreting remote-sensed data about the land from aerial photographs and satellite information is not, by itself, sufficient for resource mapping. The remote-sensed data need to be combined with digital versions of the traditional topographic map in order to allow aerial photography and satellite data to be *geo-referenced*. Geo-referencing refers to the ability to locate as precisely as possible where things are situated on the land, both in relative and absolute terms—including locating on a map what portion of the ground is represented by an aerial photograph or satellite image and rectifying any geometric distortions on the remote-sensed image caused by the angle of photography and/or lens distortion. A number of companies sprang up in BC to develop digital computer mapping and GIS solutions in response to needs identified by government ministries and other industry clients. By the 1980s, this had led to a chaotic situation in which various digital mapping companies developed their own unique and proprietary ways of digitally encoding map data for their computer systems, with none of the systems able to exchange data efficiently with competitors. This created an enormous complication in information management.

Government and industry were soon in a position where, even within one government ministry, geographic information was collected and processed by three or more digital mapping systems that were unable to share data. Recognizing this folly, the provincial government took leadership initiative through their Crown Lands unit to develop standards for collecting, recording, and encoding geographic data digitally that would allow different software systems to communicate with each other, facilitating smooth digital data exchange. The end result has been the development of the province's Spatial Archives and Interchange Format (SAIF), which is an open standard that has now been formally accepted by the province and has been promoted internationally through the International Organization for Standardization (ISO). Additional information about SAIF can be found at *http://home.gdbc.gov.bc.ca/fmebc/*.

Topographic Mapping

By the 1980s, it was generally accepted that the original complete topographic coverage of the province at a scale of 1:50,000 was out of date and at a scale not suitable for more detailed resource inventory and planning needs. Therefore, in 1987 the provincial government went into partnership with a consortium of mapping companies called the Digital Mapping Group Limited to form the Terrain Resource Information Management (TRIM) program. The mandate for this program was to produce an up-to-date larger scale digital topographic database. Products of this TRIM program are *TRIM files* (Figure 2.2). A total of 7,027 digital *TRIM file sets* cover the province at a scale of 1:20,000, with map sheet boundaries based on quartering the original 1:50,000 National Topographic System (NTS) sheets (Sebert, 1999). Each file set consists of several files containing positional and representational topographic base data, including information about elevation. The difference between positional and representational map data is that positional map data give exact coordinates of where features are located on the ground, while representational map data are shown in positions to satisfy cartographic visualization.

The 1:20,000 TRIM set was completed in December 1996, about 10 years after initiation of the program. Given unanticipated cost overruns and a difficult provincial fiscal climate in the latter stages of the program, some funding for this initiative eventually had to come from cost-sharing agreements with end-user clients (BC, 1995). TRIM data sets can be accessed and purchased digitally through an on-line system called LandData BC, described in more detail below. Purchase price for any one of the 7,027 TRIM sets at 1:20,000 will vary depending on what files are ordered and who the user is (there are various discount schemes). However, users must budget multiples of hundreds of dollars per digital set, and should be prepared to purchase multiple sets if their study area spans boundaries of BC's topographic tile structure. More information about TRIM data is available at *http://home.gdbc.gov.bc.ca/TRIM/trim*.

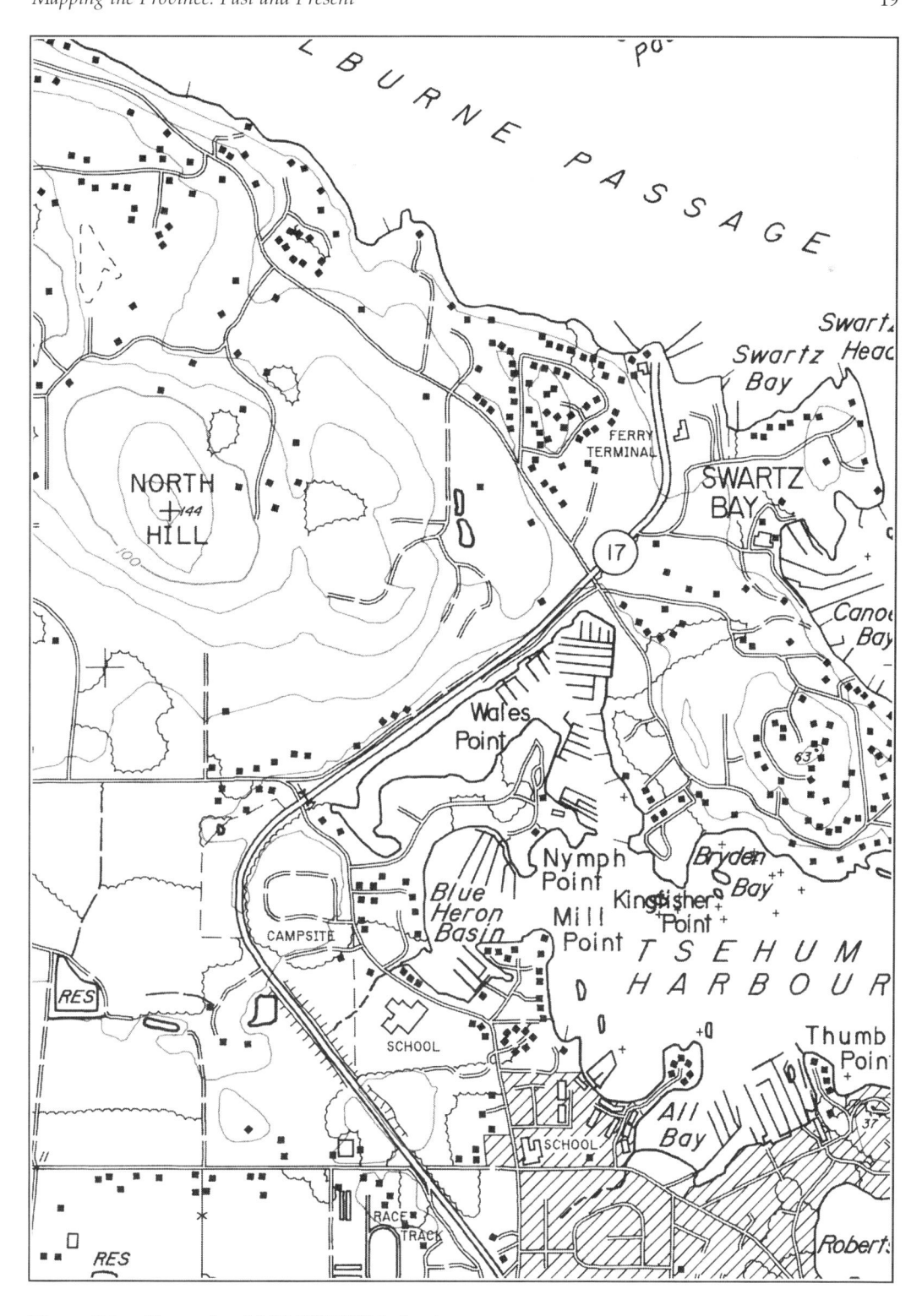

Figure 2.2 Example of 1:20,000 TRIM sheet

TRIM data are marketed by the provincial government as a "precisely specified, carefully controlled, fully structured, rigorously checked, three-dimensional digital mapping program compiled from contemporary aerial photography" (BC, 1999). Despite this statement, TRIM data are not without flaws, a primary one being that the aerial photography in some maps is up to 15 years old with little, if any, ground verification. The latter makes this digital initiative out-of-date for resource management purposes. Recognizing the need for a revised version of TRIM has already translated into the TRIM II program. Based on new 1:40,000 aerial photography, TRIM II consists of updating the original 1:20,000 TRIM data to new specifications, producing orthophotos for each 1:20,000 map sheet, and limited 1:10,000 and 1:5,000 digital map products. Initial plans are for TRIM II data to be produced using a cooperative partnership model, with key partners being the Ministry of Forests, the Ministry of Environment, Lands and Parks, Forest Renewal BC, and forest operators. For more information about TRIM II access check *http://www.landdata.gov.bc.ca*.

Beyond the 1:20,000 TRIM data, the province also makes available digital topographic coverages at scales of 1:250,000 and 1:2,000,000. A single file covers the province at 1:2,000,000, while 84 files are required for the 1:250,000 coverage. In addition, the province markets a number of map products that are derived from these base maps. Some of these products are bundled together to form what is known as *British Columbia's Digital Atlas Program* (*http://www.env.gov.bc.ca:80/gdbc/bcatlas.htm*). One of these products is a digital model of BC's terrain, entitled the *Gridded Digital Elevation Model (DEM)*. Elevation data captured from aerial photographs and other surveys for TRIM data compilation were utilized to interpolate a set of elevation heights equally spaced on a grid. Grid spacings are available at 25, 100, or 500 metres. These digital elevation data are available as point data, or as colour or grey scale images in Tagged Image File Format (TIFF). Additional products developed from TRIM data are introduced later in the chapter.

Geographic Data BC and LandData BC

One of the challenges the government faced was how to market and distribute digital TRIM data and related digital geographic information products. For many decades, the traditional topographic paper maps were distributed and sold by the province's Surveys and Resource Mapping Branch through an initiative called MAPS BC. The search for a solution to market and distribute digital geographic information eventually led the government to replace the Surveys and Resource Mapping Branch with a unit called Geographic Data BC (*http://www.home.gdbc.gov.bc.ca*). Geographic Data BC's mandate includes the development and management of land-related information and associated systems to support economic development and effective resource management.

Geographic Data BC, in partnership with industry, has developed a data access and distribution system called LandData BC (*http://www.landdata.gov.bc.ca*) put into production in June 1998. LandData BC is an Internet-based access and distribution infrastructure for spatially referenced data. LandData BC includes a downloadable spatial browser and viewer, a comprehensive catalogue of available digital and analogue data, and an order management module. In partnership with BC Online, a revenue management service is also offered for private industry partners marketing value-added products based on TRIM for data custodian partners. In 1999, LandData BC was serving 65 different data products from several different sources to approximately 500 registered customers (BC, 1999). These products include TRIM and TRIM II data. MAPS BC counter sales have since been closed, with all its services and retail sales activities transferred to LandData BC.

Geodetic Control and Surveying Challenges

An interesting obstacle was encountered by the province when setting out on the original TRIM program in 1987. The problem focused on which geodetic framework to use when starting the revised topographic mapping. In order to understand this problem, some background explanation is required.

The world is a complex three-dimensional object. To facilitate mapping, this complex shape is generalized by geodesists into a mathematically defined simple geometric shape of best fit. Without going into excessive detail, Canada, the US, and Mexico reached an agreement in 1927 on which simplified geometric shape to use and how to fit it to the true shape of the earth, calling this the North American Datum 1927 (NAD27). Thereafter, all topographic mapping, nautical charting, and other baseline mapping initiatives surveyed and mapped locations in North America to this geodetic datum.

With the advent of more precise measuring techniques, including satellite technology, it became possible to refine our understanding of the true shape of the earth. By the latter part of the middle of the 20th century we had to acknowledge that NAD27 was based on a relatively poor fit of the true shape of the earth. This led to development of a revised geodetic reference system and a new geodetic datum — the North American Datum 1983 (NAD83). Here comes the problem. Within the province, the geographic survey coordinates of a feature on the ground, surveyed to NAD27, may be out by quite a distance from the same feature's coordinate surveyed to NAD83. Imagine you have a map showing a lake surveyed to NAD27 and wish to construct a logging road adjacent to the lake. You survey the ground for the logging road to NAD83 using contemporary surveying technology. When you subsequently map your road survey coordinates on the original NAD27-based map, you may well find that the map shows the road in the lake. This, of course, is unacceptable.

The question the government faced in 1986 was whether the new TRIM program should be mapped to the old NAD27 to facilitate compatibility with all mapping already undertaken for the province, or whether it should take advantage of NAD83 to reflect better the true shape of the earth. In 1990, NAD83 became the official datum for provincial mapping coordinates and, in the end, TRIM was surveyed to NAD83. Of course, this implied that the TRIM mapping initiative is incompatible with all previous mapping. Tremendous efforts have subsequently gone into developing and implementing translation routines to convert NAD27 to NAD83 coordinates. Today, a frequent mapping mistake is to combine NAD27 with NAD83 data without the appropriate conversions. This can imply considerable errors, especially in large scale mapping exercises. Remember the logging road in the lake?

The official switch to NAD83 in 1990 also required revision to BC's original geodetic reference framework. This revised geodetic control, known as Management of Survey Control Operations and Tasks (MASCOT), became operational in 1994. The MASCOT database defines the geo-spatial reference system (latitudes, longitudes, and elevations) in the province through some 50,000 geodetic control monuments and benchmarks. Although horizontal coordinates are referenced to NAD83, elevations are based on the Canadian Vertical Datum (CVD28). The MASCOT database was made available to the public by way of an on-line Internet Web access in 1995 (enhanced in 1996) at *http://www.pwccanada.com:8001/mascot*.

The GPS has revolutionized the determination of coordinate location on the surface of the earth. Taking advantage of a system of satellites that transmit locational data, hand-held GPS receivers allow anyone to determine where they are to within tens of metres in three dimensions. For more precise determination of location (metre or centimetre precision), it is necessary to access additional data to correct for deliberate distortion built into the satellite transmissions for military purposes. In BC, the provincial government has established a network of nine active control points distributed throughout the province that measure and broadcast this distortion. The stations are in Williams Lake, Penticton, Victoria, Port McNeil, Invermere, Fort St. John, Fort Nelson, Dease Lake, and Terrace. These base stations, called the British Columbia Active Control System (BC ACS), continuously monitor data from all available GPS satellites. Observation data for post processing are made available through Land Data BC or by way of a Bulletin Board Service (250-480-1382). Observation data may be purchased in one-hour packets or under a variety of subscription options. BC ACS allows GPS users to reference their data accurately on NAD83 and CVD28. In addition, services can be purchased from other private GPS control point stations established throughout the province. A common mistake that is made these days is to use non-differential GPS to determine and record position to within a metre's precision without subsequently postprocessing the data to correct for distortion.

A logical extension of BC ACS is the provincially supplied Global Surveyor System (*http://www.pwccanada.com:8001/mascot/*). This system provides real time differential GPS positioning for 1 to sub-10 metre accuracy by computing and broadcasting range corrections for GPS satellites in view across the province. The corrections are computed at the active control points located at Williams Lake and Terrace, transmitted to the communications centre in Ottawa, broadcast via MSAT satellite beacon, and received at the roving GPS receiver by a small MSAT communications receiver. Service is available on a subscription basis (BC, 1999). This system allows high-end differential GPS to correct for distortion in real time in the field.

Other Geographic Information Initiatives

BC has a substantial collection of aerial photographs. Geographic Data BC coordinates and manages the province's annual aerial photography programs on behalf of other government agencies, notably the Ministry of Forests and the Ministry of Environment, Lands and Parks. The average year sees the completion of 58,000 line kilometres and acceptance of 50,000 frames of aerial photography. The average annual expenditure is in the order of $2 million. The aerial photograph archive currently contains approximately two million photographs (BC, 1999). Analogue aerial photography products can be accessed and purchased through Land Data BC. Geographic Data BC is exploring the feasibility and practicality of storing and distributing aerial photography products in digital form.

A number of thematic land use and land cover mapping initiatives are ongoing in BC. Geographic Data BC is coordinating the Baseline Thematic Mapping (BTM) initiative, alternatively known as Present Land Use Mapping (PLUM). This initiative takes advantage of the Landsat satellite imagery, combining it with TRIM's digital elevation model and planimetry to map different land use classes at the 1:250,000 scale. Twenty different land use classes had been mapped by the beginning of the new millennium, with representation products available through LandData BC. Geographic Data BC continually seeks partnerships with other agencies, such as the Canadian Space Agency, the Canadian Centre for Remote Sensing, and federal ministries, to explore a variety of other land use and land cover mapping projects.

Efforts to produce maps of biophysical habitat and terrestrial ecosystems are ongoing. The maps are produced by delineation of aerial photographs according to described standards followed by standard field sampling and verification procedures. Mapping scales range from 1:2,000,000 (showing BC's ecoregion classification system) to 1:5,000 (showing estuarine wetlands). Data about the rarity, conservation status, and location of rare and endangered animals, plants, plant communities, and record trees in the province are available from the Conservation Data Centre at *http://www.elp. gov.bc.ca/rib/wis/cdc/index.htm*.

A comprehensive model of the stream networks in BC is available through the province's watershed atlas initiatives by the Ministry of Environment, Lands and Parks. The *TRIM Watershed Atlas* (TWA) takes advantage of the TRIM digital elevation model and planimetry to create an ordered network and heights of land for each watershed. The TWA is available through LandData BC (*http://www.landdata.gov. bc.ca/*). The Fisheries Branch of the BC Ministry of Environment, Lands and Parks has linked a comprehensive aquatic attribute database to a computerized 1:50,000 base map of aquatic features for the province based on the 1:50,000 scale federal national topographic map series (1,173 maps). The atlas differentiates approximately 250 watershed groups for the province, defined as "large drainage areas." A joint program between the federal and provincial governments is the Floodplain Mapping Program, identifying and mapping areas that are highly susceptible to flooding (*http://www.elp.gov.bc.ca/wat/fpm/fpminfo.html*).

Official names of BC's landscape features, natural areas, and communities are the responsibility of the Geographical Names Office of Geographic Data BC. These names are accessible from the British Columbia Geographical Names Information System (BCGNIS) (*http://www.gdbc.gov.bc.ca/bcnames/*). The Geographical Names Office is a member of and operates in accordance with the Canadian Permanent Committee on Geographic Names.

BC is working on a digital map of its road network. The Digital Road Atlas (DRA) is being developed cooperatively by Geographic Data BC, Emergency Communications for Southwestern BC, Elections BC, and Natural Resources Canada. The atlas will be based on data from the province's Transportation Centreline Network (TCN) created by the Ministry of Highways, urban street files from the Geography Division of Statistics Canada, TRIM planimetric data, and information about forestry roads supplied by the Ministry of Forests, updated with GPS positioning, and augmented with navigation and address data. More information about the status of the Digital Road Atlas can be found at *http://home.gdbc.gov.bc.ca/DRA/default.htm*.

There are numerous other mapping and geographic information initiatives in BC. This chapter has attempted to focus on major province-wide initiatives with a long life span. Many of the other mapping initiatives have a regional or project specific focus. Not all initiatives are carried through to completion, and many products disappear from public access through time. In today's world, the best way to stay up-to-date about what geographic information is available is to access and search one of several key websites. The following sites may be good starting points. An obvious site is Geographic Data BC at *http://home.gdbc.gov.bc.ca/*. Useful leads may be found by searching the web pages of the BC Archives at *http://www.bcarchives.gov.bc.ca/index.htm*. The BC Stats website at *http://www.bcstats.gov.bc.ca/* may also prove helpful. The Land Use Coordination Office's Geographic Information Service (LUCO GIS) is custodian of several GIS datasets pertaining to land use planning and other activities in BC. Their website is intended to provide access to some of these data (see *http://www.gis.luco.gov.bc.ca/*). Also highly recommended is Glenn Letham's Spatial News at *http://www.spatialnews.com*.

PRESENT AND FUTURE CHALLENGES

We live in exciting times. Technology and information play fundamental roles in contemporary society. Innovations in both technology and information practices continue to create new opportunities and challenge existing mapping and geographic information initiatives. Society has expectations of government, industry, and academia to deliver high quality, current analogue and digital information about the province in a format that is as easy to access as possible. While expectations are high, what is less well understood by the public is that collecting, processing, and distributing geographic information is very costly and time consuming. This is especially true when trying to cover the geography of a province as large and diverse as BC.

The relationship between information, information technology, and society is also under critical review by the public, academia, and government. The public is questioning the ethics and motivations behind data collection and distribution. Contemporary debates pit society's right of access to information against an individual's right to guaranteed privacy and confidentiality. The problem is that it is increasingly feasible in today's world of digital information technology to combine diverse datasets to build profiles about individual citizens of the province, or to locate endangered species that require protection from abuse.

How are BC's authorities and experts that are in charge of mapping responding to this problem? The province now has legislation through Bill 50, and an associated Information and Privacy Commissioner, to address the questions of right to information access and privacy protection. The Information and Privacy Office has already had to rule on several cases relating to geographic information, with many more expected.

One of the questions the Commissioner has faced is: "What constitutes 'fair cost of access' to geographic information?" The two sides of this question are society's expectation of access to information at minimal cost to ensure affordability and equity, versus the provincial government's search for 'cost-recovery' and 'sale for profit' in an era of fiscal deficit. The question has arisen in part as a response to land use planning in the province. Stakeholders and interest groups questioning the government's land use planning decisions have asked for access to the same data that the government collected and used to assist it in its decision making processes. Stakeholders and interest groups want access to these data to confirm statements made and to evaluate proposed and alternative planning scenarios. They have expressed unwillingness to pay the government tens of thousands of dollars for TRIM files and related information, arguing that the taxpayer has paid for these data once already through taxation. The debate over "fair cost of access" remains unresolved. What appears to be the trend, however, is for government to seek private industry partners actively to form joint geographic information ventures. The motivations for this are, in part, to reduce direct costs to the taxpayer and to foster private industry, but also to justify government charge-back fees.

The challenges of compatibility, simplicity, and efficiency of access to digital geographic data are being addressed by the province, industry, and the user community on an ongoing basis. Today's digital mapping solutions remain expensive and complex to use. This creates an uneven playing field where those with technology and technology know-how have a great advantage. Community mapping initiatives all over the province are looking for ways to overcome these barriers. At the same time, government and industry continue to search for ways to standardize provincial geographic information collection and distribution to facilitate data compatibility and sharing.

A powerful spatial data translation utility called the Feature Manipulation Engine (FME) has been developed by SAFE Software (*http://www.safe.com*). FME was spawned from work directed to investigate the problems associated with the sharing of data between the Ministry of Forests and forest operators, as well as other government agencies and the private sector. The first version of FMEBC is available free of charge at *http://home.gdbc.gov.bc.ca/fmebc/software.htm*. It is useful for translating between MOEP, SAIF, Intergraph Design (IGDS), and Arc Shape formats. A much broader and more powerful commercial version of FME may be licensed directly from SAFE Software. Land Data BC uses an embedded version of FME as its translation engine. Another effort to standardize, rationalize, and consolidate geographic data collection, storage, and distribution in the province is the BC Ministry of Forests Integrated Spatial and Attribute Corporate Database (INCOSADA) initiative at (*http://www.for.gov.bc.ca/isb/incosada/*).

It is clear that contemporary provincial mapping and geographic information initiatives are technology dominated. Considerable energies are dedicated to asking and answering questions concerning how to capitalize on and manipulate technology to facilitate mapping needs. The danger in all this is that technology issues can begin to drive perceived or real mapping requirements, perhaps at the expense of addressing what the end-users of maps and related geographic information actually need. Exciting technological developments should not lose sight of end-user needs and working environments, the needs of the households in BC who cannot afford computers, or the citizens of the province who are computer illiterate.

In the excitement of collecting and digitally encoding geographic information, we must not overlook allocating efforts and resources into what it is that the information tells us about the province. The last comprehensive thematic atlas published for BC dates back to 1979 (Farley, 1979). A new atlas for BC, telling a comprehensive story of the province's geography and its people through maps, words, and multimedia is long overdue.

Acknowledgements:

Information about mapping before the 20th century is based in large parts on Gilmartin (1987). A note of thanks to my research student, Jeremy Holmes, for assisting in the collection of background information for this chapter, and to Diana Hocking and Colin Wood for commenting on earlier drafts of this manuscript.

REFERENCES

Andrews, G.S. (1954). Surveys and mapping in British Columbia resources development, *Transactions of the Seventh British Columbia Natural Resources Conference*. Victoria: British Columbia Natural Resources Conference.

BC (1991). Provincial Government cartographic activity report. *Canadian Institute of Surveying and Mapping Journal*, 45(1), 105-107.

BC (1995). Cartographic activity report. *Geomatica*, 49(1), 102-105.

BC (1999). Cartographic activity report. *Geomatica*, 53(2), 221-242.

BC Natural Resources Conference (1956). *British Columbia atlas of resources*, Victoria.

Farley, A.L. (1960). The historical cartography of British Columbia. Madison: University of Wisconsin, Department of Geography, unpublished PhD dissertation.

Farley, A.L. (1979). *Atlas of British Columbia*. Vancouver: The University of British Columbia Press.

Gilmartin, P.P. (1987). Landmark maps in British Columbia's past. In C. Forward (Ed.), *British Columbia: Its resources and people* (pp. 25-40). Victoria, BC: Western Geographical Press, Western Geographical Series, Vol. 22.

Lamb, W.K. (1978). Maps relating to the Vancouver Expedition. *Association of Canadian Map Libraries Bulletin*, 28.

Lamb, W.K. (1988). Vancouver's charts of the northwest coast. In B. Farrell and A. Desbarats (Eds.), *Exploration in the history of Canadian mapping: A collection of essays* (pp. 99-112). Association of Canadian Map Libraries and Archives.

McGrath, G., and Sebert, L.M. (Eds.) (1999). *Mapping a northern land: The survey of Canada 1947-1994*. McGill-Queen's University Press.

Pearson, D.F. (1974). An historical outline of mapping British Columbia. *The Canadian Cartographer*, 11(2), 114-24.

Sandilands, R.W. (1988). The history of hydrographic surveying in British Columbia. In B. Farrell and A. Desbarats (Eds.), *Exploration in the history of Canadian mapping: A collection of essays* (pp. 113-132). Association of Canadian Map Libraries and Archives.

Sebert, L.M. (1999). Provincial topographic mapping. In G. McGrath and L.M. Sebert (Eds.), *Mapping a northern land: The survey of Canada 1947-1994* (pp. 116-139). McGill-Queen's University Press.

Spittle, J.S. (1973). Early printed maps of British Columbia: A preliminary report on the maps, plans and charts printed and published in the Crown Colony between 1858 and 1871. *Association of Canadian Map Libraries Proceedings*, 7.

Spittle, J.S. (1988). Early printed maps of British Columbia: Maps printed and published in New Westminster, 1861-1866. In B. Farrell and A. Desbarats (Eds.), *Exploration in the history of Canadian mapping: A collection of essays* (pp. 193-204). Association of Canadian Map Libraries and Archives.

Thompson, D.W. (1966). *Men and meridians*, Volume 1. Ottawa: Queen's Printer.

Thompson, D.W. (1967). *Men and meridians*, Volume 2. Ottawa: Queen's Printer.

Thompson, D.W. (1969). *Men and meridians*, Volume 3. Ottawa: Queen's Printer.

Plate 3 Summer rock slides in the Coast Range ▶

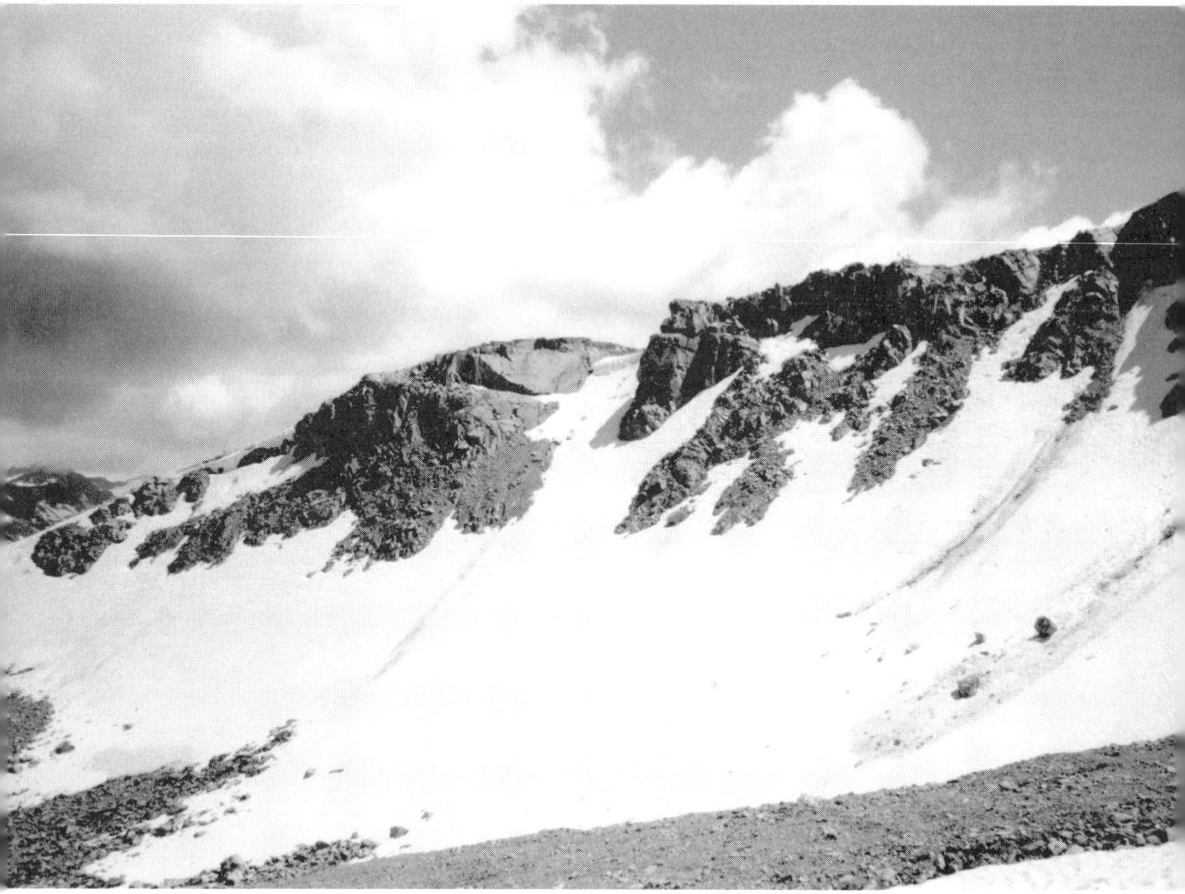

Landforms and Natural Hazards

Harold D. Foster
Department of Geography, University of Victoria

Landforms

British Columbia lies within the Cordilleran and Interior Plains regions of Canada, two of the country's five major physiographic subdivisions (Holland, 1964). The Canadian Cordillera is predominantly rugged and of high relief and includes all of the mainland and offshore islands west of the eastern margins of the Rocky Mountains. Only in the northeast does the province extend beyond the Cordillera into the Interior Plains region. There the relief is one of plateaus, plains, and prairies (Figure 3.1).

The huge area (947,800 sq km) of BC is both geologically and geomorphologically varied.[1] Located near the junction of the Pacific and North American plates, two of the six large elements that make up the majority of the earth's lithosphere, BC is an integral part of the circum-Pacific 'Ring of Fire.' The junction between the two plates is composed predominantly of transform faults. As a result, the Pacific and North American plates slide past one another, neither creating nor destroying the lithosphere (Press and Siever, 1982). Such movements are, however, associated with numerous shallow-focus earthquakes. Two smaller plates, the Juan de Fuca and Explorer, occur in BC's southern offshore waters. There, the leading edge of the North American Plate overrides the smaller plates, forcing them into the mantle where they are absorbed (Yorath, 1990).

The variety of geological environments in BC is immense, the bulk being composed of folded, faulted, and metamorphosed rocks, ranging in age from the Precambrian to the Recent and in type from sedimentary to volcanic and intrusive. That part of BC lying west of the Rocky Mountain Trench was involved in the Coast Range Orogeny, lasting from early Jurassic time through to post-Lower Cretaceous. This was associated with major mountain building and folding and faulting on a regional scale, together with the intrusion of granitic batholithics in the Insular, Coast, and Columbia mountains and elsewhere. Subsequent erosion removed the covering sedimentary rocks, exposing the underlying batholithic cores. Contemporaneous deposition of Upper Cretaceous and early Tertiary sediments also occurred in two basins. To the west was a depression that included Vancouver Island, the Queen Charlotte Islands, and the Gulf of Georgia. A second basin was located in what is now the Rocky Mountain region. The Rocky Mountains, therefore, now occupy the site of a former geosyncline, a recipient of deposition during the Palaeozoic and Mesozoic eras. The post-Palaeocene Rocky Mountain Orogeny terminated this sedimentary process and ended in the formation of the Rocky Mountains. During the Tertiary, most of the province was subjected to extensive erosion. Differential uplift and erosion in the Pliocene caused extensive rejuvenation and deep river incision, establishing the present arrangement of mountains, plateaus, and plains (Holland, 1964). On several occasions, this regenerated topography was later subjected to extensive Pleistocene glaciations. At its peak, during the Wisconsin, the Cordilleran Glacier Complex was a continuous and interconnected mass of valley and piedmont glaciers and an ice sheet that, although centred in BC, stretched northwest to the Aleutian Islands and south to Mount Adams, near the Columbia River, a distance of 3,780 km. The shed lay between the Coast Mountains and the Rocky Mountains, where the ice was at least 2,280 m thick. Other smaller ice caps formed on Vancouver Island and on

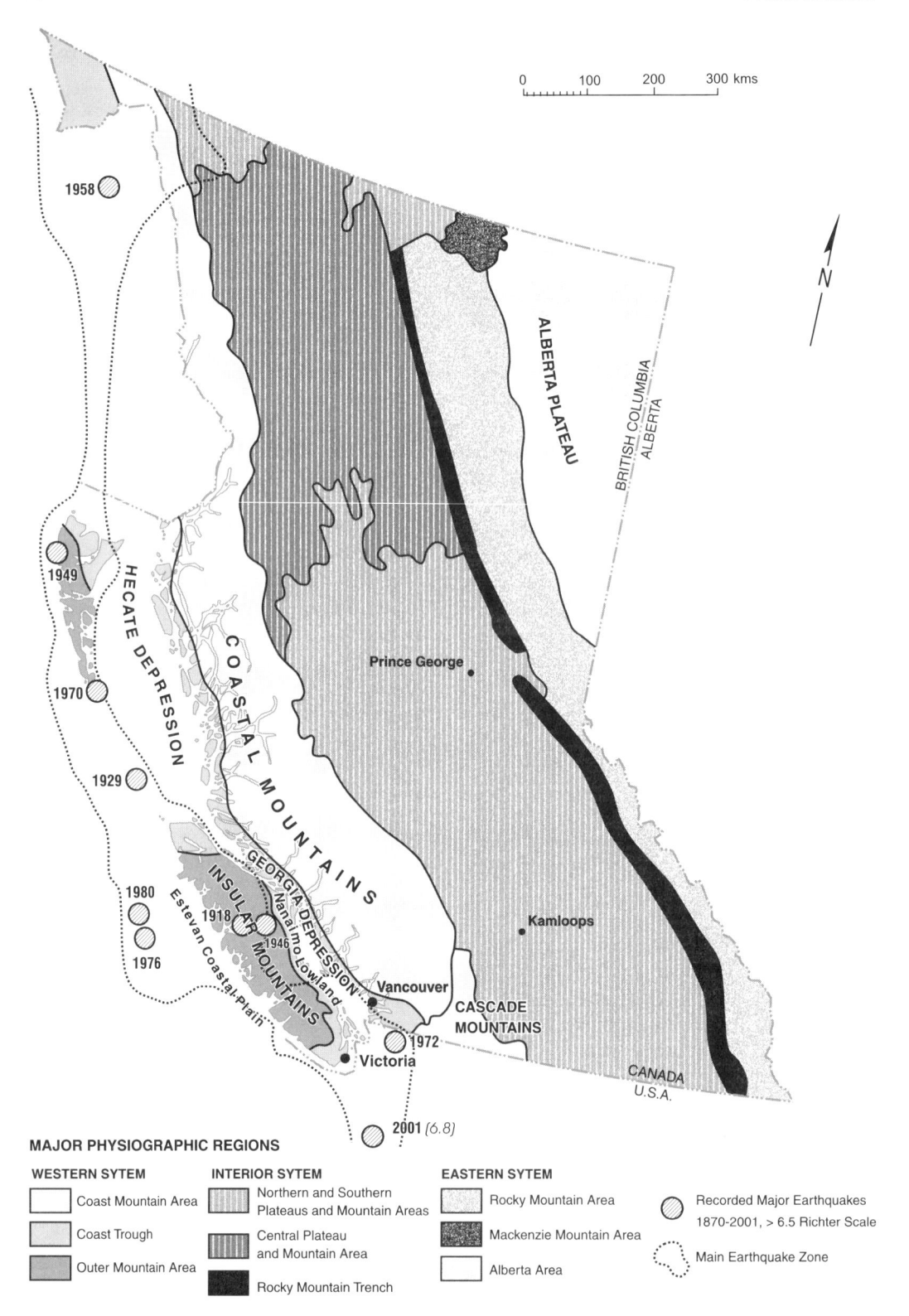

Figure 3.1 Landforms

the Queen Charlotte Islands (Flint, 1957). As a result of such Pleistocene glaciations, the province is now marked by a wide range of striking glacial erosional and depositional features, including U-shaped valleys, fjords, and large deposits of till and glacio-fluvial and glacio-marine sediments.

The generally high relief of BC and the westerly atmospheric circulation to which it is subjected result in major variations in precipitation. This ranges from as little as 25 cm annually in parts of the province's interior to over 500 cm along the coast. Interior river basins receive most of their annual precipitation as snow during the winter months. This stays in storage until late spring or summer, when higher temperatures release it to stream flow. Mountain areas also support a multitude of glaciers and ice caps. These are found predominantly in the northwest and southwest of the Coast Mountains, one of the largest being the Llewellyn Glacier, south of Atlin Lake.

It is clear, from this brief summary of the physical geography of BC, that the province has experienced a most varied geological and geomorphological history. Its active seismicity; heavy rainfall; high snowfall; steep, glaciated slopes; folded, faulted, and jointed rocks; and unstable sediments are associated with a diversity of natural hazards. How these are managed provides the focus for the remainder of this chapter.

Natural Hazards

There is no area of BC that is free from natural hazard risk. However, associated losses can be reduced by planning for greater safety through the adoption of numerous disaster mitigation strategies. This process of deliberate risk management usually involves the operation of complex decision-making networks, termed "safety delivery systems" (Foster, 1981). Figure 3.2 is a heuristic model of such a system. It illustrates that the reduction of risk from major natural hazards almost always involves the cooperation of a variety of participating groups. These include: international, national, regional, and local governments; the scientific community; financial institutions, such as insurance companies and banks; developers; architects; realtors; the media; the owners and renters of private homes and commercial buildings; and the general public.

Regardless of the place or the hazard under consideration, the acceptable level of risk has been defined either implicitly or explicitly. The management of every safety delivery system then tries to achieve this target by the adoption of strategies intended to ensure that losses from the hazards for which it is responsible do not rise above this threshold. Naturally, the acceptable level of risk from particular hazards varies from country to country and indeed from region to region. As a result, societies evolve in a manner that allows them to operate within specific levels of tolerance for natural and man-made events. Boundaries to what is, in effect, acceptable risk are defined either by laws or common practice. Regulations, such as public health and building codes, usually identify the maximum event that should be guarded against and consequently govern the losses that must be accepted. The associated level of safety reflects a variety of factors, including the availability of capital and manpower, past experience, needs, wants, and priorities.

Such safety delivery systems are dynamic. Social goals may alter and as a result the public may demand greater protection from earthquakes, floods, hurricanes, or other hazards. Most displays of dissatisfaction with a particular safety delivery system take place after a disaster, which clearly demonstrates that existing standards are too low (Buchanan, 1983). As a consequence, the law or associated codes and regulations may be altered and the safety delivery system involved modified to meet new objectives. In addition, change and associated improvements in security can be achieved by the provision of incentives designed to promote the adoption of innovation. The incentives that are provided to different groups within the safety delivery system may be in the form of capital (e.g., grants and subsidies), income tax credits, accelerated depreciation, or tax exemptions. They can also involve the provision of

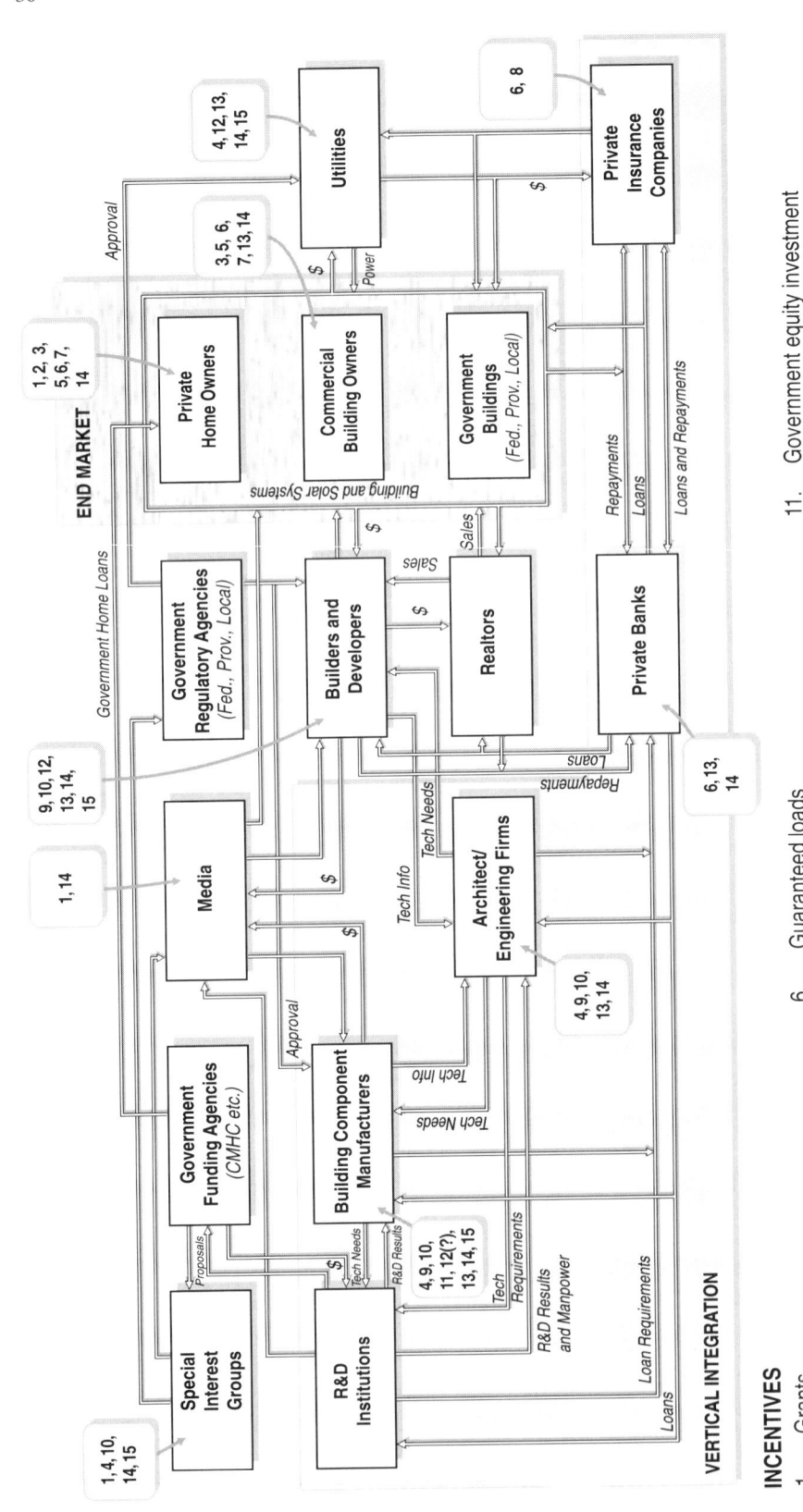

Figure 3.2 Hazard response system

INCENTIVES

1. Grants
2. Income tax credits
3. Income tax deductions
4. Research and development
5. Low cost loans
6. Guaranteed loads
7. Accelerated depreciation/rapid amortization
8. Government insurance and reinsurance
9. Government procurement
10. Demonstration programs
11. Government equity investment
12. Tax exempt bonds
13. Information dissemination
14. Education and training programs
15.

information through research, development, demonstration, and education and training programs. The points where these incentives can best be utilized to reduce losses are also illustrated in Figure 3.2.

Regardless of which hazard is involved, in theory at least, every safety delivery system's management can choose whether or not to implement four basic groups of mitigation strategies (Foster, 1981). Typically, these involve measures to modify or remove either the hazard or the infrastructure at risk, or they seek to accommodate accepted losses with minimum social disruption. In practice, however, the choice of strategies may be limited by such factors as: a lack of scientific knowledge about the hazard and its probable impact; an absence of appropriate technology; excessive cost, or legal and social objections to implementation. The selection of mitigation strategies is also influenced by the training of those involved in managing the safety delivery system and the perceptions and attitudes of various special interest groups and the general public who are served by it. In addition, some hazards strike so rarely, as, for example, meteorites, or cause so little damage that no safety delivery system exists for them. In such cases, the typical response by those adversely affected is to bear the loss.

British Columbian Safety Delivery Systems: Case Studies

A multiplicity of delivery systems have evolved in the province in attempts to increase public safety and to protect property in BC. These networks include those seeking to reduce the damage caused by floods, snow avalanches, earthquakes, and *tsunamis*. Examples of such systems are described in detail here in an effort to illustrate how they have developed and the basic principles involved in their operation.

Flood Safety Network

Experience has shown that floods are the most damaging of BC's natural hazards. This is because access to drinking water was a major factor in the initial location of many settlements. Silt deposition on flood plains also provided fertile agricultural soils, while river transport facilitated trade and forest clearing. As a result, many cities in BC were sited on river banks, estuaries, or lakesides (see **Figure 5.1**). Subsequent growth, therefore, often took place on flood plains, leading to escalating losses from floods. Areas threatened by flooding on Vancouver Island include Port Alberni, Campbell River, Courtenay, Duncan, and Lake Cowichan. By far the greatest risks are being taken in the Fraser Valley. During the 1948 flood in this area, dykes failed and 2,000 homes were destroyed; 16,000 residents had to be evacuated and 10 perished. A recurrence today could be expected to cause an estimated $1.8 billion in damages throughout the Fraser Valley (*http://www.elp. gov.bc.ca/rib/wat/fpm/flood/brochur2.html#3*). While the Fraser River reached a height of 7.62 m at Mission during the 1948 flood, the greatest flood of record was in 1894 when the river crested at 7.92 m at the same location. However, at that time settlement was sparse and damage restricted (Andrews, 1993).

Other more recent floods of note occurred in Kamloops in 1972 and in the Vancouver-Squamish-Brackendale areas in 1980 and 1981. In Kamloops damage reached $8 million, as 200 houses were inundated, while in the Squamish floods losses totalled $13 million and $2 million in successive years. Serious flooding also took place in North Pemberton in the winter of 1984, damaging 175 homes (Scanlon, Conlin, Duffy, Osborne, and Whitten, 1985). Starting the second week of November 1990, the Salmon River on Vancouver Island overflowed twice in 2 weeks, resulting in the evacuation of Sayward on both occasions. In October 1991, serious flooding occurred in the Nass Valley, while the Fitzsimmons Creek flood, near Whistler, caused approximately $4 million in damage in the same year (Ward and Skermer, 1992). Although such damage is considerable, far larger losses can be anticipated. This great loss potential was described in the conclusions of the federal-provincial Fraser River Joint Advisory Board Report in 1976. That publication stated:

Greater floods than that of 1894 can and will occur, but the specific year or years of their occurrence cannot be predicted. There is a 1-in-3 probability that the 1894 flood will be equalled or exceeded during the 60-year period from 1973 to 2032.

Flooding can occur in BC for a variety of reasons. Over most of the province, maximum river discharge occurs during the snowmelt-generated spring freshet period of May to July. The rivers of Vancouver Island, however, carry maximum flows in the winter months, as a direct result of high rainfall. A less common phenomenon is flooding caused by the outbursts of glacier-dammed lakes, or *jökulhlaups*, which have occurred from Tulsequah, Flood, Summit, and Ape lakes in the Coast Mountains (Clague, 1987). In addition, there have been dam failures in BC from the beginning of the century until as recently as May 1995.

When trying to reduce the risk of serious floods, some key questions must be addressed. Where are floods most likely to occur? When will they take place? How can we prevent them, or mitigate the damage that they cause? A major flood safety delivery system has developed in BC during the past 105 years, since the first legislative response to this hazard took place. At that time, the passage of the *Drainage, Dyking, and Irrigation Act* was stimulated by the 1894 major spring freshet which caused widespread inundation along the Fraser and the Thompson River flood plains.

The first scientific effort to systematically identify those areas of BC most likely to suffer serious flooding only began in 1974 with establishment of the BC Floodplain Development Control Program. A year later the federal government established a National Flood Drainage Reduction Program. These two attempts to identify areas at high risk of flooding and discourage development in them were melded in December 1987 with the federal/provincial Agreement Respecting Floodplain Mapping (Andrews, 1993). This restricted both governments from developing designated floodplains, discouraged provision of financial assistance to others wishing to do so, and encouraged local authorities to restrict such construction. It also required floodproofing measures be incorporated into any new floodplain development for it to be eligible for future disaster assistance. In August 1994, an Amending Agreement extended this arrangement until March 31, 2003. Additional funding was provided until March 31, 1998 to phase down the mapping program by completing several high priority prospects. Nevertheless, existing floodplain maps will be kept up-to-date.

The Floodplain Mapping Program, promoted by those two federal/provincial agreements, uses remote sensing, ground and river surveys, and computer modelling to map potential flood areas. Recommendations to designate the area in question as a floodplain are then made to a steering committee consisting of provincial and federal members. To date, 169 floodplain areas have been designated and more than 840 associated map sheets produced. Details can be found at *http://www.env.gov.bc.ca/wat/fpm/fpmhome.html* and are available from Crown Publications Inc. The maps delineate the areas that can expect flooding, on average, a minimum of once every 200 years. Such floods can occur at any time of the year; the indicated flood levels may be exceeded and portions of the floodplain can expect flooding more often. While the Agreement's costs are shared and each map is a joint publication, the province assumes the responsibility of ensuring that the maps are accurate.

Therefore, the question "where are floods most likely to occur in BC?" has largely been answered. "When are they most likely to occur?" raises a completely different set of issues. Predicting floods requires a great deal of accurate data. To forecast river or lake flood levels, two primary types of information are needed: hydrologic and meteorologic. The former includes data on river levels and flows, soil moisture, lake levels and snow depth, snowpack water equivalent, and snow-covered area. The latter includes readings of precipitation, temperature, wind speed direction and duration, evaporation, and weather forecasts (Andrews, 1993). A variety of agencies and individuals are involved in collecting this data and the procedures involved are becoming more automated and sophisticated as instrumentation is being linked directly to forecast centres by satellite. This allows access to data in real time, making it available to forecasters within seconds of being recorded. Computer links also allow for information sharing. For example, the computer systems of the Atmospheric Environment Service of Environment Canada can be accessed for meteorological data, weather forecasts, and radar maps (Andrews, 1993).

Since many floods in BC result from rapid snowmelt, it is essential for flood forecasters to have accurate snowpack information. The BC Ministry of Environment, Lands and Parks, therefore, monitors snowpack using about 250 sampled snow courses and 50 snow pillows. The latter are reinforced plastic bags, approximately 3 m in diameter, that are filled with antifreeze solution and left on the ground in remote locations. As snow accumulates and buries a pillow, the pressure inside it increases. All pillows are connected to Data Collection Platforms which relay information on snow water equivalent (proportional to the weight of the snow), temperature, and precipitation, via satellite, to the BC Ministry of Environment, Lands and Parks, where it is analysed and the information made publicly available.

The responsibility for monitoring snowpack and predicting the probability of flooding lies with the River Forecast Centre of the Resources Inventory Branch of the Ministry of Environment, Lands and Parks which bases its predictions on hydrologic and meteorologic data collected throughout the province. Although not limited to the Fraser and Thompson river basins, it is for them that such flood predictions are most significant. Should floods occur, local governments are responsible for the initial response within the municipal boundaries, although they may request help from other organizations. The provincial government will assume control when a local government's capacity to respond adequately is overwhelmed. Similarly, the province may request assistance from the federal government during major flood events. That is, as long as the capacity to deal effectively with a flood or other emergency situation exists, the operational responsibility for management remains at the lowest level of government possible. In 1992, the Inter-Agency Emergency Preparedness Council (1998) identified key ministries for hazard response in BC who were obliged to prepare response plans for the designated hazards, in consultation with the Provincial Emergency Program (PEP). In the case of flooding, although the Ministry of Environment, Lands and Parks is responsible for providing flood forecasts and bulletins, the Ministry of Transportation and Highways is the key ministry and has the responsibility of directing and coordinating provincial flood-fighting operations in the case of major floods. If required, it will be assisted by the PEP and Emergency Preparedness Canada (EPC).

When major floods occur, both the federal and provincial governments have agencies ready to respond. EPC is responsible for coordinating the emergency planning of federal departments, agencies, and Crown corporations. It also links their efforts with those of the BC government. EPC also provides funds for approved emergency planning projects and sponsors courses and conferences at its study centre in Arnprior. One of the most important functions of the organization is the administration of the federal Disaster Assistance Program (DAP). When a disaster occurs of sufficient scale to place an undue burden on any provincial economy, aid may be sought from the federal government. The BC government applied for aid under the DAP as a result of both the 1980 Terrace and 1980-81 Squamish floods.

Although EPC plays a significant role during major flooding, most of the rescue work is coordinated by the PEP of the Ministry of the Attorney General (*http://www.pep.bc.ca/index.html*). The PEP is assisting in setting up a province-wide emergency communications network and in the training of personnel capable of responding to emergencies. Emphasis is also placed on encouraging municipalities to prepare disaster plans for their own jurisdictions. The value of the PEP was demonstrated during the period from October to December 1981 when major storms created debris-torrents in the Howe Sound area. Several threatened communities were evacuated by PEP personnel, reducing loss of life.

It is not enough to know where and when floods are likely to occur; efforts must also be made to mitigate floodplain damage. The strategies available for achieving this can be grouped into two broad categories: structural and non-structural. The former usually have an engineering focus and seek to protect existing development by confining flood waters and lessening their impacts. They include dams, storage reservoirs, dykes, and diversion channels. Non-structural approaches to floodplain management, in contrast, seek to be preventative rather than corrective, and attempt to reduce damage on floodplains by restricting development in high risk areas. Strategies include floodplain regulation, land use bylaws, subdivision regulations, flood proofing, and tax adjustments.

Both structural and non-structural strategies for reducing flood losses are now widely applied in BC. Initially, far greater emphasis was placed on the former approach. The first legislative response to flooding, for example, was the *Drainage, Dyking, and Irrigation Act*, which was passed in 1894, stimulated by the elevated spring freshet that caused widespread inundation on the Fraser and Thompson flood plains. Other more recent structural flood-related legislation includes the *Flood Relief Act* and the *Fraser Valley Dyking Board Act*, both of which were passed in 1948 as a direct response to the major Fraser River flood of that year (Buchanan, 1983). The *Flood Relief Act* provided for a cooperative federal-provincial aid, relief, and rehabilitation program in the Fraser Valley. It also established a cost sharing program in which the federal government provided 75% of the cost of the repair and construction of dykes and created the authority on which dyking boards rested, such as those set up in Chilliwack, Sardis, and Mission. Due to the damage and the threat of subsequent flooding, dyking repairs were urgently needed in the Fraser Valley. To address this problem, the province established the Fraser Valley Dyking Board through the 1948 *Act* of the same name. This body acted quickly to repair the dyking system and to increase its height. Fortunately, this was achieved prior to the 1950 freshet, which resulted in the third highest water level on record at Mission. As a result of this prompt action, no flood damage resulted. Research into the flood hazard on the Fraser River culminated with the 1967 report of a Canada-BC Committee, which prepared a plan for protection that would cost $33 million to implement. This led to a federal/provincial agreement (May 24, 1968) to improve the protection from the spring freshet on the Fraser. Subsequently, this was expanded to provide a comprehensive flood control program for the area. In 1976, a further $60 million was made available by each level of government and the program was extended until March 31, 1984 and has since been renewed (Andrews, 1993).

Over the past 30 years, this program has established a complex system of dykes to protect the majority of the Fraser Valley floodplain. In some places it has provided pumping capacity and main drains to prevent local runoff from causing flooding behind the dykes. This system is designed to protect against the highest floods of record caused by spring snowmelt runoff. It successfully handled the very high 1972 freshet, while sea dykes endured the record high sea levels of 1982 (Andrews, 1993).

In total, there are 140 dyking systems in BC. Most are owned and operated by 90 local authorities, dyking districts, and municipalities, but there are also 20 provincial systems. On the Lower Mainland alone there are 600 km of dyking, 400 floodboxes, and 100 pumpstations, while in the province as a whole, dyke length totals over 1,000 km and protects 120,000 hectares of floodplain (*http://www.elp.gov.bc.ca/rib/wat/fpm/flood/brochur2.html#2*). In addition, flood control on the Fraser is assisted by the Nechako River diversion and by reservoirs for hydroelectric developments on the Bridge and Stave rivers (Andrews, 1993).

There are approximately 3,000 dams operating in the province, some 400 of which would probably cause life loss should they fail. These dams range from small, privately-owned irrigation dams to BC Hydro's 242 m high Mica Dam. To prevent further flooding resulting from dam failure, the Provincial Dam Safety Program was instituted by the Comptroller of

Water Rights in 1967. As part of this program, dams are inspected by safety officers, who are responsible for ensuring that they do not pose an unacceptable risk to life, property, and/or the environment (*http://www.env.gov.bc.ca/wat/dams/brochur1.html#1*).

Although dykes, reservoirs, pumping stations, diversions, and other structural methods may reduce flood frequency and magnitude, it is widely agreed that flood management also requires a non-structural approach. This agreement was the impetus for the previously described Floodplain Mapping Program. Indeed, the provincial Water Management Branch began administering a Floodplain Development Control Program as early as 1974. This was implemented as part of the federal government's national flood damage reduction effort. The BC program seeks to identify high risk areas and make recommendations on floodplain management, as well as to review subdivision applications, community plans and bylaws to see if they increase the risk of flood damage.

As discussed earlier, in December 1987 the Canada/BC Agreement Respecting Floodplain Mapping combined federal and provincial efforts in this area. Both governments agreed that flood damages had to be reduced by carefully considering all practicable structural and non-structural alternatives. Effectiveness, costs, associated benefits, and environmental impacts were to be considered. The Agreement intends that preference be given to measures that prevent vulnerable development in flood risk areas (Andrews, 1993). This is why such areas must be mapped and designated. Throughout Canada, the federal Flood Damage Reduction Program, of which such floodplain mapping agreements are a part, requires that local authorities be encouraged to zone according to flood risk in designated areas. In addition, local levels of government are prompted to incorporate flood hazard information into municipal planning through their official plans, zoning bylaws, subdivision plans, and flood and fill regulations (Andrews, 1993).

Despite all federal and provincial efforts to reduce flood damage, losses continue to mount. Consequently, both governments have begun to demonstrate a new willingness to widen the types of incentives available to those involved in the flood safety delivery system. Indeed, the recent agreement by federal and provincial governments that the best way to prevent flood damage is often to stop development in high-risk areas represents a major change in philosophy. It is also becoming increasingly likely that the payment of relief to victims will be tied to more stringent conditions, often precluding reconstruction on high risk sites.

Avalanche Safety Network

In BC, westerly flowing mild, humid air creates a snow pack that can adhere to extremely steep slopes, up to 60 degrees. This climatic phenomenon is particularly prominent in the coastal ranges and the Selkirk Mountain Range, and creates the potential for very large, destructive avalanches, rarely found in mountain ranges where the climate is colder and drier (Pearce and Hightower, 1993).

As a consequence, with the exception of infectious pathogens, avalanches have caused more deaths in the province than any other natural hazard (Freer, 1980). Between 1950 and 1979, for example, 267 such fatalities occurred, and snow avalanches continue to pose risks to the province's infrastructure, transportation system, and recreationists. The worst avalanche recorded to date took place on March 4, 1910, when a work train was derailed and buried in Roger's Pass, resulting in 66 deaths. In 1915 the Britannia Mine was struck, killing some 30 men. Similarly, in 1965, the Granduc Mine, north of Stewart, was hit by an avalanche that killed 26 miners. In the same year, an avalanche also destroyed housing in Ocean Falls; seven lives were lost. However, only after the North Route Café near Terrace was destroyed on January 22, 1974, killing a further seven people, did BC take the first steps in setting up a comprehensive safety delivery system for this hazard. This involved establishing a Department of Highways Avalanche Task Force. One of its major achievements was the development of an ***avalanche hazard index***. This was designed to indicate the probability of a vehicle being caught in a snow slide and was based in part on traffic volume, as well as the magnitude and frequency of avalanches to which a particular stretch of road is subjected (BC Department of Highways, 1974). Such an index was necessary since, during a typical 1970s winter, 3 vehicles were completely buried, 13 partially buried, and 18 trapped by avalanches on BC's road system (Buchanan, 1983).

Snow avalanches continue to be a major problem in parks and other mountainous recreational areas in BC. Skiers, particularly those who fly into remote areas by helicopter, and snowboarders who go outside boundaries, snowmobilers, hikers, and climbers are frequently killed. To illustrate, between February 1978 and April 1984, there were 28 damaging avalanches in BC that were responsible for a total of 35 fatalities and 56 injuries, the majority of whom were recreationists (Shaerer, 1987). Such losses continue to mount. On January 2, 1988, for example, nine fatalities occurred in three separate recreation-related accidents.

It has been recognized for many years that the optimal way to prevent avalanche damage to infrastructure is to restrict building in high risk zones. As early as 1906, the *Land Registry Act* included particular clauses that were eventually used to reduce risk in new subdivisions—including risk from avalanches. This Act stated that, in the case of land that was outside a municipality, the approving officer could examine the site and conduct studies to determine whether the proposed development was "against the public interest." If this was discovered to be the case, permission to subdivide could be refused. In 1979, the *Land Titles Act* was amended, giving the approving officer a clearer mandate to refuse development "if he considers that the land is subject, or reasonably expected to be subject, to flooding, erosion, landslip, or avalanche . . ." (Buchanan, 1983).

Naturally, since such legislation exists, the province is obliged to determine and manage avalanche risk. For example, any subdivision or ski area development proposal for a region that might be susceptible to snow avalanches is generally referred, by the approving officer, to the Snow Avalanche Section of the Ministry of Transportation and Highways. This Section evaluates the site and makes recommendations based on the degree of risk involved. Other related programs are also administered by the Section. All of the highways in BC have been risk mapped for avalanches and avalanche hazard atlases have been produced to identify high risk sites along all major highways. Highway managers can utilize these maps to reduce losses in their jurisdictions. The Section is heavily involved in increasing awareness regarding the snow avalanche threat and has developed an avalanche management program for the province's road system and organized seminars for approving officers, land use planners, and forest management personnel. The Section has constructed numerous weather stations to monitor snow conditions and it supplies rescue equipment and volunteers in emergencies.

There is also some federal government involvement in avalanche management in BC. Parks Canada (1998), for example, administers risk management programs within the national parks; however, the provincial Snow Avalanche Section is responsible for the extremely high hazard Rogers Pass section of the Trans-Canada Highway. Numerous research projects have been carried out in this area by members of the National Research Council of Canada, Division of Building Research, often in cooperation with the provincial government (Shaerer, 1972). In very high risk areas such as Rogers Pass, active hazard reduction takes place. Extensive avalanche defences have been built to modify the magnitude and intensity of the impact of snow on the Trans-Canada Highway. In addition, artillery and explosives have been used to increase the frequency and hence decrease the severity, of avalanches.

Efforts to protect BC's infrastructure and major highways and rail systems from avalanches do not necessarily provide safety in all mountainous areas. Freedom is an important Canadian value, so emphasis is placed on user education and issuing warnings, rather than prohibition. Several private and public organizations try to minimize avalanche-related losses among skiers, climbers, hikers, and snowmobilers. They include the US National Operational Hydrologic Remote Sensing Center, which provides snow cover maps of the province on the Internet (*http://www.nohrsc.nws.gov/canada/bc/q1r_new.gif*), and the BC Ministry of Environment, Lands and Parks, which, as previously described, monitors the provinces snowpack throughout the snow season.

Several organizations use this and other snow- and weather-related data, and disseminate avalanche bulletins by telephone, fax, mail, or the Internet. These include the Canadian Avalanche Association (*http://www.avalanche.ca*), which provides an Avalanche Information Bulletin containing up-to-date information on weather, snowpack, and avalanche risks in the South Coast Mountains, the North Columbia Mountains, the South Columbia Mountains, and the Rocky Mountains. Parks Canada also issues an Avalanche Report for its national parks in BC and Alberta, namely Kootenay, Yoho, and Banff (*http://www.discoveralberta.com/ParksCanada-Banff/AvalancheInfo*). The web site of the Northwest Weather and Avalanche Center (*http://www.nwac.noaa.gov*), which is administered by the US Department of Agriculture - Forest Service, also carries information on BC's current avalanche potential, as does that of the Cyber Space Avalanche Center (*http://www.csac.org/Bulletins/*).

A 5-step avalanche rating scale is used in BC: 1 is relatively harmless; 2 could kill a person; 3 destroys a car; 4 destroys a railway car; 5 destroys a forest of 40 hectares. Avalanche danger descriptions are: low (unlikely); moderate (possible); considerable (probable); high (likely); and extreme (certain).

When education and warnings fail, various search and rescue facilities may be needed. The federal contribution to this effort is coordinated by the National Search and Rescue Secretariat (NSS) (*http://www.nss.gc.ca*). Within non-federal jurisdictions the PEP plays a lead role. Some recreationists carry a personal locator beacon, such as the F1-ND Avalanche Beacon, which, in an emergency, transmits to the COSPAS-SARSAT satellite system. The NSS coordinates the Canadian contribution to this monitoring system and is responsible for Canada's registry of personal locator beacons. In worst case scenarios, the Cyber Space Avalanche Center maintains an up-to-date global data bank containing statistics and reports on avalanche fatalities and serious injuries.[2]

In BC, it is fortunate that there is relatively little development in high risk avalanche zones. As the growth of the population continues and winter sports increase in popularity, this situation may change. It is necessary, therefore, for all avalanche tracks to be identified and their history determined so that this information can be incorporated into land use planning. The whole area of personal risk-taking during recreation, especially the benefits and costs of helicopter skiing, also require more research.

Seismic Safety Network

The Pacific coast is Canada's most seismically active region. Each year, seismologists working for the Geological Survey of Canada, at its Sidney, Vancouver Island office, record more than 1,000 earthquakes. The majority of these have epicentres associated with active faults that lie in the Pacific. Indeed, in the past 70 years, more than 100 earthquakes of magnitude 5 or greater have been recorded in the offshore region. Had any of these occurred on land, they could have caused damage (*http://www.pgc.nrcan.gc.ca/seismo/eqinfo/eq-westcan.htm*). The earth's surface is constantly changing because it consists of plates that move relative to one another, at speeds of about 2 to 10 cm per year. Such plates can slide past, diverge, or collide, and the west coast of Canada is one of the few regions on the planet where all three types of movement are taking place. The result of such movements is significant earthquake activity. This can occur along the offshore faults, in association with the subducting ocean plate, or within the continental crust.[3] Moving inland from the coast and its active plate boundaries, however, earthquake frequency and magnitude decreases with very little significant seismic activity taking place in Saskatchewan (*http://www.pgc.nrcan.gc.ca/seismo/eqhaz/canq.htm*). Of particular interest in BC is the Cascadia subduction zone, which extends from the west of the northern tip of Vancouver Island to northern California. Here the oceanic Juan de Fuca plate is moving about 2 to 5 cm per year toward North America and sliding beneath it. Evidence from crustal deformation measurements suggests that this movement is not smooth and that the two plates are currently locked, building up strain in the earth's crust. This squeezing is responsible for the approximately 300 small earthquakes experienced each year in southwestern BC, and the rarer damaging crustal earthquakes, such as the magnitude 7.3 earthquake on Vancouver Island in 1946. These earthquakes, however, are not sufficient to release all the strain, and every few centuries giant, megathrust earthquakes occur (magnitude >8) on the Cascadia subduction zone.[4] While such megathrust earthquakes have not yet been observed in the short written history of western Canada, there is excellent evidence from First Nations' oral history, buried soils, *tsunami* deposits, and silt turbidities (landslide) layers on the ocean floor that they occur at approximately 500 year intervals. Indeed, Japanese *tsunami* records suggest that the last time a giant megathrust earthquake occurred on the Cascadia subduction zone was January 26, 1700 at about 9:00 p.m. (Hyndman et al., 1997). With the exception of a collision with a substantial asteroid or comet, giant megathrust earthquakes are the most significant of the natural hazards that threaten BC, and indeed Canada.

It will not take a magnitude 8 or 9 megathrust earthquake, however, to cause extensive damage to BC's infrastructure. A recent study by the Munich Reinsurance Company of Canada reviewed the economic and insurance implications of a magnitude 6.5 earthquake with an epicentre at 123°W, 49°N at a depth of 10 km below the Strait of Georgia. It would cause damage in southwestern BC totalling between $14 billion and $32 billion, only $6.7 billion to $12 billion of which would be insured. It could result in some 6,240 minor injuries, 832 serious injuries, and 207 fatalities. Neither the provincial or federal economies, nor the Canadian insurance industry could absorb losses of this scale without serious dislocation (Canadian National Committee for the International Decade for Natural Disaster Reduction, 1994).

The reality of the seismic threat in BC has given rise to a wide variety of activities associated with earthquake prediction, mitigation, and response. While, as yet, no specific earthquake warnings are issued by any level of government, the National Building Code included seismic zoning maps in its 1953, 1970, and 1985 editions. New maps are being prepared for release in the next edition of the Code, probably in the year 2000 or 2001. In the current building code, there are two seismic zoning maps for Canada, one showing maximum horizontal ground velocity and the other maximum horizontal ground acceleration. Both are probabilistic, giving the likelihood of a given horizontal acceleration or velocity being exceeded in a specific time period. The probability used in the National Building Code is 0.0021 per annum; that is, a 10% probability of an earthquake causing ground motion greater than the expected value during a 50 year time period. Contours delineate zones that are most likely to experience similar shaking intensities (*http://www.pgc.nrcan.gc.ca/seismo/eqhaz/seishaz.htm*). These two maps do not predict earthquakes, but they provide a guide to probable ground motion that can be expected in an area in a given time period and are used to ensure new buildings can withstand it.

In the 1970s, many scientists believed they were on the verge of a new era that would see the practical prediction of earthquakes. Indeed, the Japanese designated earthquake prediction as a national project in 1965 and since that time have spent about $1.4 billion in attempting to develop an accurate predictive methodology (Kunii, 1997). However no warning was issued prior to the 1995 earthquake in Kobe (magnitude 7.2). Earthquake prediction to date has relied on observations of environmental changes that occur prior to ground movement. Such precursors are then used to forecast earthquakes, or are used in conjunction with predictive models. Possible earthquake precursors are thought to include ground tilt, changes in water table height, seismic wave activity, gas releases from water wells, and changes in the intervals between eruptions of periodic geysers (Carnegie Institution of Washington, *http://www.carnegieinstitution.org/news_960704.html*). No predictive models have proved accurate enough to warrant widespread application and, as a result, there are no such systems in BC.

While, as yet, there is no method for accurately predicting earthquakes, some warning systems are in operation. In 1995, many people in Mexico City had approximately a 20 second warning that an earthquake had occurred before they felt its impact. Automatic radio-controlled sirens in the city were triggered by earthquake sensors, located near the epicentre, some 300 km away. This system worked because these sensors transmitted their radio warning signals at the speed of light, far faster than the speed that earthquake waves travel. A similar type of warning system has been installed in Japan to stop automatically bullet trains. While no such system is operative in BC, a small, personal earthquake warning system, Quake Alert, is being distributed in the province. This is based on the principle that earthquakes generate both pressure or "P waves" (that travel about 8 km per second) and much more damaging shear or "S waves" (that travel at some 4.8 km per second). The Quake Alert sounds an alarm when significant "P waves" are detected. In the Loma Prieta earthquake, it took about 10 seconds for the earthquake's "P waves" to reach San Francisco, and some 20 seconds for its "S waves" to arrive. Under these circumstances, people would have had 10 seconds to get out of the way of objects that were likely to fall, or to hide underneath protective desks or other heavy furniture (*http://www.equakealert.com/*).

The warning aspect is very different for a *tsunami*, a series of ocean waves generated by rapid displacement of large volumes of water by coastal slumps or landslides, meteor impact, volcanic eruptions, or thrust-type submarine earth movement. Although occurring in other oceans, *tsunamis* have been recorded most often within the Pacific basin where, between 1900 and 1970, 138 were reported, 34 of which were locally destructive, while 9 also caused damage at great distances from their sources. The effects of such waves in coastal areas can be very destructive. In 1964, for example, 122 people died and 200 were injured by seismic sea waves generated as the result of earth movements centred in Prince William Sound, Alaska (Hansen and Eckel, 1966). This was the largest of the 10 seismic sea wave trains recorded on the west coast of BC during the 65 years of operation of the Tofino tide gauge. Therefore, it is not surprising that it caused widespread damage to many Vancouver Island coastal settlements. The greatest impact occurred at Port Alberni, where the first wave arrived without any official warning. Including damage to the MacMillan Bloedel and Powell River Company plants in Port Alberni, estimates of the total losses reached as high as $10 million. Houses were displaced up to 300 m and logs moving at speeds in excess of 30 km per hour were driven into buildings. As a consequence, 58 properties were completely destroyed, and 320 dwellings suffered damage.

The proven risk of destruction by *tsunamis* along Canada's west coast and elsewhere in the Pacific Rim has led to development of a complex safety delivery system comprising organizations and individuals drawn from almost the entire Pacific Rim. They are involved because the *tsunami* warning network now operating in BC is an integral part of a larger international system covering the Pacific Ocean. The headquarters of the Pacific Tsunami Warning System is in Ewa Beach, Hawaii, and its data is supplied by at least 30 seismological and 50 tide stations, including the seismological station at the Pacific Geoscience Centre in Sidney and tide gauges at Bamfield, Winter Harbour, and Langara Island on Canada's west coast. When an earthquake registering about 6.5 or greater on the Richter scale is observed at a participating seismological station, this information is immediately relayed to Ewa Beach. There, the epicentre's location is determined by analysing data from several stations. If it is suspected that a *tsunami* may have been generated, tide stations in the area are requested to monitor their gauges for evidence of anomalous readings. If the existence of a *tsunami* is verified, warning bulletins are sent to all participating countries, including Canada. The arrival time at various Pacific coastal points is then estimated from travel time charts prepared for each tide station in the system. These travel times are considered accurate to within about 2.3 percent. Except when they are close to the epicentre, threatened areas can then be evacuated and mobile infrastructures and fittings removed. The time required for a Pacific-wide *tsunami* to reach BC's coast will vary from some 5½ to 18 hours, depending on its origin. Warnings may also be received from the Alaskan Tsunami Warning Center, located in Palmer, Alaska. The PEP is the designated dissemination agency for *tsunami* bulletins, issued by either the Pacific or Alaskan warning centres, and has the responsibility for deciding on appropriate action in respect to BC's coasts, including the need for evacuation (Provincial Emergency Program, 2001, *http://www.pep.bc.ca/hazard_plans/ tsunami2001/Tsunami_Warning_and_Alerting_ Plan-2001.pdf*).

Much earthquake- and *tsunami*-related damage can be avoided by determining local variations in risk and ensuring that planning prevents development where the risk is high. Wuorinen undertook an early effort to produce an earthquake microzonation for Victoria in the early 1970s (Wuorinen, 1974). Subsequently, this microzonation was used to set insurance rates and improve the accuracy of the City of Victoria's disaster plan. This map sought to develop a three-dimensional view of Victoria by identifying bedrock outcrops and the nature of sediments exposed in engineering trenches and boreholes. It was postulated that ground motion, and hence damage, would be greatest on fill (artificial ground) and least where the bedrock was at, or close to, the surface. Wuorinen (1979) subsequently produced a similar microzonation for the Saanich Peninsula. A comparable map was prepared for Greater Vancouver in 1979 by the Ministry of Environment. It identifies three simplified geological zones that are incorporated into the National Building Code of Canada for use in the design of large buildings. These zones consist of:

- compact or stiff soils less than 15 m thick and bedrock;
- compact or stiff soils more than 15 m thick and loose or soft soils 15 m thick; and
- loose or soft soils more than 15 m thick.

It is believed that the first of these zones has the lowest seismic risks and the third has the highest. This map is still available on the BC Ministry of Energy and Mines web site (*http:// www.em.gov.bc.ca/Mining/Geolsurv/Surficial/ quake/eq6.htm*).

The BC Geological Survey is undertaking urban seismic microzonations (Monahan and Levson, 1997). These have been completed for Chilliwack and Coquitlam and are underway for Greater Victoria. In the Greater Victoria region, for example, 15 seismic cone penetration tests and 4 spectral analyses of surface wave tests have been conducted in an effort to help predict soil and sediment susceptibility to amplification. In addition, a three-dimensional view of the stratigraphy of the region was obtained by consulting 5,000 geotechnical borehole logs, several hundred water well records, and nearly 3,000 engineering drawings for municipal water and sewer lines. Three hazard maps resulted from this research: a combined amplification and liquefaction hazard map, a slope instability map, and a composite hazard map. The latter combines all three hazards and reflects the greatest of these, identifying high-risk areas for regional planning purposes. It displays 10 degrees of risk, ranging from very low to very high (Monahan, Levson, McQuarrie, and Bean, 1998).

In addition, the Geological Survey of Canada will provide seismic hazard calculations for building sites in Canada (*http://www.pgc. nrcan.gc.ca/seismo/eqhaz/seishaz.htm*). The peak horizontal ground acceleration and velocity are given for exceedance probabilities of 5, 10, 22, and 40% over 50 years. All that is required is the latitude and longitude of the site, name of the construction project, and a nominal fee.

Progress is also being made toward predicting the coastal areas most likely to be inundated by major *tsunamis*. Whitmore (1993), for example, has modelled expected *tsunami* amplitudes and currents along the North American coast for Cascadia subdirection zone earthquakes and a detailed *tsunami* zoning map has been prepared for Alberni.

Beyond their value in ensuring that new buildings, as far as possible, avoid high risk locations, seismic and *tsunami* microzonations are useful in predicting the scale of future earthquake associated disasters. The author and a colleague (Foster and Carey, 1976) produced what appears to have been the world's first simulation of the impact of a series of earthquakes on an urban centre. This research project focused on Victoria and involved the stages now commonly found in predictive models. The first step required the production of a seismic microzonation map (Wuorinen, 1974). This was followed by the identification of the buildings in Victoria and their assignment to 24 classes, ranging from one- to three-storey wood-framed residential to steel frame bridges. Once this was achieved, the world's seismic literature was searched to identify how each type of building had reacted to ground motions of differing Modified Mercalli Intensity during actual earthquakes. This data permitted the development of a matrix linking building type to expected damage. All of this information was computerized, allowing production of a series of maps that identified the patterns of expected damage from earthquakes of different magnitudes. The use of a matrix relating deaths and injury to the degree of building damage subsequently allowed Foster (1980) to predict the human casualties likely to be associated with such earthquakes. This type of simulation is now quite common; of particular interest are those for Los Angeles, San Francisco Bay, and Tokyo, produced by Risk Management Solutions, Inc. (1995a,b,c).

Emergency Preparedness Canada (EPC), along with a consortium of companies led by Nobility Inc. of Vancouver, is developing the *Natural Hazards Electronic Map and Assessment Tools Information System* (NHEMATIS) (*http://www.nobility.com/apps/index.htm*). NHEMATIS produces simulations of damage that may be created by specific hazards in various regions of Canada. It is able to simulate earthquake destruction, for example, in the Greater Vancouver region. The validity of Keenan's (1994) plea for a more effective seismic retrofit policy in BC are confirmed by these simulations.

The two major provincial statutes authorizing implementation of emergency management programs in BC are the *Emergency Program Act* (1993) and the *Emergency Program Management Regulation* (1994). The former assigns roles and responsibilities to the PEP, provincial government ministries, and local governments. For example, it requires local governments to develop plans to prepare for, respond to, and recover from earthquakes and other disasters. In addition, provincial ministries and government corporations are required to plan emergency and business continuation strategies. PEP's main roles are to aid in preparation of the plans and coordinate or assist in coordinating the provincial government's response to a major disaster, such as a damaging earthquake (BC Office of the Auditor General, 1997). As a result of these Acts and earlier provincial legislation, disaster plans have been prepared at various levels of government throughout BC. To illustrate, PEP issued a *British Columbia Earthquake Response Plan*, in interim form, in 1992. This provides a general overview of the implications of earthquakes of varying magnitudes. It also describes the responsibilities, organization, and nature of operations necessary for earthquake emergency response and identifies and assigns critical emergency functions to the ministry with the greatest resources, capability, and expertise in that area. Each supporting ministry, for example Human Resources, Health, Attorney General, Transport and Highways, is responsible for the detailed planning that is needed to maintain and manage that function.

The plan recognizes that three levels of government—local, provincial, and federal—may be involved in responding to earthquakes. As with other disasters, local governments are assigned the role of first responder. If their resources are insufficient to deal adequately with the situation, the Provincial Emergency Coordination Centre would be activated in Victoria by PEP. In order to coordinate the province's involvement, one or more Provincial Field Response Centres would be set up to give assistance in local areas. All ministries and agencies involved in the response effort would have centre representation. If provincial emergency resources were exhausted by a major earthquake, the federal government would be requested, by the province, to assist.

The *Emergency Program Act* of BC is complemented by two pieces of federal legislation, namely the *Emergencies Act* and the *Emergency Preparedness Act*. The latter established EPC, and also authorized the federal government to enter into agreements with provinces regarding emergency planning and response. In 1988, the *Canada-British Columbia Memorandum of Understanding of Emergency Preparedness* was signed, and it is this agreement that would oblige the federal government to assist the province if a major earthquake caused extensive damage. When a catastrophic earthquake is considered to have taken place, the national Earthquake Support Plan allows EPC to mobilize recovery personnel and their equipment, pending a request from BC for federal aid (BC Office of the Auditor General, 1997).

During the 1990s, a series of disaster exercises were conducted to assess and improve the effectiveness of this approach to earthquake preparedness. These included ORACLE, an evaluation of the Ministry of Health and Ministry Responsible for Seniors' internal response plan; CANATEX 2; and Thunderbird 1 and 2.

CANATEX 2 was a 12 day exercise held from May 2 to 13, 1994 involving the federal government and the BC and Alberta provincial governments. It required response to a magnitude 8.5 earthquake caused by a 400 to 600 km rupture of the Cascadia subduction zone, some 15 km off the coasts of BC, Washington, and Oregon. It was planned to test the BC Earthquake Response Plan (interim), together with both the National Earthquake Support Plan and the Alberta Support Plan. Most provincial ministries, crown corporations, and utilities took part, as did 14 Lower Mainland municipalities, the Vancouver Port Corporation, and the Vancouver International Airport Authority. The federal involvement included 21 departments and agencies. Other organizations such as the Red Cross and Salvation Army also participated.

The government of BC has also conducted two internal earthquake response exercises. Thunderbird 1 was held in November 1993, had a duration of 3 days, and simulated damage from a magnitude 7.3 earthquake with an epicentre 90 km north of Vancouver. Thunderbird 2 took place in November 1996 and tested the ability of the Provincial Field Response Centre and ministry, agency, and municipal emergency operations centres to respond to an earthquake seriously affecting Victoria (BC Office of the Auditor General, 1997).

Nevertheless, a recent performance audit conducted for the BC Office of the Auditor General concluded that "governments in British Columbia are not adequately prepared for a major earthquake." A variety of weaknesses were identified, including the need for development of more detailed simulations and scenarios; better coordinated retrofitting of the infrastructure; a new public communications strategy; clearer definition of the role of insurance; and improvements in provincial and local government disaster plans.

Conclusions

In *British Columbia: Its Resources and People*, this author wrote:

> It can be seen from this brief review of geological and geomorphological hazard management in British Columbia that safety delivery system improvements are possible. Losses are increasing and there is still the potential for major earthquake or flood generated disasters. Legislation has been ad hoc, often crisis stimulated, and has tended to deal with hazards in a fragmented manner. Perhaps new comprehensive legislation is needed. This might seek to address all major hazards, promote total risk mapping and provide for greater integration of existing safety delivery systems. Insurance might also be used to ensure that those taking the highest risks do not continue to do so at public expense (Foster, 1987).

Some of these comments are still valid, and others are not. Certainly, in the decade or so since these observations were first made, disaster planning has improved greatly in BC. This has been partly due to the passage of new, comprehensive provincial legislation, such as the *Emergency Program Act* (1993) and the *Emergency Program Management Regulation* (1994). The PEP has also been active in development of province-wide disaster response strategies, such as the *BC Earthquake Response Plan* (1999) (*http://www.pep.bc.ca/hazard_plans/eqplan99/eqplan99.html*). Furthermore, the Inter-Agency Emergency Preparedness Council has clarified ministry responsibilities in the event of a disaster (*http://www.pep.bc.ca/iepc/mandate.html*). Both industry and universities are also more involved with emergency and disaster management. Examples of the latter trend include the on-line Emergency Preparedness Information Exchange (EPIX) (*http://hoshi.cic.sfu.ca/epix*) operated by the Centre for Policy Research on Science and Technology at Simon Fraser University, the Disaster Recovery Information Exchange (DRIE) (*http://www.drie.org*), and EPC's Safe Guard Program (*http://safeguard.ca/english/index.html*).

While the disaster planning situation in the province is improving in some ways, in others it is not. Growing population pressures are encouraging the spread of new construction on higher risk sites. This must be prevented by greater vigilance at the local government level. In addition, there is a trend toward more high-risk recreational activities in mountain and coastal areas. It is still also very unlikely that Canada's insurance industry would be able to meet its obligations in the event of a high magnitude earthquake affecting southwestern BC. The disaster preparedness situation in the province, therefore, while better, is still far from ideal.

REFERENCES

Andrews, J. (1993). *Flooding: Canada water book*. Ottawa: Ecosystem Science and Evaluation Directorate, Economics and Conservation Branch.

BC Department of Highways (1974). *Avalanche task force: Report on findings and recommendations*. Victoria, BC: Department of Highways.

BC Office of the Auditor General (1997). 1997/98 Report 1: Earthquake preparedness. Victoria, BC: Office of the Auditor General.

Buchanan, R.G. (1983). *An assessment of natural hazards management in British Columbia*. Victoria: University of Victoria, Department of Geography, unpublished M.A. thesis.

Canada-British Columbia, Fraser River Joint Advisory Board (1976). *Fraser River upstream storage review report*. Victoria: Queen's Printer.

Canadian National Committee for the International Decade for Natural Disaster Reduction (1994). *Canadian National Report*. Prepared for the IDNDR mid-term review and the 1994 World Conference on Natural Disaster Reduction, Yokohama, Japan, 23-27 May, 1994.

Clague, J.J. (1987). Catastrophic outburst floods. *Geoscience Canada*, 16(2), 18-21.

Flint, R.F. (1957). *Glacial and pleistocene geology*. New York: John Wiley.

Foster, H.D. (1980). *Disaster planning: The preservation of life and property*. New York: Springer Verlag.

Foster, H.D. (1981). Reducing disaster losses: The management of environmental hazards. In B. Mitchell and W.R.D. Sewell (Eds.), *Canadian resource policies: Problems and prospects* (pp. 209-232). Toronto: Methuen.

Foster, H.D. (1987). Landforms and natural hazards. In C.N. Forward (Ed.), *British Columbia: Its resources and people* (pp. 43-63). Victoria, BC: University of Victoria, Department of Geography, Western Geographical Series, Vol. 22.

Foster, H.D., and Carey, R.F. (1976). The simulation of earthquake damage. In H.D. Foster (Ed.), *Victoria: Physical environment and development* (pp. 221-240). Victoria, BC: University of Victoria, Department of Geography, Western Geographical Series, Vol. 12.

Freer, G.L. (1980). Investigating snow avalanches. In Ministry of Transportation and Highways, *Geological hazard evaluation for highway personnel* (pp. 59-66). Victoria, BC: Queen's Printer.

Hansen, W.R., and Eckel, E.B. (1966). The Alaska earthquake, March 27, 1964: Field investigations and reconstruction effort. In R.W. Tank (Ed.), *Focus on environmental geology* (pp. 46-65). London: Oxford University Press.

Holland, S.S. (1964). *Landforms of British Columbia: A physiographic outline*. Victoria, BC: Department of Mines and Petroleum Resources, Bulletin No. 48.

Hyndman, R.D., Rogers, G.C., Dragert, H., Wang, K., Oleskevich, D., Henton, J., Clague, J.J., Adams, J., Bobrowsky, P.T. (1997). *Seismology: Giant megathrust earthquakes.* Ottawa: Natural Resources Canada, Geological Survey of Canada. http://www.pgc.nrcan.gc.ca/seismo/hist/mega1.htm.

Keenan, K.M. (1994). Establishing a seismic retrofit policy: Implications for buildings with historical significance in the Lower Mainland of British Columbia. Unpublished MA Thesis, School of Community and Regional Planning, UBC.

Kunii, I.M. (1997). It just isn't working. *Time Asia*, 150 (11), Sept. 15, 1997. http://www.pathfinder.com/time/magazine/1997/int/970915/earthquake.html.

Monahan, P.A., and Levson, V.M. (1997). Earthquake hazard assessment in Greater Victoria, British Columbia: Development of a shear-wave velocity model for the quaternary sediments. In D.V. Lefebure, W.J. McMillan, and J.G. McArthur (Eds.), *Geological fieldwork 1996* (pp. 467-479). British Columbia Geological Survey, Paper 1997-1.

Monahan, P.A., Levson, V.M., McQuarrie, E.J., and Bean, S.M. (1998). Seismic microzonation mapping in Greater Victoria, British Columbia, Canada. Paper submitted to the ASCE Geotechnical Earthquake Engineering and Soil Mechanics Conference, Seattle, Washington, August 3-6, 1998.

Pearce, L., and Hightower, H. (1993). *British Columbia hazard, risk and vulnerability analysis.* Vol. 1. Vancouver: Disaster Preparedness Resources Centre, University of British Columbia.

Press, F., and Siever, R. (1982). *Earth.* San Francisco: W.H. Freeman, pp. 441-463.

Provincial Emergency Program (2001). *British Columbia's tsunami warning and alerting plan.* Victoria, BC: Ministry of Attorney General.

Risk Management Solutions Inc. (1995a). *What if the 1906 earthquake strikes again? A San Francisco Bay scenario.* Menlo Park: Risk Management Solutions Inc.

Risk Management Solutions Inc. (1995b). *What if a major earthquake strikes the Los Angeles area?* Menlo Park: Risk Management Solutions Inc.

Risk Management Solutions Inc. (1995c). *What if the 1923 earthquake strikes again? A five-prefecture Tokyo region scenario.* Menlo Park: Risk Management Solutions Inc.

Scanlon, J., Conlin, D., Duffy, A., Osborne, G., and Whitten, J. (1985). *The Pemberton Valley floods: BC's tiniest village responds to a major disaster.* Ottawa: Emergency Communications Research Unit, Carleton University.

Shaerer, P.A. (1972). Terrain and vegetation of snow avalanche sites at Rogers Pass, British Columbia. In O. Slaymaker and H.J. McPherson (Eds.), *Mountain geomorphology* (pp. 215-222). Vancouver: Tantalus.

Shaerer, P.A. (1987). *Avalanche accidents in Canada: A selection of case histories 1978-1984.* Ottawa: National Research Council of Canada.

Ward, P.R.B., and Skermer, N.A. (1992). *The 50-year flood in Fitzsimmons Creek, Whistler, British Columbia.* Geotechnique and Natural Hazards. Vancouver: BiTech Publishers.

Whitmore, P.M. (1993). Expected *tsunami* amplitudes and currents along the North American coast for Cascadia Subduction Zone earthquakes. *Natural Hazards*, 8(1), 59-73.

Wuorinen, V. (1974). A preliminary seismic microzonation of Victoria, BC. Unpublished MA Thesis.

Wuorinen, V. (1979). A methodology for mapping total risk in urban areas. Unpublished PhD Thesis, Department of Geography, University of Victoria.

Yorath, C.J. (1990). *Where terranes collide.* Victoria: Orca Books.

ENDNOTES

[1] The total area of BC is: land - 929,730 km^2; water - 18,070 km^2; for a total of 947,800 km^2. This is 9.5% of the Canadian total of 9,970,610 km^2.

[2] Avalanche training courses are now part of ski resort operations in BC. However, many accidents occur because skiers and boarders cross safety barriers into danger zones, looking for the "perfect run."

[3] BC's complex typography and seismic activity derive from its location at the boundaries of major crustal/tectonic plates. Fragments (terranes) of different plates may be pushed up against other plates (accreted).

[4] The most recent noticeable earthquake (6.8) in southern BC had an epicentre near Olympia in Washington State. It occurred relatively deep in the crust, so its effects were less significant than would have been the case had it been closer to the surface.

Climate

Stanton Tuller

Department of Geography, University of Victoria

INTRODUCTION

All of climate is energy in one form or another. The controls of the amounts and types of energy found in an area include land and sea distribution, other variations in local surface type, local relief, elevation, latitude, and the effects of advection. These controls combine to give BC a great deal of climate variation on both the regional and micro scales.

The purposes of this chapter are to describe and explain the regional variations in the present climate of BC as indicated by the 1961-1990 climatic normals, and to identify some of the important controls. BC's climate will be placed in the spatial context by drawing comparisons with the rest of Canada. Temporal variations will be mentioned to illustrate that atmospheric conditions are not static, but change over a range of time scales. Emphasis will be on the lowland, valley bottom areas that contain most of the population and recent climate data.[1]

Other summaries of the climate of BC as a whole can be found in Chapman (1952), Kerr (1952), Kendrew and Kerr (1955), Schaefer (1978), Chilton (1981), and McGillivray (2000).

VARIATION AND CHANGE OVER TIME

Atmospheric conditions are not static over time but vary over a wide range of time scales. BC covers a large area, hence the magnitude and timing of climatic change and variation may not be uniform over the entire province (e.g., Clague, 1981; Mathewes, 1985; Ryder and Thomson, 1986; Hebda, 1995). The following summary highlights some of the general patterns. While past climates and the times indicated may be different for a specific area, it serves to provide a context for understanding contemporary climates.

The maximum extent of ice during the last stage of Wisconsin glaciation was reached about 15,000 years before the present (BP) (Clague, 1981). Ice covered virtually all of BC and reached into northern Washington and the southern margins of the Puget Sound lowland. Relatively cool conditions prevailed over the next 4,000 to 5,000 years as deglaciation progressed. Clague (1981) suggests moist conditions, whereas Mathewes (1985) indicates the possibility of a dry era before 12,000 BP and a moist one from about 12,000 - 10,500 BP.

By about 10,000 BP the climate of BC was warm and dry, compared with both the last 10,000 years as a whole and modern conditions. Eventually, a decrease in temperature and increase in precipitation led to conditions similar to the long-term averages of the "modern" era. Suggestions on the actual timing vary. For example, vegetation associations determined from pollen analysis indicate maximum temperatures and driest conditions in the 10,000 - 7,000 BP interval (Mathewes and Heusser, 1981; Hebda, 1995). Mathewes (1985) has cooling beginning about 7,000 BP with current conditions reached in the 4,500 - 3,000 BP interval over most of BC. Clague (1981) suggests temperatures were higher than modern values until about 6,600 BP in south-central BC and 5,200 BP in the mountains of the south coast. The northwest, however, had warm conditions until about 2,500 BP and lacked the dryness of the early part of the warm interval found in other parts of BC. There was a period of widespread alpine glacier advance about 3,500 - 2,000 BP (Clague, 1981; Ryder and Thomson, 1986). Other periods of glacier expansion occurred 5,800 - 4,900 BP and in the last 1,000 years (Ryder, 1978).

Climate was relatively warm in the southern Rockies about 1,000 years ago (Luckman, 1994). However, low summer temperatures became dominant in the period from the late 1100s to the mid-1300s (Luckman, Briffa, Jones, and Schweingruber, 1997). Ryder and Thomson (1986) indicate alpine glacier advances starting in the Coast Mountains before 1100. The period from the late 1700s through much of the 1800s was cold throughout the province. The beginning of the period varies, however. Glacial advances are indicated in the southern Rockies and on Vancouver Island during the early 1700s (Smith and Laroque, 1996; Luckman et al., 1997). The 1800s had some of the lowest temperatures in the recent history of the province. Many glaciers reached their maximum recent extent during this interval. Luckman and colleagues (1997) report relatively warm summers in the southern Rocky Mountains from the mid-1300s to mid-1400s and during the mid-1700s.

Instrumental data are available over the last century. The late 1800s through early 1920s and late 1940s through mid-1950s were relatively cool over most of BC (Powell, 1965a; Schaefer, 1976; Moore, 1991; Gullett and Skinner, 1992; Raphael, 1993; Luckman, 1998). The relatively low temperatures in the late 1940s and early 1950s were accompanied by lower than average total hours of bright sunshine (Powell, 1965b). The 1930s through early 1940s, and especially the 1980s to the present, are relatively warm periods. In fact, air temperatures in the 1990s are the warmest in the last several hundred years (Luckman et al., 1997).

Although there are cycles in the data, the general trend in air temperature has been upward over the last 100 years. Gullett and Skinner (1992) report overall trends of +0.4°C/100 years in their Pacific region (covering coastal BC), 0.5°C/100 years in their South BC Mountains region (includes the bulk of the central and southern Interior) and 0.8°C/90 years in their Yukon/North BC Mountains region. Most of the increase in the Pacific and South BC Mountains region has been in the daily minimum temperature. There was little to no trend in the daily maximum (Environment Canada, 1995). Luckman (1998) cites a change of +1.4°C/100 years in the central Rockies, with the greatest change occurring during the winter season.

The early part of the 20th century had higher than average precipitation, as did the late 1940s and 1950s. The late 1920s and early 1940s were relatively dry (Powell, 1965a; Tuller, 1990; Environment Canada, 1995; Luckman, 1998). Precipitation in the 1930s and from 1960 to the early 1990s shows little uniformity throughout the province, with some areas/stations showing comparatively high values and others low values. Tuller (1990) found the year-to-year variation in precipitation at Victoria and Agassiz has been greater since 1950 than it was before that year. Environment Canada (1995) also shows less persistence of dry and wet periods in recent years.

There are many possible controls of climatic variation over a range of time scales. A few of these include periodic earth orbit variations (Milankovitch cycles), changes in solar output, differences in atmospheric dust content and changes in radiatively active gases (e.g., carbon dioxide, methane, halons, nitrous oxide) (Lamb, 1972; Hartmann, 1994; Hengeveld, 1995). These all influence climate through their effect on ground surface and atmospheric radiation budgets.

The climate of an area is also affected by atmospheric circulation patterns related to the positions of high and low air pressure systems, location of storm tracks and advection of warm or cold air. Changes in circulation engendered by mountain building has been suggested as being a possible cause of long-term climate variations.

Much of the year-to-year and decadal variability of climate has also been associated with changes in atmospheric circulation. For example, winters with an intensified Aleutian low pressure centre that is located somewhat east of its mean position combined with an amplified high pressure ridge over western Canada creates a preponderance of southwesterly airflow over BC. This type of circulation, called "the positive Pacific North America (PNA) pattern" (Wallace and Gutzler, 1981), advects warm air over the province creating warmer than normal winters (Yarnal and Diaz, 1986; Shabbar and Khandekar, 1996) and below average snowpacks, particularly in the south (Moore and McKendry, 1996). It often accompanies the *El Niño* pattern of tropical Pacific sea surface temperature (Horel and Wallace, 1981; Yarnal and Diaz, 1986; Shabbar and Khandekar, 1996; Shabbar, Bonsal, and Khandekar, 1997). However, the characteristics of *El Niño* events and their connections with middle latitude circulation and weather vary from occurrence to occurrence (Trenberth, 1997) so that actual BC weather can also vary (Yarnal and Diaz, 1986).[2]

The pressure patterns with their vertical air movement combined with their influence on winter storm tracks can also affect precipitation. The positive PNA pattern can produce drier winters over BC, especially in the south (Shabbar, Bonsal, and Khandekar, 1997). However, the effect on precipitation is far from consistent and is sensitive to even small variations in the positions of the pressure systems and storm tracks.

Similar associations with middle latitude circulation have been found with another pattern that shows much longer persistence in its stages. This has been called the Pacific Decadal Oscillation by Mantua, Hare, Zhang, Wallace, and Francis (1997) and the North Pacific Oscillation by Gershunov and Barnett (1998). The recent positive phase of this oscillation extending from 1977 through to at least the early 1990s saw warmer than average winter temperatures in BC and somewhat lower than average winter precipitation, snowpacks, and streamflow at a number of stations (Moore and McKendry, 1996; Mantua et al., 1997).

Air pressures higher than normal over the northeastern Pacific accompanied by lower pressures over western Canada inhibit warm air advection, reducing air temperature. This negative PNA pattern is more frequent during *La Niña* years and the negative phase of the North Pacific Oscillation (which lasted from 1947 to 1976).

In summary, the 1961-1990 period dealt with in this chapter has been warm compared with the last 1,000 years, but not unusually warm compared with 10,000 to about 6,500 years ago.

SOLAR AND NET ALL-WAVE RADIATION

The initial source of energy for all other climatic elements is solar radiation. Spatial variation in solar radiation is the driving force that produces the observed patterns of many other climatic processes and elements.

The southern Interior of BC receives the most solar radiation throughout the year (for example, Summerland CDA, Figure 4.1). This part of the province combines the positive effects of low latitude, relatively high elevation, and low amounts of atmospheric water vapour (Table 4.1) and cloud cover (Department of Transport, 1968) compared with other regions. The southern Interior is followed by areas of the south coast whose location in the lee of mountains limits cloud cover (Nanaimo at Departure Bay and Vancouver at UBC). This region is also at relatively low latitude, but has a lower elevation and more water vapour to absorb incoming solar radiation than does the southern interior. Solar radiation is generally less in central and northern BC than it is in the south. Of the six stations presented here, Fort Nelson has the lowest total during winter when the latitudinal gradient of solar radiation is at its annual maximum. Stations on the outer coast (e.g., Sandspit) have lower solar radiation than stations in the central Interior (e.g., Prince George) in all seasons. Sandspit's total is even less than Fort Nelson's in summer when the latitudinal gradient is reduced and the effects of lower elevation and greater cloud cover become dominant.

The minimum mean monthly solar radiation occurs in December at all stations (Figure 4.1). This is the month of the winter solstice and of extensive cloud cover in all regions of the province. Northern stations receive their maximum solar radiation in the month of the summer solstice, June. The annual peak is delayed until July at southern stations, when less cloud offsets the effects of lower solar altitude, shorter days, and a more humid atmosphere.

BC generally receives less solar radiation than other regions of southern Canada in winter (Atmospheric Environment Service, 1982; 1987b). One factor is that BC is at higher

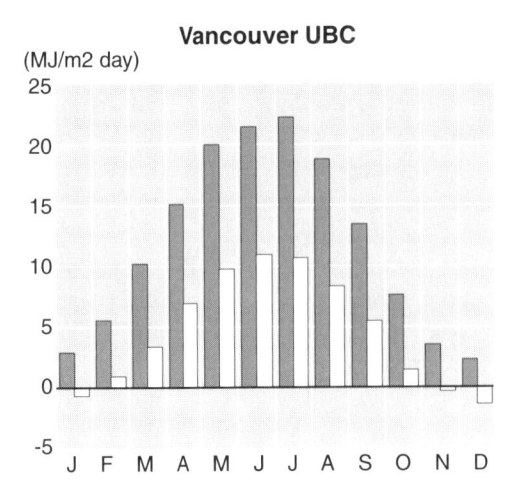

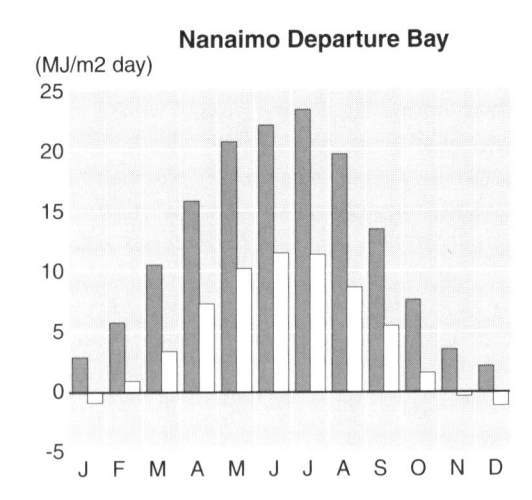

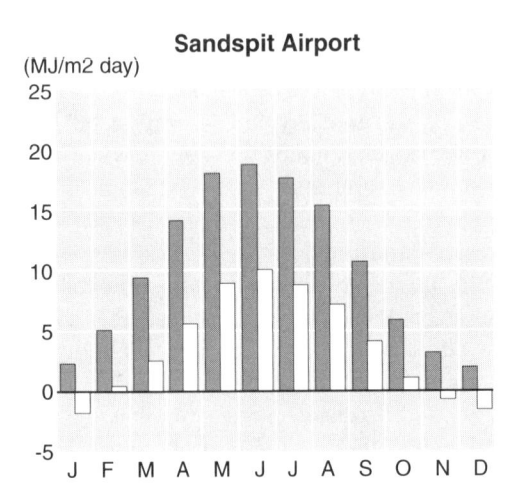

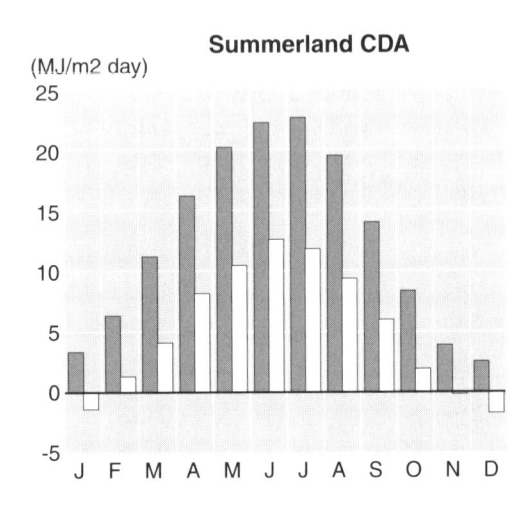

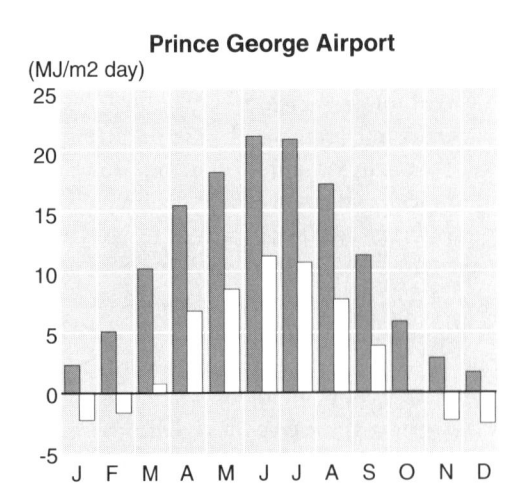

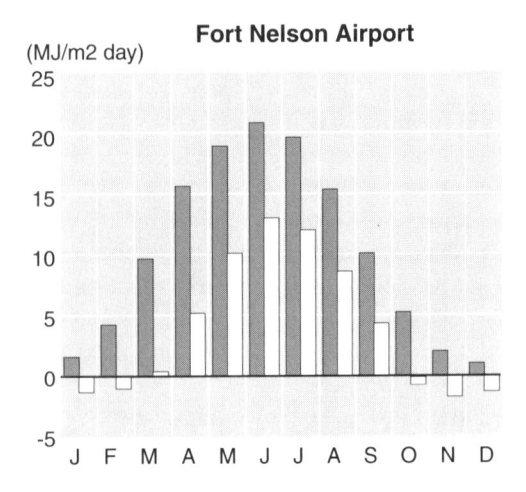

Figure 4.1 Mean monthly solar (black) and net all-wave (gray) radiation at selected stations

Climate

Table 4.1 Mean vapour pressure at selected stations (kPa)

Station	Elevation (m)	January	April	July	October
Coastal					
Sandspit Airport	5	0.68	0.76	1.28	1.00
Prince Rupert Airport	34	0.57	0.72	1.28	0.93
Victoria International Airport	20	0.70	0.83	1.31	1.02
Vancouver International Airport	3	0.67	0.86	1.44	1.06
Southern Interior					
Penticton Airport	344	0.42	0.63	1.19	0.76
Kamloops Airport	345	0.37	0.58	1.14	0.74
Cranbrook Airport	939	0.31	0.52	1.02	0.61
Northern Interior					
Smithers Airport	523	0.31	0.51	1.12	0.69
Prince George Airport	676	0.31	0.49	1.11	0.65
Fort St. John	695	0.21	0.44	1.16	0.56
Fort Nelson Airport	382	0.09	0.42	1.23	0.50

Source: Atmospheric Environment Service (1993).

latitude than southern Ontario, southern Quebec, and the Atlantic Provinces. Also, many BC stations, especially those on the coast, are at lower elevations and have more cloud cover than stations on the Prairies. During the summer, however, when the effects of latitude are reduced, southern BC stations receive more solar radiation than those in the Atlantic Provinces and Quebec, and slightly more than some southern Ontario stations.

Net all-wave radiation (net radiation) is the net amount of radiant energy (both solar and long-wave) available on the earth's surface. Values were calculated for the six stations used to show the patterns of solar radiation. Mean monthly surface albedos representative of the regions surrounding the stations presented by Hay (1979) were used for all stations except Prince George, where they were estimated by the author. Summer albedo ranged from .14 at Fort Nelson to .25 at Nanaimo, Sandspit, and Vancouver. January albedo ranged from .26 (Vancouver) to .55 (Fort Nelson).

A number of equations that estimate the amount of downward, clear sky, atmospheric long-wave radiation were tested against data from Canadian stations that measure global and reflected solar radiation and net all-wave radiation. The equation of Idso and Jackson (1969) was selected for use during months when the air temperature was below freezing and that of Satterlund (1979) was used for the rest of the year. Clear sky values were corrected for the effect of cloud cover using the method and cloud type coefficients attributed to Bolz (Geiger, 1966). Cloud cover data were taken from the Federal Department of Transport (1968) and cloud type distribution was taken as that expected at each station. Upward terrestrial (long-wave) radiation emitted by the earth's surface was computed using a ground surface radiant temperature that varied from 2°K above air temperature during midsummer to 2°K below air temperature in midwinter.

The mean monthly net all-wave radiation at all stations is negative during the November-January period that surrounds the winter solstice (Figure 4.1). It is also negative at Prince George and Fort Nelson in February when surface snow cover produces a high albedo. Fort

Nelson receives relatively low amounts of solar and downward atmospheric long-wave radiation and has a slightly negative net all-wave radiation in October. The variations in net solar and net long-wave radiation are about equal between stations and usually counter each other in winter. Therefore, the difference in net all-wave radiation between stations is small. In general, however, it is slightly higher at the two south coast stations (Vancouver and Nanaimo). Summer differences in net all-wave radiation are produced primarily by the differences in solar radiation. The absolute range among stations in net solar radiation is about 3.5 times that in net long-wave radiation. The stations with the highest summer net all-wave radiation are those with either a high solar radiation (e.g., Summerland CDA), or a low albedo (e.g., Fort Nelson).

AIR TEMPERATURE

Air temperature is controlled by vertical and horizontal energy transfers that affect the amount of sensible heat contained in a parcel of air. Vertical energy transfers which increase air temperature are absorbed solar and long-wave radiation and sensible heat flux density from the ground. Air advected from areas with other radiation and energy budget regimes is the horizontal transfer. The pattern of air temperature in BC can be viewed as a response to: latitude, which influences the radiation budget; elevation, which primarily controls the density of the air and its efficiency in absorbing solar and long-wave radiation; and the contrasting surface energy budgets of land and ocean surfaces.

The July mean daily maximum, the temperature representative of the daytime when people are most likely to be outdoors, is used to show the pattern of summer air temperature. The July mean daily maximum air temperature is highest in the interior valleys of south central BC (Figure 4.2; Atmospheric Environment Service, 1984; 1993). It decreases to the west (cool ocean influence), north (higher latitude), and east (higher elevation). The dominant controlling factor is the land-sea influence. During the summer the oceans have a lower surface temperature than do land surfaces, a result of abundant ground heat flux density and evaporation along with upwelling of cool subsurface water along the immediate coast. Mean July sea surface temperatures at stations on the outer coast range from about 11°C to 13°C (Institute of Ocean Sciences web site, *http://www.ios.bc.ca/ios/osap/data/lighthouse/bcsop.htm*). The resulting lower rate of heat transfer to the air through long-wave radiation and sensible heat flux density produces a lower air temperature. The lowest July daily maximum air temperatures, therefore, are found on the outer coast.

The difference in summer warmth between interior and coastal stations is somewhat overestimated by the July temperature. July is usually the warmest month at interior stations, but August is often warmer at stations on the outer coast. The longer delay in time of annual temperature peak is a result of greater heat storage in the ocean and is a common feature differentiating maritime and continental temperature regimes.

The range of summer temperatures found in BC is emphasized by comparison with the rest of Canada. July mean daily maximum air temperatures in lower elevation, southern Interior valleys are among the highest in Canada. Those on the outer coast, however, are among the lowest in southern Canada. Only coastal Labrador has stations with comparable values (Atmospheric Environment Service, 1984).

The ocean-land influence on air temperature is reversed in winter when the ocean surface is warmed by heat stored during summer or brought in by currents from warmer regions. The January mean sea surface temperature at stations on the outer coast ranges between about 6°C and 8°C (Institute of Ocean Sciences web site, *http://www.ios.bc.ca/ios/osap/data/lighthouse/bcsop.htm*), much higher than land surface temperatures at this time of year. The resulting heat transfer to the air gives outer coastal stations in the south the highest January mean daily air temperatures (Figure 4.3).

Air temperatures in the Interior are below freezing with the lowest values occurring in the north. Northern stations frequently come under the influence of cold Arctic air and receive much less solar radiation than stations in the south (Figure 4.1). The coastal mountain ranges limit the exchange of air between coastal and interior regions. Coastal stations are better exposed to relatively warm southwesterly air flows. The Coast Mountains limit the inland penetration of mild oceanic air at low levels and, at the same time, are a barrier against the movement of cold continental air to the coast. Continental air that does reach the coast must descend during its migration and would undergo some adiabatic warming. The variation in air temperature throughout the province is greater in winter than in summer (Figures 4.2 and 4.3).

Mean winter air temperatures on the coast are the highest in Canada. Interior stations in the far north are as cold as those found on the Prairies. Thus, BC during both winter and summer has temperature regimes that span the range found in the whole of southern Canada (Atmospheric Environment Service, 1984).

AIR PRESSURE

There is a direct relation between air temperature and the pressure of the air in the upper troposphere. Mean *upper air* pressure decreases from south to north over BC following the latitudinal temperature gradient.

Sea level air pressure is a product of air density and vertical movement. During winter, cold, dense continental air creates high sea level air pressure over the land (Atmospheric Environment Service, 1987a). Lower pressure is found over the ocean with its warmer, less dense air and uplift associated with cyclonic storms over the Pacific. The highest mean winter sea level air pressure in the province is found in the northeast and the Rocky Mountain Trench area. The lowest is found on the outer north coast (Atmospheric Environment Service, 1976; 1987a). The general air pressure gradient runs east to west.

The sea level air pressure gradient reverses in summer. The warmer land now has lower sea level air pressure than the ocean. The subtropical high pressure cell with its subsiding air moves northward and extends its influence along the BC coast (Neiburger, Johnson, and Chien, 1961). The highest mean sea level air pressure is found along the outer coast, and the lowest in the northeast and in the warmest valleys of the southern interior (Atmospheric Environment Service, 1976; 1987a). The northeast is well removed from the influence of the subtropical high pressure cell and far enough north to be located near the principal summer storm track (Klein, 1957; Reed, 1960; Reitan, 1974). The low pressure in the Interior valleys is primarily a result of the high air temperature. The midsummer air pressure gradient is directed from the southwest to northeast and its magnitude is only about one-half that of winter.

WIND

Mean *upper air* winds over BC come from the western quadrant throughout the year, parallelling the pressure gradient created by the latitudinal gradients of solar radiation and temperature in the mid-latitudes. Mean 500 mb geostrophic winds over the southern part of the province are from the west in both summer and winter. Those over the north are generally from the west-northwest in January and west-southwest in July (Lahey, Bryson, Wahl, Horn, and Henderson, 1958). The mean speed of the 500 mb geostrophic wind is greater in winter than summer in response to the increased solar radiation, air temperature, and, thus, upper air pressure gradients in this season. The speed is greater over the southern part of the province than over the north. The approximate mean January speeds are about 61 kilometres per hour (km/h) in the south and 36 km/h in the north. July values vary from 36 km/h in the southeast to 11 km/h in the northwest. The upper air westerlies are important in imparting the west-east direction of travel to weather systems that pass over BC.

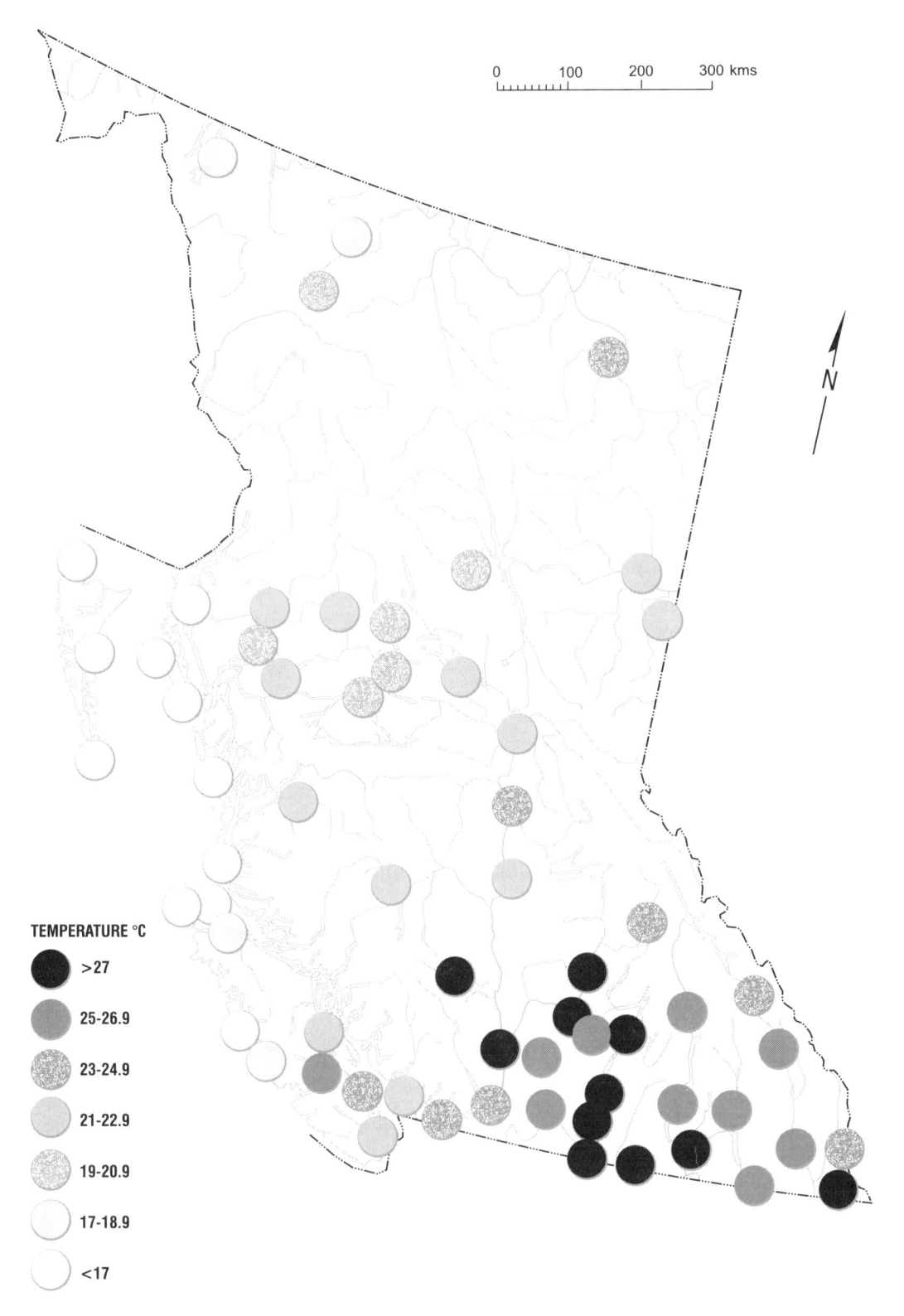

Figure 4.2 July mean daily maximum air temperature (1961 - 1990 normal)

Climate

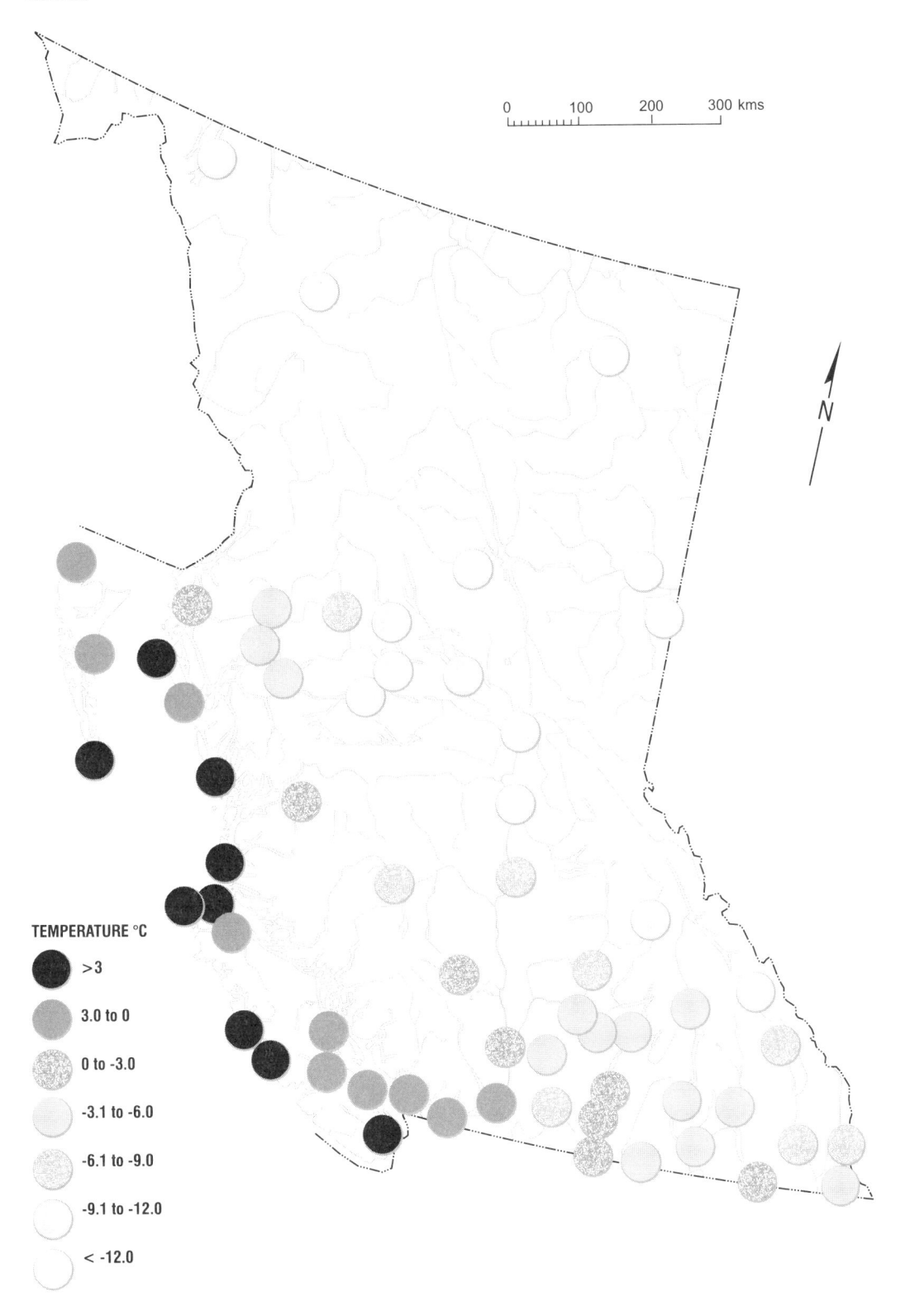

TEMPERATURE °C
- >3
- 3.0 to 0
- 0 to -3.0
- -3.1 to -6.0
- -6.1 to -9.0
- -9.1 to -12.0
- < -12.0

Figure 4.3 January mean daily air temperature (1961 - 1990 normal)

The mean winter pressure pattern would create *surface* winds with a southerly or easterly component over the central and southern parts of the province. However, surface winds at valley bottom stations are greatly influenced by local relief. Winter winds at most stations follow this pattern, but the actual distribution varies from station to station. Northerly winds are common in northern BC. Calms are relatively frequent at valley bottom stations in winter when cold, stable air can accumulate and decouple the surface air from the winds at higher elevation. These situations with stable, stagnant air create high air pollution potential.

Surface winds following the generalized mean pressure gradient in summer would have a northerly or westerly component. Calms are generally less frequent during summer than winter at interior stations where greater instability reduces the chance of calms. Most coastal stations, however, have more calms in summer, the season with fewer cyclonic storms and a smaller mean pressure gradient.

The seasonal pattern of wind speed varies widely from station to station. In general, however, the highest mean monthly wind speeds occur in winter at most coastal stations and the lowest in late summer or early fall (Atmospheric Environment Service, 1993). The annual range is less and the annual cycle is more variable at interior stations. The late summer-early fall minimum is seen at many stations, but a few have a winter minimum. The month with the maximum mean wind speed is variable with winter and spring months being the most common.

Well-exposed coastal stations are as windy as any place in Canada. Cape St. James, a very well-exposed station on the southern tip of the Queen Charlotte Islands, has a mean annual wind speed of 32 km/h and a January mean of 40 km/h (Atmospheric Environment Service, 1993). It has recorded a maximum speed of over 120 km/h in every month from September through April. Its maximum recorded wind speed through 1991 was 177 km/h. Mean annual wind speeds at most valley bottom, interior stations are lower than those at stations in the rest of southern Canada.

Humidity

The term *humidity* is used here to describe the actual quantity of water vapour in the atmosphere. The vapour pressure, the partial pressure of water vapour, is the measure of humidity that is used.

The major source of water vapour for all of BC is the Pacific Ocean. Stations near the coast are closest to this source and have the highest humidity throughout the year (Table 4.1; Atmospheric Environment Service, 1993). Inland stations that receive more frequent incursions of low level Pacific air have higher humidity than those that are more sheltered.

Two additional controls of humidity are elevation and air temperature. Atmospheric water vapour decreases rapidly with elevation. The Okanagan and Thompson river valleys (Penticton and Kamloops Airports, respectively) have higher humidity than does Cranbrook Airport located at higher elevation on the margins of the Rocky Mountain Trench (Table 4.1). The amount of water vapour the air can hold is affected by the air temperature. The low winter air temperature at northern stations puts an upper limit on winter atmospheric water vapour and combines with distance from an effective source of moisture to produce low winter humidity.

Coastal stations in BC have the highest winter humidity in Canada (Atmospheric Environment Service, 1987a). The rest of the country is predominantly under the influence of dry continental air in this season. Winter humidity in the southern interior is similar to that of the Atlantic Provinces and southern-most Ontario. Northern BC has a humidity regime like that of the Prairies.

Summer humidity in BC is relatively low. Evaporation from the eastern Pacific is limited by its low surface temperature. Even coastal stations have lower summer humidity than do those in much of Ontario and Quebec, the Maritimes, and southern Manitoba, which are influenced by air from warmer water surfaces (Atmospheric Environment Service, 1987a).

Although humidity near the surface is much higher in summer than in winter, the zonal transfer of tropospheric moisture from the Pacific Ocean is greater in winter, a result of the higher westerly wind speed. The maximum inflow of moisture during winter occurs over southern and central BC, whereas the maximum in summer occurs over the northern part of the province (Hare and Hay, 1974). The transport of moisture and the total amount of water vapour in the air are more important factors in precipitation than is the surface humidity.

PRECIPITATION

Precipitation measured at ground level (neglecting dew) is a result of the available water vapour in the air and dynamic lifting mechanisms that produce the cooling necessary to convert water vapour into water droplets or snowflakes large enough to fall to the surface. In most cases the presence or absence of the lifting mechanisms is the most important control of the distribution of precipitation over an area the size of BC.

The most important lifting mechanism for precipitation in BC is the mid-latitude cyclonic storm. Cyclonic storms affecting the province originate primarily in the central and western Pacific (Klein, 1957; Reitan, 1974). Those formed in the western Pacific reach the coast in their old age or occluded stage and usually bring light to moderate, but often long duration, precipitation. Those from the central Pacific are younger and more vigorous. An occasional intense storm migrates from south to north along the west coast of North America, reaching southwestern BC. Many Pacific cyclones are followed by unstable marine air that brings unsettled weather and showers to the coast (Hare and Hay, 1974).

The most obvious feature of the distribution of annual precipitation is the high amount on the windward sides of the major north-south trending mountain ranges (Figure 4.4; Atmospheric Environment Service, 1993). Mountains on the outer coast that are perpendicular to the westerly and southwesterly flow that accompanies much of the precipitation in the province have particularly strong effects (Walker, 1961). These well exposed stations on the outer coast have the highest annual precipitation in Canada. Stations in the rainshadow of the Coast Mountains have only about one-tenth the annual precipitation recorded at well exposed stations on the windward side of the range. Low precipitation is especially evident in the narrow valleys. The interior mountain systems also show the orographic influence. The Pacific air that reaches these, however, generally is drier air from higher elevations that passes over the Coast Mountains and thus orographic precipitation is not as extreme as on the coast. It must be remembered that the lowland and valley bottom patterns depicted in Figure 4.4 do not reveal the much higher precipitation that occurs on the higher slopes. The Selkirk Mountains provide a good example of orographic effects in the interior (Kendrew and Kerr, 1955). Revelstoke, on the windward side of the range, has an annual total precipitation of 950.2 mm, but Brisco, on the leeward side, receives only 448.1 mm. Two stations on the upper slopes of the Selkirks, Glacier National Park Rogers Pass and Glacier National Park Mt. Fidelity, receive 1,612.0 and 2,159.2 mm, respectively.

Precipitation in northern BC is limited by the dry Arctic air that is common, especially in winter and spring, and by the north's isolated location with respect to the southwesterly flow of moist Pacific air that accompanies much of the precipitation in the southern part of the province.

Precipitation follows a marked seasonal cycle at stations on the coast. Southern stations have a distinct maximum in winter (Figure 4.4). This coincides with the greatest frequency of mid-latitude cyclonic storms. The monthly maximum usually occurs in December which is more humid than January (Hay, 1971; Tuller, 1972), although storm frequency may be somewhat greater in the latter month. Maximum precipitation shifts to the fall on the far northern coast. Cyclonic storms are relatively numerous during that season and precipitable water vapour is much higher than it is in midwinter. Summer is the dry season all along the

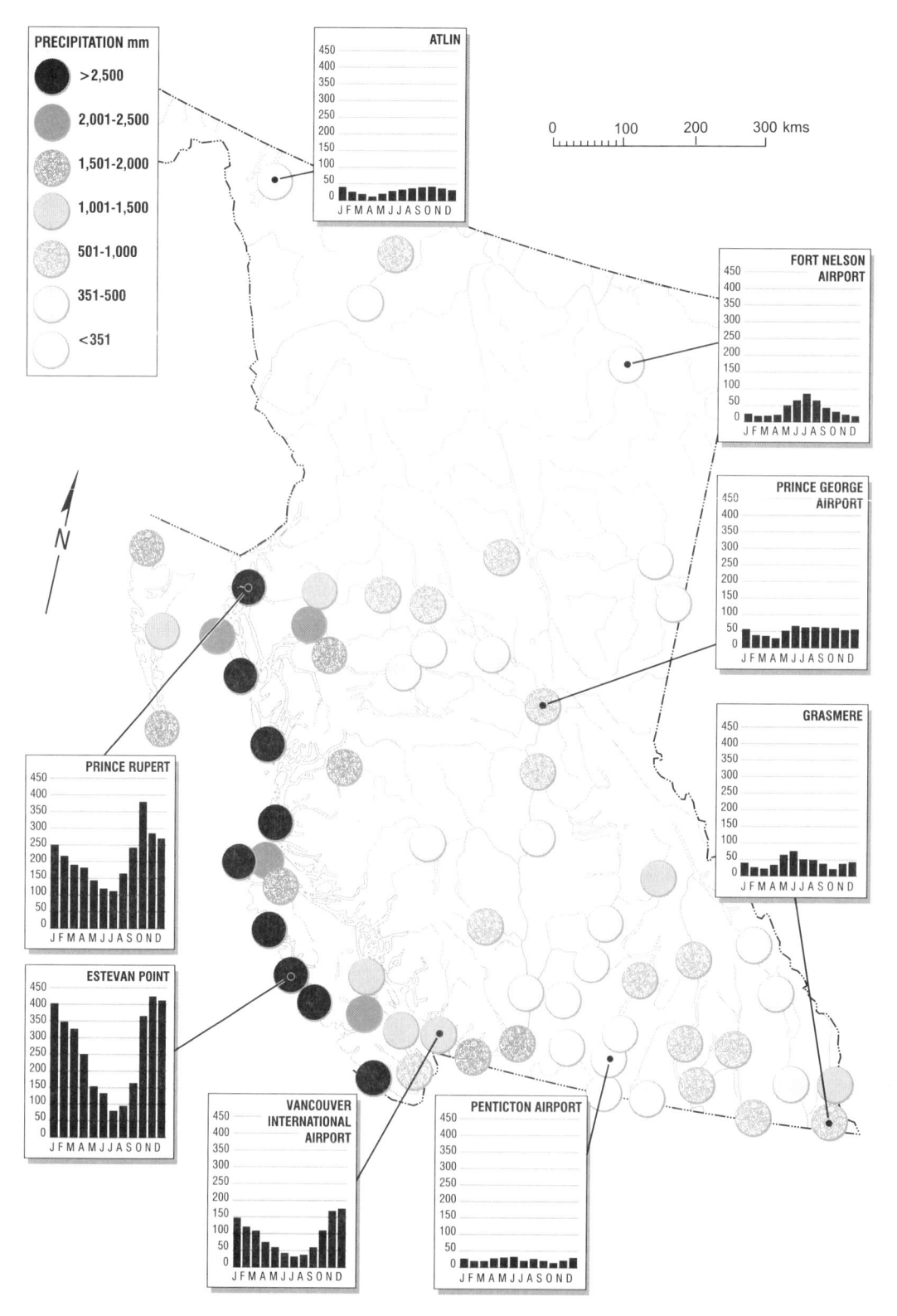

Figure 4.4 Annual precipitation (1961-1990 normal) and monthly distribution at selected stations

Climate

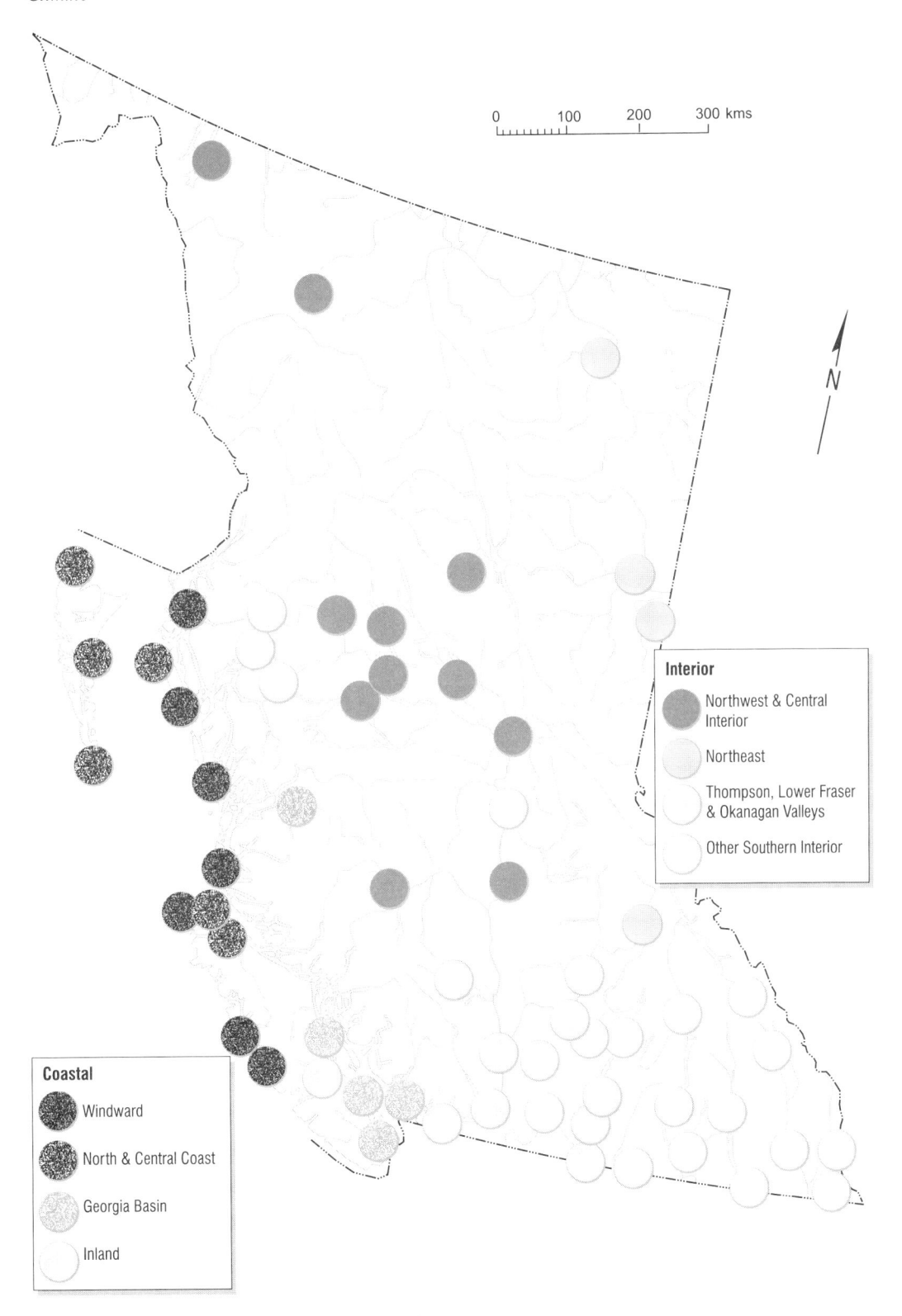

Figure 4.5 Temperature-precipitation regions

coast, with July being the driest month at most stations. Cyclonic storm frequency is low during the summer and the subtropical high pressure cell, with its subsiding air and subsidence inversion, frequently influences the south coast.

The northern Interior displays the opposite seasonal pattern. The greatest precipitation occurs in summer when more moisture is available and the air is more unstable than in other seasons. July is the wettest month at most stations (Figure 4.4). The driest season is spring, April being the driest month at many stations. Spring is the time between the cyclonic storm regime of winter and the instability of summer. Dry Arctic air dominates northern BC in that season (Bryson and Hare, 1974).

The most even distribution of precipitation throughout the year is found in the southern Interior. Most stations have a primary maximum in winter (cyclonic storm regime), a secondary maximum in summer (instability and convective precipitation), and a relatively dry spring and fall. The bulk of annual precipitation throughout the province is associated with frontal systems (Walker, 1961), and even in the Interior they act as important trigger factors for summer convectional showers.

High intensity rainfall is not common at lowland and valley bottom stations in BC. The Peace River region and the outer coast have the highest values. Over most of the province the *15 minute extreme rainfall* is less than one-half of that in southern Saskatchewan, Manitoba, Ontario, and Quebec (Atmospheric Environment Service, 1986).

One-day rainfall intensities can be relatively high on the outer coast, however, when orographic effects combine with a vigorous cyclonic storm to produce heavy, sustained rain. The majority of well-exposed stations have recorded over 150 mm of precipitation in one observing day and a few, where orographic effects are pronounced, have received over 200 mm (Atmospheric Environment Service, 1993). Even higher values can be expected on the upper slopes. The outer coast has the highest one-day rainfall intensity of any region in Canada (Atmospheric Environment Service, 1986).

The large variation in winter temperature and precipitation throughout the province gives rise to a large variation in snowfall regimes. Snowfall is irregular in occurrence and generally melts quickly along the south coast. Mean annual snowfall varies from about 25 to 100 cm and falls on 5 to 15 days per year during the October-March period. The annual snowfall on the south coast is the lowest in southern Canada (Atmospheric Environment Service, 1986). Annual snowfall on the north coast can range up to about 100 cm at lowland stations well exposed to ocean influences and up to 200 cm on cooler sites at higher elevations or in protected inlets. These values are similar to those on the Prairies, but a continuous snow cover throughout the winter is not expected. Snow in the interior, however, can be expected to persist; although in light precipitation areas a great deal of drifting can occur, leaving some areas bare of snow. The annual total reflects the distribution of annual precipitation. The dry valleys of the southern interior receive between 50 and 100 cm of snow per year. The Rocky Mountain Trench receives between 100 and 200 cm, but Revelstoke averages 445 cm. Annual snowfall varies from about 130 to near 400 cm at northern interior stations.

May-September Climatic Water Balance

The climatic water balance is the difference between the atmospheric supply of water (precipitation) and the demand for water through potential evapotranspiration (PE, the amount of water that would be evaporated if surface moisture was not a limiting factor).

Growing season (May-September) climatic water balance was determined using mean monthly total precipitation (Atmospheric Environment Service, 1993) and potential evapotranspiration (PE) computed via the Priestley and Taylor (1972) method. Available energy (net all-wave radiation minus ground heat flux density) is the control of PE in the Priestley and Taylor formula. Ground heat flux density was taken as 5% of net all-wave radiation at the beginning of the period declining to zero at the end. Regional variations are illustrated by the six stations used in the net all-wave radiation analysis.

Station-to-station differences in May-September PE (Table 4.2) reflect the differences in net all-wave radiation. Values range from a high of 489 mm at Summerland to a low of 327 at Sandspit Airport. Through extrapolation of the individual station results to larger regions, one would expect the greatest PE to occur in the southern Interior valleys, followed by the lower Fraser Valley and southeastern Vancouver Island. Northeastern BC would have a relatively high growing season PE. The minimum would occur on the west coast, especially in those areas with frequent summer cloud or fog.

Summer is relatively dry and sunny in most of BC. Potential evapotranspiration exceeds precipitation, leading to a climatic moisture deficit (Wallis, 1982) that must be alleviated by soil moisture, ground water, irrigation, or some other source of water to ensure adequate growth of shallow-rooted plants. The major exception is the exposed west coast, which has relatively low PE and sufficient summer precipitation. Computed climatic moisture deficits range from 14 mm at Sandspit to 346 mm at Summerland (Table 4.2). July is the month of maximum deficit at all stations except for Fort Nelson Airport, where it is June.

Table 4.2 May-September climatic water balance at selected stations (rounded off to the nearest mm)

Station	Potential evapo-transpiration	Precipi-tation	Climatic water balance
Summerland	489	143	-346
Nanaimo	433	183	-250
Fort Nelson	425	302	-123
Vancouver	413	246	-167
Prince George	370	297	-73
Sandspit	327	313	-14

Sources: Atmospheric Environment Service (1993) [Precipitation] and computed by author [Potential Evapotranspiration and Climatic Water Balance]

TEMPERATURE-PRECIPITATION REGIONS

A simple, regional classification of climate was derived using readily available data—the 12 monthly values of each of the 1961-1990 normals of total precipitation and mean daily air temperature (Atmospheric Environment Service, 1993). Principal components analysis reduced the 24 original variables to three uncorrelated factors representing precipitation, summer temperature, and winter temperature. Cluster analysis using Ward's (1963) method and discriminant analysis were employed to combine stations into discrete groups based on the similarity in factor scores. The combination of principal components analysis and grouping procedures is a common method of objectively determining climate regions on the basis of the climate data itself (e.g., McBoyle, 1971; McBoyle, 1972; Powell and MacIver, 1977; Willmott, 1978; Goossens, 1985; Anyadike, 1987; DeGaetano and Shulman, 1990; Fovell and Fovell, 1993; Baeriswyl and Rebetez, 1997).

The 63 stations used in this analysis divide nicely into coastal and interior groups (Figure 4.5). The temperature difference between the two groups follows the well-known maritime/continental dichotomy. The coast has higher annual total precipitation (Figure 4.4, Table 4.3) than does the interior and also has a distinct seasonal cycle with a winter maximum and summer minimum.

Four separate temperature-precipitation regions comprise the coastal zone. The first region includes stations located on the outer coast on the windward side of the mountains (Figure 4.5). The maritime temperature effect and pronounced orographic uplift are major influences on the climate of this **Windward** coast region. The result is high precipitation throughout the year, mild winter temperatures and cool summers (Figures 4.2, 4.3, and 4.4; Table 4.3).

Stations either in a rainshadow location or without extreme orographic uplift are included in the other three coastal regions. The first is the **North and Central Coast**. This region has a temperature pattern similar to the windward coast but reduced orographic uplift producing less precipitation (Figure 4.4, Table 4.3).

Table 4.3 Mean data for temperature-precipitation regions

Region	January mean daily temperature (°C)	July mean daily temperature (°C)	Annual total precipitation (mm)
COASTAL			
Windward Coast	3.4	13.5	2901.3
North & Central Coast	3.4	13.1	1820.6
Georgia Basin	2.9	17.1	1089.3
Inland	-1.2	16.8	1813.5
INTERIOR			
Northwest & Central Interior	-11.5	14.1	467.1
Northeast	-15.3	16.0	590.8
Thompson, lower Fraser & Okanagan valleys	-2.9	20.9	365.1
Other South Interior	-6.1	18.2	568.6

The next coastal region includes stations in the **Georgia Basin**. Rainshadow effects of Vancouver Island limit precipitation compared with other coastal regions. The low latitude gives the region a high annual air temperature for BC.

The **Inland** coastal region includes stations located at a distance from the shoreline in coastal valleys that still come under the marine influence. This region contains stations at varying distances from the coast, a range of latitudes (Figure 4.5), and a variety of exposures to uplift factors. Hence, a diversity of climatic conditions is represented. Lower winter temperature is the major feature distinguishing this inland coastal region from others on the coast (Table 4.3).

Compared to the Coast, the Interior has a colder winter and a large annual air temperature range (Figures 4.2 and 4.3, Table 4.3). Precipitation at the valley bottom stations included here is low compared to the coast (Figure 4.4, Table 4.3); convective precipitation, however, results in both summer and winter maxima.

Interior stations fall into three major regions that can be given locational names: the Northwest and Central Interior, the Northeast Interior, and the Southern Interior regions (Figure 4.5). The Southern Interior is further divided into two categories that reflect the influence of more localized controls.

Winter temperatures are low in the **Northwest and Central Interior** region but the dominant features of this region's climate are relatively low precipitation and low summer air temperatures (Table 4.3).

Cold winters are the significant distinguishing characteristic of the **Northeast Interior** region, which has a greater frequency of Arctic air masses and less influence from marine air than is experienced in other parts of the province (Figure 4.3). The cold winters combined with moderate summer air temperatures give this region a large annual air temperature range (Table 4.3).

The Southern Interior includes two groups of stations. These groups are determined by station site factors and do not form contiguous regions. Stations in the **Thompson River, Lower Fraser and Okanagan valleys** are at relatively low elevations and in rainshadow locations. Their climate is distinguished by very low precipitation and the highest summer air temperatures in the province. **Other Southern Interior** stations are at somewhat higher elevations and more exposed to atmospheric uplift. A wide range of sites creates a diversity of atmospheric conditions but this climatic region can be described as having warm, but not hot, summers and cool winters. Precipitation is variable because of the range of site conditions but, on average, it is low.

CONCLUSIONS

BC is characterized by a wide range of climatic conditions. The range of latitude and elevation, contrasting land and sea influences, different sources of advected heat and moisture, and the effects of mountain ranges and relief all combine to give the province a great diversity of climates even at the regional level as discussed in this chapter. This diversity of climates provides a range of opportunities and challenges for successful human occupancy. Except for tropical and polar climates, there should be a climate that appeals to nearly everyone somewhere in BC.

REFERENCES

Anyadike, R.N.C. (1987). A multivariate classification and regionalization of West African climates. *Journal of Climatology*, 7, 157-164.

Atmospheric Environment Service (1976). *Station, sea level and vapour pressure normals based on the period 1953-1972.* Downsview, Ontario: Environment Canada, Atmospheric Environment Service.

Atmospheric Environment Service (1982). *Climate normals, Volume 1, Solar radiation, 1951-1980.* Ottawa: Environment Canada, Atmospheric Environment Service.

Atmospheric Environment Service (1984). *Climatic Atlas Canada, Map Series 1, Temperature and degree days.* Ottawa: Environment Canada, Atmospheric Environment Service.

Atmospheric Environment Service (1986). *Climatic Atlas Canada, Map Series 2, Precipitation.* Ottawa: Environment Canada, Atmospheric Environment Service.

Atmospheric Environment Service (1987a). *Climatic Atlas Canada, Map Series 3, Pressure, humidity, cloud, visibility, and days with thunderstorms, hail, smoke/haze, fog, freezing precipitation, blowing snow, frost, snow on the ground.* Ottawa: Environment Canada, Atmospheric Environment Service.

Atmospheric Environment Service (1987b). *Climatic Atlas Canada, Map Series 4, Bright sunshine and solar radiation.* Ottawa: Environment Canada, Atmospheric Environment Service.

Atmospheric Environment Service (1993). *Canadian Climate Normals 1961-1990, British Columbia.* Ottawa: Environment Canada, Atmospheric Environment Service.

Baeriswyl, P.-A., and Rebetez, M. (1997). Regionalization of precipitation in Switzerland by means of principal component analysis. *Theoretical and Applied Climatology*, 58, 31-41.

Bryson, R.A., and Hare, F.K. (1974). Climates of North America. In R.A. Bryson and F.K. Hare (Eds.), *Climates of North America* (pp. 1-47). New York: Elsevier.

Chapman, J.D. (1952). *The climate of British Columbia.* Paper presented to the Fifth British Columbia Natural Resources Conference, 1952.

Chilton, R.R.H. (1981). *A summary of climatic regimes of British Columbia.* Victoria: BC Ministry of Environment.

Clague, J.J. (1981). *Late Quaternary geology and geochronology of British Columbia, Part 2: Summary and discussion of radiocarbon-dated Quaternary history.* Geological Survey of Canada, Paper 80-35.

Department of Transport (1968). *Climatic normals, Volume 3, Sunshine, cloud, pressure and thunderstorms.* Toronto: Department of Transport, Meteorological Branch.

DeGaetano, A.T., and Shulman, M.D. (1990). A climatic classification of plant hardiness in the United States and Canada. *Agricultural and Forest Meteorology*, 51, 333-351.

Environment Canada (1995). *The state of Canada's climate: Monitoring variability and change.* SOE Report No. 95-1, Ottawa: Environment Canada.

Fovell, R.G., and Fovell, M.-Y. (1993). Climate zones of the conterminous United States defined using cluster analysis. *Journal of Climate*, 6, 2103-2135.

Geiger, R. (1966). *The climate near the ground.* Cambridge, Mass.: Harvard University Press.

Gershunov, A., and Barnett, T.P. (1998). Interdecadal modulation of ENSO teleconnections. *Bulletin of the American Meteorological Society*, 79, 2715-2725.

Goossens, C. (1985). Principal component analysis of Mediterranean rainfall. *Journal of Climatology*, 5, 379-388.

Gullett, D.W., and Skinner, W.R. (1992). *The state of Canada's climate: Temperature change in Canada 1895-1991.* SOE Report No. 92-2, Ottawa: Environment Canada, Atmospheric Environment Service.

Hare, F.K., and Hay, J.E. (1974). The climate of Canada and Alaska. In R.A. Bryson and F.K. Hare (Eds.), *Climates of North America* (pp. 49-192). New York: Elsevier.

Hartmann, D.L. (1994). *Global physical climatology.* San Diego: Academic Press.

Hay, J.E. (1971). Precipitable water over Canada: II. Distribution. *Atmosphere*, 9, 101-111.

Hay, J.E. (1979). *An analysis of solar radiation data for British Columbia.* Victoria: BC Ministry of Environment.

Hebda, R.J. (1995). British Columbia vegetation and climate history with focus on 6 ka BP. *Géographie Physique et Quaternaire*, 49, 55-79.

Hengeveld, H. (1995). *Understanding atmospheric change: A survey of the background science and implications of climate change and ozone depletion*. 2nd edition. SOE Report No. 95-2, Ottawa: Environment Canada.

Horel, J.D., and Wallace, J.M. (1981). Planetary-scale atmospheric phenomena associated with the Southern Oscillation. *Monthly Weather Review*, 109, 813-829.

Idso, S.B., and Jackson, R.D. (1969). Thermal radiation from the atmosphere. *Journal of Geophysical Research*, 74, 5397-5403.

Kendrew, W.G., and Kerr, D. (1955). *The climate of British Columbia and the Yukon Territory*. Ottawa: Queen's Printer.

Kerr, D. (1952). Climate of British Columbia. *Canadian Geographical Journal*, 45, 143-158.

Klein, W.H. (1957). *Principal tracks and mean frequencies of cyclones and anticyclones in the Northern Hemisphere*. Washington: US Government Printing Office.

Lahey, J.F., Bryson, R.A., Wahl, E.W., Horn, L.D., and Henderson, V.D. (1958). *Atlas of 500 mb wind characteristics for the Northern Hemisphere*. Madison: University of Wisconsin Press.

Lamb, H.H. (1972). *Climate: Present, past and future, Volume 1, Fundamentals of climate now*. London: Methuen.

Luckman, B.H. (1994). Evidence for climatic conditions between ca. 900 - 1300 A.D. in the southern Canadian Rockies. *Climatic Change*, 26, 171-182.

Luckman, B.H. (1998). Landscape and climate change in the central Canadian Rockies during the 20th Century. *The Canadian Geographer*, 42, 319-336.

Luckman, B.H., Briffa, K.R., Jones, P.D., and Schweingruber, F.H. (1997). Tree-ring based reconstruction of summer temperatures at the Columbia Icefield, Alberta, Canada, AD 1073-1983. *The Holocene*, 7, 375-389.

Mantua, N.J., Hare, S.R., Zhang, Y., Wallace, J.M., and Francis, R.C. (1997). A Pacific interdecadal climate oscillation with impacts on salmon production. *Bulletin of the American Meteorological Society*, 78, 1069-1079.

Mathewes, R.W. (1985). Paleobotanical evidence for climatic change in southern British Columbia during late-glacial and Holocene time. In C.R. Harington (Ed.), *Climatic change in Canada 5, Critical periods in the Quaternary climatic history of northern North America* (pp. 397-422). Ottawa: National Museums of Canada, Syllogeus 55.

Mathewes, R.W., and Heusser, L.E. (1981). A 12,000 year palynological record of temperature and precipitation trends in southwestern British Columbia. *Canadian Journal of Botany*, 51, 707-710.

McBoyle, G.R. (1971). Climate classification of Australia by computer. *Australian Geographical Studies*, 9, 1-14.

McBoyle, G.R. (1972). Factor analytic approach to a climatic classification of Europe. *Climatological Bulletin*, 12, 3-11.

McGillivray, B. (2000). *Geography of British Columbia*. Vancouver: UBC Press.

Moore, R.D. (1991). Hydrology and water supply in the Fraser River basin. In A.H.J. Dorcey and J.R. Griggs (Eds.), *Water in sustainable development: Exploring our common future in the Fraser River Basin* (pp. 21-40). Vancouver: Westwater Research Centre, University of British Columbia.

Moore, R.D., and McKendry, I.G. (1996). Spring snowpack anomaly patterns and winter climatic variability, British Columbia, Canada. *Water Resources Research*, 32, 623-632.

Neiburger, M., Johnson, D.S., and Chien, C-W. (1961). *Studies of the structure of the atmosphere over the eastern Pacific Ocean in summer, 1. The inversion over the eastern North Pacific Ocean*. Berkeley: University of California Press.

Powell, J.M. (1965a). *Annual and seasonal temperature and precipitation trends in British Columbia since 1890*. Department of Transport, Meteorological Branch.

Powell, J.M. (1965b). Changes in the amount of sunshine in British Columbia, 1901-1960. *Quarterly Journal of the Royal Meteorological Society*, 91, 95-98.

Powell, J.M., and MacIver, D.C. (1977). *A summer climate classification for the forested area of the Prairie Provinces using factor analysis*. Edmonton: Northern Forest Research Centre.

Priestley, C.H.B., and Taylor, R.J. (1972). On the assessment of surface heat flux and evaporation using large scale parameters. *Monthly Weather Review*, 100, 81-92.

Raphael, C. (1993). Temperature trends at Prince George, British Columbia (1943-1991). *Western Geography*, 3, 71-83.

Reed, R.J. (1960). Principal frontal zones of the Northern Hemisphere in winter and summer. *Bulletin of the American Meteorological Society*, 41, 591-598.

Reitan, C.H. (1974). Frequencies of cyclones and cyclogenesis for North America, 1951-1970. *Monthly Weather Review*, 102, 861-868.

Ryder, J.M. (1978). Geology, landforms and surficial geology. In K.W.G. Valentine, P.N. Sprout, T.E. Baker, and L.M. Lavkulich (Eds.), *The soil landscape of British Columbia* (pp. 11-33). Victoria: BC Ministry of Environment.

Ryder, J.M., and Thomson, B. (1986). Neoglaciation in the southern Coast Mountains of British Columbia: Chronology prior to the late Neoglacial maximum. *Canadian Journal of Earth Sciences*, 23, 273-287.

Satterlund, D.R. (1979). An improved equation for estimating long-wave radiation from the atmosphere. *Water Resources Research*, 15, 1649-1650.

Schaefer, D.G. (1976). *Climatological impacts of Peace River regulation and a review of the possible effects of climatic change on agriculture in the area*. Report prepared for B.C. Hydro and Power Authority.

Schaefer, D.G. (1978). Climate. In K.W.G. Valentine, P.N. Sprout, T.E. Baker, and L.M. Lavkulich (Eds.), *The soil landscape of British Columbia* (pp. 3-10). Victoria: BC Ministry of Environment.

Shabbar, A., Bonsal, B., and Khandekar, M. (1997). Canadian precipitation patterns associated with the Southern Oscillation. *Journal of Climate*, 10, 3016-3027.

Shabbar, A., and Khandekar, M. (1996). The impact of El Niño Southern Oscillation on the temperature field over Canada. *Atmosphere-Ocean*, 34, 401-416.

Smith, D.J., and Laroque, C.P. (1996). Dendroglaciological dating of a Little Ice Age glacial advance at Moving Glacier, Vancouver Island, British Columbia. *Géographie Physique et Quaternaire*, 50, 47-55.

Trenberth, K.E. (1997). Short-term climate variations: Recent accomplishments and issues for future programs. *Bulletin of the American Meteorological Society*, 78, 1081-1096.

Tuller, S.E. (1972). Mean monthly and annual precipitable water vapour in Canada. *Weather*, 27, 278-289.

Tuller, S.E. (1990). Precipitation trends at Victoria, British Columbia. *Climatological Bulletin*, 24, 158-167.

Ward, J.H. (1963). Hierarchical grouping to optimize an objective function. *American Statistical Association, Journal*, 58, 236-244.

Walker, E.R. (1961). *A synoptic climatology of parts of the Western Cordillera*. Montreal: McGill University, Arctic Meteorology Research Group, Publication in Meteorology No. 35.

Wallace, J.M., and Gutzler, D.S. (1981). Teleconnections in geopotential height field during the Northern Hemisphere winter. *Monthly Weather Review*, 109, 784-812.

Wallis, C.H. (1982). *Calculating irrigation requirements for Eastern Vancouver Island*. Victoria: BC Ministry of Environment.

Willmott, C.J. (1978). P-mode principal components analysis, grouping and precipitation regions in California. *Archiv für Meteorologie, Geophysik und Bioklimatologie*, 26B, 277-295.

Yarnal, B., and Diaz, H.F. (1986). Relationships between extremes of the Southern Oscillation and the winter climate of the Anglo-American Pacific coast. *Journal of Climatology*, 6, 197-219.

ENDNOTES

[1] Data is derived from Weather Service of Canada. Every 10 years the climate normals for specific conditions (e.g., temperatures) for BC are published. In this chapter the author has also calculated statistics based on this data (noted in text).

[2] *El Niño* is the occurrence (around Christmas) of warm water along the Pacific coast of Ecuador and Peru. It affects weather patterns throughout the Pacific Basin. In BC it brings milder, wetter winters (e.g., 1993-94). The opposite condition, known as *La Niña*, brings cold water flows to the Pacific coast.

Plate 4 BC has a large number of wild streams and rivers: Nairn Falls ▶

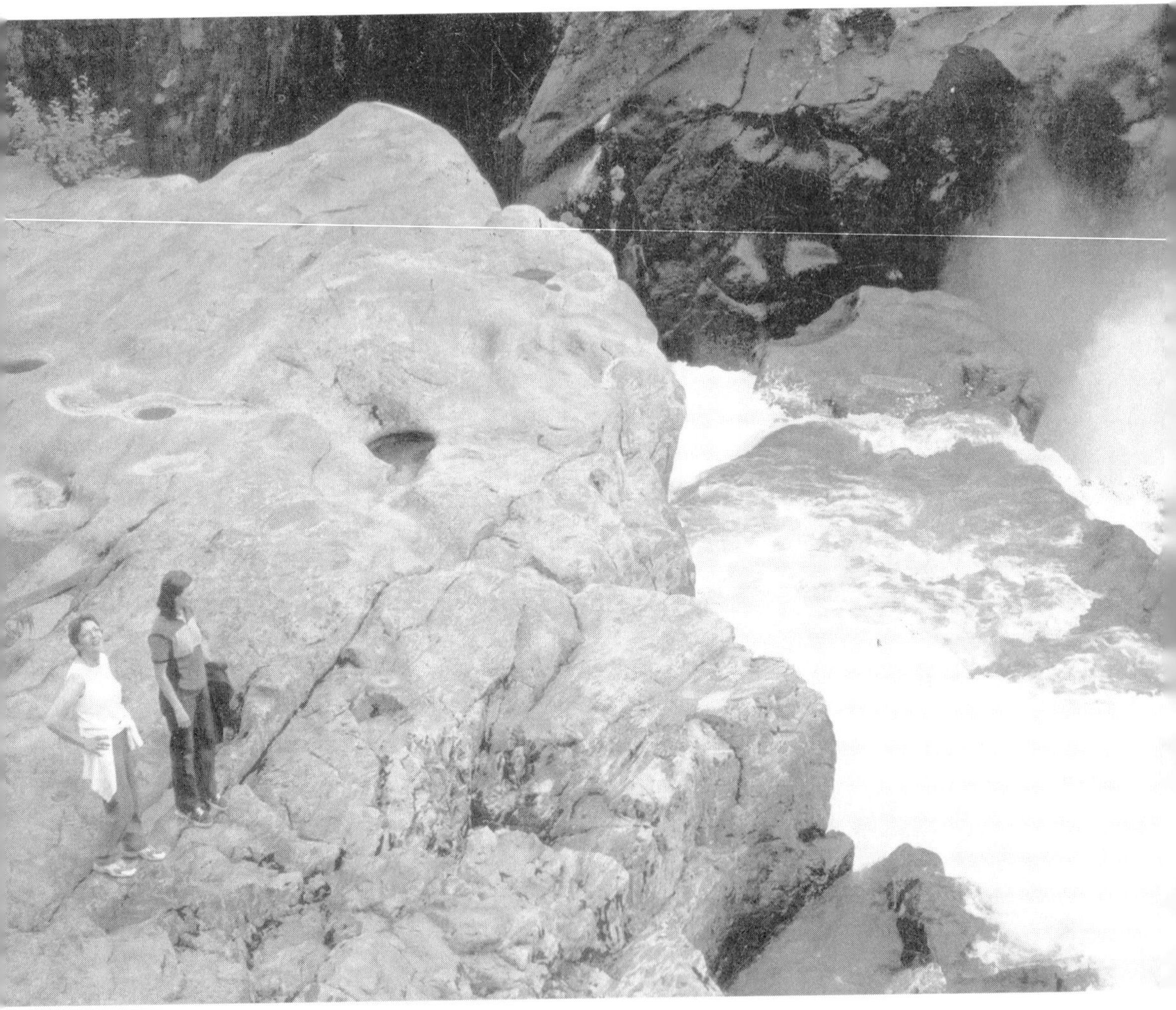

Water Resources

Sandra Smith

Department of Geography, University of Victoria
updated from W.R.D. Sewell (1987)

Introduction

More than almost any natural resource, water acts as a powerful conditioning factor in economic, social, and political affairs. In Canada, the availability of water has played a critical role in shaping settlement patterns, the structure of economic activity, relationships between various levels of government, and to an increasing degree the quality of life. In this respect British Columbians are extremely fortunate. Collectively they have access to more than one-third of Canada's precipitation runoff, which itself amounts to 9% of the world total. With a relatively small population for a large area, BC's water endowment is even more generous.

With such a wealth of resources, one might justifiably conclude that the province has no problems with water, either now or in the foreseeable future. Such, however, is not the case. Nature is stingy, as well as being generous, and does not bestow her bounty in a uniform way. Water availability, in fact, varies considerably from one part of the province to another. Besides this, there are many possible uses for water, some of which can be developed harmoniously and others which result in serious conflicts. Other issues arise from the division of responsibilities for water management between the various levels of government, including the fact that some rivers cross international or inter-provincial boundaries, and that social values attached to water resources have changed over time. A consequence has been that BC water management issues have been the subject of considerable discussion and some ensuing legislation in recent years.

This chapter begins by describing the nature and distribution of BC's water resources. The various uses to which these assets have been put and the problems that have emerged as a result are then discussed. The development of water resources, of course, has taken place within an institutional framework of laws, public policies, and administrative agencies. This framework is outlined, focusing particularly on current institutional arrangements. The chapter concludes with comments on challenges the province's water managers will have to face in the near and more distant future.

BC's Water Wealth

Anyone flying over BC cannot fail to be impressed by three major features of the environment: the massive, rugged mountain ranges; the numerous narrow steep-sided valleys; and the myriad rivers which in many cases flow for hundreds of kilometres from their headwaters to the ocean. These features, combined with the large area (947,800 km^2) of the province and its location on the Pacific coast, are responsible for its huge water wealth.

As indicated in Tables 5.1 and 5.2, several of the province's rivers are very large in terms of their length, drainage area, and discharge. In addition, there are over 16,000 lakes, ranging from small mountain tarns to bodies of water more than 500 km^2 in area (Cannings, 1998). The locations of the major streams and lakes are shown in Figure 5.1.

It has been estimated that, collectively, the rivers of BC discharge some 781 trillion m^3 per year. This is obviously an extremely favourable endowment, however this figure needs to be interpreted with caution. Water tends to be rather uneven in its spatial distribution and it varies considerably in its availability over time.

Table 5.1 Length of major rivers

River	Length (kilometres)
Fraser	1,368.5
Columbia	750.3
Skeena	579.6
Stikine	539.3
Liard	483.0
Nass	378.3
Peace	281.7

Source: Farley, A.L. (1979). *Atlas of British Columbia*. Vancouver: University of British Columbia Press.

There may, in fact, be poverty in the midst of plenty, or, alternatively, so much water that it becomes an embarrassment. Both features are present in BC. They arise in part from the nature of the province's terrain and in part from seasonal variations in precipitation.

About 75% of BC's land area is more than 1,000 m above sea level. More than half of it is over 1,300 m above sea level. As shown in Figure 5.2, high mountains lead to major differences in precipitation and hence runoff across the province. The Northern Cordillera acts as a barrier to moisture-bearing winds from the Pacific. Precipitation is frequently extremely heavy at the coast, sometimes in excess of 750 cm, but declines rapidly as one moves from west to east. It is especially heavy on the western slopes of the mountain ranges, but much lower on the eastern slopes which create a rain shadow effect. There are several interior areas where annual precipitation is less than 50 cm, and a few places where it is as low as 12.5 cm. Spatial variations in precipitation in the province are depicted in **Figure 4.4**.

Not only are there important spatial differences in precipitation, but there are seasonal variations as well. Broadly speaking, in the coastal regions winters tend to be very wet and summers relatively dry. In much of the Interior of the province precipitation is fairly evenly distributed throughout the year, although the spring is often quite dry. In the coastal regions a portion of the winter precipitation is in the form of snow and part is in the form of rain, especially at lower elevations. In the Interior much of the winter precipitation is in the form of snow. The factors of terrain and climate result in strikingly different seasonal stream flow patterns across the province, as illustrated by the hydrographs for the Fraser River, the Cowichan River, the Yakoun River, and the Liard River portrayed in Figure 5.3. The earlier peak of the Liard River may be compared with the peak on the Fraser River while winter flooding occurs on the Cowichan River. The Yakoun River hydrograph shows a

Table 5.2 Drainage area and mean annual flow of major rivers

River	Drainage Area (km^2)	Mean Annual Flow (m^3/sec)	Years of Record
Fraser at Hope	217,000	2710	85
Columbia at International Border	155,000	2820	59
Liard above Beaver River	119,000	1410	27
Peace near Taylor	97,100	1450	46
Stikine near Wrangell	51,600	1610	13
Skeena at Usk	42,200	897	70
Nass above Shumal Creek	18,500	824	62

Source: Environment Canada. Water Survey of Canada. *Surface Water Data Up to 1996.* CD-ROM, 1996.

Water Resources

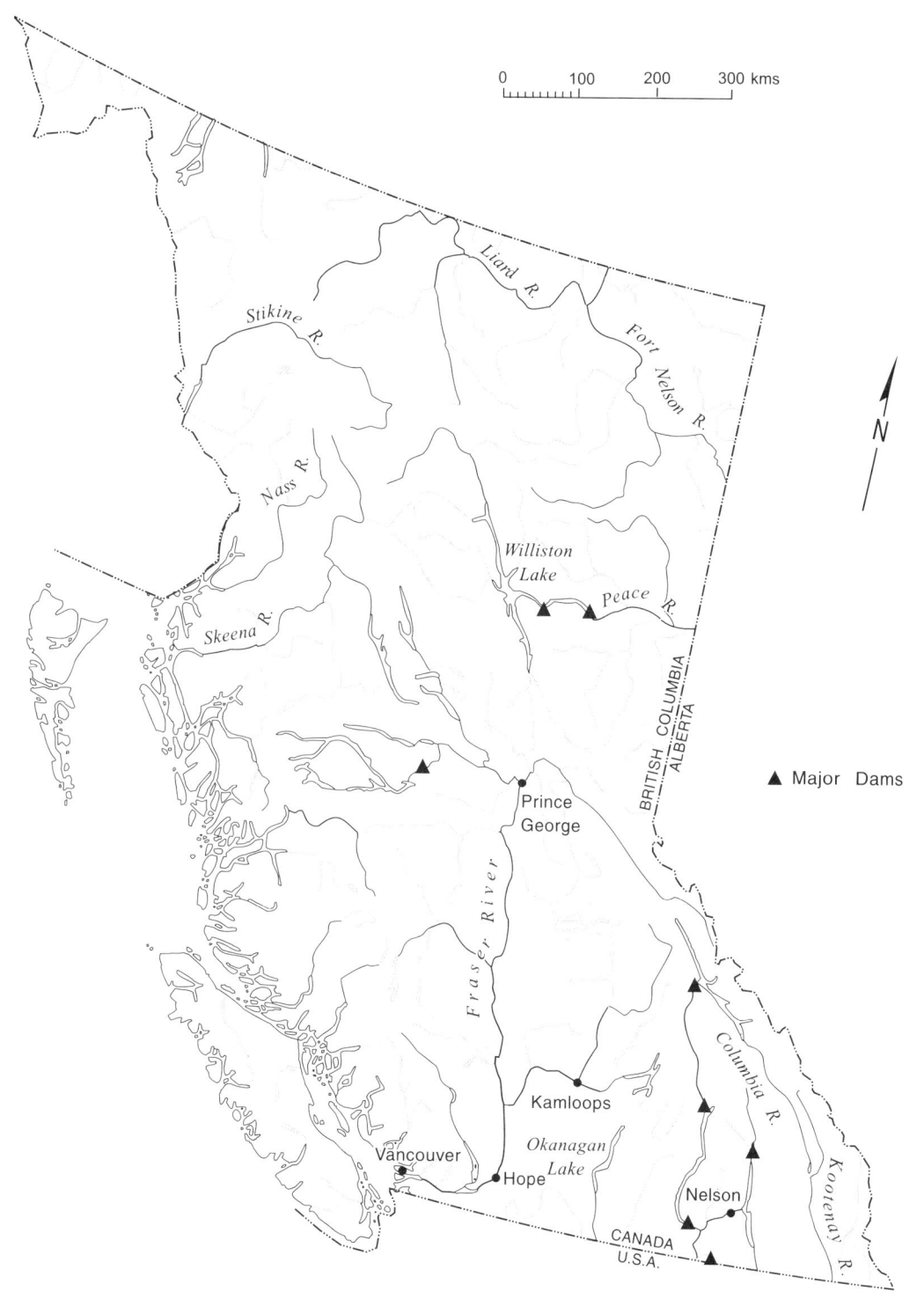

Figure 5.1 Major rivers and lakes

situation where mountain snow-melt is not a major factor.

Beyond the seasonal fluctuations, there are often major variations from year to year. For example, the maximum recorded flow of the Fraser River at Hope was 15,200 m^3 per second on May 31, 1948, and the lowest was 340 m^3 per second on January 8, 1916. Similarly, the highest flow recorded on the Skeena River at Usk was 9,340 m^3 per second on May 26, 1948, while the minimum was 51.8 m^3 per second on March 1, 1950 (Resource Inventory Section, Ministry of Environment, Lands and Parks, 1996).

Of interest currently is the possible impact of *El Niño* and global warming on recorded flows. The average temperature difference between *El Niño* winters and normal winters is about 1 to 1.5°C, with higher temperatures most noticeable in southern BC. In general, *El Niño* winter conditions are slightly drier and there is much less snow in the southern half of the province, especially on the Pacific coast where snowfall can be 50% below normal (Environment Canada, 1999, *http://weatheroffice.com/default.asp?page=ElNino/default.htm*). To date, the impact of global warming is difficult to assess. One study suggests that for the BC coast there is a trend toward lower stream flows in spring and fall, and higher flows in winter (Whitfield, 1998).

These major spatial and temporal variations in runoff have several implications for human activity. They may mean that water may not be where it is needed when required. A consequence may be to limit the economic growth of a region, either because the water is not there or is too expensive to bring in from elsewhere. Another implication may be that rivers occasionally overflow their banks, causing major losses of property and possibly of life as well. Hence, a major challenge has been to cope with seasonal and other variations in streamflow.

The relative abundance of perennial streams and the generally easy access to many of them has resulted in most of the water withdrawals being made from surface sources. The provincial Ministry of Environment, Lands and Parks estimates that water for use in homes, farms, industries, and power generation is provided by over 24,000 rivers, creeks, and lakes, while groundwater aquifers provide water supplies for over 600,000 people throughout the province (*http://www.elp.gov.bc.ca/wat/wrs/strategy/strategy.html#11*). As yet, there are only rough estimates of the total magnitude of the province's groundwater resources.

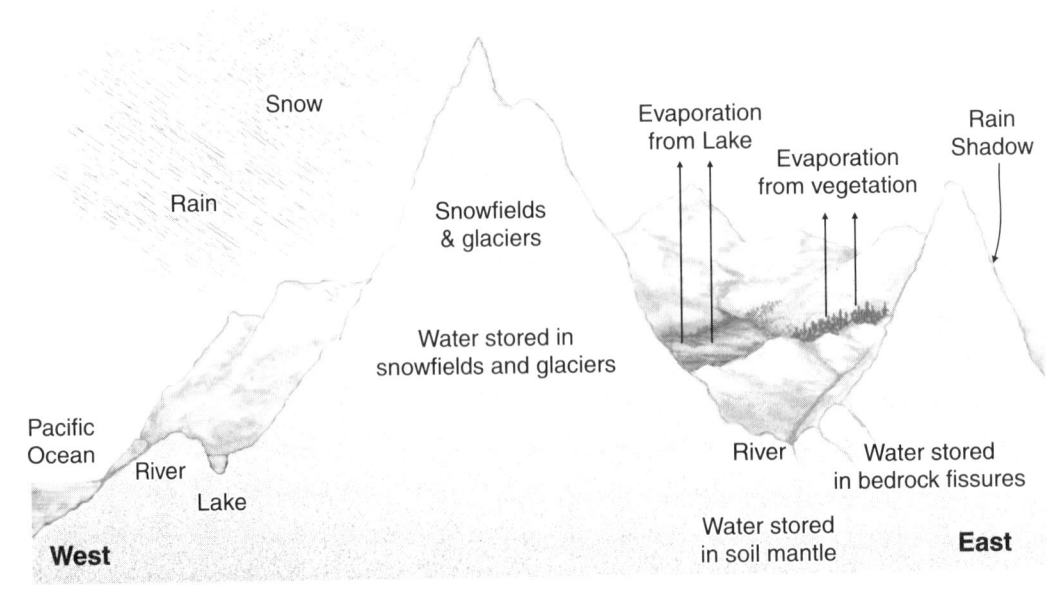

Figure 5.2 The hydrologic cycle in BC

Water Resources 69

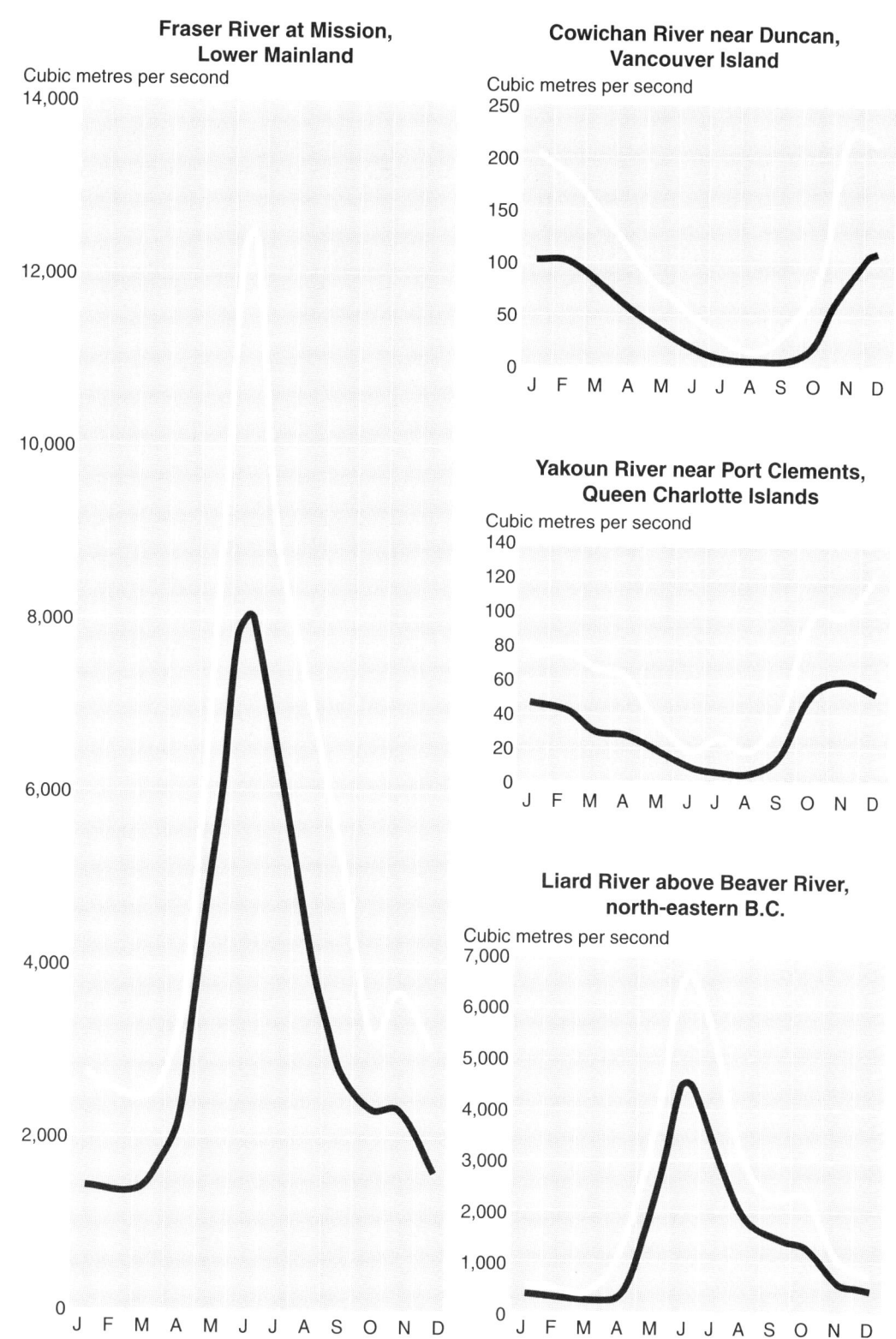

Fraser River at Mission, Lower Mainland
Cubic metres per second

Cowichan River near Duncan, Vancouver Island
Cubic metres per second

Yakoun River near Port Clements, Queen Charlotte Islands
Cubic metres per second

Liard River above Beaver River, north-eastern B.C.
Cubic metres per second

Figure 5.3 Hydrographs of selected rivers

WATER USES

Compared with people in many parts of the world, British Columbians are heavy water users. In Vancouver, water use for all purposes now exceeds 650 litres per person per day (Greater Vancouver Water District, 1999, http://www.gvrd.bc.ca/services/water/know/index.html). In BC, water use for all purposes accounts for the withdrawal of some 380 litres per person per day. Canadians use 326 litres per person per day at home, twice as much water as the average European (Environment Canada, 1999, http://www.ec.gc.ca/agenda21/98/wateruse.html).

For the sake of convenience, water use can be classified into withdrawal, consumption, and instream categories. Withdrawal uses are those that involve abstraction from a water body, such as for use in a household or factory, or on a farm. Part of this withdrawal may be 'consumed' in the sense that it does not return directly to the water body, either because it is incorporated physically into the product (such as in beer or soft drinks) or because it is evaporated into the atmosphere. In some situations water may be transferred to another watershed. It should be noted that water withdrawals do not always equal total water use or demands due to the fact that in some instances a given volume of water is 'recycled' or used more than once. This has been increasingly the case in certain manufacturing and mining industries. Thus, for Canada as a whole, a total of 57,935 million m^3 (MCM) per year are withdrawn to serve a demand of 4,352 MCM (Environment Canada, 1991, http://www.ec.gc.ca/water/en/manage/use/e_wuse.htm). Instream uses are those that take advantage of the water where it is, as in navigation, migration and spawning of fish, hydroelectric power generation, recreational pursuits, or simply for aesthetic appreciation.

Data for water intake (amount consumed) for BC and other parts of Canada are set out in Table 5.3. These data show that the manufacturing sector is the largest water user in the province, reflecting the huge quantities that are withdrawn by the forest products industry, and especially by pulp and paper plants. It should be noted, however, that water use in the manufacture of pulp and paper has declined significantly between 1975 and 1997, from 160 m^3 per tonne of pulp to 69.8 m^3 (http://www.ec.gc.ca/agenda21/98/wateruse.html). The second largest user is municipal, while agriculture, in which irrigation has become increasingly important, lies just slightly behind in third place. The pattern of withdrawals differs from that of Canada as a whole, particularly reflecting the relatively minor role that the cooling of

Table 5.3   Surface water intake* in Canada, 1991 (MCM per year)

Region	Population in 1991 (000)	Thermal power	Manu-facturing	Municipal incl. rural residential	Agri-culture	Mining	Regional total
Atlantic	2,322	2,126	601	356	15	77	3,175
Quebec	6,895	1,005	1,616	1,703	100	74	4,498
Ontario	10,084	23,095	3,457	1,660	186	87	28,485
Prairies	4,626	2,025	447	685	3,014	50	6,221
BC**	3,282	106	1,161	698	676	75	2,716
National total	27,296	28,357	7,282	5,102	3,991	364	45,096

*Water intake = amount consumed + amount returned to surface water

**Sectoral data for Yukon and Northwest Territories included with British Columbia

Source: Environment Canada, 1998, http://www.ec.gc.ca/water/en/info/pubs/fs/e_FSA4-1.htm.

thermal power stations plays in BC compared with Ontario, the Atlantic Provinces, or Quebec. Most of BC's power is generated by hydroelectric plants, an instream use. Water withdrawals for all purposes, consumptive and non-consumptive, across the province are shown in Table 5.4.

Table 5.4 Annual BC water withdrawals for all purposes by region

Region	Withdrawal (MCM)
Vancouver Island	26.6
Lower Mainland	48.8
Southern Interior	15.8
Kootenay	369.0
Cariboo	2.7
Skeena	15.9
Northern Interior	163.3
Okanagan	2.8

As might be expected, the heaviest abstractions are concentrated mainly in the Lower Mainland, an area of major urban agglomeration, or where manufacturing is focused: the Kootenays and the Northern Interior. Among the most important uses in the province are those for which no withdrawal is made—the instream uses. Total allocation under licence as of August, 1996 was 645 MCM per year, of which 622 MCM was for hydro-power allocation and 17.7 MCM for non-consumptive instream flow allocations such as conservation licences (BC, Environment, Lands and Parks, 1998).

Many of the major rivers and inland lakes support runs of anadromous fish and furnish a habitat for other species of fish (see **Chapter 18**). In addition, water-based recreation has expanded very rapidly in popularity in recent years, both for British Columbians and for a growing tourist industry. In 1997, recreational angling contributed an estimated $1.2 billion annually in direct and indirect benefits to the provincial economy (BC, Agriculture, Fisheries and Food, 1997).

EMERGING PROBLEMS AND ISSUES

Water resources have clearly played an important role in BC's economic development and the evolution of a quality of life of which its citizens are justly proud. Over the years, however, several problems and issues have emerged, some of which are reaching critical proportions. These difficulties stem largely from:

- spatial and temporal distribution of the resource;
- rapid expansion of population, urbanization and industrialization; and
- changing social values.

Water Quality

Declining water quality has become an increasingly pervasive issue. It results both from expanding urbanization, industrialization, and historically from an attitude that the use of water for the disposal of wastes should be regarded as free. These conditions presented few difficulties when major polluters were located far away from the larger established centres of population. There were no major outbreaks of water-borne, vector related diseases nor fish kills of a significant magnitude. There seemed to be little to worry about. Things changed as a result of the explosive growth of population and polluting industries, and in part as a consequence of increasing awareness and concern by the public at large about environmental deterioration. Today, efforts to protect water quality by regulating "end of pipe" point discharges from industrial and municipal outfalls have been successful in many areas but major efforts are still required to control pollution from non-point sources, which are the many diffuse and unregulated origins associated with urbanization, agriculture, and other forms of development.

Examples include: threats to drinking water supplies of the Abbotsford-Sumas Aquifer from nitrogen leachate caused by spreading high nitrogen poultry manure on fields; closure for public bathing of Burnaby's Deer Lake due to high fecal coliform counts; and the loss of salmonid populations in the Brunette River basin. Road construction during timber harvest continues to contribute to non-point source water pollution, as do prescribed burning and fertilizer and pesticide application associated with logging activities. These practices have the potential to affect drinking water in BC's 450 community watersheds, other water supplies, and fish and fish habitat.

Microbiological contamination also presents a significant problem for drinking water supplies. The incidence of intestinal infections in BC is much higher than elsewhere in Canada. Of these infections, 30% were water-related. Boil water advisories, which indicate when water is unsafe for human consumption, increased 6-fold between 1986 and 1992 (Province of BC and Environment Canada, 1993).

Water Pricing

At present, the pricing of water in BC does not promote sustainable development by taking into account the economic value of water, or in terms of ensuring sustainable use. Water costs only a few cents or less per 1,000 gallons (BC, 1993) and is not priced to ensure that adequate infrastructure is maintained. In the Greater Vancouver Water District customers pay some of the lowest rates in Canada (McNeill, 1992). While rainfall in the Greater Vancouver area is prevalent in the winter, the period of peak demand in the summer requires reliance on storage reservoirs. As the population of the area grows and existing water systems age, new storage and distribution systems will be needed and construction of reservoirs comes with a significant cost to the environment. Currently, water is not metered in many cases and the cost of such future infrastructure is not factored into the cost of water. This situation is found particularly where water is supplied by small management authorities.

Groundwater

Groundwater supplies drinking water to 22% of the province's population, and accounts for 9% of the total water consumption in BC (Hess, 1986). Groundwater use is more difficult to manage than surface water, presents difficulties in determination of the extent and pattern of aquifers, and is difficult to rehabilitate once contaminated. Yet BC is the only province in Canada that does not license use of or drilling for groundwater.

There are many examples of groundwater problems, including: well interference where large capacity wells lower the water levels of neighbouring wells (Surrey); artesian wells which flow freely, thus wasting water and lowering water levels (Okanagan, Gulf Islands, Surrey); groundwater/surface water conflicts (Cherry Creek in Kamloops, Chimney Creek in Williams Lake); excessive groundwater withdrawals in coastal areas resulting in salt water intrusion (Gulf Islands); and poor well construction practices and health and public safety risks associated with uncapped and abandoned wells (Province of BC, 1993).

Water Export

Whether BC's water should be made available for export became a very contentious issue in the early 1990s. The provincial government adopted a policy in 1984 which generally opposed water export from interior streams but permitted bulk export from coastal streams (streams which emptied into the ocean). A moratorium was later placed on the consideration of licences for extraction from coastal streams (1991 until 1994). By 1993 there were:

- six licences for bulk marine shipment and 15 applications to expand these operations;
- a number of licences for bottling mineral and surface water but no restriction on size of container and no requirement to bottle in BC;
- several significant bottling operations from groundwater sources; and
- a proposal to divert water from the North Thompson River into the Columbia River in order to supply markets in the US.

Droughts and Floods

As noted earlier, water in BC is not always available when and where it is wanted. This is especially so in regions that receive on average less than 80 cm of precipitation per year, but for various reasons have developed activities that have become dependent upon at least that amount, such as irrigated agriculture or salmon fishing. From time to time the Okanagan, Cariboo, and Kootenay regions have suffered long periods of below average runoff and agricultural production has suffered as a consequence. Sometimes the parks and gardens of Vancouver and Victoria have withered as a result of prolonged periods of drought and occasionally salmon have been unable to reach their spawning grounds because water levels have been too low. However, compared with certain other regions in Canada, notably the Prairies, BC has only minor problems with respect to drought, particularly of a long-term nature.

A much more pervasive problem is that of floods. There are few municipalities in BC that do not have some sort of flooding problem. Areas that are particularly flood prone include the basins of the Fraser, Squamish, and Columbia rivers, and various locations on Vancouver Island. The problem is especially severe in the lower Fraser Valley, with the flood loss potential continuing to grow as a result of population growth and industrial expansion. This is emphasized by studying the results of the flood of 1990 where, during heavy winter storms, floodwaters from the Nooksack River in Washington State flowed into Canada just south of Abbotsford causing $1.5 million damage in the West Sumas Prairie area.

The largest flood of record on the Fraser River occurred in 1894. Were this flood to reoccur, it would directly affect a substantial part of the province's manufacturing industry, much of its horticulture and dairy farming, as well as many residents who live in areas that depend on dykes for protection. For example, the City of Richmond alone has a 1996 population of 145,867. When the last major flood occurred in 1948 it cost some $20 million in damages that were compensated, mostly for property losses, rehabilitation, and repairs in the Lower Fraser Valley. Actual losses were much larger. If a similar flood occurred today and protective works did not hold, losses would be many times that amount, perhaps as much as $1.8 billion (Fraser Basin Management Board, 1996) (see **Chapter 3**).

Protection of Fisheries

Preservation of fisheries has been the focus of some of the sharpest conflicts in water use. In the past there were a number of examples, such as the proposal to use certain fish migration streams for the development of hydroelectric power, as in the case of a further diversion of the Nechako River into the Kemano River proposed to enable an increase in power output on the latter, or the proposed McGregor Diversion on the Fraser River and the Site C project on the Peace River (see **Chapter 18**). Today environmentalists and other interest groups are calling for increased protection of fish resources, as well as expressing concern about flood control, recreational and other implications of water regulation at power and other water control facilities (Rosenau, 1998). In short, although BC possesses a vast wealth of water resources, there are rapidly growing problems to be faced in their management. While some of these are rooted in the nature of the resource itself, an increasing number stem from conflicts among users and among different levels of authority. Ultimately the solutions must be found in a flexible and sensitive institutional framework.

THE INSTITUTIONAL FRAMEWORK

Over the past century a complex set of institutions has evolved for the management of BC's water resources. These consist of laws, policies, and administrative arrangements that are intended to allocate water among competing users and to furnish various water-related goods and services. These institutions have been modified over time, in response to the emergence of new problems, the improvements of technologies, and the introduction of new concepts and ideas. However, changes have been particularly profound in recent years given downsizing of federal and provincial government services.

Federal Government Activities

Jurisdiction over BC's water resources is shared between the federal and provincial governments. This division of authority has had an important influence over the manner in which the resources have been developed. Historically, the federal authority has helped shape water management in BC in five major ways—namely, by:

1. carrying out programs designed to improve navigation or enhance fishery stocks;
2. imposing regulations either to maintain or improve water quality, especially where fishery stocks are involved, or to ensure that the national interest is maintained in the development of international or interprovincial streams;
3. undertaking cooperative data collection programs with respect to water quantity and quality;
4. participating in water resources planning; and
5. cooperating in various schemes of development, notably those concerning flood control or treatment of municipal wastes.

Thus, between the 1950s and the 1980s the federal government has been active in such programs as the Salmonid Enhancement Program, the Fraser River Flood Control Program, and the Floodplain Mapping Agreement. Its International Joint Commission has been called upon to ensure the national interest in relation to streams crossing international boundaries and assistance has been given for planning studies such as the Okanagan Basin Study.

A growing concern for water issues in Canada led the federal government to instigate an Inquiry on Federal Water Policy. In 1987, a federal water policy was adopted which sought to protect water and encourage its efficient management through realistic pricing, science leadership, integrated planning, legislative renewal, and public awareness (Environment Canada, 1998, *http://www.ec.gc.ca/water/en/policy/pol/e_pol.htm*). It has been suggested that the adoption of this policy was the high point of federal interest in water as an individual resource (Pearse, 1998). Subsequent years have seen a declining federal interest in water and a move towards protecting the integrity of ecosystems and improving economic performance. Environment Canada's Inland Waters Directorate, which derives its mandate mainly through the *Canada Water Act, 1970*, has been significantly downsized and dispersed through various regions and other government departments. Table 5.5 sets out federal administrative agencies and legislation concerned with water in BC.

In 1998 the federal government initiated a review of its role through the development of *[Towards] a Federal Freshwater Strategy*, which is a strategy that is expected to foster a "national vision" for water management based on sustainable development, protecting freshwater ecosystems, and using water efficiently. Federal water policy appears to be pursuing the following directions, at least in the immediate future:

- narrowing of federal interest, particularly where funding is concerned (e.g., project construction or development of floodplain mapping);
- promoting water-efficient technologies in the use of existing water supplies;
- giving priority to environmental issues at the interprovincial level (such as management of the MacKenzie River) and at the international level (such as climate change);
- developing partnerships to deliver water-related programs;
- providing leadership in freshwater science and data collection, albeit with considerably reduced funding; and
- reforming the outdated *Canada Water Act* and *Canadian Environmental Protection Act*.

Indications of this activity include the joint publication, with BC, of information relating to protection of the ecosystem (Canada, Department of Fisheries and Oceans, 1994-1997), the introduction of amendments to the *Canadian Environmental Protection Act* to fast-track the evaluation and control of toxic substances (Environment Canada, 1998, *http://www.ec.gc.ca/press/cepa98_n_e.htm*), and granting of funds under the Agenda 21 program, for example, to

Table 5.5 Federal government administrative agencies and legislation concerned with water in BC

Agency	Legislation
ENVIRONMENT CANADA	Canada Water Act Canadian Environmental Protection Act Environmental Assessment Act International Rivers Improvement Act Migratory Birds Convention Act Canada Wildlife Act International Boundary Waters Treaty Act Environmental Contaminants Act National Parks Act Pest Control Products Act
FISHERIES AND OCEANS CANADA	Fisheries Act Department of Fisheries and Oceans Act Ocean Dumping Control Act
TRANSPORT CANADA	Canada Shipping Act Navigable Waters Protection Act
NATIONAL HARBOURS BOARD	National Harbours Board Act Harbour Commissions Act
NATIONAL ENERGY BOARD	National Energy Board Act
HEALTH AND WELFARE	Department of Health and Welfare Act
INDIAN AND NORTHERN AFFAIRS	Department of Indian Affairs and Northern Development Act Northern Inland Waters Act

For further information see *http://www.Canada.justice.gc.ca/loireg/index_en.html*.

address drainage and wastewater issues affecting water quality in the Baynes Sound area (Environment Canada, 1998, *http://www.ec.gc.ca/press/action6_b_e.htm*). Following significant public calls for the development of a policy on water export, the federal government, in November 1998, introduced amendments to the *International Boundary Water Treaty Act* of 1911 to prohibit "bulk" removals from boundary waters, particularly the Great Lakes.

Provincial Government Activities

While the federal government exercises a degree of control over water use and has assisted materially in overcoming several problems, the major direction for water management in BC comes from the provincial government. This authority arises from the *Constitution Act* (1982) which assigns the responsibility for the majority of natural resources, public lands, and property to the province. Water, being subject to property, and land being taken to include water, is therefore subject to provincial management. The provincial authority allocates water among competing users, draws up plans for development, sets priorities, and does most of the regulation to ensure that water quality is maintained. The province also relates water management to the development of other resources and assesses its environmental impacts and other consequences.

The major provincial agency dealing with water matters is the Ministry of Environment, Lands and Parks, but it shares that responsibility with other ministries (Table 5.6). The Ministry has two divisions: regional and headquarters. While the regional division is responsible for integrated operational activities, the headquarters' Water Management Program now covers a wide range of purposes of water management, including the provision of standards, programs, and strategies in the areas of water allocation, water use plans, water quality, groundwater management, public safety, water utility regulation, and appeals.

Under the provisions of the *Water Act*, the Water Management Program issues licences for water withdrawal. Those wishing to obtain a licence make an application to the Comptroller of Water Rights, that is, the Regional Water Manager. The proponent must indicate timing and quantity of the intended abstraction as well as the appurtenance to which the licence would be attached. Providing there is no objection from other licence holders, a licence is granted for payment of a fee. Such fees vary considerably in magnitude. An irrigator in the Okanagan, for example, withdrawing some .01 m^3 per second (100 acre feet) must pay $55 dollars for this amount. In contrast, if BC Hydro required a flow of 150 million acre feet, the fee would be an estimated $242 million (BC Ministry of Environment, Lands and Parks, 1993b). On the basis of current fees and rentals for 42,037 licences, power revenue was $320 million due to extremely high power production in 1997-1998, while revenue from other sources was $6.3 million (BC Ministry of Environment, Lands and Parks, 1998).

The Ministry also carries out responsibilities with respect to water quality management. Quality objectives are set for various water bodies (BC Ministry of Environment, Lands and Parks, 1996) and permits issued to those who intend to discharge wastes into water bodies. The permits specify the conditions under which the discharge may be made, including the volume that may be released. A third function of the Ministry is the prosecution of those who do not meet the requirements of the permit. Efforts to seek compliance have intensified significantly in the last 10 years. Hence, although they are not all water-related, it is noted that for the period October 1, 1998 to March 31, 1999 there were 58 operations listed as failing to meet environmental standards, including 19 under the category of municipal sewage and 14 for industrial effluent (BC Ministry of Environment, Lands and Parks, 1999, *http://www.elp.gov.bc.ca/main/newsrel/fisc9900/november/nr174.htm*).

A separate section of the Environment, Lands and Parks headquarters' division provides Resource Inventory including inventory, mapping, and inventory-related information (for example, streamflow, snowpacks, floodplain mapping, and water quality).

The Ministry of Fisheries was established in February 1998; fish conservation and protection issues and management of BC's freshwater recreational fishery are within the purview of the Fisheries Program of the Ministry of Environment, Lands and Parks.

Like the federal government, the provincial government reached a high point in 1993 with regard to its expressed interest in water management policy with the publication of the discussion paper *Stewardship of the Water of British Columbia*. The paper suggested a phased program to accomplish the following goals:

- selected regulation of groundwater;
- development of a more prudent water pricing policy;
- enabling better stream management practices;
- commitment to water management planning;
- introduction of a wide range of water allocation tools which would improve the current system and allow reallocation of existing water rights in the public interest;
- enabling comprehensive floodplain management strategies;
- ensuring the consideration of water quality protection and drinking water quality measures in decisions involving land and water use;
- greater emphasis on protecting aquatic environments and conserving water; and
- development of a policy on water export.

Table 5.6 BC government administrative agencies and legislation concerned with water in BC

Agency	Legislation
ENVIRONMENT, LANDS AND PARKS	Ministry of Environment Act
	Water Act
	Waste Management Act
	Environment Management Act
	Environment and Land Use Act
	B.C. Fisheries Act
	Pesticide Control Act
	B.C. Wildlife Act
	Water Protection Act
	Fish Protection Act
	Land Act
	Park Act
	Environmental Assessment Act
	Emergency Program Act
MUNICIPAL AFFAIRS	Municipal Act
FORESTS	Forest Act
	Forest Practices Code
HEALTH	Health Act

For further information see *http://www.qp.gov.bc.ca/bcstats/index.htm*.

In 1995, the government introduced the *Water Protection Act*, which provided new limits on the export of water and prohibition of the transfer of water between major watersheds (for example, the previously proposed McGregor Diversion or Peace River Site C). These included:

- all water, including groundwater, is vested in the Province of BC;
- licences and approvals are required for water removal, including removal from BC;
- water removal from BC may only occur in containers of 20 litres capacity or less, unless specifically grandparented; and
- large scale transfers between major watersheds are prohibited.

The scheme also depended upon the provisions of the newly adopted *Environmental Assessment Act* to ensure that any significant water project would be subject to environmental assessment.

In addition, regulations were introduced in 1995, pursuant to the *Water Act*, which set out environmentally sensitive standards for activities that modify the nature of a stream or its flow and for activities or construction that occur within the bed and banks of a stream.

Beyond the *Water Protection Act*, several legislative and other measures for the protection of water have been taken in recent years. The *Forest Practices Code* introduced guidelines that are important for the protection of water quality in two forms. The *Community Watershed Guidebook* sets out recommended procedures for forestry practices on Crown land in 450 watersheds designated as "community watersheds." In addition, the *Code* sets out best management practices for harvesting adjacent to streams on lands leased from the provincial government.

The *Fish Protection Act* was passed, providing enabling powers for such measures as: no new bank-to-bank dams on provincially-significant rivers; better protection of water flows for all fish in the province by improving the water licencing process; designation of "sensitive streams" where fish stocks are at risk; improved riparian protection for urban streams; expansion of the definition of threatened and endangered species to allow such designations for fish and aquatic plants and invertebrates; strengthening of the powers of local governments to protect the environment, including fish habitats; designation of water management areas to address conflicts; allowing water licences to be granted to community-based interest groups for the purpose of protecting water flows for fish and promoting stream stewardship activities; and establishment of new, creative sentencing provisions. Many of these powers are yet to be enacted through regulations but, in the interim, numerous excellent publications in *The Stewardship Series* have been prepared in conjunction with the federal government to assist in promoting concepts of *stream stewardship* (Canada, Department of Fisheries and Oceans, 1994-1997).

Another new initiative is the preparation of Water Use Plans that will involve stakeholders in the management of water use conflicts at BC Hydro facilities. BC Hydro holds 88 licences of which 70 were granted before 1962. Most of these licences do not provide conditions relating to the protection of fish. The new process will define the detailed operating parameters to be used by hydro facility managers in day-to-day operations, clarify how rights to provincial water resources should be exercised taking into account multiple users of the resource including instream uses, and provide the opportunity to consider costs and benefits of alteration to existing operating rules.

In November 1999 the BC Ministry of Environment, Lands and Parks released *A Freshwater Strategy for British Columbia* in which they set out priority actions to be completed over the next 3 years. To encourage healthy aquatic ecosystems these included implementation of *Fish Protection Act* measures, improvements to the community watershed protection process under the *Forest Practices Act*, completion of 12 Water Use Plans, development of Pollution Prevention Plans in partnership with business and industry, initiation of Performance Based Regulations for industrial discharges, development of a Non-Point Source Action Plan at the local government level, and various water education and stewardship initiatives. The protection of human health and safety will be undertaken through coordinating government action on protecting drinking water, ensuring pro-active floodplain management, and regulating dams in regard to public safety and providing standards in this regard. Sustainable social, economic, and recreational benefits of water will be provided through improving water allocation operations, implementing water management planning under the *Fisheries Protection Act*, and pursuing groundwater legislation and other protection measures.

Water management in BC is clearly complex, involving four levels of government when local government and First Nations are included, as well as myriad agencies, interest groups, and the public. Formal mechanisms have been established for bringing various interests together, such as the Fraser Basin Council. The Council's mandate is to integrate social, economic, and environmental dimensions of sustainability through facilitating shared decision-making. Water-related issues dealt with by the Council include: attempting to resolve concerns over access to the residual flow of water in the Nechako River following construction of the Kenny Dam which supplies power to aluminum operations in Kitimat, BC; establishing partnerships regarding needed improvements to water quality in Shuswap Lake; developing a nutrient management plan in the Fraser Valley; and developing a flood hazard management strategy for the lower Fraser Valley (Campagnolo, 1998).

Another example of intergovernmental co-operation is seen in the *Integrated Flood Hazard Management Strategy* published in 1996. This focused on flood protection works, land use planning and management, and emergency response and recovery (Fraser Basin Management Board, 1996). Among the directions proposed were placing a high priority on the maintenance of existing dykes, clarifying and strengthening partnerships between four levels of government, strengthening flood hazard management in local and regional land use plans, and supporting preventative measures in order to reduce future compensation claims. An increased role for local government is emphasized with regard to coordinating flood hazard management activities.

Inter-jurisdictional agreements also assist water management. For example, the Canada-BC Water Quality Monitoring Agreement between Environment Canada and the Ministry of Environment, Lands and Parks has ensured that water quality has been monitored at selected locations throughout the province since 1985. Less formal mechanisms also exist, such as referrals between government agencies and considerations given to water management during the preparation of the province's Land and Resource Management Plans (LRMPs).

THE CHALLENGES AHEAD

Most visitors to BC would acknowledge that British Columbians have managed their water resources well and compared to certain other parts of North America this would be a reasonable conclusion. The large majority of British Columbians have access to cheap, safe, and potable water supplies, and industry and agriculture have adequate supplies of electricity and water. Water-related epidemics and fish kills from point sources of pollution are limited while the province is renowned for its outstanding water-based recreation opportunities.

Water management in BC in the 20th century has moved from the early settlers' single purpose projects in the form of farmers' dykes and irrigation systems to management systems that emphasize sustainability and stewardship. The institutional focus has changed from the allocation of water and construction of large projects such as dams and dykes to the determination of ways in which a sustained and healthy water resource can be achieved. Most frequently, this achievement is being sought through partnerships at the local level and/or between the various levels of government. Such arrangements will be significantly challenged to address the issues at hand.

The mid-1970s was an era of intense institutional change in water management in BC at both federal and provincial levels, but subsequently the pace slowed. The late 1980s saw considerable activity at the federal level in the development of the Federal Water Policy, but more recently there has been a significant lessening of interest and decrease in funding as attention has been refocused on the protection of the ecosystem and the encouragement of sustainability. At the provincial level, interest in the adoption of comprehensive legislative measures for the management and protection of water was at its peak in the first half of the 1990s, but since that time political interest has somewhat diminished.

Assuming that the goal is a progressively more comprehensive and effective level of water management, it is interesting to compare some examples from BC's current water management scheme with the initiatives of other Canadian provinces as organizations are reoriented to achieve sustainable development (Shrubsole and Mitchell, 1997). As Table 5.7 shows, there is still much to be done to achieve comprehensive water management. At the federal-provincial level the issue of climate change will require significant attention, as will issues such as water export, providing leadership in freshwater science and data collection, and reforming outdated legislation.

There is still a serious need for some form of regulation regarding groundwater in BC. Such regulation could, at the very least, introduce a formal program of inventory and of controls such as requiring permits for new wells, certification and licensing of well drillers and pump installers, and standards for drilling construction and abandonment of wells.

Control of non-point sources of pollution requires extension of appropriate management measures to private land where timber harvesting will occur, improving non-point-source pollution management in agriculture, and facilitating more effective stormwater management. The *Fish Protection Act* requires significant action before it will become effective, including the designation of sensitive streams and development of protection policy directives and the enabling and preparation of water management planning. The flood hazard management strategy developed for the Lower Fraser Valley requires implementation and extension to other areas. The issue of water pricing requires thorough review and appropriate implementation not only to ensure sustainability but also to address the issue of inadequate infrastructure for water supplies. BC's *Water Act*, although effective, remains outdated legislation. Finally, the need for public involvement in the development of new water management policies and in the implementation of strategies has never been greater.

As water management changes from the delivery of outputs (often assisted by the federal government) to sustainable water management, there are certain principles that provide guidance (Shrubsole and Mitchell, 1997). These include placing emphasis on an ecosystem approach, anticipating and preventing problems by relying on the *precautionary principle*, striking partnerships and involving stakeholders, building capacity at the local level in order to encourage efficiency and effectiveness, and utilizing integrated planning initiatives. The need for institutional leadership coupled with effective power-sharing is essential to achieve a sustained and healthy water resource based on these principles.

Table 5.7 Adoption of themes of Canadian water management in BC

Other Provinces	British Columbia
Development of water policies	*Stewardship of the Water of British Columbia*, 1993
	A Freshwater Strategy for British Columbia, 1999
Adoption of an ecosystem approach	*Fish Protection Act*, and joint publication with the federal government of "Stewardship" publications
	Forest Practices Code
	Environmental Assessment Act
Increased attention to groundwater management	*Water Protection Act* confirmed ownership of groundwater by Crown
	Pilot projects on Pender Island and Hornby Island
	Drafted Code of Practice for Construction, Testing, Maintenance, Alteration and Closure of Wells
Growing use of partnerships and stakeholders, including First Nations	Fraser Basin Council
Introduction of demand management practices	Development of water conservation guidelines
Attention to the issue of water export	*Water Protection Act*

REFERENCES

BC Ministry of Agriculture, Fisheries and Food (1997). *The BC fisheries strategy. Towards a 'made-in-BC' vision to renew the Pacific salmon fishery.* Victoria: Queen's Printer.

BC Ministry of Environment, Lands and Parks (1993a). 1-Groundwater management. In *Stewardship of the water of British Columbia.* Victoria: Queen's Printer.

BC Ministry of Environment, Lands and Parks (1993b). 3-Water pricing. In *Stewardship of the water of British Columbia.* Victoria: Queen's Printer.

BC Ministry of Environment, Lands and Parks (1996). *Water Quality Status Report.* Victoria: Ministry of Environment, Lands and Parks, Water Quality Branch.

BC Ministry of Environment, Lands and Parks (1998). Personal communication. Gary Robinson: Updating of water licensing information. Victoria: Ministry of Environment, Lands and Parks, Water Management Program.

BC Ministry of Environment, Lands and Parks, and Environment Canada (1993). *State of environment report for British Columbia.* Victoria: Ministry of Environment, Lands and Parks.

Campagnolo, I. (1998). *Shared decision making in a not so "Brave New World" of sustainability.* Victoria: Canadian Water Resources Association, Keynote Address at the 51st Annual Conference.

Canada Department of Fisheries and Oceans (1994-1997). *The Stewardship Series.* Ottawa: Department of Fisheries and Oceans, and Victoria: Ministry of Environment, Lands and Parks.

Cannings, R., and Cannings, S. (1998). *The world of fresh water.* Vancouver: Greystone Books.

Day, J., and Affum, J. (1993). *Toward sustainable water planning and management in British Columbia* (prepared for The British Columbia Round Table on the Environment and the Economy). Victoria: Queen's Printer.

Foster, H., and Sewell, D. (1981). *Water: The emerging crisis in Canada.* Toronto: James Lorimer.

Fraser Basin Management Board (1996). *Integrated flood hazard management strategy.* Vancouver: Fraser Basin Management Program.

Hess, P. (1986). *Groundwater use in Canada.* Ottawa: Environment Canada. National Hydrology Research Institute, Inland Waters Directorate.

McNeill, R. (1992). Water pricing and sustainable development in the Fraser River Basin. In A. Dorcey (Ed.), *Perspectives on sustainable development in water management* (pp. 417-429). Vancouver: University of British Columbia Westwater Institute.

Pearse, P. (1998). *Water management in Canada. The continuing search for the federal role.* Victoria: Canadian Water Resources Association, Keynote Address at the 51st Annual Conference, mimeo.

Resource Inventory Section, Ministry of Environment, Lands and Parks (1998). Personal communication. Robin McNeill and Robin Wyman: Updating of Flow Information and Hydrographs based on Environment Canada data.

Rosenau, M., Conlin, K.R., Penner, R., Fields, D., Delaney, P., Mullen-Dalmer, D., and Turmel, B. (1998). Water use plans: A mechanism involving stakeholders to manage water-use conflicts at hydro facilities. In Y. Alila (Ed.), *Mountains to sea: Human interaction with the hydrologic cycle* (pp. 154-159). Canadian Water Resources Association 51st Annual Conference Proceedings, Cambridge, ON.

Sewell, W.R.D. (1987). Water resources. In C.N. Forward (Ed.), *British Columbia: Its resources and people* (pp. 199- 225). Victoria, BC: Department of Geography, University of Victoria, Western Geographical Series, Vol. 22.

Shrubsole, D., and Mitchell, B. (1997). *Practising sustainable water management: Canadian and international experiences.* Cambridge, Ontario: Canadian Water Resources Association.

Whitfield, P., and Taylor, E. (1998). Apparent recent changes in the hydrology and climate of coastal British Columbia. In Y. Alila (Ed.), *Mountains to sea: Human interaction with the hydrologic cycle* (pp. 22-29). Cambridge, Ontario: Canadian Water Resources Association, CWRA 51st Annual Conference Proceedings.

Plate 5 Summer vegetation patterns in the southern Interior near Penticton (looking northwest) ▶

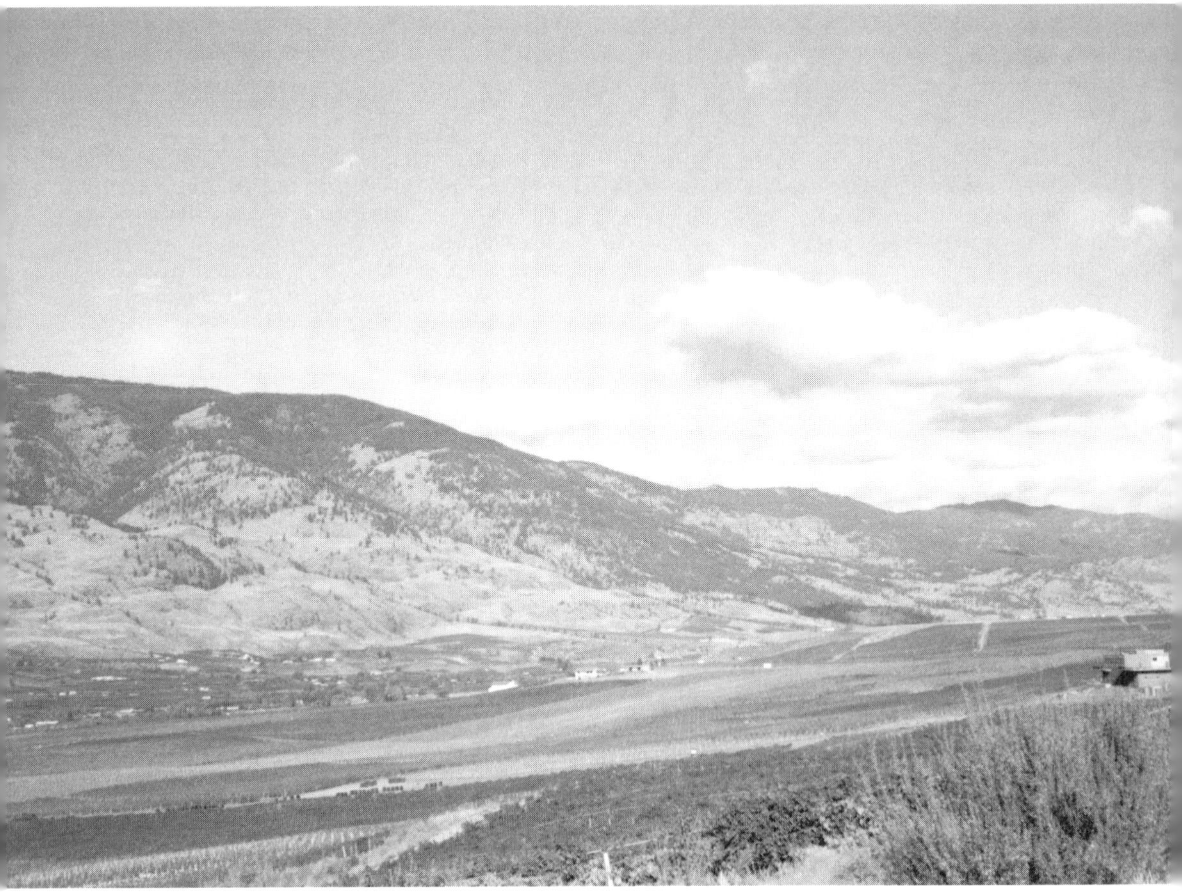

Vegetation

Michael C.R. Edgell

Department of Geography, University of Victoria

An enduring image of BC is that of a mountainous province covered with an endless sea of coniferous forest, interrupted only by widely scattered alpine areas and in the southern Interior by open sagebrush grasslands. However, this image belies the floristic diversity and vegetation complexity of the province. In addition to conifers, over 2,000 species of flowering plants are found within its boundaries. Admittedly, forests do cover about 44% of BC, and evergreen conifers dominate over 90% of these forests; furthermore, deciduous trees are a significant component of many forest types that, encompassing such wide latitudinal and longitudinal extent and topographic diversity, are anything but uniform in structure and floristics.

Introduction

BC is the meeting point of three great North American forest realms. The forests of the Pacific slope are part of a continuous 3,600 km coastal belt of tall coniferous forests extending from northern California to Alaska, variously dominated throughout their range by coast redwood, Doulas-fir, western red cedar, western hemlock, and sitka spruce. Extending across the southern two-thirds of the province, from the lee slopes of the Coast Mountains to the Rockies, are diverse mixed coniferous forests that stretch southward through the Cordillera to Mexico. Finally, across the northern third of the province there is a belt of forests that are structurally and floristically akin to the vast boreal forests extending eastward to Labrador. To this forested mosaic must be added considerable areas of treeless alpine tundra and, in the central Fraser, lower Thompson, lower Similkameen, Nicola, and Okanagan valleys, the dry sagebrush grasslands and open savannas that are northern extensions of the Palouse Prairie and Sonoran desert of the United States.

Each of these major realms contains many different vegetation types, reflecting complex, long-evolving, and selective interactions between plants and environment during the last 12,000 to 15,000 years. The dominant influences governing these interactions are climatic and soil diversity that are, in turn, dependent on the topographic complexity and latitudinal-longitudinal extent of the province. Even a cursory glance at a vegetation map indicates the obvious northwest-southeast zonation of vegetation types aligned parallel to broad climatic and topographic contrasts. At a more detailed level, differences in local climate, soil types, and drainage impart finer textures and contrasts to the vegetation cover.

These plant-environment systems, however, are not merely static reflections of present climate, topography, and soils. They are dynamic, responding both to internal succession processes inherent in the vegetation itself, and to externally imposed environmental changes that have influenced the availability and distribution of suitable habitats or migration routes during the late and post-glacial period. Environmental changes continue: there is now overwhelming evidence that human-induced global climatic change is a reality. This change includes possible shifts in temperature and precipitation patterns that could have significant long-term impacts on plant-environment systems in BC (Hebda, 1991).

The broad outlines of this extraordinarily complex vegetation cover can be examined from two viewpoints—the floristic and the ecological. The first of these provides a picture of the geographical distribution of taxonomic groups—the flora—and in particular the species. In contrast the ecological viewpoint focuses on the discrete vegetation assemblages in the landscape—the plant communities—that have evolved (and continue to evolve) through time from selective interactions between the flora and the environment.

FLORISTIC PATTERNS

Generally, the climatically mild southern areas of the province are floristically more diverse (having more species per unit area) than northern areas. The coast-interior ecotone of the southwest corner contains 60% of all tree species in BC; the south Kootenays are almost as rich (Krajina, Klinka, and Worrall, 1982). At least four geographical *floristic elements* or groups of species are found within BC. These elements reflect first, the influence of species' origins with respect to general continental floristic regions, and second, their organization into distinctive spatial patterns in the province according to their ecological requirements, availability of suitable habitats, migration, and establishment and competition with other species. Selected examples of these four elements are shown in Figure 6.1.

The boreal-transcontinental element (Figure 6.1a) consists of species that are widespread in the boreal sub-arctic or temperate zones across North America. In BC they have a decidedly northern and eastern distribution. Some species, such as tamarack (*Larix laricina*), jack pine (*Pinus banksiana*), and many shrub willows, are restricted to the far northern or northeastern sections of the province. Others, such as white and black spruce (*Picea glauca, P. mariana*), extend farther south into the Interior Plateau.

Species centred in the mountain and valley complexes east of the coastal divide form a continental element (Figure 6.1b). The distribution of some species in this group, such as Engelmann spruce (*Picea engelmanii*) and whitebark pine (*Pinus albicaulis*), overlap the southern edges of the boreal element. Others, such as ponderosa pine (*P. ponderosa*), western larch, and sub-alpine larch (*Larix occidentalis, L. lyallii*), are southern or southeastern in distribution and are widespread farther south in the western US. Distribution patterns in this group are complex because of the topographic diversity of the Interior mountain and valley systems. Many species, including sumac (*Rhus glabra*), poison ivy (*R.radicans*), sagebrush, and some wormwoods (*Artemesia* spp.), that are limited to or centred in the drier interior areas, are also included in the continental element.

The Pacific element consists of species restricted to lowland and mountain areas west of the coastal divide (Figure 6.1c). This element contains two major sub-groups. First are those species, such as yellow cedar (*Chamaecyparis nootkatensis*), amabilis fir (*Abies amabilis*), sitka spruce (*Picea sitchensis*), and red alder (*Alnus rubra*), that are widespread throughout the high precipitation zones of the coast. Second is a distinctly southern or Gulf Islands group that includes garry oak (*Quercus garryana*), arbutus or madrone (*Arbutus menziesii*), hairy manzanita (*Arctostaphhylos columbiana*), and a number of flowering plants such as Easter lily (*Erythronium oreganum*) that are restricted to the drier rain shadow areas of the southwest coast.

An important group of trees and shrubs exhibits a dual or disjunct distribution pattern, occurring in both the coast region and in the wetter Columbia and western Rocky Mountain areas of the Cordillera. This Pacific-Cordilleran element contains, in addition to those shown in Figure 6.1d, such species as western red cedar (*Thuja plicata*), Pacific yew (*Taxus brevifolia*), cascara (*Rhamnus purshiana*), and the appropriately named shrub, devil's club (*Oplopanax horridum*). Some of the flowering plants of the Gulf Islands region also show a disjunct distribution, reappearing in the drier areas of the southern interior.

In contrast to these floristic groupings are species that are more ubiquitous in their distribution. They include a variety of races of lodgepole pine (*Pinus contorta*), which is the most widely distributed conifer in the province; sub-alpine fir (*Abies lasiocarpa*), which

Vegetation

Figure 6.1 Selected examples of the floristic elements

occurs in boreal as well as sub-alpine forests; Douglas-fir (*Pseudostuga menziesii*), which in its coastal and interior forms extends from west to east across the southern third of the province; and trembling aspen (*Populus tremuloides*) and paper birch (*Betula papyrifera*), which, although of limited occurrence on the coast, are widely distributed through the rest of the province.

The actual range occupied by a species is often smaller than its potential range because of competition from other species or barriers to plant migration. Thus, no true firs (*Abies*) have colonized the Queen Charlotte Islands, although the islands are climatically suited to both amabilis fir and probably sub-alpine fir. Members of the genus *Populus* are also absent from the Queen Charlotte Islands, apart from an isolated stand of black cottonwood (*Populus trichocarpa*). Conversely, some species may occur in small isolated areas, or refuges, outside of their main ranges, such as arbutus on the west coast of Vancouver Island at Kyuquot Sound. Isolated patches of Rocky Mountain juniper (*Juniperus scopulorum*) in northwestern BC and tamarack in the Prince George area are hundreds of kilometres from their respective major ranges. In some parts of the province, especially the more densely settled areas that have been occupied for many years, the native flora has been augmented or, in some cases, even replaced by successfully established exotic species. Approximately one-third of the species on the Saanich Peninsula have been introduced, mainly from Europe; 36% of the grasses (*Poaceae*), 60% of mustards (*Brassicaceae*), 50% of legumes (*Fabaceae*), and 44% of asters/sunflowers (*Asteraceae*) are of foreign origin (Szczawinski and Harrison, 1972). The two latter families in particular include persistent and invasive weeds. Scotch Broom (*Cytisus scoparius*) has run rampant on the coast following its introduction in the 1850s and is well established in the Kootenays. It is capable of supplanting native species in disturbed or dry sites and it is difficult to eradicate due to its aggressive growth habits, efficient seed dispersal, and nitrogen-fixing ability. In the southern Interior, two members of the introduced *Asteraceae* genus *Centaurea* or knapweeds (*C. nigra, C. repens*) have invaded thousands of hectares of grazing land, seriously reducing rangeland carrying capacity.

VEGETATION PATTERNS

Floristic maps, while giving an indication of what species may be found where, give no impression of the actual plant communities in the landscape or the qualitative nature of the vegetation cover of the province. Species are not evenly distributed within the ranges shown in Figure 6.1. Rather, within its range each species is distributed in the landscape according to its ecological requirements. This distribution, in response to the environmental complex of topography, climate, soil, drainage, competition, fire, and human disturbances is multidirectional and multidimensional. However, it is not random. Species with similar ecological requirements and the ability to coexist through at least part of their life spans will tend to group together in habitats. Other groups of species will occupy different habitats. These groups are called *plant communities* and collectively they constitute the vegetation of a given area. Thus, alpine tundra vegetation is composed of a mosaic of communities variously dominated by species groups of lichens, mosses, grasses, heaths, or broad-leaved herbs. The vegetation of the Gulf Islands is frequently characterized by relatively dry and open woodland and savanna communities in which there are varying proportions of Douglas-fir, lodgepole pine, arbutus, garry oak, and colourful spring-flowering herbs.

The pattern of communities in the landscape and their collective expression as the vegetation is, therefore, much more complex than that of individual species. The utilization of a hierarchical *biogeoclimatic* classification system, proceeding from generalized to more detailed categories, is one way of understanding this complexity (Krajina, 1969; Meidinger and Pojar, 1991). At the most generalized level, the vegetation of the province can be divided into four formations (Table 6.1). *Mesothermal* or moder-

Vegetation

Table 6.1 Simplified classification and selected climatic characteristics of biogeoclimatic units

	Biogeoclimatic Units		Climatic Characteristics		
Formation	Region	Zone	Accumulated Degree Days Above 5°C	Mean Annual Precipitation (cm)	Elevation (m)
Mesothermal Forest	**Pacific Coast Temperate**	a. Coastal western hemlock	1060-2205	100->450	0-670
	sub-montane/montane:	b. Coastal Douglas fir	1790-2121	65-125	8-225
	a. wetter				
	b. drier				
Microthermal Forest	**Southern Cordilleran Temperate**	a. Interior cedar-hemlock	1267-2140	50-140	315-1085
	sub-montane/montane:	b. Interior Douglas fir	903-2366	30-120	120-1130
	a. wetter	b. Montane spruce	890-1300	38-66	1128-1550
	b. drier	b. Ponderosa pine	1500-2440	32-60	240-950
	Coast Mountains Boreal	Mountain hemlock	c.920	170-500	400-1800
	sub-alpine				
	Cordilleran Boreal	a. Engelmann spruce/sub-alpine fir	630-800	50-200	865-1860
	sub-alpine	b. Spruce/willow/birch	c.500	45-70	900-1700
	a. southern-central				
	b. northern				
	High Latitude Boreal	a. Boreal white and black spruce	709-1268	38-60	390-840
	sub-montane/montane:	b. Sub-boreal spruce	884-1500	44-150	480-1250
	a. northern	b. Sub-boreal pine-spruce	690-1040	46-52	910-1200
	b. central				
Alpine	All Areas Above Tree Line	Alpine tundra	0-250	70-300	>1000 (N) >2350 (S)
Semi-Arid Cold Steppe	Southern Cordillera Semi-Arid	Bunch grass	1770-2515	20-33	300-700

ate temperature) forests grow in mild and sub-humid to very humid sub-montane or montane regions of the coast. *Microthermal* (cold temperature) forests occupy a wide range of montane and sub-alpine cold, humid, snowy winter climates, although summers may be warm and dry. *Grassland* or *steppe* occurs in cold winter, warm summer, and low precipitation areas where tree growth is limited to the most favourable sites. *Alpine tundra* occupies high elevation areas where extreme climatic harshness precludes normal tree growth.

Each of these formations can be further subdivided into regions that more specifically define climatic types resulting from the longitudinal transition from maritime to continental, the latitudinal change from temperate to sub-boreal or boreal and altitudinal influences (Table 6.1). The altitude of the tree line varies considerably across the province. It is about 2,250 m in the continental southeast, 1,600 to 1,800 m in the maritime southwest, 1,400 m in the northeast, and 1,000 m on the north coast (Figure 6.2). Due to this variation, the terms *sub-montane*, *montane*, and *sub-alpine* used to delimit zones and vegetation types below the tree line encompass different altitudinal ranges in each of the regions.

Within each region are one or more biogeoclimatic zones (Table 6.1). Each zone is characterized by a combination of relatively uniform climate, soil, and vegetation. The communities that collectively make up the vegetation of any zone are dominated by a number of characteristic major species. *Climax* communities, occupying *mesic* habitats that are intermediate in moisture and nutrient status and dominated by species that can regenerate on these habitats, are assumed to reflect the overriding influence of climate. These assumed climax communities are used to characterize each biogeoclimatic zone.

The biogeoclimatic zones of BC, all but two of which are forested, provide the framework for the following overview of vegetation in the province (Figure 6.3). At the level of dominant species, the concept of the biogeoclimatic zone is a useful summary, but it does have some disadvantages. Communities of very wet (*hygric*) or dry (*xeric*) environments are often as

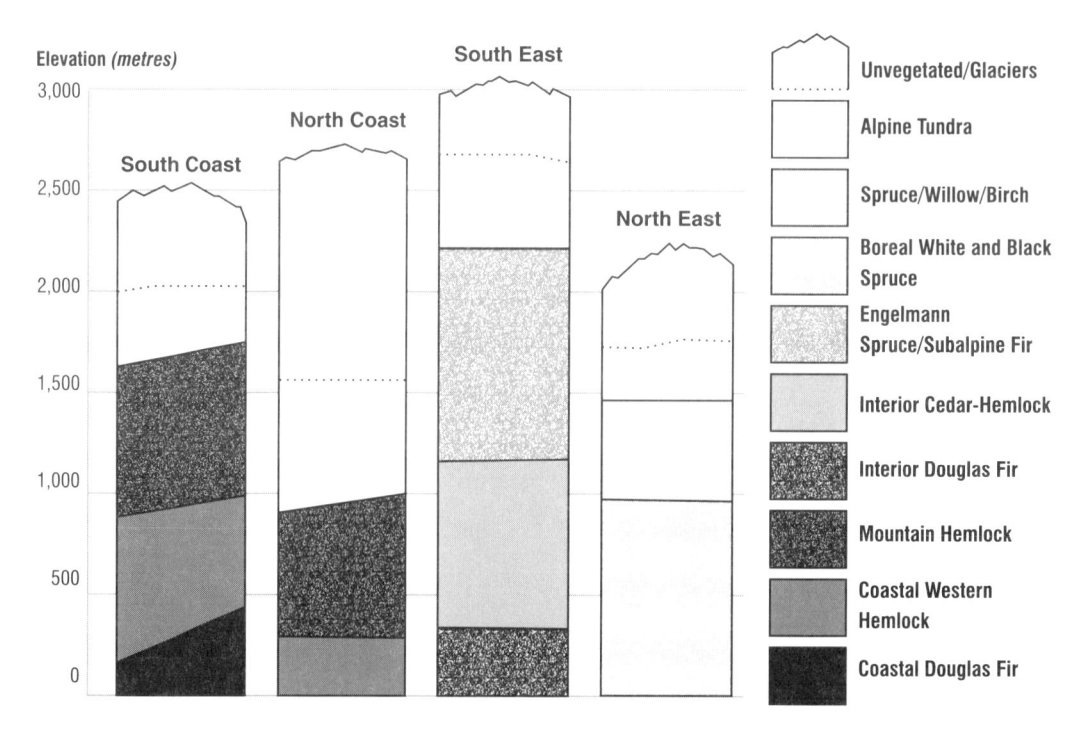

Figure 6.2 Treeline and altitudinal variation of selected forest zones

Vegetation

Figure 6.3 The generalized pattern of biogeoclimatic zones

abundant as those of mesic ones, so that it is necessary to subdivide each zone into smaller sub-zones and associations to more truly reflect what is seen in the landscape. More importantly, in many areas of the province climax communities are the exception rather than the rule. They have been replaced by regrowth or *seral* communities following the destruction of the original communities by agricultural clearing, logging, grazing, drainage, and/or other human activities. These seral communities in, for instance, the coastal Douglas-fir and the interior ponderosa pine and bunchgrass zones are more important landscape elements than the few remaining patches of climax vegetation.

MESOTHERMAL FORESTS

These forests, the most luxuriant of which are the coastal rain forests, occupy sub-montane to montane elevations (0-1,000 m in the south; 0-300 m in the north) on the Pacific slopes of the Coast and Insular (island) Mountains. Winters are mild and wet and summers generally cool, although in the rain shadow of the Olympic and Insular Mountains on the southwest coast, summers are warm and dry. Mesothermal forests contain two biogeoclimatic zones.

Coastal Western Hemlock Zone

Occupying the wettest outer and more northerly parts of the coast, rain forests dominated by western hemlock (*Tsuga heterophylla*) also extend inland along the major valleys of the Coast Mountains. Although western hemlock is the characteristic species throughout the zone, western red cedar is often co-dominant. Coastal Douglas-fir (*Pseudostuga menziesii var. menziesii*) occurs as a seral species in the south, while amabilis fir becomes important farther north. A narrow fringe on the west coast is characterized by sitka spruce and this species becomes more important on the north coast and in the Queen Charlotte Islands. On extreme exposed coasts of northern Vancouver Island, the northern mainland, and the western Queen Charlotte Islands, stunted forests or woodlands of western hemlock, lodgepople pine, and yellow cedar form complex mosaics with peat bogs. Apart from the characteristic tree species, other features of these forests are a very dense shrub layer consisting mainly of salal (*Gaultheria shalon*) and *Vaccinium* species, an abundance of bryophytes, and a paucity of herbs. Away from the exposed coasts, the zone contains the most productive forest land in Canada and has been extensively logged since the 1960s, particularly on the south and central coast. Regrowth stands, frequently dominated by red alder, are widespread.

Coastal Douglas-fir Zone

Forests in which Douglas-fir is, or was, a dominant constituent are limited on the coast to the rain shadow area of Georgia Strait at elevations up to 250 m on eastern Vancouver Island, the Gulf Islands, and restricted areas of the Lower Mainland. Climatically, the zone is characterized as *modified Mediterranean*, with a well-marked summer dry period of varying intensity. Douglas-fir originally was a fire climax species in many of these forests, maintained by periodic (3 - 500 year) forest fires. Nearly all of the original old-growth forests were harvested, as they, along with the drier forests of the western hemlock zone, were almost the only forests utilized by the coastal forest industry up to the 1940s. A mosaic of regrowth communities covers those areas not permanently cleared for agriculture or urban development. Western red cedar, grand fir (*Abies grandis*), lodgepole pine, arbutus, Pacific dogwood (*Cornus nuttallii*), and bigleaf maple (*Acer macrophyllum*) are mixed with Douglas-fir, depending on habitat differences and succession stage. In the drier sub-zone centred on the Gulf Islands and southeast Vancouver Island, arbutus becomes more prevalent and garry oak occupies open woodlands or grassy savannas that support a rich and attractive flora of spring-flowering forbes. These mixed, floristically rich, open forests and woodlands are among the most aesthetically pleasing and diverse in the province. In the face of urban and suburban development, however, they are disappearing quickly, and garry oak ecosystems have been declared an endangered ecosystem (BC Ministry of Environment, Lands and Parks, 1993; Hebda and Aitkens, 1993).[1]

MICROTHERMAL FORESTS

Collectively, these forests are the most widespread in BC, occupying the boreal latitudes and montane to sub-alpine elevations of the Cordillera and Coast Mountains. All areas have cold, often snowy winters and short, although sometimes dry and hot, summers. Because of the wide latitudinal and longitudinal range and associated climatic, topographic, and floristic diversity, microthermal forests are extremely varied. With the exception of wetter types in the Columbia Mountains and Skeena drainage system, they are structurally and floristically distinct from the coastal mesothermal forests.

Montane Forests

Interior Cedar-Hemlock Zone

Occupying the lower valley slopes of the Columbia Mountains and parts of the southern Rocky Mountain Trench in the southeast and the mid-sections of the Skeena drainage system in the northeast, these forests are occasionally called the *Interior wet belt*. Winters are cool and wet due to orographic effects on eastward-moving air masses that still retain enough moisture to produce heavy precipitation. Although the precipitation is lower than that on the coast, vegetation structure and floristics are very similar. Logging has removed many of the original climax communities of western red cedar and western hemlock because the quality and volume of timber in these forests are second only to those of coastal stands. Spruces, sub-alpine fir, western larch, interior Douglas-fir (*Pseudostuga menziesii* var. *glauca*), and western white pine (*Pinus monticola*) are widespread, both in the remaining climax and many seral stands. In terms of conifers, the southeast section of this zone has the greatest variety of any forest type in the province; and in terms of overall floristic richness, the West Kootenay forests are exceeded only by those of southeast Vancouver Island.

Interior Douglas-fir Zone

Apart from isolated areas in the southern Rocky Mountain Trench, this zone essentially extends westward from the interior cedar-hemlock zone across the montane elevations of the southern Interior Plateau, as far north as Williams Lake and the Chilcotin River valley. It lies, therefore, in the rain shadow of the Coastal Mountains and although temperatures suggest a long growing season, the dry summers often impose severe water stress. Like those of the interior cedar-hemlock zone, interior Douglas-fir forests extend southward into Washington, Oregon, Idaho, and Montana. Although the zone is named for the interior form of Douglas-fir occupying open to closed forests over large areas, forest types are complex due to both environmental and human influences. With the development of the interior forest industry since the 1960s, much of this zone has been logged. Regrowth stands dominated by ponderosa or lodgepole pines frequently replace Douglas-fir forests. Trembling aspen, spruce, and western larch are common. Grand fir, western hemlock, and western white pine occur in the wetter areas. In marked rain shadow areas, dry grasslands are common and have been extended by fire and persistent grazing, especially in the southern Chilcotin.

Montane Spruce Zone

This zone occupies a narrow mid-elevation range between the Engelmann spruce-subalpine fir and interior Douglas-fir zones in the south-central Interior. Extending south from the Fraser Plateau, the montane spruce zone is characterized by cold winters and short, often dry and warm summers. Although the zone is named for spruce, many of the forests are composed of even-aged regrowth stands of lodgepole pine—a result of repetitive wildfires. Sub-alpine fir and Engelmann spruce do regenerate under the lodgepole pine canopy, but rarely attain *climax* status because of repeated disturbance. In more favourable sites or southern areas, Douglas-fir, trembling aspen, and sub-alpine fir are more extensive.

Ponderosa Pine Zone

Generally lying between 350 and 900 m along the lower valley walls and bottoms of the southern Interior and the southern Rocky Mountain Trench, this is the driest and (in the summer) the warmest of the province's forest zones. Typically, it occurs between the lower elevation bunchgrass and higher elevation interior Douglas-fir zones. Although classified as forest, productivity is low and logging is now of little importance. Cattle grazing, however, is an important use of the ecosystems in this zone. The vegetation is a mosaic of forests, savannas, and grasslands—the result of complex interactions between habitat variation, fire, and human influences. In addition to Ponderosa pine, interior Douglas-fir occurs in gullies and on north-facing slopes, and trembling aspen forms dense stands along streams and seepage zones. Some stands of Ponderosa pine are open and park-like, with an understory of bluebunch wheatgrass (*Agropyron spicatum*), fescues (*Festuca* spp.), and balsamroot (*Balsamorhiza sagittata*). Many of these stands are the legacy of past logging or fire, and with the advent of fire suppression, are frequently being replaced with denser, closed stands, often containing much lodgepole pine. Variations in soil and topography, supplemented by fires, have produced widespread grasslands that grade into those of the more extensive lower elevation bunchgrass zone.

Sub-alpine Forests

These forests occupy the altitudinal zones between montane forests and the tree line throughout BC, both in the Pacific and Cordilleran regions. Elevations range from 400-1,000 m in the northwest Coast Mountains to 1,250-2,250 m in the dry continental sub-alpine regions of the southeast.

Mountain Hemlock Zone

This is the mildest sub-alpine zone, restricted to the Coastal and Insular Mountains above 900 m elevation in the south and 400 m in the north. It is characterized by very heavy snowfalls that last into spring and prevent soils from freezing but also result in a short growing season. Mixtures of mountain hemlock (*Tsuga mertensiana*), amabilis fir, and yellow cedar, the latter especially on wetter soils, dominate the forests. Sub-alpine fir and whitebark pine are present near the timberline and Douglas-fir and western white pine intrude in southern regions at lower elevations. Tree growth is retarded at higher elevations and closed forests give way to a parkland of trees in favoured habitats interspersed with more open areas of alpine heath or meadow. Like the lower elevation coastal western hemlock zone, these forests are rich in mosses, however the shrub layer of salal is replaced by one dominated mainly by *Vaccinium* spp., *Rhododendron albiflorum*, and mountain heathers, *Phyllodoce* and *Cassiope* spp. These become more abundant in the parkland zone transitional to alpine tundra where floristically rich and colourful herb meadows develop in moist, sheltered habitats. Although tree growth rates are low at the upper elevations, more accessible stands have been cleared and some logging has extended to the tree line.

Engelmann Spruce-Sub-alpine Fir Zone

This zone occupies an inverted U-shaped crescent in the southern two-thirds of the province, extending from the Rockies to the southern part of the Skeena and Omenica Mountains and thence southward along the eastern slopes of the Coast Mountains. It is the highest in elevation of the forest zones in the province, lying between 1,250 and 2,250 m in the southeast and 900 and 1,700 m in the north. The dry continental climate results in less protective snow cover than in the mountain hemlock zone and soils may become frozen. In such a wide latitudinal range there are many tree species, although old-growth mixtures of Engelmann spruce and sub-alpine fir are the most widespread. To the south, the zone grades into the two montane forest zones and is characterized also by whitebark pine and alpine larch. In the north, Engelmann spruce is replaced by hybrid Engelmann-white spruce in transitions

Vegetation

to boreal and sub-boreal forests. Throughout the zone, as in so many other forests, lodgepole pine is an important seral species. Parklands are common at the upper limits of tree growth, varying from grasslands on dry slopes through heaths to lush herb meadows in more favoured areas.

Spruce-Willow-Birch Zone

Restricted to sub-alpine elevations of 1,000-1,700 m north of 57° and occupying areas above the boreal forests but below tundra, this zone is centred on the Cassiar, Skeena, and Omenica Mountains. It extends west to the St. Elias Mountains and east across the northern Rockies to the Alberta Plateau. Due to a combination of altitude and elevation it is climatically the most extreme of the forest zones in BC. Over large areas it is occupied by a scrub of willows and birch, with only scattered sub-alpine fir. At lower elevations, forests of white spruce and sub-alpine fir contain occasional black spruce, lodgepole pine, and aspen, the latter especially on sheltered south-facing slopes. Some areas show the interesting phenomenon of an inverted tree line. Large valleys, into which cold air drains and accumulates, sometimes causing permafrost, are too harsh for tree growth and are vegetated only by grasslands, heaths, or low shrubs. Trees that, in turn, are replaced by shrubs at the more exposed higher elevations occupy the lower slopes of the valleys, away from cold air drainage. To the east of the Rockies, this zone is influenced by wildfires and regrowth stands are widespread.

Boreal Forests

Forests typical of the great trans-Canadian boreal formation are restricted in BC to sub-montane and montane elevations (200-950 m) north of 54°. Three zones are recognized, one a true boreal forest and the other two transitional to more southern microthermal forests.

Boreal White and Black Spruce Zone

This zone is centred on the Alberta Plateau region east of the Rocky Mountains but north of 57° extends also to valleys west of the Rockies. The climate is controlled by Arctic air masses, resulting in a very short growing season, harsh winters, and generally poor soil development often associated with permafrost and/or poor drainage. Besides the two spruces, forests are characterized also by sub-alpine fir, lodgepole pine, tamarack, trembling aspen, balsam poplar (*Populus balsamifera*), and birches. Poorly drained sites contain muskeg, tamarack (only northeast of the Rockies), and black spruce. True forests, in which white spruce and trembling aspen are the most important species, are limited to the better-drained or alluvial sites, where the balance between species is largely influenced by fires—an integral component of the boreal environment. The generally poor growth of and limited access to these forests mean that large areas are still unlogged; aspen, however, represents an important resource.

Sub-Boreal Spruce Zone

Lying to the south of the true boreal forests, this zone extends from 52° to 57° in the central Interior at elevations immediately below the Engelmann spruce-sub-alpine fir zone and dominates much of the Nechako and Quesnel Plateaus and the upper Fraser basin. It is transitional to both the sub-alpine and more southern Interior Douglas-fir zones. Climatically, the zone is less severe so that the forests are more productive than those of the boreal white and black spruce zone. White spruce, hybrid Engelmann-white spruce, and sub-alpine fir are dominant. Seral stands of lodgepole pine and aspen are widespread and lower, wetter areas are occupied by paper birch and black cottonwood. The productive forests in this zone are a crucial resource for the interior forest industry, and since the 1970s have been among the most heavily and destructively logged in the province. Regrowth stands—the result of fire as well as logging—are widespread.

Sub-Boreal Pine-Spruce Zone

Formerly included in the previous zone, these forests occupy the drier, colder, high elevations of the Fraser and Nechako Plateaus east of the Coast Mountains, with a major concentration in the northern Chilcotin. Climatic harshness and a long fire history have produced vast even-aged stands of lodgepole pine, often with extensive lichen-dominated groundcover, interspersed with vast wetland habitat. White and hybrid spruce occur in more favoured areas, and black spruce in the northern sections.

Semi-Arid Grassland/Steppe

The combination of continentality and rain shadow effects that produces the ponderosa pine zone is intensified along the lower valleys of the southern Interior. Here, in the southern Okanagan, lower Thompson, Nicola, mid-Fraser, and lower Chilcotin valleys, the warmest and driest climate in BC supports open grassland and shrub-steppe ecosystems. These ecosystems collectively form the bunchgrass zone, the smallest of the province's biogeoclimatic zones, occupying less than 1% of the province's area.

Bunchgrass Zone

The lower elevations in these valleys were originally occupied by grassland dominated by bunchgrass species of *Agropyron* and *Poa*, and in the driest areas by sagebrush (*Artemesia tridentata*) shrub steppe. Overgrazing has significantly altered these original communities and they are now often dominated by *increaser* or invading species such as rabbit bush (*Chrysothamnus nauseosus*), pussytoes (*Antennaria* spp.), cactus (*Opuntia fragilis*), and *Centaura* spp. Tree growth is marginal and limited to drought and fire-resistant ponderosa pine, supplemented by Douglas-fir and aspen on soils with better water supply. Above 700-1,000 m, tree cover increases and grasslands grade into communities of the ponderosa pine and interior Douglas-fir zones.

ALPINE TUNDRA

At elevations ranging from 1,000 m on the north coast to 2,250 m in the southeastern mountains, increased climatic severity ultimately prevents tree growth and the open parklands of the upper sub-alpine grade into alpine tundra.

Stunted or *krummholz* trees sometimes extend into the lower elevations of the alpine tundra but true tundra communities are dominated by low-growing shrubs, herbs, grasses, mosses, and lichens. They often form complex mosaics in response to minor differences in topography, exposure, bedrock geology, and length of snow cover. Only lichens or xeric mosses will grow in the most extreme habitats and thin grasslands of *Festuca* and *Carex* species are frequent on dry exposed slopes. Denser plant cover includes shrub communities dominated by dwarf willows, *Vaccinium*, *Cassiope*, *Phyllodoce*, and *Dryas* and, in sheltered or moist areas, luxuriant herb meadows. Adaptions to extreme desiccation, cold and physical abrasion include prostrate growth of many shrubs and the well-known cushion form of a wide range of different plants. Large areas are bare of plant cover and alpine ecosystems in general are fragile and prone to damage from the heavy recreational use that they often attract.

CONCLUSIONS

The varied and rugged topography, together with the regional and altitudinal variations in environment, result in a rich and diverse pattern of vegetation in BC. Despite the large area of the province, the mountainous terrain and the dry, semi-desert conditions in the southeast result in only about 44% of the area being forested. Much of the vegetation has been changed during the last century. The forests have been modified by harvesting and replanting with human-preferred species that have higher market value. Agriculture and ranching have also contributed to the change in meadow and grassland communities. However, greater care in forest harvesting methods, road construction, herbicide applications, and an expanding appreciation of the natural (native) vegetation now bode well for the future. The designation of about 13% of BC as parks and reserves is also commendable. In the long view, however, it is highly probable that the change in global climatic conditions will have an impact on the vegetation patterns in BC.

REFERENCES

BC Ministry of Environment, Lands and Parks (1993). *Garry oak ecosystems at risk*. Victoria: Wildlife Branch.

Hebda, R.J. (1991). Global climatic change and the impact on BC plants and vegetation. *Bioline*, 10(1), 11-15.

Hebda, R.J., and Aitkens, F. (Eds.) (1993). *Garry oak meadow colloquium*. Proceedings: Victoria.

Krajina, V.J. (1969). Ecology of forest trees in British Columbia. *Ecology of Western North America*, 2, 1-146

Krajina, V.J., Klinka, K., and Worrall, J. (1982). *Distribution and ecological characteristics of trees and shrubs of British Columbia*. Vancouver: University of British Columbia, Faculty of Forestry.

Meidinger, D., and Pojar, J. (Eds.) (1991). *Ecosystems of British Columbia*. British Columbia Ministry of Forests, Special Report Series, No. 6

Szczawinski, A.F., and Harrison, A.S. (1972). *Flora of the Saanich Peninsula*. Victoria: Provincial Museum, Occasional Papers No. 16.

ENDNOTE

[1] The last major undisturbed garry oak stands (located on Saltspring Island) will become protected with the designation of the Gulf Islands National Park.

Plate 6 Murals depicting significant local historical events can be seen in many communities ▶

TRAVEL
INFOCENTRE
HORSESHOE BAY HOTEL
CLEMENT'S DRUG STORE

Geopolitical Development: An Overview

Paul F. Thomas

Department of Geography, University of Victoria

INTRODUCTION

This chapter surveys particular geopolitical highlights associated with the formation and evolution of BC, from the time of European contact to the present. For convenience, this geopolitical development is subdivided into pre-Confederation and post-Confederation intervals.

The pre-Confederation period—predominantly Eurocentric in flavour, can be subdivided into three crucial phases characterized in turn by:

1) the antecedent, 'great power' rivalries in the Pacific Northwest;
2) the role of the Hudson's Bay Company, and its leading actors, as instruments of British imperial interests;
3) the circumstances and agencies propelling BC into a confederation with Canada.

The discussion of the post-Confederation interval revolves around a case study that deals with the geopolitics of BC's hydro-power development during the 1950s and 1960s. Although this phase epitomizes an unprecedented political mania for economic, infrastructural development on the mega scale, it also induced its opposite, namely an equally unprecedented explosion of public environmental awareness.

The ensuing *economy versus environment* tensions triggered new sets of concerns that persist to this day. In that respect, those two decades of *hydro-power, power politics* signalled BC's coming of age and a part of 'ecotopia.' Indeed, those decisive decades irrevocably betokened the province's greatest quantum leap toward a greater, albeit incomplete, local locus of control. That leap stands as a marked contradistinction to the region's earlier dominance by Eurocentric and eastern North American, geopolitical scripts far more oblivious to the voice of the people than today.

For micro studies that explore the subtexts, subtending the necessarily broad brush-strokes of this chapter, the reader is respectfully referred to *BC Studies*, a specialized quarterly engaged with the past and present of BC's cultural, economic, and political life

ANTECEDENT GEOPOLITICAL ACTORS AND INTERESTS IN THE PACIFIC NORTHWEST

Fur Trade and Polity

When Canada was made a 'dominion' through the legislative provisions of the *British North America Act* in 1867, the Latin expression, *a mari usque ad mare* [from sea to sea] was used to describe its east-west extent. At that time, such a motto was really inapt since Canada did not yet fully extend from the Atlantic to the Pacific Ocean. The new nation was still missing all of present-day British Columbia and all of the Hudson's Bay Company's (HBC) territories lying east of the Rockies and extending to the Great Lakes and the Arctic. However, in 1869 the prairie territories of the HBC were directly transferred to Canada. Two years later, in 1871, the separate British colony of BC, which earlier had been *de facto* HBC territory, also became a part of Canada. This truer sea-to-sea dominion in effect politically transmogrified into a nation the earlier trading territories over which the HBC had at one time or another held monopolistic sway. This later constitutional mode of nation-building could also be regarded as simply another variant of the *imperialist project*, that is, as a more efficient geopolitical codification of colonial acquisitions in the service of transnational commercial interests.

Founded as a London-based English corporation in 1670, the HBC was conceptually an embryonic precursor to the multinational corporations of today, and arguably driven by comparable economic imperatives. Awarded a monopoly over trade in the region watered by rivers flowing into Hudson Bay, the HBC's principal objective was to exploit the fur trade and by so doing perhaps stumble upon a Northwest Passage to the Pacific. In the 1750s, conflicts with the French intensified over control of profitable fur sheds and trading routes. These conflicts were resolved by the British conquest of French-Canada in 1763.

However, the ensuing imperialist drive westward into a vast unknown interior, and ultimately to the Pacific Ocean, was to prove unamenable to monopolistic control. By 1783 a rival group of speculators formed the North West Company (NWC) of Montreal. A few decades later, the fierce competition with the HBC was trending toward a depletion of the choicest fur-bearing animals and smaller profit margins. A corporate takeover seemed to be in order. In 1821, the two companies merged under the name of the HBC, whose monopoly was renewed and guaranteed by licence. Their newly combined territory extended to the Pacific Ocean in the west, and the Arctic Ocean to the north. The merger was to have a fixed term of 21 years. Renewed in 1838, the trading monopoly was allowed to expire in 1859, after which the HBC could retain title to its property rights. These rights (except for the forts and trading posts) were finally transferred in 1870 to the Dominion of Canada for a sum of £300,000 and a land grant of 2,835,000 hectares.

The Role of Great Power Rivalries

The British

Were it not for the perceptions and actions of various geopolitical actors, British Columbia need not have become British in the first place, nor a part of Canada. Clearly, the HBC was an important geopolitical actor, present at BC's birth and at its later union with Canada. On the one hand, the HBC was a local proxy for British imperial interests. On the other hand, its interests were not always congruent with those of the British colonial office. The desire to expand overseas trade had already been a precipitating motive in the formation of the earlier *English East India Company* in 1600 which aimed to control trade in Asia, Africa, and America. Their adventurers were to establish the first English outposts in North America.

In 1778 the first Englishman, Captain James Cook, set foot on the Pacific coast north of 48°N latitude when his ship landed at Nootka Sound on Vancouver Island where he was welcomed by Nootka Chief Maquinna. In that same year Cook also mapped the Alaskan coast, returning with sea otter pelts which his crew sold in China at the very high price of $100 per pelt— a sum equal to 2 years wages for the average sailor. Fifteen years later Sir Alexander Mackenzie became the first European overland explorer to reach the Pacific, after an east-west traverse of British North America (Figure 7.1).

Russians and Americans

In the late 1700s, Russia and Spain also intensified their geopolitical interest in the Pacific Northwest coast of North America. Peter the Great recruited the services of Danish sea captain Vitus Bering to explore the seas between eastern Siberia and Alaska. As a result of Bering's discoveries, Peter's imperialist successors initiated a lucrative Alaskan fur trade with the local natives without establishing a permanent Russian colony, until they were forced to do so in 1784. The compelling reason was the strength of foreign competition, especially from the British, who were able to offer higher quality goods at a cheaper cost to the local Aleutian peoples. By 1799, the Russian Tsar Paul I had created his own version of the HBC known as the Russia America Company. Granted a monopoly of the coastal North American fur trade, this new fur trading company was empowered to claim and settle all territories already occupied by Russians north

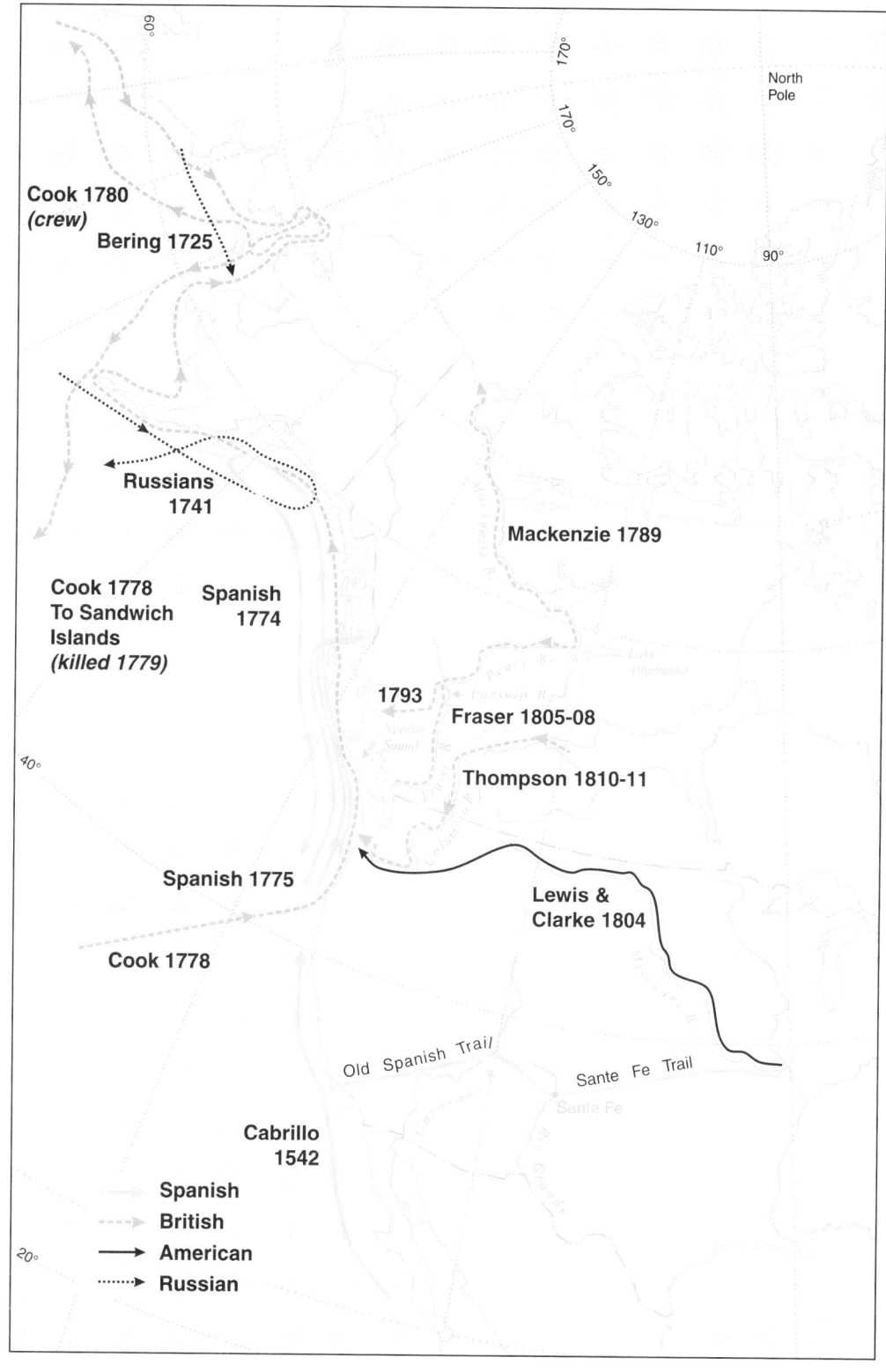

Figure 7.1 European exploration in northwest North America

of 55°N latitude. Nor were they to regard that line as a constraint to further southward penetration. Later they were able to maintain a settlement near Bodega Bay, California for 30 years. Eventually, in 1841, that settlement was sold to German entrepreneur John Sutter, who soon found the gold that precipitated the 1848 California Gold Rush. Meanwhile, in keeping with the imperialist norms of the times, the Russians, through the spreading of disease and guns, were able to reduce the Aleutian population under their jurisdiction by 90%. That is to say, a pre-contact population of about 20,000 inhabitants was reduced to 2,000 persons by the time Russia's Alaskan territory was sold to the US in 1867.

Long before that sale, the Russian navy had been attempting to enforce a 160 km offshore oceanic swath as their exclusive territorial sea. This oceanic limit, however, had proved to be no serious barrier to penetration by British and American naval vessels. The resulting disputes were resolved by conventions. In 1824, the US agreed to recognize the 54°40'N latitude as the southern limit of the Russian empire in America. In 1825, Britain and Russia agreed that the 141°W meridian would demarcate the eastern limit for the vast bulk of the latter's Alaskan territory, with the exception of the southern coastal strip contiguous with the present Pacific Panhandle as far as 54°40'N. At the same time, Russia conceded trading rights along the Alaskan coast to both the US and Britain for 10 years. This concession arguably forestalled, then and there, any Russian expansion that might have curtailed the expanse of present-day BC. In any case, by the late 1850s the Russians were defeated by the British and French during the Crimean War in a contest of the great European powers of the day. As a result, the Russians were readily persuaded that, given the costs of their recent war, they could no longer afford the luxury of maintaining a colony in North America. Accordingly, the Russians initiated talks with the Americans who, by the time the dust of the American Civil War had settled, took possession of Alaska in late 1867 on the strength of a promise to pay $7.2 million. In 1868, American ratification of that promise definitively excised Russia's 126-year toehold on the North American continent. The Russian presence, however, had simply been displaced by an even greater threat to Britain's territorial claims in the region. This fresh threat was that of an American bear hug now squeezing—for the first time—from the northwest, as well as from the south.

The Spanish

In order to forestall the southward creep of Russian traders searching for seal and sea otter pelts along the Pacific coast to the north of California, the Spanish, clearly understanding that "possession was 9/10ths of ownership," established a number of *presidios* (military posts) and missions to signal their effective occupance of coastal California. They also sent exploratory expeditions into northern Pacific waters toward Alaska in 1774, 1777, 1778, and 1790, with the option of claiming any new territories of promise that might present themselves. In 1789, the Spanish, while in the process of constructing a fort at Nootka Sound in present-day BC, were interrupted by a British naval vessel carrying officers and Chinese artisans instructed to build a trading post at the very same site. The British contingent was immediately taken captive and dispatched to San Blas in southern Florida, thereby precipitating a *casus belli*. Diplomacy, however, managed to prevail. The prisoners were returned and the Spanish resumed building their fort in 1790. Later that same year, the *Nootka Convention* was signed whereby Nootka Sound was to remain open to all European powers. In addition, both Spain and Britain were to have equally unfettered trading access to unclaimed portions of the Pacific Northwest. Britain intensified its exploration of the region through naval captain George Vancouver,[1] who spent the 3 years from 1792 to 1795 surveying the coast. This action led to a revised *Nootka Convention* in 1792. Therein, Spain and Britain agreed not to maintain a permanent base at Nootka Sound, and barred any third power from doing so. Soon thereafter Spain became involved in Europe's Napoleonic wars—as did Russia; and as a pragmatic matter of policy was compelled to direct its geopolitical attentions away from the North Pacific. In 1819, Spain surrendered all of its interests in the Pacific Northwest, north of 42°N (California's present northern boundary), to the US. In exchange the latter promised to respect Spanish claims south of that latitude.

The French

Having learned of Cook's voyages and Russian activities from the 1770s onward, the French took some exploratory interest in the Pacific Northwest. However, after conceding French Canada to the British by the Treaty of Paris in 1763, their land base for any possible overland exploration had been eliminated. A naval expedition to Alaska was then attempted. It failed when its leader was lost at sea in 1788. The onset of the French Revolution in 1789 put further expeditionary efforts on hold. By 1815, at which time the Napoleonic Wars had been settled, France had already long since sold off the residue of its North American holdings to the US through the Louisiana Purchase in 1803. It gave Napoleon Bonaparte of France $15 million. In exchange he relinquished a land area of 2.1 million km^2, which roughly comprises the middle third of the present-day continental US lying west of the Mississippi River. As a result, France was no longer a North American power to be reckoned with. The Louisiana Purchase provided more *Lebensraum,* or "living space," for the US by eliminating the possibility of conflict between French interests and those of westward-moving American settlers. The risk of BC's antecedent territories falling under American political jurisdiction was thereby greatly exacerbated.

The Role of Naval Power

During the period outlined above, when the number of European geopolitical actors contending for toeholds in the Pacific Northwest was at its peak, the leading factors colouring the shape of these contentions were *naval power, geographical space relations,* and *environmental/ resource perceptions.* Britain, having the more powerful navy, was better able to project its sea power than France, which was unable to hold on to French Canada and any major interests in India after 1763. However, by the mid 19th century, implicit British naval doctrine viewed the projection of any naval power to the Pacific coast of North America as being far less utile than it had been on the Atlantic seaboard, which it had been unable to hold toward the end of the American Revolution (c. 1783). By the mid 1800s, the Americans would have acquired far more proximate overland access to their western shores, which the British could not counter by any sea power in the Pacific. At a time when only a single British merchant vessel might do an annual run around Cape Horn to the Pacific Northwest, was it not expecting too much to dispatch a strong naval squadron that would be at risk of encountering the perennially violent storms that assailed the southern tip of South America?

Similar considerations coloured British geopolitical attitudes toward Russia and Spain. Russia, via its budding Siberian, and subsequent Alaskan bases, appeared to have easier access to the Pacific coast further south. In the Pacific, confrontations with Russia would have proven very costly and so had to be avoided. Closer to its home base however, Britain had a much stronger hand. The British navy could easily blockade any Russian vessels in the Black Sea, and proceeded to do just that during the Crimean War. It was by such roundabout means that the Russians were pressured to give up their North American colony. Although Alaska was apparently proximate to Pacific Siberia, it was far from the Russian heartland of the Moscow-St. Petersburg-Odessa triangle.

The British attitude toward Spanish interests in the Pacific Northwest was similar. As with their situation vis à vis the Russians, the British would have had to service extremely long lines of communications and therefore preferred to avoid confrontation in the Pacific. The Spanish, for their part, were more experienced with tropical and subtropical navigation than with the mid- and northern latitudes. Although, theoretically, they may have had more proximate bases in California, or even on the Pacific Coast of South America, which avoided the necessity of passing Cape Horn, the Spanish also were afraid of stretching their power too thinly, given their other military commitments in Europe, as well as the broadly scattered, global character of the Spanish Empire itself. Well aware of the flaws in the Spanish geostrategic armour, Britain was prepared to exert its naval muscle in the North Pacific and in effect forced Spanish interests to back off.

Winners and Losers

By the mid 19th century, it appeared that the greatest net gains in geopolitical control of the Pacific Northwest would likely be obtained by the US and Britain. The waning interests of France, Spain, and Russia were leaving the stage, more by default than by design, to Britain and the US, who would, by their actions or inactions, define the boundaries of present-day BC. The matter would no longer be predominantly coloured by considerations of sea power. The US was emerging as a major land power. Land-power interests would also eventually come to the fore in the Pacific region of British North America.

THE CLASH OF BRITISH AND AMERICAN INTERESTS IN THE PACIFIC NORTHWEST

British and American Perceptions of Alaska and the Pacific Northwest

As implied earlier, British North America's western boundary (which was later to become BC's western boundary) had been, in effect, demarcated by a bilateral treaty dated February 28, 1825, whereby Britain conceded virtual control of the Alaskan territory to Russia in exchange for exclusive rights to what is now mainland BC, Yukon, and a portion of the Northwest Territories (NWT).[2] The Alaskan territory, as we have seen, was sold to the US in 1867/68, thus placing American interests and a possible threat of American hegemony on the northwest frontier of British territory. The province of BC did not yet exist; nor was there any compelling reason in the first four decades of the 19th century for it to exist. Nor was it clear that the vaster interior portion of the territorial domain antecedent to BC even needed to be British. The perception of this territory's value at imperial headquarters in London was refracted through the lenses of British sea power and of the commercial interests dependent upon that sea power which had not yet escaped the fur staples trap.[3] Those interests were primarily littoral. The mainland interior was perceived as a barrier to transportation and communication possessing little value in its own right except as a source region for furs. The fur-shed value of the interior could presumably be enhanced if efficient conduits to coastal trading depots could be developed. The NWC of Montreal, as alluded to earlier, had the necessary motivation and instrumentality for finding such conduits in the person of Alexander Mackenzie, who became the first white man to traverse North America north of Mexico. His exploits would intensify a ferocious rivalry with the HBC for control of transcontinental fur transhipment routes.

Land Exploration and its Purpose

The 1793 overland traverse of the Pacific west by Alexander Mackenzie stimulated parallel exploits by others following in his wake. In 1808, Simon Fraser in tracing the Fraser River established the first non-coastal trading posts west of the Rocky Mountains. Four years later, in 1812, David Thompson, arguably the greatest of the fur-trade explorers, became the first white man to traverse the Kootenay region. In doing so, he traced the Columbia River from its source to its mouth (see Figure 7.1). The HBC acted expeditiously to take advantage of these new conduits, even merging with the NWC in 1821 to prosecute the fur trade more efficiently. Even so, the enlarged HBC was under instructions from its political masters in London to avoid attracting new settlement for its own sake. The priority was to be the fur business. Settlement was to be capped at the minimal threshold level that would permit efficient maintenance and provisioning of a limited number of trading posts.

To the south of the British Pacific Northwest a somewhat different set of politically sanctioned *environmental-use perceptions* would emerge. After acquiring the Louisiana Territory from France in 1803—the principal geopolitical achievement of his office—American President Thomas Jefferson commissioned the explorers Meriwether Lewis and William Clark to travel as far west as possible. By 1805 they had reached the Pacific Coast after having negotiated the savage Columbia River. Apprised by the reports of Lewis and Clark that followed their exploits, American fur traders also began taking an interest in the Pacific region, parallelling, and then later clashing with those of the NWC further to the north. By 1811, the first American trading post was constructed at the mouth of the Columbia River. It was named Astoria, after Jacob Astor, the founder of the *Pacific Fur Company* (PFC). Astoria soon began to compete with the NWC's *Fort George*, the precursor to the present-day city of Prince George on the upper Fraser River. Strange to say, the British were also to call Astoria, *Fort George*, after they had purchased it together with the other forts and assets of the PFC, from Jacob Astor's traders in 1813.

Today such abandonment of territory seems to be out of character with the American national mythos of *manifest destiny*, conveniently mobilized for justifying the expansionary ambitions of the US from the time of its political rupture from Britain in 1783. However, some 30 years later, Britain was engaged in a military rematch with the Americans known as the War of 1812 (1812-1815). With Astoria under the threat of attack from the British navy, Jacob Astor opted for a cash sale rather than risk the destruction of his company's assets in the Pacific Northwest.

In 1821 the British government, desirous of consolidating their territorial bridgehead in the present day state of Washington, instructed the HBC and NWC to amalgamate, with the former Fort Astoria becoming the Pacific headquarters for a now expanded HBC. However, the Columbia River, which flowed down to the coastal post of Astoria, also comprised the last leg of the Oregon Trail that had been broached by Lewis and Clark. The Oregon Trail was to become a transit corridor for an ever surging influx of agricultural settlers following in the wake of renewed fur-trading activity on the part of the Americans.

Geostrategic intuitions and lost opportunities

In 1825, mindful that most British exploration had taken place north of the Columbia River and that he needed to shorten and strengthen his 'defensive perimeter,' the HBC's chief factor for the Pacific Northwest, John McLoughlin, moved his headquarters from Astoria to Fort Vancouver (the present-day Vancouver, Washington, sited on the Columbia River across from Portland, Oregon). In doing so, he effectively surrendered the mouth of the Columbia, as well as its southern bank to future American occupation. Nevertheless, this move gained certain situational advantages. Firstly, McLoughlin acquired a forward gateway to the interior (from the standpoint of British naval support proceeding from the Pacific Ocean). This forward outpost, at a major bend in the Columbia River, also put him 80 km south of Astoria's latitude as well as 150 km upstream, where he would have a narrower north-south bridging challenge should the British ever wish to extend their southerly salient even farther south into the easily negotiated Willamette River valley. A more interior location further upstream, however, was contraindicated due to the presence of numerous rapids on the Columbia a short, upstream distance to the east (Figure 7.2).

Unravelling of the HBC Mission Focus and its Implications

It was at this juncture that the *mission focus* of the HBC gradually began to unravel. Whereas the Americans perceived the Willamette Valley as an environmental Mecca for agricultural development and settlement for its own sake, the HBC, for their part, viewed such possibilities as a distraction from its central mission of collecting and trans-shipping furs. Even so, McLoughlin needed to maintain and provision his enterprise. His new location proved ideal for harvesting the river salmon as a very

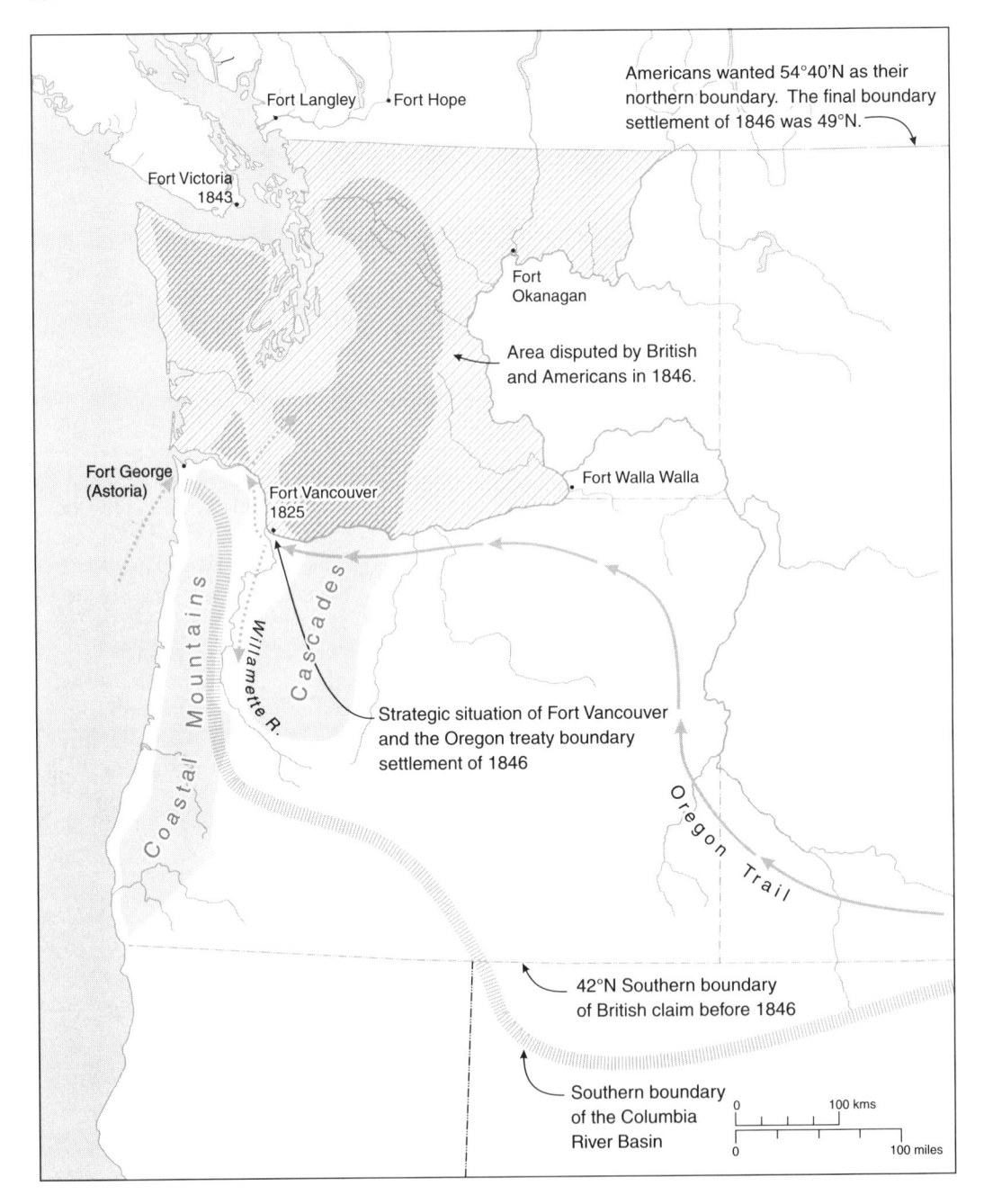

Figure 7.2 American and British claims in the northwest region of North America

inexpensive source of food for his people. In addition, timber could be readily cut and floated for use in ship repairs and warehouse and shelter construction. Soon the HBC would find it profitable to export salmon and big timbers to European markets unfamiliar with such items. Within a few decades, the monocultural focus of the HBC would be altogether overtaken by a proliferation of alternative, economic distractors, whittling away at their fur trade business. Although agriculture, fishing, and timber cutting would continue to expand, it would be mining—and gold mining in particular—that would become the midwife for present-day BC.

Relations with First Nations

Attendant upon the heels of the HBC's shortening of its 'defensive perimeter,' different patterns of sequent occupance developed on either side of this interim British-American boundary. Americans were far less dismissive of agricultural development that brought more settlement and greater missionary zeal in its train. The missionaries not only attempted to Christianize the local native Americans but also to impose an agricultural lifestyle upon a native people accustomed to nomadic ways. Such cultural clashes led to physical clashes. In response to an engineered perception or discourse that "the Indians were massacring whites," many American settlers began calling for the extermination of Native Americans. A more corporate discourse of "management, stability, property and order" seemed to be the norm in British HBC lands to the North (but the reality was a different order of harshness[4]). There, the cooperation of the natives was indispensable to the viability of the fur-trading system. They had taught the whites not only how to trap and preserve the furs, but also how to build canoes, provision themselves, move over great distances, and so forth. Their continuing good will was essential. The fur-trading system was co-extensive with the range of the beaver. Most of British North America was beaver country while most of the US was not; hence its lesser need for depending on native Americans for the economic activities that the eastern seaboard and its diaspora had in mind. Had McLoughlin opted for greater agricultural activity at Fort Vancouver, Washington, it is an open question whether the Columbia River would be BC's southern border today. A few decades later, the HBC's fur-trading would be displaced anyway, by other economic activities, including agriculture; McLoughlin could not, of course, have had this foresight. Otherwise, armed with such prescience, he could have encouraged more agricultural settlement for the sake of a more effective occupance of his cleverly chosen, geostrategic situation. Although Americans—given their greater critical mass—were pouring in at a faster rate, the British would arguably have been in a stronger political position to resist the Americans on the matter of the Oregon question. Had they fully succeeded, all of the north bank of the Columbia would arguably be in Canada's hands today.

The Oregon Treaty and *Manifest Destiny* Revisited

Less than two decades after McLoughlin's strategic move to the site at Fort Vancouver which commanded egress from the Willamette River, American settlers started trickling southward, up the river's valley. They were part of the *Great Migration* from the east. In 1843 they followed the Oregon Trail, settling along the Columbia and the river that discharged into it, namely the Willamette. Although their number was less than 1,000, these arrivals immediately created their own provisional government for what was termed *Oregon Country*. Such was the brash ethnocentrism of the mid-19th century American psyche, that the general population had imbibed ever deeper the messianic script, that heaven itself had intended for the entire Pacific seaboard of North America to be deeded to the US as a matter of divine right. Within a year, expansionist political sentiment had taken up the battle cry, *"fifty-four forty or fight,"* calling for the British to cede all of their western territory lying south of 54°40'N latitude (that is, south of Alaska) to the Americans or risk military conflict. James Polk, elected

American president in 1844, took up this cry with a view to taking over most of today's BC. It must be understood that the Americans in the West began giving free land grants long before that practice was started in Western Canada. The British, on the other hand, still prisoners of a limited environmental perception that saw little value in their territorial holdings beyond fur, gave ground. In view of the declining fur trade and certain competing preoccupations in Europe, the British in 1843 voluntarily moved their Pacific headquarters from Fort Vancouver to Victoria on Vancouver Island. An amicable compromise was reached by the Oregon Treaty of 1846 (ratified in 1848) which established the 49th parallel as the northern boundary for the US.

The Pig War and its Larger Geopolitical Significance

As a comical, quasi-tragic sidelight to boundary setting, the island of San Juan in the southern Straits of Georgia was not clearly assigned to either side. With both British and American nationals residing on the same island, tensions peaked again in 1859 when an American killed a British neighbour's pig that was apparently rummaging in his garden. The escalation of the dispute, jocularly known as the "Pig War," involved joint occupation of the island by British and American garrisons for 12 years. Eventually, the German emperor was brought in as arbitrator in 1872 and awarded all of the San Juan islands to the US.

Although this incident seems silly from the parochial standpoint, its potential geopolitical implications at the time were far more ominous given the concomitant events of the period that were gradually predisposing BC's confederation with Canada in 1871. The year 1867 witnessed not only the creation of the Dominion of Canada, but also the Alaska Purchase and a recrudescence of American manifest-destiny power politics that could now be backed by military muscle. Instead of being disbanded after the end of the Civil War in 1865, the US Cavalry had found a new role for itself in exterminating native Americans on the western frontier.[5] This role was readily legitimated by socially constructed demands for "law and order" in the face of "Indian savages." The cavalry's forces could be quickly brought in, thanks to the coming of the railroads in the west, the military efficacy of rail transport having already been proven in the east during the Civil War. By 1869, one could travel by rail from the east coast to Sacramento, California, with further western branch lines soon to follow.

In essence, the British hold on the Pacific West had come under a much greater threat of extirpation by the pincers-grip of the newly acquired American Alaska on the north, and the American controlled Washington Territory to the south, the Washington Territory being a fission product of the former Oregon Territory. With the State of California already inducted into the American union in 1850, the Americans were optimally poised to regard the entire Pacific seaboard north of Mexico as prospective American territory. Their capacity for a territorial grab was not merely rhetorical, but also military.

Post civil-war, anti-British feelings were also running high, owing to Britain's role in having built and provisioned Confederate ships during the war. One such ship, the *Alabama*, had sunk, destroyed, or captured more than 60 Union vessels before it was sunk by a US warship in 1864. After the Alaska purchase, the American Congress hounded Britain for war damages. One suggestion was that the cession of Britain's Pacific west coast might satisfy the *Alabama Claims*. Fortunately for the future Province of British Columbia, the legal arguments dragged on through international tribunals until 1885, when a mutually agreeable monetary settlement was finally reached.

GEOPOLITICAL ACTORS AND BC'S PRECURSOR TERRITORIES PRIOR TO CONFEDERATION WITH CANADA

Role of the HBC and its Leading Agents

The primary territory on which the NWC and its senior rival, the HBC, had organized their trade was roughly co-extensive with the realm of the beaver; that is, vast areas in the northern half of North America perceived to be unsuitable for agriculture, or at least unlikely to draw enough settlement to drive out the beaver. In the west, the NWC being first in the field had initial advantages in organizing and exploiting the Pacific coast drainage basin. In 1821, the need for economic rationalization in the face of duplicate organization and depleting fur resources persuaded London to impose a merger of the two rival fur-trading companies. This new company simply retained the name of the HBC. The later political entity of Canada was to be, in effect, co-extensive with, and a political legitimation of, the HBC's territorial holdings.

Victoria, the Crown Colony of Vancouver Island and the Appearance of Sir James Douglas as Local Actor

In view of competition from the Americans in the south, in 1843 the Hudson's Bay Company moved its headquarters from Fort Vancouver on the Columbia River, to Victoria at the south end of Vancouver Island (see Figure 7.2). This new western depot was more readily defensible by British naval vessels which could be based nearby in a fine natural harbour at Esquimalt. This location decision, together with the situational perceptions and further 'regional-planning decisions' (so to speak) of the geopolitical actor making them, would within less than four decades conduce to the emergence of present-day BC within Canada. That actor was Sir James Douglas, who would later be called *the father of British Columbia*. Originally inducted as an apprentice with the NWC at the age of 16, Douglas became an HBC employee at the time of the merger in 1821. After serving under McLoughlin at Fort Vancouver, he became Chief Factor in the area by 1839. Anticipating American control of the lower Columbia, Douglas commissioned the blazing of a trail from New Caledonia[6] following a path from its regional situation in the northerly Fraser River basin, southward to Fort Langley in the lower river delta. This trail facilitated the transport of furs from the northern interior of the mainland to their ultimate trans-shipment point at Victoria, which would become the main Pacific depot of the HBC. With British fears of Americans expanding north of the 49th parallel, in violation of the Oregon Treaty, Vancouver Island was leased to the HBC for 10 years beginning in 1849, with Douglas as Chief Agent for HBC operations. At the same time, the island was also designated the Crown Colony of Vancouver Island and given its own governor in the person of Richard Blanshard. This system of dual autocracy soon had to be abandoned as the chief executive officer of a powerful commercial interest, that is, the HBC, easily outmanoeuvred Blanshard, the Queen's representative. As a consequence, Blanshard departed within 17 months of his arrival.[7] Douglas was then appointed to succeed Blanshard as governor, so that by late 1851 he had become the economic as well as the political master of Vancouver Island.

Breakout from the fur-staples trap

Vancouver Island's establishment as a self-governing (albeit autocratic in form) British colony in 1849 was contingent upon its attainment of a viable level of settlement by 1854. Three factors, however, discouraged settlement. Firstly, the price of land on Vancouver Island was too high, considering that it was free south of the 49th parallel. Secondly, agricultural expansion was now permissible for the first time—in addition to fur-trading. In order to encourage settlement for its own sake, markets for agricultural surplus south of the border were closed owing to prevailing tariff policies. As a result, agricultural output would tend to be pegged at such levels as were merely necessary and sufficient to provision the fur fort and its harbour. Thirdly, the California gold rush of 1849 constituted a much stronger magnet for population growth. Fortunately, the discovery of coal at Nanaimo in 1852 catalysed an export business based on markets in San Francisco. This boon was arguably instrumental in starting a geo-economic breakout from the fur-staples trap. Coal could fuel local transport as well. It also enabled Esquimalt to become the major fuelling station of the British navy on the entire Pacific coast of the Americas. Furthermore, a side benefit to the export of coal was its value in redressing inbound/outbound imbalances of cargo. Consequently, the use of unprofitable ballast for outbound cargo was greatly reduced. The multiplier effects generated from a more rapid accumulation of monetary capital attributable to coal, together with the in-migration of workers for the coal industry, fostered increases in population growth. The desirable expansion of agriculture for local use was, in its turn, thereby stimulated (see Figure 7.3 for the situation of Esquimalt).

Gold, the New Geostrategic Dynamic and the United Colony of British Columbia

Arguably, the most severe blow to what had been the fur-trade monoculture came with the discovery of placer gold on the Fraser River in 1856. The earlier discovery of gold in the Queen Charlotte Islands in 1852 had led to Britain's geopolitical codification of those islands as the *Dependency of Queen Charlottes*, with a view to pre-empting possible American occupation. This new 'vital interest' had also coloured Britain's formal ratification of James Douglas as Governor of Vancouver Island. As a strong, territorially-minded personality, Douglas understood that the naval vessels that were based in Esquimalt were within closer, symbolical, protective range of the Queen Charlotte Islands than any forces that the Americans could send at that time. Gold galvanized comparable territorial imperatives on the mainland when, in 1858 alone, an influx of 30,000 persons sought to capitalize on the Fraser gold findings. With men and goods passing through Victoria, local land and food prices ballooned. American capital, goods, and technology also opportunistically invaded the town, triggering the perception of a threat to British sovereignty. The economic threat to the HBC was quite tangible. Gold miners could simply buy furs directly from the aboriginals at will, thereby bypassing the HBC. The HBC monopoly on fur-trading was unravelling.

By 1859, Lord Lytton, the British Secretary of State for the Colonies, had formally created the mainland *Crown Colony of British Columbia*, with James Douglas as its first governor. Douglas was allowed to retain his governorship of Vancouver Island. At the same time, he was forced to sever his ties to the HBC. Ironically, it was he who had, through his HBC offices, prudently claimed the land and mineral resources of the Pacific region *for the Crown*, going so far as to license miners and to prevent foreign vessels from sailing up the Fraser River beyond Fort Langley. His imperial masters stated, however, with Machiavellian panache, that Douglas had been more intent upon protecting HBC interests than those of the Crown. Adducing that rationale, they swiftly extinguished the company's rights and privileges west of the Rockies (without publically admitting that its monopoly had unravelled anyway). At the same time, in recognition of his ability and zeal, Douglas was promoted as local political czar for the same territory. By the time Vancouver Island and the mainland colony were merged into the single *United Colony of British Columbia* in 1866, Douglas had already been deposed (c.1863), this time with the honour of a knighthood. It was Dr. John Helmcken, a former HBC surgeon as well as son-in-law of James Douglas, who negotiated the terms of union, as he had been Speaker of the Legislative Assembly of Vancouver Island. The single British colony of British Columbia had now become both the *de facto* and *de jure* political heir to the HBC's economic empire west of the Rockies. The geopolitical outcome of a united colony had been largely shaped by further gold discoveries and additional geostrategic initiatives taken by Douglas during his last few years of high political office.

One of his key initiatives was the improvement of the Fraser River trail, beginning in the winter of 1858, to ease the plight of miners who were being forced to pay exorbitant rates for supplies. Placer gold mining was also problematic in that the sluice technology needed to maintain profitability was highly capital-intensive for the times, so that the first-wave labour pool could not be economically sustained. To counter the economic depression following the gold boom of 1858, Victoria was declared a free-trade entrepôt. Once again an inbound/outbound cargo imbalance resulted. As outbound

Geopolitical Development: An Overview

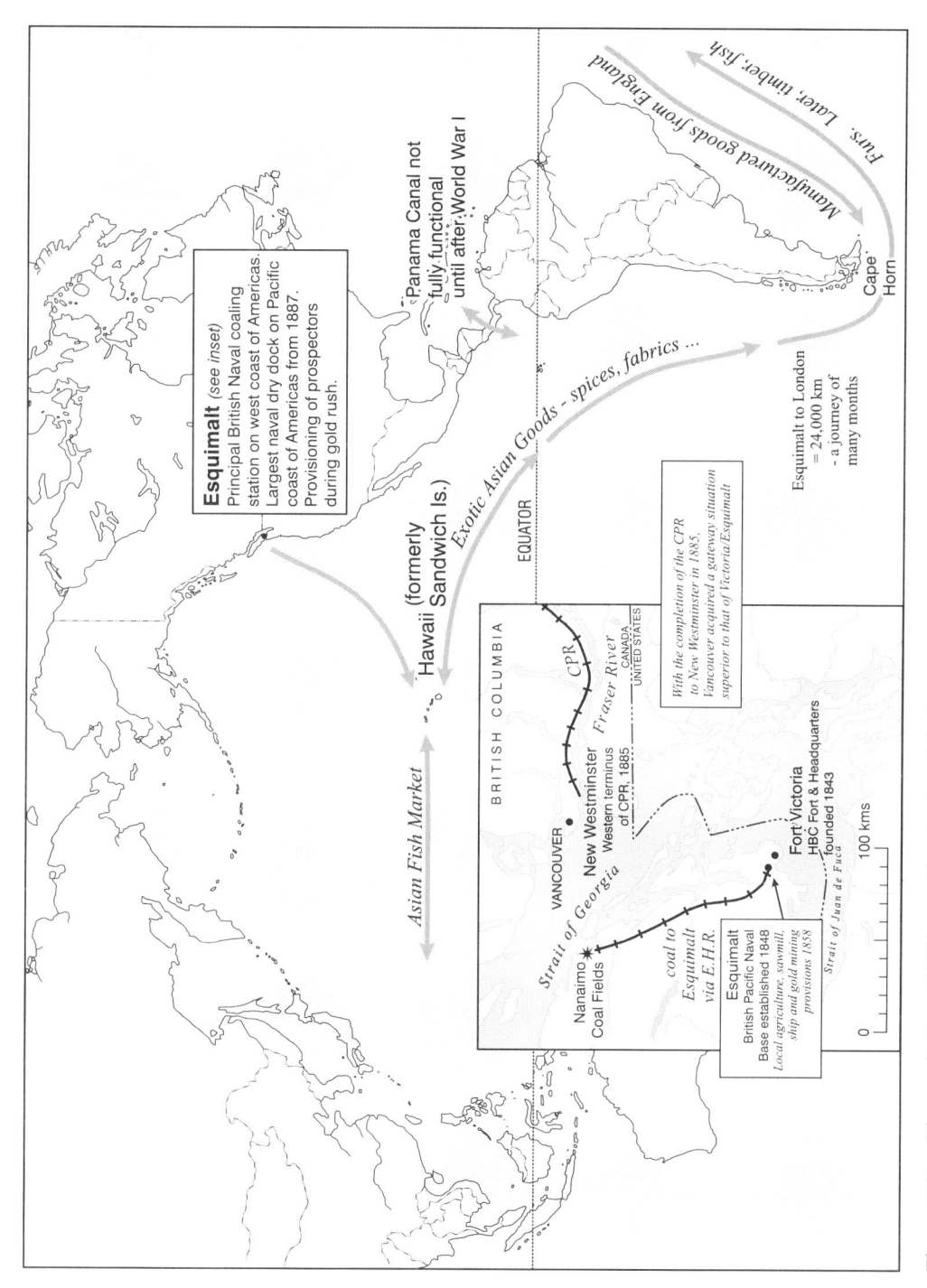

Figure 7.3 The evolution of BC's position in the global transportation and trading systems

gold provided negligible ballast in terms of weight, other staple industries—in addition to coal—were now stimulated to increase profits for outbound export cargoes. With furs no longer Douglas' main concern, he gave more attention to timber. Timber provided spars for both naval and commercial ships, building materials for local housing, and beams, joists, and posts for firstly the coal, and later the gold-mining industries. Within the decade following the regnum of Douglas, further economic diversification was evidenced by whaling, the marketing of fish oils in Hawaii, fish canneries on the lower Fraser, saw milling, soap making, brewing and distilling, and an iron foundry in Victoria.

The Cariboo Road

The preliminary road-building initiatives of Douglas were to prove very fortuitous when more gold was discovered at the Quesnel fork of the Fraser in the Cariboo in 1860 (Figure 7.4). With more in-migration and supplies to Victoria and New Westminster (which had been declared the capital of the combined colony in 1858), Douglas commissioned a contingent of British army engineers to survey and construct a proper *Cariboo Road* which would improve and extend his original pack trail along the lower Fraser River to Barkerville. The road had to be finished by private contractors and was finally extended to Barkerville—the heart of gold country—by 1865, 2 years after Douglas had lost office. By the time the road was completed, the placer gold had been exhausted with its capital-intensive successors of high-tech hydrology and tunnelling, once again decimating the work force. The costs of the Cariboo Road had been a major factor in the political demise of Douglas. Britain was not interested in subsidizing cost over-runs which eventually resulted in a $1.38 million debt. Douglas (not unlike a number of subsequent BC politicians) had overestimated the tax and royalty revenues that would be available to pay for his transportation/communications vision. On the other hand, the public debt created by Douglas had a positive side. It helped catalyse the 1866 union of Vancouver Island and the mainland colony of British Columbia (informally referred to as New Caledonia before 1858) into the single United Colony of British Columbia. After all, Vancouver Island wanted a share of the mainland's gold revenues. At the same time, the mainland colony would benefit by Vancouver Island's sharing of infrastructural development costs. In addition, Britain welcomed a simplifying of its span of control over its Pacific North American holdings. After a 2-year tug of war as to whether the capital of the combined colony would continue to be at New Westminster on the mainland, or on Vancouver Island, the issue was resolved in favour of Victoria, the earlier capital of Vancouver Island. The condition that it give up its free port status was readily accepted. As governor of the mainland as well as governor of Vancouver Island, Douglas had earlier strongly tilted toward Victoria as a personal place of residence, viewing the costs of developing the more rugged New Westminster site as being too demanding of colonial revenues. Although the old-guard political elites at Victoria prevailed in 1868, the net result—due to Victoria's insularity—was a duplication of costly government services on the mainland.

When all was said and done, Douglas had served his purpose. Gold had now displaced furs as the driving mechanism for economic development. Following the 1858 gold rush into the Fraser River valley, prospectors had been pushing northward to the Nass, Stikine, and Peace river basins. In 1862, the *Stikine Territory* was established. Its creation was a harbinger of Douglas' demise. The following year, 1863, the Stikine Territory became part of the lower mainland colony and Douglas was out of office. With its appetite whetted by gold, Britain's interest in greater, hands-on, political control of the Pacific Northwest had been transiently rekindled, and then re-asserted in the creation of the combined colony of 1866. In eastern British North America, the *Dominion of Canada* was created the following year in 1867, by uniting the former colonies of *New Brunswick*, *Nova Scotia*, and (central) *Canada*—which had been created by the prior 1841 union of *Lower Canada* and *Upper Canada*.

Geopolitical Development: An Overview

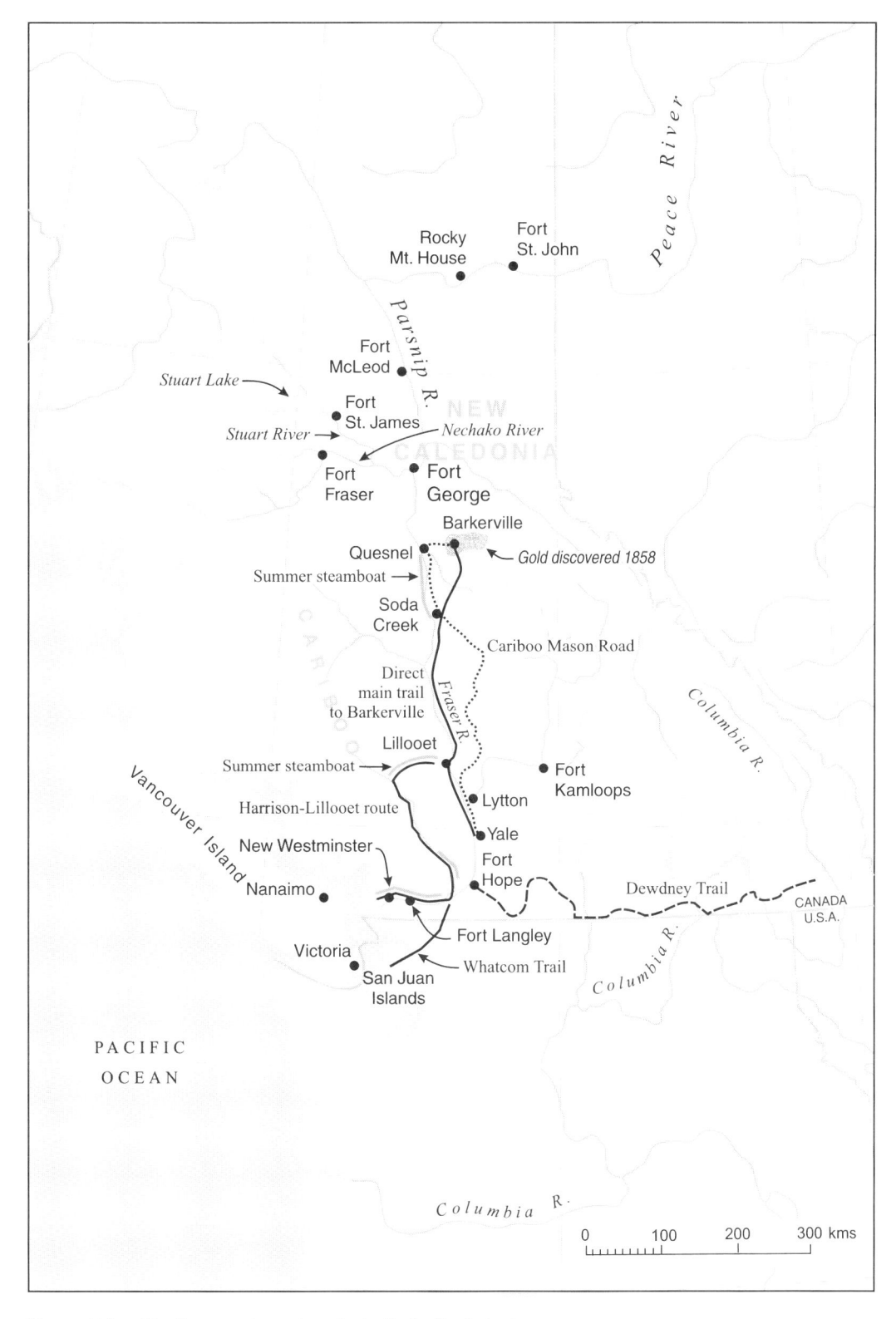

Figure 7.4 Trading posts and early trails in the Interior

UNION WITH CANADA

Concurrently with the creation of the *Dominion of Canada*, the financial position of the *United Colony of British Columbia* (BC) had become precarious. There were three geopolitical options, namely: 1) to join the United States; 2) to join the newly created Dominion; 3) to maintain its status quo as a British colony. The issue of relationships with the aboriginal population did not affect any of those options at that point in time. With the rapid decline in the relative importance of the fur economy in favour of gold-mining and other economic activities, dependency on the aboriginal people also declined. At the same time, the interest of the colonists in the coastal fishing industry (which could utilize traditional aboriginal know-how) came later, in the 1870s.

The Case for Joining the US

At first blush, the possibility of BC's annexation by the US appeared quite strong. The union of 1866 had failed to solve the economic problems of the combined colonies. Even with a tariff wall in place to protect local enterprise, the US was still BC's most important trading partner. With annexation the tariffs would disappear, thereby stimulating even greater economic activity. Although a locally based British naval squadron could conceivably patrol the coast at a less than optimal level, credible British force could not be projected into the mainland interior. On the other hand, the 49th parallel was proving to be a permeable membrane for burgeoning American settlement south of the border. Now that the American Civil War was over a certain malaise was resurfacing with respect to the boundary settlement of the 1846 Oregon Treaty. As indicated earlier, the Alaska purchase of 1867 led many Americans to perceive BC as the middle layer of a sandwich whose upper and lower layers were already US property. In view of the unsettled *Alabama Claims*, that mid-layer was arguably ripe for ingestion by American military forces that had not been fully demobilized after the conclusion of the Civil War in 1865. BC also felt ignored by its parent, Britain, which in its turn did not perceive a need for any substantive inputs beyond the *ipse dixit*s, or legal rhetoric, of the colony's new constitution. If Britain was displaying the apathetic face of an absentee landlord, the Americans were evincing an ebullient hands-on approach in developing the settlement of Sitka in Alaska. If the Americans were to be encouraged to do similar things for BC as a whole, would not greater economic benefits redound to the benefit of both parties? With eastern Canada over 3,000 km away and the communications obstacles so great, would not linking BC's fortunes to the rest of British North America bring more difficulties than benefits? The matter was brought to a preliminary test vote in 1869 when a petition advocating union with the US was circulated in Victoria. The petition received only 105 out of a possible 5,000 eligible signatures. Despite the apparent economic advantages for the general populace, BC apparently preferred the Union Jack, or British flag, to the Stars and Stripes that emblazoned the jaws of the American vice. Were BC to continue as a separate colony of Britain, the squeeze of the American vice would likely only intensify. Accordingly, some now deemed it prudent to explore the pros and cons—and even the feasibility—of BC joining the Dominion of Canada.

Factors Influencing Union with Canada.

Vested Interests of the Local Establishment

Although it seemed more economically advantageous for BC's population at large to cast their lot with the muscular Americans, a more decisive factor was the economic interests of BC's ruling elite. Arguably, it was these same interests which were scripted by the "spin doctors" of the day into the geopolitical discourse of *sentimental preference* for the Union Jack and *fear of domination* by American values. In essence, the senior level of the BC's governing and administrative apparatus wanted guarantees that its 'perks,' especially by way of salary and influence would be maintained. The Americans could not do so, however, as any new governing and administrative apparatus would have to be American in form as well as spirit. After all, had they not fought a war of independence from Britain less than a century earlier? So why should they preserve British political forms in BC if that colony were to become an American state? Britain, for its part, could hardly be expected to sustain defectors to its North American geopolitical rival. If BC were to join the Dominion of Canada, would BC's elite interests be protected? The bottom line was 'yes.' On July 7, 1870, the government of Canada undertook to provide lifetime pensions at two-thirds of salary for BC's ruling elites. The one-third salary reduction was intended to induce the recipients to seek such alternate governmental employment as would obviate the necessity for the pension having to be paid out. In any case, Ottawa was able to provide alternative employment in keeping with previous status and salaries to most of the persons affected. In effect, the path to BC's union with Canada had been negotiated with very little loss to the pecuniary interests of BC's preconfederation officialdom. A principal device had been the carrot of the 'buyout' or 'golden handshake.'

Aligning Local Perceptions with British Geopolitical Interests

In the course of BC-Canada courtship rituals, the geopolitical interests of Britain and Canada rather than those of the BC establishment of 1870 turned out to be the paramount deciding factors. Britain did not want BC to fall into American hands. At the same time, Britain did not want to be saddled with assuming the costs of preventing such a worst-case scenario. Prussia was looming as a European power to be reckoned with, so that the British could not afford overseas entanglements. After all, travel by water from Britain to the Pacific Northwest still necessitated a circuit around Cape Horn —a total distance of 24,000 km. Revenues that might be gleaned from BC gold had an uncertain future. The colony was far less important to the vital interests of the British Empire than was India, whose resources and markets were impacting so conspicuously on the English standard of living at home. Naturally, Britain would be very pleased were BC to join Canada which, after all, was still a British dominion. Although such a political coupling had been previsioned, a certain amount of see-sawing and uncertainty would occur before it could come to pass. Following the political exit of James Douglas in 1864, Frederick Seymour had succeeded him as governor of the mainland colony. Within 2 years he had become the first governor of the United Colony of British Columbia, but not before being summoned to London for consultation with the British Colonial Office. He was a professional colonial administrator who had been parachuted into BC by Britain, after having served the imperial interests in Tasmania, and later in the West Indies. Although the 1866 act that united Vancouver Island and the mainland colony into the *United Colony of British Columbia* had incorporated his personal administrative recommendations, Seymour still had other problems. As a recently arrived interloper, he lacked the breadth and depth of regional knowledge possessed by his predecessor. Although he was constructively involved in treaty talks with coastal aboriginal groups, he had no direct knowledge of the Dominion of Canada, and was indifferent to the idea of a political union with that entity. Thus, further progress toward confederation seemed unlikely, until Seymour unexpectedly died in mid-1869. In fairness to Seymour, it should be noted that he had come to BC to make the union between Vancouver Island and the mainland colony work and to establish a workable administrative structure for BC, before concerning himself with BC-Canada relationships. However, he had arrived in the colony prior to the American purchase of Alaska. With the US controlling Alaska, Britain had to make its Pacific *Realpolitik* vis à vis the Americans more explicit to its own colonial representatives.

Seymour's death, therefore, gave Britain an opportunity to appoint a new governor with instructions to facilitate BC's confederation with Canada. The instructions were consistent with British imperial policy under Gladstone, England's prime minister at the time. That policy favoured bestowing a strong measure of local independence from the British homeland while at the same time encouraging the highest level of mutual cooperation among the various North American colonies. The intention was to foster a level of self-sufficient cohesion that was still compatible with a voluntary allegiance to the crown. The new governor was Anthony Musgrave, who did have some indispensable knowledge of eastern Canada. Not only had he just served as governor of Newfoundland, but he was also personally acquainted with Sir John A. MacDonald, the Prime Minister of the Dominion. Understanding that he was not to impose a union despotically, but to achieve one amicably, he carefully cultivated the loyalty of BC's pro-British, power elite, leaving it with the conviction that he would not fail to speak up for the pecuniary interests of so gentlemanly a class.

Pros and Cons of Union with Canada

Local perceptions of problems associated with union oscillated in response to events and the availability of new information. Seymour had been, not unreasonably, leery of the new administrative headaches for BC that getting involved with Canada might bring. In addition to the distance of 3,200 km to (central) Canada, there was the matter of the intervening prairie territories of the HBC that lay between Canada and BC. How could a union of non-contiguous territories be possible? Should not the Prairies, then part of the North West Territories, be integrated with Canada first, to provide spatial continuity of superordinate, governmental administration? The British Colonial Office was well aware of the non-contiguity issue and forestalled its further use as an impediment to confederation by adroitly overseeing the transfer of the HBC territories to Canada. In 1870, *Rupert's Land*, that is, the HBC territory in North America was sold to Canada for the sum of £300,000. The HBC was also to retain one-twentieth of the fertile lands to be opened for settlement, plus title to the lands upon which its trading posts were sited. The Bank of Montreal acted as the government's banker. The negotiations had begun in 1867, the birth year of Canada. By 1869, Seymour had died. The land-retention portion of the arrangement was significant to the future development of Canada as it facilitated the construction of the first trans-Canadian railway.

Recycling of Corporate Elites as Geopolitical Actors

Although the HBC was no longer a major geo-economic player, its former holdings would be transformed, by 1871, into the political region of present-day Canada. In other words, the government of Canada had displaced the HBC as the central geopolitical actor. Also significant was the persistence of what might be called the HBC's political-economic, *savoir-faire infrastructure*.[8] This sapiential apparatus was manifested by the advent of a new order of geo-economic activity overseen by an elite corporate directorate, operating behind the scenes. In 1863, this elite group had already acquired control of the HBC in London, England on behalf of the Grand Trunk (railway) Interests. In effect, after the sale of Rupert's Land to Canada, the interests of the Grand Trunk people and the interests of the imperial government in London had converged. In the new economic order that would follow, the former fur-trading infrastructure would be replaced by railways and the infrastructure of machine civilization. Nevertheless, the former HBC's *savoir-faire infrastructure* would prove to be of immense subsequent importance. Lord Strathcona (D. A. Smith), who had been an important HBC official, was to play a leading role in the construction and management of the Canadian Pacific Railway (CPR), which was to capitalize on its land grant. In BC, the volatility associated with the gold economy would be stabilized by the advent of railways, steamships to the orient, and the mixed blessings of manufacturing. The HBC would become an important retailer operating through a chain of department stores. Its geopolitical pre-eminence had now been displaced by an interlocking directorate of corporate and governmental interests representing the Bank of Montreal, the CPR, the Canadian government, and least, but not insignificantly, the HBC.

Local Actors of Influence

Amor De Cosmos – An Unwitting Tool for Distant Geopolitical Actors

Before Musgrave's arrival as governor, a leading activist spearheading the discussion on acceptable terms for confederation with Canada was the colourful eccentric, Amor De Cosmos, who was to become a singularly ineffective Premier of BC in 1872. Born William Smith, De Cosmos was an idea man in the extreme and can be considered the *intellectual father* for the union of Vancouver Island with the BC colony, responsible government, and confederation with Canada. His had the political misfortune of thinking and acting too independently of others—so much so that by the time of his death in 1897 he was popularly regarded as insane. In any case, as we have seen, the final disposition of BC's fate was determined by the *force majeure* of more privileged, geopolitical scriptwriters based in London and Ottawa. People like De Cosmos simply and unwittingly strengthened the hands of the major external players by rendering public opinion favourable to what the outlines of their grand plan called for anyway. Local issues stimulated by De Cosmos included: construction of a robust wagon trail to connect with central Canada; a more responsive government structure; trade-reciprocity with the US; and relief for the provincial debt. Straw votes were taken on the confederation question. Americans in BC were allowed to vote on the questions, but aboriginal peoples and the Chinese were disenfranchised. The ground swell was promising but, as we have already seen, Governor Seymour was not interested.

BC's Confederation Team

Musgrave, on his own authority, selected three official delegates to represent BC's interests in exploratory parlays to take place in Ottawa. Their mission was primarily to ascertain the kinds of concessions—if any—that BC could extract from Ottawa as a condition of union. The three delegates selected were: J. Trutch, BC's Chief Commissioner of Lands and Works; R. Carrall, elected member for Cariboo; and J. Helmcken, elected member for the city of Victoria. De Cosmos was bypassed as he was considered a loose cannon. Interestingly, the three delegates actually represented a broad spectrum of opinion and economic interests regarding confederation. Carrall, an anti-American spokesperson for investment interests in the Cariboo, was at the outset the most enthusiastic booster of union with Canada. Trutch and Helmcken initially preferred a continuation of BC's status quo as a Crown Colony to a union with Canada. Trutch, however, was open to the possibility of union with Canada, provided that an all-Canadian transcontinental railway line was forthcoming. Representing vested commercial and transportation interests in the lower mainland, he was fearful of absorption by the US if the Americans were to build a second transcontinental railroad abutting the BC border just south of the 49th parallel, the first one having just been completed to Sacramento, California in 1869. On the strength of that latter achievement and the promise of the first, William Henry Seward, the American Secretary of State who negotiated the Alaska Purchase, had made a political foray into Victoria during the summer of 1869. There he tried to drum up support for what would be considered today as a variant of "Project Cascadia," that is, a common political association between BC, Oregon, Washington, *plus Alaska*! Owing to local economic stagnation, German and Jewish immigrants in Victoria appeared keenly interested in the idea.

John Helmcken

John Sebastian Helmcken was arguably the father of BC's confederation with Canada. He was an inspired choice for a delegate as he was perhaps the most likely political representative to put the general good ahead of his interests. The year of his arrival in the Pacific West he deftly extinguished a smallpox epidemic that had broken out at Esquimalt harbour. By 1865, this devoted individual who had been the first white medical practitioner in BC, was popularly regarded as the leading physician in the area "from San Francisco to the North Pole and between Asia and the Red River." Not really political by nature, he had been parachuted into elite political circles soon after his arrival on the west coast by Governor James Douglas, whose eldest daughter he had married.

As the first Speaker of Vancouver Island's elected House of Assembly—a position he held from 1856 until 1866—he negotiated the terms of union with the mainland colony. Upon creation of the United Colony of BC he became the Legislative Speaker for all of BC. He had been elected to the Legislative Council of BC on an anti-confederation ticket, with support from a number of persons calling for annexation with the US. He felt that BC's paramount needs for immigrants and trade could not be met by Canada. He was too pessimistic to seriously entertain the possibility of Ottawa spending money on a colony whose population was so small. So, federal expenditure on a transcontinental railway line would not likely be forthcoming. Nevertheless, Musgrave shrewdly suggested that Helmcken help draft the terms under which confederation would be more palatable to himself and his compatriots. If those terms were not acceptable, then—as Musgrave jokingly observed—he at least would get a change of scenery, see the country, and be well fed at Ottawa's expense.

Helmcken had no prior first hand knowledge of Canada when he set off with his delegates for Ottawa in May 1870. Their routing involved a 5-day paddle-steamer trip from Victoria to San Francisco, then train trips via Central Pacific and Union Pacific rail lines through the US, to southern Ontario. Fortuitously, the year 1870 was also the first year to witness transcontinental rail travel in North America. Thus Helmcken and his companions could directly experience the reality and feasibility of train travel, as opposed to its mere possibility (or impossibility, if all the phantom obstacles to railway construction present in Helmcken's mind were factored in). The reality of riding the rails with speed and comfort instantly turned Helmcken into a pro-confederation advocate. If the Americans could build a rail line across difficult western terrain, then for Helmcken, a comparable BC-Canada link should also be economically and politically feasible.

Tying the Geopolitical Knot

When Helmcken and his confreres arrived at their destination, they were somewhat startled by Ottawa's willingness to accept most of BC's draft terms for Confederation (see box). Doubtless, they were unaware of the prior facilitative discussions between Ottawa, London, and Musgrave. Moreover, Helmcken's arrival happened to coincide with an eruption of concern over Fenian raids[9] into Canada, a concern that put Ottawa into a very concessionary frame of mind. Consequently, negotiations were speedily and satisfactorily concluded within 3 weeks. Upon Helmcken's return to Victoria with the terms of BC-Canada confederation in hand, he was greeted by an incredulous public that was actually startled by Ottawa's unexpected promise to construct a transnational railroad.[10] In November of 1870, elections were held to elect a more representative and 'responsible,' 'predominantly elective' Legislative Council. All pro-Confederation candidates were elected. On January 5, 1871, the new Legislative Council convened to hear Governor Musgrave present the proposed terms for confederation with Canada which were then passed unanimously without debate.[11] Joseph Trutch, one of the three delegates sent to Ottawa in June of 1870, was once again dispatched there in April 1871 to ensure that the terms BC had so recently agreed to would not be altered in any way by the Canadian Parliament. Ironically, on his own initiative Trutch offered his Ottawa hosts a political loop-hole by suggesting that their commitment to construct a railway need not be regarded as a "cast iron contract"—a comment that generated considerable abreaction in Victoria (see *Colonist*, June 1, 1871.) Fortunately, the terms of union had already been accepted in Ottawa prior to Trutch's political gaffe, having passed the Commons and the Senate before his arrival. By May 16, an Imperial Order-in-Council was in place. It decreed that BC was to be admitted as a new province of Canada effective July 20, 1871. The federal authorities then selected Trutch to replace Anthony Musgrave as the new Lieutenant-Governor of BC, with instructions to make local government in

BC even more representative. July 20 having been declared Confederation Day in BC, it was celebrated with considerable fanfare and public rhetoric, in keeping with the *British-sentiments discourse* of the times.

Post-Confederation Geopolitical Highlights

BC evolved geopolitically as a function of an economic history that, at first, reflected the geostrategic and geo-economic interests of external actors. *Effective occupance* was predicated on maintaining effective lines of communications, which in their turn were necessitated by the exploitation of a succession of natural resources. The first valuable staples of furs and gold catalysed development of an embryonic transportation grid. These early staples were followed in their turn by coal, timber, salmon, base metals, and so forth. Greater political control and stability required a greater economic integration that could only be provided by improvements in transportation. Critical to such integration was the completion of the Canadian Pacific Railway (CPR) in 1885, which reoriented BC to eastern North America. Less than four decades later, the effective opening of the Panama Canal in 1920 (after a 6 year closure from the 1914 completion because of World War I) meant that shipping routes around

---

Terms of Union

The final terms of the BC-Canada confederation agreement of July 1871 were principally as follows:

1. Ottawa would absorb BC's current debt, estimated to be $1,045,000.

2. The need for a linking wagon road from BC to the Great Lakes would be bypassed through the construction of a railroad to be commenced within two years and finished within 10 years. [As it happened, scandal-plagued Prime Minister Sir John A. MacDonald, the railroad's biggest booster, was out of office between 1873 and 1878, so that the CPR was not completed until 1885.] BC was to gift a 20 mile swath of land on either side of the rail line, in return for a $100,000 federal grant in perpetuity.

3. BC was given three federal Senators and six seats in the House of Commons—a reduction from the "four and eight" formula originally tendered. This political representation and any future subsidies were to be based upon an attributed provincial population of 60,000 persons rather than the number of 120,000 initially proposed by BC. Ottawa's figure was very generous, considering that BC's total population in 1871 was in the order of 37,000, of which no more than 10,000 persons were non-aboriginal. BC was also permitted to introduce 'responsible government' at its pleasure.

4. Ottawa would financially subsidize the construction of a federal dry dock at Esquimalt.[12] In return, Helmcken would drop his demand for a separate BC tariff. The subsidy consisted of a 10-year interest free loan on a capital sum not to exceed £100,000 (about $400,000).

5. Pensions would be guaranteed for any colonial civil servants and non-elective Legislative Councillors, who might lose their positions as a result of the new confederation arrangements.

A number of other matters such as nature and frequency of mail services, and 'Indian policy' [i.e., the political emasculation of the aboriginal population, as well as Chinese immigrants], were also agreed to.

Cape Horn to Europe could be short-circuited. After World War II, further road and rail building intensified, under provincial government policies that effectively placed the increasingly integrated economic/transport infrastructure at the service of externally-controlled multinational resource corporations. From the 1980s on, as Pacific-Rim trade displaced trans-Atlantic trade in importance, Asian interest in BC's resources, and other economic opportunities, was vigorously courted. Some of this interest proved problematical when it entailed illicit international activities such as drug smuggling, or refugee-boat landings allegedly orchestrated by international criminal gangs.

Thanks to greater public awareness, in recent decades a number of interjurisdictional skirmishes over environmental and resource-control issues have arisen. BC has challenged Alaska, Ottawa, and Washington State over Pacific coast fishing rights. Groups of BC fishers seem perennially at political loggerheads with some First Nations bands over local fishing rights and privileges. *Greenpeace*, an environmental activist movement, has used global mass media to publicize problematic issues of forest management in ways that have threatened the economic interests of multinational forest companies. Risks of oil spills and other forms of water pollution from foreign vessels plying BC's coastal waters continue with little abatement. The BC government was in conflict with the federal government and the US regarding nuclear-powered submarines based at Nanoose Bay on Vancouver Island.

First Nations

Ever-increasing depletion of natural resources by white immigrants—beginning in the several decades prior to Confederation—seriously deformed the traditional economy of the aboriginal populations, even as they tried to counter-manipulate their white trading partners. The resulting intercultural stresses produced political consequences that are still in the process of being sorted out today. The issues are technically of a geopolitical character, inasmuch as they entail relations between nations, namely that of the aboriginal "First Nations" people and Canada, as well as BC. The matter is further complicated by the existence of centuries-old, pre-contact rivalries for hegemony among the various aboriginal groups, some of whom imposed slavery on other groups.[13]

Suffice it to say here that the natives' initial attempts at adaptation could hardly succeed before the 1990s, as long as they played the white man's game, using the white man's rules. Until the 1990s, BC took a *native rights* approach that was quite distinct from that taken by other provinces. BC simply avowed that no land claim treaties had ever been signed with any First Nations. In fact, since the creation of the Crown Colony of Vancouver Island in 1849, the HBC and the British government—both acting conjointly through James Douglas—had recognized the existence of *aboriginal title*. By 1858, when the mainland had become a Crown Colony, Douglas suddenly opted for a process of 'assimilating' natives by giving them legally meaningless 'homesteading rights' to vacant (unsurveyed) land. Any exercise of homesteading rights simply legitimated the crown's prior claim to all unsurveyed land. As late as 1991, the BC Supreme Court also maintained that if there were any aboriginal property rights to begin with, they must have been extinguished in 1871 when BC entered Confederation. In 1993, the BC Court of Appeal qualified that view by declaring aboriginal rights to maintain a traditional lifestyle to be non-extinguishable. Such rights were therefore technically negotiable. In order to facilitate negotiating mechanisms, a BC Treaty Commission was created. Eventually, Ottawa agreed to provide money for any cash settlements, while BC would pay in kind by providing crown land and natural resources as and if required. A *First Nations Summit* was also established as an umbrella aboriginal body to oversee negotiations. That body was opposed by the longer-established *Union of British Columbia Indian Chiefs*. A major breakthrough, however, came to pass with the signing of the *Nisga'a Final Agreement* in 1998 (Canada, BC, Nisga'a Nation, 1998). **See Chapter 8, *Land Claims*, in this present volume for more details.**

The Geopolitics of Hydroelectric Power

After World War II, activist provincial governments in BC tried to use infrastructural projects, on a hitherto unprecedented mega scale, as tools for social and economic development. Their main goal was to attract foreign investment and so facilitate the outflow of resource exports, with a view to enhancing BC's economic prosperity—according to the discourse of the day. The premiership of W.A.C. Bennett, 1952-72, is particularly important in that regard, with the vast augmentation of the hydro power sector representing the capstone of BC's infrastructural achievements. That achievement required development of the Columbia River's power potential. However, as it is an international river, development of its power had geopolitical ramifications that continue to the present day. The power developments also awakened a slumbering public awareness of a number of environmental issues, each possessing its own geopolitical subtext; issues that are beyond the scope of this chapter.

Exploiting an International Resource

The Columbia River Basin, shared by BC and the US, drains an area of 670,810 km^2, which is larger than the area of France. About 15% of that, or 102,305 km^2, takes up the corner of southeastern BC (Figure 7.5). The larger American portion is shared primarily among the four states of Washington, Oregon, Idaho, and Montana, with fringes of the basin also impinging upon the three other states of Nevada, Utah, and Wyoming. Today, the Columbia system is the most important riverine, electric-power producer in North America, accounting for one-third of all American hydro production. This situation, of course, evolved through the concatenation of several geographical, political, and historical factors, including the roles of two non-contemporary (and arguably self-styled) historical heroes—Franklin Delano Roosevelt (FDR) and W.A.C. Bennett.

In 1930, FDR was contemplating entering the American presidential race of 1932. The Great Depression had just begun and FDR, while considering possible planks for his upcoming election campaign, came across the idea of damming the Columbia River at Grand Coulee, about 150 km downstream from Spokane, Washington. His political imagination was fired by the possibility of creating employment through a vast mega-project that would provide flood control, water for irrigation, and hydroelectric power. Upon becoming President in 1932, he authorized the construction of the then-largest concrete structure in the world. With a final installed capacity of 6.48 Gigawatts, the Grand Coulee Dam's power installation is, to this day, the leading producer of electricity in the US, ranking third in the world for installations of its type.

The public consciousness of the FDR years was first mired in the basic employment issues of the 'dirty thirties,' and later the frenzied war effort of the 1940s. The Grand Coulee megaproject had proven indispensable for the war effort, having made possible the development of six industrial plants (especially the Kaiser Corporation) that produced aluminum for 40% of America's military aircraft. In the postwar boom of the 1950s, these plants were working at full capacity to meet an burgeoning domestic demand for consumer goods. As a result, the broader spectrum of environmental and ecological awareness that has emerged in the past 25 years did not colour pre-1970 political thought in the same way—either in the state of Washington or in neighbouring BC. If BC of the 1950s were to emulate the American mega-project model, would not a comparable economic prosperity be forthcoming?

World War II had also seen a hitherto unprecedented level of international cooperation between the US and Canada. For example, the year 1942 witnessed the construction, in only 7½ months, of a military solution to a civilian's dream; that is, a highway from Dawson Creek, BC, through the Yukon to Fairbanks, Alaska. Known as the *Alaska-Canada* or *Alcan* Highway, and later simply the Alaska Highway, its construction easily overrode input from politicians in Victoria, Vancouver, Seattle, Juneau, and Anchorage on the grounds that common

Power Generation

British Columbia

1	Seven Mile	.5GW
2	Keenleyside	*storage*
3	Revelstoke	1.8
4	Mica	1.74
5	Duncan	*storage*
6	Bennet	2.7
7	Peace Canyon	.7

Columbia River Power

Washington

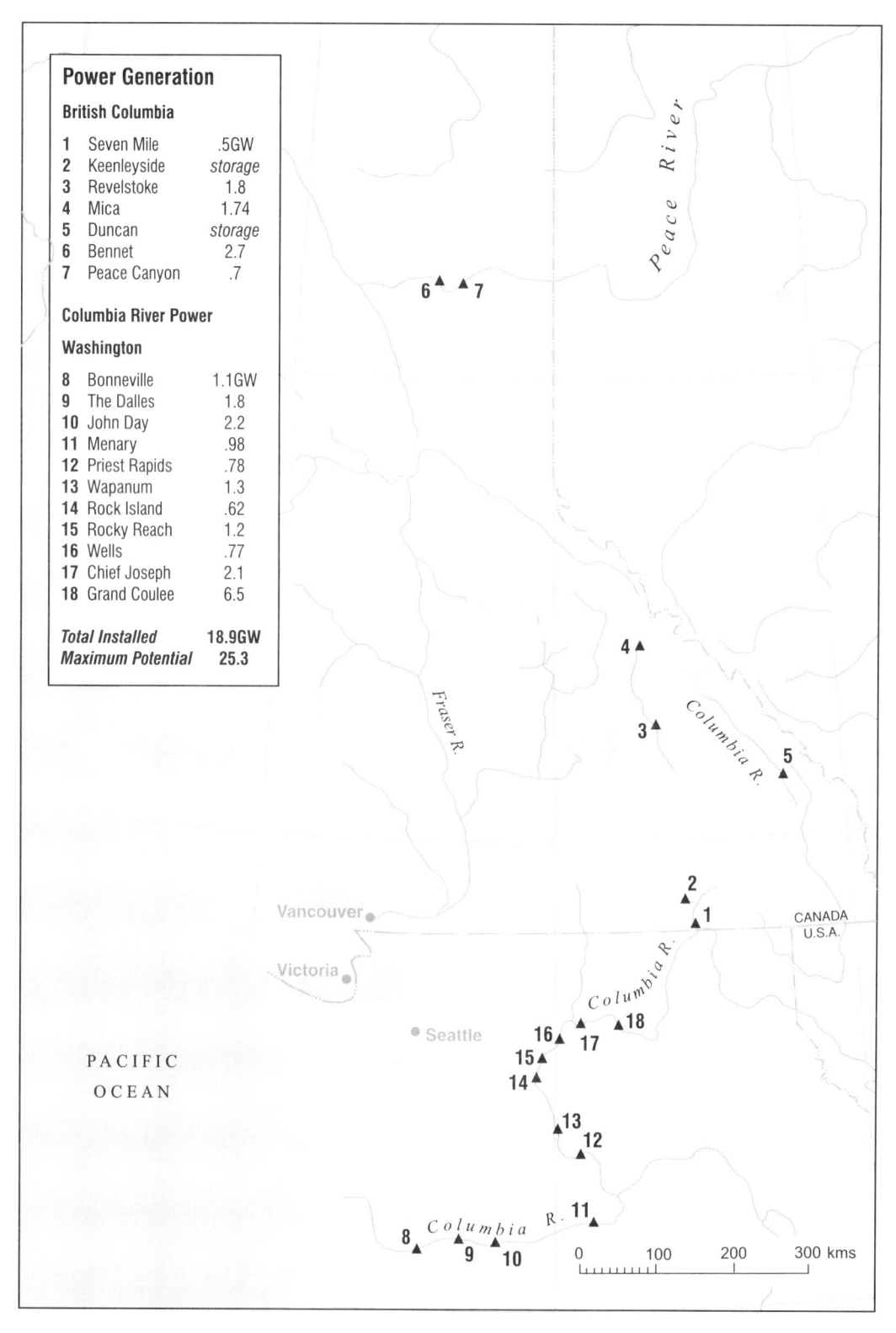

8	Bonneville	1.1GW
9	The Dalles	1.8
10	John Day	2.2
11	Menary	.98
12	Priest Rapids	.78
13	Wapanum	1.3
14	Rock Island	.62
15	Rocky Reach	1.2
16	Wells	.77
17	Chief Joseph	2.1
18	Grand Coulee	6.5

Total Installed	**18.9GW**
Maximum Potential	**25.3**

Figure 7.5 The Columbia and Peace rivers' power systems

military and geostrategic considerations in times of emergency had to take priority over parochial interests. For similar reasons, when China displaced Japan as the enemy during the Korean War (1950-53), the Alaska Highway underwent a major upgrade.

If appeal to *national emergency* could invoke the construction of an international highway then, given the Columbia River's episodic history of disastrous flooding over the decades, management of the Columbia Basin could perhaps be internationalized, so as to obtain some approximation to the unitary oversight that had earlier made the Tennessee Valley Authority so successful. Some enabling international mechanisms already existed, albeit in inchoate form. In 1909, Canada and the US had signed the *Boundary Waters Treaty*, which was intended to forestall disputes with respect to water use anywhere along the 6,400 km separating the two nations. In its immediate wake, an International Joint Commission (IJC) was also created with the larger mandate of dealing with *any other issues of mutual concern*. The problems of the Columbia Basin were intermittently raised for the next few decades until the IJC created the International Columbia River Engineering Board (ICREB) in 1944, with a view to soliciting usefully detailed, concrete proposals for taming the Columbia River. Once the economic priorities associated with World War II abated, a number of proposals did indeed come forward as the various stakeholder groups debated competing dreams.

Once the war had ended, a traditional antagonism between big money and the public interest resurfaced in BC in 1947. In that year, Premier John Hart's coalition government was compelled to recognize the principle of public ownership of electrical energy. At that time, the province's production of electricity was controlled by three private companies, namely: 1) West Kootenay Power and Light (owned by COMINCO, a CPR subsidiary); 2) East Kootenay Power and Light; and 3) BC Electric (BCE), the most profitable operation serving the Lower Mainland and Vancouver. However, Hart's political opposition —the socialist Cooperative Commonwealth Federation party, precursor to the current New Democratic Party (NDP), having garnered 37.6% of the popular vote, were proving to be a thorn in his side. To preempt their thunder, he established the BC Power Commission, a public utility that in the long run might be able to provide electrical power, at cost, to parts of the province that the private corporations thought too unprofitable to serve. That idea had been much bruited by W.A.C. Bennett, a Conservative member of Hart's Liberal-Conservative coalition who shortly thereafter ran as an independent candidate in 1949, before becoming Premier of BC 3 years later.

With W.A.C. Bennett's election as Premier on August 1, 1952, the geopolitical tug-of-war over the Columbia Basin intensified to unprecedented levels. Given the Columbia River's propensity to flood, an American proposal to build a control dam across the Kootenay River (a tributary of the Columbia) at Libby, Montana had been brought before the IJC in 1951. Inasmuch as the proposed Libby Dam, although 105 km south of the Canadian border, would create a finger lake (Lake Koocenusa) extending some 40 km into Canada, IJC referred discussion of the technical options and their implications to the ICREB. The latter body, in its turn, bogged down in the details of cost-sharing and, while recognizing mutual advantages for Canada and the US, was unwilling to specify how any downstream benefits received by the Americans might be practically divided with BC. As a result, the Libby Dam proposal, without a comprehensive framework agreement that satisfied all the major players, could not proceed. In 1954, Kaiser Aluminum (US) entered discussions with BC about a proposed reservoir dam to be built on the Columbia north of Castlegar to increase hydroelectric potential on the American side. However, progress in the discussions was quashed by the Canadian federal government on the grounds that it alone had the authority to negotiate international treaties where shared natural resources were concerned.

Premier Bennett was determined to obtain the best feasible deal—in accordance with his personal ideological understanding of 'best'— for his province when it came to sharing the

Columbia's potential benefits. He was not about to be sidelined by constitutional arguments limiting his jurisdiction. He saw in the Columbia's potential a catalyst for kickstarting his grandiose economic development agenda for BC. That agenda entailed unprecedented, mega-scale improvements to the province's existing infrastructure in transportation and hydroelectric power. Its intent was to foster long-term industrial development, and secure employment and a higher standard of living for BC's citizenry. In the attainment of that agenda, whether or not one retrospectively agrees with it, Bennett proved himself to be a consummate geopolitician in playing off the various Canadian and American interests both governmental and corporate until he got what he wanted for BC.

A proper delineation of Bennett's complex web of political gamesmanship is a fascinating story in itself, but beyond the scope of the present discussion [see Swainson (1979) and Mitchell (1983) for further details]. Nevertheless, some of the key elements of his geopolitical strategy and tactics merit some mention.

The *Two Rivers* Policy and its Geopolitical Underpinnings

W.A.C. Bennett's development agenda for BC was strongly coloured by what has been termed his "northern vision," which in turn seems to have been rooted as an unconscious, dynamic component in the man's psychic make-up, manifesting as "intuition," or keen awareness of possibilities, whenever "northern BC" entered his sphere of conscious ratiocination. As to how this psychic vector became implanted is more a question for developmental psychologists than for geographers. Although born in New Brunswick, Bennett, at the age of 18, had moved to the Canadian Peace River region which straddles both sides of the northern border separating BC from Alberta. There he attempted to assist his father in developing an agricultural enterprise on a small parcel of land. The father had been given this land by the federal Soldier Settlement Board as compensation for his services to Canada during World War I. The son, however, was ineligible for a land grant. The temperaments of the dull, unimaginative father and visionary son soon clashed. While the father revelled in the isolation of the region, the son dreamt of a railway system that would reconnect him to the hustle and bustle of vibrant central places. The son shortly left to seek fame and fortune in Edmonton. It is believed that he never saw his father again. However, in his private memories the Peace River country and his father seemed to have become inextricably linked, with the vastness of the former perhaps representing the potential of a father's love that was never realized. Perhaps if he were to somehow develop the Peace River country, Bennett might somehow earn his father's affection.

Some three decades later, when Bennett had become Premier of BC, the idea of developing the Peace River country still persisted as a splinter in his brain. The idea resurfaced in 1956 when he requisitioned a speculative, technical report examining the feasibility of building an electric monorail up the Rocky Mountain trench that would eventually connect with lines through the Peace River country, then to Yukon and Alaska. The findings made Bennett realize that BC lacked both the critical population density and the potential volume of rail freight to justify such an undertaking. However, the report exercise had put him in touch with potential sources of international financing. More importantly, it forced him to assess the potential energy resources that would have to be developed to run his putative monorail. He therefore commissioned a follow-up engineering report in 1957 to examine the *Power of the Peace*. It concluded exactly what Bennett wanted to hear; that is, that the Peace River system had the potential to become one of the world's major hydro developments. It seemed to him that if he were to develop its potential, then all the other socio-economic spinoffs that he sought to flesh out his vision of the north might eventually be forthcoming. His political reasoning now required that the development of this hydro power potential displace the earlier monorail idea as his holy grail.

It may seem that the Peace River issue was not a geopolitical one, inasmuch as the harnessing of new power could proceed completely within the bounds of provincial jurisdiction, without calling into play relations with external geopolitical entities. However, the hurdle of obtaining venture capital could not be surmounted without reference to extra-provincial entities. The mandarins in Ottawa were not interested in providing cost-sharing assistance. The Peace River development was not one they could control with any hope of obtaining the level of political credit and visibility for the federal authorities that could be reaped from co-sponsoring international development of the Columbia Basin. Private international capital for the Peace project might be forthcoming, but given BC's tradition of private ownership of provincial electrical resources, Bennett was loathe to surrender control of his pet projects. After all, he too sought such personal political credit as might advance his subsequent visions of development. Like all his visions, they were merely awaiting time and chance, while simmering on his back burner.

Bennett wanted to be a major player where the development of the Columbia Basin was concerned. High level discussions had taken place between Canadian Prime Minister St. Laurent and American President Eisenhower in 1956; but BC was cut out of the loop. St. Laurent soon fell out of office and his successor, John Diefenbaker, would not deal with Bennett until 1958, when his Conservative party had obtained a clear majority government in Ottawa. All the while Bennett was fearful that if any international agreements were reached on the Columbia Basin, any new Columbia power benefits that might be allocated to Canada would simply preempt the possibility of developing the potential power of the Peace. A complex array of other problems were presenting themselves. In presenting their feasibility studies, the American Corps of Engineers tried to persuade members of the American negotiating team not to enter into any dam cost-sharing arrangements with the Canadians. The treaty proposal (that was eventually signed) required that three flood control dams be built on the Canadian side of the Columbia system. The Corps of Engineers argued that Canada would have had to build the dams anyway, so why should the US contribute to construction costs? Bennett saw this tack as an American ploy to steal downstream flood control and power benefits. The American military were of course also concerned, for reasons of national security, about putting themselves in a position of dependency with respect to a strategic resource. After all, signing a treaty might limit the number of future dams the US could build on its side of the border. General McNaughton, the most influential and openly anti-American of the Canadian negotiators, countered by threatening to divert Columbia River water into the Fraser River to enable Canada to "go it alone." The threat, although actually impractical and potentially suicidal (and laughable were it to be asserted in the present decade) produced salutary results from the Canadian standpoint. At the same time, McNaughton was not helpful to Bennett as he was emphatically opposed to having the Peace developed before the Columbia.

W.A.C. Bennett as Geopolitical Actor

Bennett, determined to be a major geopolitical player in his province's water resources, proceeded unilaterally with his "Peace Project First" initiatives. To do so, he had to stall progress on the Columbia negotiations. He likely feared that once any treaty was signed Ottawa could expropriate the Canadian side of the Columbia Basin in the name of the national interest. BC would thereby be left in a mendicant position more in keeping with its traditional hinterland status vis à vis the Canadian heartland. As for obtaining financing for the Peace project, Bennett calculated that he would have to *pre-sell* the hydroelectric power. Given the then-recent technology of 500KV transmission lines, he could theoretically connect to a power grid in the Seattle area and perhaps thereby even export power to California. Ottawa had its own ideas as to what could, and what could not, be exported to the US, and invoked export regulations in an attempt to forestall Bennett and his vision of the Peace.

Indeed, a *National Energy Board Act* was passed in 1959 to delineate federal policy with respect to power exports. Even here, Bennett proved himself to be the superior tactician. Observing that federal regulations—in recognition of rainfall variability from year to year—applied only to what was termed *regular, continuous, and firm power*, Bennett arranged for a key power site in the Peace system to produce *peak power*, which could then be sold to the US as *surplus* or *dump* power, so as to bypass federal regulations. A problem with dump power, however, was its tendency to be sold at lower commercial rates and without the benefit of reliable longer term contracts.

Bennett also had the problem of an unreliable provincial market for hydro power, since the market was still essentially in the hands of private corporations. The BCE, BC's major producer of electrical energy of the day, refused to commit itself to buying Peace Power. It preferred to wait for a "slice of the Columbia River action" instead, wherewith, as a private corporation, they could have some ownership. The BCE also feared that by committing, in advance, to buying Peace Power, they would be preempted from getting their hands on Columbia power later. The BCE at the time was also run by Bennett's political rivals who were anxious to drain away all visible support, be it popular or corporate, for the Peace Project. The BCE was also secretly buying up shares in the Peace River Corporation, a legal entity that had been created to raise venture capital, with a view to scuttling their value and thereby sabotaging the project. After all, the BC government had hinted that such power might be sold to the public at cost. If so, how could the BCE be expected to make a profit?

There were other complications. General McNaughton, fearful that the Americans might proceed on their own on their side of the Columbia, was anxious to obtain an international agreement. A federal-provincial liaison committee had been created to give the impression that BC's views mattered. However, Prime Minister Diefenbaker indicated to Bennett that the federal government wanted a major say regarding any Columbia-project benefits to Canada. In return for this control, BC would only be loaned 50% of the costs (plus interest) of building any water storage dams. No assistance would be given for any power-generation or transmission costs; and all downstream energy was to be returned for use in Canada. The latter provision was really a patronage fillip for the BCE who would thereby obtain cheap power in return for their political support of Diefenbaker and his federal Tory party.

Bennett proceeded strategically on all fronts so as not to lose whatever Columbia benefits he might squeeze out of both the Canadian and American governments. At the same time, the Peace project still had to come first. To bolster that priority, he made it clear that he did not want any downstream power on the Columbia returned to Canada. What he wanted was the return of a cash payment for such power to help finance his Peace scheme. He also wanted to avoid the costs that would be incurred in building the transmission lines that would return the raw power itself. Such costs alone were estimated to be $100 million. He also wanted to avoid the possibility of such power competing in cost and convenience with the Peace power that he envisaged.

Still fearing that Ottawa might expropriate BC's interests in the Columbia, Bennett stopped funding site feasibility and cost estimates for that basin and instead, by way of creative bookkeeping, reallocated this funding to detailed engineering and cost studies for harnessing the power of the Peace. However, the international hydro power politics intensified, and in Washington, DC on January 17, 1961 a formal treaty was signed by Prime Minister Diefenbaker for Canada and President Eisenhower (representing his recently elected successor, J.F. Kennedy) for the US. However, Ottawa had not yet outmanoeuvred Bennett, who knew the treaty still had to be ratified by all stakeholders. As BC's conditions had not yet been fully addressed, ratification could be stalled. In August of 1961, Bennett delivered his *master stroke* by introducing Bill 5, the *Power Development Act*, into the BC legislature. This Act expropriated the BCE (by compensating its parent company—the *BC Power Corporation*), transforming it into a crown corporation into whose provenance all assets and liabilities of the Peace River Power Development Corporation (PRPDC) were also transferred. The PRPDC was just a convenient paper entity, expressly created for legitimating feasibility studies and for raising capital.

This larger, newly created crown corporation called the *BC Hydro and Power Authority* was to finance the actual development of Peace Power by issuing parity bonds. Bennett then tabled the *Report of the British Columbia Energy Board on the Columbia and Peace Power Projects*. The report had great credibility as the board's chair, Gordon Shrum, a physicist seconded from the University of BC, was in effect acting as an independent commissioner. Its findings, very conveniently, indicated that public costs of developing Peace Power would be virtually identical to those for the Columbia. The report also noted that, since the end result of having two different projects would be the production of more power than BC could absorb in the short term, the excess power should be sold to American markets. The report then recommended that, owing to their greater proximity, the Columbia treaty downstream benefits should be sold first. In order to do so, without interference from Ottawa, it was strongly recommended that control over the disposition of downstream benefits be vested in BC, before final ratification of the Columbia Treaty.

The federal government was geopolitically stymied. In 'provincializing' the province's hydro resources, Premier Bennett had also scored political points with its citizens by indicating that the federal government, via its self-serving tax regulations, had for its own purposes "long skimmed off the taxes" paid by the previously privately-owned power monopolies. Now that the shoe was on the other foot such financial haemorrhaging of potential provincial revenues would stop. As if by nemesis, Prime Minister Diefenbaker's own political power base across Canada began to haemorrhage instead. At the beginning of 1963, the American contingent to the IJC indicated the US' willingness to pay cash for downstream benefits on the Columbia. Later that year, Diefenbaker lost political office; and on June 3, 2 months after the federal Liberal party had regained power, Ottawa also agreed to the sale of downstream benefits. A deal was signed between Ottawa and BC on July 8, 1963. Unfortunately, a fly in the ointment still remained with respect to the legality of the process whereby Bennett had expropriated the BCE.

Prior to its expropriation, the BCE had been the largest remaining privately-owned power company in the nation, with a reputation for overcharging its customers. Despite public approval of the expropriation, BCE had immediately countered with a legal challenge before the Supreme Court of BC. Two years later, on July 29, 1963, BCE won a ruling that the expropriation had been illegal since it had originally been incorporated as a private utility under federal, and not provincial jurisdiction. BCE had been covertly assisted in its lawsuit by certain multinational corporations based in other countries who, under the guise of protecting the value of their stockholdings in BCE, were determined to financially undermine Bennett's government in BC. With his legendary *legerdemain* however, Bennett quickly orchestrated an arrangement whereby, on September 25, the BCE was simply persuaded to settle for a larger compensatory emolument. Five days later he called a surprise provincial election. His principal opponent was David Fulton, a former federal cabinet minister from the defeated Diefenbaker government. His platform called for cancellation of the Columbia Treaty, without providing an alternative aphrodisiac for the public mood which Bennett had more skilfully cultivated. Unsurprisingly, the result of Fulton's challenge was re-election of Bennett's party by a landslide. Bennett then used this fresh public mandate adroitly to pressure the Americans into meeting his floor price of 5 mills /kWh (as opposed to figures of about 4 mills/ kWh that had been touted earlier) for downstream power benefits. The Columbia Treaty was finally ratified on January 22, 1964 in Washington, DC. A new prime minister, Lester B. Pearson, signed for Canada. President Lyndon Johnson, who had just succeeded the assassinated John F. Kennedy, signed for the US.

The Columbia River Treaty

On September 16, 1964, during a special ceremony at the Peace Arch border crossing in BC, President Johnson presented Premier Bennett (clearly the hero of the hour) with a cheque for $273.3 million as a 'return of cash value' for the Columbia's downstream power benefits (estimated to be 1.325 Gigawatts over 30 years). In addition, BC was to receive $69 million, in three instalments, for downstream flood-control benefits, in effect giving BC a total cash return of $342.3 million. The treaty was regarded as a 60-year deal. However, its terms could be revisited after 30 years. The start-date for renewal was not to be based upon the date of ratification, namely 1964 plus 30 years, but rather on the completion-dates of the various treaty dams plus 30 years. BC was to construct three treaty dams, named the *Duncan*, the *High Arrow* (later renamed the *Keenleyside*), and the *Mica* (see Figure 7.5). In return, the Americans could build the Libby Dam on Montana without either compensating BC for raising the level of the Kootenay River on the BC side, or claiming any compensation for having done so. The Duncan was completed in 1967 and the Keenleyside in 1968, just one week after the Bennett dam on the Peace River. The Mica, the largest of the treaty dams, was not contracted for until 1967. It was completed for flood control purposes by 1973 and generating power by 1977. The first two dams were built for *flood control* purposes only. The Mica, by the terms of the final treaty, was allowed to be retrofitted to take power generators. The initial retrofit yielded 1.74 Gigawatts of power. Final retrofitting later allowed a total output of 2.65 Gigawatts. The other two Canadian dams could also be retrofitted as occasion required, in which case BC would have to compensate American downstream power users for any resulting diminution of their installed hydro power capacity. In 1983, BC completed a fourth major dam on the Columbia at Revelstoke which by 1984 possessed 2.7 Gigawatts of installed capacity. This dam re-uses the water from Mica and is considered to be outside of the treaty arrangements.

Columbia Basin Trust: Geopolitics of Public Relations and Renewal

According to the 30-year renegotiating provisions, the three dams were due to come up for treaty renewal in 1998, 1999, and 2003. The *Columbia Basin Trust* was created in 1996 by way of establishing a mechanism for modifying and renewing the original treaty provisions. Under new provisions, all of the former downstream hydro benefits were to be returned to BC as electricity (using existing transmission lines) rather than cash. Of those benefits, 78.5% of the power was to be returned by the border town of Blaine, Washington and 21.5% via Nelway and Waneta in the Kootenays starting no sooner than April 1998. This arrangement represents a considerable savings in transmission line costs as compared to what would have been required in 1964 had BC elected to take power instead of cash. The power returned to BC is rated at 1.4 Gigawatts and is projected to be worth about $30 billion (in 1999 dollars) for the second 30-year term of the 60-year treaty. It is unlikely that BC will be able to use all of this extra power, so provisions are being made for possible resale back to the US. However, to comply with the North American Free Trade Agreement (NAFTA), the US, via a 1997 agreement, is also free to sell power in BC at competitive rates. BC nevertheless anticipates being able to sell much of its surplus power to the US at a discount with a view to attracting further industrial development. Selling discounted power at less than cost to the US would, however, be problematic because NAFTA rules specifically contraindicate the sale of state-subsidized goods and services. As for upgrading existing treaty dams on the Canadian side, only the Keenleyside dam has been mooted for a first-time projected retrofit in 2002 to give an installed capacity of 0.150 Gigawatts. That figure—in deference to the far greater political influence of environmentalists in the 1990s—was reduced from the 0.220 Gigawatts initially proposed. Smaller-scale power upgrades to private installations owned by West Kootenay Power at Waneta and Brilliant, which services various mining operations in southeastern BC, are still awaiting approval. Such proposals must now be reviewed by the Columbia Basin Trust, which has a much broader environmental protection mandate than the 1964 treaty. Indeed, a projected Unit 5 to increase hydro output at Revelstoke's non-treaty dam was indefinitely suspended in 1999. A much broader cost-accounting basis for non-power downstream benefits by way of flood control and other environmental enhancements means that, starting in 2003, BC should receive a far greater income stream than it did the first time around. The value of these benefits is projected to be $200 million per year or $6 billion for the remaining 30 years of the treaty; that is, 87 times—in dollar terms—what had been received during the first 30 years. [After adjusting for inflation the real return is probably closer to eight times as much.]

W.A.C. Bennett lost the Premiership of BC to David Barrett, leader of the NDP in 1972. Bennett's political successors argued that his megaprojects had been accomplished at the expense of human values, and that he had sold BC "down the river"— that he had come out bested by the Americans in the Columbia Treaty negotiations. However, Barrett, for his part, proved himself to be no less a hydro zealot than Bennett. In claiming political capital for the public ownership of power resources as being very appropriate to his socialist mandate, Barrett ironically turned out to be the one who may have been overbuilding. More ironically, it had been Bennett who, under the guise of an anti-socialist discourse, had been the first to socialize those same resources, even at the cost of being labelled another "Fidel Castro." Barrett also saw BC Hydro as his central tool for the social and economic development of the province. He spent unprecedented sums in constructing transmission lines, expanding generating capacity, increasing staffing levels and extending the uses of the new power at a speed which even BC Hydro regarded as faster than necessary (BC Hydro Pioneers, 1998).

Hindsight discloses that under the development parameters of the day, forests and farmlands were inundated, trout streams lost and winter rangeland for big game gone. The Mica Dam alone is said to have cost the loss of 60,000 truckloads of logs. But the real benefits of flood control and irrigation were not inconsiderable. Most objective, retrospective accounts regard W.A.C. Bennett as having driven the hardest geopolitical bargain possible for BC at the time.[14] For the Americans, the Columbia Project was but one of many enterprises on their platter. Presumably they could afford a larger margin of negotiating error than Bennett could. Even so, they "had to pay cash on the barrel head to build the upstream dams ...to sell bonds to get the money, to build transmission lines to California [to ensure a market for the power], to mortgage half the electricity that could be produced from water stored in Canada, to take a 30-year mortgage and then to pay a premium for the flood damage that would be avoided downstream" (Boyer, 1974, p. 833). As for the long term prospects that might arise out of the Columbia Basin Trust, such generalizations are too hazardous to venture at this time. Discussion records concerning a number of pending critical nuances are not yet in the domain of readily available public knowledge. The original Columbia River Treaty signalled the importance of hydro energy as a staple to be exported, rather than as an economic input for increasing the *value-added* of provincially produced finished goods for export. Thereby, BC was for a very long time marked as hinterland region, whose importance continued to be merely "the hewing of wood and the drawing of water." It remains to be seen whether the new Columbia Basin Trust arrangements will counter that perception in any significant way.

SUMMARY AND REFLECTIONS

BC is the composite of a multi-layered complex of spatial and human/temporal factors; at a basic level, it displays the interplay of physical geography and changing human perceptions of the same, coloured conceptions of merchantable natural resources and awareness of situational possibilities. The associated mental images reflected both the existing technological wherewithal, and the power of organized human effort, whether corporately, or politically controlled.[15] This continuing interplay of active and passive factors has cartographically impressed its patterns of sequent economic, social, and political occupance on the map of BC.

The early post-contact rivalries among the great European powers of the day and the intercultural stresses arising from the interaction of the aboriginal peoples with the Europeans in a sense prefigured, at low-intensity and local scale, the present internecine power plays, on the contemporary world stage, for the control of strategic material and situational resources. Though the scales of contention may differ, the contemporary geopolitical discourse has many parallels with the colonial one. Admittedly, present-day BC has a far greater spatial field of interaction with the rest of the world, as the present discourse of *globalization* keeps reminding us. Nevertheless then, as now, events in BC often reflected decisions taken elsewhere.

Sometimes one wonders whether Canada is merely a land, rather than a nation, and whether BC need ever have become a part of Canada. Given the natural, *north-south* grain of North America, one also wonders why the *east-west* project of Canada should ever have succeeded. Part of the answer lies in the fur-trade, for it was the first economic driver in the creation of Canada. Intense, resource-depleting competition between the London-based HBC and the Montreal-based NWC induced the latter corporation to project its fur-trading interests far beyond the Great Lakes. The exploration stimulated by that commercial imperative resulted in a new chain of fur forts strung across the Athabaska River basin and high Canadian Prairies through the Cordillera as far as the Pacific. When the HBC absorbed the NWC, it absorbed the Far West, thereby consolidating the territory that would become the polity of *Canada*. In essence, *Canada* is the political legitimation of the HBC's fur-trading territory. The inclusion of BC was needed to maintain congruence between the political entity and its corporate precursor, thereby pre-empting a possible American takeover of the Far West. The eventual completion of the CPR in 1887 to Vancouver simply ratified that fact in an effective, concrete way. It also marked the decline of the relative importance of naval power in maintaining effective occupance of the Canadian Far West. The insular port situation of Victoria succumbed to that of Vancouver which was now possessed of direct, facile access to a vast continental hinterland.

Of course, even before BC joined Canada in 1871, other resources were displacing furs as drivers for the province's geo-economic and geopolitical development. The Gold Rush of 1858 required improvement of transportation access to the mainland interior and administrative oversight over potential gold revenues so the Crown might protect its share. Provisioning spinoffs entailed development of other resources: particularly coal, timber, agriculture, fish and, later, metallic minerals. The development of BC, as for Canada as a whole, was always principally resource-driven. The difference was only in the nature of the resources. The construction of the CPR was the first mega-project to impact on BC, and proved a great boon for the exploitation of timber resources and metallic minerals. However, that was not a homegrown project. The biggest homegrown mega-project in BC history was the Columbia River power project, conceived in the 1950s and completed in the 1960s—with tag ends persisting to the present. Its ripple effects included a rise in the politics of environmental awareness and a clamour for greater economic diversification that emphasized greater value-added manufacturing. These political trends were modulated by the world oil crisis of the mid 1970s. By the late 1980s, the *information revolution* did allow some degree of economic diversification, with *globalization* becoming the buzz word of the 1990s.

Hindsight suggests that the Columbia River hydro-power mega-project appears to have provided greater ballast for a governing political party than any other single initiative in the history of BC. Premier W.A.C. Bennett retained his office from 1952 to 1972—a total of 20 years. That time-interval compares very favourably with the average political longevity of 4.1 years for the 32 premiers who held office over the 130 years from Confederation to the present. If one considers only the decade 1991-2000, the contrast is even more remarkable. That period produced five different premiers, for an average life-span of only 2 years. W.A.C. Bennett has been characterized as a benevolent despot; but a number of premiers who followed him were no less despotic and arguably less benevolent, with far fewer concrete achievements trailing on the clouds of their rhetoric. Other premiers attempted to emulate Bennett's successes with mega-projects of their own, such as the NE Coal project, the Coquihalla Highway, and the fast ferries program to link Vancouver Island with the mainland. Most of these later projects ran into serious cost over-runs or outright failure. The mere existence of BC's bountiful endowments does not guarantee their judicious use. Practical intelligence, personal integrity, vision, and a disciplined bounding of that vision to limited, manageable objectives have distinguished this province's most memorable geopolitical actor from all of his successors.

REFERENCES

Boyer, D. (1974). The Columbia River: Powerhouse of the NorthWest, *National Geographic*, December 1974.

Barman, J. (1996). *The West beyond the West*. Toronto: University of Toronto Press.

BC Hydro Pioneers (1998). *Gaslights to Gigawatts*. Vancouver: Hurricane Press.

BC Ministry of Aboriginal Affairs (1999). *Nisga'a Final Agreement*. Victoria: Government of BC.

Canada, BC, Nisga'a Nation (1998). *Nisga'a Final Agreement*. Ottawa and Victoria: Government Printing Office.

Department of External Affairs, Canada (1964). *The Columbia River Treaty: Protocol and Related Documents*. Ottawa: Government of Canada.

Carty, R. (Ed.) (1996). *Politics, policy and government in British Columbia*. Vancouver: UBC Press.

Donald, L. (1997). *Aboriginal slavery on the Northwest coast of North America*. Berkeley: University of California Press.

Foster, H., and Sewell, D. (1981). *Water: The emerging crisis in Canada*. Toronto: Lorimer.

Gillespie, G. (1999). Captain George Vancouver: 200 years dead on May 12th, 1998, *BC Historical News*, Spring 1999, 2-3.

Grant, D.J. (1980). *T.D. Pattullo's Northern Empire: The Alaska Highway and the proposed annexation of the Yukon Territory, 1933-1941*. Unpublished M.A. Thesis, Victoria, University of Victoria.

Harring, S.L. (1998). *White Man's law: Native People in nineteenth century Canadian jurisprudence*. Toronto: Osgoode Society for Canadian Legal History.

Harris, J. C. (1998). Social power and cultural change in pre-Colonial British Columbia, *BC Studies*, 115/116, 45-82.

Harris, J. C. (1997). *The resettlement of British Columbia: Essays on colonialism and geographical change*. Vancouver: UBC Press.

Innis, H. (1999). *The fur trade in Canada*. Toronto: University of Toronto Press.

Jackson, K. (Ed.) (1983). *Ideology of the NDP in BC*. Victoria: BC Project.

Johnston, H. (1996). *The Pacific province: A history of British Columbia*. Vancouver: Douglas & McIntyre.

Krutilla, J. (1967). *The Columbia River Treaty*. Baltimore: John Hopkins.

Mackie, R. (1997). *Trading beyond the mountains: British fur trade on the Pacific 1793-1843*. Vancouver: UBC Press.

MacLachlan, M., and Sutter, W. (Eds.) (1998). *The Fort Langley Journals 1827-30*. Vancouver: UBC Press.

Mitchell, D. (1983). *W.A.C. Bennett and the Rise of British Columbia*. Vancouver: Douglas & McIntyre.

Mouat, J. (1997). *The business of power*. Victoria: Sono Nis.

Muckle, R. (1998). *The First Nations of British Columbia: An anthropological survey*. Vancouver: UBC Press.

Sewell, W. R. D. (1968). The Columbia River Treaty: Some lessons and implications. In R. Irving (Ed.), *Readings in Canadian geography* (pp. 340-351). Toronto: Holt, Rinehart, .

Shelton, W. (Ed.) (1967). *British Columbia and confederation*. Victoria: University of Victoria.

Swainson, N. (1979). *Conflict over the Columbia*. Montreal: McGill-Queen's University Press.

Tennant, P. (1996). Aboriginal Peoples and Aboriginal title in British Columbia politics. In R. Carty (Ed.), *Politics, policy and government in British Columbia* (pp. 45 - 64). Vancouver: UBC Press.

US Department of Commerce (1998). *Statistical abstract of the United States*, 118th edition.

Wicks, L. (1999). BC Minister of Labour, 1952-1961. Personal Interview regarding W.A.C. Bennett.

Williston, E., and Keller, B. (1977). *Forests, power and policy*. Prince George, BC: Caitlin.

Endnotes

[1] That Captain George Vancouver was able—in three summers and with rudimentary means—"to chart the most intricate 10,000 miles of coastline on the planet" is a remarkable feat of surveying for which he received sparse credit in his lifetime. For recent attempts to redeem his reputation, see Gillespie (1999).

[2] An interesting sidelight to the treaty was an implicit recognition of a role played by the Ukrainian Cossacks in developing the Siberian and Alaskan fur trade. That role was somewhat analogous to that of the French voyageurs in developing the proto-Canadian fur trade. This recognition was betokened by having Petro Poletica, a Cossack aristocrat, sign the treaty as plenipotentiary for Russia, while Lord Canning signed for England. This token was no doubt double-edged as it could also be interpreted as a *de jure* legitimation of Russia's *de facto* destruction and absorption of the Ukrainian Cossack Hetmanate (state) which had occurred a few decades earlier.

[3] For the first definitive treatment of the role that fur staples played in the economic development of Canada, see Innis (1999). This work is an abridged update of a 1930 classic which arguably established Harold Innis as the father of Canadian economic geography. For a detailed understanding of how the fur trade played out in proto-BC as a variant of the discourse of commercial capitalism, it is necessary to peruse the works of J. Cole Harris. See "Strategies of Power in the Cordilleran Fur Trade," c. 2 of Harris (1997).

[4] It can not be blithely said that the British fur traders were more virtuous than the Americans in their dealings with the natives, as those dealings were also predicated on violence. This violence, however, was of a different order more akin to psychological terrorism. For example, they might threaten to unleash smallpox on the natives, or to blow up noncompliant individuals with gunpowder (see Harris, 1998, p. 58). Ironically, the reality of a smallpox outbreak in the Victoria area in 1862 wiped out 20,000 persons, or one-third of the native population. Sadly, although the pre-contact native population in the geographic space antecedent to BC had been 80,000, that figure had declined to about 25,000 by the time of BC's confederation with Canada. In effect, 68% of the native population had been liquidated by disease, firearms, and alcohol. These injuries were in addition to the concomitant cultural genocide, discussion of which is beyond the scope of this article. Harris (1997) points out that the rhetoric of "law and order" was more sympathetic to the natives than the actual operation of the white man's legal apparatus that did not balk at the judicial execution of problematical individuals. See also Harring (1998).

[5] It has been observed that the *modus operandi* of the HBC was not too dissimilar from that of a private army. The HBC's overt objective, however, was not to 'eliminate an enemy'—as was the case with a US cavalry intent on operationalizing the discourse of 'the best Indian is a dead Indian.' Rather, the intent was to impose Eurocentric concepts of time-management, scheduling, routing, cost economies, etc., on both the HBC employees and the natives with whom they dealt—and to do so with military-style sanctions and with military efficacy. See Harris (*ibid*).

[6] The term *New Caledonia* requires some elaboration. It was the label that Simon Fraser gave to the central and highland plateau area of BC for the NWC in 1806. The name initially designated a fur-trading district having its headquarters at Fort St. James on Stuart Lake. During the 1858 Gold Rush, it came to denote the area of gold-discoveries in the upper Fraser River basin reached by the Cariboo Road that followed the Fraser northward from its delta. For a short interval beginning in 1858, the British Colonial Secretary, Lord Bulwer-Lytton used the term *New Caledonia* to refer to the British western North America. He dropped the term in favour of *British Columbia* when it was discovered that the French had an island colony named New Caledonia in the South Pacific.

[7] One of the irritants had been Blanshard's inability to sanction the apparent liberality of Douglas's Indian policies. Douglas was himself a mulatto who had married a woman with some Indian blood.

[8] Cole Harris refers to the HBC's entire *gestalt* configuration of material arrangements, accumulated practices, and superstructure [in the Marxian sense of values, assumptions, intentions, and ideas] as constituting *the colonial fur trade discourse*. See Harris, 1997 (p. 281). *Savoir-faire infrastructure*, might therefore represent such abstracted elements of Harris' discourse as might be *transferable* to successor economic activities that could benefit from the HBC's earlier physical and administrative networking capabilities.

[9] The Fenians were members of an Irish-American movement created in 1857 with the objective of procuring the independence of Ireland from Britain. Inasmuch as its membership included 10,000 American Civil War veterans, spoiling raids across the border into Canada that were intended to pressure the British into making concessions to the Irish became readily conflated with fears of American annexation. On the one hand, this external threat helped to unite the British colonies of North America. On the other hand, the Dominion authorities were trying to argue that their treasury had been depleted by the costs of countering Fenian raids, so that there was no money available to construct a transcontinental railroad (see Shelton, 1967, p. 135).

[10] Helmcken at this time thought the railway would be constructed as far as Vancouver Island. The actual rail routing to be followed could not be announced for quite some time, owing to Ottawa's need to maintain secrecy, until certain rights of way had been purchased from the Province of Ontario.

11 The leading BC newspaper of the day sardonically reported that a new legislative body, "created ... for the express purpose of deciding the great question of Confederation [did so by] giving a unanimous vote in silence..." See *Colonist*, January 19, 1871.

12 The construction of this dry dock was one of Helmcken's conditions for BC entering confederation that the federal authorities initially resisted. Ottawa was fearful that other seaboard provinces might follow suit and also demand federally subsidized dry docks. BC, of course, wished to maintain and enlarge the economic spinoffs stemming from Pacific maritime traffic along the temperate Pacific coast, especially with respect to the British naval presence at Esquimalt, which had appeared in 1848 as a reaction to British-American tensions over trading rights. From 1854-1856, thanks to both the Crimean War and the development of coal-mining at nearby Nanaimo, Esquimalt became the major fuelling stop for the British navy on the Pacific coast of the Americas. That function was reinforced by completion of Fisgard lighthouse in 1860 as a response to the Fraser Gold Rush that lured so many fortune-seekers from California by water. After 1871, however, the good diplomatic offices of Ottawa had to be invoked to represent BC's interests regarding the British naval presence. In becoming a province, BC had lost jurisdiction over foreign relations. The major dry dock, completed in 1887, marked the high watermark of British naval presence on the west coast. In 1905, owing to the recently concluded Boer War in South Africa, Britain recalled its imperial forces from its far-flung outposts. The defence of Esquimalt was left completely in the hands of Canada. The base was subsequently taken over by the Royal Canadian Navy, which had to be created from scratch in 1910. A new federal dry dock was built between 1921 and 1927. In 1942 it was used to refit the Queen Elizabeth, the largest liner of its day, as a troop ship to transport 15,000 soldiers at a time to the European theatre of war. To this day, it remains the largest graving dock on the west coast of North America.

13 A current representative political document is: Canada, British Columbia, Nisga'a Nation, *Nisga'a Final Agreement*, 1998. See also Harring (1998) and Tennant (1996). For an appreciation of aboriginal slavery see Donald (1997).

14 Derrick Sewell (1964) appeared not to have been excessively critical of the final terms of the Columbia Treaty. He acknowledged that comprehensive river-basin planning was an ideal that was difficult of international implementation at the best of times—as indicated by experience from other jurisdictions. The consideration of the full range of economic and technical possibilities entailed by the concept of comprehensive water resource management invariably became constricted by cost, time, and a host of institutional factors, not the least of which was the dearth of Canadian personnel (at the time) capable of evaluating the various possibilities. Were Sewell living today, he might arguably add that alternative options must be assessed in terms of the broadest possible cost/benefit parameters. Such would no doubt include social, as well as environmental, cost-accounting procedures.

15 Halford Mackinder attached great importance to *organized* human effort, labelling it as the "going concern" indispensable for any geopolitical undertaking. See his *Democratic Ideals and Reality* (New York: Norton, 1948).

Plate 7 A totem display in Stanley Park, Vancouver shows the variation in tribal carving styles ▶

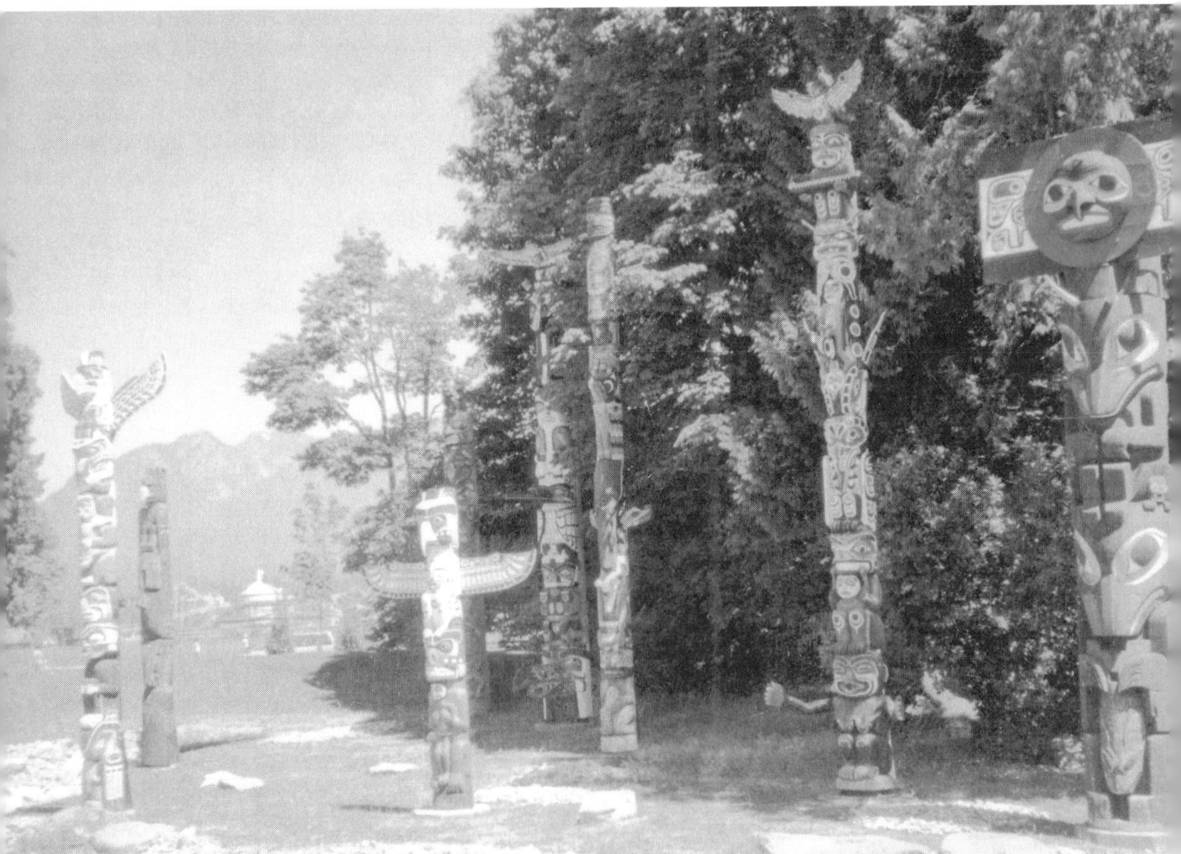

Geography and Treaty Negotiations

Frank Duerden

School of Applied Geography, Ryerson University, Toronto

INTRODUCTION

Treaty negotiations in BC are rooted in geography. Historic land use patterns determine the legitimacy and extent of land claims; legal decisions have to be interpreted in resource management contexts; questions of spatial allocation and equity are an important component of land selection, and a range of techniques from the evaluation of land and resource potential, to the application of GIS technology to depict various scenarios for treaty outcomes are employed in the negotiation process (Duerden and Keller, 1992; Ray, 1993). Expectations regarding outcomes are greatly influenced by the broader geographic contexts in which treaty negotiations sit. This includes the geography of BC's population distribution, the structure of its space economy, and the geography of resource management issues such as conservation and management of forests, fisheries, and wilderness that are often conflated with First Nations' interests.

Given that treaties were initially negotiated in order to facilitate the settlement of southern Canada by Europeans, it may seem strange that treaty negotiations have yet to be concluded in BC, especially given that the Calder Decision, which gave impetus for claim negotiations in northern Canada, was the outcome of litigation brought by the Nisga'a. It was not until 1990 that the Government of BC agreed to negotiate modern treaties. The fact is that successive provincial governments had argued variously that First Nations were inferior, that the *Proclamation Act* of 1763 (which gave birth to the treaty process) only related to lands east of the Rocky Mountains, and that even if First Nation rights existed, they had been extinguished through explicit government actions and the passage of time.

Thus negotiations in BC are occurring somewhere close to the end-point in modern treaty negotiations in Canada, a process that has seen the question of the rights to over 50% of the nation's surface area resolved over the past 30 years (Notzke, 1994; Wolfe, 1995; Young, 1995). Unlike other areas where comprehensive land claim negotiations have been concluded, however, there are, large non-native populations, extensive land and resource alienation, and as a result a plethora of interests clamouring to be accommodated in the treaty process (Cassidy and Dale, 1988). This chapter proceeds by briefly examining the background of treaty negotiations in BC, then focuses on the manner in which the geography of the province may impact land allocation and cash compensation, the major components of settlements. It is clear that once they are signed and implemented, treaties will bring new spatial jurisdictions with significant implications for resource management. The probable form of these is examined and the economic expectations regarding settlements critically reviewed in this chapter.

THE LEGAL AND HISTORICAL CONTEXTS

The *Proclamation Act* was the basis for treaty negotiations in Canada. It essentially asserted that the expansion of non-Native interests in British North America could only take place pursuant to negotiations between the government (in the initial instance Britain, and later the federal government) and representatives of

First Peoples. Modern land claim negotiations resulted from the fact that, while the treaty process had facilitated settlement and economic development in southern Canada east of the Rocky Mountains, in northern Canada and in BC, Euro-American interests were asserted without negotiated accommodation of First Nations' interests. As recently as 1970, treaty negotiations had taken place for less than half of the surface area of Canada, but the pace at which outstanding land claims have been settled over the subsequent 30 years is impressive, with comprehensive land claim settlements covering virtually all of Canada north of latitude 60°. Today BC, with 9.5% of the nation's land mass, is by far the largest region in which the question of First Nations' land rights has not been resolved.

There were numerous reasons for this shift in the government's willingness to settle outstanding grievances. These included a series of landmark Supreme Court decisions (Calder, Baker Lake, Sparrow, etc.) that legitimized First Nations' arguments, increased public awareness of the issue, and elevated concerns that uncertainty about ownership of land and resources and consequent litigation by First Nations could deter major development projects in northern Canada. The *Calder* (1973) decision acknowledged the notion of Aboriginal Title; the *Baker Lake* case laid down the tests for establishing the legitimacy of a land claim; and the *Sparrow* case recognized the continuance of First Nation resource rights. Comprehensive land claim settlements were initially focused on the north and generally covered components addressed in traditional treaties, namely land, financial compensation, and various management rights. The purpose of negotiations (from the standpoint of government) was to establish with certainty and finality the disposition of land and resources; in other words, which lands belonged to First Peoples and which belonged to the Crown. In the course of negotiations, First Nations would relinquish claims to land and resources throughout the areas that they had traditionally used and occupied (known as "Traditional Territories") in return for certain ownership of lesser amounts of land, cash, and a range of rights related to resource management and self-government. In the Yukon land claim settlement, for example, First Nations surrendered claims to some 450,000 km^2 of land in return for direct ownership of 41,500 km^2 (8% of the Territory's surface area) and $190 million cash. Although the land/cash format of this agreement reflects traditional treaties, the actual provisions are considerably different from those of earlier treaties. Yukon Natives obtained some 7 km^2 of land per capita compared to allocations in traditional treaties that were a maximum of only 2.4 km^2 per capita, and generally averaged .2 km^2 (Duerden, 1996).

When the Europeans arrived on the coast of what is now BC in the late 18th century they were on the margin of a land inhabited by a wide range of well organized and sophisticated societies, with 10 major linguistic groups, and a range of cultural traditions and resource management practices (Figure 8.1). Although their relative population sizes differed widely, a reasonable analogy would perhaps be with the size and cultural diversity of Western Europe. This diversity and cultural richness was not recognized by the new settlers, partly because they arrived on the coastal margin and had no understanding of the geography of the region that was eventually to become BC. The perspective was strongly Euro-centric and the various native groups encountered were noted for the way their appearance and life-style differed from that of the European, rather than the way in which they differed from each other.

Initially, the Europeans were in southern coastal regions and only moved inland and northwards as resource demands changed, the assertion of their interests coming in successive waves of resource exploitation—the fur trade, mining, and forestry. Numerous explanations have been forwarded to account for the fact that various new (indeed alien) activities were very rapidly established. One argument is that some activities were welcomed by the Natives and that, in the early stages of development, they in fact were exploiting the fur traders. Given the fact that Natives vastly outnumbered Europeans at the outset of colonization, that they controlled the supply of furs

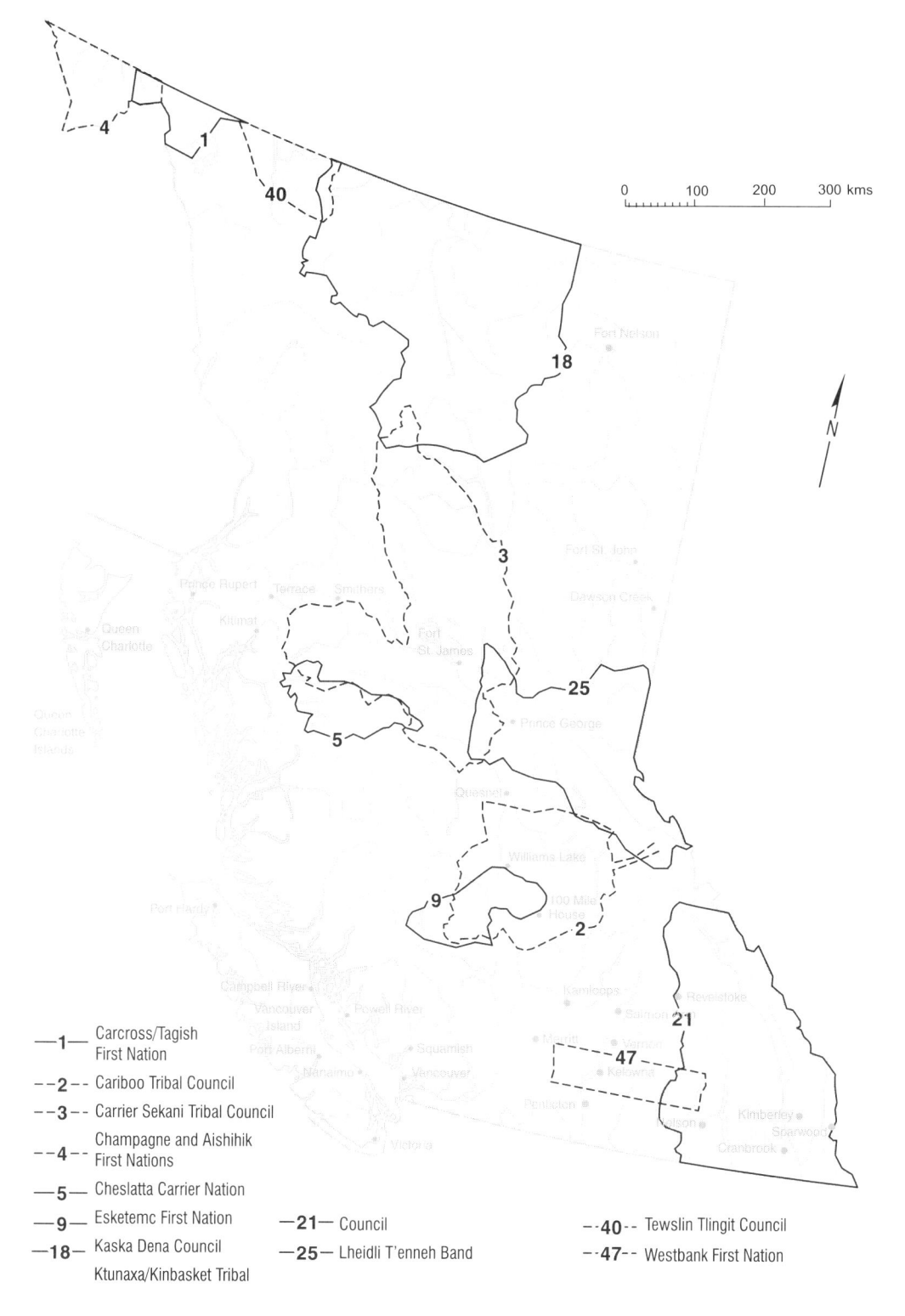

Geography and Treaty Negotiations in British Columbia

— 1 — Carcross/Tagish First Nation
– –2– – Cariboo Tribal Council
– –3– – Carrier Sekani Tribal Council
– –4– – Champagne and Aishihik First Nations
— 5 — Cheslatta Carrier Nation
— 9 — Esketemc First Nation
— 18 — Kaska Dena Council
Ktunaxa/Kinbasket Tribal
— 21 — Council
— 25 — Lheidli T'enneh Band
– –40– – Tewslin Tlingit Council
– –47– – Westbank First Nation

Figure 8.1 Examples of tribal land claims in BC. Note their total extent and the boundary overlap issue (nb. this is not an exhaustive list)

and knew the land while the Europeans did not, it is surmised that it would have taken willing acquiescence by First Peoples for the fur trade to flourish (Fisher, 1977). Other explanations include the notion that Natives misunderstood the intentions of Europeans, or that their intentions were misrepresented and that the promise of material gain was a powerful inducement to accommodate European interests. Yet another perspective is that First Peoples were powerless to prevent colonialism, and this became increasingly true as the demographic balance between Natives and Europeans shifted dramatically in the 19th century. Disease and other impacts brought by the newcomers had a devastating effect on the Native population. Tribal groups collapsed, land use patterns changed, and entire communities disappeared from the landscape. Estimates of the size of the Native population on the eve of contact are as high as 300,000 (Tennant, 1990); by 1881 it was down to 50,000, approximately half of the total population of the province. Twenty years later it constituted less than 30% of a total population of 170,000.

Although the *Proclamation Act* had obliged British representatives to negotiate with First Nations in order to facilitate expansion of their interests in Canada, the only treaty negotiations in BC were in southern Vancouver Island (Douglas Treaty) and the northeast (Treaty #8), and the prevailing wisdom became that because BC was west of the Rocky Mountains, the *Proclamation Act* had no validity and so there was no obligation to negotiate treaties. Ultimately a system of negotiated treaties was abandoned in favour of an imposed solution in which First Nations were allocated lands reserved for their use; the balance of the land in BC was designated "Crown Land." Land and resources were appropriated as required for industrial production, the popular view being essentially that industrial land uses took precedence over all others because cash revenue uses were superior to traditional subsistence pursuits. The *Forestry Act* (1912) exemplifies this point. Its guarantee of a 35 year supply of timber to pulp mills had strong spatial implications because the rate of exploitation greatly exceeded renewal, bringing timber harvesting into increasing conflict with First Nations' land and resource interests.

First Nations' resource use at every level was impacted by the demands of industrial society. The growth of the forest industry was largely facilitated by the leasing of what had been designated as Crown Land to lumber companies, and as global urbanization brought increased demand for construction materials and newsprint, expansion of forest exploitation accelerated. Ancestral lands and traditional territories were overrun, modification of forest ecosystems resulted from deforestation, and in some areas the introduction of agriculture had an amplified impact. Agriculture brought with it alien attitudes towards animals as, for example, "wild" animals were increasingly viewed as predators. Fishing was transformed from a subsistence activity into an industrial and commercial one, stressing fish stocks. BC's growing immigrant population competed with Natives for wildlife resources. Mining scarred landscapes and introduced a host of toxins to previously pristine rivers; eventually, demands for hydro-power from emerging industries and growing populations modified major drainage systems and displaced populations. At the regional level, control over resource management and resource allocation effectively passed to the Ministry of Forests, with regional Chief Foresters managing land use.

That these changes were debilitating for BC's Native population is a crass understatement. Disease, demoralization, and loss of traditional lands and way of life had taken a heavy toll. First Nation populations remained a shadow of their pre-contact sizes until well into the 20th century. It is well documented, but perhaps not widely known, that in the face of adversity BC First Nations conducted a sustained and skilful lobby to reassert their rights utilizing a full range of political and legal initiatives, including direct petitions to the British government (the first of which was in 1909), lobbying of politicians, and litigation based on the argument that their lands and resources were appropriated illegally. It was not until 1973 that they met with significant success, when the Supreme Court ruled that Frank Calder, a Nisga'a Native, had title to ancestral land in northern BC, because in the absence of treaty negotiations he had never surrendered rights to his land and because by entering into negotiations with Canada's original peoples to obtain access to their lands, the British government had inferred that such rights existed. The precise nature of this title remained undefined and the judges were split on the issue of the continuance of *Aboriginal Title*, but the decision cast into doubt the legality of occupancy of, and resource use on all lands in Canada that had been occupied without meeting the conditions of the *Proclamation Act*.

Initially this did little to move the negotiation agenda ahead in BC, but it was a significant factor in the federal government's decision to pursue comprehensive land claim negotiations in northern Canada and open negotiations with the Nisga'a.[1] The provincial government, however, was intransigent and refused to participate in negotiations. It was another 15 years (1990) before a combination of factors, including uncertainty created by the Calder Decision, pressure from the federal government, sustained and effective agitation by BC First Nations, an accumulation of law suits (Guerin v. the Queen, Sparrow, Delgamuukw), and the need to facilitate resource development, led the Province to the negotiation table. It would appear that the BC government paid a high price for its prevarication and the subsequent slow pace of negotiations. In 1997, the Supreme Court of Canada not only upheld the notion that *Aboriginal Title* was possibly unextinguished throughout most of the province, but also defined it as applying to a comprehensive range of land and resources (for an excellent review of the background to Delgamuukw see Culhane, 1998).

Treaty negotiations commenced in 1990, in a world far removed from that in which initial contact and occupancy took place; a world where vast areas of land had been appropriated or alienated, towns and cities existed where there was formerly wilderness, and a plethora of interests competed for land and resources. By 1991, although the Native population had made a spectacular recovery, numbering some 130,000 and exceeding pre-contact levels, it constituted only 4.5% of BC's total population of 3,724,500. With approximately 75% of the province's population living in the Lower Mainland and on southern Vancouver Island, it is only a few rural and northern regions that have anything approaching a demographic balance between aboriginal and non-aboriginal populations. Land claim settlements have to be reached with 66 First Nations who between them are claiming rights to some 93% of the surface area of BC. These groups each have geographies, cultures, languages, and economies that differ considerably both from each other and from those of the non-Native population of the province. The negotiation process has to address these distinct geographies, and ideally government must reconcile First Nations' interests and those of the general population of BC. Negotiations are taking place against a backdrop of a multiplicity of resource issues that in themselves may not be seen as claim issues, but that have become conflated one way or another with First Nations' land rights. These include forest conservation, fisheries, wilderness area management, and sustainable development. First Nations, whose vital interests are associated with these resources, have been sought (or cited) as allies by some environmental and other interest groups.

THE GEOGRAPHY OF LAND CLAIM SETTLEMENTS[2]

There are some 66 First Nations groups in BC who for the most part are differentiated from each other by differences in culture, the geographic context in which they are found, and their degree of urbanization. Resource dependency and resource management practices vary between groups and there are varying degrees of preparedness for participation in treaty negotiations—a time consuming and detailed task addressing all aspects of First Nations' life and drawing on its most skilled human resources. In comprehensive land claim negotiations in northern Canada, umbrella organizations represented all First Nations and initial negotiations took place between these organizations (such as the Council for Yukon Natives, or Tungavik Federation of Nunavut) and government to produce an *umbrella land claim agreement*. This agreement would address all issues, including global land quantum, cash compensation, co-management agreements and self-government. Subsequent negotiations took place at the community level to produce locally sensitive agreements which conformed to the provisions of the *Umbrella Agreement*. Although the regions in which agreements were reached were large, the issues and diversity of experiences, geographies, and interests were not as diverse as in BC. There were also far fewer First Nation groups and much greater unity between those groups than is found in BC. As a result, the approach in BC is to negotiate on a Nation by Nation basis and currently 52 First Nations have entered the process, of which 33 have signed Framework Agreements that outline the components subject to negotiation. Only two, the Nisga'a and Sechelt, have completed the process (Figures 8.2a and 8.2b).

For government, the salient outcome that is sought from treaty negotiations is the certainty that the nature of land ownership in BC is clearly defined for all time, removing any threat of litigation, minimizing land use conflict, and creating an environment conducive to investment and development. For First Nations the desired outcome is that settlement will provide some compensation for historic grievances, a basis for self-determination, a base for economic development, and access to opportunities denied them in the past. The basic components of contemporary treaty negotiations are very similar to those found in traditional treaties, with First Nations surrendering claims to interests in land and resources over wide areas in return for retaining certain ownership of lesser amounts of land, cash, and a range of defined rights. However, modern treaties that will inevitably provide precedents for BC are much more generous than traditional treaties, providing much larger allocations of land and more generous cash settlements. There is also far more on the modern negotiating table than there was in traditional negotiations, including environmental assessment, land use planning and resource management rights, all of which are essentially modern concepts. These components that often take the form of co-management agreements with government and First Nations jointly involved in decision making can be viewed in two ways. From the standpoint of First Nations they provide opportunity to enhance control over resources and influence decision-making throughout Traditional Territory in a manner they never could before. To government, such agreements provide a forum for ameliorating conflict and facilitate balanced stewardship of resources.

While the precise nature of agreements will vary from place to place to reflect local circumstances, for the most part, land-claim agreements have common spatial components manifest in new patterns of land tenure and the emergence of First Nations as major resource management decision makers. These components essentially mean that modern treaties will impose a new jurisdictional geography on the landscape of settlement regions which can have as many as four spatial components.

Traditional Lands: contains all the lands in which the First Nation has interests. It is identified by mapping out areas of historic and contemporary use and occupancy and is the region in which land selection will be made and the region throughout which the First Nation has special interest in controlling land use. From a geopolitical standpoint, the boundary of this region may also serve as the boundary for self-government purposes and for a variety of sub-agreements involving co-management.

Rural Lands: large blocks of land that the First Nation owns in the interest of all beneficiaries. Ideally, the resources of such lands (both renewable and non-renewable) make a major contribution to the economic base of First Nation communities. These lands may be identified as "priority lands" by mapping out land use potential, contemporary use, and areas of sensitivity. Ownership of such lands generally (but not always) includes sub-surface rights.

Site Specific Lands: small areas identified by individual First Nation members or families and held by them as a residence, cabin, or hunting camp. Some Site Specific areas may be identified because they also satisfy certain collective interests. This category includes such things as graveyards, meeting sites, and areas of archaeological importance. There may be a large number of these (in excess of a hundred), depending on the size of the claimant group.

Community Lands: usually lying within a community, they are relatively small (subdivision or block size). They may provide housing for First Nation members, or generate revenue from such ventures as tourism or the operation of commercial premises. These assume special importance as revenue generators in highly urbanized areas.

Other sub-agreements that provide for the extension of First Nations' land/resource interests beyond retained lands through their Traditional Territory can be identified: special land classification, harvesting agreements, joint management agreements, special land classification, environmental assessment agreements, and land use planning agreements.

Special Lands: are specifically identified as areas in which both the First Nation and government have an interest, dedicated to specific uses such as parks or conservation areas, and managed jointly by government and a First Nation. Surrendered lands of special value to a First Nation (for example, for harvesting a particular species or as an important wildlife habitat) may be included in this category.

Harvesting Agreements: are ideally designed so that First Nations have priority use of wildlife resources. They are usually structured to give harvesting priorities and management rights to a First Nation throughout a Traditional Territory, guaranteeing first priority for subsistence harvests. Generally, these agreements do not give First Nations absolute management rights, but provide shared management (co-management) of resources with government. However, they often specify exclusive harvest rights for specific species and are geographically sensitive, addressing not only general management issues, but also management of resources of special interest to individual First Nations. For example, in the treaty settlement offer made to the Snuneymuxw First Nation by the government, the group is guaranteed a pink salmon harvest of 5,600 fish biannually, while the fish allocation provisions in the Sechelt Agreement lay out complex, quantified terms for fisheries management. Forest harvest agreements in proposed settlements in BC generally take the form of joint management agreements in Traditional Territory off settlement land, while on settlement lands First Nations have exclusive forest management rights, but management practices must meet or exceed provincial standards. The Nisga'a agreement outlines with great precision the volume of timber that may be harvested from settlement lands for each of the first 9 years of the final settlement.

Joint Management Agreements: may address the topic of management and control of land-based activities as diverse as heritage resources, forest resources, and trap-line allocation within traditional boundaries in a co-management framework.

Environmental Assessment and Land Use Planning Agreements: follow a co-management model, with First Nation representatives sitting on planning commissions and environmental screening panels. Where land use planning has been incorporated into land claim agreements (such as in the Yukon and NWT), attempts are made to identify planning regions that are co-terminus with Traditional Territories and First Nation representatives share management of the planning process with the region's broader population. Subsequently, long term plans are developed to ensure that land uses are compatible with regional goals. In the *environmental assessment process* (ideally) proposed activities impacting a First Nation's Traditional Territory are screened for potential environmental impacts and compatibility with existing uses. In some northern settlements, First Nations have won the exclusive right to screen activities on retained lands, however there is a "meet or beat" clause, where standards have to meet or exceed those met elsewhere. Similar provisions are found in all of the agreements, framework agreements, and government settlement offers currently in BC.

The various levels of control outlined above vary both in the spatial extent (area) of jurisdiction and the degree of control. Three levels of control are recognized, ownership of land (retained lands), management of resources on the land (harvesting agreements), and management. It becomes evident that the actual degree of control that a First Nation can exert decreases as the nature of control becomes less specialized and the region under consideration increases in size. At the highest level of control is ownership, the ultimate form of control, insofar as the First Nation can choose to accept or reject proposed land uses and has all the rights that accompany ownership. At a somewhat lower level, there is involvement with other parties in co-management of specific resources throughout Traditional Territory (for example, wildlife), and finally there is involvement in land use regulation on a large regional scale with a range of agencies and stakeholder groups, generally in co-management regimes.

There are two significant implications from the schema outlined. First, the range of agreements are so complex that their performance can only be viewed as an outcome of in terms of the synergy between the various components. In other words, whether an agreement is successful or not has to be seen in the light of its various components working together to satisfy the specific needs of individual First Nations. The complexity provides considerable scope for agreements to be brokered that reflect the peculiar geographies of regions in which negotiations are taking place. Thus, the preoccupation with fish harvests for the coastal Sechelt, with forest harvest rights for the virtually landlocked Nisga'a, and with parks management issues (alongside fish and forests) for the Nuu-chah-nulth and Dididat, whose traditional territories encompass Pacific Rim National Park. Secondly, implemented agreements could have a marked impression on land and resource management practices at the regional level, partly because of changes in land tenure and partly because co-management agreements will give First Nations a potentially strong voice in decision making for a wide range of resources.

Land is fundamental to treaty negotiations. Loss of lands and the resources they contain is the central First Nations' grievance. Reassertion of control over a land base holds the promise of providing a diverse resource base for economic development and a basis for cultural and spiritual regeneration. It is thus not surprising that questions surrounding the quantity, quality, and location of retained lands are critical to the land claim processes. They assume special importance in BC because it has far higher population densities, more mature infrastructure development, and a much higher incidence of alienated land than other regions in which modern treaty negotiations have taken place. While other comprehensive claim negotiations generally provide strong precedents for BC, especially in the area of co-management of resources, extrapolation of land quantum from these settlements to BC could have some interesting ramifications and usefully serves to demonstrate the importance of viewing the components of settlements synergistically. For example, in Quebec if the per capita allocation in the James Bay settlement (the least generous of the comprehensive settlements) were used as a basis for calculating total land quantum, the province's Native population would retain some 70,000 km^2. If the average quantum from the Yukon settlement were used as a precedent, this figure would rise to some 522,000 km^2—over 50% of the province's surface area.

The question of how much land would be retained as an outcome of treaty negotiations is further compounded by the question of how such lands would be distributed throughout BC. One simple approach would be to allocate land across First Nations according to population size; another would be to allocate it proportionally to the size of the territory each First Nation had traditionally occupied. The rationale for the first approach is that population size is a good reflection of current (and presumably future) needs; for the second it is that the larger a First Nation's territory, the larger its legitimate claim. If, for example, the Quebec projection cited above were used as a basis for determining total quantum in BC, the Sechelt First Nation would receive 1,124 km^2

of land using traditional territory as a basis for allocation and 398 km² if population size were used. The Nisga'a would have received 9,097 km² and 2,147 km² respectively.

Although such scenario building has a certain fascination, a "one size fits all" systemic approach to land allocation is very much at odds with the contemporary geography of BC and ignores the reality that treaty outcomes are highly complex with provisions that should be viewed holistically. While vast areas of northern and central BC are largely rural and characterized by low population densities, the south (Vancouver, the lower Fraser Valley, and southern Vancouver Island) contains 75% of the population. Settlement of land claims through the surrender of lands on which there are long-established third party interests would alienate non-Native populations and make such an approach politically unacceptable. As a result, it is the federal government's policy that lands owned by third parties are generally not available for selection in treaty negotiations, meaning that there is relatively little potential treaty land in southern BC.[3] However, the highly urban character of southern BC means that lands available for allocation generally have high monetary value and have considerable potential for revenue generation compared to lands elsewhere in the province. It is highly simplistic to assume that variations in economic rents created by the province's population distribution provides an easy solution to the land allocation problem, but it does provide some basis for offsetting land quantum deficiencies with land quality in urban areas, and offsetting revenue generating deficiencies with land quantity in rural areas.[4]

Comparison of some of the elements of the Nisga'a Framework Agreement in rural northern BC with the Sechelt agreement in the urban south shows how local circumstance and geography play into negotiation outcomes. The Nisga'a, with a population of 5,400, are located in one of the more isolated parts of the province, characterized by low population densities, with a First Nation's economy based on a range of terrestrial resources and a non-traditional economy largely based on forest resources. The Sechelt, numbering some 985, are located within commuting distance of Vancouver, in an area where there are strong urban and recreational residential pressures; their traditional economy was (and is) essentially marine-based, while the local economy can perhaps be best described as strongly tertiary, providing services catering to an urban-oriented population. Nisga'a Traditional Territory encompasses approximately 24,000 km² compared with about 4,000 km² for Sechelt. While the Sechelt region is replete with alienations and third party interests, thus making allocation of large blocks of land difficult, there is a relative dearth of such in northern BC. The Sechelt will retain some 19 km² (Figure 8.2a) of land pursuant to settlement compared with the Nisga'a allocation of 1,992 km² (Figure 8.2b). However, 35% of the Sechelt lands are defined as *urban* in character and will potentially command substantial economic rents. Differences in financial compensation awarded to the two claimant groups also serve to offset variations in land quantum to a limited degree.[5] While the Sechelt cash settlement is $42 million compared to the Nisga'a award of $190 million, on a per capita basis the

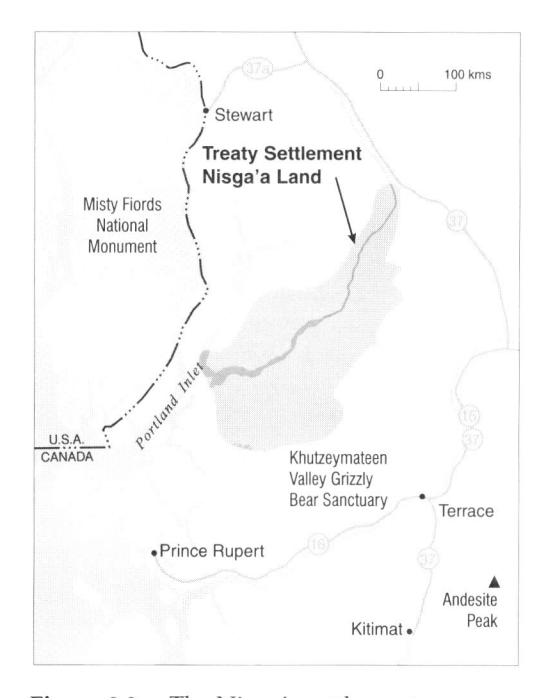

Figure 8.2a The Nisga'a settlement

Figure 8.2b The Sechelt's traditional territory

former far outstrips the latter ($42,000 vs $34,000), and if viewed globally when adjusted for population provides $7.84 million more than the Nisga'a agreement. Other salient differences between the agreements include provisions that reflect differences in geographical context and histories. The Sechelt agreement, for example, has a substantive section addressing ocean fishing, while the Nisga'a has one dealing with forest resources. Self-government provisions differ between the groups, with the more urbanized Sechelt adopting an essentially municipal model and the Nisga'a, with substantive traditional lands and widely flung population, adopting what could be described as a strong form of regional government.

While the preceding examples show that the contemporary geography of BC has a significant impact on inter-regional variations in land quantum, at the intra-regional level land quality is a major determinant of a treaty's ability to fulfil the needs of individual First Nations. This is because a retained land base is required to satisfy a multiplicity of needs, from traditional pursuits to provision of an adequate economic base for future development. A central First Nations' concern is that land quality is distributed so they retain a fair resource base,[6] while governments have concerns that land selection strategies could have major negative impacts on the interests of non-Native residents. As a result, rules (or conventions) may be developed for land selection. Such rules had their basis in comprehensive claim negotiations in northern Canada and tried to ensure that retained lands were not concentrated in a very few large blocks, leading to resource monopolization by First Nations, or that First Nations did not control both sides of river valleys (thus potentially tying up riparian rights and controlling waterways), and that lands containing existing third party interests would not be subject to negotiation.[7] The Coolican Commission, established to review comprehensive claims policy in the mid 1980s, conceded that these rules effectively restricted legitimate First Nations' interests (Government of Canada, 1985). This point was practically underlined by events surrounding the collapse of comprehensive negotiations in the Yukon in 1985, when investigation revealed that the resource values of much of the retained land were of little utility, either from the standpoint of traditional pursuits or revenue generation. In later negotiations in the Yukon, First Nations obtained the right to retain lands that fairly represented the character of their traditional territory. This was guaranteed by *an agreement* (ultimately entrenched in the final agreement) stating that retained lands should fairly represent the geography and resource base of the region in which land selections take place. Thus, if a traditional territory contains a mix of agricultural potential, good quality forests, and minerals, retained lands would contain an appropriate (but not disproportionate) mix of these resources.

Land Claims and Economic Development

Historic grievances, cultural links to place, and legal arguments variously have been long-standing foundations of land claims processes and although they may provide excellent social reasons for resolving the treaty question, they also have very persuasive economic implications. Major legal decisions regarding First Nations' rights in BC have strong implications for the existing economic order. The *Sparrow* case was perceived to be a threat to the established commercial fishing industry and *Calder*, and then (resoundingly) *Delgamuukw*, brought into question the ownership of resource lands. In practical terms, expectations about the economic benefits of settlements are perhaps the most important consideration driving the treaty process. Government, for example, casts the process in a benefit-cost framework, arguing that the certainty that settlement brings will encourage investment, create a more stable business climate, and thus contribute to both regional and provincial economic development (see, for example, ARA Consulting, 1995). Three major studies commissioned by government depicting the benefits and costs of settlements demonstrate net benefits to the province as a whole, although the most recent of these (Thornton, 1999), which suggests benefits to the province of about $3.5 billion, also strikes a note of caution regarding extrapolation from limited data and assumptions regarding First Nations' human resources. First Nations view settlement as a basis for economic self-determination, providing compensation for historic damage done to their traditional economies and for the removal of resources from their lands without permission or recompense. It provides monies and a resource base to participate in the modern economy together with the opportunity to eradicate the socioeconomic imbalance between themselves and much of the rest of the province's population.

The resource lands of rural BC are a major component of the provincial economy; at the regional level they are the dominant economic base in many areas. Uncertainty regarding land ownership, sustained litigation with unpredictable outcomes, and civil disobedience to protest activities like development of logging roads on First Nations' lands are costly to established industries and seen as a deterrent to new investment. Certainty about land and resource ownership is the outcome governments seek from treaty negotiations, both settling outstanding grievances for all time and making a stable environment for growth and development beneficial to the population as a whole. Other economic benefits seen to flow to the province (and to some extent to the federal government) pursuant to treaty settlements come in the form of First Nation expenditures and programme cost savings. It is expected that the cash compensation aspect of settlements may have local multiplier effects. Expenditures currently directed at First Nations would decrease as improved economic conditions in First Nations' communities result in lower economic dependency ratios and improved health, and as First Nations assume responsibility for programmes currently administered by government.

From the standpoint of First Nations, treaty settlements provide some redress for past exploitation of their lands and resources and opportunities for development and economic self-determination. The cash compensation components of settlements should provide capital for investment in First Nations' ventures, with retained lands providing resources and locational opportunities (for tourism facilities for example) that would be the foundation for First Nations' enterprises. In some areas First Nations' economies may be enhanced through resource revenue sharing agreements in which income generated from resource development within a group's traditional territory is shared with the Nation. A number of geographic factors will have significant bearing on the ability of treaty settlements to fulfil these expectations. Retained lands must have economic potential, either in the form of resources (such as minerals, good soils for agriculture, and timber) or in the form of access to commercial opportunities (tourist potential, high traffic corridors), and a guarantee of land quality in framework agreements is important.

The ability of the cash compensation component of settlements to provide a basis for sustained economic development depends to some extent on the geography of investment, and here First Nations may be faced with some difficult decisions. The objective is to develop a basis for long term revenue at the community level, putting money into the hands of the individual beneficiaries who together constitute First Nation populations and generally have high expectations regarding the benefits that would flow from settlement. An obvious approach would be to invest in projects at the community level, creating local employment and a secondary multiplier effect, thus alleviating some of the poverty associated with Native reserves. While for some First Nations there are excellent local investment opportunities associated with their location, many are remote areas where a high level of risk may be attached to investments, reflecting distance to markets, volatility of natural resource markets, or (as in the case of tourism) seasonality and weather. Investment in ventures at the local level may also be bedevilled by lack of education and training, especially skilled labour, and an alternate strategy may be to invest in capacity building. Risk associated with local investment could mean that economic benefits are not passed to future generations, while capacity building may reap long-term rewards, but would defer immediate economic returns. An alternative strategy would be to invest in stable long term securities, such as bonds or blue-chip stocks, that would generate guaranteed annual returns and minimize risk. This would be manifest in a flow of capital from rural BC to urban heartlands, with local economic benefits and immediate rewards traded for guaranteed returns and future benefits. While this approach guarantees revenue over the long term, it detracts from addressing immediate problems and the potential to create at least short-term economic opportunities in the First Nation's territory.

Although the economic impacts of settlements have been characterized as positive by government, many in rural BC are perhaps not as optimistic. Currently, much of BC's commercial natural resource base is controlled by non-First Nation interests, and while this makes a substantial contribution to the overall economy of BC, its role is even more important at the regional level where forestry, fisheries, and tourism are dominant economic bases of a myriad of small communities. A perception from within these communities is that the changes in land tenure and resource regulation practices that would accompany treaty implementation would not help the community economies which are already weakened by declining fish stocks and environmental concerns regarding forest harvest practices. This concern has contradictory underpinnings. One argument is that the balance of economic power would swing toward First Nations' interests as they developed resources on retained lands; another is that, for a variety of reasons ranging from lack of entrepreneurial skills to a conservationist ethic, resources would remain undeveloped. This latter concern has been somewhat reinforced by the tendency to conflate First Nations' land and resource interests and environmentalism. In some cases this has occurred due to environmental pressure groups appropriating what they perceive to be indigenous environmental and conservationist values giving rise to concerns that increased First Nations' control over resources will result in further economic decline. Indications are, however, that First Nations are vitally interested in promoting development. Nuu-chah-nulth has made it clear that it wants participation in limited logging in Clayoquot; the Nisga'a Agreement contains a detailed forest harvest plan.

Conclusions

In the preceding narrative it is argued that, while there is a systematic, rigorous approach to the negotiation of treaty settlements in BC, the complex provisions of treaties combined with the province's varied geographies offers considerable scope for outcomes that will vary significantly from nation to nation. While settlements will require accommodation of a wide range of interests, they also hold the promise of a better quality of life for beneficiaries. Realization of such promise depends on the extent to which individual First Nations take a proactive stance toward implementation of final agreements and maximize their benefits. Whether movement through negotiation to implementation will occur in the foreseeable future is debatable. Acceptance of the legitimacy of native claims in BC was the culmination of a long struggle. Progress toward final settlements over the past few years has been halting and promises to be a very lengthy process, subject to the vagaries of public opinion and dependent on the goodwill of governments.

REFERENCES

ARA Consulting Group (1995). *Social and economic impacts of aboriginal land claims settlements: A case study analysis*. Ministry of Aboriginal Affairs, Government of BC.

Cassidy, F., and Dale, N. (1988). *After native claims?* Lantzville, BC: Oolichan Books.

Culhane, D. (1998). *The pleasure of the Crown*. Burnaby, BC: Talonbooks.

Duerden, F. (1996). Land allocation in comprehensive land claim agreements. *Applied Geography*, 16(4), 279-288.

Duerden, F., and Keller, P. (1992). GIS and Native claims. *Operational Geographer*, 10(4).

Fisher, R. (1977). *Contact and conflict: Indian European relations in British Columbia 1774-1890*. Vancouver: UBC Press, 1992.

Government of BC (1999). *Nisga'a Treaty*. Victoria: Ministry of Aboriginal Affairs.

Government of BC (1999). *Sechelt agreement in principle*. Victoria: Ministry of Aboriginal Affairs.

Government of Canada (1985). *Living treaties, lasting agreements*. Ottawa: Department of Indian Affairs and Northern Development.

Notzke, L. (1994). *Aboriginal peoples and natural resources in Canada*. North York, ON: Captus Press.

Ray, A.J. (1993). The historical geographer and the Gitksan-Wet'usuwet'en comprehensive claim: The role of the expert witness. In G. Cant, J. Overton, and E. Pawson (Eds.), *Indigenous land rights in Commonwealth countries* (pp. 81-88). Proceedings of a Commonwealth Geographical Bureau Workshop, Christchurch, February 1992. Canberra: Commonwealth Geographical Bureau, Ngai Tahu Maori Board and Department of Geography, University of Canterbury.

Tennant, P. (1990). *Aboriginal peoples and politics. The Indian land question in British Columbia 1949-1989*. Vancouver: UBC Press.

Thornton, G. (1999). *Financial and economic analysis of treaty settlements in British Columbia*. Victoria: Ministry of Aboriginal Affairs, Government of BC.

Wolfe, J. (1995). First Nations' sovereignty and land claims. In B. Mitchell (Ed.), *Resource and environmental management in Canada* (pp. 55-80). Toronto: Oxford University Press.

Young, E. (1995). *Third World in the first*. London: Routledge.

ENDNOTES

[1] Uncertainty regarding in whose favour the courts might rule in interpreting the precise Aboriginal Title was a spur to negotiate rather than litigate. Did Aboriginal Title merely mean that First Nations had the right to harvest traditional resources using traditional methods? Or did it mean that they had absolute rights to all resources in non-treaty areas?

[2] There is some confusion in the popular mind regarding the term "land claim." For most Canadians it is interpreted as meaning that First Nations are claiming land from the government. The First Nation perspective, however, is that they never surrendered land to government in the first instance, and the process could be characterized as one in which government is claiming land. These semantic differences are important, the notion of First Nations as claimants tending to reinforce the more negative stereotypes of First Peoples.

[3] Despite this well established policy, some groups opposed to the treaty process continue to use the threat of land confiscation to create unease among the general population regarding the outcome of negotiations. There may be circumstances in which government will buy out a third party interest and transfer it to a claimant group.

[4] These differences are illustrated in the Carrier-Sekani Tribal Council's (west of Prince George) who want a settlement that includes a forestry project, job training, and technical expertise development to manage a forest area effectively (i.e., public land). In contrast, the Snuneymuxw First Nation (Nanaimo region) are interested in a settlement that includes part of Gabriola Island (which is in private ownership). Their claim is that there is ample proof that it was formerly tribal land and a reasonable settlement would be 1,200 ha. Gabriola Island residents do not share this view (February 2001).

[5] As this volume was going to press the Sechelt announced that they were withdrawing from negotiations because the land quantum agreed to in their Agreement in Principle was inadequate.

[6] In "modern" treaty processes there are examples, from both Alaska and the Yukon, of land allocations to First Nations in which retained lands were of low quality compared to the general quality of land available in regions under negotiation. In the case of the Yukon, mal-distribution of land quality was a factor that contributed to the collapse of negotiations in 1985; the problem was addressed when negotiations resumed in 1986.

[7] Although there are some exceptions to this rule they are very few, and generally involve buying out third party interests.

Plate 8 Dragon boat racing in Victoria's Inner Harbour ▶

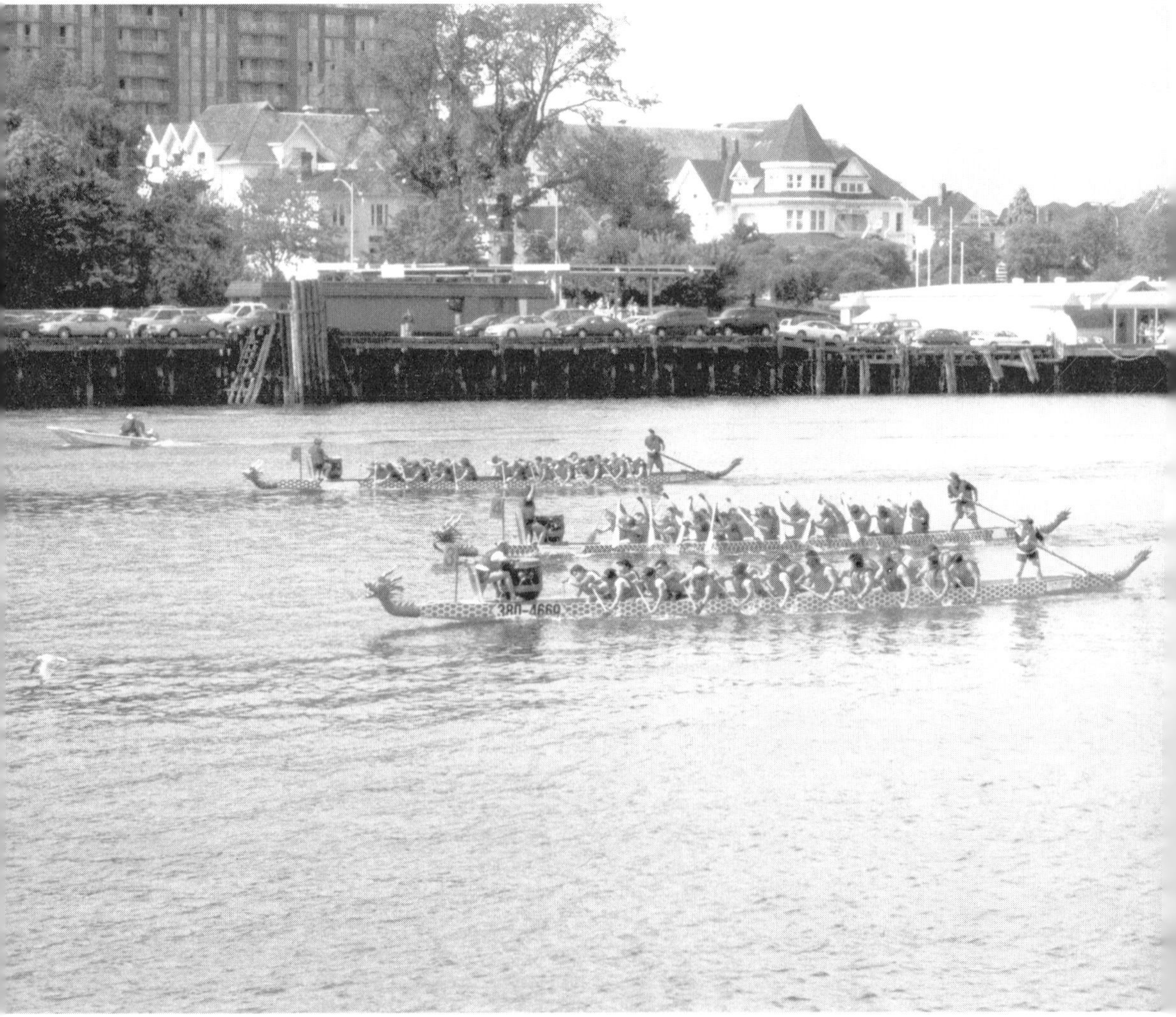
380-4660

Chinese: The Changing Geography of the Largest Visible Minority

David Chuenyan Lai
Department of Geography, University of Victoria

The Chinese were among the earliest immigrants to enter BC during the historical era. They remained the largest visible immigrant minority in the province for more than a century. When the province was still a frontier colony of the British Empire, the Chinese were employed to build trails and wagon roads, clear dense bush and forests for urban development, reclaim deltas and flooded plains for arable farming, and build the section of the Canadian Pacific Railway (CPR) in the colony. They provided the much-needed labour in coal-mining, fish-canning, lumbering, and many other industries. In spite of their contributions, they were not accepted by the host society for nearly a century. This chapter has two themes: the evolution of the history and geography of Chinese settlement in BC from 1788 to 1999, and an examination of how the Chinese immigrants suffered from discrimination in employment, education, citizenship rights, and occasionally with violence. The chapter will also describe their struggle to join the mainstream of the western community, and eventually gain acceptance and recognition.

EARLY IMMIGRANTS AND DISCRIMINATION, 1788-1884

The Chinese landed on Vancouver Island as early as 1788, that is, 70 years before the Colony of BC was established and 83 years before it became a province of Canada. In his memoirs of voyages from China to the northwest coast of North America, Captain John Meares, a British fur trader, mentioned that he recruited 50 Chinese smiths and carpenters from Macao and Guangzhou (Canton) in South China in the spring of 1788 and took them to Nootka Sound on Vancouver Island (Meares, 1790). Throughout the summer the Chinese craftsmen helped him build a small fortress and a 40-ton schooner, the *North West America*, the first sailing vessel built in BC. Their craftsmanship, obedience, and diligence impressed Meares so much that the next year he brought in 70 more Chinese to Nootka Sound. He wrote in his memoirs that "if hereafter trading posts should be established on the American coast, a colony of these men should be a very important acquisition." His remarks were prophetic. The supply of cheap Chinese labour was nearly indispensable in assisting European settlement.

After the Anglo-Spanish fighting in Nootka Sound in 1789, Spaniards took possession of the area and imprisoned the Chinese workers. What happened to them is still a mystery (Meares, 1790). For nearly 70 years, there was no written evidence of further Chinese arrivals until the summer of 1858 when Chinese travelled north from the US after hearing about gold strikes in the lower Fraser River.

Gold Rushes

The first group of Chinese immigrants from San Francisco arrived at Victoria by boat (*Victoria Gazette*, 1858). Very soon, more Chinese labourers came by ship directly from Hong Kong; this marked the first wave of Chinese immigration to the colony of Vancouver Island (created in 1849) and the colony of BC (created in 1858).

During the pioneer days the governments of both colonies found it impossible to obtain labourers, especially white labourers, to do public work. Most people coming to BC at the time were seeking fast fortunes, and would not work for low wages. Therefore, the colonial government relied on Chinese labour contractors to import Chinese labourers for building trails and wagon roads, draining swamps, digging ditches, and other heavy manual labour. As a consequence, hundreds of Chinese labourers were widely scattered along the banks of the Fraser River and its tributaries and in other gold mining areas on the mainland.

Nearly all Chinese immigrants were single young men who were poor and unemployed in their villages in China. They came to *Gim Shan* (the "Gold Mountain," referring to BC) to seek wealth through hard work or good fortune. If they succeeded in making a fortune— in fact, they rarely did—they would return to China immediately. They did not feel at home in BC because the Caucasians were completely different from them in speech, dress, food, and customs. As a result, they segregated themselves from the host society, dominated by British and Americans, and confined themselves in Chinatowns. Many considered Westerners to be barbaric aggressors of Chinese territory (e.g., the Opium Wars, 1839-1842). They did not behave in the Confucian way. The host society, on the other hand, thought of the wretched Chinese labourers as sojourners, and generally despised and ostracized them for not conforming to western society. The colonial government estimated that in 1862 the total population of the colonies of Vancouver Island and British Columbia, excluding the native Indians (now called First Nations), stood at about 11,000, of which 7,700 were whites, 2,300 were "coloured" (now called Blacks), and 1,000 were Chinese (United Kingdom, 1862).

The Fraser gold rushes had virtually ended by the mid-1860s and the colonies of Vancouver Island and British Columbia were in financial straits. To reduce expenditures, in 1866 the two were merged into the United Colony of British Columbia, with a combined population, excluding native Indians, estimated at 8,410, of which 6,408 were white, 1,759 Chinese, and 243 "coloured" (United Kingdom, 1868). About 40% of the Chinese were focused in the Cariboo District, and 26% in the lower Fraser River between Hope and Lytton. Many of them were looking for work in logging camps, ranches and farms, fish canneries, and coal mines. Many also worked as domestic servants or cooks for white families, or operated laundries and tailoring stores serving the general public. Those depending on cheap labour felt Chinese labourers were indispensable and beneficial to the economy of BC. However, this view was not shared by many white labourers. They believed their livelihood was being threatened and put pressure on the colony government not to employ Chinese. The simmering resentment against Chinese labourers began to boil in the early 1870s when the economy of the colony continued to deteriorate. From the late 1870s onward no politician in the province would receive support from white workers if he did not speak out against Chinese labour.

Labour Unrest

Anti-Chinese groups soon formed to protest Chinese immigration. A Victoria newspaper, *The Colonist* (*TC*), reported (May 16, 1873) that an Anti-Chinese Society in Victoria demanded revision of the *Sino-British Treaty of 1860*, which allowed the immigration of Chinese to Canada.[1] In 1878, the Workingmen's Protective Association (WPA) was formed with goals of "the mutual protection of the working classes of British Columbia against the influx of Chinese, and the use of legitimate means for the suppression of their immigration" (WPA, 1878). Politicians such as John Robson, Arthur Bunster, and Noah Shakespeare, playing upon white workers' fear of Chinese competition for jobs, bamboozled their constituents and gained publicity by denigrating Chinese labourers. Portraying themselves as the champions of white labour protectors, these demagogues scooped the votes of local white workers and eventually achieved their political aspirations.

A classic example is Noah Shakespeare, a coal miner from Nanaimo.[2] In the late 1860s he moved to Victoria, where he printed and delivered *The Standard* (*TS*), a local newspaper, and later ran a photography gallery for a few years before taking an active part in politics (MacDonald, 1917). After being elected a city councillor in 1874, he succeeded in convincing council to insert a clause in all city contracts which stipulated that white labour only should be employed (*The Colonist*, 1874). A year later, he persuaded council to pass a bylaw to prevent employment of Chinese labour on any city works (*The Standard*, 1875a). A reader wrote a letter to *The Standard* stating that the bylaw was un-Christian and that Shakespeare had introduced it merely for political gain, as he aspired to a seat in the legislature (*The Standard*, 1875b). The editor of the newspaper also claimed that Shakespeare's sympathy for white labour was insincere (*The Standard*, 1875c). However, he was soon viewed by many local white workers as a white labour protector, and re-elected to city council again and again, retaining this position for 4 years before being elected Mayor in 1882 (Parker, 1912). In 1876, he spearheaded a petition to the Dominion Parliament requesting that Ottawa prevent the entry of Chinese into Canada, "removing what threatened, at no distant date, to render British Columbia the dumping ground for the worst class of Asiatics" (Kerr, 1890, p. 284). In 1879, the Workingmen's Protective Association was reorganized and renamed the "Anti-Chinese Association," with Shakespeare as president. He strongly opposed employment of Chinese in the construction of the Canadian Pacific Railway and decided to run as a Member of Parliament in July 1882. In all of his public speeches he slandered the Chinese and called them "an unmitigated evil (who) came here to settle...paid light taxes...no interest in the country...no benefit to any civilized community" (*The Colonist*, 1882). He won the election and displaced Arthur Bunster as the MP for Victoria (1882-1887) (BC Directory, 1892). Throughout his lifetime in Victoria he orchestrated an anti-Chinese movement.

However, Shakespeare was not the only agitator. From 1871 when BC joined confederation, the Chinese question became a political issue. Editorials, feature articles, and letters to the editor were published in *The Colonist* and *The Standard*, newspapers that played a significant role in the early life of the city of Victoria. Beyond providing international, national, and local news, the newspapers recorded details of the debates of the provincial legislature and city councils as well as discussions at public meetings. They functioned as provincial and municipal forums, critics, and defenders. As a result, comments in the popular newspapers had a profound effect on the formation of public opinion about the Chinese. John Robson, editor of *The Colonist*, opposed the coming of Chinese labourers and advocated measures to discriminate against them. Amor De Cosmos, editor of *The Standard*, had no strong objection to Chinese immigration and usually maintained a favourable attitude towards them. The two newspapers held different opinions when the legislative assembly passed the *Qualification and Registration of Voters Amendment Act* which disfranchised both the Chinese and the native Indians (BC, 1872). The Attorney General referred the Act to the Dominion Government for approval as he felt it might be unconstitutional to exclude those Chinese who might be British subjects, for example, Hong Kong-born Chinese (*The Standard*, 1874a). *The Standard* had always supported the Chinese right to vote but it changed its stand during the provincial by-election in Lillooet District in November 1874. William Saul, who was supported by *The Standard*, was defeated by William Brown by three votes (*The Standard*, 1874b). Believing that eight Chinese voters had cast their ballots in favour of Brown, *The Standard* demanded that their votes be disqualified (*The Standard*, 1874c). *The Colonist*, which had previously been advocating the disfranchisement of the Chinese, wanted the Chinese votes to stand because they had been cast for Brown.

Ironically, a year later the attitudes of the two newspapers toward the Chinese right to vote changed. Councillor J.D. Drummond, supported by *The Standard*, and Councillor C. Morton, supported by *The Colonist*, were both running for mayor during Victoria's civic election in January 1875. After Drummond won the election, *The Standard* hailed the victory, declaring that the Chinese population had availed themselves of the privilege of the liberal franchise (*The Standard*, 1875d). *The Colo-

nist, on the other hand, did not recognize the Chinese right to vote because it estimated that of 92 Chinese votes, "Lummond" got 77 because he promised them "plentee workee," and shoved them into the ballot-stalls (*The Colonist*, 1875). The editor of *The Colonist* demanded the exclusion of Chinamen from the franchise. The Chinese voters were, therefore, pawns in the political game of the two rival newspapers.

On April 22, 1875, the provincial government obtained royal assent for the *Act to Make Better Provision for the Qualification and Registration of Voters*, whereby no Chinaman or Indian would be eligible to vote in any legislative assembly election (BC, 1876). The following year an *Act to Amend the Municipal Act of 1872* was passed, by which "no Chinese or Indians shall be entitled to vote at any Municipal Election for the election of a Mayor or Councillor" (BC, 1877).

Settlements in 1881

The national census included BC for the first time in 1881. It listed 4,350 Chinese in BC, and 23 Chinese in other provinces. In other words, virtually all the Chinese in Canada were found in BC. This explains why the white public in the province worried far more about the influx of Chinese immigrants and was more antagonistic toward the Chinese than were those elsewhere in Canada. The census also reveals that Chinese were the third largest ethnic group in the province, following First Nations and the British and other Europeans (Table 9.1). If the First Nations were excluded, then the British accounted for nearly 62% of 23,798 immigrants in BC, followed by the Chinese (18%), French (3.8%), and German (3.6%).

Nearly 78% of the Chinese in the province lived on the mainland and most were concentrated in gold-mining towns like Keithley and

Table 9.1   Ethnic composition of population in BC, 1881

Ethnic group	*Number of persons*	*Percent of provincial total*
Native Indian	25,661	51.88
British	14,660	29.64
English	7,297	
Scottish	3,892	
Irish	3,172	
Welsh	299	
Other Europeans	2,832	5.73
French	916	
German	858	
Scandinavian	236	
Spanish and Portuguese	144	
Italian	143	
Dutch	94	
Other Groups	441	
Chinese	4,350	8.80
African	274	0.55
Unspecified	1,682	3.40
Total	*49,459*	*100.00*

Source: Census of Canada, 1881.

Quesnellemouth in the Cariboo District, and Yale, Hope, and Lytton in the lower Fraser River area. Victoria's Chinatown was the largest, with a Chinese population of almost 600, and was the distribution centre for Chinese merchandise to other Chinatowns in the province. New Westminster's Chinatown was the second largest and most of its 200 Chinese residents were engaged in the fish-canning industry. The third Chinatown was in Nanaimo where the Chinese residents were mostly coal-miners (Figure 9.1).

"Necessary Evil"

An influx of Chinese workers into BC in the early 1880s occurred in response to the demand for labourers to build the BC section of the Canadian Pacific Railway. This served to exacerbate the labour tensions of the previous decades. In Ottawa, Amor De Cosmos, an MP for Victoria and previous champion of Chinese labour, changed his position at this time (May 12, 1882) and asked the Canadian government not to employ Chinese labour because he feared Chinese labourers would soon outnumber white people in BC (Canada, 1882a). This assertion might reflect the stereotypical view of the provincial Sinophobes. According to the 1881 Census, white people accounted for 35% of the provincial population whereas Chinese represented only 9%. Andrew Onderdonk, the railway contractor, initially promised to use white labour only, but later found it impossible to obtain enough workers. When he advertised labouring positions in Victoria at $1.50 per day for labourers, and $125 per month for overseers, only 39 out of 142 applicants were deemed satisfactory (Lai, 1998). He would need at least 10,000 strong men to build the railway, so he had to look elsewhere for much of his labour force. He turned to Chinese labourers whom he knew were cheaper and more hard-working; he paid them only $1 per day. In response to De Cosmos' complaint, Prime Minister Macdonald said:

If you wish to have the railway finished within any reasonable time, there must be no such step against Chinese labour. At present it is simply a question of alternatives—either you must have this labour, or you cannot have the railway (Canada, 1882b).

Many British Columbians considered Chinese labourers an evil, but not having a railway would be worse. Thus, they had no choice but to accept the lesser of two "evils" and tolerate the employment of Chinese temporarily.

By 1882, the total labour force on the railway had reached about 9,000: 6,500 Chinese and 2,500 white. Almost the entire railway line from Port Moody to Craigellachie was graded by Chinese labourers with white foremen. There is no report of the number of deaths of white and Chinese workers because, in those days, reporting work accidents was not required by law, and because the number of deaths *directly* related to railway construction accidents was not high. Most of the Chinese labourers died from winter cold, illness, malnutrition, and lack of medical attention (Lai, 1998). Andrew Onderdonk estimated that between 500 and 600 Chinese workers died during the construction of the line—three Chinese for every kilometre of track. Upon completion of the CPR in 1885 and the Esquimalt and Nanaimo Railway a year later, many Chinese workers were thrown out of work. With starvation staring them in the face, they entered almost every type of employment and took any job at reduced wages. They were viewed by white workers as a menace to their livelihood and a detriment to their well-being.

On February 18, 1884 the BC Legislature passed three acts: prohibiting Chinese immigrants from landing in the province; preventing Chinese from acquiring Crown lands; and requiring every Chinese over 14 years of age to pay a $10 annual fee for a residence licence (BC, 1884). These acts were soon disallowed by a Dominion Order-in-Council; however, they prompted the Dominion government to set up a Royal Commission in July 1884 to investigate the issue of Chinese immigration in the province.

The Commission Report revealed that BC had a Chinese population of 10,492, of which

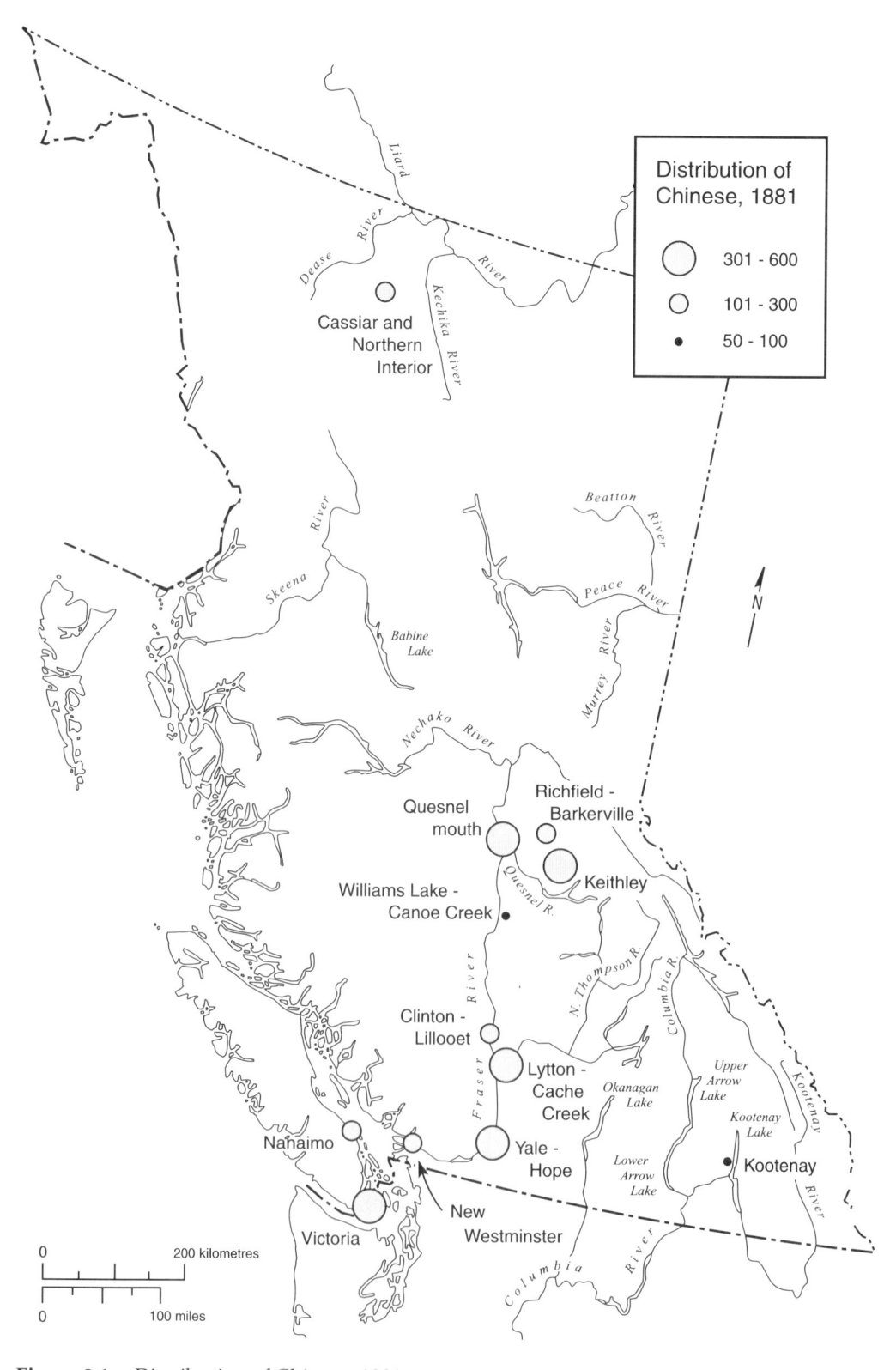

Figure 9.1 Distribution of Chinese, 1881

there were nearly 28% railway workers, 16% gold miners, 7% coal miners, and 35% other labourers (Canada, 1885a). Less than 2% were merchants, restaurant keepers, doctors, and teachers. Only 1.5% were females, 88 of which were married women and girls, and 70 were prostitutes. The remaining 10% included boys under 17 and new immigrants whose age and sex were not recorded in the report. This population was widely dispersed in southern BC, with about 35% (3,510) living in makeshift tents along the route of the railway line. The largest established Chinese settlement was in Victoria, with a Chinese population of 1,767, followed by New Westminster (1,680), Wellington (754), and Quesnellemouth (506). Small communities of Chinese were scattered in the Cariboo and Lillooet districts. The City of Vancouver had not yet been incorporated and its predecessor, the small village of Granville, had only one Chinese grocery store and two laundrymen.

THE PERIODS OF RESTRICTION AND EXCLUSION, 1885-1946

Based on the recommendations of the 1884 Royal Commission Report, the Dominion government passed the *Chinese Immigrant Act* in July 1885 to end its traditional free and non-restrictive policy toward Chinese immigration. In an effort to discourage immigration, this new legislation, enacted on January 1, 1886, required every person of Chinese origin entering Canada to pay a head tax of $50 (Canada, 1885b). The poor and unemployed of China earned about $2 a month at this time. In Canada they could earn 10 times that, which was a great incentive for coming here. They believed they had no choice but to borrow money to pay the heavy head tax and the passage to Canada, with the hope that by labouring hard they might eventually earn enough to pay off their debts and obtain a better life for themselves and for their children. Once here, they discovered that their larger income did not stretch very far. At that time they could earn less than $19 a month.

After deducting rent, food, clothing, and other expenses, a labourer could barely save about $3 a month. Nevertheless, they persisted. At least they were working and there was the promise of the future. Consequently, the $50 head tax did not deter Chinese immigration and neither did subsequent tax increases—to $100 in 1901 and $500 in 1903 (Canada, 1900, 1903). The number of Chinese immigrants increased from 77 in 1905 to a record high of 7,445 in 1913 (Canada, 1900-1917). Most of these immigrants settled in Vancouver and Victoria.

Violence in Vancouver

The history of Vancouver's Chinatown began with violence and fear. Vancouver, incorporated on the former site of Granville Village on April 2, 1886, was a frontier town on the densely wooded side of Burrard Inlet. John McDougall, a contractor, brought a group of Chinese labourers from Victoria to clear the forested Brighouse Estate on the southern shore of Coal Harbour. Many unemployed white workers in the city were infuriated when they learned that the contractor preferred to hire Chinese labourers because they were willing to work for about half the wage (Roy, 1989). On January 8, 1887, R.D. Pitt, a member of the Knights of Labour, led a mob to rush the estate, pull down the Chinese labourers' tents and order them to return to Victoria (*The Colonist*, 1887a). City Council and the few police officers there did not intervene. Later in the month, four anti-Chinese public meetings were held at City Hall where it was decided that the Chinese must not be allowed to establish themselves in Vancouver (Roy, 1976). Notices posted by "The Vigilance Committee" warned that "all Chinamen must leave the city limits on or before the 16th January instant.... And we warn the authorities not to interfere with us if they value their lives" (*British Columbian*, 1887; *The Colonist*, 1887b). The Chinese living in the burgeoning Chinatown located on Dupont Street on the north shore of False Creek were very worried about the warning, but did not know what to do.

An Anti-Chinese League that was formed in Vancouver on February 2, 1887 urged local businesses not to deal with Chinese labour. Despite the widespread anti-Chinese feeling in Vancouver, the contractor for the Brighouse estate again brought in Chinese labourers from Victoria to clear the land. On the afternoon of February 24, members of the Anti-Chinese League marched to the estate and once again the camps were stormed. They assaulted the Chinese labourers and threw their bedding and clothing into a fire (*British Columbian*, 1887). There was an unconfirmed report that four Chinese were tied together by their pigtails and thrown into the icy waters of Coal Harbour (Plate 9.1). Some agitators in the mob raided Chinatown, looting houses and setting fire to some buildings (Roy, 1976). Many Chinese escaped to the bush; a few jumped into False Creek where they almost died of exposure. The few police officers did not or could not stop the violence. After the mob had left, the Chinese immediately barred the doors and windows of their houses, quickly packed their belongings onto wagons, and left hastily for New Westminster (*The Colonist*, 1887c). They did not feel safe in Vancouver as the city's police could not protect them.

When Victoria received news of the violence the provincial government worried that the outside world might consider Vancouver an unruly frontier town and that the violence would discourage potential investors and white immigrants from coming to Vancouver. Accordingly, the provincial government suspended the police powers of Vancouver and dispatched 35 special provincial constables from Victoria to restore order (*The Colonist*, 1887d). With this police presence, the Chinese returned to Vancouver where they re-established their Chinatown on Dupont Street (renamed Pender Street East in 1904) and around its intersections with Shanghai Alley, Canton Alley, and Carrell Street. By mid-March about 80 Chinese were

Plate 9.1 "An unconfirmed report that four Chinese were...thrown into the icy waters of Coal Harbour"

working on the Brighouse Estate and 90 at other locations without incidence (Roy, 1976). Nevertheless, the violence in Vancouver set a precedent for outbursts in other parts of the province. Between 1898 and 1906 four outrages were committed by mobs of irate whites who forced Oriental newcomers out of town: first in the Slocan Valley, then at Atlin in the northwest, next at Salmo in the Kootenays, and finally in Penticton (Ward, 1978).

With the advantages of its deep harbour and location as the western terminus of the CPR, Vancouver gradually replaced Victoria as the major seaport and urban centre on Canada's Pacific coast. Vessels plying between Asia and Canada by-passed the island city to call at Vancouver. Consequently, new Chinese immigrants began to land at Vancouver first and the city's Chinese population increased rapidly from 1,103 in 1891 to 2,840 in 1901, only 138 fewer than Victoria's (Canada Census, 1891 and 1901). After 1901, Vancouver's Chinese population outnumbered that of Victoria and its Chinatown replaced Victoria's as a major target for racial hostility in BC.

Reacting to the continuing influx of Chinese as well as Japanese into Vancouver, the Asian Exclusion League organized an Anti-Oriental Parade and held a mass meeting in City Hall on the evening of September 7, 1907 (Adachi, 1976). While the meeting was still in progress, "a gang of hoodlums" marched into Chinatown, wrecking stores and smashing windows before moving on to raid the Japanese quarter (Roy, 1989, p. 191ff). After the riot, the Chinese staged a passive protest by withdrawing their services as domestic servants and as hotel, restaurant, and laundry workers. Order was not restored for several days.

By 1911, Vancouver's Chinese community, with a population of 3,871, was the largest in the province, followed closely by Victoria's at 3,458 persons. About a thousand Chinese were working in the coal mines of Comox District and another thousand in fish-canning in the Skeena River valley (Figure 9.2). With the exception of a few hundred Chinese miners or trappers in the Cariboo District, the majority of the Chinese had settled down in the valleys of the lower Fraser, Okanagan, and Kootenay. Chinese was still the largest visible minority in the province, accounting for 5% of the total population, followed by the Japanese (2.2%), "Hindu [sic]" (0.6%), and "Negro [sic]" (0.1%) (Table 9.2).

Educational Segregation

By this time Chinese immigrants wanted their children to study with white children in public schools and grow up like them in Canada, but they had to face considerable opposition. In Victoria in 1903, for example, the school board carried out educational segregation that placed all of the 15 junior Chinese pupils in a separate room in Rock Bay Elementary School (Lai, 1987). (The few senior Chinese children were left in other public schools to study with white children.) Five years later the school board placed all of the Chinese pupils from First Primer (Grade One) to Second Reader (Grade Four) in the segregated Fisgard Street Chinese School in Chinatown, and permitted them to study with white children after they had finished their Second Reader. The partial segregation proved to be detrimental to the Chinese children as they had no opportunity to practice their spoken English with English-speaking children. When they entered the Junior Third Reader (Grade Five), they found it difficult to communicate with their white classmates.

The prejudice against the Chinese children remained so strong that in 1921 the "Special Committee on the Problem of Oriental Aggression" of the Victoria Chamber of Commerce felt that "white children sitting side-by-side with Orientals tended to develop the idea of social equality," and so recommended to the school board that all the Chinese children be segregated from white children in public schools (*The Colonist*, 1921). The school board estimated that of approximately 230 Chinese pupils in Victoria, about 90 were already in a segregated school, leaving 140 mostly senior Chinese students not yet segregated. Accordingly, when the school term began on September 5, 1922, all of the Chinese students in Boys' Central

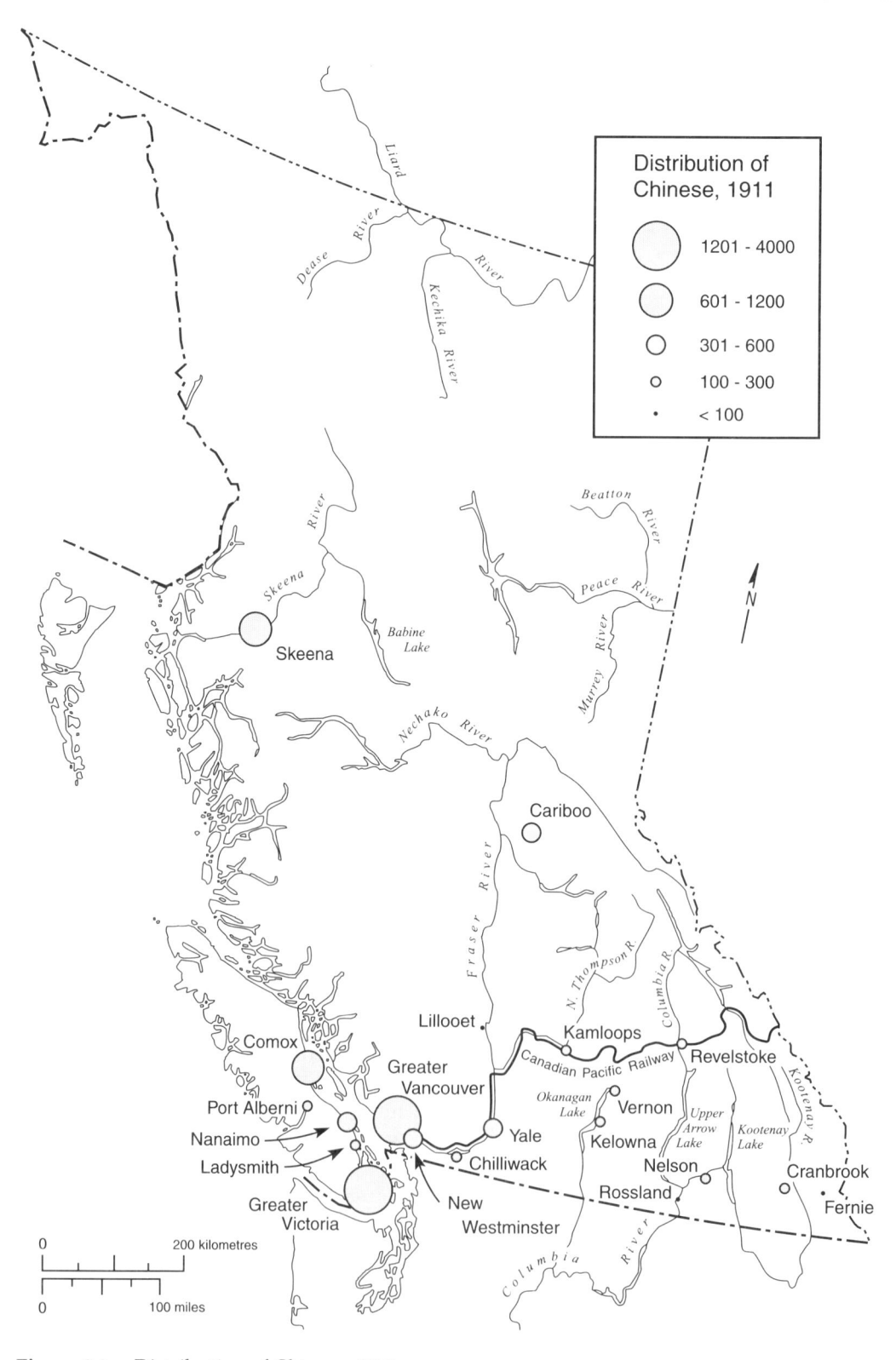

Figure 9.2 Distribution of Chinese, 1911

Table 9.2 Ethnic composition of population in BC, 1911

Ethnic group	Number of persons	Percent of provincial total
British	252,683	64.4
English	133,186	
Scottish	74,493	
Irish	40,642	
Welsh	4,362	
Other Europeans	66,231	16.9
French	15,968	
German	11,880	
Scandinavian	9,721	
Spanish and Portuguese	8.907	
Italian	7,015	
Dutch	6,896	
Other Groups	5,844	
Native Indian	20,134	5.1
Chinese	19,568	5.0
Japanese	8,587	2.2
Hindu	2,292	0.6
Negro	473	0.1
Unspecified	22,512	5.7
Total	*392,480*	*100.0*

Source: Census of Canada, 1911.

School and George Jay School were taken to a segregated school (*Victoria Times*, 1922). To protest the segregation, they returned home and began a strike. An umbrella organization in the Chinese community, the Chinese Consolidated Benevolent Association (CCBA), immediately hired a lawyer to negotiate with the school board, and at the same time organized an Anti-Segregation Association (ASA) to enforce the strike until the school board changed its policy. The Chinese community in Vancouver soon set up an Anti-Segregation Support Group Association, providing the ASA with financial and moral support. Other Chinese communities in the province also responded to the ASA's appeal and donated generously. In addition, the ASA urged the Chinese government to protest on its behalf to the British and Canadian governments (CCBA, 1922). The issue had by then become a national concern because Canada was in the process of signing a trade agreement with China. If the school board of Victoria persisted with its segregation policy, a boycott of Canadian-made goods in China was possible. When the school term began in September 1923, the school board, under pressure from Ottawa, the churches, and public opinion, informed the CCBA that all senior Chinese pupils would be returned to their original schools to study with white children, but the junior pupils would still be placed in segregated schools during the first 4 years of their elementary education. The CCBA accepted this partial segregation and called off the year-long strike.

Exclusion from Entry

As previously stated, the number of Chinese immigrants to Canada continued to increase, in spite of a heavy head tax. Between 1886 and 1924, a total of 82,369 Chinese entered the country, and their head tax amounted to $23,782,650. Under the *Chinese Immigration Act* of 1903 the province in which a Chinese immigrant landed would keep half of his head tax and the federal government the other half. Most Chinese immigrants entered Canada at Vancouver and Victoria, and as a result BC received the largest share of the proceeds. Strong opposition to Chinese immigration in the province remained unabated in spite of financial benefits from the head tax, and the fact that the Chinese population in other provinces grew while it declined in BC, for example, from 98% of the national total in 1891 to 59% in 1921 (Table 9.3).

In 1921, the Chinese population in Canada stood at 39,567, representing only 0.45% of Canada's total population. Nevertheless, under pressure from the government of BC, the federal government eventually carried out a more drastic and inhuman policy to end the migration. On June 30, 1923 Ottawa passed the new *Chinese Immigration Act*, notoriously known as the *Chinese Exclusion Act*, by which no person of Chinese origin or descent would be permitted to enter Canada. Between 1925 and 1947 only 12 Chinese were allowed entry. Not only did this isolate Chinese people in Canada from their parents, wives, and children in China, but it also stopped the growth of Chinese communities across Canada for the

Table 9.3 Number of Chinese in BC and in Canada from 1881 to 1996

Census year	British Columbia	Canada	Percent of national total
1881	4,350	4,383	99.2
1891	8,910	9,129	97.6
1901	14,885	17,312	86.0
1911	19,568	27,831	70.3
1921	23,533	39,587	59.4
1931	27,139	46,519	58.3
1941	18,619	34,627	53.8
1951	15,933	32,528	49.0
1961	24,227	58,197	41.6
1971	44,315	118,815	37.3
1981	96,915	289,245	33.5
1991	196,725	652,630	30.1
1996	312,330	921,585*	33.9

Source: Censuses of Canada, 1881-1996.

*This figure does not include 7,770 respondents who claim to be "Taiwanese" and 780 respondents who claim to be "Tibetan."

next two decades. The Chinese population was further reduced as a growing number of elderly Chinese passed away or retired to China, and a large number of unemployed Chinese returned to China during the Depression of the early 1930s. The loss in population was not offset by the birth rate. Intermarriage was extremely rare as it was not socially accepted either in the Chinese community or in the host society. By 1941, Chinese accounted for only 2.3% of BC's population, dropping to the second position for the first time, replaced by the Japanese (2.7%) as the largest visible minority (Table 9.4). The Chinese community in Greater Vancouver was by far the largest, with a total population of 8,580, followed by that of Greater Victoria with 3,452 (Figure 9.3). Other Chinese communities were found in New Westminster, Nanaimo, Kamloops, and other major towns or cities.

During the Exclusion, a Canada-born generation of Chinese emerged. They received a western education, considered Canada their home, and became more associated with the

Table 9.4 Ethnic composition of population in BC, 1941

Ethnic group	*Number of persons*	*Percent of provincial total*
British	571,336	69.9
English	321,948	
Scottish	152,677	
Irish	83,460	
Welsh	13,251	
Other Europeans	175,512	21.5
Scandinavian	41,560	
German	22,407	
French	21,876	
Russian	16,474	
Italian	13,292	
Dutch	12,737	
Polish	8,744	
Ukranian	7,563	
Finnish	6,332	
Austrian	4,624	
Other Groups	19,903	
Native Indian and Innuit	26,999	3.3
Japanese	22,096	2.7
Chinese	18,619	2.3
Other Asians	1,757	0.2
Negro	473	0.1
Unspecified	1,542	0.2
Total	817,861	100.0

Source: Census of Canada, 1941.

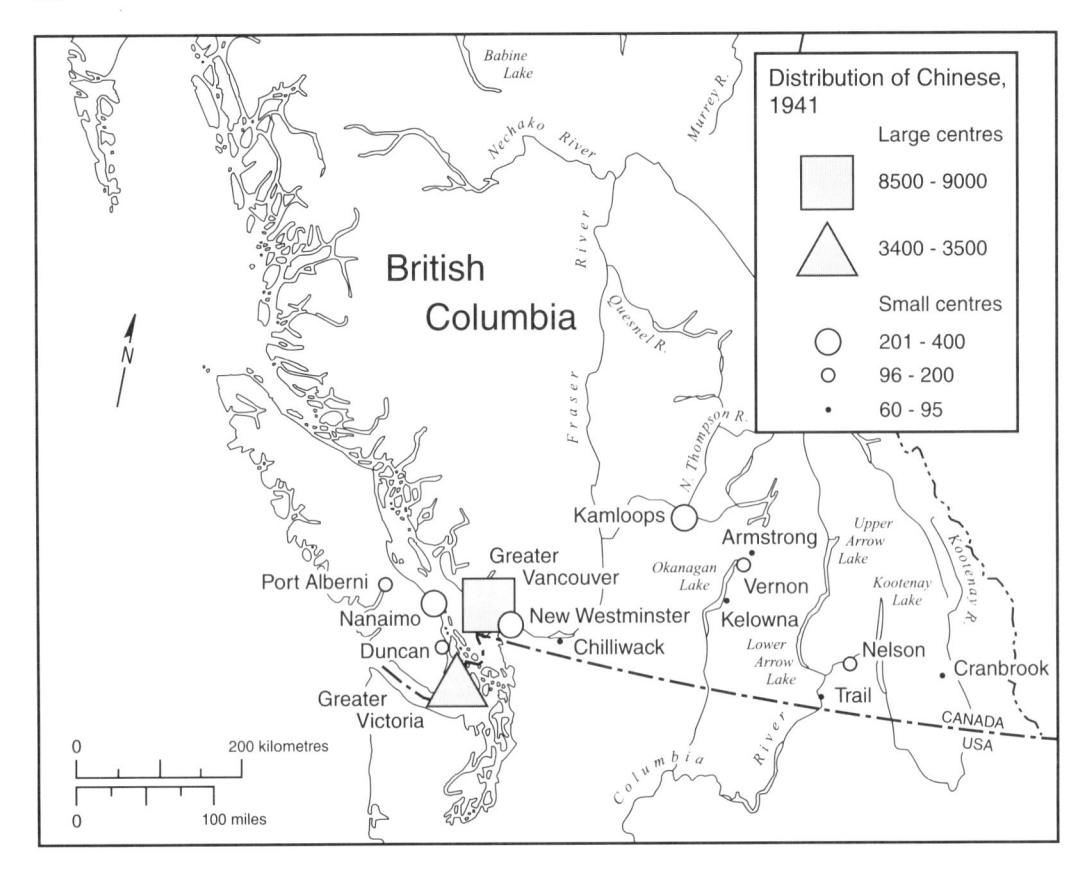

Figure 9.3 Distribution of Chinese, 1941

host society. For example, a group of locally-born Chinese students in Victoria established the Chinese Students' Athletic Club, a basketball team, in 1931 (CSA, 1950). The club won so many championships that it became known throughout the Pacific Northwest and Canada and was chosen to represent Canada in the North American Oriental tournament for 2 years. The club always participated in charity events such as the Cariboo Games for the benefit of the Red Cross.

Conversion to the Christian faith is another indicator of Chinese assimilation or integration into the host society. In 1941, for example, about 20% of Chinese in Vancouver were Christian. Naturalization may also be considered a good index of assimilation. In 1931, 18% of Chinese in Toronto were naturalized, while only 3% of Chinese in Vancouver and Victoria were naturalized (Wickberg, 1982). The small percentage of naturalization in BC was mainly because prejudice against Chinese was strongest in BC and its judges were more likely to turn down a Chinese application for citizenship.[3] Furthermore, Vancouver and Victoria chinatowns were so well established and self-contained that most of their Chinese residents could survive with little or no contact with white society.

Although the Canadian-born or naturalized Chinese had tried hard to integrate into the fabric of the Canadian way of life, they were still ostracized by the host society. For example, Chinese were not permitted to swim in the city-owned Crystal Pool in Victoria. As lakes and beaches are far away from Chinatown and the water is usually icy cold, Chinese children had no place to learn to swim. As a result no Chinese Boy Scouts could attain the King's Scout badge, the highest honour in scouting, because swimming is one of the requirements.

One of the most discriminatory laws was the insertion of a new section of the Dominion Franchise Bill in 1920, which decreed that:

> ...persons who by laws of any province of Canada are disqualified from voting a member of the legislative assembly of such province in respect of race, shall not be qualified to vote in such province of this act (Canada, 1920).

The disfranchisement had not only stripped the Chinese of their citizenship right in a free society but also seriously limited their future commercial activities and opportunities for employment. For example, under the *Liquor Licence Act* of 1899, licences to sell liquor would not be issued to anyone who was not on the voting list. Similarly a professional society could implement any measure to discriminate against the Chinese without specifying the type of race they wanted to exclude. For example, Chinese people could not be lawyers or pharmacists in Canada because any person whose name was not on the voting list would not be eligible to become a student or apprentice in those fields.

The question of Oriental franchise became a political issue after the mid-1930s. Under the influence of the international socialism movement, socialist and labour groups formed the Cooperative Commonwealth Federation (predecessor of today's New Democratic Party) in 1933 and soon became a rising political party in BC. A large number of its members wanted to enlist the support of Asian workers; as a result, it dropped its anti-Oriental stance and supported the enfranchisement of the Oriental people. During the 1935 federal election, Liberals in BC appealed to white racism and warned the voters that:

> ...a vote for any CCF candidate is a vote to give the Chinaman and Japanese the same voting right that you have (Angus, 1935, p. 389).

As a result, only three CCF members out of BC's 15 seats were elected to the Parliament.

Unwanted Soldiers

After the outbreak of the war in Europe in 1939, young Canadians were called for compulsory military training under the *National Resources Mobilization Act*. BC's premier, T.D. Pattullo, immediately wrote to Prime Minister King urging him not to call up Chinese or Japanese for fear of their demand for equality and franchise in return for military service, and saying that such a demand would never be tolerated in BC (Roy, 1978). Accordingly, Prime Minister King announced in January 1941 that Canadians of Oriental origin would not be called for compulsory military service. In spite of this, some patriotic Chinese Canadian youths took the military training and volunteered their service in the army although they were not considered to be or treated as Canadian soldiers.

After Japan's bombing of Pearl Harbour on December 7, 1941, Japan became Canada's enemy and China became Canada's ally. Chinese Canadians volunteered their services in the Red Cross and other services and enthusiastically supported the Victory Loan Drive, oversubscribing their quotas. As the war went on, prejudice against Chinese lessened. In August 1944 the Canadian government decided to call up Chinese Canadians for compulsory military training. Thirteen Chinese were recruited in the Special Operations Executive and trained to be special agents with the objectives of infiltration, sabotage, subversion, and guerrilla warfare in Asia. More than 100 Chinese were grouped under Force 136 and trained in parachute jumping warfare and commando techniques to fight behind Japanese lines in Asia (Wong, 1944).

The recruitment provided a valuable opportunity for the Chinese to demand enfranchisement. Reverend Andrew Lam, together with other Chinese youth leaders, immediately formed the Chinese-Canadian Association and appealed to church groups and service clubs for their support for enfranchisement (Lee, 1976). In 1945, the legislature amended the *Provincial Elections Act* and enfranchised Orientals and native Indians who served in the armed forces. Consequently, at least 50 Chinese veterans of World War I and about 400 Chinese then serving in the forces were granted the vote (Lee, 1976). Two years later, enfranchisement was extended to all Chinese-Canadians in Canada.

Post-War Immigrants and Integration, 1947-1999

Ottawa repealed the Exclusion legislation and abolished many discriminatory laws and regulations against the Chinese on May 14, 1947. Naturalized Chinese Canadians were permitted to sponsor their wives and children for admission into Canada, and the admission classes were broadened through the 1950s and early 1960s. As Chinese were permitted to enter Canada again, the Chinese population in BC grew gradually from 15,933 in 1951 to 24,227 in 1961. However, the Chinese population had dropped from a record high of 9% of the provincial total in 1891 to less than 2% in 1961 (Table 9.5).

On October 1, 1967, the federal government introduced for the first time a non-discriminatory immigration policy based on merits like education and occupational skill rather than on race. Many of the Chinese immigrants that were subsequently admitted into Canada were professional people such as doctors, engineers, and teachers. Under the Immigrant Investor Program (IIP), introduced in 1986, Chinese entrepreneurs and investors entered Canada with a large amount of capital and invested heavily in Canadian business and industry. By doing so, they created jobs and contributed directly to Canada's economic growth. According to Employment and Immigration Canada, BC had 13% of $2 billion in subscriptions made under the IIP between 1986 and 1993, and benefited economically from this flow of capital.

New immigration policies have resulted in a great change in the ethnic composition of BC. British people, traditionally the dominant ethnic group in the province, accounted for about 40% of its 3,689,755 residents in 1996 (Table 9.6).[4] Chinese Canadians, with a population of 312,330, represented only 8.5% of the province's total population, but they were and are still the largest visible minority.[5]

Chinese communities today are much more diversified than they were before World War II.

Table 9.5 Chinese population growth in BC, 1881-1996

Census year	Chinese	Provincial total	Percentage of total
1881	4,350	49,459	8.80
1891	8,910	98,173	9.08
1901	14,885	178,657	8.33
1911	19,568	392,480	4.99
1921	23,533	524,582	4.49
1931	27,139	694,263	3.91
1941	18,619	817,861	2.28
1951	15,933	1,165,210	1.37
1961	24,227	1,629,082	1.49
1971	44,315	2,184,620	2.02
1981	96,915	2,713,615	3.60
1986	125,535	2,883,367	4.35
1991	196,725	3,282,061	5.99
1996	312,330	3,689,755	8.46

Sources: Censuses of Canada, 1881-1996; Statistics Canada, *The Daily: Ethnic Origin*, 3 December 1987; Canada Year Book, 1999, p. 98.

Table 9.6 Major ethnic groups in BC, 1996

Major ethnic group	Number of persons
European	
British	1,779,120
German	498,380
French	339,750
Scandinavian	253,740
Dutch	176,235
Ukranian	168,765
Italian	117,895
Polish	102,390
Visible Minorities	
Chinese	312,330
East Indian	141,370
Filipino	49,185
Japanese	33,245
Vietnamese	21,095
Korean	19,610
African origin	19,435
Punjabi	18,950
Canadian	817,485

Source: Census of Canada, 1996.

Prior to the exclusion of entry, more than 90% of the Chinese in Canada had come from the Four Counties (Taishan, Xinhui, Enping, and Kaiping), the Three Counties (Panyu, Nanhai, and Shunde), and Zhongshan Counties on the Zhujiang Delta in Guangdong Province, China (Lai, 1978). Since the 1960s, most of the Chinese immigrants have come from Hong Kong, China, Taiwan, and other parts of Asia such as Vietnam, Singapore, Malaysia, and Indonesia. For example, between 1991 and 1996, 30,565 immigrants came to live in Richmond, a suburban municipality of Metropolitan Vancouver, and an analysis indicates that the top three places of birth for them were Hong Kong (44%), China (17%), and Taiwan (13%) (Census Hotfacts, 1998).

Suburbanization and Theme Malls

New Chinese immigrants are heterogeneous, not only in terms of origin, but also in terms of wealth, education, and cultural background. Many are better educated and more affluent than their predecessors. Most have settled in the large cities, especially the affluent suburbs. In 1996, for example, nearly 96% of the Chinese Canadians in BC resided in Metropolitan Vancouver (288,795) and Metropolitan Victoria (10,010) (Figure 9.4). Almost half of Metropolitan Vancouver's Chinese Canadians live in its suburban municipalities and transformed their communities' ethnic composition.

In BC, the demographic change caused by Chinese immigrants is most apparent in Richmond, a suburban municipality of Metro Vancouver. In 1996, 34% of its 148,867 residents were Chinese Canadians—the second largest ethnic group after the British (45%) (Table 9.7). Most were concentrated near the town centre on No. 3 Road between Blundell and Cambie roads (Figure 9.5). In the 1980s, a few Chinese business concerns in two small plazas on Park Road began to advertise the area in a Chinese newspaper as Richmond's New Chinatown (Lai, 2000). At that time, a strip plaza consisting of two commercial and office buildings was built by a Hong Kong company and officially opened on September 17, 1987 as Richmond's New Chinatown by Premier Bill Vander Zalm and Mayor Gil Blair of Richmond (Lai, 2000). Since then many new shopping centres in the form of plazas or enclosed malls have been built by Chinese investors and were designed specifically to cater to Chinese and other Asian immigrants (Plate 9.2). They are commonly called "Chinese Malls," "Asian Malls," "Asian-themed malls," or "ethnic shopping centres" by the public because of their distinct Chinese characteristics. These malls have numerous billboards or store signs written in Chinese characters, and many of them are divided into small strata-titled units similar to condominiums or apartment buildings. Most of the customers are Chinese; accordingly, many of the stores use the names of popular stores in Hong Kong, Taiwan, or China in order to attract more

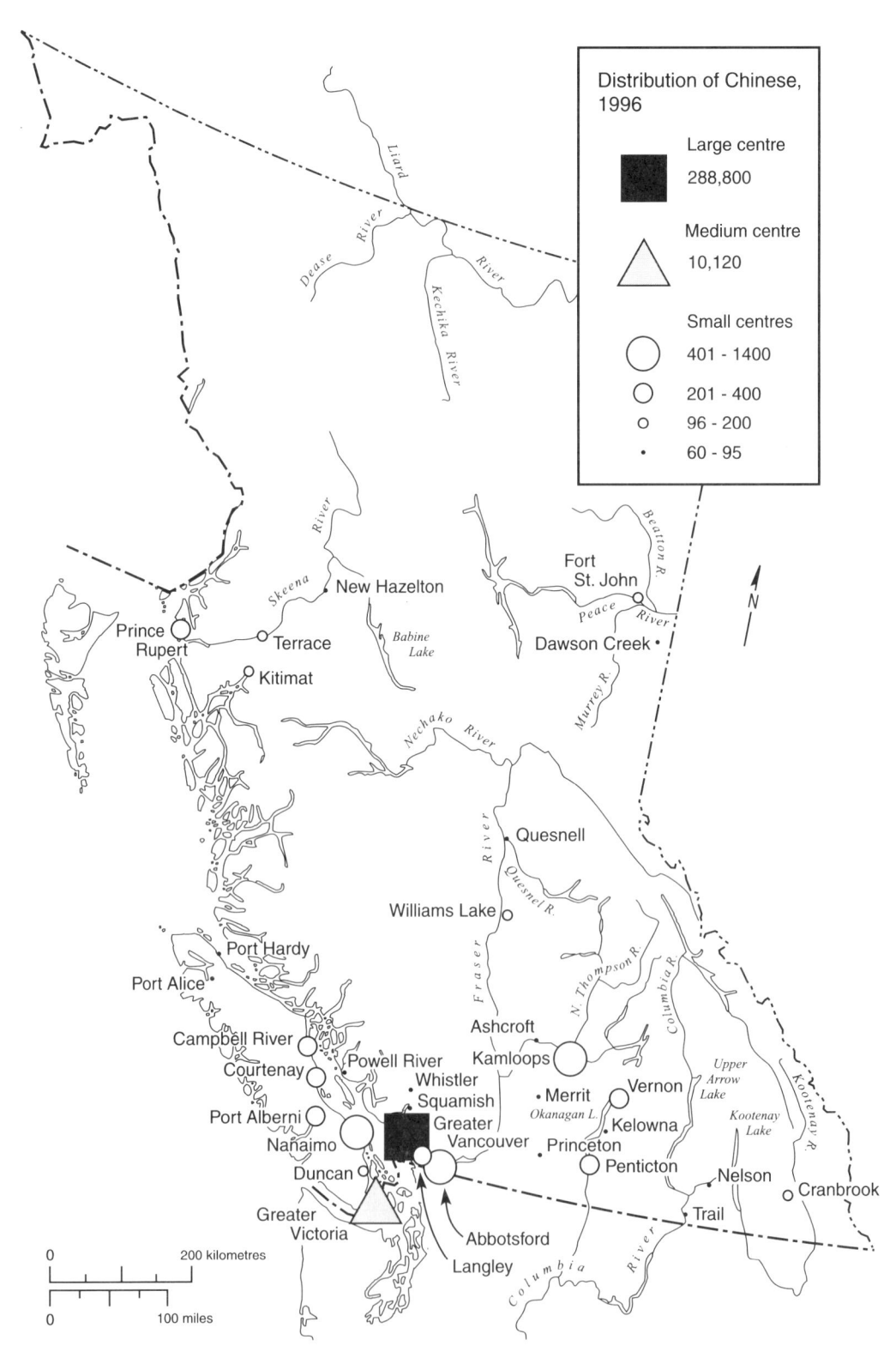

Figure 9.4 Distribution of Chinese, 1996

Table 9.7 Major ethnic groups in Richmond, 1996

Major ethnic group	Number of persons	Percent of city total
European		
British	66,795	44..87
German	11,440	7.68
French	7,350	4.94
Ukrainian	4,770	3.20
Dutch	4,175	2.80
Jewish	3,465	2.33
Polish	3,400	2.28
Russian	2,505	1.68
Italian	2,460	1.65
Visible Minorities		
Chinese	50,215*	33.73
East Indian	8,635	5.80
Filipino	5,035	3.38
Japanese	3,665	2.46
Punjabi	870	0.58
Korean	790	0.53
Vietnamese	670	0.45
Black	545	0.37
Pakistan	295	0.20
Canadian	20,045	13.47

Source: Census of Canada, 1996.

* This figure does not include 470 respondents who claim to be "Taiwanese."

Chinese customers from these places. Based on the visual display and the characteristics of customers, the author identified 49 Asian-themed malls in the Central Business District of Richmond (Figure 9.6). Similar types of Asian-themed malls have also been built in other suburban municipalities, such as the Crystal in Burnaby (Plate 9.3), the Henderson Place in Coquitlam (Plate 9.4), and Asian Centre in Surrey (Figure 9.7). Asian-themed malls such as the Sun Wah Centre and Chinatown Plaza (Plate 9.5) have also been built inside Vancouver's Chinatown. Most of these malls were built and financed by Chinese investors and entrepreneurs.

Integration and Recognition

Most of the post-1967 Chinese immigrants and Canadian-born Chinese have adapted easily to the Canadian way of life and are integrated into the host society, as indicated by the level of voluntary community service and political participation. Chinese Canadians have been appointed to serve voluntarily as Canadian Citizenship Presiding Officers, Human Rights Commissioners, and members of many official advisory committees (Plate 9.6). An increasing number of Chinese Canadians have joined various political parties in BC and run for office. For example, Douglas Jung, a war veteran and

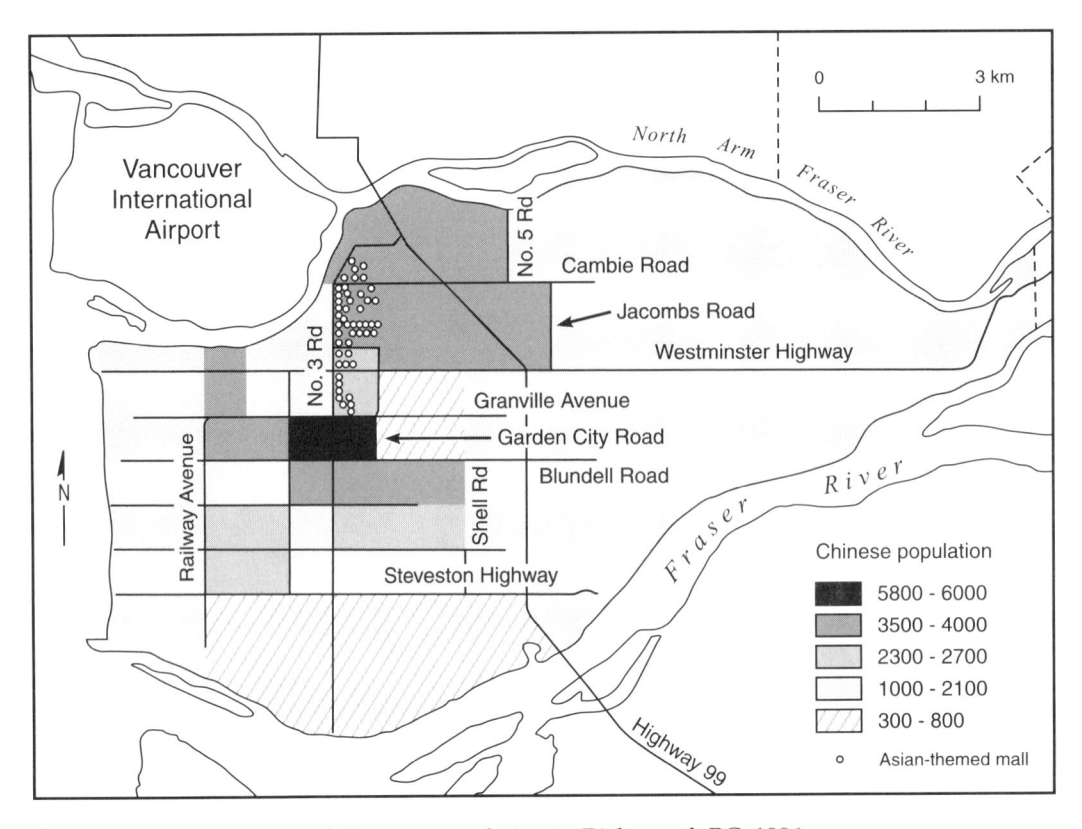

Figure 9.5 Distribution of Chinese population in Richmond, BC, 1996

a lawyer in Vancouver, entered federal politics as a Progressive Conservative and in 1957 became the first Chinese Canadian to be elected a Member of Parliament. Peter Wing was elected Mayor of Kamloops in 1966 and became the first Chinese Canadian mayor in BC. Jenny Kwan and Ida Chong are not only the first *female* Chinese Canadians, but also the only Chinese Canadians to be elected Members of BC's Legislative Assembly. Between 1957 and 2000, a total of 29 elected politicians in BC were of ethnic Chinese origin (Table 9.8). In the municipal elections of 1999, one mayor and nine councillors of Chinese ethnic origins were elected or re-elected. Alan Lowe, an architect, was elected Mayor of Victoria and became the first Chinese Canadian mayor of the provincial capital. By far the most significant event in the province was the appointment of Dr. David See-Chai Lam, an immigrant from Hong Kong, to the post of Lieutenant Governor (1988-1995).

Unlike their predecessors, many Chinese Canadians today care not only for the Chinese community, but donate their time and money for the benefit of all groups. For example, the Honourable Dr. David and Mrs. Dorothy Lam, Mr. Cheung-Kok Choi, Dr. Peter Eng, Mr. Harry Lou-Poy, Dr. Ronald and Mrs. May Lou-Poy, and Mr. Milton Wong have contributed millions of dollars to the three universities in BC, channelling their idealism into education and culture. Their donations have been duly recognized, although community-focused contributions by many other Chinese philanthropists have not yet received appropriate public attention.

Contributions of Chinese pioneers are now being recognized by the Canadian government. On June 16, 1980 the Parliament of Canada unanimously passed a motion recognizing "the contribution made to the Canadian mosaic and culture by the people of Chinese background." Two years later, a bronze plaque was installed

Plate 9.2 Aberdeen Centre at Hazelbridge Way, Richmond, BC

by the Historic Sites and Monuments Board of Canada at the museum in Yale in honour of the "necessary evil"—the Chinese railway workers (Lai, 1998, p. 10). Another significant official recognition was the unveiling of a plaque on the beach of Commando Bay on the eastern side of Okanagan Lake on September 17, 1988 in honour of the "unwanted soldiers." The text of the plaque reads:

COMMANDO BAY (1944)

DEDICATED TO THE FIRST CHINESE-CANADIANS IN CANADA'S ARMED FORCES DURING WORLD WAR II WHO VOLUNTEERED FOR SPECIAL OPERATIONS WITH BRITISH INTELLIGENCE (SPECIAL OPERATIONS EXECUTIVE) AND WHO COMPLETED THEIR INITIAL INTENSIVE PARAMILITARY TRAINING AT THIS SITE.

The plaque was erected in order to commemorate the services of the 13 Chinese Canadians who were trained intensively on the site from May to September in 1944 under Major H.J. Legg and Lieutenant-Colonel F.W. Kendall.[6] Prime Minister Brian Mulroney sent his congratulations to these Chinese Canadians who had volunteered for the extremely dangerous and hazardous missions and stated that "their contribution in war inspired overdue recognition for every Chinese Canadian in peacetime. Such a legacy will never lose its value" (Wong, 1944).

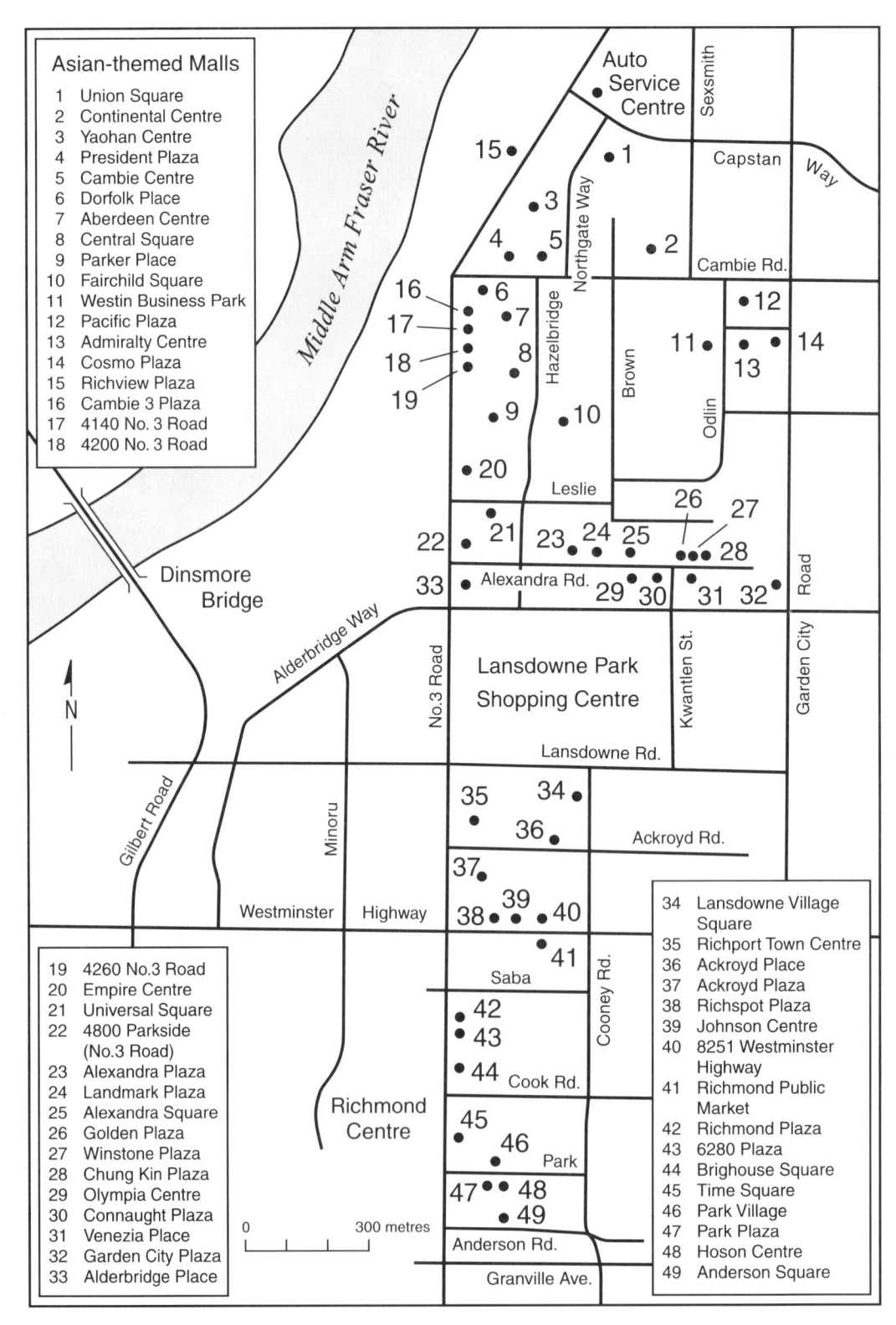

Figure 9.6 Asian-themed malls, Richmond, BC, 2000

Asian-themed Malls

1. Union Square
2. Continental Centre
3. Yaohan Centre
4. President Plaza
5. Cambie Centre
6. Dorfolk Place
7. Aberdeen Centre
8. Central Square
9. Parker Place
10. Fairchild Square
11. Westin Business Park
12. Pacific Plaza
13. Admiralty Centre
14. Cosmo Plaza
15. Richview Plaza
16. Cambie 3 Plaza
17. 4140 No. 3 Road
18. 4200 No. 3 Road
19. 4260 No.3 Road
20. Empire Centre
21. Universal Square
22. 4800 Parkside (No.3 Road)
23. Alexandra Plaza
24. Landmark Plaza
25. Alexandra Square
26. Golden Plaza
27. Winstone Plaza
28. Chung Kin Plaza
29. Olympia Centre
30. Connaught Plaza
31. Venezia Place
32. Garden City Plaza
33. Alderbridge Place
34. Lansdowne Village Square
35. Richport Town Centre
36. Ackroyd Place
37. Ackroyd Plaza
38. Richspot Plaza
39. Johnson Centre
40. 8251 Westminster Highway
41. Richmond Public Market
42. Richmond Plaza
43. 6280 Plaza
44. Brighouse Square
45. Time Square
46. Park Village
47. Park Plaza
48. Hoson Centre
49. Anderson Square

Chinese: The Changing Geography of the Largest Visible Minority 169

Plate 9.3 The Crystal at 4500 Kingsway, Burnaby, BC

Plate 9.4 Henderson Place at Pipeline Road, Coquitlam, BC

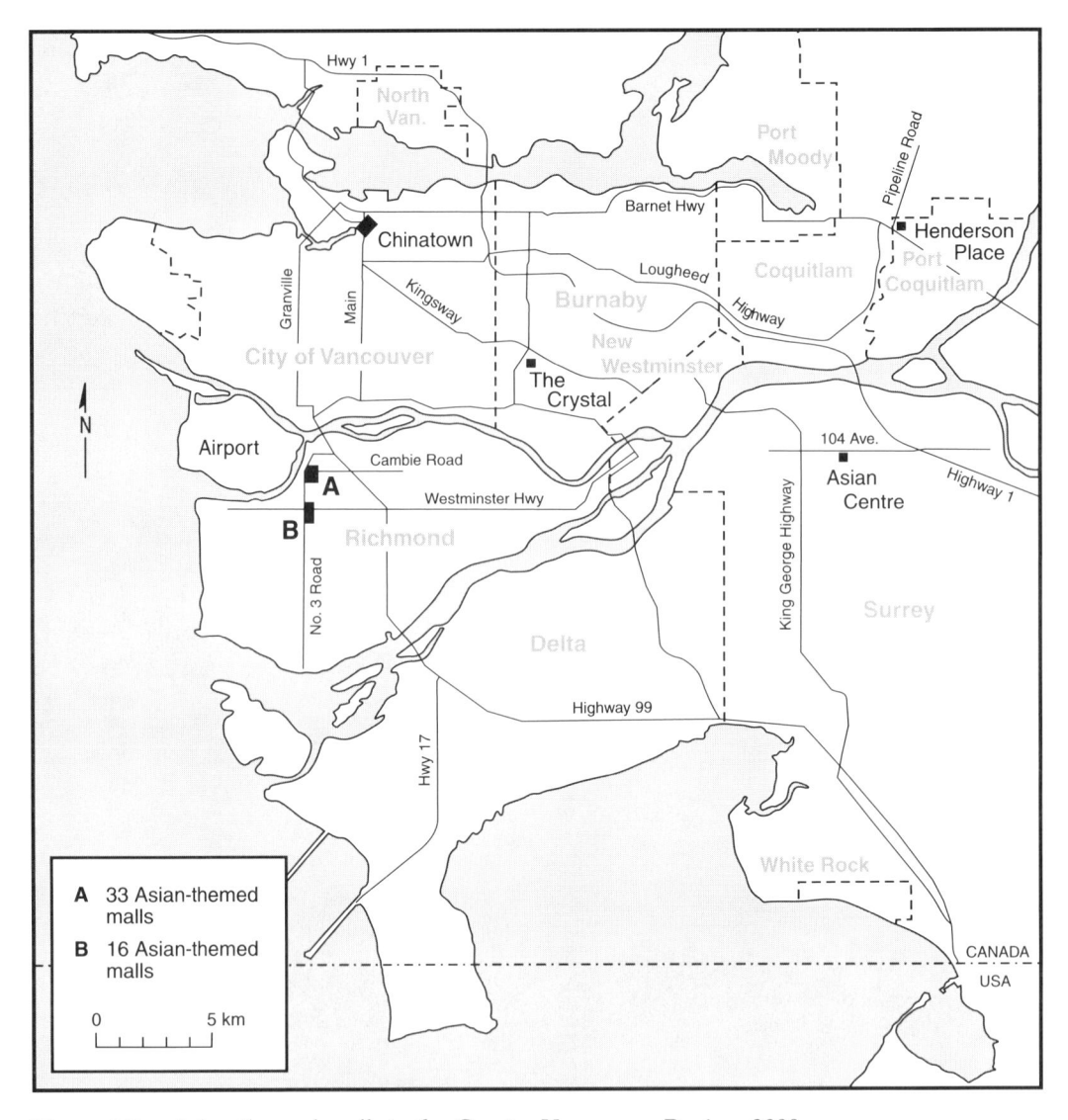

Figure 9.7 Asian-themed malls in the Greater Vancouver Region, 2000

Epilogue

Chinese Canadians have never accounted for more than 9% of BC's total population, though they have virtually been the largest visible minority. From the time that it became a province of Canada in 1871, discrimination against the Chinese became a hallmark of BC's white citizens for decades. Chinese Canadians have travelled a long and difficult journey from ostracism to acceptance by the host society. The "Dark Age" period of their migration history in BC is now at an end and their contributions to the province have been recognized. Chinese Canadians should continue to participate in the activities of the host society, join in the mainstream of Canadian society, and help to build a strong multi-cultural society so that all Canadians may live in peace and harmony.

Plate 9.5   Chinatown Plaza at Keefer Street, Vancouver, BC

Acknowledgements:

The author is grateful to the Vancouver Centre of Excellence for Research on Immigration and Integration in the Metropolis for funding this research, and to Dr. Dan Hiebert for the provision of 1996 data on ethnic origins in BC and in Census Tracts and Enumeration Areas in Richmond, BC.

Plate 9.6   David Chuenyan Lai, C.M., a Chinese Canadian appointed as a Canadian Citizenship Ceremony Presiding Officer

Table 9.8 Elected politicians of Chinese ethnic origin in BC, 1957-2001

Name	Position	Period
Douglas Jung	Member of Parliament (Vancouver)	1957-62
Art Lee	Member of Parliament (Vancouver)	1974-78
Raymond Chan	Member of Parliament (Richmond)	1993-00
Sophia Leung	Member of Parliament (Vancouver-Kingsway)	1997-
Jenny Kwan	Member of Legislative Assembly (Mount Pleasant)	1996-
	Councillor (Vancouver)	1993-96
Ida Chong	Member of Legislative Assembly (Oak Bay-Gordon Head)	1996-
	Councillor (Saanich)	1993-96
Richard Lee	Member of Legislative Assembly (Burnaby North)	2001-
Patrick Wong	Member of Legislative Assembly (Vancouver-Kensington)	2001-
Peter Wing	Mayor (Kamloops)	1966-71
Ed Lum	Mayor (Saanich)	1988-93
	Councillor (Saanich)	1965-73
Harry Chow	Mayor (Colwood)	
	Councillor (Colwood)	1985-87
Alan Lowe	Mayor (Victoria)	1999-
	Councillor (Victoria)	1991-92
Dorothy Kostrzewa (nee Cheung)	Councillor (Chilliwack)	1969-78 1987-
Ben Lee	Councillor (Kelowna)	1973-89
Bill Yee	Councillor (Vancouver)	1982-86
Richard Lee	Councillor (Merritt)	1984-86
Sandra Wilking (nee Wong)	Councillor (Vancouver)	1988-90
Jack Mar	Councillor (Central Saanich)	1988-93
Joe N. Leong	Councillor (Kamloops)	1990-93 1996-
Tung Chan	Councillor (Vancouver)	1991-93
Maggie Ip	Councillor (Vancouver)	1993-96
Ken Eng	Councillor (North Saanich)	1996-98
Derek Dang	Councillor (Richmond)	1996-
Stan Lim	Councillor (Golden)	1996-
Donald Lee	Councillor (Vancouver)	1996-
Daniel Lee	Councillor (Vancouver)	1996-
Daniel Chiu	Councillor (Coquitlam)	1999-
Lyndia Hundleby (nee Chin)	Councillor (Esquimalt)	1999-
Jackie Ngai	Councillor (Saanich)	1999-
Lindsay Wong	Councillor (Rossland)	1999-

REFERENCES

Adachi, K. (1976). *The enemy that never was*. Toronto: McClelland & Stewart.

Angus, H.F. (1935). Liberalism stoops to conquer. *Canadian Forum*, 15, 389.

BC (1872). Statutes of British Columbia. Victoria, BC: Government of BC.

BC (1876). Statutes of British Columbia, p. 3. Victoria, BC: Government of BC.

BC (1877). Statutes of British Columbia, p. 567. Victoria, BC: Government of BC.

BC (1884). Statutes of British Columbia. 2nd Session, 4th Parliament, Chapter 2 (p. 3), Chapter 3 (p. 5-6), and Chapter 4 (p. 7-12). Victoria, BC: Government of BC.

BC Directory (1892). p. 188. Victoria, BC: William Ltd.

British Columbian, New Westminster, 11 January 1887.

Canada (1882a). House of Commons Debates, 12 May 1882, p. 1476. Ottawa: Government of Canada.

Canada (1882b). House of Commons Debates, 12 May 1882, p. 1477. Ottawa: Government of Canada.

Canada (1885a). Royal Commission on Chinese Immigration: Report and Evidence, p. 398. Ottawa: Government of Canada.

Canada (1885b). Statutes of Canada, "An Act to Restrict and Regulate Chinese Immigration into Canada," Chap. 71, 207-12. Ottawa, 48-9 Victoria.

Canada (1900). Statutes of Canada, "An Act to Restrict and Regulate Chinese Immigration into Canada," Chap. 32, 215-221. Ottawa, 63-4 Victoria.

Canada (1900-1917). Department of the Interior, Superintendent of Immigration, Annual Reports, 1900-1917. Ottawa: Government of Canada.

Canada (1903). Statutes of Canada, "An Act to Restrict and Regulate Chinese Immigration into Canada," Chap. 8, 105-111. Ottawa, 3 Edward VII.

Canada (1920). Statutes of Canada, Chap. 46, Sect. 369.

Canada Census (1891 and 1901). Ottawa: Government of Canada.

Canada Census (1996). Census of Canada: British Columbia, Population. Ottawa: Government of Canada.

Census Hotfacts (1996). City of Richmond, Vol. 6, No. 2, p. 1.

Chinese Consolidated Benevolent Association (1922). Annual Report, 1922-23, Minutes of Meeting on 27 November 1922.

Chinese Students Athletic Club (1950). *20th Anniversary Celebration and Re-union, 1931-1950 Souvenir Program*. Victoria: Chinese Students' Athletic Club.

Kerr, J.B. (1890). Biographical dictionary of well-known British Columbians—with an historical sketch. Vancouver: Kerr and Begg.

Lai, D.C-Y. (1978). An analysis of data on home journeys by Chinese immigrants in Canada, 1892-1915. *The Professional Geographer*, XXIX(4), 361.

Lai, D.C-Y. (1987). The issue of discrimination in education in Victoria, 1901-1923. *Canadian Ethnic Studies*, XIX(3), 49.

Lai, D.C-Y. (1998). *Canadian steel, Chinese grit: No Chinese labour, no railway*. Vancouver: National Executive of Canadian Steel.

Lai, D.C-Y. (2000). The impact of new immigration policies on the development of new Chinatowns and new Chinese shopping plazas in Canada. *Asian Profile*, 28(2), 101-102

Lee, C.F. (1976). The road to enfranchisement: Chinese and Japanese in British Columbia. *BC Studies*, 30, 44-76.

MacDonald, D.D. (1917). *The BC orphan's friend*, Historical Number 1847-1914. Victoria, BC.

Meares, J. (1790). *Voyages made in the years 1788 and 1789, from China to the north west coast of America*. London: J. Walter.

Parker, C.W. (Ed.) (1912). *Who's who and why: A biographical dictionary of notable men and women of Western Canada*, Volume 2.

Roy, P. (1976). The preservation of peace in Vancouver: The aftermath of the anti-Chinese riot of 1887. *BC Studies*, 31, 44-59.

Roy, P. (1978). The soldiers Canada didn't want: Her Chinese and Japanese citizens. *Canadian Historical Review*, LIX(3), 341-358.

Roy, P. (1989). *White man's province - British Columbia politicians and Chinese and Japanese immigrants, 1858-1914*. Vancouver: University of British Columbia Press.

The Colonist (1874). 21 August. Victoria, BC.

The Colonist (1875). 14 January. Victoria, BC.

The Colonist (1882). 1 July. Victoria, BC.

The Colonist (1887a). 13/14 January. Victoria, BC.

The Colonist (1887b). 15 January. Victoria, BC.

The Colonist (1887c). 27 January. Victoria, BC.

The Colonist (1887d). 2 March. Victoria, BC.

The Colonist (1921). 29 November. Victoria, BC.

The Standard (1874a). 29 January. Victoria, BC.

The Standard (1874b). 20 November. Victoria, BC.

The Standard (1874c). 24 November. Victoria, BC.

The Standard (1875a). 13 January. Victoria, BC.

The Standard (1875b). 22 July. Victoria, BC.

The Standard (1875c). 2 August. Victoria, BC.

The Standard (1875d). 16 August. Victoria, BC.

United Kingdom (1862). *The Colony of Vancouver Island and the Colony of British Columbia: Blue Books*. London: Colonial Office.

United Kingdom (1868). *The Colony of British Columbia: Blue Book.* London: Colonial Office.

Victoria Times (1922). 6 September.

Ward, W.P. (1978). *White Canada forever: Popular attitudes and public policy toward Orientals in British Columbia.* Montreal: McGill-Queen's University Press.

Wickberg, E. (Ed.) (1982). *From China to Canada: A history of the Chinese communities in Canada.* Toronto: McClelland and Stewart.

Wong, M. (1944). *The Dragon and the Maple Leaf: Chinese Canadians in World War II.* London, Ontario: Pirie Publishing.

WPA (1878). *A constitution of the Workingmen's Protective Association.* Victoria, BC: Archives of British Columbia.

ENDNOTES

[1] Since it was first published in December 1858, the *British Colonist* had been published under the name of the *Daily British Colonist*, the *Daily British Colonist* and the *Victoria Daily Chronicle*, the *Daily Colonist*, and now the *Times-Colonist*. For brevity, the newspaper is referred to as *The Colonist*. Similarly, the *Daily Standard*, also known as the *Evening Standard*, is referred to as *The Standard*.

[2] Shakespeare was councillor in 1875, 1878, 1880, and 1881.

[3] For a general statement of naturalization certificate policy, 1915-1930, see Public Archives of Canada, RG 25, G1, Vol 1867, file 263, part I, P.C. 1378.

[4] The 1996 Census asked people their ethnic origin, permitting them to specify up to four groups. Hence, people who gave multiple origins were double or triple counted in Table 9.6. For example, a person who has a German father and a Chinese mother might give "German," "Chinese," and "Canadian" in his/her answer to the ethnic origin question. If all the categories of ethnic groups in BC were added up, the total population would exceed many more than the actual population of the province.

[5] The population figure of Chinese Canadians did not include 4,095 Taiwanese, 65 Tibetans, and Chinese who were listed in the census as "Canadian" only.

Spatial Economy

Colin J.B. Wood

Department of Geography, University of Victoria

Introduction

BC's way of life and economy evolved rapidly over the last 150 years, from the arrival of the Hudson's Bay Company in its quest for furs and the subsequent exploitation of the rich resource base to the emergence of Vancouver as the third largest city in Canada and an important economic centre of the Pacific Rim region. The development of the economy from exporting raw and semi-processed materials—first furs and gold, then timber, fish, agricultural products, and finally hydrocarbons and electrical power—is a microcosm of Canada as a whole, designated by Harold Innis in the 1930s as the "staples economy" (Hayter and Barnes, 1990). Indeed, lumber, pulp, and coal remain BC's major exports today, with well established markets in the US and Pacific Rim (Figure 10.1). However, from the 1970s on, the economy has matured significantly in terms of *diversification* with the evolution to, on the one hand, production of luxury yachts and natural foods and essences, and on the other hand, a dynamic service sector that includes a thriving tourism and hospitality "industry," high tech (producing both products and services), and film production. This chapter briefly outlines the growth of the provincial economic system and then describes the key elements of BC's economic geography. Many details concerning individual resource industries such as mining, energy, agriculture, and tourism are covered in other chapters in this volume.

The Growth of the Economy

In the 19th century, the northwest region of North America was one of the most isolated areas in the world. A steady trickle of British settlers came to the colony, interspersed with brief periods of frenzied growth booms associated with the gold rushes. The exploitation of coal seams on Vancouver Island and the development of sawmills and canneries along the coast formed the initial elements in the resources-based economy that gradually emerged, together with initial urban nucleations formed around the original fur trading posts, or the new resource processing centres.

A second impetus for growth came with the boom in railway construction and completion of the trans-continental Canadian Pacific Railway (CPR) in 1885 which played an instrumental role in the settlement of BC. To help finance its construction in BC, substantial land grants were allocated to the CPR on southeast Vancouver Island, along the proposed route between the Rocky Mountains and the coast terminus, and in the coal/metal mining region of southeast BC (Seager, 1996). The early 1900s also saw the Grand Trunk (later the CN) railway crossing the central Interior forming a link between the Prairies and the new ocean port at Prince Rupert. A third main railway axis came in the form of a north-south connection between Vancouver and Prince George—the Pacific Great Eastern, later to become the provincially-owned BC Railway. A fourth link between the mining region of southeast BC and Vancouver (Kettle Valley Railway) was also completed.

Continental and then global demands for BC's raw materials gradually increased, first with the trans-Canadian rail link (the main benefit negotiated by BC for joining Confederation) and then the northwest US rail system, and the opening of the Panama Canal in 1914 (effectively 1920). Resource exploitation generated relatively high incomes and profits, providing an impetus for infrastructure growth, with

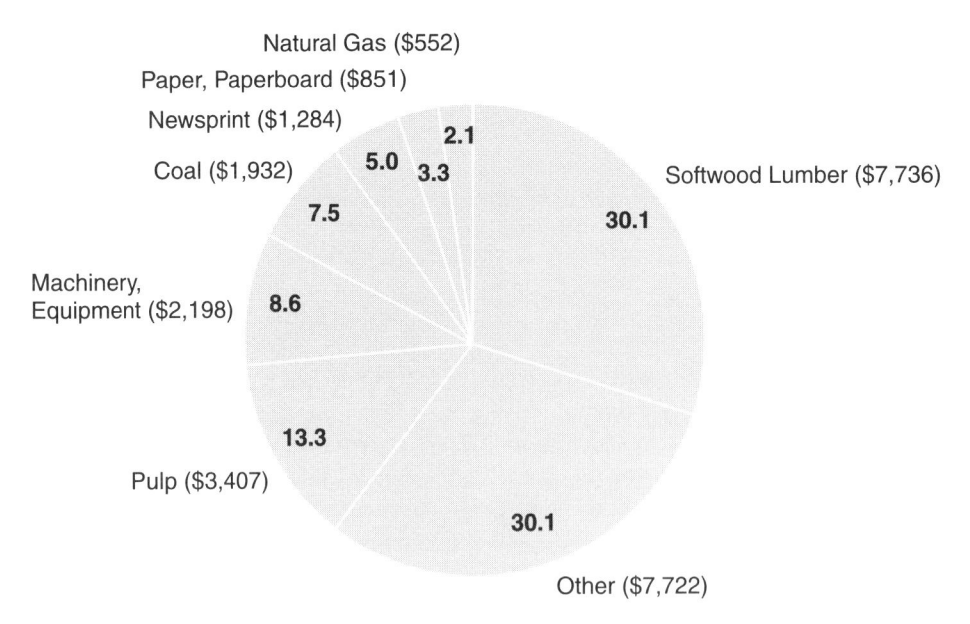

BC Exports by Product/Commodity

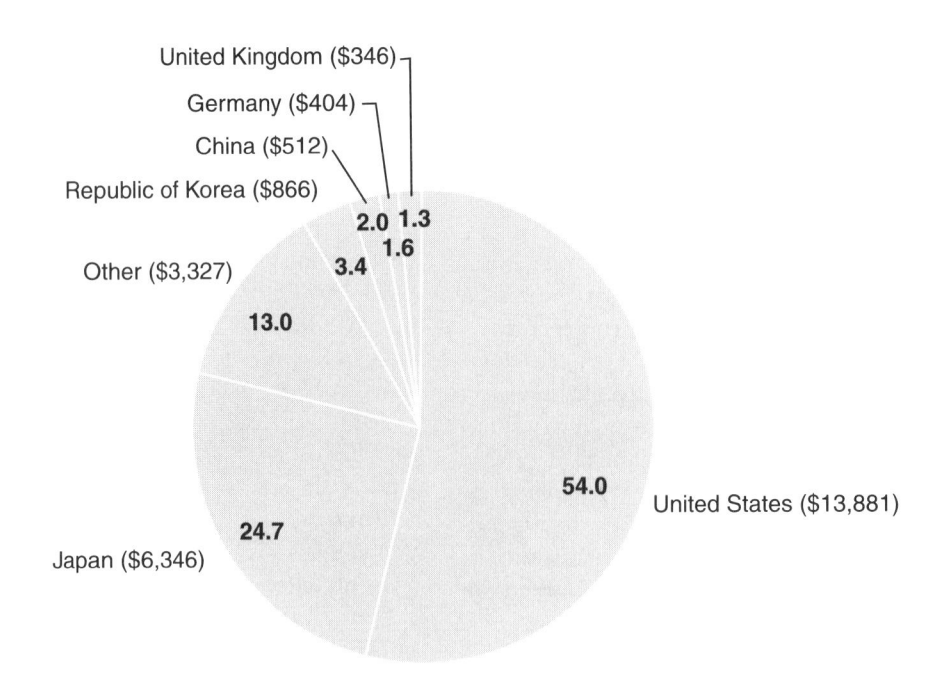

- Natural Gas ($552) — 2.1
- Paper, Paperboard ($851) — 3.3
- Newsprint ($1,284) — 5.0
- Coal ($1,932) — 7.5
- Machinery, Equipment ($2,198) — 8.6
- Pulp ($3,407) — 13.3
- Softwood Lumber ($7,736) — 30.1
- Other ($7,722) — 30.1

BC Merchandise Exports by Country, 1996

- United Kingdom ($346) — 1.3
- Germany ($404) — 1.6
- China ($512) — 2.0
- Republic of Korea ($866) — 3.4
- Other ($3,327) — 13.0
- Japan ($6,346) — 24.7
- United States ($13,881) — 54.0

Figure 10.1 The main elements of BC's economy as shown by export categories and trading partners

spin-off linkages in support and producer service industries. Capital investment was attracted from Britain, the US, and Europe. Workers and their families were drawn from eastern Canada, Europe, and Asia to blast the rock, hew the timber, plough the land, and raise the children of the next generation. In contrast, First Nations people began a precipitous decline in numbers that would not rebound until the 1940s, with many of their traditional claims to resource use being usurped.

Unlike frontier regions such as California, without a large and varied agricultural base due to the mountainous terrain, BC did not develop an evenly spreading pattern of central places with the possibilities of economic diversification. The evolution of the small, resource-oriented companies into large scale mining and forestry operations with their insatiable appetite for capital and technological innovations saw their rapid, chrysalid-like emergence into large corporations through amalgamations and buy-outs. Generally they were neither concerned with local research activities nor diversification. Consequently, most urban centres evolved as assembly points for raw materials or initial resources processing centres—characterized as *single enterprise communities*—and stayed relatively small in size.

Victoria and New Westminster were the initial administrative and commercial urban centres on the south coast, chosen for their defensive sites and strategic significance in relation to the Pacific, and access to water and the Fraser River Valley's links to the Interior (see **Chapter 7**). The choice of Vancouver as the transcontinental rail terminus in the late 19th century set in motion the processes for its sustained growth. It possessed more favourable locational attributes as a rail, oceanic, and coastal shipping/transhipment point than the other two. With a larger natural harbour, space for industrial development, and a powerful corporate lobby in the form of the CPR, it grew quickly. The installation of grain elevators by the 1920s consolidated its position for bulk cargo exports from the Prairies. Victoria kept a grip on to its role as provincial capital, experiencing a slow growth rate as a tourist and retirement city; New Westminster was eventually absorbed into the greater Vancouver urban region. Kamloops and Prince George initially grew as rail centres; Nanaimo exported coal; and Kelowna was a lakeport. They gradually evolved as regional commercial centres during the period of post-war highway improvements and mega project development—commonly known as the Bennett era.

This generalization of BC's economy and community into a simple geographic *core and periphery* understates the province's complex, underlying socio-political milieu, for the relations of workers, capital, and the state have a remarkable history, which substantially influenced, for example, the role of the province in the regional economy (Warburton and Coburn, 1988; Johnston, 1996). This dynamic continues into the contemporary political forum with the swings in control of the provincial government between labour-based (New Democratic Party) and pro-capitalist/bourgeois, anti-labour coalitions (Liberals, Conservatives, Social Credit, Reform). These parties are different from and in many respects independent of the similarly-named federal parties (Fisher and Mitchell, 1996). The generalization also masks the social distance between the rough and ready mining towns and the more genteel fruit farming region of the southern Interior.

The Bennett Era

The post-World War II era saw the ascendency of the remarkable WAC Bennett, premier of BC from 1952-1972 (see **Chapter 7**). During his premiership, the BC government embarked on major hydroelectric power and transportation infrastructure projects. Essentially a populist with a power base in the hinterland, he "helped induce in BC a tradition of distrust of large powerful organizations such as big business, big labour, or big government—particularly the federal government in far off Ottawa" (Fisher and Mitchell, 1996, p. 265). The highway, bridge construction, rail extension, ferry expansion, and modernization schemes were essential formative elements in the evolving economic geography of the province of BC, and necessary precursors to the onset of diversification. Notwithstanding the small "c" conservative ideology of his party, these investments were (and remain) publically owned.[1]

1990s

At the end of the 20th century, it was clear to many observers that the economy of BC was evolving. Davis and Hutton (1992, p. 2) suggested it had grown to a "mature, advanced, export-oriented staple economy in transition," in many ways atypical of a resource dependent economy. This can be attributed to: a varied resource base with more processing; locational and specific quality advantages in forest products; relatively cheap energy; an urbanized, well educated population located in five main nuclei; a developed physical and social infrastructure in the south that attracts capital investment and migrants; non-excessive terms of trade that permit the growth of high incomes fought for by the union movement; and an environment that, for example, encourages resort development and attracts wealthier retirees who bring pension and investment incomes. To this can be added the desire by many Hong Kong residents to live in a western, capitalist democracy in the face of the takeover of the People's Republic of China in 1997.

Nevertheless, there have been concerted expressions of the need to diversify the economy in order to overcome the boom and bust cycle of the commodity/primary, raw material oriented sectors. Suggestions in the 1970s focused on encouraging manufacturing in its traditional forms, reflecting perhaps a lack of innovative thinking in itself and a lack of awareness of the trends already occurring in the world economy. The need for promoting the growth of value-added industries such as secondary manufacturing (e.g., wooden house components) has been a frequent refrain. Although Allen (1986) and others claim that BC lacks a suitable market base for evolution to a manufacturing stage of development, some secondary, value-added manufacturing does take place, clearly at odds with their interpretation and more in line with the modern reality of a global market place and the diminished importance of transportation costs in the final product price. Periodically surfacing in government and business circles is the desire to set up a small, integrated steel works to encourage shipbuilding and a secondary steel-using manufacturing sector, but it has yet to reach the drawing board stage. This idea is partly to fill the vacuum created by the meagre spin-off in secondary activities by the forest products industry, as forest companies have a very poor record in research and development (Hayter, 1996). Without this impetus from BC's major resource/manufacturing industry, it would seem difficult to envisage the evolution of secondary, value-added manufacturing capabilities.

During the 1990s, federal fiscal policies increasingly impinged on the provinces. The federal government's desire to reduce deficits and control inflation and provincial spending resulted in downloading to provincial responsibility much of the former federal involvement in health care and post-secondary education. In addition, federal hiring freezes, for example, seriously affected the role of the RCMP in non-urban areas of BC, the coastguard and lighthouse system, and even the Pacific Naval fleet. With only token federal Liberal representation in the province, together with the west's perception of Ottawa's obsession with Quebec, friction between the governments has resulted.

Late 1990s and into the New Millennium

With a GDP of approximately $110 billion (1999 market prices; $90 billion at 1992 prices), BC is the third largest provincial economy in Canada; it ranks higher than many nation states (ranked approximately 54th globally, including major corporations and nation states); it contributes about 14% of Canada's GDP, which is approximately 108% of the national average of provincial contributions. BC functions within the Canadian, North American (NAFTA), and global economic systems—all of which have had substantial shocks in form and function in the last 3 decades, are responding to the demise of protective regulation and subsidy as they are challenged and "dismantled" through NAFTA and WTO pressure, and are attempting to survive the vicissitudes of Asian meltdown.

GENERAL FEATURES OF THE ECONOMY

The historical evolution of BC within the Canadian mosaic, its geographic location, and its resources endowment—together with the ascendency of unique political figures such as WAC Bennett—give it a distinct identity in the regional economic subsystems of North America (Figure 10.2). This section outlines the main elements of the economy—the government's role, and features of production and consumption. Space limitations preclude a more detailed evaluation of the service economy, although it is well covered by Hutton (1999) (see also **Chapter 12**).

- Although commodities are still a dominant part of BC's exports ($25.6 billion in 1996), they are a declining percentage of the total economy (13% of GDP and 11% of the workforce) (Stats Canada); in short, the economy is now mainly *driven by the service or tertiary sector*. Imports include motor vehicles, fuel, consumer/manufactured goods, and food.
- Private corporations undertake resource exploitation (except hydro). However, as the resource base is considered unalienable, publicly-"owned" domain (since 1896, with the exception of outstanding First Nations' territorial claims), the provincial government sets the terms and conditions for resource exploitation (except ocean fisheries, a federal jurisdiction) through, for example, forest tenure arrangements. This has recently led to American complaints about the true market price of the raw material (the *stumpage rate* issue) and undervaluation.
- Operating in the Canadian quasi-cartel banking system means that much of the capital supply system, banks, and the financial system as a whole are controlled from eastern Canada. There is, however, a strong Credit Union presence in BC accounting for about 30% of bank transactions and ensuring local reinvestment. Moreover, recent immigrants, especially from Hong Kong, bring investment capital. However, despite restructuring to make the Canadian banking system more competitive, it is unlikely that financial control will move from Ontario (Dobialas, 1996).
- BC, along with Alberta, Saskatchewan, and Ontario as "have" provinces, generally contributes more than it receives in federal *transfer payments*. This has to be balanced against the federal government's management and protection of Canada's Pacific coast with three military bases at Abbotsford, Comox, and Esquimalt, and a Coastguard/helicopter base at Sidney, which have significant regional multiplier effects; the activities of the federal Department of Fisheries and Oceans, fisheries research/conservation; and the Pacific Forest Research Centre.[2]
- The federal government also injected $1.8 billion into coal mining development in northeast BC (now closing down due to low coal prices). It has also been involved in recent years in infrastructure development: airports, railways, and housing construction (CMHC); the Western Diversification Program; and various other growth stimulation projects such as tourism promotion.[3]
- A substantial section of the basic infrastructure is publicly owned (provincial government): electric power (except southeastern BC, Kootenay Power Co.); roads and ferry system; automobile insurance; hospitals and health care; education system infrastructure; BC rail (2,400 km); airports (formerly federally controlled) via municipal or local companies.
- Most of the large resource corporations, West Kootenay Power, main telephone system (Telus), Vancouver professional sports franchises (except the BC Lions Canadian Football team), and large retail chain stores are mainly American-owned, with some recent Norwegian involvement in the forest sector; there are Japanese controlling interests in some hotel chains. The media are mainly eastern Canadian-owned.

Government

The provincial government plays a significant role in the regional economy, having an annual budget of over $20 billion (Table 10.1).[4] Its importance lies in: ownership of most of the

180   British Columbia

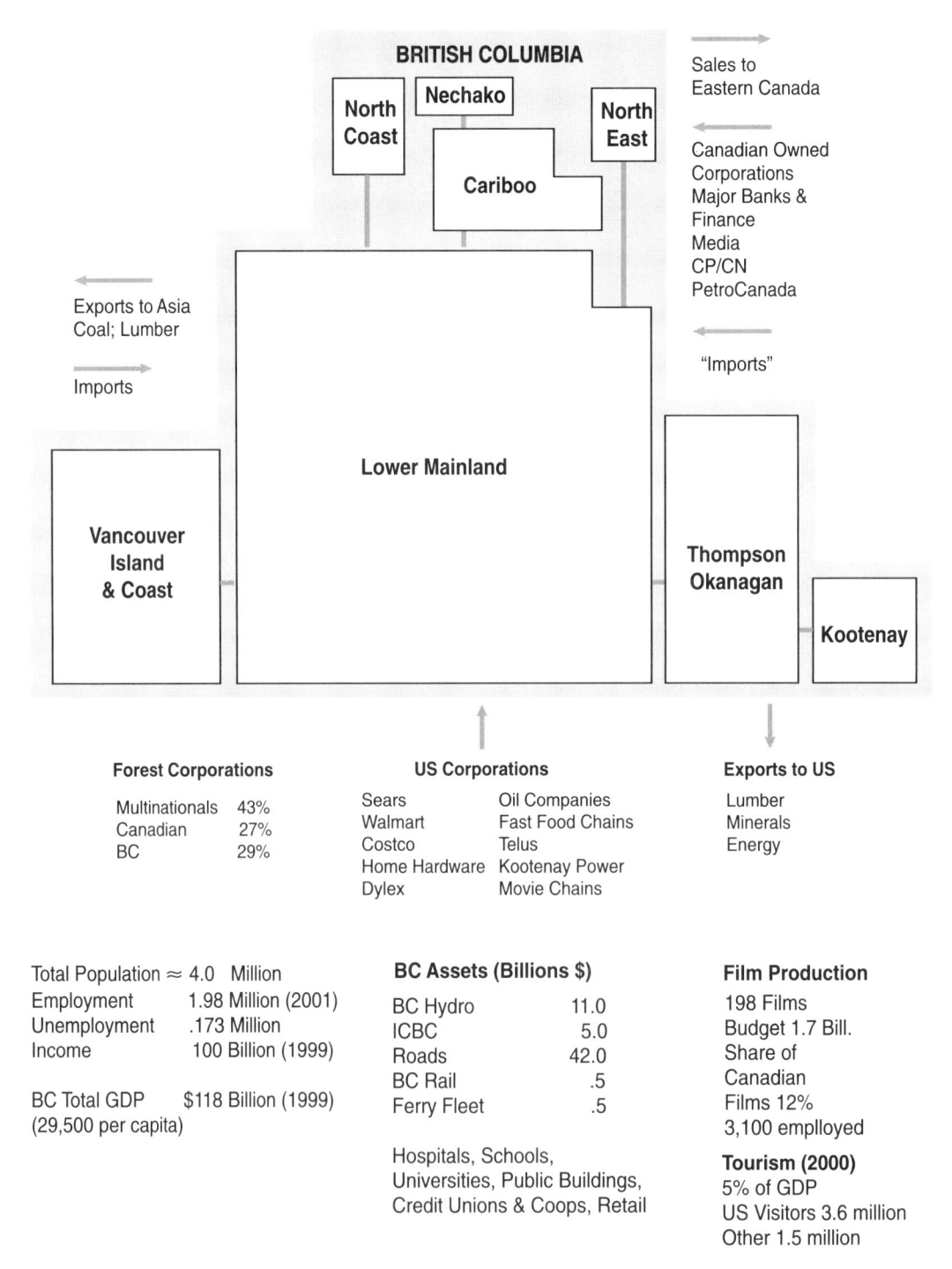

```
                    BRITISH COLUMBIA          →
                                              Sales to
        North    Nechako     North            Eastern Canada
        Coast               East              ←
                                              Canadian Owned
                 Cariboo                      Corporations
                                              Major Banks &
                                              Finance
                                              Media
                                              CP/CN
                                              PetroCanada
←
Exports to Asia
Coal; Lumber                                  ←
→                                             "Imports"
Imports

                 Lower Mainland

Vancouver                            Thompson
Island                               Okanagan
& Coast
                                              Kootenay
```

Forest Corporations	**US Corporations**	**Exports to US**
Multinationals 43%	Sears Oil Companies	Lumber
Canadian 27%	Walmart Fast Food Chains	Minerals
BC 29%	Costco Telus	Energy
	Home Hardware Kootenay Power	
	Dylex Movie Chains	

Total Population ≈ 4.0 Million
Employment   1.98 Million (2001)
Unemployment   .173 Million
Income   100 Billion (1999)

BC Total GDP $118 Billion (1999)
(29,500 per capita)

BC Assets (Billions $)

BC Hydro   11.0
ICBC   5.0
Roads   42.0
BC Rail   .5
Ferry Fleet   .5

Hospitals, Schools,
Universities, Public Buildings,
Credit Unions & Coops, Retail

Film Production
198 Films
Budget 1.7 Bill.
Share of
Canadian
Films 12%
3,100 emplloyed

Tourism (2000)
5% of GDP
US Visitors 3.6 million
Other 1.5 million

Figure 10.2 The cartogram shows the relative size according to incomes/population of the eight major regions. Arrows indicate external linkages. Tables indicate general characteristics of the economy and current dynamic sectors.

Table 10.1 BC government accounts, 1998/99

Revenues ($billions) grouped by main categories (amounts rounded)

Taxes		13.1
Personal	5.40	
Corporate	1.10	
Social Services	3.20	
Property	1.30	
Fuel	.6	
Other	1.40	
Natural resources		1.8
Petroleum	.36	
Minerals	.04	
Forests	1.00	
Water	.30	
Other revenue		1.8
Government enterprises		1.3
Liquor	.60	
Hydro	.30	
Lottery	.36	
TOTAL		20.3

Expenditures ($billions)—Ministries spending close to or greater than $1 billion

Health	7.4
Education	4.2
Advanced education	1.6
Children and families	1.5
Human resources	1.5
Attorney general	.9
Other	3.6
TOTAL	20.7

Source: *BC Financial and Economic Review*, 1999.

NB: Preliminary data for 1999/2000 suggest a small surplus due to hydro and gas export revenues.

province (94%) in the form of Crown Lands, except in the settled south and in areas currently subject to First Nations' treaty negotiations; transport infrastructure, roads, rapid transit, ferry system, 30% of the rail system, auto insurance, provision of education, health care, and social services; ownership of a large part of the hydroelectric power system; regulator of and revenue collector from the resource industries; provision of a range of training, information, and economic development promotional services.

The roles of governments and multinationals in the economy is a contentious issue in the wake of "Thatcherism," the Washington Consensus (1990), WTO, and the "siege of Seattle." The particular mix favoured is part of the ideological base of each political party, their policies and objectives, and how they respond to the provincial electorate. Canada has generally opted for more government than our neighbour to the south for a variety of reasons (Lipset, 1990). Provincial economic policies are also constrained by confederation and thereby subject to national political and fiscal policies. The particular difficulty for BC governments is a mix of the following factors:

- the long run (relative) decline in commodity prices in the 20th century which influence revenues adversely; vagaries of commodity export markets—Asian meltdown;

- the increasing costs of health and education, which are regarded as fundamental services, require high skill levels, are labour intensive, are not amenable to many forms of automation and economies of scale, as in the corporate sector, and suffer from the pressures of rising expectations—translated as, is everyone entitled to triple bypass heart surgery? Should everyone be entitled to free or subsidized post-secondary education?;

- an aging population with low birth rates;

- federal general fiscal policies such as interest rate manipulation and downloading of responsibilities.[5]

Recent BC governments have laid out and implemented economic plans that emphasize diversification, investment in renewable resources, education, regional strategies, infrastructure development, high tech, film production, and tourism (BC, 1999). One of the most important influences on the provincial economy remaining within the jurisdiction of the federal government is control of immigration. Population dynamics have a major influence on virtually all aspects of life in the province, such as migration to cities and its impact on housing demand, yet its direction is left mainly to market forces and federal control.[6]

Production (manufacturing)

Inevitably, the production process is one of the most studied phenomena of our age in terms of its importance, managerial arrangements, worker involvement, and the socio-political ramifications of profit allocation. The system's evolution from Fordism/Taylorism production modes to flexible systems set within a dynamic and unpredictable system of technological change and financial and political instability is generally recognized by academia and most corporations, but not always by governments (Malecki, 1991). Various localized effects of global changes are present in the BC production system, but detailed studies of them are few; their impacts on BC communities are discussed in detail by Barnes and Hayter (1997). It has also been realized that economic activity can be divided into two categories—the *basic* or export earning sector of a metropolis/region and the *non-basic* or service sector. The former brings in earnings from products sold outside the region, while the latter recirculates incomes and helps the regional economy to function (Malecki, 1991).[7] BC's growth now appears to be pushed by the service sector—although manufacturing is still important, suggesting that the whole process has become more complex than previously thought.

Employment in BC is currently about 2 million, with the "goods producing" (primary, construction, and manufacturing) sector employing 23.8%. The resources sector is gradually losing jobs through automation, while "other manufacturing" is slowly increasing, mainly in metropolitan areas. Overall, BC has enjoyed growth (1985-2000) with the value of manufacturing shipments rising from $19.8 billion to $33.7 billion, an increase of 5% per year. Single enterprise towns mainly located in the periphery of the province still contribute significantly to the manufacturing sector (pulp and paper), but this is where labour is losing to automation. The Standard Economic Categories (SEC) sectors are shown in Table 10.2 and should be compared with employment (Figure 10.3).

Forest products still dominate manufacturing, accounting for close to 47% of shipments

Table 10.2 Manufacturing activity in BC by shipment values and categories, 1991 and 1998 ($billions)

	1991	1998
Wood products and furniture	6.2	10.5
Pulp and paper	4.0	5.8
Food and beverages	3.7	4.3
Chemical and petroleum	2.6	2.3
Metal/metal fabrication	1.9	2.9
Transport	.7	1.6
Machinery	.6	1.1
Printing	1.0	1.3
Electrical	.4	1.3
Clothing/textile	.3	.4
Plastic	.4	.7
Other	.2	.6

Source: Statistics Canada (data rounded to 1 decimal place).

by value (1999 figures). This sector has lost jobs as workers are either replaced by automation and mechanization of operations, as seen in Chemainus, or the whole operation is closed down, as in Gold River, or cut back, as in Port Alberni and Powell River. The growth in other manufacturing stems from: the increased population and larger local market base; the low Canadian to US dollar; the skilled, educated workforce; Asian immigrants; and ancillary support from the provincial and federal governments. Given the uncertainty of both production inputs and markets, producers must be flexible, employing a range of strategies to achieve this at different stages of the production process, according to what appears to work for the particular company involved (Rees and Hayter, 1996). Even in the (relatively small) clothing industry in Vancouver, flexibility is a key element of the technology employed (Mather, 1993). The form and dynamics of the industrial geography of the Vancouver region that evolved in the second half of the 20th century are discussed in detail by North and Hardwick (1992) and Hutton (1998).

Figure 10.3

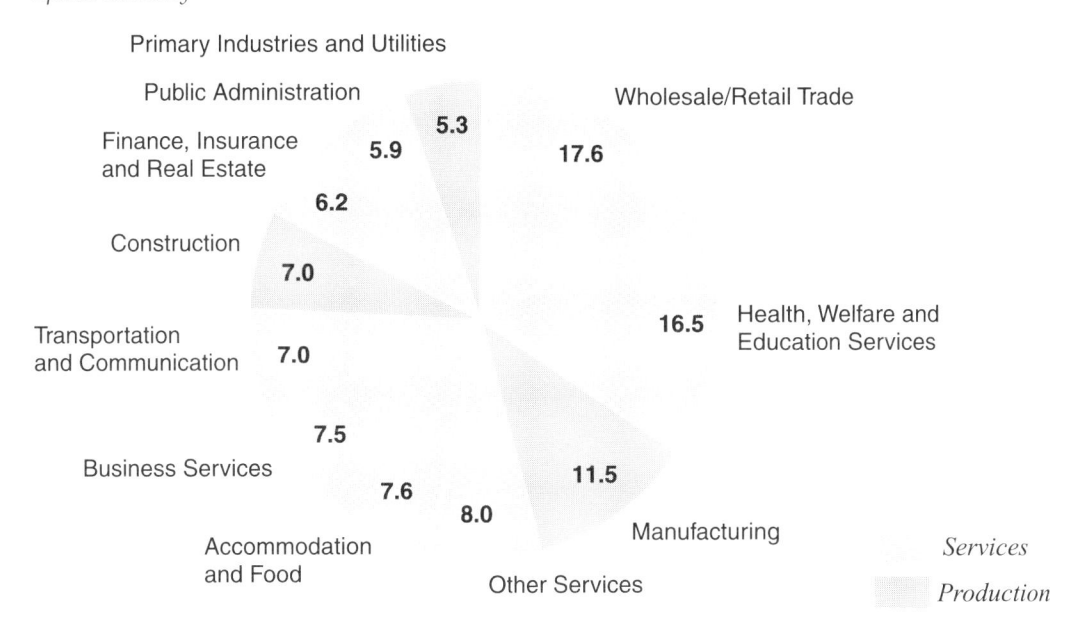

Primary Industries and Utilities: 5.3
Public Administration: 5.9
Finance, Insurance and Real Estate: 6.2
Construction: 7.0
Transportation and Communication: 7.0
Business Services: 7.5
Accommodation and Food: 7.6
Other Services: 8.0
Manufacturing: 11.5
Health, Welfare and Education Services: 16.5
Wholesale/Retail Trade: 17.6

Legend: Services / Production

Figure 10.3 Employment by sector, late 1990s (Statistics Canada, Labour Force Survey, BC Stats)

Employees and Consumers

Flexibility is not solely the concern of entrepreneurs and how they arrange production. The pulp and paper industry in BC eliminated 2,000 jobs from 1985 to 1998 through closure, "downsizing" (i.e., firing), and automation. In Powell River, about 1,000 jobs were eliminated in the pulp mill between 1983 and 1998. Through union initiative, a reduction in overtime was introduced among the labour force; this move kept 89 jobs threatened by lay-offs. The switch by workers to a basic 40-hour shift created 22 new jobs. A survey showed that 88% liked the lower work hours, even though there was a reduction in their total income (White, 1999).

The nature of the BC economy is well portrayed by the categorization of the labour force into its constituent subgroups (Figure 10.3).[8] Clearly, the resource industries are still important in the economy, particularly in the smaller, single industry towns, but are a declining employer in total numbers and as a percentage of the workforce and its degree of unionization.[9] Mechanization and automation increased output levels and maintained profits, however they also resulted in "pink slips." While manufacturing shipments grew in value (and hence profits) by approximately 5% per year, weekly earnings during the same period increased by 4% per year. During the same period, housing costs in metropolitan areas in BC increased at very high rates, giving Vancouver the highest average housing prices in the country.[10] This forces entry level house buyers such as young families to locate in outlying suburban areas, thus adding to the commuting problem. It has also resulted in more financing of consumption by credit, to the advantage of the banks. The greatest percentage of employees (and hence consumers) in BC are located in the southwest portion of the province, in the main metropolitan regions. The largest single employer located *in one place* is the University of British Columbia, underlining the importance of universities/research centres as significant growth poles in the contemporary environment of regional and urban dynamics.[11] The 1997 Census survey of household spending gives some insight into the nature of consumers in BC and basic spatial variations (Table 10.3). While household incomes are approximately 3.5% higher than the national average, there are some geographic differences reflecting regional demographic and economic levels. Incomes in

Table 10.3 Household incomes in Canada and BC and expenditures in BC, 1997

	Canada	BC	Vancouver	Victoria	Rest of BC
Number of households	11 million	1,482,850	713,660	139,000	630,190
Average income ($)	50,954	52,925	55,708	51,057	50,095
Expenditures in BC (percent of income)					
Food		11.0	11.0	11.0	
Shelter		20.8	21.5	21.0	
Transport		12.3	12.0	10.7	
Recreation		9.8	7.4	8.5	
Taxes		22.0	22.0	22.0	

Source: Statistics Canada.

Vancouver are 10% higher than the provincial average, corresponding to its role as a hub for head offices and professional services; Victoria is 4% lower, reflecting the higher proportion of retired seniors, government employment, and lower wages of the hospitality sector; the remainder of BC is 5.5% lower than the provincial average.

The single most important expenditure for households is shelter. Home ownership in the province stands at 66.3%, slightly above the national average of 65.9%. Auto ownership, the second most expensive item in household budgets, once again is higher than the national average (79.4%) at 84.5%, with about 13 automobiles per 10 households.

ECONOMIC GEOGRAPHY

BC's economic geography is a product of the interplay between the rich resource base, the organization of producers, consumers/workers, and government. It is a regional variation of the western capitalist political economy stemming from its historic circumstances and geographic location on the northwest edge of North America. The economic geography of the inner core and outer periphery are shown in Figures 10.4 and 10.5 and outlined below.

- the *core* of urbanized settlement is focused in the southwest on the Vancouver, Nanaimo, Victoria triangle, with the three centres initially growing as resource processing foci exploiting the advantage of the deep natural harbours, then evolving higher-order service functions, with Vancouver emerging as the economic hub and Victoria designated as the provincial capital. Vancouver, and then Victoria, developed metropolitan characteristics. Second level cores evolved in the south central Interior-Okanagan (Kelowna), Kamloops, Prince George, and the port towns of Nanaimo and Prince Rupert. The metro regions of the southwest are the dynamo of the province.

- a *periphery* of low population with small, mainly "company towns," where the chief activity is resource extraction and primary processing of raw materials—Powell River (pulp), Trail (base metals), Alberni (pulp). Some centres evolved as transportation nodes, favourably located at route junctions, which often predated the resource extraction/processing activity (e.g., Kamloops). Whistler is atypical in that the resource is the attractiveness of the mountains for winter skiing and summer hiking. Along the outer coast, parts of the inner coast, and in some riverside locations in the Interior are small, mainly First Nations settlements of considerable antiquity, where the focus is on a (frequently declining) fishing industry and small-scale logging operations. Many would assert that modern capitalism has erased their traditional, pre-capitalist subsistence ways; others show that much survives (Kennedy and Bouchard, 1983). Treaty agreements may herald a new era in First Nations' economic sufficiency; the traditional reality is that many young First Nations people drifted to the cities looking for work, but unfortunately with few skills for urban occupations.

- a well-developed transportation *infrastructure* that, despite rugged terrain and occasionally extreme winter conditions, generally works efficiently, serving local, regional, continental, and international traffic, enabling Vancouver to be Canada's Pacific gateway.

Changes in the Urban System

The urban system is the outgrowth of more than a century of economic and administrative forces as BC evolved from a colonial trading outpost to a regional economy. Settlements were initiated as points of concentration where the raw materials of forest, mines, fisheries, and farm were assembled, together with a labour force and system of management to process logs, ores, salmon, beef, apples, and so on for export from the region. Gradually moulded onto this role were local then regional retail and service functions. In turn, this subsystem became integrated into the national and now global systems through company take-overs as, for example, national and international chain stores bought out local retail operations. After almost a century of growth, many urban centres have evolved internal economic and social differentiation. Further, the urban system is set within a national system that is itself undergoing substantial changes (Simmons, 1991). A detailed account of the historical evolution of the BC urban system is set out in the First Edition (Forward, 1987).

Cities in BC are varied in character and distinctive compared with the uniformity of cities in other regions of Canada. The range of physical settings and the more cosmopolitan and better-educated population give a greater individual variety. Since Forward's analysis in the late 1980s, further changes to the provincial urban system have occurred, brought about by varied rates of regional growth due to migration, an economic system in transition, and time/space convergence through technological changes in transportation and its associated linkages (Hutton, 1997; 1998). Variations in growth in the urban system between 1981 and 1998 are illustrated in Table 10.4. The aura of rapid growth around the metropolitan poles reflects the decentring processes of metropolitan economic transition and the high cost of land and housing in Vancouver and Victoria. In contrast, in the periphery there is a certain degree of stasis in other centres and stagnation in the southeast region.

Metropolitan Region

The dominant elements of the spatial economic geography of Greater Vancouver (i.e., the core metropolitan region) are illustrated in Figure 10.4, which details the main forms of land use and the activity foci, which generate employment, retail, and institutional services—interaction and hence traffic and circulation activity. Dominant elements are: the waterfront zones as areas of industrial activity for storing or processing raw materials for local use and/or for transhipment; the main residential areas associated with the core settlements of the original villages that grew into municipalities, and then suburbs. Mall construction from the late 1950s consolidated the suburban cores, but challenged the viability of the original village retail cores. Many of the latter have been recently redeveloped in order to give a more interesting and physically attractive appearance than the malls. Downtown Vancouver has retained and increased its role as the commercial and business centre through its increasing international status/activities, increased residential component and renovation/gentrification of inner areas. Regional and municipal planning policies have had a pronounced effect on this regional economic geography (see **Chapter 13**) to produce a vibrant core and metropolitan region (Wynn, 1992; Davis, 1997).

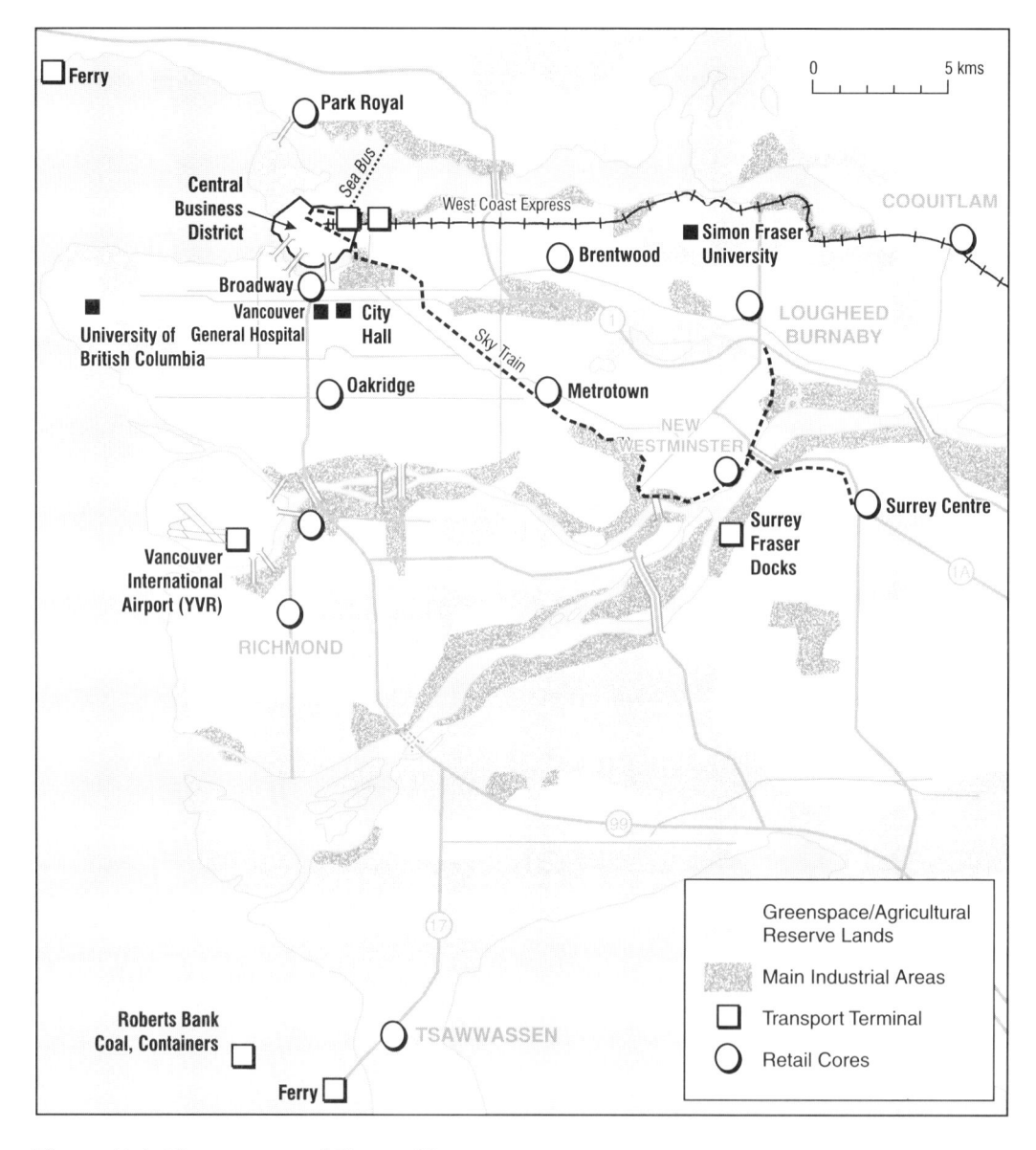

Figure 10.4 The core area of Greater Vancouver

TRANSPORTATION

BC's railways, highways, ferries, coastal freighters, barges, and airlines, see a constant movement of freight and passengers at the local, regional, continental, and global scales for the core area is a gateway and transhipment point to the continent (Figure 10.5). Pipelines and the electric power grid systems move energy from the Interior, the northeast, and Alberta to the south and southwest. Automobiles are the major form of transport for individuals and trucks for local and long distance, high value freight. In the metropolitan areas there are well developed transit systems that are expanding and improving the quality of service for commuting and regional travel. A well integrated transportation system is necessary for the development and effectiveness of an advanced economy; indeed, BC's way of life revolves

Spatial Economy

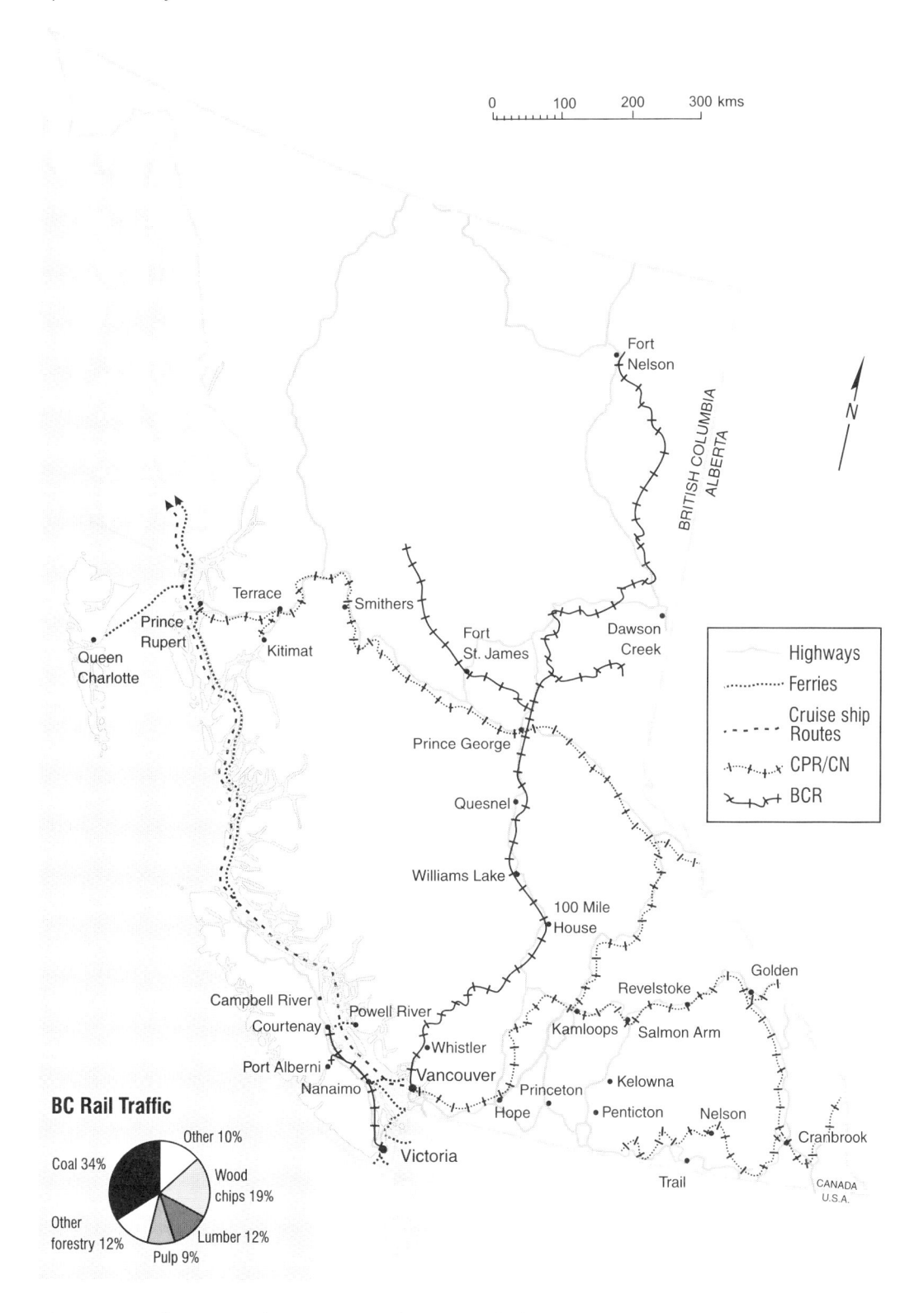

Figure 10.5 The main urban centres and transport linkages

around its diverse yet integrated transportation facilities. The southwest core is the hub of Western Canada and the Pacific "gateway" (Prince Rupert also) for continental, coastal, and local traffic. The sheltered, ice-free harbours and the safe movement of shipping along the inner coast help make Vancouver an ideal terminus and transfer point between land and sea and then air.

Shipping

The province's *raison d'être* derived from the global strength of the British navy and merchant fleet during the 19th century. Its protection and integration with the colonial commercial system made possible the emergence of a maritime economy oriented to both trans-oceanic and coastal links, a situation later reinforced through confederation and the transcontinental Canadian rail connection in the late 19th century, along with the construction of grain elevators by the 1920s. The rise to importance and export viability of the forest products industry is partly attributable to the cheap movement of raw materials along the coast using log booms and barges and ocean freighter loading facilities at coastal mills. Coastwise barge traffic is still an important medium for the movement of wood chips, construction aggregates, and fuel.

Vancouver, the main port for the region, is the busiest foreign tonnage port in Canada and one of the top three in North America for foreign cargo, handling annual freight of 70 million tonnes—20% of the Canadian total (1998 figures). Prince Rupert usually moves about 60 million tonnes, mainly wheat and coal exports, but will suffer as the Tumbler Ridge coal mines are closed. New container facilities at Roberts Bank, just a few kilometres south of Vancouver, are a marked improvement to the system in the face of fierce competition to be the first marine access point to western North America from Asia. Much of the original ownership, management, and security of port facilities was a federal jurisdiction. Recent federal "downloading" of these responsibilities has left some unresolved management issues in its wake.

Passenger traffic continues to increase, both on the provincially-owned ferry system and foreign-owned tourist cruise ships. Originally part of the CPR rail empire, the ferry system eventually became a provincial responsibility, again through the foresight and drive of WAC Bennett. Now one of the largest ferry fleets in the world, it transports 156 million passengers and 8 million vehicles annually (Table 10.5). Journalist Alan Fotheringham once wryly suggested that if guns were mounted on the fleet it could sink the Canadian navy in an afternoon (Royal Canadian Navy, Pacific Squadron 66,000 tonnes, fastest vessel top speed 28 knots; BC ferry fleet 190,000 tonnes, top speed of fastest vessel 35 knots); perhaps it could.

Although first generation vessels were expanded (stretched length and height) and new ferries purchased, the fleet suffers from the classic public utility conundrum of producing a sufficient profit to replace aging capital—the fleet and docks—yet providing a reasonably priced fare tariff (a ludicrous argument is that the system is an extension of the highways and should therefore be significantly subsidized from general revenues—or even free). It is politically attractive, whatever the party in office, to hold fare structures lower than is economically realistic. Main routes with high passenger/truck volumes run at a profit, while smaller, low volume, inter-island ferries run at a significant loss. A corporate-run (private) system answerable only to shareholders would have no hesitation in downsizing timetables and eliminating some runs completely.

Ocean cruising is one of the fastest growing sectors of the tourist industry, with Vancouver emerging as the main "gateway" port on the Alaskan summer cruise route, with close to 900,000 passengers in 1998, having the link advantage with Vancouver airport.

Railways

The rugged terrain with its mountains, canyons, lakes, and deeply-indented coastline has challenged generations of engineers and construction workers as ribbons of steel were laid in BC. Three rail companies—CPR, CN, and

Table 10.4 Average population and rank of cities by periods and 1996

Rank	1870–1891	1901–1921	1931–1951	1961–1981	1996
1	Victoria 11,900	Vancouver 146,000	Vancouver 420,600	Vancouver 1,059,100	Vancouver 1,831,600
2	Vancouver 8,300	Victoria 37,300	Victoria 79,500	Victoria 195,000	Victoria 304,000
3	Nanaimo 3,600	Nanaimo 6,200	Trail 13,200	Prince George 45,800	Abbotsford 136,000
4		Prince Rupert 5,300	Chilliwack 13,000	Kelowna 44,800	Kelowna 136,000
5		Trail 5,200	Abbotsford 11,900	Kamloops 43,900	Kamloops 85,000
6		Kamloops 4,100	Powell River 7,800	Nanaimo 41,100	Nanaimo 85,000
7		Chilliwack 3,300	Kamloops 7,400	Abbotsford 35,400	Prince George 75,000
8		Vernon 3,200	Prince Rupert 7,200	Chilliwack 33,900	Chilliwack 66,000
9		Fernie 3,000	Penticton 7,000	Port Alberni 26,600	Courtenay 55,000
10		Cranbrook 2,900	Port Alberni 6,900	Vernon 21,900	Vernon 55,000
11		Revelstoke 2,500	Nanaimo 6,900	Courtenay 20,500	Penticton 41,000
12		Ladysmith 2,200	Nelson 6,300	Trail 19,500	Williams Lake 38,000
13		Kelowna 2,100	Kelowna 6,300	Penticton 18,400	Duncan 36,000
14		Courtenay 1,600	Vernon 6,100	Prince Rupert 16,000	Campbell River 35,000
15		Grand Forks 1,400	Ocean Falls 4,500	Powell River 14,500	Mission 32,000
16		Merritt 1,000	Cranbrook 3,100	Terrace 12,000	Port Alberni 27,000
17			Prince George 3,100	Cranbrook 12,000	Quesnel 25,300
18			Courtenay 3,000	Dawson Creek 11,900	Terrace 20,000
19			Mission 2,800	Mission 11,900	Powell River 20,000
20			Summerland 2,800	Kitimat 10,900	Cranbrook 19,000
21			Fernie 2,600	Campbell River 9,900	Prince Rupert 17,000
22			Revelstoke 2,600	Fort St. John 8,900	Salmon Arm 16,000
23			Duncan 2,300	Nelson 8,500	Fort St. John 15,000
24			Dawson Creek 2,100	Salmon Arm 7,500	Kitimat 12,000
25			Spallumcheen 1,900	Kimberley 7,000	Dawson Creek 11,000
26			Ladysmith 1,700	Quesnel 6,400	Summerland 11,000
27			Salmon Arm 1,700	Castlegar 6,100	Nelson 9,700
28			Grand Forks 1,400	Squamish 6,000	Whistler* 9,200
29			Creston 1,400	Summerland 5,800	Merritt 7,800
30			Merritt 1,200	Williams Lake 4,900	Kimberley 7,000

Note: Populations are rounded to the nearest hundred and a city had to be listed in at least two of the three census years to be included (totals are census agglomerations). * designated a "resort municipality" in 1975.

Sources: Censuses of Canada 1871–1981; 1996.

BC Rail—operate close to 7,000 km of track in the province. The development of these rail systems is inextricably tied to most of the history and much of the current economy of BC (Forward, 1987; Johnston, 1996). After the speculative overbuilding in the early part of this century, the system has been pruned down and now mainly moves freight from the Interior of BC and from central and eastern Canada to the ports and vice versa. BC Rail, with 2,314 km of track, moves freight from the Interior to the coast. Originally the Pacific Great Eastern (a British-owned subsidiary), it was acquired outright by the province in 1918, saving it from financial collapse; it also owns and operates wharves and port loading facilities and is the fourth largest rail system in Canada (Garden, 1995; Wedley, 1998). The opening of the northeast coalfield at Tumbler Ridge (Figure 10.5) in the 1980s to exploit the high grade metallurgical coal, mainly for export to Asian markets, necessitated a new rail line and considerable infrastructure. It was probably the most extensive addition to the North American rail system since the early 20th century. Much of this section might be mothballed as the coal mines are closing operations. As unit trains for coal movement have become heavier and faster, upgrading the tracks has been an almost continuous process. The composition of freight for BC rail is shown in Figure 10.5.

The increase in freight movement was paralleled until recently by the disappearance (save for a few transcontinental trains, a daily run on Vancouver Island's Esquimalt and Nanaimo Railway, and a daily service on the BC Railway between Vancouver and Prince George) of passenger traffic due to air and bus competition. As a rule, rail companies prefer not to have mixed traffic, especially since large sections of their systems are single tracks and are more conducive and profitable for unit and container freight trains. A revival of rail transport in the 1980s in the metro areas with the construction of SkyTrain rapid transit in Greater Vancouver (now undergoing expansion), and then the West Coast Express commuter service between Abbotsford and Vancouver in the 1990s suggests a significant future for this form of travel given the rising cost of gas and increasing air pollution concerns in the Fraser Valley. The metro rail systems built early this century could not compete with the rapid expansion of automobiles, buses, and new roads in the 1930s, so passenger services were abandoned. The daily passenger rail service between Vancouver and Seattle, now revived and upgraded, indicates renewed interest in this form of long distance travel. Recently there have been media reports that CN is probably merging with US rail interests to form a continental rail corporation, which would impact on BC.

Table 10.5 BC ferry fleet (1999)

Type (number of vessels)	Year built	Length (m)	Gross tonnes	Passenger capacity	Vehicle capacity	Service speed (knots)
Spirit class (2)	1993-4	168	18,790	2,100	470	19.5
Queen of the North (1)	1969	125	8,889	800	157	22
Queens – large (4)	1962-4	130	8,700-9,350	1,340-70	286-376	19-21
Queens – mid (6)	1964-81	130-39	4,500-7,000	1,170-1,465	192-362	16-19
Queens – small (6)	1960-92	96-115	2,856-5,864	389-989	80-138	14-18
Other mid-size (6)	1965-1982	74-84	1,100-1,400	394-450	50-70	12-14
Other small (12)	1956-1975	13-60	21-841	38-293	0-49	8.5-20
Total: 37 vessels – 190,000 tonnes						

Source: BC Ferries Corporation website, *http://bcferries.com*.

Vehicles and Roads

There are now more than 2 million vehicles registered in BC, with a ratio of approximately 63% automobiles to 36% trucks/commercial (the Canadian average is about 75-25); almost 50% of autos are registered in the Vancouver region (Stats Canada, 1997). A recent transportation survey conducted in Saanich, a large suburb in the Victoria Capital Regional District that is perhaps typical of metropolitan areas in BC, showed that 83% of respondents used autos most frequently for travel, with "convenience" listed as the primary consideration (CRD Trends, 1999). The survey shows that despite the very good transit system in Greater Victoria, a majority still prefer to use automobiles. However, a comparison between Vancouver and Seattle of average commuting distance (11 vs 15 km respectively) can be attributed partly to Vancouver's more compact urban form (due in part to the ALR) and better transit system for commuting (Murray, 1991). This suggests that, while there is a long way to go in terms of improving matters of energy efficiency, pollution, and so on in the province, urban governments have made more progress here than many North American cities in terms of sprawl management and its consequences (Bula and Ward, 2000). There are, however, many problems associated with our desire for rapid, comfortable personal mobility. Transportation is a major, ongoing issue (congestion, travel times, safety, air pollution, cost) in the metropolitan regions of BC, with planning initiatives currently underway at the regional district and municipal planning levels (see **Chapter 13**). For example, in the safety category, traffic fatalities in the 1990s averaged 600 per year, with 50,000 injured. Estimates of the total cost of each fatality alone are $1.3 million. Aggressive government and police actions in the late 1990s reduced the accident rate by several percentage points even though the population is increasing (BC Auditor General, 1997).

While there are still large areas of BC without paved roads, most of the province, especially in the south, is well served with good highways of which 42,000 km are paved and 39,000 km unpaved, plus 2,691 bridges (1999). As with the rail system, there is constant upgrading of the road infrastructure responding to the growing economy. There is a 5% annual increase in the provincial trucking industry and expanding tourism/leisure traffic. Unlike other forms of transportation, which are monopolized by a few large private and government corporations, the trucking business has a large number of independent truck companies.

Air

Air passenger and freight traffic grew rapidly from the late 1950s as flight technology and airplane size developed, ushering in the age of mass air travel. It was prompted also by the sheer size of BC and Canada and the relatively high incomes in BC to pay for this form of travel. Vancouver (YVR) is the main air traffic centre or "hub" for northwest North America. It handles local, regional, continental, and trans-Pacific (Asia) and trans-polar (Europe) traffic. Victoria (YYJ) is more of a regional hub, but handles some continental and international regular and charter traffic (Table 10.6).

Table 10.6 Traffic growth at Vancouver and Victoria airports

	Passengers (millions) 1999 (1992)	Freight (kg) 1999 (1992)
Vancouver	9.9 (5.8)	260,000 (144,000)
Victoria	1.8 (.68)	n/a

Source: Vancouver and Victoria airport authorities

It is probable that Vancouver airport injects between $1.5 and $2.0 billion into the Lower Mainland economy annually. Much can be accounted for by the growth of Vancouver as an international gateway. Recent boosts to YVR have come from: tourism through "open jaw" tickets for the Rocky Mountains experience; as a connection for the Alaska cruise ship runs; as a hub for the winter ski packages; and due to "open skies" policies in the US that deregulated carrier access to/from that country.[12]

Transition

Many of the changing features of BC's economic geography clearly indicate the impact of global and continental conditions that will continue to reshape and restructure both Vancouver's role in the regional economy and the evolving socio-political dynamic of BC as a whole (Barnes and Hayter, 1997). The main features and trends are indicated in Table 10.7, where the economic dominance of the southwest *core* is readily apparent. Resource extraction, while still important, is being overtaken by activities such as finance, commerce, tourism (see **Chapter 12**), high technology, and film production.

In contrast, for many small, single-enterprise towns in the *periphery*, reduced labour demands in the forest industry through automation, and for many coastal villages the closures in the fisheries, pose serious problems for their economic survival. These communities are working hard to explore initiatives with fish farms, tourism, ski resorts, private universities, and retirement subdivisions to name a few (Reed and Gill, 1997; Halseth, 1999). The creation of a new university in Prince George appears to be a successful growth pole strategy that might be emulated in other parts of the province with other service industries. The major indicators of system restructure are highlighted in Table 10.7.

Several authors have reported that growth in the Vancouver metropolitan region is driven by an expanding population, influx of capital, and the expansion of service activities, especially high tech and media. Vancouver's employment has grown at the rate of 5% per year, compared with 2.5% for Toronto and 1.9% for Montreal (Hutton, 1998). Clearly, the region is moving away from a dependence on the rest of the province for much of its economic activity. High tech and film production are two examples of the activities which require technical skill and ingenuity, certain kinds of venture capital, and which entail participation in the global market place. The central role of tourism in the BC economy, an activity that is often an important element in the forms of transition taking place in many economies, is discussed in **Chapter 12**.

High Tech

By 2000 there were more than 52,000 people (3.5% of the workforce) employed in the *high tech* sector, with a service to manufacturing sector ratio of 75% to 25%. Approximately 65% is

Table 10.7 Indicators of transition in the BC and Vancouver spatial economies

Feature	BC	Vancouver
Global integration	High % exports	Gateway function
Service economy	Service 76% employment Service exports	Transaction/innovation
Urban change	Growth in Fraser Valley towns as spin off and commuting centres	Decentring/multinucleation
Urban decline	Small, single enterprise towns Search for alternative economic base	Less dependency on periphery
Urban restructure	Urban periphery malls	Redevelopment of CBD

(based partly on Hutton 1998, Halseth 1999)

concentrated in Vancouver. Services can range from producing specialized software, computerized design, to medical diagnosis; manufacturing high tech can range from advanced, fuel cell systems (Ballard Systems) to global positioning beacon systems (Table 10.8).

Table 10.8 High tech employment

	Percentage of high tech workforce
Information technology products	30
Information technology services	18
Communications technology	15
Manufacturing (various)	9
Medical/life sciences	8
New media	5
Other	15

Source: Boei and Fong (2000).

Case Study

Founded in 1969, MacDonald Dettwiler Associates (MDA) employs approximately 1,700 in Richmond, a suburb of Vancouver. Its focus originated in spatial graphics and software development associated with satellite imaging systems and remote-sensed data. The company was bought by Orbital Sciences (US) in 1995. In 1999, its revenues were about $298 million, with net earnings of $13 million. MDA now presents itself as an information corporation. It sells BC government data under contract and provides a substantial range of information products from radar imaging systems to communication systems for police and firefighters (Boei, 2000).

Film

Close to $1 billion of production took place in "Hollywood North" in 1999. There were more than 100 productions in different parts of the province, with a concentration in the Lower Mainland and Vancouver Island, underscoring the rate of growth (BC official growth rate estimate is about 21% per year) that is occurring in all sectors of the film industry and the pool of technical and support services now available in BC. It is estimated that, on average, a "shoot" spends $7 million and employs 113 people (BC Ministry of Finance and Corporate Relations, 1999). The relatively high labour input means that there is a strong local multiplier effect in the regional economy. While the attractions of the scenic and diverse natural and urban environments are part of the draw for American film makers, the cheapness of the Canadian dollar is also undeniable. To reinforce the emergence of a long term basis to the film industry, the BC government has supported studio expansion and initiated a film tax credit on labour costs for provincially-based companies. These developments also encouraged local skill development in several areas, such as animation production.

CONCLUSIONS

BC is a provincial jurisdiction physically and economically larger than many national states, where the majority of the relatively small population enjoy a level of income higher than the national average. The traditional basis of the province's prosperity is almost exclusively from the exploitation of the abundant wealth of natural resources. These activities still contribute significantly to the economy, but constitute a declining share of total output and employment. It is a serious mistake, however, to believe that the resource economy is no longer important. As other chapters describe, despite there being some issues associated with the continued sustainability of the resources sector, in the long run it will continue to be important in a world using resources faster than it is renewing them; this means that some of BC's fiscal problems associated with poor revenues from the resources sector are temporary. Nonetheless, in the face of fickle international markets, diversification is a sensible strategy for survival and prosperity. The higher standards of environmental quality that are now expected and required, while adding to the processing costs of resource corporations and their global competitiveness, maintain and enhance the ambient qualities of BC. The high quality of the environment and lifestyle are factors that attract, for example, tourism, high tech, and retirees.

Through a variety of circumstances, BC has survived the most extreme impacts of the economic restructuring of the late 20th century through greater diversification, immigration of young people and capital from Hong Kong and eastern Canada, and investment in research and education. The natural environment is a great attraction. The stability of Canada and BC attracts investment. **The population and area possess all the attributes that are indicative of a high quality of life for the majority and for the future.** The *factor conditions* for generating prosperity are present (Porter, 1990). The recurring problem of the economic and social geography of BC—congestion in the core and stagnation in the periphery—stems from rapid, concentrated growth. Achieving a balance between economic growth and the quality of life is the challenge for the new millennium. **Spreading the benefits to the smaller, single enterprise communities is part of this challenge.**

The economy of BC is unusual in the degree of provincial government ownership and participation. This has prevented undue levels of profit outflow and foreign control, but has mitigated against innovation. Some forms of privatization might be beneficial. The predilection for government megaprojects and their dubious benefits may be over. Political groups appear not to be tempted (so far) to sell off public assets in order to reduce long term debt. If they are placed on the open market, or *privatized*, it is likely that only American, Japanese, or European-based multi-national corporations would have the capital to purchase them. The radical reorganization of the New Zealand economy in the 1980s ("rogernomics") is the closest example that is relevant, given that New Zealand's economy is about the same size as BC's (Kelsey, 1995). The business class in BC generally eulogize the changes in New Zealand, suggesting that this is *the* direction for BC's political economy. While there are many benefits to be derived from increased competition, when driven by ideology rather than common sense, as in the case of both the UK and the US, it can materially increase the polarization between income groups, rather than trickle down wealth. Similarly, an economy managed by a socialist ideology can drive out initiative and wealth creation. Clearly, the challenge lies in finding the appropriate mix that leads to cooperation between the major stakeholders in the economy to develop strategies for economic resilience and enhancing the relatively high standard of living, and between welcoming foreign investment/immigration and having one's assets stripped at give-away prices. Government, and hence, public ownership and control of many assets is a major reason much of BC's wealth circulates in BC.

REFERENCES

Allen, R.C. (1986). The BC economy: Past, present, future. In R.C. Allen and G. Rosenbluth (Eds.), *Restraining the economy* (pp. 9-42). Vancouver, BC: Economic Policy Institute.

Barnes, T., and Hayter, R. (Eds.) (1997). *Troubles in the rain forest*. Victoria, BC: University of Victoria, Department of Geography, Western Geographical Series, Vol. 33.

Boei, W. (2000). MDA heads into muddy IPO waters. *Vancouver Sun*, May 31.

Boei, W., and Fong, P. (2000). High tech industry rolling in BC. *Vancouver Sun*, August 4, pp. A1-A2.

BC (1999). Status Report: BC Economic Plan (1998-2001). Victoria, BC.

BC Auditor General (1997). Trucking Safety Report. Victoria, BC: Office of the Auditor General.

BC Ministry of Finance and Corporate Relations (1999). *Financial Economic Review* (Annual), Volumes 56-59: 1996-1999. Victoria, BC: Ministry of Finance and Corporate Relations.

Bula, F., and Ward, D. (2000). How we became the world's laboratory. *Vancouver Sun*, March 4, pp. A8-A9.

Capital Regional District (1999). *Trends*, 16(2). Victoria, BC: CRD.

Davis, C. (Ed.) (1997). *The Greater Vancouver book*. Vancouver: Linkman Press.

Davis, H.C., and Hutton, T. (1992). *Structural change in the British Columbia economy: Regional diversification and metropolitan transition*. Prepared for the Economy Core Group, BC Round Table on the Environment and the Economy. Victoria, BC.

Dobialas, G. (1996). The Canadian financial system in international perspective. In J.N.H. Britton (Ed.), *Canada and the global economy* (pp. 84-100). Montreal: McGill/Queens University Press.

Dyck, I. (1989). Interpreting home and wage workplace: Women's daily living in a Canadian suburb. *Canadian Geographer*, 33(4), 329-341.

Fisher, R., and Mitchell, D.J. (1996). Patterns of provincial politics since 1916. In H.J. Johnston (Ed.), *The Pacific province* (pp. 254-273). Vancouver: Douglas & McIntyre.

Forward, C.N. (1987). Urban system. In C.N. Forward (Ed.), *British Columbia: Its resources and people* (pp. 359-379). Victoria, BC: University of Victoria, Department of Geography, Western Geographical Series, Vol. 22.

Garden, J. (1995). *British Columbia Railway*. Revelstoke, BC: Footprint Publications.

Halseth, G. (1999). We came to look for work: Situating employment migration in BC's small resource-based communities. *Canadian Geographer*, 43(4), 363-381.

Hayter, R. (1996). Technological imperatives in resource sectors. In J.N.H. Britton (Ed.), *Canada and the global economy* (pp. 101-122). Montreal: McGill/Queens University Press.

Hayter, R., and Barnes, T. (1990). Innis staple theory, exports and recession: BC 1981-1986. *Economic Geography*, 66, 156-173.

Hutton, T.A. (1997). The Innisian core-periphery revisited. *BC Studies*, 113, 69-98.

Hutton, T.A. (1998). *The transformation of Canada's Pacific metropolis*. Montreal: Institute for Research on Public Policy.

Johnston, H.J. (Ed.) (1996). *The Pacific province: A history of BC*. Vancouver, BC: Douglas & McIntyre.

Kelsey, J. (1995). *The New Zealand experiment: A world model for structural adjustment?* Auckland: Auckland University Press.

Kennedy, D., and Bouchard, R. (1983). *Sliammon life, Sliammon lands*. Vancouver, BC: Talon Books.

Lipset, S.M. (1990). *Continental Divide*. New York: Routledge.

Malecki, E.J. (1991). *Technology and economic development*. New York: Wiley.

Mather, C. (1993). Flexible technology in the clothing industry: Some evidence from Vancouver. *Canadian Geographer*, 37, 40-47.

Matthews, R. (1983). *The creation of regional dependency*. Toronto: University of Toronto Press.

Murray, P. (1991). *Transportation and urban form: A comparison of Seattle and Vancouver*. Honours Thesis, Department of Geography, University of Victoria, Victoria, BC.

North, R., and Hardwick, W. (1992). Vancouver since the Second World War: An economic geography. In G. Wynn and T. Oke (Eds.), *Vancouver and its region* (pp. 200-233). Vancouver, BC: UBC Press.

Porter, M.E. (1990). *The competitive advantage of nations*. New York: Free Press.

Reed, M., and Gill, A. (1997). Community economic development in a rapid growth setting: A case study of Squamish BC. In T. Barnes and R. Hayter (Eds.), *Troubles in the rainforest* (pp. 263-285). Victoria, BC: University of Victoria, Department of Geography, Western Geographical Series, Vol. 33.

Rees, K., and Hayter, R. (1996). Flexible specialisation, uncertainty and the firm: Enterprise strategies in the wood remanufacturing industry of the Vancouver Metropolitan Area, British Columbia. *Canadian Geographer*, 40(3), 203-218.

Savoie, D. (1992). *Regional economic development*. Toronto: University of Toronto Press.

Seager, A. (1996). The resource economy, 1871-1921. In H.J. Johnston (Ed.), *The Pacific province: A history of BC* (pp. 205-252). Vancouver/Toronto: Douglas & McIntyre.

Simmons, J. (1991). The urban system. In T. Bunting and P. Filion (Eds.), *Canadian cities in transition* (pp. 100-124). Toronto: Oxford University Press.

Statistics Canada (1997). *Road motor vehicles: Registrations*. Ottawa.

Warburton, R., and Coburn, D. (Eds.) (1988). *Workers, capital and the State in British Columbia*. Vancouver: UBC Press.

Wedley, J.R. (1998). A development tool: W.A.C. Bennett and the P.G.E. railway. *BC Studies*, 117, 29-50.

White, J. (1999). *Working less for more jobs*. Vancouver: Communications, Energy and Paperworkers Union.

Wynn, G. (1992). The rise of Vancouver. In G. Wynn and T. Oke (Eds.), *Vancouver and its region* (pp. 69-148). Vancouver: UBC Press.

ENDNOTES

1. The first wave of provincial public ownership of utilities was in the early 20th century (Ontario Hydro) slowly followed by other provincial governments (1950s) who also realized their revenue and export potential. Post-W.A.C. Bennett projects: Northeast coal $3 billion (1980-90); Expo $1 billion (1986); Coquihalla $1 billion (1985); SkyTrain $1 billion (first phase 1980s); Fast ferries $.45 billion (1998).

2. Federal centres in BC also contribute to research on: agriculture; forests; geoscience; and astronomy.

3. The federal government has a long history of regional development projects aimed at the have-not regions, the merits of which have been much debated (Matthews, 1983; Savoie, 1992).

4. The relative decline in resources and federal transfer revenues has led to the search for other sources such as gaming—which may incur increased social costs. The main order of expenditures are similar for most provinces.

5. National fiscal policies generally tend to favour core areas of jurisdictions (i.e., central Canada).

6. While priding itself on helping developing countries, the developed world is also taking many immigrants who are essential to the development of less developed countries, thereby exacerbating their problems.

7. Regional economic theory and concepts like *growth poles* have often been misused through misunderstanding and political largesse.

8. The contribution of women (home/family/rearing the next generation) is grossly underrepresented in official accounting systems (Dyck, 1989).

9. Trade unions have responded by trying to unionize the notoriously difficult service sector companies. Many are US-owned with anti-union policies.

10. Average house prices May 2000 and (increase in the previous 12 months): Vancouver - $301,000 (8%); Calgary - $173,000 (5%); Winnipeg - $88,000 (0%); Toronto - $228,000 (5%); Montreal - $123,000 (2%); Halifax - $126,000 (6%) (*CMHC Housing Facts*, 5(5), 4). House prices in Vancouver clearly reflect the impact of the concentration of immigration and migration.

11. Vancouver Airport employs more people in one place, but they have several different employers.

12. While this section focuses on the large commercial carriers, much of the recent development of BC and the continuing survival of small communities relies on the small companies using float planes.

ADDENDUM

The new provincial Liberal government (2001) is faced with decreased revenues and increased operating costs. A policy of program and job reduction is under way.

Land Recreation

Bruce Downie

PRP Incorporated, Victoria, BC

INTRODUCTION

The importance of outdoor recreation in modern society makes British Columbia both a valued place to live for residents throughout the province and a desirable destination for those from elsewhere in Canada and around the world. The diversity of BC's outdoor recreational opportunities can satisfy almost any interest and the quality of the experience ranks highly amongst other locations.

This chapter provides an overview of land-based outdoor recreation in BC, identifying specifically its significant characteristics and directions for the future. This broad task begins with the development of a framework for outdoor recreational activities according to their fundamental determinants. A second aspect of the context for understanding outdoor recreation in this province will be a review of the major providers of recreational opportunities. Finally, some trends in outdoor recreation will be identified which point the direction for planning and development for the future.

AN OUTDOOR RECREATION ACTIVITY FRAMEWORK FOR BC

Relationship of Recreation to Landscape and Climate

The province's diversity in outdoor recreation stems from its varied landscape and climate. The nature of the landscape is a major determinant in the range of potential recreational activities. High mountain peaks and valleys, coastal wetlands, broad lowland valley bottoms, lakes and rivers, rolling plateau, and open prairie all contribute to the extensive recreational opportunities this province offers.

There are other dimensions to this diverse landscape that also add to its recreation potential: the biological variety and abundance of plants and animals; the remoteness and feeling of wilderness over such large areas; and the rich cultural heritage of the people. This richness of diversity creates some remarkable recreational settings (Peepre, 1994).

Variations in climate also widen the spectrum of available outdoor recreation activities. Major seasonal changes provide both summer and winter activities. Types and amounts of precipitation in both seasons also affect the nature of the recreational environment. Dry conditions improve useability, while wet environments raise water levels or snow accumulations.

Landscape and climate also have a significant effect on recreation in BC because of their dominant influence on settlement and development in general. Facilities and access are key aspects of the nature and extent of outdoor recreation. The mountainous landscape of much of the province has influenced all forms of development, so much so that large portions are inaccessible by road and therefore limited in the amount and type of recreation that takes place there. Thus wilderness activity opportunities are plentiful over most areas of the province, yet access to them is more limited (Figure 11.1).

Recreation Framework–Season–Activity

A number of other determinants can be identified that provide a framework for recreational activities. Of greatest significance are differences based on the level of facility requirements and on whether it is a short-term day time or an extended overnight activity. An organizing framework for recreation activities is illustrated in Table 11.1. Other factors, such as whether pursuits are passive or active, may distinguish one from another, but are not thought to contribute significantly to the presentation of an overall framework.

Examples within the framework are discussed below. They illustrate the nature of the relationship between the framework factors and the patterns of recreational activity experienced in the province. They also highlight the nature and significance of the economic impact of the outdoor recreation industry.

Facilities Based - Winter - Skiing/Snowboarding

There is no question that skiing and snowboarding are a prominent factor in BC's recreation appeal (Figure 11.1). The province's landscape offers ample opportunity for these activities. High mountain ranges oriented north-south across the prevailing winds provide good slope conditions with high snowfall accumulations. Moderate temperatures, especially in coastal and most southern areas of the province, allow comfortable conditions for recreation. Cross-country skiing takes advantage of the more undulating terrain and requires good, although not as heavy, snowfall accumulations, and also benefits from comfortable temperature ranges. Downhill ski resorts also provide cross-country trail areas. The plateau areas of the Interior offer excellent cross-country ski conditions at the numerous facilities in the region (Nordic Group International, 1988). Heli-skiing and ski-touring, the backcountry versions of the facility-based activities discussed here, are also well suited to the province's mountainous landscape and enjoy extensive participation.

Locations for downhill skiing and snowboarding are not determined only on the basis of natural conditions, but also on the ability to provide facilities and access to the area. Facilities are typically privately owned, although the land base, while often also privately owned, is in some cases held under lease agreement from Crown Lands. In some instances these are within provincial parks (e.g., Cypress, Seymour, and Manning provincial parks) with some very controversial results (Steig, 1997).

The largest and most successful resort areas are situated in close proximity to major population areas and provide easy road access to a large complex of on-site facilities. In return, such developments generate significant economic benefits for the adjacent community, particularly if it can respond positively to the opportunity (John Gow Consultants Ltd., 1987). The activity itself requires significant infrastructure support, and short winter days encourage a range of associated entertainment facilities for after ski hours.

The success of the Whistler ski resort is a remarkable example—growing from "nothing" to a resort village that offers more than 30 lifts, 36 hotels, 27,500 rental beds, 75 restaurants, 22 pubs/nightclubs, and 180 retail shops, and is consistently rated as the best ski resort in North America. In 1996, development and expansion projects costing $194 million were completed at Whistler Village. This development of ski resorts as "destination" vacation spots has resulted in increased numbers of residents, visitors, merchants, hospitality agencies, businesses, and investors expanding the breadth of facilities and services.[1]

An estimated 60 alpine ski areas operate in BC, 20 of which provide 95 percent of the business volume and activity. In 1996/97 the sector: generated more than 4.5 million skier days; reached estimated skier expenditures in excess of $500 million; provided 8,500 person years of employment; had resort assets of $400 million; and, had associated real estate assets of more than $2 billion (BC Ministry of Employment and Investment).

Cross-country ski trails have been developed and managed by public agencies, non-profit associations, clubs, and private sector operators. While many sites have been developed and maintained on private lands, a large portion of facilities exist on Crown Lands even though operations may be undertaken by an outside group (BC Ministry of Forests, 1994). This is becoming even more prevalent as public agencies encourage greater private sector

Table 11.1 Recreation Activities Framework

	Land Based				Water Based	
	Air	Facilities-based	Non-motorized	Motorized	River	Lake
Winter						
Day use	heli-skiing	downhill skiing cross-country skiing	spelunking snowshoeing cross-country skiing fishing/hunting	snowmobiling fishing/hunting		
Overnight use			camping ski-touring snowshoeing fishing/hunting	snowmobiling fishing/hunting		
Summer						
Day use	sky-diving ultralight hang-gliding	golfing cycling	walking hiking picnicking nature study horseback riding mountain biking rock climbing spelunking fishing/hunting	atv's fishing/hunting	swimming canoeing kayaking rafting tubing	swimming canoeing boating
Overnight use		cycle touring	backpacking nature study trail riding mountain biking mountain climbing fishing/hunting	fishing/hunting	canoeing kayaking rafting	canoeing boating

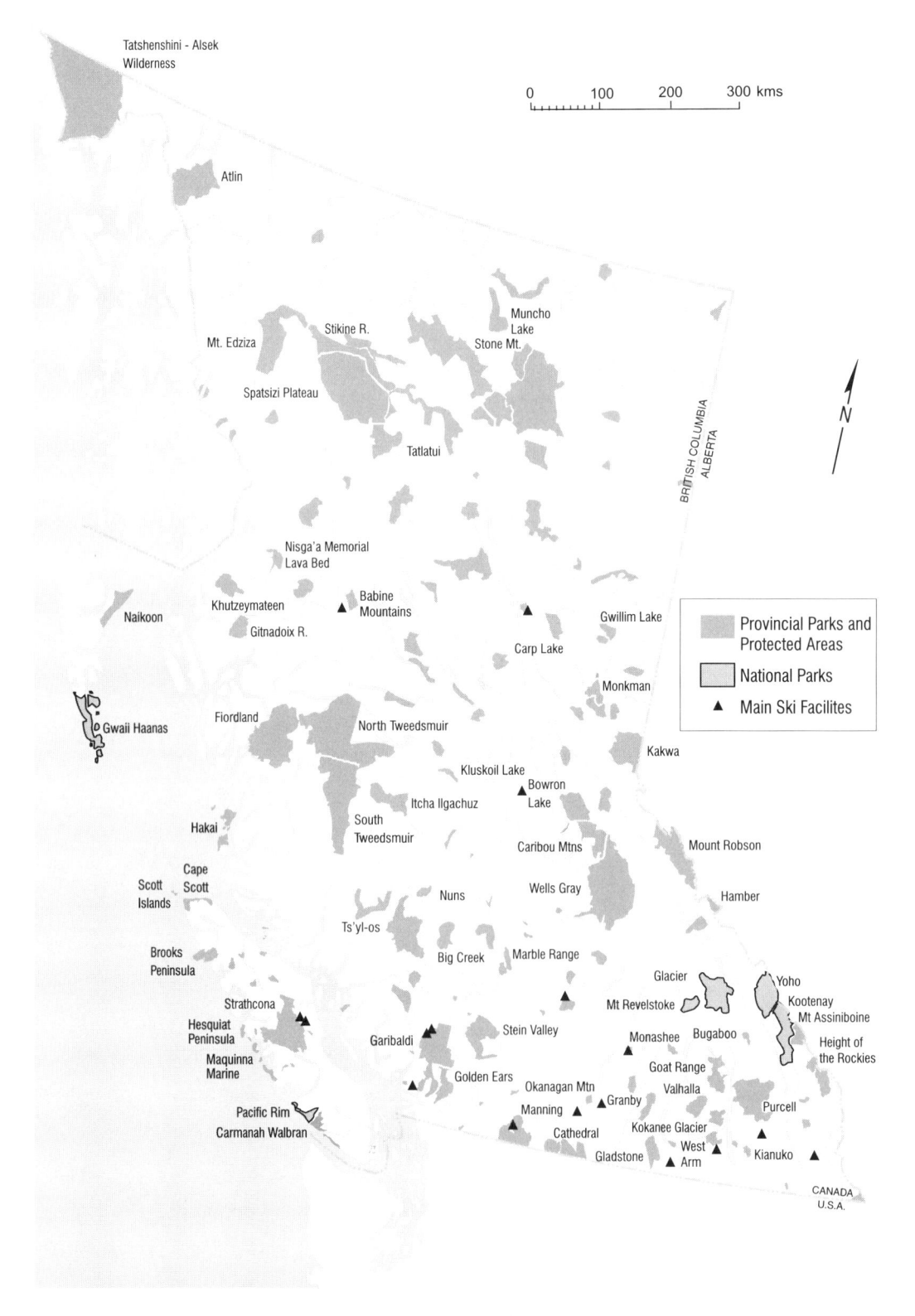

Figure 11.1 Ski facilities and national/provincial parks

and volunteer involvement in a wide variety of public services (Nordic Group International, 1988). Compared with downhill skiing facilities, cross-country ski areas do not have the same impact due to significantly reduced infrastructure requirements. Nevertheless, many cross-country ski areas are well developed and built with a full range of private sector service facilities, often in conjunction with downhill ski resorts both inside provincial parks (e.g., Manning Provincial Park) and outside (e.g., Whistler). Economic viability requires that such private facilities, if they are not tied to a major downhill ski resort, be linked to another year-round recreation resort or facility such as a guest ranch or hot spring resort (Nordic Group International, 1988).

Concentration of facilities is very closely related to the major population centres which are the market base for such operations. Lower Mainland users represent approximately 50% of the total cross-country skier visits at commercial facilities throughout the province, with the Cypress area alone accounting for nearly 33% of the total provincial use (Nordic Group International, 1988).

The demographic profile of participants in skiing largely fits with the perception of the general public. Downhill skiing/snowboarding is a young person's activity. The dominant age group for cross-country skiing, on the other hand, is definitely older and has much greater potential for expansion. Differences in survey categories make accurate comparisons difficult, but it appears that about half of BC's cross-country skiers are over 40 (much closer to the profile of the Canadian population), compared with almost 75% of downhill skiers being under 35 (Nordic Group International, 1988; Campbell Goodell Consultants Ltd., 1989). From an income perspective, downhill and cross-country skiers are comparable, indicating that income levels of downhill skiers are notably high considering their younger age and reportedly lower levels of education. The other noteworthy variation is gender. Male participation in downhill skiing is significantly higher, while participation rates in cross-country skiing are reportedly either about gender equal or dominated by women, depending upon the survey referenced (Nordic Group International, 1988; Campbell Goodell Consultants Ltd., 1989).

Accounting for an estimated 90% of the global market, BC is also the world leader in heli/snowcat skiing. The majority of the operations are based in the Rockies, the Columbia Valley, the Cariboo, or the South Coast. Growth has been dramatic. In the last decade total revenues from heli/snowcat skiing increased from $18 million to $72 million. The clientele is predominantly European (60%) and American (30%) (BC Ministry of Employment and Investment, 1999).

All told, recreational skiing in BC is a leading industry, especially considering its relationship to other tourism activities, both in the active winter season and a broader range of activities developed in mountain resort locations which are extensively used in the summer season as well.

Facilities Based – Summer – Golf

Golf is a facility-based recreational activity that is enjoying increasing popularity—its growth in BC has been significant over the past two decades and a large number of expansions and new course developments supported this demand (Pacific Analytics Inc., Strategic Concepts Inc., and The Tourism Research Group, 1993). The longer outdoor activity season on the west coast, along with major population concentrations, encourage a greater intensity of activity in the Lower Mainland and on Vancouver Island compared to other areas of the province, although the Okanagan and the Rocky Mountain Tourist Region also demonstrate a strong activity level. There are a number of reasons for this growth, especially within BC (International Sports Inc., 1993a). Golf is an appealing activity for older people, a very significant factor in BC's aging population, and is attractive to women as well as men. Recent estimates suggest that over 5 million Canadians play golf (20% of the population) and 15% of them reside in BC (Royal Canadian Golf Association, 1999).

Golf also appears to be relatively recession proof, appealing to a large and affluent market that exists both locally and internationally. The appeal of the activity is supported by BC's very attractive natural backdrop and the province is recognized by the PGA as a golf destination. In addition, golf courses contribute to green belt space in the urban context, thus improving the residential atmosphere in many communities. This can be a significant attraction for new business and industry to locate in a community.

However, there are also some significant constraints related to golf course development and activity (International Sports Inc., 1993a). Golfing has been perceived as an elitist activity with high participation costs that involves the affluent, white male population sector. In addition, golf courses consume a relatively large land area with low intensity of use on lands that typically have high use capacity, and there is no means whereby activity intensity can be increased on a given site. They also present some significant environmental challenges and impacts, especially related to habitat loss, water consumption, and introduction of fertilizers and biocides. As a result, new sites are difficult to locate and acquire to serve local demand. The tourist resort type of development has greater flexibility of location, although the tourism component of golfing activity still remains relatively low, estimated at about 13% (Pacific Analytics Inc. et al., 1993).[2]

Golf courses can be categorized into three groups: member-controlled, organized as non-profit societies; privately-owned, owned by an individual or corporation as profit-making ventures; or municipal, owned by the municipality for the benefit of taxpayers. Results of a 1990 survey indicated the scale of facility development, which had experienced a sharp rise over the previous three years responding to a high pent-up demand and was projected to continue significant growth over the next two decades. For example, in a later study, Vancouver Island alone was reported to have an additional 12 new golf course developments in the planning stages, two of which involve hotel and resort components (International Sports Inc., 1993).

Use levels and corresponding economic impacts of golf as a recreation and tourism activity in BC are very significant. In 1990 the total number of rounds played (18 hole equivalents) was 5,740,000, of which 770,000 (13.4%) were recognized as tourist participation. This translated into a total revenue in the golfing industry of $150 million, representing a growth rate of 45% during the period from 1987 to 1990 (Pacific Analytics Inc. et al., 1993).

Non-Motorized - Winter / Summer - Commercial Hunting

Like many jurisdictions, BC has a history, going back to the early part of this century, of requiring the services of licensed guide outfitters for non-resident hunters. In 1948, the practice of defined *Guiding Territories* replaced the gentleman's agreement approach to operating areas. Guiding Territories are legal entities managed by the Wildlife Branch, each having a range of associated management regulations, including reporting regulations, restrictions, and quotas. Resident hunting has priority over non-resident hunting; therefore, where availability of a certain species is limited, guide/outfitter allocations may be significantly impacted by resident hunter harvest.

Although guide/outfitter operations do include related activities such as sport fishing, trail riding, and wildlife viewing, 90% of their operations are directly related to hunting (DPA Group Inc., 1991). Game species, most of which are found in all guiding regions of the province (although variable in their concentration) include: deer, moose, elk, caribou, goat, sheep, grizzly bear, black bear, and cougar. Hunting seasons vary according to the specific animal, but the two main seasons are spring and fall. Typically, an outfitter's base camp is supplemented with one or more out-camps, accessible by air, boat, or horse.

A key element of BC's reputation as a premier location for big game hunting is the wilderness experience embodied in each client's visit. The province's extensive wilderness provides not only a rich wildlife resource, but also the experiential elements that are so essential to a visitor's appreciation of their trip. Guide outfitters are not just selling a hunt, but a complete experience. It is not surprising, therefore, that most of the issues facing guide outfitting in the province focus on these components: wildlife quotas; conflict with other users (e.g., resident hunters, other wilderness users); and impacts by resource activities (e.g., logging, mining, access roads) (DPA Group Inc., 1991a).

As might be expected, the demand, the length of the trip, and the associated costs of hunting trips are highly variable depending upon the species being sought, with deer and black bear being at the low end of the time/cost spectrum and sheep and grizzly being at the high end.[3] Survey results recorded that a total of 10,210 hunting clients were hosted by BC guide outfitters for a total of 72,200 hunter days (an average of 283 client days per operation), representing a total revenue of $22.1 million. The dominant client group are males (82%) between the ages of 35 and 54 (56%) from the US. It is also interesting to note that in the survey results, the average length of time the respondents had hunted was 31 years (DPA Group Inc., 1991).

In conjunction with commercial hunting, the same factors that make hunting an extremely attractive activity for non-residents also create extensive resident hunting activity. The system is managed through the Wildlife Branch of the Ministry of Enviroment, Lands and Parks and has a major impact both on recreational activity in the backcountry and on the provincial economy. Records for the 1999-2000 season show that about 435,000 resident and 17,000 non-resident hunting licences were issued.[4]

Non-Motorized – Summer – Ecotourism Nature / Adventure

The category 'Ecotourism Nature/Adventure' is very broad and includes many of the non-motorized summer activities listed in Table 11.1. Detailed data on individual activities are difficult to acquire, and combined data often include a range of other activities not specifically included in the assessment. Nevertheless, some general indicators are apparent. This subsector is a key component of the overall outdoor recreation sector within BC. Results of recent studies show the province to have enormous ecotourism potential and a very highly positive perception in the market place (HLA Consultants and the ARA Consulting Group, 1995).

The focus of this sector is on nature-related activities. Walking, hiking, and trekking figure prominently, along with canoeing and camping. While adventure components such as mountain biking and climbing are less significant in overall participation numbers due to the physical demands of the activity, their participation rates are increasing (HLA Consultants and the ARA Consulting Group, 1995). These activities are widely dispersed throughout the province, from urban and near-urban areas, including parks and coastal trails, to remote backcountry wilderness. The most significant factors determining types of participation are access and ability.

Ecotourism participants are typically 25 to 54 years of age, well educated, members of nature-related clubs or organizations, readers of nature-related magazines, and willing to spend significant amounts of money on this form of recreation or vacation. Their impact in BC is huge. It is estimated that of the 21.5 million overnight visitors in 1998, over half took part in land-based, outdoor recreation activities, contributing over $700 million to the provincial economy (Tourism BC, 1998; Tourism BC, 1999).

An Outdoor Recreation Administrative Framework For BC

Another important organizing structure that can help put the recreation spectrum in BC in its proper context is one illustrating the relationship among the providers of recreation opportunities. Providers of outdoor recreation are either public or private (Table 11.2). The Crown Land base available for recreation throughout the province is 82 million hectares—about 92% of the total area of the province (BC Ministry

Table 11.2 Recreation activity and/or facility providers

	Public sector	Private sector
Land	parks and protected areas lakes rivers Crown Land (e.g., provincial forests)	private land (e.g., ranches, cottages, resorts)
Services/Facilities	picnic areas campgrounds interpretive facilities trails (e.g., hiking, riding, cross-country skiing) backcountry shelters specific activity facilities (e.g., beach facilities, food concessions, equipment rentals)	accommodation (e.g., cabins, lodges, hotel/motel, camping) trails (e.g., hiking, riding, cross-country skiing) resorts specific activity facilities (e.g., skiing, guide outfitting areas)

of Environment, Lands and Parks, 1997). Of this Crown Land, approximately 84% is classified as Provincial Forest, 12% has Protected Area Status, and the remainder is in urban/industrial use (BC Ministry of Forests, 1994).

However, the degree of facility support and, therefore, the intensity with which such a land base is used for recreation is relatively low compared to that which the private sector provides in support of outdoor recreation opportunities. In particular, major facilities providing accommodation, access, and specific activity support for intensive use areas are commonly the role of the private sector and account for a significant segment of outdoor recreation activity in excess of the ratio reflected in land ownership. However, it should be noted that in many instances private sector facilities and services operate on Crown Land.

Public Providers: Parks

Parks are a major component of public lands dedicated to recreation activity. Less significant in terms of their overall size than other forms of Crown Land, they do not always have recreation as the primary goal of their land use dedication, but they are dominant in the public perception of recreation opportunities. Parks reflect jurisdictional differences depending on the level of government responsible. National, provincial, and regional park systems are well developed in BC and play a major role in the spectrum of recreation opportunities available to residents and visitors (Figure 11.1). While regional parks are less developed beyond the metropolitan regions, they are a critical component of the recreation opportunities for major population centres like the Lower Mainland and Victoria (Osborn, 1991; CRD Parks, 1992), and are becoming increasingly important in other centres, such as central Vancouver Island and the Okanagan.

Within every park system, regardless of the jurisdiction, there is a dual mandate of protection and recreation and a continuum of balancing the components of the mandate (BC Ministry of Environment, Lands and Parks, 1997; Canada, 1997; CRD Parks, 1999). Thus each authority has a responsibility to protect key resources and to provide opportunities for people to experience and enjoy those areas dedicated as parks. Although each one has a broad mandate, there is both a general emphasis and one that differs from one system to the next. National parks are envisioned as having a goal that is focused on *protection of the representative and unique natural features of the*

Canadian landscape with all public appreciation and recreation positioned secondarily to that focus. Provincial parks are increasingly moving toward a similar philosophical position (BC's Park Legacy Panel, 1999), although, in practice, current policy is dedicated to providing recreational opportunities with a balance between the conservation and recreation objectives within the mandate. In regional parks, recreation is widely acknowledged as a dominant objective; however, due to the nature of recreational activities the protection aspects are still strongly recognized.

National Parks

Recognizing the need for outdoor recreation opportunities to be consistent with maintaining ecological integrity, only those activities that promote appreciation of park resources while respecting ecosystem integrity are felt to be acceptable in national parks. Activities are assessed for their appropriateness with respect to both the system as a whole and to specific applications on an individual park basis. Mechanisms for adequately assessing recreation impact and activity suitability in parks have been developed in recent years in response to concern over ecosystem integrity (Payne and Graham, 1993; Parks Canada, 1994a, Parks Canada, 1994b).

National parks are intended to represent the 39 terrestrial natural regions of Canada as defined within the system plan. Seven of these regions are present in BC. Of these seven, four are represented by existing parks. Of the three remaining regions, two are entirely within BC and one is shared with the Yukon. Prospects for completion of the system are good in one region and low in the other two.

In spite of their small size (a combined total of 11,436.9 km^2), the six national parks in BC attract considerable visitor use, especially Pacific Rim National Park (Parks Canada, 1995). While use data does not necessarily exceed the other parks in the province, use of the Rocky Mountain parks is highly affected by the Trans Canada highway corridor and the attraction of Banff and Jasper. Users of Pacific Rim National Park are truly west coast destination oriented.

A number of significant issues face Parks Canada in BC. First, completing the system will be difficult due to several circumstances, including a high level of committed land in some key areas yet to be represented and arduous negotiating conditions with differences in attitudes toward national park establishment among key players (Canada, BC, and First Nations).[5]

Another major issue is reflected in the visitor data. High visitor use levels in relatively very small park areas put pressure on ecosystem integrity within the park. Pacific Rim Park already has a reservation system in its campgrounds and on the West Coast Trail. Both show significant signs of overuse, even under the reservation system (Parks Canada, 1994). The problem is compounded by developments within the park, such as the regional highway running through it, and extensive forest resource harvesting taking place around the edges. Such circumstances present situations where park areas appear incapable of sustaining the ecosystem they are attempting to represent (Theberge, 1993).

Provincial Parks

The protected areas system contains both parks defined under the *Parks Act* and other protected areas defined under the *Environment and Land Use Act*. In recent years efforts have been undertaken to expand the system through significant system planning inputs to the regional land use planning processes (Downie, 1997). The land use recommendations have resulted in establishment of many new protected areas. Since 1992, parks and protected areas have doubled to over 12% of the land base. This area includes the current total of 780 provincial parks, recreation areas, and ecological reserves.[6]

The parks system provides extensive visitor facilities and support services for recreational activity (representing a capital investment of $378 million) and in 1998 recorded a total of 26,262,000 park visits (BC Ministry of Environment, Lands and Parks, 1999, *http://www.elp.gov.bc.ca/bcparks/facts/stats.htm*). There is a wide variation both in park size and use. Highly used parks are those that focus on relatively intensive recreational activities and provide facility support, such as beach activity and camping (e.g., Rathtrevor, Cultus Lake, Bear Creek) or skiing (e.g., Cypress). Very high satisfaction ratings (94%) have been recorded in park user surveys, and visitors especially appreciate the 'sense of security,' 'cleanliness of restrooms,' and 'cleanliness of grounds' (BC Parks, 1990; BC Parks, 1996). Obviously, there is a very different user market taking advantage of a huge area of backcountry embraced in the park system where facilities are minimal or not provided and access is limited. As a comparison, visitor use in 1998 in the entire northern region of the province was recorded at about 2.7 million visits compared to the 6.4 million visits on Vancouver Island and 8.2 million visits in the Lower Mainland (BC Ministry of Environment, Lands and Parks, 1999, *http://www.elp.gov.bc.ca/bcparks/facts/stats.htm*).

The protected areas system also has a huge economic impact. Significant efforts have been made to understand and quantify that impact better. The Coopers and Lybrand study (1995) identified some important elements emerging (Note: the data used as the basis of the study was for 1993, at which time there were 407 provincial parks and 131 ecological reserves covering a combined area of 6.5 million hectares, or about 7% of the province; and number of visits totalling 22.8 million). First, the expenditures on parks totalled over $430 million (90% from park visitors), creating almost 10,000 jobs. This economic impact was distributed throughout the province, with 75% originating outside the Lower Mainland and Victoria. Secondly, park users value their park and recreation experience more highly than the direct costs they incur. Lastly, it was concluded that parks have values that are not directly related to use and cannot be quantified. These values, including option and existence values, were noted to be significant (Coopers and Lybrand Consulting, 1995).

The protected areas system is struggling under considerable pressure from influences such as: the massive expansion of protected area lands; increasing collaborative needs with respect to establishment, planning, and operations with industry; local people and First Nations; and high levels of service demands and significantly decreased staffing levels, capital funding, and operating budgets. To develop a course of action that would effectively carry the agency through such difficult times into a better position in the future, the Minister of Environment, Lands and Parks sought outside opinion. In September 1997, the BC's Parks Legacy Panel was appointed to review the situation of BC Parks and make recommendations for change. A host of recommendations resulted from the process, the most significant of which addressed concerns over maintaining the ecological integrity of the system, and the current inadequate funding to protect and operate it (BC's Parks Legacy Panel, 1999). A wide range of strategies for addressing these and other issues was presented in the Panel's report, including control of visitor use levels and commercialization, restricting intrusions by other resource users, increasing interpretive and education programming, changing administrative structures, increasing revenue generation, and improving legislation. BC Parks has taken up the challenge of the vision presented by the panel and is working to implement many of the recommendations.

Regional Parks

In recent years there has been notable growth of regional parks systems throughout the province of BC. The change is seen to be part of the increasing importance of the converging factors of lifestyle, environmental quality, and locally accessible recreation opportunities. These trends are appearing in urban areas, where the demand for close to home, open space with high quality recreational experiences and a greater emphasis on public education in a natural setting is intensifying. Over the last decade, the major urban centres of Vancouver and Victoria saw their regional parks systems expand significantly and take on a much higher profile in the communities they serve. Planning and expansion of regional parks systems are also evident in many other areas around the province such as the Okanagan and central Vancouver Island.

The Victoria Capital Regional District (CRD) serves as an example of this trend and the significance that these parks systems have for recreation in local communities. In 1987, the CRD parks system included 16 parks covering 2,690 ha and was administered with a comprehensive budget of approximately $1.13 million (Downie, 1987). By 1998, the system had increased to 24 parks covering 8,483 ha which supported over 2 million visitors, including over 19,000 participants in interpretive programs and over 3,700 students in school-based programs. The system enjoys widespread public support, not only from the over 250 volunteers that contribute to the operation of the parks, but also by the general public. The 1998 comprehensive budget had risen to $4.5 million with the support of municipalities and the public for increased tax revenue dedicated to parks (CRD Parks, 1999).

The key components of the system continue to be some of the well established, large park areas such as East Sooke, Elk/Beaver Lake, and Mount Work.[7] However, indicative of recent initiatives to broaden the system and provide greater linkages throughout the CRD is the development of the Galloping Goose Regional Trail, a major trail corridor for walking, cycling, and horseback riding winding its way over 60 km between Victoria and Sooke. Current efforts are focused on developing *greenways* throughout the region, in addition to coastal and drainage corridors that will serve both as protection zones for remnant ecological communities, as well as recreational corridors (see **Chapter 13**).

Public Providers: Provincial Forests

While protected areas attract a large percentage of the outdoor recreational activity in the province, they include only a small percentage of the Crown Land available. The majority of the land area of the province is held by the Crown and designated as *Provincial Forest*. While resource activities are managed on this land, there are also opportunities for a wide variety of recreational activity. In many locations facilities have been developed in support of activities such as camping, boating, fishing, hiking, trail riding, snowmobiling, and cross-country skiing. In other areas, only resource roads provide access to backcountry areas where facilities are non-existent and users are on their own to explore.

With such a widespread and unstructured land base available, documentation of the full extent of visitor use is difficult. Visitor use is monitored at many sites where facilities have been developed; because of the attractiveness of these areas, use estimates are helpful. In 1993, the number of visitor days was estimated to be 45 million, a figure that is approximately double the visitor use levels of provincial parks (BC Ministry of Forests, 1994). The level of activity is very significant, and these backcountry areas target a segment of the visitor spectrum that prefers less structure, fewer facilities, and fewer people than the more intensively used park areas.

Blending recreational use with resource activity is the principal challenge within provincial forests (BC Ministry of Forests, 1994). Significant work around recreation inventory and planning has been incorporated into forestry planning in recent years. The consideration of recreational opportunities has become a mandatory component in forest harvesting operations, with the benefit of drawing greater attention to such opportunities and building greater recreation planning expertise within the Ministry of Forests and the forest companies.

Private Sector Providers

Commercial recreation companies abound in BC. For the purpose of this discussion, they can be divided into two main groups: those that operate and depend on their own private land for the success of their business; and those that depend on the use of Crown Land to sustain their operations.

In the first group, destination resorts are the most common example. Many such facilities are based on a particular activity and setting, and cater to a clientele looking for a full service operation. Ocean beach lodges with the attraction of a spectacular setting and the comfort of well-appointed accommodation, good food, and a relaxing atmosphere (such as Tigh-Na-Mara Resort in Parksville or Crystal Cove Beach Resort in Tofino) are an example. Similar resort complexes are developed at freshwater locations offering both beach and lake activities, and often providing activities such as golfing, horseback riding and hiking trails, or special features associated with the site. Examples of this include the Harrison Hotsprings Resort and Lake Okanagan Resort. Others have more extensive private land on which to operate and provide activities that use the character and setting of their locations. Guest ranches that provide horseback holidays in the summer and cross-country skiing in the winter illustrate this category. 108 Mile Ranch is one example of many such facilities that successfully operate in the Cariboo.

The second group of commercial operators are those which from a very small location provide outdoor recreation services over a wide area through the use of public land. In many instances, there are very formal arrangements with the government over the use of Crown Land by the private company for the provision of public recreation services. Such is the case of guide/outfitters, for example, who operate over large areas of Crown Land under a lease arrangement. Outfitting areas are individually leased, allowing outfitters to invest in facilities and advertise opportunities with the assurance of knowing their territory will not be infringed upon by others or by incompatible activities. Another example of this type would be lodge operations that exist within parks, such as Lake O'Hara Lodge in Yoho National Park. Extensive facilities have been built by a private operator on a site leased from the park. The attractiveness of the setting is extremely marketable, and services cater to individuals who are interested in hiking the surrounding trails within the park.

The second group also includes many companies whose relationship with administering land agencies is much less formal. Often a simple area-specific permit, or even just a business license, is all that is required to offer outdoor recreation services in the market place.

River rafting companies like Canadian River Expeditions operate trips on rivers around BC, including the Tatshenshini and Chilko; outdoor adventure companies organize hiking, cycling, and canoeing trips in a variety of locations all over the province; whale watching companies operate out of centres like Victoria and Tofino; and tour companies offer cruises to various locations in the Queen Charlotte Islands. The extent of the outdoor recreation private sector enterprise is enormous.

Trends In Outdoor Recreation

To understand trends in outdoor recreation, it is essential to look at the variables influencing participation in the spectrum of activities that exists in BC today. The dominant factors have been fairly constant. Participation is not static even throughout adulthood. Age, education, income, discretionary time, gender, and household composition are significant factors, each with their own relationship to participation (Coopers and Lybrand, 1996). Special mention should be made of certain observations:

- occupation is not an important indicator;
- income is not a strong indicator on its own, but when combined with age and education is more significant;
- increase in education correlates with increase in recreation activity, but shows a negative correlation with respect to certain activities such as home activities, fishing and hunting; and,
- ethnicity is becoming an increasingly important factor in outdoor recreation demand in BC.

The changing nature of Canada's demography is also an important consideration in understanding trends. These four features are critical: a slowing of population growth; gradual then accelerated aging of the population; increasing influence of immigration; and, a preponderance of internal migration (Balmer, 1994). Considering these factors and those relating to participation as discussed above, a number of trends can be identified.

Trend #1:

Growing Importance and Levels of Outdoor Recreation Activity

There is an abundance of evidence in support of the importance of outdoor recreation for BC residents today (Balmer, 1994; BC Parks, 1994; BC Parks, 1994a; BC Parks, 1996; CRD Parks, 1992). Not only do studies indicate very high levels of participation, but that the number of people recreating outdoors has risen substantially in recent years. Much of this activity is reportedly close to home and pursued on a regular basis as part of a healthy lifestyle. Regional parks have consistently recorded growing use of and support for the urban-based park lands they administer (CRD Parks, 1992), and municipalities continue to experience growth in the development and use of other forms of recreational facilities (Osborn, 1991).

However, these same attitudes and participation patterns extend to more distant activity areas and a broader range of outdoor activities. Use of the provincial parks system has grown from about 15 million visits in 1985 (Coopers and Lybrand, 1995) to 26.3 million visits in 1998 (BC Ministry of Environment, Lands and Parks, 1999, *http://www.elp.gov.bc.ca/bcparks/facts/stats.htm*). Recreational use of provincial forests was recorded at 40.9 million user days in 1991 (BC Ministry of Forests, 1991) and estimated at 45 million by 1993 (BC Ministry of Forests, 1994).

A number of factors influence this trend, the most significant being the overall growth of population within the province. At the same time, increasing levels of education and household income are also recognized as important factors in outdoor recreation participation rates (Balmer, 1994).

Trend #2:

Growing Importance of Natural Environments

Evidence also suggests that natural environments are of utmost importance. Survey respondents believe that protection of natural environments is the most important benefit of parks, and as a result there is considerable public interest in creating more parks and protecting the natural environment. For example, in a Capital Regional District public survey (CRD Parks, 1992), 92% of respondents stated "outdoor recreation was important to them compared to other interests," 92% identified a natural environment as important to their outdoor recreation experience, 90% agreed with the conservation and outdoor recreation roles of CRD Parks, and 70% agreed to increases in their taxes in support of protecting more parkland. Similar results have been found in surveys of public opinions with respect to provincial parks where over 90% of respondents ranked "preservation of natural environments and protection of wildlife" as the most important benefits (BC Parks, 1990; BC Parks, 1994a). Consistent with this important recognition of the value of parks to their recreation experience, it has been documented that people are more likely to use parks now than they were a decade ago, and are visiting them more often.

Trend #3:

Paradoxical Growth of Passive and Active Activities

Significant growth is indicated at both ends of the active/passive spectrum (Balmer, 1994). The population of BC is aging, and passive recreation activities will appeal to this growing sector of society. This older portion of the population has been influenced by attitudes toward healthy living and exercise. Although pursuits will be less active than in previous years, a healthier older population will still have a strong incentive to be active in the outdoors. Many of the fastest growing pursuits in the province are those well suited in some ways to the interests and abilities of the aging population, including wildlife viewing, nature study, going to the beach, golfing, bird watching, and walking for pleasure.

At the other end of the spectrum, increases in active outdoor activities can be understood to compensate for the more common sedentary work styles of the information age. In addition, young adults are not as commonly constrained by young family commitments in making weekend and holiday plans. Thus, faster growth rates are found for self-powered activities such as windsurfing, canoeing, kayaking, skating, mountain-biking, and walking for exercise, in addition to new and exciting activities such as snowboarding and rollerblading.

Trend #4:
Paradoxical Growth of Activities Requiring Safety and Risk Management

Another spectrum that is noteworthy in recreation trends is the safety versus risk continuum (Balmer, 1994). To a certain extent, this too reflects the demographic characteristics described above. Active seniors are concerned about safety, preferring to find secure footing, healthy food, and nearby health-support services. Another aspect of the safety question is the increasing concern for property theft, vandalism, and personal security while in the outdoors.

It is not only seniors who are concerned about the safety end of the spectrum, however. Newcomers to Canada and foreign visitors want to experience the outdoors, but may have little familiarity with nature and the environment. They look for activities to engage in that are relatively easy and that can take place in secure facilities. Even among society in general, our highly urbanized lifestyle has little experience with the natural environment and needs introductory experiences and education. Supporting this uncertainty is the higher public profile around search and rescue and liability issues. In response to these concerns, there is measurable interest in taking the urban experience into the wilderness both from a security and a convenience perspective. Support for cabin or cottage accommodation in provincial parks grew from 38% in 1983 to 55% in 1989 (BC Parks, 1991).

At the other end of the spectrum are high growth rates for adventure activities such as rockclimbing, and many aspects of adventure tourism including hiking, trekking, kayaking, horseback riding, and rafting.

Trend #5:
Paradoxical Growth of Environmentally Friendly Activities and Activities Requiring Large Scale or Intensive Development

A final development that shows increasing activity is the spectrum relating to environmental awareness and impact of recreational activities (Balmer, 1994). At one end are those activities that promote wise use, minimal impact, and increased knowledge and awareness. At the other end are the big development scenarios, including large-scale development of infrastructure and utilization of the latest in technological wizardry.

There is no doubt that society has improved its awareness of ecology and the environment. School curricula and experiential learning advanced conservation dramatically in the past 20 years. Now there is a clear emphasis on environmental learning as an integral part of the recreation experience (e.g., elderhostel), and such activities as wildlife viewing, nature study, and bird watching are examples of this fast growing sector (Ethos Consulting et al., 1991). Beyond the educational component, environmentally friendly activities (those that study rather than harvest nature) are growing in popularity, as are people-powered activities (e.g., cross-country skiing, canoeing) rather than motor-powered (e.g., power boating, snowmobiling, driving for pleasure) (HLA Consultants and the ARA Consulting Group Inc., 1995).

However, at the development end of the spectrum, there are still high pressures and demand for extensive infrastructure, including ski resorts, golf courses, roads, accommodation, and services (BC Ministry of Employment and Investment, 1999). In addition, the technology drive within the leisure industry market appears to be endless. New technologies have spawned activities with widespread environmental implications. Examples are the jet ski, mountain bike, windsurfer, snowboard, and rollerblade. There also continues to be strong interest in and demand for motorized access to wilderness in activities such as heli-skiing, heli-hiking, fly-in fishing and hunting, and all terrain vehicle (ATV) use. This pressure might be expected to continue with the affluent elderly looking for comfortable access to a shrinking and increasingly valued outdoors both on road and off-road. Will the future see the helicopter RV, amphibian car, the go-anywhere ATV (land, water, snow)?

Trend #6:
Growth of International Tourism

There is every evidence that recent increases in international tourism will continue into the future, having a very significant impact on the outdoor recreation system of BC. Reference to such trends has been identified in a number of earlier areas of this chapter, such as the analysis of the skiing and ecotourism markets (Campbell Goodell Consultants Ltd., 1989; Coopers and Lybrand Consulting, 1995; HLA Consultants and the ARA Consulting Group Inc., 1995) (see **Chapter 12**).

The international tourism market is driven by a combination of social, demographic, and economic factors. International visitors tend to be older, with professional and technical occupations, and more education. Scenic beauty is the main attraction to BC and visitors typically participate more as sightseers, walkers, pleasure drivers, and developed campers. Stays tend to be short vacations or weekends, particularly add-ons to business trips, usually because of the scheduling difficulties of two working adults. Within BC, their preference is for full service, near urban destinations (HLA Consultants and the ARA Consulting Group Inc., 1995).

Common characteristics of the demands of this group of visitors include trends towards:

- an emphasis on participation and learning—seeking fun, excitement, and the chance to feel the authentic culture and atmosphere of where they are;
- healthy lifestyles—including types/quality of food, and outdoor activities;
- more sophisticated and more demanding itinerary planning—do-it-yourself customized holidays to replace the group tour; and
- the 'greening' of tourism—increased sensitivity to impact of activities and services

Addressing these needs has significant implications for the outdoor recreation system in BC. Examples such as the resort complex development of Whistler or the interior guest ranch are significantly driven by this type of outdoor recreation interest and will continue to be a major growth area in the future (DPA Group Inc. and McLaren Plansearch Corp., 1988; Ethos Consulting, 1991; McLaren Plansearch Corp. et al., 1987; Coopers and Lybrand Consulting, 1995).

CONCLUSIONS

BC has both the opportunity and the challenge of being a world class environment for outdoor recreation. The quality that makes the province such a desirable place to live also attracts millions of visitors to share in the wealth of opportunity to experience the outdoors in a beautiful and comfortable setting. Maintaining the integrity of the outdoor experience while providing for the needs of a wide range of participants is a major challenge. Meeting the challenge will have major positive benefits for the people and economy of the province. Failing to meet it could have significant negative impacts on the quality of the environment and the lifestyle of British Columbians. The future holds great potential if there is sound planning and a commitment to the quality of both outdoor recreational experiences and the environment that supports it.

REFERENCES

Balmer, K.R. (1993). The future of outdoor recreation: An emerging BC 'cultural trademark.' In *Outdoor recreation in British Columbia: Supply and demand, issues and trends—Background papers*. Prepared for Protected Areas Strategy, Victoria, BC.

BC Ministry of Employment and Investment (1999). *Investment opportunities: Mountain resorts and tourism*. Victoria, BC: Ministry of Employment and Investment.

BC Ministry of Environment, Lands and Parks (1997). *Ministry of Environment, Lands and Parks: Annual report, 1997*. Victoria, BC: Ministry of Environment, Lands and Parks.

BC Ministry of Forests (1989). *Managing wilderness in provincial forests: A policy framework*. Victoria, BC: Ministry of Forests.

BC Ministry of Forests (1991). *Outdoor recreation survey 1989/90: How British Columbians use and value their public forest lands for recreation*. Victoria, BC: Ministry of Forests.

BC Ministry of Forests (1994). *Forest, range, and recreation resource analysis*. Victoria, BC: Ministry of Forests.

BC Parks (1990). *Public opinions about BC parks: Summary report*. Victoria, BC: BC Parks.

BC Parks (1991). *Camping trends in British Columbia 1980-1990: A summary*. Research Services, BC Parks. Victoria, BC: BC Parks.

BC Parks (1994). *Recent trends in outdoor recreation by British Columbians 1989-1994: A summary*. Research Services, BC Parks. Victoria, BC: BC Parks.

BC Parks (1994a). *BC residents: Importance of outdoor recreation, camping experience, and vacation preferences 1989 - 1994: A summary*. Research Services, BC Parks. Victoria, BC: BC Parks.

BC Parks (1996). *Provincial park use by British Columbians 1991 - 1996: A summary*. Research and Evaluation Services, BC Parks. Victoria, BC: BC Parks.

BC Parks (1996a). *1996 park data handbook*. Victoria, BC: BC Parks.

BC's Park Legacy Panel (1999). *Sustaining our protected areas system: Final report of the Legacy Panel*. Victoria, BC: Parks Legacy Secretariat.

Campbell Goodell Consultants Ltd. (1989). *The market potential for ski vacations in British Columbia: Executive summary*. Report prepared for Industry, Science and Technology Canada, BC Ministry of Regional Development, and BC Ministry of Tourism and Provincial Secretary. Victoria, BC: Queens Printer.

Canada – Department of Canadian Heritage (1997). *National parks system plan*. Ottawa, ON: Parks Canada.

Coopers and Lybrand Consulting (1995). *Economic benefits of BC parks*. Victoria, BC: Ministry of Environment, Lands and Parks.

Coopers and Lybrand Consulting (1996). *Current and future economic benefits of BC parks*. Victoria, BC: Ministry of Environment, Lands and Parks.

CRD Parks (1999). *1998 annual report*. Victoria, BC: CRD Parks.

CRD Parks (1992). *1992 CRD parks householder survey report*. Victoria, BC: CRD Parks.

Downie, B.K. (1987). *Capital Regional District regional parks system plan (4 vols.)*. PRP Parks: Research & Planning Inc. Victoria, BC: PRP Inc.

Downie, B.K. (1998). Parks: A British Columbia perspective. In J.S. Marsh and B.W. Hodgins (Eds.), *Changing parks: The history, future and cultural context of parks and heritage landscapes* (pp. 238-249). Toronto, ON: Natural Heritage/Natural History Inc.

DPA Group Inc. (1991). *Guide outfitters of BC: Opportunity analysis*. Report prepared for the Research Services Branch, BC Ministry of Tourism and Provincial Secretary. Victoria, BC: Queens Printer.

DPA Group Inc. (1991a). *Strategic plan for the guide outfitters of British Columbia*. Report prepared for Industry, Science and Technology Canada, BC Ministry of Tourism, and BC Ministry of Regional Development. Victoria, BC: Queens Printer.

DPA Group Inc., and McLaren Plansearch Corp. (1988). *Fishing lodges and resorts in British Columbia: Marketing and development initiatives*. Report prepared for BC Ministry of Tourism and Provincial Secretary. Victoria, BC: Queens Printer.

Ethos Consulting (1991). *Natural resource-based tourism in Northwestern BC*. Report prepared for Industry, Science and Technology Canada, Ministry of Development Trade and Tourism. Victoria, BC: Queens Printer.

Ethos Consulting, Tourism Research Group, BioQuest International, and Henderson and Associates (1991). *The commercial wildlife viewing product: A discussion of market and development potential*. Victoria, BC: Ministry of Tourism.

HLA Consultants, and the ARA Consulting Group Inc. (1995). *Ecotourism – Nature/adventure/culture: Alberta and British Columbia market demand assessment: Main report*. Vancouver, BC: Queens Printer.

International Sports Inc. (1993). *Golf industry opportunities in BC: A discussion paper*. Victoria, BC: Ministry of Small Business, Tourism and Culture.

International Sports Inc. (1993a). *Golf resort development strategy*. Victoria, BC: Ministry of Small Business, Tourism and Culture.

John Gow Consultants Ltd. (1987). *Ski market study*. Report prepared for the Department of Regional Industrial Expansion (Canada) and the BC Ministry of Tourism, Recreation and Culture and BC Ministry of Economic Development. Victoria, BC: Queens Printer.

McLaren Plansearch Corp., Tourism Research Corp., and Addison Travel Marketing (1987). *Guest ranches of British Columbia: Product and market analysis*. Victoria, BC: Ministry of Tourism, Recreation and Culture.

Nelson, J. (2001). Time runs short for national treasure. *Times Colonist*, March 26th, p. A7.

Nordic Group International (1988). *British Columbia cross-country ski area study*. Report prepared for the Canada-British Columbia Tourist Industry Development Subsidiary Agreement. Vancouver, BC: Queens Printer.

Osborn, L. (1991). *Demand for outdoor recreation in the Lower Mainland* (Major Parks Plan Technical Report No. 1). Burnaby, BC: Greater Vancouver Regional District.

Pacific Analytics Inc., Strategic Concepts Inc., and The Tourism Research Group (1993). *The golf industry in BC: Financial results and economic impacts, 1987-1990*. Victoria, BC: Ministry of Tourism.

Parks Canada (1994). *Managing the West Coast Trail: 1993 survey summary*. Calgary, Alberta: Parks Canada.

Parks Canada (1994a). *A proposed framework for assessing the appropriateness of recreation activities in protected heritage areas*. Ottawa, ON: Department of Canadian Heritage.

Parks Canada (1994b). *Allowable outdoor recreation activity profiles: A tool for visitor and risk management*. Ottawa, ON: Department of Canadian Heritage.

Parks Canada (1995). *Parks Canada visitor use statistics: 1993-1994*. Ottawa, ON: Parks Canada.

Payne, R.J., and Graham, R. (1993). Visitor planning and management in parks and protected areas. In P. Dearden and R. Rollins (Eds.), *Parks and protected areas in Canada* (pp. 185-210). Toronto, ON: Oxford University Press.

Peepre, J.S. (1994). Outdoor recreation in BC: What do we value and what should we protect. In *Outdoor recreation in British Columbia: Supply and demand, issues and trends—Background papers*. Prepared for Protected Areas Strategy, Victoria, BC.

Royal Canadian Golf Association (1999). Golf participation in Canada. Quick facts 1999. http://www.rcga.org/membership/membership-quickfacts.htm.

Steig, K. (1997). Cypress Provincial Park: A questionable future. *Parks and Wilderness Quarterly*, 8(4).

Theberge, J.B. (1993). Ecology, conservation, and protected areas in Canada. In P. Dearden and R. Rollins (Eds.), *Parks and protected areas in Canada* (pp. 137-153). Toronto, Ontario: Oxford University Press.

Tourism BC (1998). *BC visitor study*. Victoria, BC: Tourism BC.

Tourism BC (1999). *1996 tourism performance*. Victoria, BC: Tourism BC.

ENDNOTES

[1] The resort town of Whistler has maintained its attractiveness through strict but sensible development and design guidelines and high quality construction requirements. As a result, it now has the cachet of being an international destination ski resort rather than another tacky tourist spot. However, it has also evolved into a year-round resort with a range of outdoor activities available.

[2] In an amendment to the ALR legislation in 1988, golf courses became a permitted use of ALR reserves. This resulted in a rush of applications as a back-door way of obtaining subdivision approvals. This amendment was rescinded in 1991 by a new government.

[3] Grizzly Bear hunting in BC is a controversial issue. Further studies are necessary to determine the merits of hunting policies and the possible impact of international environmental pressure groups.

[4] A serious ongoing issue is poaching of animal parts for the (illegal) Asian traditional medicine market.

[5] Efforts are currently underway for a federal-provincial initiative to establish a new national park and/or protected area in the Gulf Islands region to protect the Garry Oak and coastal ecosystems. Most land in this area is privately owned, so it is necessary to have a substantial fund for land purchases (Nelson, 2001).

[6] The total protected area of BC is now slightly more than 12% of the total land mass—a remarkable "first" in North America. Amendments to the protected areas legislation and new designations brought the total of Class A parks and ecological reserves to 691 (March 2001).

[7] Increasing recreation pressures are especially noticeable on the lakes and rivers within the settled areas of the province, where fishers, rowers, swimmers, and jet-skis compete for space. See Carr (1998) for a recent study of these issues in the CRD region.

Plate 10 Alpine centres such as Whistler have evolved into year round resorts ▶

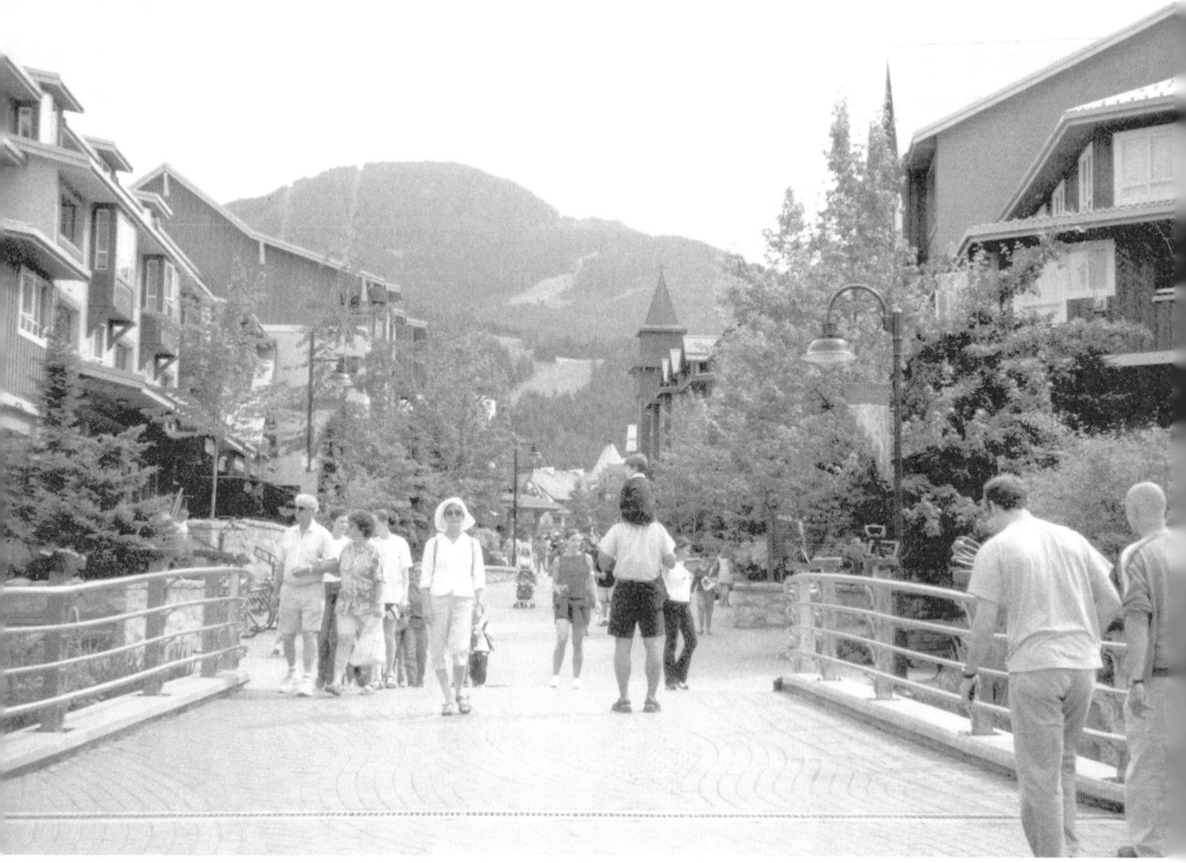

Tourism

Rick Rollins

Malaspina University College, Nanaimo

Introduction

The tourism industry in BC grew remarkably over the past 15 years. This chapter examines this development and its problems and then reviews strategies for the future. The perspective adhered to is that tourism is an emerging resource industry much like forestry and fisheries, but with some important differences (Murphy, 1985). First, tourism in BC depends heavily on the quality of the natural environment, but these resources are not the complete product. In addition to attractive scenery, one must consider the cultural heritage, such as the contribution of First Nation's culture, to the appeal of the province as a tourism destination. While the natural and cultural environments of the province are significant generators of tourism travel, the competitive value of the industry in BC is also shaped by the tourism infrastructure, including hospitality services, transportation services, and tourism marketing and information services. Much attention is directed at understanding the market place for tourism and the market forces influencing tourism consumption because tourism is an industry in a competitive global environment.

Second, tourism is unique in that people travel to use the resource, rather than exporting the resources to another place to be used. Since tourists are compelled to travel to the resource, be it scenery, heritage, or other attraction, people living in or near a tourist attraction are often brought into direct contact with tourists. Tourists and local residents often visit the same major attractions, such as beaches, parks, and museums, and use the same services, such as restaurants, service stations, stores, and banks. Hence, whether individual residents and businesses feel they are part of the tourism industry, they are part of the tourism "product."

Third, although tourism has been described as a renewable resource industry that can be sustained into the future, this cannot be taken for granted. When a tourism destination area becomes popular, the associated volume of visitors cannot fail to result in some change to the physical environment (Mathieson and Wall, 1982; Hammit and Cole, 1987) and the social environment (Keough, 1989; Rollins, 1997). The amount of change, kind of change, and control of change are important issues.

From these brief observations it is apparent that tourism is a complex resource industry. It incorporates fundamental elements of leisure behaviour within a setting that has both environmental and cultural components. To add to this complexity, there is some debate regarding how to define tourism: does tourism only refer to travel for pleasure, or does it include business travel; does tourism refer to the activity of non-residents of BC who visit the province, or does it include the travel of BC residents within the province; does tourism refer to travel to and within the province, or does it include travel of BC residents to places outside the province? This is not just an academic debate: any attempt to describe the tourism industry or to measure the benefits and costs of tourism development will be shaped by the way the activity is defined.

For the purposes of this chapter, tourism is defined as:

> ... *the travel, the activities, and services used by any person who travels more than 80 km or stays overnight in a fixed or non-fixed roof accommodation whether it be for the purpose of business or pleasure.*
>
> (Tourism BC, 1996)

This definition of tourism includes regular vacations, weekend and recreational travel that takes people beyond their local community, and tourist activities associated with business travel—particularly conventions. It includes facilities and services that may be designed primarily for resident use, yet are used by tourists during their stay, as well as accommodation and attraction facilities associated with the industry.

THE SIGNIFICANCE OF TOURISM

At the beginning of the second millennium, tourism has emerged as one of the major industries in the world, with significant economic impact and employment. By 1982, some 280 million international tourist trips were taken annually (Murphy, 1984), and by 1996 this number had increased to 595 million (Roberts, 1998). The total economic impact of global travel in 1996 was estimated as $US 3.6 trillion, or 10.6% of the gross global product.

In 1997, receipts from tourism in Canada amounted to $12 billion. BC's tourism has grown in conjunction with tourism's world wide expansion. Today, the tourism industry accounts for more than 5% of economic activity in BC and is ranked as the province's third largest export behind softwood lumber and pulp (BC Stats, 2001). In the late 1990s, tourism generated about two-thirds as much direct gross domestic product (GDP) as the forest sector, and about two-thirds more direct GDP than mining (BC Ministry of Finance and Corporate Relations, 1997). The growth of tourism in the provincial economy is illustrated in Table 12.1, showing tourism GDP from 1987 to 2000. Tourism GDP rose 2.3% during 1997, which was the smallest increase since 1991. 1997 was the fifth consecutive year that BC's tourism sector grew faster than the economy as a whole. The tourism sector's 1998 growth rate of .7% compares to .4% for the entire provincial economy.

In 2000, over 22 million people travelled to tourism destinations in BC (Table 12.2), spending $9.5 billion. Of this number, 50% were BC residents travelling within the province, 22% were from other provinces, and 28% originated in other countries. Non-resident travel to BC is particularly significant in terms of revenues generated, accounting for over 70% of tourism revenues (Table 12.2). With regard to the North American market (visitors from the US and from Canadian provinces and territories), increased trends likely reflect the influence of an aging and affluent group of "baby boomers" seeking specialty "getaways" and adventure. BC is uniquely positioned to capture this growing market, offering both urban sophistication and a "wilderness experience."

In 2000, a total of 250,000 (or about one in eight) workers in BC were employed in tourism related businesses (Table 12.3), an increase of 6% since 1997 (BC Stats, 2001). The food and beverage sector accounts for almost half of all tourism jobs, however the area experiencing the fastest growth is adventure tourism and recreation, up 11.1% to 13,000 jobs. Tourism is a labour intensive service industry. While other industries are resorting to further automation in an effort to remain competitive in world markets, tourism needs workers to provide a world class product and service. Also significant is the relatively high proportion of

Table 12.1 Tourism GDP in BC: 1987 to 1999 (millions of dollars)

Year	Tourism GDP ($ million)
1987	2,643
1988	2,816
1989	3,054
1990	3,237
1991	3,353
1992	3,482
1993	3,662
1994	4,066
1995	4,322
1996	4,568
1998	4,200
1999	5,000

All tables from BC Stats, 2000.

Table 12.2 Overnight visitor volumes and revenues by market areas in BC, 2000

Market area	Visitors in 2000 (thousands)	Percentage	Revenues ($ millions)	Percentage
BC residents	10,761	50.0	2,476	26.5
Other Canadians	4,914	21.9	2,834	30.5
US visitors	4,967	20.2	2,321	24.8
Overseas visitors	1,739	7.9	1,696	18.2
Total	22,445	100.0	9,327	100.0

Table 12.3 Tourism-related employment in BC, 1997

Tourism industry sector	Employment	Percent
Food and beverage	115, 297	49
Transportation	47.060	20
Accommodation	30,589	13
Attractions	21,177	9
Adventure and recreation	14,118	6
Travel trade	7,059	3
Total	235,300	100

young people employed in tourism professions (45%) compared to youth employment in other sectors of the economy (Tourism BC, 1997).

The major attractions of the province, and of the country in general, are the scenic landscapes, open spaces, and outdoor recreational opportunities—all of which have a strong appeal in an urbanized world (Tourism Canada, 1987). The size, terrain, and coastal location of BC create a variety of vegetation types that support diverse wildlife species and offer a wide range of land- and water-based recreation activities. These include skiing, sailing, river rafting, ocean kayaking, fishing, hunting, and camping. However, most visitors seem content with general sightseeing through the car windows—enjoying the scenic value of the landscape, without necessarily venturing very far into the natural landscape. Despite the province's "supernatural" appeal and the widespread appeal of such attractions, most traffic focuses on four of the province's tourist regions (Table 12.4). This imbalance is caused by the varying degrees of accessibility and opportunity for multi-purpose trips within BC. Since most tourists other than those on cruise ships travel by car, good highway connections tend to channel visitors into certain regions. The effect of this phenomenon can be seen in Table 12.4. The four regions with the highest visitor levels straddle the Trans-Canada Highway: Vancouver Coast and Mountains; Vancouver Island; Thompson-Okanagan, and BC Rockies. Another reason for the uneven distribution of

Table 12.4 Room revenues by region (million$)

Tourist region	1999	2000*
Lower Mainland	778	830
Vancouver Island/Coast	238	246
Thompson-Okanagan	166	183
Kootenay	53	63
Cariboo	41	43
North	18	20
Northeast	24	28
Total	1329	1427

*estimated

visitor activity is the overwhelming attraction of water. Vancouver Island and the Vancouver-Lower Mainland area offer seascapes, boating, salmon fishing, whale-watching, and beach activities, and the Thompson-Okanagan offers lake activities and river rafting (Figure 12.1).

The natural and cultural resources of BC combine to create a tremendous potential for the tourism industry—one which both individuals and governments are eager to grasp. Tourism has not only been one of the strongest growth industries since the 1950s, but has also shown unexpected resilience during downturns in the rest of the provincial economy. For example, the first 6 months of 1998 were described as a recession for the province, but during that period total international visitation was up 3.2% compared to the same period in 1997 (Tourism BC, 1998). In fact US visitation, fuelled by a favourable exchange rate for the US dollar, was up 10%, overshadowing a 16% drop from the Asia/Oceanic region. Hence, tourism and tourism-related activities have begun to receive greater attention and investment. Between 1991 and 1997, the number of tourism-related businesses grew from 10,000 to 16,500 (Tourism BC, 1997).

TOURISM BC: THE ROLE OF THE PROVINCIAL GOVERNMENT

Tourism BC—formerly a division within the Ministry of Small Business, Tourism and Culture—became a Crown Corporation in 1997, charged with the responsibility for coordinating strategic tourism marketing and of supporting consumer and market research to bring the right products to market.[1] Specifically, the corporation is responsible for the following:

- marketing British Columbia as a tourism destination;
- providing information services for tourists;
- encouraging enhancement of standards of tourism accommodation, facilities, services, and amenities;
- enhancing professionalism in the tourism industry;
- encouraging and facilitating the creation of jobs in the tourism industry;
- collecting, evaluating, and disseminating information on tourism markets, trends, employment, programs, and activities and on availability and suitability of infrastructure and of services that support tourism programs; and
- generating additional funding for tourism programs.

Tourism BC developed a number of particularly successful programs. To support the consumer purchasing process, it operates the toll-free, *Super Natural British Columbia Travel Information and Accommodation Reservations* service. This service is used by more than 700 industry operators, including hotels, campgrounds, and conference centres. Tourism BC supports the tourism *infocentres* located in most cities and towns in the province to provide face-to-face travel information to visitors. It also developed a number of training programs to improve the standard of customer relations in the tourism industry. One example, the Superhost Program, has proven so successful that it has been developed for use in several other countries. Tourism BC provides an Accommodations Inspection program and a quality star rating system, including a listing of approved accommodation properties in the annual *BC Accommodations Guide*. It sponsors many studies and reports, some of which have been referenced in this chapter. One prominent study is the Tourism Growth Management Strategy (Tourism BC, 1996).[2]

TOURISM MARKETS AND MARKETING STRATEGIES

While tourism in BC has experienced remarkable growth in recent years, the industry operates in a highly competitive global environment. To remain competitive, it is necessary to develop well planned marketing strategies (Butler, 1980; Tourism BC, 1996). Some of the marketing strategies developed by Tourism BC (1997) are now described.

Tourism

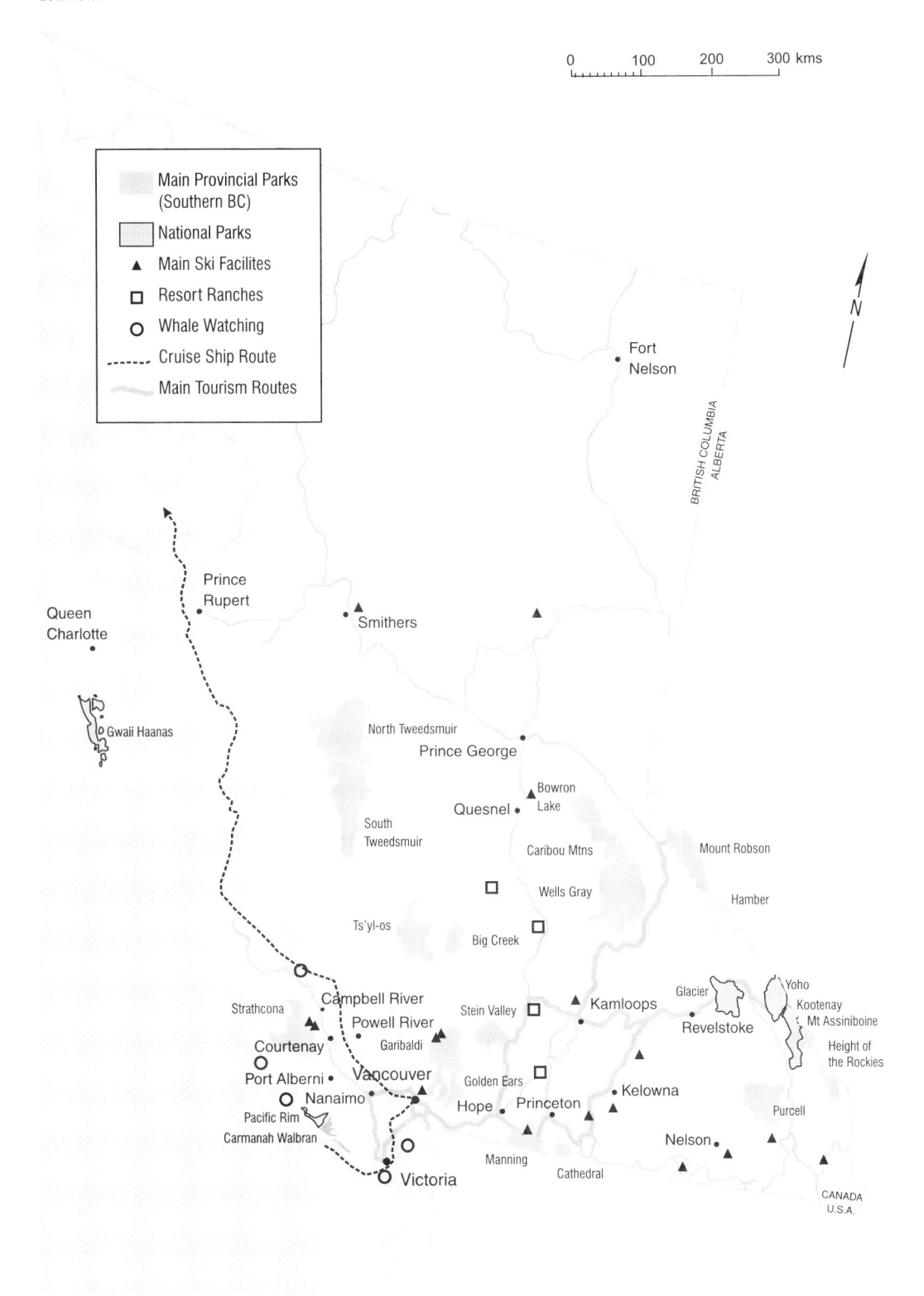

Figure 12.1 Geographic patterns of tourism

The BC Regional Market

The short haul regional market, consisting mainly of visitors from Alberta, Washington State, and Oregon State, is the largest source of visitor revenues and offers the opportunity to develop repeat business and distribute revenues more equitably throughout the province. Accounting for almost 27% of visitor revenues, the BC resident market is the engine that drives the industry throughout the year (Table 12.2). The major strategy for this market is to encourage development of the getaway travel market in shoulder seasons to all areas of the province, from Oregon, Washington, and Alberta, featuring the following products: golf, general touring, city sightseeing, theme events, marine activities, and fishing. Alpine ski products will be promoted to support the winter product. Touring and soft adventure will be encouraged for all seasons.

The North America Long Haul Market

This market includes regions outside of the Pacific North West, the most significant of which are California and Ontario. The growth in the US market was stimulated by, among other factors, the *1995 Open Skies Agreement*, which deregulated air traffic between the two countries. This resulted in a near doubling, to 20, of the number of major US markets with direct air service to BC, and had a beneficial effect on the development of Vancouver as the home port for the Alaska cruise industry. For this market, the major strategy is to promote getaways with an urban focus on general sightseeing and touring. During the winter, the focus is on skiing opportunities at Whistler/Blackcomb, the Thompson-Okanagan, and the BC Rockies, as well as regional winter products around the province.

The Asia-Pacific Market

The largest market in this group is Japan, but other significant markets include Hong Kong, Taiwan, South Korea, Australia, and New Zealand. Volumes of Asian visitors have increased dramatically since 1984, but competition for these travellers is extremely strong, especially from the US and Australia. These travellers are interested in nature and soft adventure, providing BC with an opportunity to capitalize on its natural surroundings. The focus for this market is to encourage visitors to explore areas of the province that do not have capacity constraints. Product features include general touring and soft adventure activities such as hiking, whale watching, horseback riding, and golf. Also important is the expansion of the shoulder season through niche products such as winter illumination and blossom tours, as well as skiing opportunities.

The European Market

This market consists mainly of the United Kingdom, Germany, Switzerland, France, and the Netherlands. More UK residents are coming independently; fewer are visiting friends and relatives as their main trip purpose. Despite relatively high unemployment and economic uncertainty, Germans remain committed to travel as a necessity rather than as a luxury. Overall, this group continues to grow faster than short haul traffic, due to increasing affordability. These travellers are becoming more price sensitive and booking lead times are becoming shorter. The priority for this group is to introduce them to new areas within BC with a focus on soft adventure products as well as more rugged experiences such as guest ranch stays, white water rafting, and heli-hiking. In winter, these visitors will be encouraged to experience ski resorts throughout the province, as well as non-ski winter opportunities.

TOURISM PRODUCTS

Another important consideration is the tourism product as seen from the perspective of the traveller. From this orientation the industry can be divided into eight major product areas (Tourism BC, 1996). These product areas will be described in terms of capacity, utilization, estimates of growth, and estimates of revenue.

Cruise Ships

Vancouver has emerged as the west coast centre for the summer/fall cruise ships that ply the spectacular Inside Passage to Alaska (Figure 12.1). Passengers can "fly and cruise" either one way or both ways. The one millionth passenger was carried in the 2000 season. Over the last 5 years the industry has grown significantly at the rate of 12.3% per year, with a high proportion of passengers coming from all over North America and Europe (via Vancouver International Airport) (Figure 12.2). A smaller number of cruise ships call in at Victoria's outer harbour. Clearly the southwest region of the province has benefited immensely from this activity with direct and indirect gains being injected into the economy.

There are 23 internationally owned ships that travel the route between Vancouver and Alaska. The television program *The Love Boat* helped popularize cruise holidays. However, the Princess Cruises Line based in Los Angeles has two new 99,000 tonne vessels which will not join the Alaska run: they are too big to get through the Panama Canal.

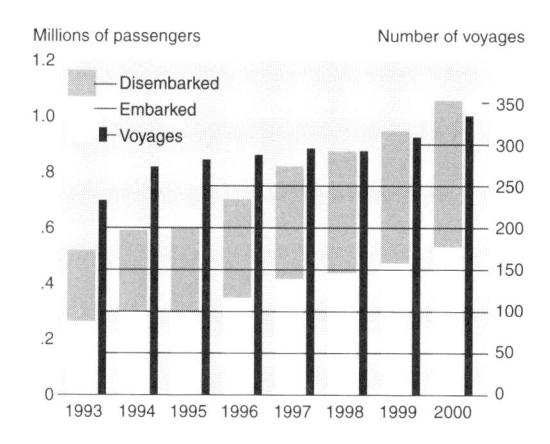

Figure 12.2 Cruise ship data

Skiing

The ski industry includes alpine, Nordic, and heli-skiing. The province has 46 alpine facilities, the majority of which operate at between 17% and 40% utilization. There are 29 developed Nordic facilities, and 24 heli-ski/snowcat facilities. Approximately 5.5 million alpine and Nordic ski visits and 64,500 heli-ski and snow-cat visits occurred in 2000. Estimates of annual revenues from the combined ski industries are between $600 million and $700 million. However, despite these economic benefits, there are numerous concerns about the ski industry. One is the need to balance visitor use between weekdays and weekends, and between peak and shoulder seasons. Another problem is that ski slopes alter the appearance of alpine areas in ways that some people find unacceptable. Beyond the visual changes, ski developments create environmental changes by altering the forest cover, building ski lodges and other facilities, and bringing large numbers of people into a natural setting. Sometimes these changes in the environment have an impact on wildlife populations. In addition to environmental impacts, large numbers of visitors can cause stresses in local communities. These stresses can take several forms, such as line-ups in stores and traffic congestion.

Sport Fishing

Sport fishing includes both the fresh and salt water fishing experience for tourists. These experiences may be pursued independently or through purchase of a guide charter or lodge package. There are 291 lodges in the province, providing 6,278 units. In addition, there are 142 marinas and 1,300 charter guides. Many of the salt water lodges are over 80% utilized. Total visitor volume includes 2.7 million total salt water angler days and 4.6 million freshwater angler days. Estimates of yearly revenues range from $556 million to $675 million.

At times the sport fishing industry is in conflict with the commercial fishing industry and First Nations' fisheries. For example, when salmon numbers are low, great pressure is put on all fisheries. The reasons for the decline in salmon are not well understood, but some factors include over-harvesting; damage to spawning streams from logging and urban growth, and pollution (see **Chapter 18**). Hence, there is a great deal of uncertainty regarding continuous access to fish resources. This inhibits opportunities for expansion and new facility development. Another form of uncertainty for the sport fishing industry is the difficulty in securing long term tenure arrangements on Crown Lands where the prime locations for fishing lodges are usually found.

Golf

BC's golf industry can accommodate 1,518,000 rounds of golf per day. On average, the overall provincial utilization is 77%. Just under 50% of this utilization can be attributed to tourism. Estimates of yearly revenues range from $110 million to $131 million. The golfing industry suggests that there needs to be four to five resort courses in a region in order to promote it as a golf resort destination. This has now been achieved in most regions of the province.

Outdoor Activities

The outdoor product includes both independent and package outdoor experiences involving land- and/or water-based activities. These activities are diverse. Land-based activities include camping, backpacking, horseback riding, and hunting. Water-based activities in ocean environments include sailing, scuba diving, whale watching, and ocean kayaking. Freshwater activities include water-skiing, whitewater rafting, and canoeing. The outdoor product also includes passive outdoor vacation experiences on lakes, ocean waterfronts, and some backcountry areas. These passive pursuits include sightseeing, birdwatching, and photography.

There are 950 outdoor operators in BC, and 573 outdoor accommodation properties, providing 8,688 units. In addition, there are 410 parks providing 10,829 sites. The number of parks is increasing dramatically in the province as a result of completion of the Protected Areas Strategy (see **Chapter 11**). Many of the outdoor accommodation properties, including park facilities are fully booked during the peak summer months. Estimates of use levels include 1.2 million visitors for land- and water-based activities and 2.793 million visitors to provincial parks. Estimated revenues range from $813 million to $953 million.

One issue with the outdoor product is the conflict that sometimes occurs between people pursuing multiple activities in a single setting. Motorized pleasure boats are viewed as noisy and intrusive by people travelling in kayaks, and cross country skiers often feel the same about snowmobiles. Many outdoor activities have significant risk elements that need to be managed in order to sustain the quality of the product. For example, provincial regulations regarding whitewater rafting were introduced following a number of accidents and deaths on rivers in the province. Some people are concerned about the ethics and environmental impacts associated with hunting. For most outdoor-related tourism activities, the quality of the outdoor product is highly dependent on natural settings, so changes in settings from logging, mining, urban development, and other developments make the outdoor product very vulnerable. In summary, the major concerns for the outdoor product include uncertainty regarding the long term sustainability of the resource, access to natural areas, and long term tenure of built facilities in some natural areas. Further, there is a lack of high-end accommodation outside of the Vancouver-Victoria area.

The Touring Product

The touring product includes group travel, independent package tours, and independent touring wherein the traveller visits multiple destinations. An example of group travel is a seniors group travelling to Harrison Hotsprings; an independent package tour might consist of a motor coach tour of various attractions on Vancouver Island; and a family from California travelling to BC in a camper vehicle is an example of an independent tour. Hence the touring product consists of several components, including travel routes, attractions, accommodation options, and companies or agencies who specialize in assembling tours and touring information. The number of units in accommodation properties along touring routes is 34,460, and the number of attractions is about 600. There are 308 licensed motor coach carriers operating 1,850 motor coaches. These facilities and services are often fully booked in the peak season. About 4.1 million touring visitors are accommodated each year in this sector. Estimated revenues vary from $1,159 million to $1,479 million.

One concern with the touring product is the social impact of high visitor volumes on host communities. For example, some destinations, such as Victoria, Tofino, and Bamfield, can seem to be overwhelmed by tourists during peak seasons. A related concern is traffic congestion and other strains on transportation systems. The ferry system serving Vancouver Island and the Gulf Islands is often severely congested during the summer months, resulting in people having to wait in line through several sailings. Other concerns for the touring product include: the lack of accommodation facilities outside the Victoria/Vancouver/Whistler area; the lack of mid-range accommodation facilities in Vancouver; and the availability of motor coaches during peak season.

The Urban Product

The urban product includes tourists visiting Vancouver and/or Victoria and participating in urban tourist activities such as restaurants, concerts, sporting events, and museums. The number of urban accommodation properties is 25,497 units as well as 3,347 campsites available in Vancouver-Victoria. These accommodations are near fully booked during the peak summer months. Vancouver receives about 5.8 million and Victoria about 3.5 million urban visitors each year. Estimated annual revenues from the urban product vary from $1,866 million to $2,060 million.

One problem regarding the urban tourist product arises when particularly high visitor volumes create undesirable impacts on host communities. Severe traffic congestion was one negative impact of Expo 86 in Vancouver. Victoria also can experience crowding during the peak season, or when special events occur, like the Commonwealth Games.

The Business and Convention Product

The convention product encompasses business travel and attendance by tourists at conventions and trade shows. The number of meeting facilities in the province is approximately 385 and the number of meeting rooms is 2,159. These properties are inadequate to meet the demand at times in the Vancouver area, but not elsewhere in the province. Approximately 445,533 delegate days were generated at four major convention centres in BC. There are about 4.7 million business and convention visitors per year. Estimates of revenues from the business convention product vary from $1,216 million to $1,403 million. A major concern for this sector is the discrepancy between overutilization within the Vancouver area, and low levels of utilization in the interior regions.

TOWARD A SUSTAINABLE TOURISM INDUSTRY

The viability of the tourism industry is affected by the quality of the tourism product. Based on observations made in several tourism destination areas, Butler (1980) described a tourism destination *cycle of evolution*, which begins with small numbers of tourists discovering a tourist destination. As the destination becomes better known, more visitors travel to the area and more tourism development occurs. Eventually, with more growth, the tourism industry becomes consolidated with a high number of tourism arrivals each year. If the quality of the tourism experience is not diminished and remains competitive with other destinations, the local tourism industry will remain viable. In many cases, however, the industry stagnates and declines. In some cases a stagnating tourism industry rejuvenates, but this is infrequent. The stagnation of the tourism industry has been linked in some cases to community concerns regarding the type of tourism development, where it occurs, and the extent to which host communities feel they have a say in tourism development (Keough, 1989; Murphy, 1985; Murphy, 1994). Many communities are critical of the behaviour that tourists exhibit in their communities, the environmental impacts associated with some tourist activities and facilities, and the perception that many of the economic benefits of tourism flow away from host communities to non-resident tourism operators and companies.

Consequently, the debate about the long-term viability of tourism enterprises has led government and industry leaders to examine *sustainable development*. The concept of sustainable development was borrowed from "Our Common Future," a highly influential publication of the World Commission on Environment and Development (WCED, 1987) that described sustainable development as "development that meets the needs of the present without compromising the ability of future generations to meet their own needs" (Murphy, 1994, p. 275). Within this context, sustainable development has been used as a philosophical or ethical framework for the tourism industry, including the following themes:

- protection and conservation of natural resources;
- maintenance of communities and way of life;
- sensitivity to local lifestyles;
- maximizing of economic benefits to host communities;
- provision of quality of tourism experiences; and
- community involvement in tourism planning.

Many of these principles have been applied in adventure tourism, but other sectors of the tourism industry have adopted them as well. For example, Canadian Pacific Hotels have developed a "green program" implemented throughout the CP chain in Canada (Hawkes and Williams, 1993). At their Chateau Whistler property, the following initiatives have been taken:

- reduction of waste, through reduced packaging, reusable linen, and electronic mail;
- recycling of all paper, cardboard, glass and tin products;
- recycling: use of recycled paper and cardboard products;
- reuse of printer cartridges, soap and wire hangers;
- introduction of lady bugs, rather than pesticides, to control aphids;
- use of cleansers which are non-toxic and biodegradable;
- use of flow taps to conserve water; and
- purchase of locally produced food supplies, where possible.

In 1996, Tourism BC, along with the major tourism industry associations in the province, developed a "growth management strategy" intended to guide tourism development and contribute to a sustainable industry (Tourism BC, 1996). Based on a number of workshops with industry and government, a vision for tourism development was articulated, as described in the following section.

Sustaining the Resource Base

With regard to resource sustainability, two perspectives are apparent: the impacts of tourism on the resource; and the impacts on the tourism industry by other resource industries. The impacts of tourism on the resource include altered viewscapes created by ski hill, marina, and resort developments. Other impacts are a direct result of visitor activities. These impacts would include loss of wildlife through over-hunting and over-fishing, and loss of wildlife habitat through road and ski hill construction. The emergence of whale-watching as a tourist activity has raised concerns about its possible impacts on whales. These concerns have been addressed in a code of ethics and practices developed by the whale-watching industry to keep whale-watching boats a safe distance from the whales. Similarly, the tourism industry is vulnerable to several impacts from other resource industries, such as the loss of scenic value due to logging or mining. Further, tourism sometimes competes with other industries for the same resources (e.g., the sport fishing industry competes for the same resource as the commercial fishing industry; and the adventure travel industry competes with the logging industry with regard to old growth forests.

Quality of the Visitor Experience

Product quality can be described along several dimensions. With regard to accommodation, a major concern is the shortage of high-end quality accommodation outside of the Vancouver area. Also related to the overall experience is the level of service, particularly in a competitive global tourism economy. Issues that affect the quality of the tourism experience in BC include transportation problems, such as ferry reservation systems and delays at border crossings. Other complaints concern hours of operation of some attractions, and the closing of visitor information centres during shoulder seasons.

The province enjoys a high quality natural setting, but it must set policies to protect it. For example, land use decisions, including visible logging and mining, are impacting the quality of the setting. Aspects of these land use conflicts are being addressed in regional planning initiatives such as the Land and Resource Management Plans (LRMPs) being developed throughout BC (see **Chapter 13**). Finally, product quality is sometimes compromised when conflicts occur between different tourist groups, such as the conflict between motorized use (e.g., jet boats) and non-motorized use (e.g., kayaks).

Improve Utilization

There is a need to increase utilization of tourism products in the regions. It seems that the quality of services and facilities is generally an issue in many non-urban areas. This is sometimes expressed as a concern about the quality of tourism operators, many of whom enter the tourism industry for lifestyle reasons, but lack an understanding of the service industry, and the complexities of operating a business in a highly competitive environment. With the increase in sophistication of markets, there is a need to increase professional standards.

The tourism product in BC is largely under-utilized, especially in areas outside Vancouver, Victoria, and Whistler, and during the shoulder and off-seasons. While this is a concern for advocates of mass tourism, there is a counter argument suggesting that what some people may describe as an under-utilized region could in fact represent a rather unique tourism setting precisely because of the low level of tourism development. For some segments of the tourism market, there is a preference to explore unique and authentic natural environments and cultural settings. For these people, a tourist destination is diminished when the natural setting becomes too cluttered with tourism facilities and other tourists, or when the cultural environment appears contrived to meet the tastes of the mass tourist. The theme of "Super Natural British Columbia" is a deliberate effort to market an image of the province as a tourism destination where mass tourism is not the norm.

While the tourism industry in BC has for the most part opted for higher value tourists rather than "mass tourists," the ability to attract and sustain high visitor expenditures will depend on product quality; quality attractions, diversity of things to do, and quality service; and economic conditions and a cheap dollar.

Maintaining Host Communities

As stated earlier, one of the essential components of a sustainable tourism industry is the support of host communities. People who reside in or near the places where tourism occurs generally support tourism for the economic benefits, employment opportunities provided, facilities created, and the less tangible feelings of pride that come with being recognized as a community other people would like to visit. However, host communities also want some assurance that life in the community will not be compromised by the presence of tourists (Lankford and Howard, 1994; Rollins, 1997; Delamere and Rollins, 1999). For example, two significant tourist events in BC had to be cancelled as a result of not attending to community concerns. The Kelowna Regatta and the Parksville Sand Castle Festival were extremely popular and brought significant tourism revenues to the host communities, but in both cases the event was discontinued due to riots and damage to property that occurred when the party atmosphere could not be controlled.

Increasingly, communities in the province have embraced tourism for its many benefits, not the least of which is the economic diversity it brings to many rural communities heavily impacted by downturns in the traditional resource economies based on forestry, mining, and fishing. Nevertheless, many communities have insisted they play a part in tourism planning, to have a say in the type of tourism development and where it occurs.

SUMMARY AND CONCLUSIONS

The study of tourism is of particular interest to geographers because of the relationship between human behaviour, culture, and the built and natural environments. Tourism can be analysed from a number of the perspectives used in the discipline of geography, including resource management, urban planning, economic geography, and spatial analysis. This chapter provides a general overview of tourism development in BC from a geographical perspective, and provides a framework for examining tourism in other places as well.

The tourism industry is an important element in the economy and communities of the province in terms of people employed and contribution to GDP. The expectation is that tourism will continue to grow and contribute to a new, more diverse provincial economy less dependent on the traditional primary industries such as forestry, mining, and commercial fishing (Gallagher, Sweet, and Rollins, 1997). It is hoped that tourism will play a particularly significant role in many of the smaller coastal and rural communities that have suffered much from the boom and bust cycles associated with the resource industries which these communities have relied upon in the past. However, if tourism is to become a sustainable industry in BC, a number of issues need to be resolved.

One of these is access. Tourism needs access to resources such as fish and land. These resource attributes are highly specific to the tourism industry. For instance, land must have certain qualities to be appropriate for a particular tourism experience. Access to resources and land for many existing operators is increasingly an uncertainty that must be addressed. Moreover, expected market growth will lead to further demand on land and resources. This is exacerbated by an approval process that has become costly, slow, and uncertain, constraining investment and opportunities for operators to exploit new markets. Some of the difficulty in access is related to unresolved land claims, a situation that ties the hands of resource managers in terms of making any long term resource commitments to the tourism industry.

A second issue relates to the nature of the tourism infrastructure in BC—specifically to a lack of high-end accommodation outside of urban areas. Tourism operators (as distinct from accommodation operators) feel they can attract a larger number of visitors who demand high-end packages, but that the quality of accommodation outside Vancouver, Victoria, and Whistler is generally a constraint. On the other hand, the urban areas of Vancouver and Victoria experience bottlenecks during peak seasons. Accommodation is scarce during some months of the year; if there is high season growth in sectors such as cruise ships and conventions, there would need to be more accommodation available. In addition, transportation within BC by air, is felt to be expensive, and ferry transportation has some bottleneck problems.

A third significant concern lies in product development. There is generally a lack of high quality attractions outside of the Vancouver/Victoria/Whistler area, therefore restricting tourism development in rural areas. Further, there seems to be a lack of product packaging. While the products are inherently attractive, if more people are to buy them, improved packaging should include the right combination of products, such as integrating transportation and other features into a single package. A related issue is seasonality in the tourism industry. Seasonality is a constraint to growth because the potential for increased business often occurs during the months when there is limited capacity for a product or for accommodation. This means that growth can take place only if there is expansion of supply—which may be uneconomical because demand is seasonal—or if there is displacement of other business. Product development is also hindered by limited access to financing. It seems that lenders do not fully understand the industry, and that both investors and operators do not necessarily appreciate the need for or have equity to invest in the business and may have a limited track record.

A fourth area of concern relates to human resource development in the industry. With the increasing sophistication of the markets and the anticipated growth in visitor volume, more high quality, well-trained staff are required. At the management level, there is a concern that tourism operators lack professional management skills. As the business environment becomes more complex, this will restrict the growth of individual companies and will tend to reduce the number of operators, particularly smaller businesses.

Turning to the issue of effective marketing, there is a lack of integrated marketing, leading to low consumer awareness. While marketing efforts exist for all products, by all operators and regions, those efforts are not necessarily integrated, and therefore the opportunity to have the greatest effect on consumers is lost. Effective marketing and product development requires reliable data. Decisions are being made in the industry without adequate information. Particularly where potential growth is concerned, lack of quantitative information on capacity, utilization, expenditures, revenues, and consumer preferences for product leads to uncertainty, which adds to risk.

The tourism industry in BC operates in a business environment, as well as in a natural environment, a built environment, and a social environment. The social environment relates to community acceptance and support of tourism activity. Community acceptance affects access to resources and land. Where potential new tourism developments are concerned, there is likely to be a community consultative process. This process may either deter potential plans being proposed or prevent them from being achieved. At a higher level of social environment, the tourism industry operates in a political arena, in which provincial and federal government policies influence the viability of tourism operations while government agencies work hard to develop the industry. Some government regulations are viewed as a constraint because, for many products, they make business more complex, more expensive, and sometimes more uncertain than it would otherwise be. For example, taxes specific to tourism seem too high. In addition to the general tax structure in BC and Canada, there are other taxes, fees, and licenses which have a detrimental, cumulative impact on the industry.

Clearly, there are several unresolved issues that need further research, public discussion, and government policy review. Notwithstanding these matters, however, the future of the tourism industry in BC looks bright.

REFERENCES

BC Ministry of Finance and Corporate Relations (1997). *British Columbia Economic Forecasts (1987-1996)*. Victoria, BC: Government of BC.

British Columbia (2001). *BC Stats*. Victoria, BC: Government of BC.

Butler R.W. (1980). The concept of a tourist area cycle of evolution: Implications for management of resources. *Canadian Geographer*, 24, 5-12.

Delamere, T., and Rollins, R. (1999). Measuring attitudes towards community festivals: Social impact priorities in Parksville. *Recreation and Parks BC*, Spring, 16-19.

Gallagher, P., Sweet, R., and Rollins, R. (1997). *Intermediate skill development in British Columbia: New policy and research directions*. Victoria, BC: BC Ministry of Education, Skills and Training.

Hammit, W.E., and Cole, D.N. (1987). *Wildland ecology: Ecology and management*. Toronto: Wiley.

Hawkes, S., and Williams, P. (1993). *The greening of tourism: From principles to practices*. Burnaby, BC: Simon Fraser University.

Keough, B. (1989). Social impacts. In G. Wall (Ed.), *Outdoor recreation in Canada* (pp. 231-275). Toronto: Wiley.

Lankford, S., and Howard, D. (1994). Developing a tourism impact attitude scale. *Annals of Tourism Research*, 21, 121-139.

Mathieson, A., and Wall, G. (1982). *Tourism: Economic, physical, and social impacts*. London: Longman.

Murphy, P. E. (1984). Tourism. In C. N. Forward (Ed.), *British Columbia: Its resources and people* (pp. 401-430). Victoria, BC: University of Victoria, Department of Geography, Western Geographical Series, Vol. 22.

Murphy, P. E. (1985). *Tourism: A community approach.* New York: Routledge.

Murphy, P. E. (1994). Tourism and sustainable development. In W. Theobold (Ed.), *Global tourism: The next decade* (pp. 274-290). Toronto: Butterworth–Heinemann.

Roberts, M. (1998). Travel and tourism. *The Economist*, January 10, 3-16.

Rollins, R. (1997). Validation of the TIAS as a tourism tool. *Annals of Tourism Research*, 24(3), 740-742.

Tourism BC (1996). *Towards a tourism growth management strategy: Tourism industry product overview.*

Tourism BC (1997). *Tourism BC 1997-1998 business plan.*

Tourism BC (1998). News Release (September 18).

Tourism Canada (1987). *Pleasure travel markets to North America: Japan, UK, West Germany, France.* Ottawa: Department of Regional Industrial Expansion.

World Commission on Environment and Development (1987). *Our common future.* Oxford and New York: Oxford University Press.

ENDNOTES

[1] Crown Corporations are government-owned entities that can operate in the private sector at arms length from the usual ministerial bureaucracy.

[2] For current information visit *http://www.hellobc.com*.

Land Use Planning

Colin J.B. Wood and Cimarron Corpé
Department of Geography, University of Victoria

Laurie Jackson
Victoria University, Wellington, New Zealand

INTRODUCTION

The 1990s were a remarkable decade in BC for the formulation and application of new and reformulated planning processes to resolve a wide range of land use and environmental issues. This activity, promulgated by a New Democratic Party (NDP) government, was partially the response of an administration elected to deal with a range of environmental issues, and partially due to its ideological belief in planning procedures and their role in effecting an efficient, fair, and environmentally sustainable land use system. These initiatives led to revisions in the existing land use planning (LUP) system and a resurgence in associated agency activities.

Under the provisions of the Canadian Constitution, LUP is primarily a provincial jurisdiction, although the federal government does exercise some influence over certain aspects (Hodge, 1991). On *Crown Land* (public land) and in a few situations on private, non-urban land, provincial ministries and agencies regulate land use and undertake planning procedures. In urbanized areas, provinces generally delegate LUP to municipalities (in BC, also to Regional Districts) through the provisions of a *Municipal Act*. During the 20th century a considerable body of land use legislation evolved in each province. Clearly, such regulations affect the workings of the market in land, property rights, and opportunities to generate revenues. Consequently, the extent and effectiveness of planning procedures has tended to vary with the political party in power, whether it favours "free enterprise" and minimal government intervention, or one that is more orientated to an orderly system seeking a balance of economic, social, environmental, and aesthetic values. Planning often appears to happen in bursts of activity and legislation, as society deals with pressing environmental and community issues. The nature of the "issue attention cycle" and "planning cycles" have been noted by several authors (Gunton, 1985).

This chapter reviews the main features of land use planning in BC. First, the conceptual basis to land use arrangements, the planning process—its development and the particular circumstances of planning for urban, rural, and wilderness environments—is introduced. Attention then turns to the evolution of LUP in BC. (A summary of the key historical events and developments in planning on Crown Land is listed in Appendix 1.) This is followed by a review of the institutional arrangements for planning in non-urban areas, mainly Crown land, and then urban areas (see **Chapter 11** for wilderness and parks). The chapter concludes with some general reflections on the LUP process in BC and the challenges facing planners.

LAND USE PLANNING

Land Use

Land is utilized for many purposes—settlements, industry, farms, forest harvesting, parks —or left unused as ecological and wilderness reserves. Variations in use can be explained in terms of a mix of physical attributes (physiography, soil quality), economic geography (location, economic rent, income generation), and forms of ownership/regulation (*fee simple*, leasing). The demand for and supply of land—the market in land—and its value and price at particular locations, is an indication of its revenue generating capabilities. For example, land in the fertile Fraser Valley generates more revenue than a similarly sized parcel in a remote upland area (the technical term for these kinds of differences is *economic rent*). The flow of investment in, profits from, and taxation applied to this system are important features in the circulation of capital through the economy and are central to the workings of capitalism and the state (Harvey, 1985; 1996). For a number of reasons—particularly the revenue factor—governments regulate many aspects of land and can also expropriate it if it is judged to be in the public interest (power of *eminent domain*). The land base and how owners, users, and regulators interact with it constitute the **land use system**. For policy makers and planners, therefore, it is important to have a basic inventory or data base of land use variables and a clear understanding of the operations of the land market in their jurisdiction.[1]

Planning

Planning is a decision making process undertaken to manage systems rationally, whereby decision makers perceive goals, formulate objectives, and set about achieving them in a systematic and "bounded" rational way (Hall, 1982). However, the motivations and behaviours of participants in the land use system can vary. For example, studies have shown that many owners do not constantly seek to maximize income from land, while a few treat it without much care for its long term value. Variation in decision making can be explained by a *hierarchy of needs*: for corporations, by profit; for non-governmental organizations, stakeholder interests or utopian values; for governments, ideally, protecting and enhancing the *public good*, and also for maintaining revenues.[2] Therefore, land use patterns are the geographic form of a complex system of competing and sometimes conflicting demands between users. As a result, some kind of planning to rationalize the process according to an interplay of economic priorities, societal demands, environmental needs, and political realities is undertaken by most governments.

How should this take place? Ideally, agencies with jurisdiction over land use determine goals, priorities, and policies, hopefully with meaningful public input to effect an efficient, fair, and environmentally sound system. Its operation, together with a statement of legal authority, goals, objectives, obligations, and set of approved procedures is generally laid out in a formal *land use plan* which shows what kinds of land use are allowed and where. Depending on the circumstances, plan formulation and implementation are undertaken by planners who draw on basic design principles, the particular attributes of the area at hand, and their own creative skills to formulate plans and communicate them to the public.

Plans should respond to the specific needs of a situation according to a defined geographic context, environmental systems, economic reality and cooperation between the planners and the public. Planning procedures themselves can range from elementary to sophisticated, from elitist to citizen driven, short- to long-range, focused on a specific issue such as transportation or wide and comprehensive, entail minimum government involvement or be all encompassed by bureaucracy. The focus may be more on the people and groups involved, often called *community planning*, or more on the environment and the ways in which it is managed. Ultimately, the worse case is where no planning takes place, whereas many would argue from experience that where there is too much, or the wrong kind, is just as bad (Porteous, 1989).

Evolution of Land Use Planning

Planning concepts, legislation, and practices evolved in the early 20th century as governments grappled with rapidly growing populations, changing technology, expanding cities, declining rural areas, and increasing demands on the environment—conditions which led to conflicts that were not effectively resolved by the market or legal systems (Hall, 1982). Many of the issues persist today, while several of the early planning ideas they prompted are still at the core of contemporary policies. To understand the context of LUP in BC it is useful to briefly review, from a geographic perspective, the development of planning in relation to three general environments—urban, rural, and natural areas such as parks and wilderness.[3]

Urban Areas

While early towns and cities in North America were laid out in an organized, usually spacious grid form, rapid industrial growth, technological/economic changes, and weak municipal organization led to deteriorating conditions for many of the inhabitants. Understandably, early 20th century planning ideas therefore possessed a strong reformist element, drawing on concepts ranging from designs for new cities to local zoning ordinances. Ebenezer Howard, a leading thinker of the time, published his "Garden City" idea in 1898, a proposal for reforming human settlements and the local economy. (The green belt idea was based on Colonel Light's 19th century plan for Adelaide, Australia). It blended urban and rural values, included *green belts*, and notions of a new community with a balance between individual and community values. Another contribution came from a contemporary, Patrick Geddes, who was the first to articulate the process of LUP as *survey-analysis-plan-action*. He also favoured citizen input and ecological planning regions, decades before universal suffrage and ecosystems became generally accepted (Hall, 1982). Thomas Adams brought many of these innovative ideas from Britain to Canada during his appointment as chief planner for the Dominion Conservation Commission (Adams, 1917; Hodge, 1985), while others spilled over from urban reform and planning movements in the US (Demeritt, 1995).

From the 1930s onward, the fledgling social sciences began to develop empirical knowledge and conceptual formulations for understanding urban systems and their characteristics, such as: urban spatial form; neighbourhoods and social organization; transportation; spatial economic variation; aesthetics of urban design; and processes of decay or revitalization. This information now provides a rich source of concepts and empirical guidelines for both plan formulation and problem solving (Hall, 1988; Levy, 1997; Bunting and Filion, 2000).

Rural Areas

The European colonization of North America dislodged the indigenous people, began extensive exploitation of the rich resources base, and established a settlement system of provinces/states, counties, townships, and individual farm lots. Land ownership and new forms of land use based on specialization and a monetary economy were also introduced.[4] Unfortunately, many of the settled areas were unsuitable for profitable farming for environmental and economic reasons. As a result, by the early 20th century, as BC was still being settled, many other rural areas of North America saw increasing poverty. As conditions worsened in the droughts and economic depression of the 1930s, the Canadian and US governments embarked on planned rural, multi-purpose projects, notably the Prairie Farm Program and the Tennessee Valley Authority scheme. These projects sought to restore the deteriorating land base, proposed new forms of rural organization, and gave an impetus to rural planning generally (Troughton, 1995).

These activities also led to the development of new technical procedures for evaluating the resource base, such as: land *capability analysis*; conservation of forest and soil through *sustained yield;* and effective accounting of public projects using *cost-benefit* methods. In this way the characteristics of natural systems and their use by society became the focus of *natural resources* studies, a core area of geography and one that is closely linked to both planning and environmental conservation (Mitchell, 1995).

Wilderness

Public interest in protecting wilderness areas increased significantly in the late 19th century.[5] A similar desire to establish urban parks also occurred (*BC Public Parks Act of 1876*). The federal designation of *National Parks* in the Rocky Mountains (1880s) was followed by the creation of Strathcona Park by the BC government in 1911. As park utilization increased, the need for plans also grew. From the 1950s onward, recreation and ecological research responded to these pressures with innovative management concepts such as *carrying capacity*, *limits of acceptable change (LAC)*, *recreation opportunity spectrum*, and *biodiversity* maintenance. LUP now includes recreation evaluation, which determines ecological and aesthetic values for conserving areas of outstanding scenic quality, recreation and tourism values, wildlife protection, and is indeed applicable to the evaluation of recreation potential for all areas (Dooling, 1984; Dearden, 1995) (see also **Chapter 11**).

Ideally, the three specialized planning environments should be integrated into regional and provincial planning scales as a geographic continuum; currently, strategic planning in BC is undertaking this complex task. It is also clear that planners now deal with a wider range of issues caused by economic change, new forms of urbanization, social dysfunction, and environmental crises. In short, comprehensive LUP is now transformed into a broader form of social action so that land use and community planning overlap. Ideally, planning in these contexts also represents a system of making choices and balance between Utopian goals and individual self interest. This general perspective can be translated into specific foci of concern and dimensions of choice.

Planning Foci

LUP is unusual in being simultaneously both a practical and Utopian process, for it deals with day to day issues—rezoning applications and resolving neighbourhood squabbles—yet also subsumes visions and strategies for broader horizons, wider interests, and future generations. Planning is increasingly seen as extending beyond land use management to being part of a community's strategic survival system in an age of fierce global competition, flexible accumulation, and economic insecurity. Ultimately, the land base is at the interface between physical and human systems; the challenge for planners is to make them compatible. The central foci for choices in both land use and community planning involve seeking a harmonious balance between:

individual rights/public good
local/regional/national levels
utility/amenity   efficiency/equity
priority/balance   element focus/system harmony
resource use/materialism — environmental conservation
progress/heritage   reactive/proactive

for both the present and future of society and the environment. The balance may also have to be between strategic shifts which can disrupt, change, and improve the system with the need to continue a system's routine management. How these choices are implemented as a form of social action depends on the public's awareness and concern translated as a political mandate to undertake them. How this has evolved in BC is the focus of the next section.

EVOLUTION OF LAND USE PLANNING IN BC

The provinces evolved variations of the Anglo-American LUP process (Kiernan, 1990; Hodge, 1991) with differences reflecting each region's unique historical, geographical, and cultural circumstances. These embryonic sociopolitical entities shared a common backdrop of: a staples-oriented economy; a core of urbanization and resource producing periphery; a federal/provincial milieu; and a set of institutional arrangements based on English (except Quebec) civil law and property arrangements (Hodge, 1985; McCann and Gunn, 1998). In addition, Canadians enjoy the advantages of a large resource base, a relatively small and peaceful population, and a friendly neighbour —factors which permit a range of policy and planning options with decisions usually conducted in a civilized atmosphere. A greater familiarity with, and acceptance of the government's role in society and the market place also evolved, compared with the US (Lipset, 1990), resulting perhaps in the greater acceptance of community values over and above personal property rights. Despite the many positive attributes we possess, it would be short-sighted to overlook the presence of ongoing problems

Land Use Planning

such as unresolved Native land claims, poor isolated regions, and instances of careless disregard for the environment.

The motivation to implement LUP in BC historically ebbed and flowed with the political party in power and its ideological position on government's role in the economy and for example, its perceptions of the appropriate size of bureaucracy and the importance of planning (Blake, Guppy, and Urmetzer, 1997). In BC, this dynamic has seen cycles between conservative and mildly socialist oriented groups, their control of the provincial and major urban governments, and either their predilection for a free market in land or for regulations and planning procedures (Figure 13.1).

The Early Phase: The System Emerges

With the onset of European colonization, the BC government established an orderly process for: regulating settlement; leasing crown land, mainly for forest harvesting and mining operations; and delegating local services and regulations to municipalities in urbanizing areas. Some land was set aside as parks. The immediate vicinity of First Nations' villages was demarcated as "Indian Reservations," coming under Dominion (federal) jurisdiction; other native territorial claims were denied or ignored since few treaties were signed. The result of this sequestration was for reservations to become islands of neglect and impoverishment. Elsewhere, population and incomes grew, urban areas expanded, and land use competition increased, especially along valley floors.

In rural BC, there were few of the problems of rural poverty and exhaustion experienced in other regions of North America (aside from Native villages). The farming area is relatively small and located in the southern valleys, east Vancouver Island, and the Peace region; moreover, farmers were generally in a less precarious economic situation. As Crown Land leases were utilized for forestry, mining, and grazing, the Ministry of Forests (MoF) emerged as the agency with the main responsibility for managing land use over most Crown Land. Apart from agriculture along the valley floors and ranching on the interior plateaux, rural

Provincial Governments

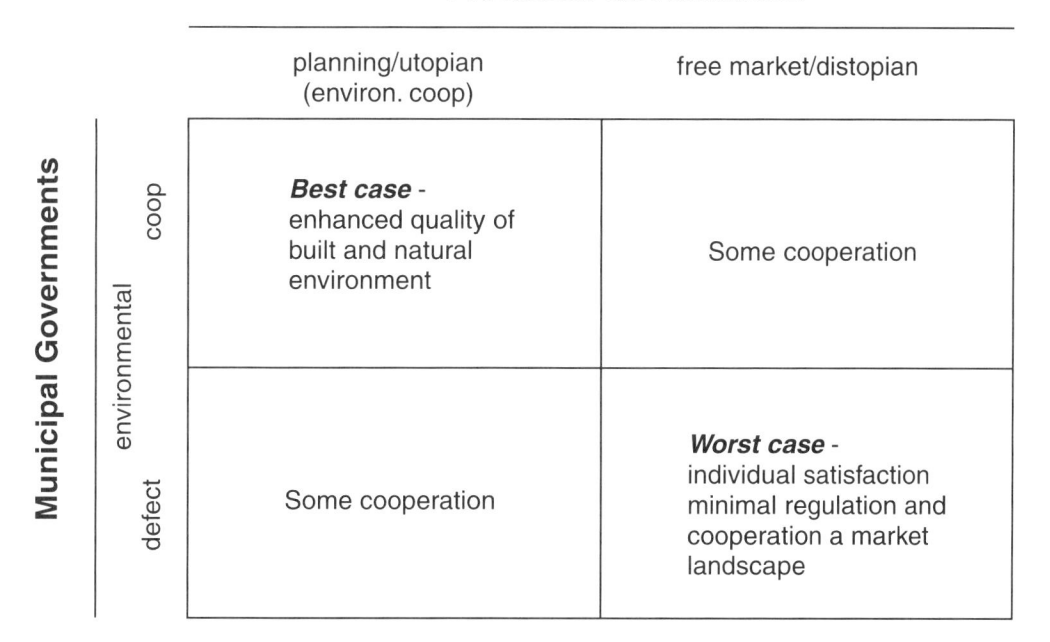

		planning/utopian (environ. coop)	free market/distopian
Municipal Governments	environmental coop	**Best case** - enhanced quality of built and natural environment	Some cooperation
	defect	Some cooperation	**Worst case** - individual satisfaction minimal regulation and cooperation a market landscape

Figure 13.1 Alternative ideological polarity of Canadian sub-national governments and their landscape impacts

economic development therefore often centred on a forest products mill, linked to timber supply from an adjacent Crown Land lease. Rural land use planning in BC became generally related to forest leases and harvesting issues, thereby maintaining the economic vitality of the smaller, single-enterprise (mainly mill) towns. However, this economic requirement has to be balanced against the demands for recreation and wilderness areas. While conflict between logging and forest preservation has dominated environmental issues in BC, nevertheless agricultural and range land management are still important regional issues in the Fraser Valley and Interior of the province (see **Chapter 17**).

Crown Land

The BC government decision in the 1880s to lease large land parcels rather than sell them resulted in the government being the largest land owner (94% of the land base), with provincial ministries supervising the leasing and use of Crown Land. The ministries of Crown Lands and Parks, Forests, and Highways all became lead agencies in regulating different aspects of land use, most of which were oriented to a single use (forest harvesting or mining) with minimal environmental regulation by today's standards. The MoF became the main agency for managing Crown Land throughout BC (see **Chapter 16**) simply because the value in the greater part of the province's land lay in its timber resources.[6] With an extensive forest coverage, few regulations seemed necessary. Indeed, it was not until almost mid-century that restocking of harvested areas became required. Eventually, sustained yield practices became part of forest policy together with a more carefully managed and monitored land use system.

Municipalities and Regional Districts

Local government in urbanized areas is organized as municipalities, typically of township size (100 km^2). Victoria and Vancouver soon spread their influence beyond their city boundaries, drawing adjacent municipalities into their orbits as bedroom communities. Both cities established water catchment areas farther afield as local water sources became inadequate. Although urban expansion by annexation of adjacent jurisdictions is not favoured in Canada, it nevertheless became necessary to coordinate many local services region-wide —initially sewage, water, land, and utilities.[7] Planning boards were established in the late 1950s to meet this role. In the 1960s they were renamed, reorganized, given a wider range of responsibilities, and extended across BC as 28 *Regional Districts* (RDs).

Federal Land

The federal government exercises jurisdiction over the offshore zone, harbours, military bases, national parks, and "Indian reservations." Wartime airfields requisitioned through emergency powers generally became federally-managed airports in the postwar era. Aside from the national parks and the offshore zone, many of these interests were recently delegated to local control and privatized. Federal areas are anomalies in the context of the provincial and municipal LUP systems as provincial regulations do not apply to them.[8] One contentious issue was the acquisition of land by the Department of National Defence (DND) for military training in the Columbia Valley (Cultus Lake area, east of Vancouver). Local resistance to the DND eventually led to abandonment of the scheme. Another ongoing controversy is the weapons testing area at Nanoose Bay on Vancouver Island which has seen protests by peace and environmental groups for many years.

Elsewhere in BC, negotiations between the First Nations and the federal and provincial governments over Native claims to traditional tribal territorial areas, compensation for loss of revenues, and constitutional arrangements are still in progress (see **Chapter 8**).

Growth and Expansion

Mega Projects Phase I (1950-1972)

Under the leadership of W.A.C. Bennett, the BC government embarked on massive infrastructure development in the form of hydroelectric dams, railway expansion (BCR), new highways/bridges, and a coastal ferry fleet.

These activities were undertaken with a *blueprint planning* approach and had minimal environmental/social impact evaluation or public consultation—partly because projects were mainly in remote areas and elite, engineered planning, driven by a growth ethic and the notion of "progress," were the unquestioned norm in the mid-20th century. Furthermore, Bennett enjoyed a strong mandate from the BC electorate (see **Chapter 7**).

In spite of the beneficial legacy of the projects, which some would argue were instrumental in the formation of BC's identity as a province, there were, however, significant environmental and human costs that would not be acceptable today (Toller and Nemetz, 1997). For example, the Bennett Dam on the Peace River had negative ecological impacts both up and downstream. On the Nechako River, the Kenney Dam was developed in the 1950s to provide power for Alcan Ltd.'s aluminum smelter at Kitimat. Although it provided the power, industry, and employment in Kitimat, it affected river levels and adjacent lands, having a traumatic impact on the Cheslatta Native Band, who were forced to move. In the 1980s, public attitudes changed to oppose proposed dams such as Site C (Peace River) and the Moran Dam (Fraser River). The remaining project on the Nechako River was a second phase of the earlier dam, designated as "Kemano II" or "Nechako completion." This project evolved into a complex controversy and litigation (1984-1990s) that eventually saw the abandonment of the half-completed second phase and a compensation pay out from the government to Alcan. The public review of large, technically complex projects presents much more of a challenge than a singular focus on economic costs and benefits (O'Riordan and O'Riordan, 1993).

Reorganization

By the 1970s, the Bennett administration (1952-1972) was out of touch with the new environmentalism and the public's desire for greater participation in substantive issues. Change came with the election of a government led by Dave Barrett (NDP). It addressed many land use planning issues, particularly through the creation of new agencies and the beginnings of wider consultation as a requirement of the planning process.

Agricultural Land Commission (1972)

The annual loss of 8,000 ha of agricultural land to urban sprawl in southwest BC and the Okanagan region combined with the impact of companies "flipping" properties prompted the new government to introduce *Agricultural Land Reserves* (ALRs) administered by an Agricultural Land Commission (ALC). All land (publicly and privately owned) that according to the Canada Land Inventory has agricultural potential was included in the reserves and became restricted solely for agriculture.[9] This legislation, the earliest of its kind in North America, represented a major landmark in the fight to control urban sprawl.

In the 1980s, with a "free enterprise" (Social Credit) government in power, a loophole was introduced whereby golf courses became a permitted use of ALRs. This resulted in a bonanza-style rush of golf course applications which included subdivisions to "make them viable." This windfall gain to developers was, in effect, government largesse to its financial supporters. Controversy over the rezoning was a factor that led to the government's replacement by a planning-oriented NDP administration (Premier Mike Harcourt). It permitted some golf course applications to be completed, but closed the loophole. The ALC is now expanded to become the Agriculture and Forest Lands Commission (AFLC, 2000). There is no direct public input into its activities, although it is advised by an appointed, stakeholder-filled panel; it recently invited submissions as input to an updating of its role and activities.

Islands Trust (1974)

The Islands Trust (IT) was mandated to protect the outstanding scenic, ecological, and amenity values of the Gulf Islands, which lie between Vancouver Island and the mainland. Most of the land on the islands is privately owned—a factor enhancing the prospect of development, especially for summer cottages. Moreover, as *unorganized areas*, there was no comprehensive land use planning taking place. The IT was given quasi-municipal authority— zoning and development approval powers—directed by an *Island Trust Council*. Council members are elected from 13 major groups of islands and in turn direct an executive committee to carry out policy. Although the islands also fall within the jurisdiction of seven different RDs, the IT mandate overrides the RDs (M'Gonigle, 1989). In the late 1980s, it appeared as though the IT's powers would be reduced and more development encouraged, but the change in government in 1991 curtailed this prospect. However, in the early 1990s a challenge to the IT's authority came from a large forest company applying to rezone their land holdings on Galiano Island into small lots. The IT refused and lost the ensuing court battle, then won on appeal.[10]

The ALC and IT have a general body of support, but garner critics nevertheless as they appear in a negative light to those individuals who believe in the supremacy of individual property rights and the opportunity for windfall gains.

Initiatives: Task Forces, Round Tables, Commissions,

Agencies like the ALC and the IT were formed in the 1970s to deal with pressing issues and are generally viewed as successful (see Appendix 1). The strategies employed to resolve other problems had a more mixed success.

Coastal Zone Management (CZM)

BC's coast is a physiographically diverse and ecologically rich region about 27,000 km in length. With the exception of the southwest, it is sparsely inhabited; nevertheless, it is under considerable pressure from an increasing number of users—aquaculture, industrial, residential, and recreational. The most important part of the coastline are estuaries—prime locations in the land/water interface for ecological processes and food chains. They are also desirable for human uses. Several jurisdictions, notably in the US, have had forms of CZM for over 30 years. However, this is not so in Canada, where localized CZM planning may occur, but there is no comprehensive legislative, agency, and planning framework (Day and Gamble, 1990).[11]

In the 1970s, conflicts between users and public concern over deteriorating estuarine habitats prompted the formation of several *ad hoc*, joint federal/provincial planning task forces to examine 11 of BC's major estuaries as jurisdiction is split between the federal and provincial governments. Two of the more pressing conflicts were over land and water use in the Lower Fraser and Cowichan river estuaries. After 8 years of task force research (1977-1985), the Fraser River Estuary Management Program (FREMP) was formed. Considered to be one of the more ambitious and successful CZM programs in Canada, it coordinates government, stakeholders', and the public's interest in the area (155 km^2), managing planning and protection of the shore according to *Area Use Designations*. Shoreline development proposals must comply with zoning; if development is possible, an environmental review is required. In 1996, a partnership was established with the Burrard Inlet Environmental Action Program; the latter was initiated in 1991 to address the management of the industrialized and heavily polluted inlet (Corpé, 2000).

The Cowichan estuary plan appears to have been less successful because agreement was not reached on revisions to the plan (mid-1990s), although a Cowichan-based Environment Committee reviews development proposals and deliberates according to strategies such as zoning and habitat restoration. A new phase of CZM came in the 1990s with the initiation of a Land and Resource Management Plan (LRMP)—a subregional planning unit (discussed later) for the Central Coast, a region of 4.78 million ha that corresponds to the Mid Coast Forest District. The plan (agreed to in April 2001) is both marine and terrestrial in focus, driven by sustainability and public consultation principles (Corpé, 2000).

Other Task Forces

Efforts to coordinate LUP on Crown Land at the regional scale occurred from the 1970s on, leading to various inter-ministry committees and agencies, and the Integrated Management of Resources Conference (1978). Loss of productive forest land, insufficient restocking, and recreational values of forest areas also became increasing issues, prompting the *Pearse Commission* and changes to the *Forest Act (1978)*. The result was an increase in forest designation from 30 to about 80% of the land base and a requirement for a strong *economic* argument for withdrawal from the provincial forest and a requirement for better inventories and comprehensive planning on Crown Land (Roberts, 1987).

Other task forces examined proposals for hydro power sites, controversy over logging in old growth areas, and the state of the timber supply. Protests by conservationists, mainly against the grip of the forest industry on Crown Land leases and the government's general, single use preference, intensified. The problem of agency-client relations and their domination by one stakeholder is not unique to BC; it occurs in many jurisdictions in North America (Fortmann, 1990). The controversy focused on allegations and obvious instances of poor logging practices, harvesting too much old growth, and insufficient parks and reserves. Protests were often triggered by landslides caused by careless logging/road building, or First Nations pressing more stridently to resolve their outstanding territorial claims. The BC government (Socred) in the 1980s, dealing with a recession, was understandably focused on promoting growth to sustain the economy and defend its revenues.

Mega Projects Phase II: Black Holes and White Ski Hills

The BC government (under Bill Bennett) tried to stimulate regional growth in the 1980s economic downturn in several ways, particularly through providing transportation infrastructure. It participated in the northeast coal project at Tumbler Ridge in 1980, to exploit the large coal deposits for the Japanese market (federal dollars were also involved). When the scheme came on stream it unfortunately coincided with a decrease in the global price of metallurgical coal so that it became a financial black hole, to the eventual tune of $3 billion. During this period, the planning function was withdrawn from the regional districts (partly to "cut costs and eliminate red tape"); planners speedily recast themselves as development officers. The provincial civil service was drastically "downsized" to the extent that the MoF could no longer accurately calculate the *Allowable Annual Cut*. Other major initiatives were Expo 86, a second tier exposition held in Vancouver, and construction of the Coquihalla Highway (toll) in the central Interior. It appears that all of these projects suffered from poor planning, substantial cost overruns and questionable accounting —a possible generic feature of all federal and provincial mega-projects. The government as facilitator did work in the promotion of tourism, partially due to joint federal/provincial support programs such as the Travel Industry Development Subsidiary Agreement which invested (1978-83) $31 million, and the Tourism Development Agreement, which invested $10 million, generating further investments of $627 million, particularly in the ski industry.

Skiing is one of the largest sectors in the BC tourism industry, resulting in significant land use ramifications (see **Chapter 12**).[12] The combination of an opportunity for profit in a growth industry, promotion by more than one government ministry, and with support from small communities where traditional forest and mining activities are in decline has led to several applications for new ski resorts, such as Garibaldi (near Squamish) and Cayoosh. However, skiing involves fragile alpine environments, which poses conflicts with wildlife, flora, and water quality. While most wildlife is hibernating during the winter period, impacts are still present. Furthermore, resorts are interested in maintaining a year-round operation with, for example, alpine hikers using lift facilities during summer months to get to alpine trails. Since resort proposals require the use of Crown Land, they are subject to the Environmental Assessment Review Process. Achieving a balance between ecological values and the economic viability of beleaguered communities is a very difficult task. Generally, economic evaluations tend to overlook the increasing marginal value of the decreasing area of wilderness. The government began to respond to concerns regarding the diminishing area of natural environment by establishing the Wilderness Advisory Committee (1985), which examined critical natural areas and the directions for conservation.

New Directions

A surge of public and government interest in the late 1980s/early 1990s led to two important developments. The first was the policy to increase protected areas from 6 to 12% of the land base; the second was to refashion the resource planning system generally. Much of this energy was an outgrowth of the tremendous work of the Commission on Resources and the Environment (CORE), which held meetings, commissioned insightful reports, revived planning at the regional level, and initiated transboundary planning activities. Another important portion of the foundation was fashioned first by the MoF with their subregional level plans at the forest district level (which become the *Land and Resource Management Plans)*, and second by the initiatives emanating from the newly formed Forest Resources Commission (1989), which reviewed several aspects of the land use planning process on forest land.

As various issues and planning processes evolved in the 1990s, clearer goal formulation, firmer direction, and coordination became necessary. This induced agencies to rethink and reshape their overall planning goals and strategies for BC, as in the Integrated Resource Planning Committee's (1993) *Statement of Principles and Process*, CORE's (1994) *Vision for Land Use*, BC Ministry of Environment, Lands and Parks' (1995) *Goals and Objectives for Strategic Planning*, and LUCO's (1993) *A Protected Areas Strategy for BC*. It also resulted in many useful studies and specifications of planning guides and templates for effective land use planning (Brown, 1996). To ensure that there was an overall consistency to these activities, a new coordinating agency, the Land Use Coordination Office (LUCO), and a new centralized Environmental Assessment Office were created.

Land Use Coordination Office (1993)

LUCO was created to develop and maintain an overall perspective on land use planning in BC through coordinating the various planning activities of different agencies. While ministries set basic strategies, LUCO is meant primarily to:

- give strategic direction and hence overall coherence;
- facilitate land use decisions by evaluating the range of possible values and impacts;
- propose effective processes and policies;
- ensure unbiased public involvement;
- liaise with the Ministry of Aboriginal Affairs over land claim negotiations; and
- coordinate the working of Inter Agency Management Committees and Community Resource Boards

(*http://www.luco.gov.bc.ca/lucoinfo.htm*)

Environment Assessment Office (1995)

One of the earliest systematic environmental impact assessments (EIAs) anywhere in the world was undertaken by Canada's federal government for the proposed redevelopment of Nanaimo's harbour (1973). Thereafter, EIA legislation was gradually introduced into the procedures of provincial agencies (Meredith, 1995). In 1995, the BC government consolidated the separate EIA procedures of each ministry under the aegis of a single agency to create a consistent and comprehensive review mechanism for development proposals. The review process now covers a wider range of potential proposals; it undertakes a more thorough evaluation of costs/benefits, socio-economic values, and potential heritage/cultural/health impacts.

The EIA is arranged as a 3-stage process. Depending on the complexity and degree of perceived impact of the proposal, evaluation may require only one stage and be quickly resolved. If a more thorough review is needed, it triggers the 3-stage set of procedures (see **Chapter 14**). Its mandate and organization indicate that there is a genuine intention to ensure that the agency is both neutral and balanced in its evaluations. Furthermore, there is a greater transparency in deliberations, with options for public involvement if warranted. Amendments to "streamline" its regulations by specifying higher thresholds for activating the process, particularly in the energy sector, were introduced in late 1998. This raised questions concerning the government's commitment to protecting the environment; however, it was an independent review that proposed the changes.

The effectiveness of any EIA review process depends on official support to enforce its provisions (Barrow, 1997). One contention is that in BC the process of forest harvesting is outside the EAO's purview (Dunster, 1991). On the other hand, a strengthening of the intention to undertake EIAs came with the agreement in 1992 between the federal and BC governments to cooperate on projects where jurisdictional complexity and overlap occurs, such as in the coastal zone. At the local level, the province holds that municipalities should take care of environmental evaluation, although if the size of a proposed development warrants it, the province can intervene under Section 4 of the *EIA Act (1995)*. The main issues here are sewage disposal and landfills. A proposed redevelopment of a former industrial site into a small town at Bamberton, a few kilometres north of Victoria, also prompted an EIA of the adjacent Saanich Inlet.

Land Use and Planning on Crown Land: The Geographic Continuum

The preceding overview briefly illustrated the phases of economic development in BC and the corresponding evolution of the various planning agencies. In the late 1970s, as a result of the revised *Forest Act*, the MoF emerged as the agency primarily concerned with planning on Crown Land at the *subregional* (district) level, and focused on new procedures for field-level management of forest harvesting operations. It was apparent, however, that a regional tier of planning was required to resolve wider controversies. The numerous studies and debates undertaken by CORE in the 1990s produced a wealth of information on both resources management and planning procedures. This included a specification of an overall planning framework for the province and the determination of areas which were priorities for land use planning (Figure 13.2). Together with the goals and objectives statements made by the various environmental agencies and the creation of the coordinating agency LUCO, it was now possible to undertake more coherent and hence effective regional planning. The Forest Resources Commission (created in 1989) examined a range of issues that pertain to land use planning on forest land, from technical evaluation issues to policies in place in other provinces (FRC, 1991a; FRC, 1991b). With this input it was possible to integrate the regional activities of the CORE process with the next tier of planning being undertaken by the MoF at the forest district level.

Regional Plans

In an attempt to resolve the "war in the woods," three regions were chosen as part of CORE's priorities for the *regional* (4 to 6 million ha) planning process because of the frequency and intensity of conflicts that occurred in those regions (Vancouver Island, East and West Kootenay, and Chilcotin/Cariboo). On Vancouver Island, the situation was particularly tense during the preparation and publication of the first draft plan (1994). Many in the forest industry could not face up to the reality of their unsustainable harvest rate (CORE, 1994). Conservationists who preferred a protected area of about 18 to 20% were disappointed with the 13% allocation, arguing that it could cap future additions. The report, a reality check for many, described by the press as "[Stephen] Owen's prescription—a bitter pill" (*Times Colonist*, 1994), was particularly vexing for logging communities in the north of the island. The final version of the plan did not emerge until early 2000, an indication of the complex issues involved (*http://www.luco.gov.bc.ca*). On the other hand, it shows that even in the most difficult and contentious situations, progress over managing the competition for public land is possible.

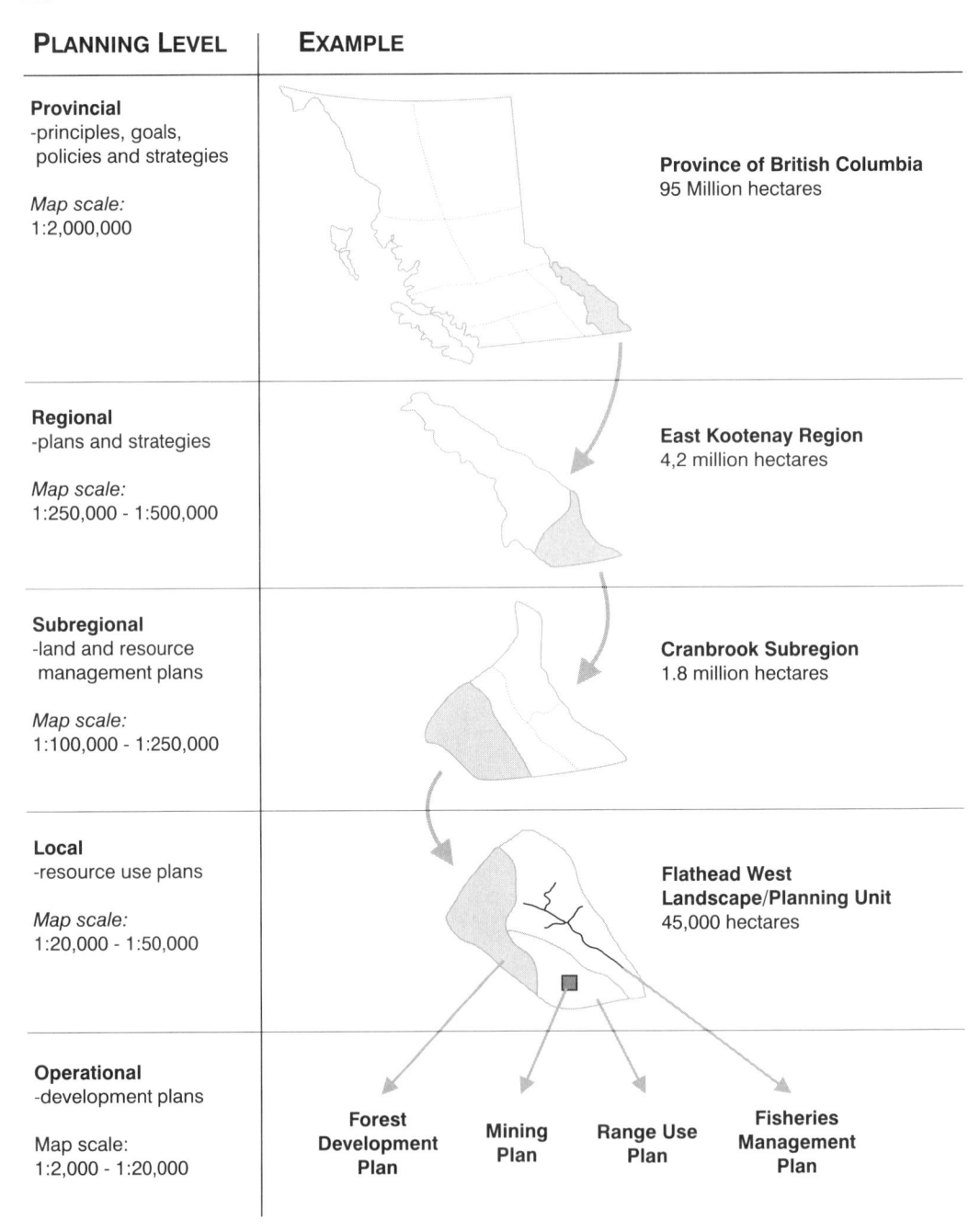

Planning Level	Example
Provincial -principles, goals, policies and strategies *Map scale:* 1:2,000,000	**Province of British Columbia** 95 Million hectares
Regional -plans and strategies *Map scale:* 1:250,000 - 1:500,000	**East Kootenay Region** 4,2 million hectares
Subregional -land and resource management plans *Map scale:* 1:100,000 - 1:250,000	**Cranbrook Subregion** 1.8 million hectares
Local -resource use plans *Map scale:* 1:20,000 - 1:50,000	**Flathead West Landscape/Planning Unit** 45,000 hectares
Operational -development plans *Map scale:* 1:2,000 - 1:20,000	Forest Development Plan Mining Plan Range Use Plan Fisheries Management Plan

Figure 13.2 The planning continuum as applied to BC (after Brown, 1996)

Land and Resource Management Plans (LRMP)

The management of approximately 85% of the province by the MoF is divided into 6 major regions comprised of 43 forest districts.[13] The regional offices implement policy directives given by the Ministry office in Victoria, and direct, support, and monitor activities at the district level. The latter are the field level operating units for the agency, which involves a wide range of work from fire suppression to Forest Code Practices compliance, restocking, and data collection.

The main focus of planning activity on Crown Lands is at the subregional level—the LRMP scale (15,000-25,000 km^2). In the case of Vancouver Island, for example, this would entail four planning subregions, also called *Resource Management Zones*. In early 2001, a total of 15 LRMPs had been completed and several plans were still in progress (*http://www.luco.gov.bc.ca/lrmp/!int-html/int-toc.htm*). While the activity is undertaken as an inter-agency procedure, the MoF is at the centre of the process. The main thrust of the planning activity, which essentially has a forward looking perspective, is built around the designation of *management zones* (which delineate consumptive and other uses), *special protection zones*, and along the coast, *marine protected areas*. Therefore, as in other LUP situations, separation and zoning are key strategies with area use designations based on appraisal by experts, public input, and special attention being given to aboriginal people and their communities' needs. The data base for the process is at the 1:250,000 scale, which permits a broader identification of systems and relationships that may span watersheds, but also attempts to maintain a sense of place and meaning for communities and hence, public input[14] (see, for example, the Okanagan/Shuswap LRMP at *http://www.luco.gov.bc.ca/slupinbc/okanshus/luco01-02.htm*).

Local

At this level (45,000 ha), the finer technical details of management predominate with the process varying according to the site's properties, the immediate locality, and the proposed land use activity. If a ski resort or any new or expanded use are proposed, planning arrangements would also trigger an EIA.

Although the focus here is on LUP, clearly the system of Crown Land leases also play an important role in the process. For example, the development of the community forest lease can lead to a different set of harvesting practices, flow of profits through the community, and emphasis on the form of long-term land use planning in the region (M'Gonigle, 1997).

Consensus Issues

The allocation of property rights to a public resource, usually in the form of long-term leases, is invariably a challenge for governments, particularly when there are competing interests whose land use activities are often mutually exclusive. Some parties believe that they have an economic right and priority to use the area. Notwithstanding the tabloids' descriptions of LUP in BC, the attempt of the government to establish a land allocation procedure with an underlying principle of sustainability where a concerted effort was made to examine a range of values, priorities, options, and stakeholders' interests is remarkable. It was a bold experiment in regional decision making and inclusiveness. Furthermore, many important lessons about the general process and practical organization of public consultation in a democracy were learned (Jackson and Wood, 1999).[15]

Arriving at decisions on land use allocation also requires a sound technical evaluation of the resource base, its characteristics, its range of values, and the feasible choice of alternatives. These frequently complex technical details are beyond the scope of this chapter, but they are dealt with in the background reports to the three regional plans mentioned previously. Much of the technical support for the planning process, particularly as far as providing options to the public is concerned, was made possible by the rapid development and use of GIS by government ministries and by the training of personnel in the Departments of Geography and the Cooperative Education Programs at universities in BC.[16]

LAND USE PLANNING IN URBAN AREAS IN BC

Most Canadians live in cities and towns and for this reason alone it makes sense that urban areas function effectively in economic, social, and aesthetic senses. The evolution, way of life, and interpretations of the variety and meaning of Canadian urban communities are detailed in several recent studies (Loreto and Price, 1990; Bourne, 1996; Bunting and Filion, 2000). The look of buildings, the grid plan, and the manifest adulation of the automobile might reasonably suggest that Canadian cities are typically "American"; however, their political, economic, and social fabrics and many of the finer details of the built form demonstrate that they are different from the US (Mercer and England, 2000). Moreover, they possess their own forms of complexity. While it is almost trite to describe urban society as complex, discussions of this aspect and the relationships between the theory of society, cities, capitalism, and the role of planners as "managers" are worth pursuing.[17] This section briefly outlines the context of Canadian urbanism and gives examples of planning activities by BC urban planners in the areas of: restructuring of the Central Business District (CBD); rezoning; transportation planning; green belt planning; and land acquisition.

Cities as Systems

A useful conceptualization of Canadian cities from a systems planning perspective that is still valid for urban LUP, particularly from a regional context and strategic viewpoint (meaning the appropriate areas of urban space, form, structure, life processes, and their connected surroundings or *urban field*) is found in Gertler and Crowley (1977) and Gertler (1996). They identify six basic needs for cities to function effectively. They are:

- resource use;
- security;
- communication;
- integration;
- culture; and
- flexibility.

Their defining characteristics are:

- a core that interacts with subcores/communities;
- mixed diversified communities;
- a mix of transport modes;
- open space and amenities distinguishing the form; and
- the regional form is a mix of urban/rural uses.

Urban Issues

The main issues occurring in Canadian urban communities that face planners are reviewed in detail by Robinson (1980), Hodge (1991), and Bourne (1996), who designate the key contenders for concern as: sprawl, congestion, controversial projects (NIMBYs), environmental quality, housing, aging, cultural diversity, economic decline, crime, governance, representation, and the consultation process.

In BC, we can also add economic viability (the fiscal base), transportation, security (e.g., organized crime and illegal drugs), and earthquake preparation as regionally significant concerns. Another less newsworthy issue is the aging physical infrastructure, such as sewers and water mains. Such problems are indicators of the inability of the urban system to meet the contemporary needs identified above by Gertler. It also suggests an underlying fiscal malaise and the way in which society manages the economic accounting and taxing of metro systems—a problem seen in its extreme form in the US, denoted by the epigram "private affluence, public squalor."

The combination of heightened awareness of the condition of the environmental "envelope" and the greater interactive relationship between planners and their communities appears more recently in the concepts of *urban bioregions* and *ecological footprints*—ideas that can shape policies to bring about sustainability and enhance the urban environment (Rees and Roseland, 1991). The gist of these concepts is embodied in the spirit and drive of *New*

Urbanism, with its revisitation of community plans and greater coordination between specialists to integrate design, movement, diversity, integration, security, and *sense of place*. The form of a community is invariably connected to its economic base which drives the system.

These conceptualizations of urban systems, specification of needs, identification of priorities, and visioning of directions for the future help set the guiding principles for urban land use planning (Perks and Jamieson, 2000). They are carried out with *planning tools* such as zoning, tax assessment, subdivision ordinances, and general design requirements as specified in community plans and set within the political and fiscal realities of municipal government (Sancton, 2000). Public input is crucial to ensure that a plan addresses community needs and has general support.

Urban Planning in BC

Most of BC's urban population live in the southwest core of the province, which is comprised of the four main urban nuclei shown in Table 13.1. Smaller, second tier cores are present in the Interior—Kelowna (Okanagan and south Interior) and Prince George (central Interior).

In addition to the generic issues identified earlier, the four centres with their coastal sites present challenges in terms of determining the best arrangements for areas of settlement, land use, transportation routes, and green belt/park conservation areas.

- There is a historical legacy whereby the CBDs of both Vancouver and Victoria are sited at the tip of peninsulas and therefore asymmetrically located in relation to the urban region. These plan forms are further complicated by sea inlets and, for Greater Vancouver and New Westminster, by the distributaries of the Lower Fraser River (**Figure 10.4**).

- Vancouver, Victoria, and Nanaimo are all hemmed in by mountains/high land and ALRs on lowlands. Shoreline landfill is an expensive and environmentally questionable option. These constraints on land supply do not give much room for manoeuvre when planning for growth.

- Site/location constraints in the Greater Vancouver area are exacerbated by the asymmetrical location of the major movement generators (the airport, UBC, SFU, riverside industry) and the absence of a freeway system penetrating the CBD area and linking the movement generators. The net result is complex traffic patterns that rely on an upgraded grid plan, street system, 21 bridges, and one tunnel. This is a recipe for congestion at any time of the day. This problem is a principal factor in Vancouver City Council's desire to have more people living where they can walk to work and the Greater Vancouver Regional District's mandate to improve transit (Translink) and plan land use arrangements that generate traffic in a more manageable way (*http://www.translink.bc.ca*) (see **Figure 10.4**).

Table 13.1 Urban nuclei of the south west region of BC

City	Origins	Growth
Vancouver	Rail terminus	Port and rail termini
	Port	Commercial
New Westminster	River port and administrative centre	Administrative: Fraser River port
		Overtaken by Vancouver
Victoria	HBC fort - port	Port - Naval Base education
	Administrative centre	Government, retirement, tourism
Nanaimo	Coal mining and port	Mid Island Centre: port

- An important aspect of urban LUP in BC that is gaining more attention by governments is earthquake preparedness. It is known that the region experiences a major earthquake about every 300 years and that it is now in the statistically susceptible period (see **Chapter 3**).

Gulf of Georgia Region

The urban centres of southwest BC are recognized as part of the wider Gulf of Georgia metropolitan region (CORE, 1992). Concern over urban growth in this area at the trans-border regional scale has led to agreements between the provincial, state, and federal governments of Canada and the US to develop joint strategic planning responses (Artibise, Vernez-Moudon, and Seltzer, 1996). The emerging "Seacouver" metropolitan region agglomeration is shown in Figure 13.3.

Small Urban Centres in the Periphery

Urban centres in the periphery of BC grew mostly as railheads and resource processing towns. Planning in these small towns tends to revolve around two recurring problems: how to function in relation to the major economic activity (mill or mine) and look for alternatives if and when closure or reduced operation occurs; and how to manage the commercial strip that develops alongside the main highway at the edge of the town.

Urban Planning Process

Altogether there are about 150 municipalities (43 have city status) that undertake land use planning according to the BC Municipal Act and may undertake an *Official Community Plan (OCP)*. Municipal operations, and hence planning, are mainly funded by the local property tax system, revenues from local licences, and annual grants from the provincial government. Municipalities also borrow to undertake major capital expenditures. The effective management of urban areas relies on a sound financial basis to municipal government. Unfortunately, many cities in North America experience fiscal crises when industries close down and leave their area, reducing the tax base, while municipal services must still be provided (Levy, 1997). Therefore, most, but not all municipal governments favour growth—that is, new subdivisions, shopping centres, industry, and commercial activity. This growth in turn employs trades persons, maintains the vibrancy of the community, and generates more revenue for the municipality.

Players in the land market, such as developers, who see profit in building new apartments or retail centres, need guidelines for the rules of the "game." Developers submit an initial proposal for consideration with municipal planners which may go through several cycles. Rezoning and development require a public hearing and discussion by council before zoning changes proceed. Depending on the degree of change or controversy, other agencies may become involved.

Dissatisfaction with *uncontrolled* urban growth on prime agricultural land in suburban and semi-rural municipalities led the provincial government to institute the ALR system described earlier. Municipalities have to arrange their land use activities and zoning according to the OCP, the ALRs, the land base, and preferences indicated in public sessions which update the OCPs. The OCPs have to be in accordance with the *Growth Management Act (1995)*. The general attitude seems to be not against growth itself, but rather for ensuring now that growth is managed in such a way as to minimize any detrimental effects and work towards sustainability. As a result, it becomes possible to see how urban LUP is now intimately tied in with economic promotion/development, local employment, and municipal fiscal viability.

In the 1980s, the BC government changed the tax assessment rules in order that municipalities could vary tax rates as incentives to attract prospective industries and businesses—a policy that is now common in Europe and North America. The benefits and costs of *reverse subsidies* is a complex issue, but is often seen as a viable financial strategy for local governments.

Land Use Planning

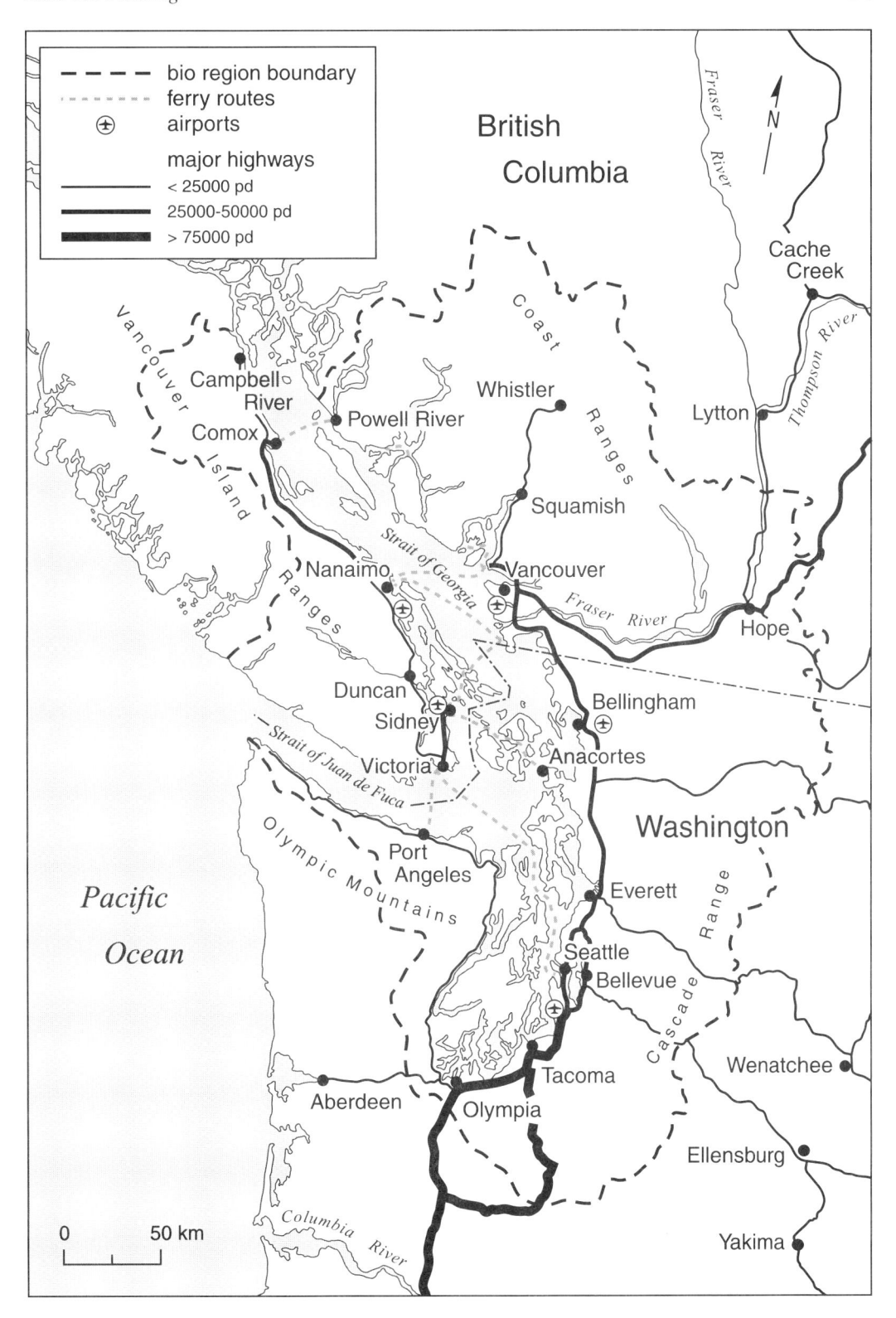

Figure 13.3 The Gulf of Georgia Region showing main urban nodes and transportation linkages

Urban Restructuring

The municipal jurisdictions of the cities of Vancouver and Victoria are a relatively small part of their urban regions. At their cores are the metropolitan CBDs, close to the port and harbour fronts. The CBDs have office, retail, and entertainment uses with some residential areas. Vancouver is the head location for corporate offices and business activity in BC, while Victoria has a smaller office core, a retail area, the Provincial Legislature, and government offices close to the CBD.

Urban planning ideas were influential in the early 20th century development of Victoria, with notably the Olmstead Brothers, and Adams and Bartholomew Associates in Vancouver being active (Forward, 1973; Wynn, 1992). As the BC economy expanded, the metropolitan regions grew, although Vancouver and Victoria did not expand beyond their city limits. Each is surrounded by other urbanized municipalities, which grew initially through suburban rail routes (1920s-1930s) and then with the automobile. Rapid expansion in the form of a mixture of single family residential, industrial, and commercial land uses came in the 1960s. Some suburban municipalities, such as New Westminster, have city status, while others, such as Delta and Saanich which have several small cores, do not (Saanich's population is greater than Victoria).

In the late 20th century, expanding population and increased economic activity were accompanied by several other developments, like *internal restructuring* (e.g., renovation of certain neighbourhoods, especially waterfront) and *regional growth* (e.g., shopping plazas, mega stores, airports in "edge" locations). Besides increased numbers, restructuring also reflects a changing economy, new and declining technologies, a new social mix, and the availability of finance for developers and entrepreneurs. Each of the four original urban nuclei are dealing with these kinds of changes by: redesigning the form and uses of their harbour front areas; the designation of high rise residential neighbourhoods in the core; unravelling traffic circulation issues; dealing with declining traditional industrial land use; coping with areas of substance abuse and prostitution; and promoting economic growth—to name a few key issues. For Vancouver, more than the others, there are social and cultural issues of greater ethnic diversity and how to incorporate this phenomenon in government and planning processes. Downtown planning has also been complicated by federal development of a large land parcel, and the provincial government selling off the former 'Expo' site to an international developer—both of which were difficult for city planners to control. Depending on one's preferences, the developments are either brilliant and globally significant or Le Corbusier's ghost resurrected as 21st century architecture.

Vancouver Restructures

Vancouver has a vibrant and brilliant core area with a mix of commerce, residential, industry, and amenity uses. In addition, it has the attraction of a remarkable physical site and setting. Planners in Vancouver play a pivotal role in the development process, a legacy of a generation of city councils interested in reshaping the city in a meaningful way. In the early 1980s, they prepared a *draft core plan* for the central commercial area and reviewed different growth options. A major engine of growth was the demand for office space, which in turn linked with housing, transport, and capacity of use. These ideas were developed a decade later in the *Central Area Plan* (1991), which set the general strategic guidelines in that the policy is to consolidate the CRD, allowing office development to continue and favouring residential, institutional uses outside this zone (Figure 13.4). This has been followed by more detailed neighbourhood level planning of the central area's 34 sub-areas (Hutton, 1998). A crucial factor in the vibrancy of the core area is the strategy to encourage more people to live downtown and ensure that the *mega projects*—large, integrated mixed-use projects—have a social housing component (20%) and housing for families (25%). Currently, there are several mega projects, with Concord Pacific Place having a projected population of 15,000 in 9,000 units (*Vancouver Sun*, 2000a) (Figure 13.4).[18]

Land Use Planning 247

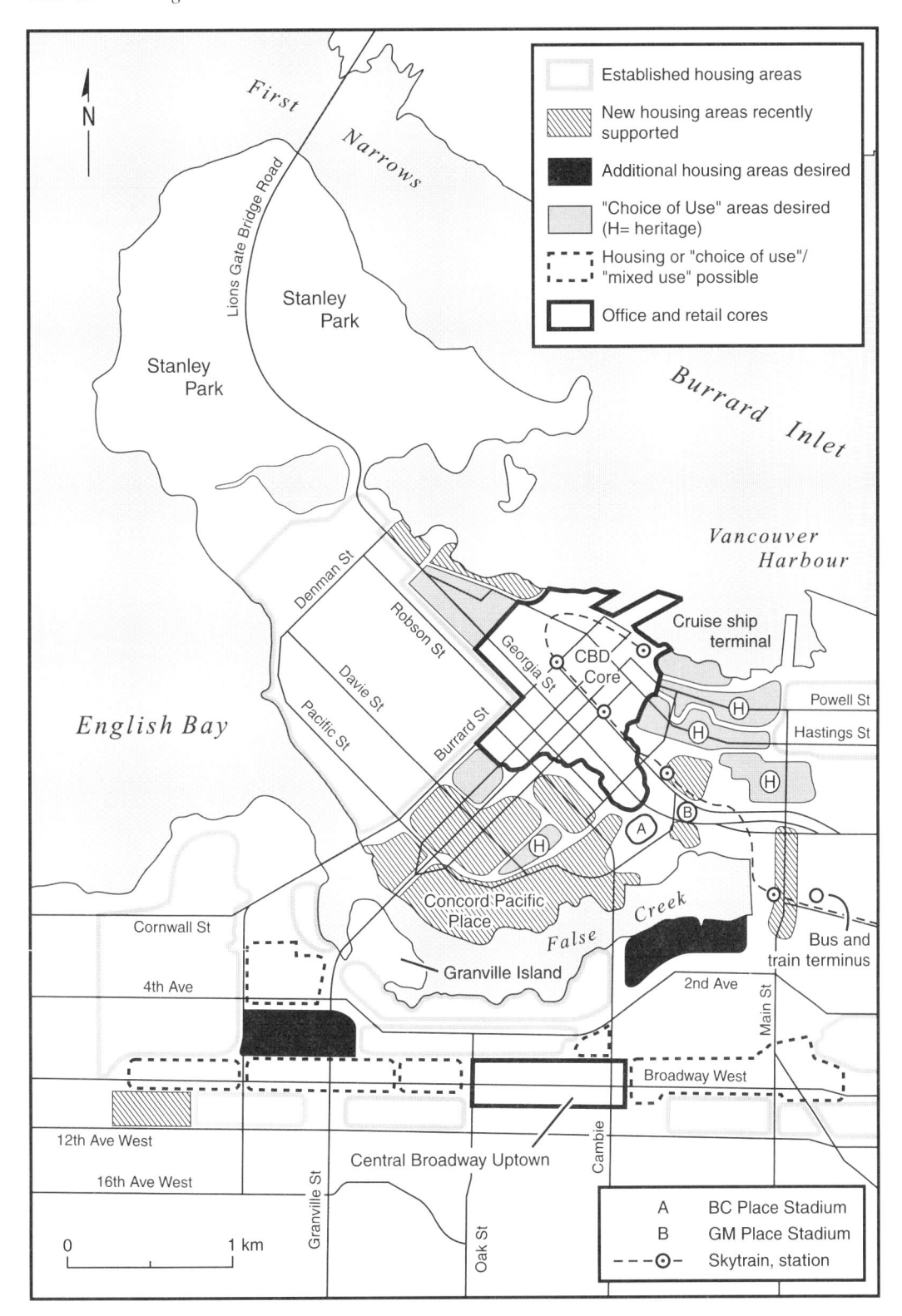

Figure 13.4 Planning for Vancouver's CBD (main source: Vancouver Draft Core Plan: updated)

Developing Options

In the early 1990s, Vancouver City Council and their planners embarked on an ambitious city-wide participation process to bring numerous voices to the planning forum to review the inevitable, difficult choices facing a growing, changing city. Using a novel form of citizen input labelled "city circles," small groups of people met (300 group meetings took place) to generate ideas for the planning staff to consider as input into *Cityplan*. This resulted in a 477 page "idea" book that helped change the direction of strategic planning in, for example, housing and transportation priorities (McAfee, 1995, 1997). Some planners, however, doubt whether the costs ($15 million, or $30,000 per page) justify the output, given the unrealistic nature of a citizen wish list, the time taken to produce it, the relatively small number of people really involved, the lack of specific solutions —all issues that strike at the heart of what a planner is meant to be doing today (Seelig and Seelig, 1997). Notwithstanding the criticisms, the redevelopment of the central core area, with its focus on residential development, is attracting attention in planning circles and generating positive comments (*Vancouver Sun*, 2000b).

Comprehensive Development Zoning (CDZ)

In 1993, the BC government made a new form of zoning (CDZ) possible for municipalities that permits one or more land use classifications at the sub-neighbourhood level as an *integrated unit*—in other words, a unique zoning area. Burnaby is one city that has adopted this approach to deal with the complexities associated with development/redevelopment such as subdivisions, or a major mixed use proposal (Ito, 1997). The main benefit is greater flexibility in the community planning process, making proposals more viable, but also ensuring that they fit in with the general plan and the immediate neighbourhood, such as through integrated amenities. Burnaby has applied CDZ to two development proposals: (A) Metro to use Development; and (B) redevelopment of the Oaklands former prison site as a residential area (Ito, 1997).

Regional Districts (RDs) and Regional Planning

A challenging social and political issue of the new millennium that has distinct geographic dimensions is how to govern and manage the needs of metropolitan regions. Currently, large urban regions tend to be fragmented into a great many jurisdictions, a situation that generally works against efficiencies in government and likely entails higher social costs. In North America, several attempts to develop workable systems of metropolitan governance are being tried, such as in Montreal (Wight, 1998). In BC, the creation of RDs in the 1960s was intended to help resolve this issue whereby the new level of local government would provide a coordinating role to its constituent municipalities, particularly in Greater Vancouver (GVRD) and Greater Victoria (CRD).

The RDs are run by a regional board with members represented by councillors delegated from the constituent municipalities in proportion to the size of the municipalities. Board decisions are implemented by an executive who have technical support, including planners. The RDs coordinate regional arrangements for utilities, waste removal, parks, many aspects of health care, social housing, and so on. The GVRD and CRD initiated regional plans in the 1970s delineating cores of settlement, areas for growth, and scenarios for the future based on varied population projections. While they gradually assumed responsibility and developed experience in managing various activities, they were stripped of much of their planning function in the late 1980s (this could only happen in BC's bizarre political climate).

In the 1990s, a new government interested in growth management and transportation planning in the metropolitan regions enhanced the RD's planning mandate, giving a renewed impetus to its regional planning role. We focus on two examples of these activities: transportation (GVRD) and green belt planning (CRD).

Greater Vancouver's Transportation: The GVRD

The great burst of interest in environmental issues, resolving transportation congestion,

Land Use Planning

enhancing community viability, and long-term sustainability prompted the GVRD to research and produce the report entitled *Creating Our Future (1990)* (Kellas, 1998). Through public consultation procedures, this visioning statement (approved by all of the constituent municipalities) provided a basis for the Liveable Region Strategic Plan (LRSP) (*http://www.gvrd. bc.ca/services/growth/lrsp/lrsp_toc.html*). The central focus of the plan addresses the linkage between land use and transportation and is meant to accord with the directives of the provincial *Growth Strategies Act (1995)*. Coordination with the municipal tier of government is made through the requirement that in each municipality's OCP a *regional context statement* is necessary to show how the local plan fits in with and supports the LRSP, or will be working toward that goal.

Plans have little value if there is no political and therefore financial support. A major step in this direction came with the BC government's decision to create the Greater Vancouver Transportation Authority, which now manages the major roads and the transit system. The new agency, which in effect is controlled by the GVRD, is required to comply with the LRSP. A crucial factor for its success is that it has various financial powers, such as revenue from the gas tax and the authority to levy tolls (Kellas, 1998). However, levying a transport tax is proving to be difficult. The role of transportation in the basic form of the GVRD perspective is shown in **Figure 10.4**.

Another feature of the GVRD planning process that augurs well for its effectiveness and accountability is the requirement for progress reports that link strategic objectives, such as expanded transportation choices, with selected annual and 5 year indicators of progress, such as rates of growth in transit use (Knight, 1998).

Greater Victoria's Green belts:
The CRD's Strategy

Popularized by Ebenezer Howard, the green belt concept became a part of regional planning thinking and practices in the mid 20th century, being adopted in the postwar development of London (England) and Ottawa. In the US, the environmentalism of the late 1960s associated with the critics of automobiles and urban sprawl, such as Tunnard and Whyte, and proponents of improved urban/environmental design, such as McHarg (1969), also supported the concept. The practice of protecting smaller green space areas using *land trusts*, which had been in place since the mid 19th century in the US, was also regaining popularity as a conservation strategy (Wright, 1994). Unlike Ottawa, the reality for other metropolitan regions in Canada is that, with many municipal jurisdictions and therefore no overall control of growth at the regional level, a green belt policy is difficult to implement. Furthermore, ecological units and their boundaries rarely coincide with political jurisdictions, thereby requiring a regional coordination of ecological management and green belt provision.

The creation of the RDs and the ALRs, and then the election in the early 1990s of a BC government interested in growth management, breathed new life into the ability to incorporate a green belt strategy in the GVRD and CRD policies. The CRD had identified preserving agricultural land and securing potential park areas combined with a managed urban growth policy as priorities in the 1983 version of its regional plan. This quasi-green belt policy, which had not really made progress, was reinvigorated in the early 1990s through the renewed interest and funding for growth management, transportation planning, and green space provision. In 1995, the CRD embarked on a Green Spaces strategy, which was later expanded to include protecting bodies of water and thus renamed the *Green/Blue Spaces Strategy (1997)* (Figure 13.5). Its components are as follows:

Green space ... ecological : scenic : outdoor recreation : renewable working land : greenways

Blue space ... waterways : lakes : marine inlets

Besides developing an overall set of strategies and objectives focusing on priorities for protection and the rationale for conservation (including public consultation through meetings and workshops), the plan also formulated

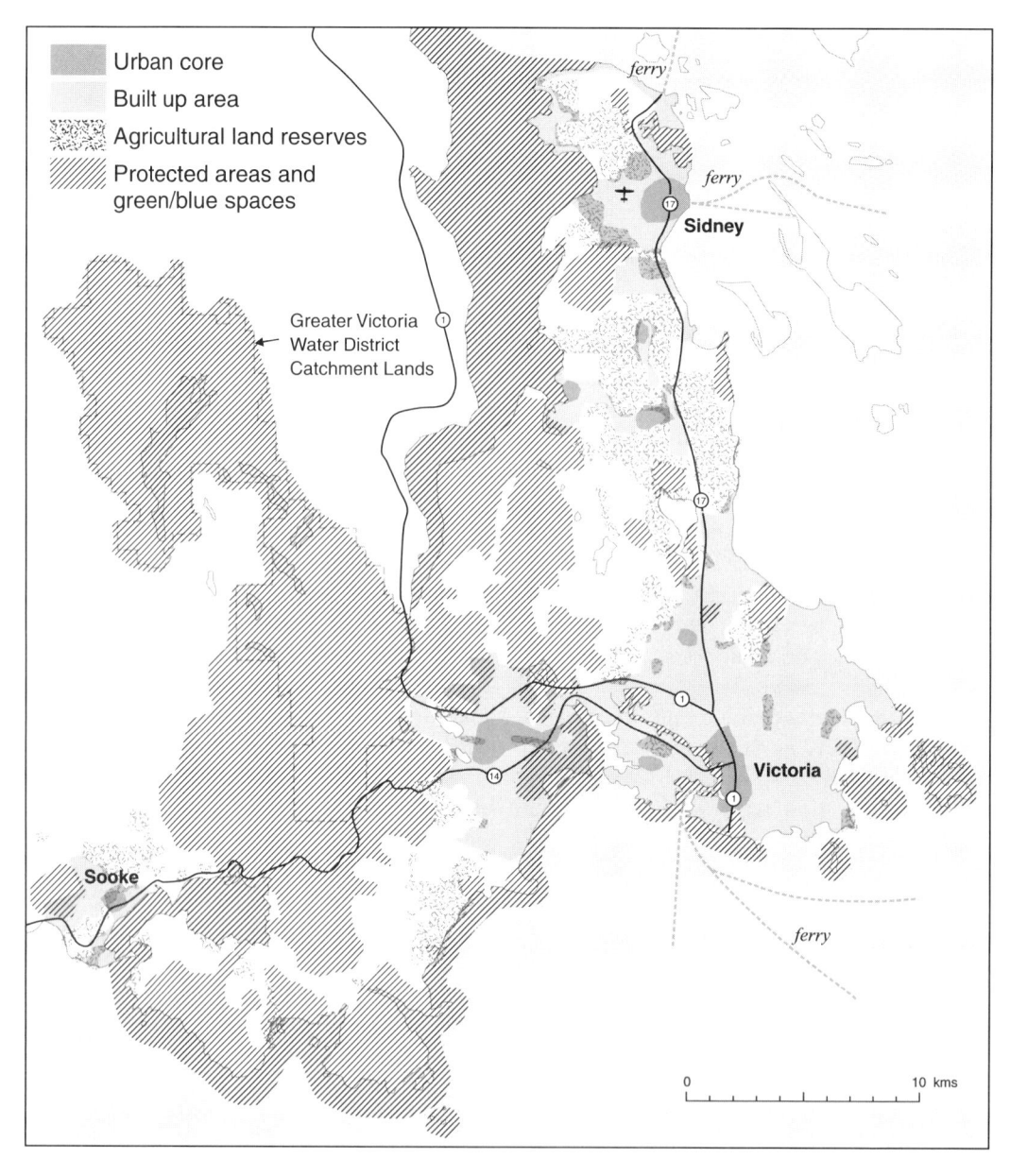

Figure 13.5 Planning for green/blue space protection in the CRD region
(source: CRD Green/Blue Spaces Plan, 1999)

a framework for a green spaces spatial system based on:

Feature	Characteristics
Green space core areas and water bodies	parks are the main natural components ecologically viable areas
Greenway corridors	linear natural features
Greenway connecting links	smaller than corridors but similar intent
Renewable resource landscapes	agriculture and forestry activity areas

Areas designated as priorities for acquisition for the Green/Blue Space Strategy and necessary to complete this form of ecologically-based system were identified in the 1999 *CRD Parks Master Plan*. The majority of properties are held in private ownership. Unless there is support and the means to undertake acquisitions, the plan becomes a paper tiger, particularly if there are other more pressing demands on municipal budgets (Capital Regional District, 1999). This situation is being successfully addressed, however, by the two following methods.

First, through the use of *land covenants* it becomes possible for NGOs to help organize the acquisition of properties through fund raising, coordination, and public awareness activities.[19] For example, in the purchase of the Ayum Creek properties in 1998, the Habitat Acquisition Trust and the Land Conservancy of BC were able to gain support, acquire funds by the purchase deadline, place use covenants on the properties, and then transfer title to the CRD (Bullen, 2000). Land trusts can often be far more effective for attracting public support and donations for acquiring land for conservation than government agencies. Second, prompted by the CRD Green/Blue Spaces Strategy, the constituent municipalities now levy funds for land acquisition. A referendum decision in 1999 enabled the levying of a modest $10 per capita. Over time this will grow to make possible further land purchases to complete the green/blue space system. The CRD sponsored workshops in the fall of 1999 to determine the rate of progress in meeting the green space goal.

While these two case studies show the land use planning activities taking place at the RD level in metropolitan regions, it is important to note that the RDs perform several other significant roles, so they are not merely a narrowly-based, supra municipal agency dealing with land use problems and transportation. Coordination of health care, public housing, and utilities are other important responsibilities of the RDs.

Economic Development

While the main narrative of this chapter is land use planning, some mention of the linkages with economic development is necessary in order to gain some insight into trends in the community environment that are influencing LUP. In the global competition for capital for investment in economic enterprises, redevelopment, and therefore jobs, it is increasingly necessary to have a "package" that includes appropriate or "facilitating" LUP. The larger urban communities in BC have a lengthy record of encouraging economic development within their jurisdictions (Baskerville, 1985). In BC, this tended to be separate from the bureaucracy of the LUP process that had gradually evolved, although it overlapped where major corporate developers such as the CPR were active. Vancouver's city council established an economic development office in the late 1970s to encourage new investment in the city. The economic downturn of the early 1980s stimulated further initiatives which included renovation and recycling of former industrial and warehouse space for office and small business use (Hutton, 1998). In the late 1980s, the provincial government changed the property assessment rules so that municipalities could offer incentives to attract new industries and businesses; this is a common policy in Europe and North America. The benefits and costs of a reverse subsidy program, while often imperfectly understood, is an economic strategy that is seen as a viable approach to improve civic finances. Other policies, such as local *import substitution* or "buy local" programs, have also featured in various inter-municipal meetings (Davis, 1989).

The small, single-enterprise communities that dot the landscape of the periphery of BC are most vulnerable to economic collapse if their mill, mine, or fishery closes, especially those communities in remote locations (Horne and Robson, 1993). Again, this is a story told and retold many times across Canada (Lucas, 1971; Halseth, 1999). Even accessible small towns like Squamish scramble to find a suitable replacement when their economic engine (a lumber mill) grinds to a halt. The processes of community economic planning invariably intertwine with LUP and the formulation of options that may attract outside investors. This planning process has to be in accordance with the values and preferences of the community, which might be difficult if distinct polarizations are present (Reed and Gill, 1997; SQUAM, 1998), or where an unusual jurisdictional situation occurs, as in Field, a small town located in the BC section of Banff National Park (Massam, 1999).

Planning in BC at the Millennium

In general, little thought was given to long-term environmental protection or sustaining resource flows as the population and development of BC grew during the first part of the 20th century. Rapid development, economic values, maximizing personal gain, and minimal regulation for the public good predominated, with the exception of some park designation and the introduction of limited conservation measures. The benefits of this era included the emplacement of transportation and renewable energy source infrastructures, expanding settlements, and relatively high incomes. The costs were: increasing pollution; poor harvesting and restocking of forest land; destroyed fish habitats; urban sprawl; deterioration of urban areas; and an alienated Native population. The latter part of the century saw considerable reform with: the environment on the political agenda; the introduction of land use planning systems; new and reformulated management agencies; corporate greening; greater accountability; and meaningful negotiations with Native peoples. Notwithstanding these changes and the progress made, the complexities of many land use, environmental, and related socioeconomic problems persist.

During the last 100 years, the context and requirement for land use and community planning has changed enormously. The current situation is one wherein the large territorial size of BC, the varied physical environments, and the competing demands for land require integrated planning at numerous geographic scales. The context for planning today is therefore one of:

- a small, highly concentrated population with relatively high incomes, located in the southwest "core" and now dominated by service industries. Small towns with single enterprises, usually forest products or mining, which comprise the "periphery" where incomes are lower;

- a relatively rapid population growth rate from in-migration, which is mainly urban and again in the southwest; the average age of the population is increasing;

- an economy—a subsystem of the national, NAFTA, and global systems—that is experiencing greater competition and instability;

- a high percentage of public ownership—94% of the land base and the basic infrastructure;

- an ongoing process of land claim settlements with First Nations;

- terrestrial and marine ecosystems that are of global significance; and

- a high level of environmental awareness, but a contradiction in that the public want a high quality environment, however they allow their vehicles and wastes to degrade the environment.

The key issues that concern the people of BC together with some of the possible planning options available are summarized in Table 13.2. As this chapter has shown, there is ongoing public interest in the quality of life in BC and solving these problems. There is a considerable body of legislation and agency expertise to address them; furthermore, a good measure of progress has been achieved.

Table 13.2 Issues facing society in BC and some possible policy and planning responses

Urban	
Governance	Amalgamation of metropolitan municipalities
Urban growth	Growth management: satellite towns
Transport	User pay -transit - system maintenance
Economic	Enterprise zones; small business nets
Social cohesion	Social housing requirement; mixing
Race relations	Integration/non-discrimination policies
Crime (local)	Neighbourhood proofing; local policing
Crime (organized)	Municipal-BC police force
Rural	
Small towns	Tax incentives; activity dispersion
Agricultural	New specialties: tax support
Isolated communities	Relocate; alternative activities
Wilderness	
Forest harvesting	Zoning; selective logging; community leases
Conservation	Ecological reserves, limits to acceptable change
General	
Relations/First Nations	Settlement/compensation/partnerships
Environmental quality	Environmental accounting; carbon tax
Safety	Earthquake and storm proofing

Conclusions

BC has a large area and a relatively small population that enjoys an environment of outstanding quality and generally a good standard of living. However, changing economic circumstances and public attitudes toward the environment and resource exploitation have caused increasing and often conflicting demands on the land resource base—issues which gained greater prominence from the 1960s onward. The change in attitudes, which resulted in direct action and often bitter protest, was timely and did result in substantive changes for the long-term viability of the environment. It is clear, however, that a reformulated system of government priorities and planning was necessary to resolve or at least ameliorate many of these controversies.

There have been cries to privatize public land holdings as another alternative to this approach by minimizing planning procedures and thereby "freeing up" the land market system, maximizing personal wealth, and relying on a trickle down process. Generally, BC governments have resisted this direction and opted for continued public ownership together with a range of planning procedures to manage the system. It was apparent by the 1990s that the legislation, policies, and planning procedures that regulated activities on both Crown and privately owned land needed revision and there had to be a directed response to public demands. The fact that provincial and municipal governments derived much of their revenue from taxing land use made the resolution of these issues even more pressing. The consequence is that substantial changes were made to LUP in BC in the last two decades, both on Crown lands and in the municipal arena—a product of legislative change, much public and media debate, economic realities, and considerable input from planners and consultants. The focus of the planning process on Crown land is the LRMP, which requires agency co-operation and public consultation. In municipal jurisdictions, the OCP is the *modus operandi.* Municipal plans now must conform also to regional growth situations—an indication of the wider strategic thinking, integration, and forward looking perspective that is now required.

If much of the dust has settled on the intense debates of the 1990s, are we any better off? One distinct advance is that the area of conserved and protected land base has increased from 6% to 12% of the total land area. Further, there is a more detailed understanding of the land resources of BC and the options that are available for the future. It is also indisputable that the public must be included in decisions. Generally, attempts to widen the degree of participation in land use planning are laudable, particularly if it is clear that there is a genuine attempt at a fair distribution of costs and benefits. This change toward openness and inclusion nevertheless runs up against the reality of increased costs and a slower pace of making decisions simply because a larger number and wider range of interests are participating. The counter argument is that these decisions will be more compatible with community needs, most likely better in the long run, more equitable, and therefore less costly for the community as a whole. A problem arises where there is no real community as such (for example, in more remote areas). The government then has the more difficult role of choosing between the arguments put forward by forest companies, mining conglomerates, resort developers, its own scientific and technical staff, and the environmentalists who live in urban areas far removed from the site of the issue. At this point we like to believe that the public interest is protected by the courts and public agencies.

Requiring agencies to be more generally accountable, more involved in regional land use planning which involves a wider clientele, and less focused on single use options is a significant step toward integrated multi-purpose land use planning; this has happened in BC over the last decade on Crown lands. In urban areas there has also been progress, where the quality of life is high even by North American standards. However, the cry has also been that municipalities roll over and make it too easy for developers or big American retail chains to get their way on rezoning applications (*Vancouver Sun*, 2000c). The municipal structure in metropolitan regions virtually ensures that there will always be one jurisdiction that will agree to a monster store, gaining the direct benefits, but only bearing a small portion of the regional costs. Such changes affect the whole region and frequently lead to a deterioration of the aesthetic quality of the urban landscape. However, surveys suggest that "jobs" are more important than the "environment" in the perspective of the public (Blake et al., 1997). In sum, estimating the distribution of the total costs and benefits needs a more thorough social and environmental accounting.

The considerable effort expended on LUP in the 1990s now means that in BC there is a clearer picture of the state of human-environmental relations in their geographic, economic, and social-political contexts than ever before. There will continue to be disagreement about who gets access to the resource base or shares in the windfall gain from rezoning, but there are procedures in place for determining and allocating a fairer distribution of costs and benefits. Further, there is better information that is more available to a wider range of parties than was the case in the past. Ideally, the best situation is not only to maintain the present arrangements which are the product of considerable public debate, but also to ensure that a process of reasonable updating takes place to maintain a resilience in the system of land management planning. This suggests that more flexibility in lease holding, with communities given the option to lease, increases the range of options. The system should not deter initiatives from the private sector, but look for ways to cooperate. Ultimately, the future of land use planning in the province depends on:

- whether the party in power in the legislature subscribes to a planning ethic or prefers a free market on Crown Land, eliminating the present agency structure. On the other hand, the direction could be community controlled leases and small business development (or the present system unchanged);

- in municipal jurisdictions, the rules of the game could be substantially altered by a BC government intent on fiscal responsibility at all levels. This would link all kinds of activities, for example, to a more developed user-pay arrangement and "free up" the system.

Appendix I: Main events in the evolution of the land use planning system: Crown land and rural areas

Early Phase

late 1800s
- Organized land settlement; Ministries formed; Indian Reserve system; urban parks established

early 1900s
- Strathcona Park 1911
- Zoning introduced in main urban centres (1930s)

Mega Projects I

1950s-70
- Dams, HEP system, highways, bridges, railways, docks
- Regional Districts formed

Reorganization

early 1970s
- Agricultural Land Reserves; Islands Trust; MoF begins systematic ecological mapping and inventory development : Environment Act : Environment and Land Use Committee (ELUC)

late 1970s
- Pearse Commission and revised *Forestry Act*: *multiple use planning* required on public forest land

- Pressure for Parks (National): Pacific Rim and Gwaii Hanaas (Queen Charlotte Islands)

Mega Projects II

1980s
- North east coal; Coquihalla Highway; Expo 86; Skytrain.

1980
- Forest and range resource analysis (*Forest Act* requirement). Detailed review of forestry resource base identifies/examines conflict over land use; details over-harvesting

1982
- Blockades over logging in the Clayoquot Sound area

- Stein Valley and Cascade Wilderness protests

New Directions I

1985
- Wilderness Advisory Committee: examines critical wilderness areas

1988
- *Dunsmuir Agreement*: on a Provincial Land Strategy - meeting of government agencies and interest groups → attempts to formulate directions

1988	• *Strangway Commission*: recommends a Round Table on environment and the economy
	• Striking the balance: Parks policy
1988	• South Moresby Land Use Agreement signed (National Park Reserve)
1989	• *Forest Resources Commission*: established to advise Ministry of Forests on land use strategies including TFL system
1990	• *BC Forest Industry*: formulates "Towards a Land Use Strategy"
1990	• Carmanah Valley Land use agreement results in Carmanah Provincial Park
1990-92	• *Protected Areas Strategy* for BC Parks, Ministry of Environment, Lands and Parks, and Ministry of Forests convene public meetings, identify goals, strategies
	• *Old Growth Proposals*; considerable public demand to protect remaining areas
1990	• *Round Table* convened - meetings, strategies for sustainability.

New Directions II

1991	• Forest Resources Commission reviews land use planning system
1992	• *Fraser Basin Management Program* - multi-government program for managing Fraser River basin - according to sustainability and consensus principles
1992	• *Protected Areas Strategy*: - determination of direction for legislative action - builds on parks and wilderness consultations - action for protected area planning.

1992	• *Commission on Resources and Environment* (CORE) - established by the BC government as an independent commission - driven by sustainability, a land use ethic, conflict resolution, regional consultation and community consensus
	  - Land Use Strategy for BC - Draft Land Use Charter
	  - Land Use Plans for: Cariboo/Chilcotin; E. Kootenay; Vancouver Island (significant conflict areas)
	  - Instruction Guides on Planning Process/Procedures

1993	• *Clayoquot Sound protests peak over old growth harvesting, 800 people arrested.*

1993	• *Integrated Resource Planning Committee*
	  - Land Resource Management (LRMP) Plans (level below major regions)
	  - Public Participation Guidelines.

1994	• CORE (DRAFT) PLAN FOR VANCOUVER ISLAND RELEASED
1994	• LAND USE COORDINATION OFFICE (LUCO)
	• *Land Title Amendment Act:* allows landowners to grant conservation covenants - later in 1990s amended to permit conservation groups to hold covenants
1995	• *Strategic Planning*: Sets out the goals/objectives - planning process - includes statements on "protecting public values," - consultation and including First Nations.
1995	• *Growth Strategies for BC:* Ministry of Municipal Affairs - directed more to urbanized regions - reviews the role of regional districts in planning arena. OCP must consider growth options
1996 to date	• continuation of the regional and LRMP plans and their publication: park and reserve committees
1997	• *Fish Protection Act* - focuses on protection of riparian (streamside) habitats
2001	• Protection of Riparian extended to southwest BC

For more details, especially on forestry, see Forest, Range and Recreation Resource Analysis report (BC Ministry of Forests, 1994, *http://www.for.gov.bc.ca/pab/publctns/frrra/frrratoc.htm*).

REFERENCES

Adams, T. (1917). *Rural planning and development.* Ottawa: Conservation Commission of Canada.

AFLC (2000). *Farms and forests for the future: A strategic plan for BC's Land Reserve Commission* (draft). Victoria, BC: Agriculture and Forest Land Commission, Government of BC.

Arnstein, S. (1969). A ladder of citizen participation. *J. of the American Institute of Planners,* 35, 216-214.

Artibise, A., Vernez-Moudon, A., and Seltzer, E. (1997). Cascadia. In R. Geddes (Ed.), *Cities in our future* (pp. 149-174). Washington, DC: Island Press.

Barrow, C.J. (1997). *Environmental and social impact assessment: An introduction.* London: Arnold.

Baskerville, P.A. (1985). *Floating free: Enterprise zones and Island development, a perspective from Victoria's past.* Islands 86 Symposium, University of Victoria.

BC Ministry of Environment, Lands and Parks (1995). *Goals and objectives for strategic planning.* Victoria, BC: Ministry of Environment Lands and Parks.

Blake, D.E., Guppy, N., and Urmetzer, P. (1997). Being green in BC. *BC Studies,* 112, 41-61.

Bourne, L. (1996). Normative urban geographies: Recent trends, competing visions, and new cultures of regulation. *Canadian Geographer,* 40, 2-16.

Brown, D.W. (1996). *Strategic land use planning source book.* Victoria, BC: Commission on Resources and Environment.

Bullen, A. (2000). *Green visions, private property, land trusts and the public in the Capital region.* Honours Thesis (unpublished). Department of Geography, University of Victoria, Victoria, BC.

Bunting, T., and Filion, P. (Eds.) (2000). *Canadian cities in transition* (2nd edition). Toronto: Oxford University Press.

Capital Regional District (1999). *Master Plan (Parks).* Victoria, BC.

Cater, J., and Jones, T. (1989). *Social geography: An introduction to contemporary issues.* London: Edward Arnold.

CORE (1992). *Land use strategy for BC: Victoria.* Victoria, BC: Commission on Resources and Environment.

CORE (1994). *Finding common ground: A shared vision for the land* (pamphlet). Victoria, BC: Commission on Resources and Environment.

Corpé, C. (2000). *Coastal zone management: The Cowichan Estuary.* MA Thesis (unpublished). Department of Geography, University of Victoria, Victoria, BC.

Day, C., and Gamble, D. (1990). Coastal zone management in BC: An institutional comparison with Washington, Oregon and California. *Coastal Management,* 18, 115-141.

Davis, C. (1989). Buy-local programs: Import substitution at the regional level. *Plan Canada,* 29, 41-51.

Dearden, P. (1995). Parks and protected areas. In B. Mitchell (Ed.), *Resource and environmental management in Canada* (pp. 236-258). Toronto: Oxford University Press.

Demeritt, D. (1995). Visions of agriculture in British Columbia. *BC Studies,* 108, 29-60.

Dooling, P.J. (Ed.) (1984). *Parks in British Columbia: Emerging realities.* Vancouver: UBC Press.

Dunster, J. (1991). *The use of EIA in forest planning and management.* FRC Background Papers. Victoria, BC: Ministry of Forests.

Fortmann, L. (1990). The role of professional norms and beliefs in the agency-client relations of natural resource bureaucracies. *Natural Resources Journal,* 30, 361-380.

Forward, C.N. (1973). The immortality of a fashionable residential district: The Uplands. In C.N. Forward (Ed.), *Residential and neighbourhood studies in Victoria* (pp. 1-39). Victoria, BC: University of Victoria, Department of Geography, Western Geographical Studies, vol. 5.

Gertler, L.O., and Crowley, R.N. (1977). *Changing Canadian cities: The next 25 years.* Toronto: McClelland and Stewart.

Gertler, L.O. (1996). The regional city of the 21st century: Looking back to look forward. *Plan Canada,* 28, 10-14.

Gunton, T. (1985). A theory of the planning cycle. *Plan Canada,* 25, 40-44.

Hall, P. (1982). *Urban and regional planning* (3rd edition). London: Allen and Unwin.

Hall, P. (1988). *Cities of tomorrow.* Oxford: Blackwell.

Harvey, D. (1985). *The urbanization of capital.* Baltimore: Johns Hopkins Press.

Harvey, D. (1996). *Justice, nature, and the geography of difference.* Oxford: Blackwell.

Halseth, G. (1999). We came for work: Situating migration employment in BC's small, resource-based communities. *Canadian Geographer,* 43(4), 363-381.

Hodge, G. (1985). The roots of Canadian planning. *American Planning Association Journal,* 51(1), 8-22.

Hodge, G. (1991). *Planning Canadian communities: An introduction to the principles, practice, and participants* (2nd edition). Scarborough, ON: Nelson Canada.

Horne, G., and Robson, L. (1993). *British Columbia community economic dependencies.* Report prepared for the BC Round Table on the Environment and the Economy.

Hutton, T.A. (1998). *The transformation of Canada's Pacific metropolis: A study of Vancouver.* Montreal: Institute for Research on Public Policy.

Integrated Resource Planning Committee (1993). *Land and resource management planning: A statement of principles and process.* Integrated resource management planning committee. Victoria, BC: Government of BC.

Ito, K. (1997). Comprehensive development zoning. *Plan Canada*, 29, 8-12.

Jackson, L., and Wood, C. (1999). The use of consensus in public involvement. *Small Towns*, 29(4), 4-11.

Kellas, H. (1998). Greater Vancouver. *Plan Canada*, 30, 30-31.

Kiernan, M.J. (1990). Land use planning. In R. Loreto and T. Price (Eds.), *Urban policy issues: Canadian perspectives* (pp. 58-85). Toronto: McClelland and Stewart.

Knight, N. (1998). An update on monitoring the GVRD's Liveable Region Strategic Plan. *Plan Canada*, 29, 30-32.

Levy, J.M. (1997). *Contemporary urban planning* (4th edition). Englewood Cliffs, NJ: Prentice Hall.

Lipset, S.M. (1990). *Continental divide*. New York: Routledge.

Loreto, R., and Price, T. (1990). *Urban policy issues: Canadian perspectives*. Toronto: McClelland and Stewart.

Lucas, R. (1971). *Minetown, milltown, railtown: Life in Canadian communities of single industry*. Toronto: University of Toronto Press.

LUCO (1993). *A protected areas strategy for BC*. Victoria, BC: Land Use Coordination Office.

McAfee, A. (1995). People participating in planning. *Plan Canada*, 27, 15-16.

McAfee, A. (1997). When theory meets practice: Citizen participation in planning. *Plan Canada*, 28, 18-22.

McCann, L., and Gunn, A. (1998). *Heartland and hinterland* (3rd edition). Scarborough, ON: Prentice Hall.

McHarg, I. (1969). *Design with nature*. Garden City, NY: Natural History Press.

M'Gonigle, M. (1989). Sustainability and local government: The case of the BC Islands Trust. *Canadian Public Administration Review*, 32(4), 524-544.

M'Gonigle, M. (1997). Reinventing British Columbia: Towards a new political economy in the forests. In T. Barnes and R. Hayter (Eds.), *Troubles in the rainforest: British Columbia's forest economy in transition* (pp. 37-50). Victoria, BC: University of Victoria, Department of Geography, Western Geographical Studies, vol. 33.

Massam, B.H. (1999). Geographical perspectives on the public good. *Canadian Geographer*, 43(4), 346-362.

Mercer, J., and England, K. (2000). Canadian cities in continental context: Global and continental perspectives on Canadian urban development. In T. Bunting and P. Filion (Eds.), *Canadian cities in transition*, 2nd edition (pp. 55-75). Toronto: Oxford University Press.

Meredith, T. (1995). Assessing environmental assessment in Canada. In B. Mitchell (Ed.), *Resource and environmental management in Canada* (pp. 360-383). Toronto: Oxford University Press.

Mitchell, B. (Ed.) (1995). *Resource and environmental management in Canada*. Toronto: Oxford University Press.

O'Riordan, T., and O'Riordan, J. (1993). On evaluating public examination of controversial projects. In Foster, H. (Ed.), *Advances in resources management* (pp. 19-52). London: Belhaven.

Perks, W., and Jamieson, W. (2000). Planning and development in Canadian cities. In T. Bunting and P. Filion (Eds.), *Canadian cities in transition* (pp. 487-518). Toronto: Oxford University Press.

Porteous, J.D. (1989). *Planned to death*. Toronto: University of Toronto Press.

Reed, M., and Gill, A. (1997). Tourism, recreational, and amenity values in land allocation: An analysis of institutional arrangements in the post-productivist era. *Environment and Planning A*, 29(11), 2019-2040.

Rees, W.E., and Roseland, M. (1991). Sustainable communities: Planning for the 21st century. *Plan Canada*, 3(3), 15-25.

Roberts, G. (1987). Land issues and monitoring in British Columbia in monitoring for change. *Land use in Canada Series* No. 28 (pp. 9-14). Ottawa: Environment Canada.

Robinson, I. (1980). *Canadian urban growth trends*. Vancouver: UBC Press.

Sancton, A. (2000). The municipal role in the governance of Canadian cities. In T. Bunting and P. Filion (Eds.), *Canadian cities in transition*, 2nd edition (pp. 425-442). Toronto: Oxford University Press.

Seelig, M., and Seelig, J. (1997). City plan: Participation or abdication? *Plan Canada*, 37, 18-22.

SQUAM (1998). *Community economic development strategy: Planning workshop brief*. Vancouver: Crane Associates.

Toller, S., and Nemetz, P. (1997). Assessing the impact of Hydro development. *BC Studies*, 114, 5-42.

Troughton, M. (1995). Agriculture and rural resources. In B. Mitchell (Ed.), *Resource and environmental management in Canada* (pp. 151-182). Toronto: Oxford University Press.

Vancouver Sun (2000a). City hall strategy aimed at enticing more residents downtown. 4/3/00.

Vancouver Sun (2000b). How we became the world's laboratory. F. Bula and D. Ward, 4/3/00, pp. 8-19.

Vancouver Sun (2000c). Wal Mart war refought in Surrey. K. Bolan, 4/3/00, p. B4.

Wright, J. (1994). Designing and applying conservation easements. *Journal of the American Planning Association*, 60(3), 381-386.

Wight, I. (1998). Canada's macro metros: Suspect regions or incipient citistates? *Plan Canada*, 38, 29-39.

Wynn, G. (1992). The rise of Vancouver. In G. Wynn and T. Oke (Eds.), *Vancouver and its region* (pp. 69-148). Vancouver: UBC Press.

ENDNOTES

1. We are referring to the modern period in this brief overview because forms of planning can be traced back to the earliest civilizations. Many of the basic ideas for land inventory systems, the GIS systems and the software that evolved from this need were developed in Canada (see **Chapter 2**).

2. One of the more difficult issues to resolve is the redistribution of costs and benefits that come from market regulation, especially where windfall gain or loss occurs through rezoning. This has been a contentious issue in many countries. For example, in BC the ALR system impacts negatively on farmers who cannot sell their land for development—traditionally their retirement fund—while the community enjoys the benefits of green belt land.

3. Planning activities can be categorized in several ways, as here or, for example, local, regional, national. While community and land use planning frequently overlap, they tend also to be more specialized sub-categories of the general planning process. Regional planning, regional economics, and regional development and analysis are also well developed sub-fields of spatial analysis and policy.

4. The 19th century expansion of settlement relied on specialized, monoculture farming over large areas to provide cheap food for the growing industrialization of Europe and eastern North America. In the long run, this is an inherently unstable land use system, as shown by the 1930s and recent agriculture trends.

5. Wilderness areas were avoided until the "Romantic Rebellion" of the 19th century. Poets and writers such as Wordsworth and Thoreau sparked an interest in nature and the wild, partly in reaction to industrial urbanism. Nineteenth century American artists like Albert Bierstadt and Thomas Moran dramatically captured the images of the wild and rugged landscape of the west, which influenced public opinion and encouraged the creation of national parks. Scientific appreciation of wilderness as ecological reserves came later.

6. It is only in recent decades that inventories have become more accurate on matters such as determining the extent and quality of timber, as the technical capabilities of the resource agencies have improved.

7. The problem is that if cities annexed land *ad infinitum*, their size, electorate, and power would rival that of the provinces. Greater Vancouver may be heading in this direction. However, Kamloops has grown by this process.

8. Victoria Airport's industrial area, for example, does not require conformity with the surrounding municipalities' zoning, or the Agricultural Land Reserves. However, the federal government also made several important contributions to land use planning in the 1970s—for example, "Preliminary Environmental Assessment: Superport Development Prince Rupert Region (1973-Environment Canada) and the Interdepartmental Task Force on Land Use Policy (1975).

9. The Canada Land Inventory was formed in 1963 to survey, map, and classify land according to a basic national system. Agricultural land is classified according to its crop/grazing potential, on a scale of 1-7, that ranks from very best (1) to not suitable for any agriculture (7). One outgrowth of this national inventory work was the evolution of the Canadian Geographic Information System approach.

10. The company had recently been taken over by a multinational corporate conglomerate that perhaps wanted to strip its assets as leverage to pay for the purchase.

11. The coastal zone has eluded the federal government as a legislative priority despite the enormous length of coastline on three oceans and the successes of our neighbour in this area.

12. Since 1980, skiing has grown at annual rates of between 5 and 10%. BC increased its market share of skiing in the northwest region of North America from 27% in 1979/80 to 45% in 1998/99, with an annual total of 5.1 million downhill skier/day visits by 1998/99, Whistler alone accounting for 40% of them (*BC Ski*, 2000).

13. As an outcome of the *Environment Management Act* of 1981, the Ministry of Environment, Lands and Parks formulated a four-tier planning system for environmental resources in 1981 with the *intention* of developing 43 subregional strategic plans (scale of 1:100,000-1:250,000) for the province. This system was adopted as the planning template by CORE and the provincial government in the 1990s. River basin (water focus) planning was also undertaken during this period.

14. The LRMPs are required to refine the broad use zones determined in the regional plans and integrate activities, help with the designation of protected areas, and employ conservation principles such as *biodiversity* management. In applying the operational rules of the Forest Practices Code, the LRMPs are meant to define the overall objectives for the operations.

15. This format for understanding community decision making according to different levels of participation was conceived by S. Arnstein (1969) as a "ladder of participation."

16. Forest Planning Canada also made important contributions to understanding consensus in forest planning (e.g., *Forest Planning Canada*, 8(2), 1992).

17. See, for example: Hall, 1982; Harvey, 1985, 1997; Cater and Jones, 1989; Levy, 1997; Bunting and Filion, 2000.

18. Restructuring near the CBD usually eliminates much of the stock of cheap, inner city housing (hotels and rooming houses) available to the urban underclass —hence Vancouver's attempts at a social housing component in redevelopment.

19. The legislation of 1994 (see appendix) gave a new impetus to conservation in the settled areas of BC, especially in the two main metropolitan regions.

Plate 11 Mining activities contribute significantly to the BC economy ▶

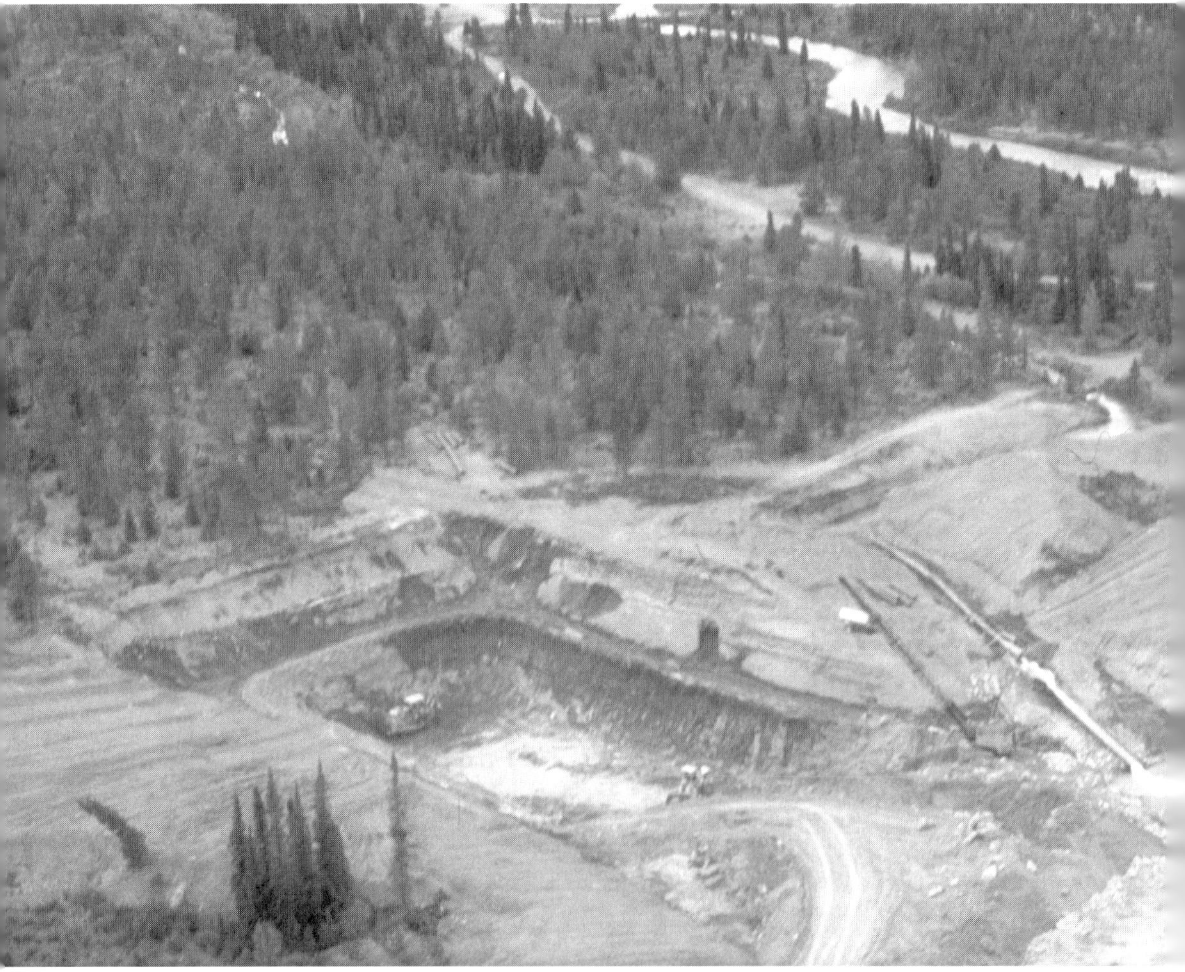

Mineral Development

Jo Harris
Jo Harris & Associates

INTRODUCTION

Rapidly advancing science is touching the lives of people throughout the world. Mineral development in BC is particularly illustrative of such change. A review of developments and trends in the province, particularly in the last decade, finds the scenario for mineral exploration, development, and production, influenced not only by international mineral prices and other economic factors, but increasingly by advances in high technology.

Mining is one of BC's oldest and most important resource industries. Mining has had a significant impact on the economic health of the province, patterns of infrastructure development and settlement, and the frontier nature of the province's lifestyles and politics. There were periods when mining dominated the economy, such as the gold rush era of the mid-19th century. Since that time it has run traditionally second to forestry among the resource industries. In the late 1990s, however, both forestry and mining fell behind the fast emerging high technology industry, which in 1998 became the largest employer, growing ten times as fast as the provincial economy.

We are no longer "hewers of wood and drawers of water." Fewer people are miners. From its former pre-eminence, mining is at times now referred to as a "sunset industry" in the province. However, by its very "boom and bust" nature and other economic and technological factors, mining has the capacity to regain importance, if not its former eminence, in the provincial economy.

High technology has contributed to fewer employees per unit produced by the mining industry. Highland Valley Copper, for example, one of the largest open-pit copper mines in the world, uses full computerization in its process, from the massive trucks and shovels in its pit, to grinding and processing of the concentrate. New computer modelling programs that enable safer, more efficient mineral extraction, developed by British Columbian and other Canadian companies, are internationally recognized for leading-edge engineering and technology.

Conventional uses for mineral products are all around us. Concrete foundations support buildings made of metal, glass, stone, brick, and granite. Copper is used for the plumbing and electrical wiring in the buildings. Roads between cities and towns are built of asphalt, while the cars that drive on them are built of steel. High technology also requires mining products. Lasers use gemstones such as sapphires and rubies, while all computers contain a minimum of 33 mineral products, including silicon for the data processing chip. Plastic contains minerals to strengthen it or make it more flexible. High temperature ceramics protect the space shuttle while moving through the atmosphere. Many of the minerals required to support the high technology industry are found, and are being developed, in BC.

Mineral exports provide foreign currencies, allowing BC residents to import goods from elsewhere, such as Korean stereo and camera equipment, Japanese electronics, food from California, and digital telephones from Singapore. These exports also affect the value of Canadian currency and our ability to travel. During the last 5 years, the export sector has been the major source of economic growth, and mining remains a significant contributor.

Prices for BC minerals are set on a world market and are often beyond the control of domestic producers, who must concentrate on reducing production costs to stay competitive. As it exports many of its products, the mining industry is particularly sensitive to changes in world markets. Consequently, exchange rate fluctuations and economic conditions in countries like Japan, which is a major importer of BC minerals, affect the value of metals, fuels, and other mineral products. The severe downturn in the Asian economies in 1997 and 1998 markedly contributed to the downturn of the provincial economy (Table 14.1).

To a large extent, prices dictate which mineral resources are developed at specific times, and the length of time mines are in production. The early gold rushes into the Cariboo, for example, could not have been sustained if not for the high price associated with the precious metal. The absence or presence of transportation systems in this large province, and associated costs, also governs the development and timing of mineral development. Building the railways parallel to and just above the US border was part of the impetus and provided the opportunity to carry coal to smelters and ocean-going steam vessels. The presence of infrastructure makes it possible to access and develop a wider range of minerals, which allows for some industry diversification and stability.

Fluctuating prices have influenced patterns of settlement. The lure of gold between 1858 and 1862 attracted the first large wave of settlers, and encouraged clearance of lands for agriculture. When the mines closed, however, communities that were established solely on the basis of the mines became ghost towns. In recent decades, this happened to the communities of Kitsault and Cassiar in the northwest, and more recently Tumbler Ridge, built in the 1980s to house the workers and families of the Bullmoose and Quintette coal mines in the northeast. Accordingly, it is recognized that new mining towns must diversify their economic base to survive in the long term. Where diversification appears less feasible, the provincial government now endorses operations such as the new Kemess South gold/copper mine near Tutade Lake, which flies in shifts of miners from Smithers, approximately 200 kilometres away.

Mines that still have reserves can be reopened periodically on the basis of higher mineral prices or technology that reduces production costs. At the turn of the century, for example, ore grades of 2% copper were considered economical, while lower grades may now be regarded as commercially viable. This allows for reopening of mines with reserves that were previously considered uneconomical.

The roots of the provincial mining industry were closely tied to the US. Many early miners in the province moved here for the gold rush and others came to work the base metal mines in the Kootenays. Even when ties to the rest of Canada improved with construction of the Canadian Pacific Railway (CPR), connections with the US, and particularly California, remained strong. Some of the technology developed in California was used in BC, and ore was transported from the province via the Great Northern Railway to smelters in Washington State and California. After the turn of the century, and particularly as gold gave way to the development of minerals such as zinc, silver, and copper, the connection diminished.

Table 14.1 Value of mineral output, 1970-2000 (rounded to nearest $ millions)

Year	Copper	Silver	Gold	Lead	Zinc	Molybdenum	Coal	Aggregates
1970	125	12	4	35	44	53	20	
1980	671	156	170	66	49	289	461	
1990	985	115	241	16	103	88	979	
2000	730	139	335	30	247	64	910	382

Source: BC Stats 2000, 2001.

Mineral Development 263

The pattern of mineral dominance continues to change. Coal, one of the first minerals developed in the province, was overtaken by gold. At the turn of the century, silver, lead, zinc, and copper mines were opened, and by 1930 these minerals had overtaken gold in importance. Copper and lead were the leading minerals in this period, but in the 1940s and 1950s zinc became more prominent and replaced copper as one of the two dominant minerals. From the 1960s to the 1980s, copper re-emerged as a leading mineral, and the development of the coalfields in the southeast and northeast of the province led to the rebirth of that mineral.[1] For the past decade, coal has been the leading mineral, now followed by silver, copper, and structural materials. Significantly, structural materials are now of greater economic importance than gold (Figure 14.1).[2]

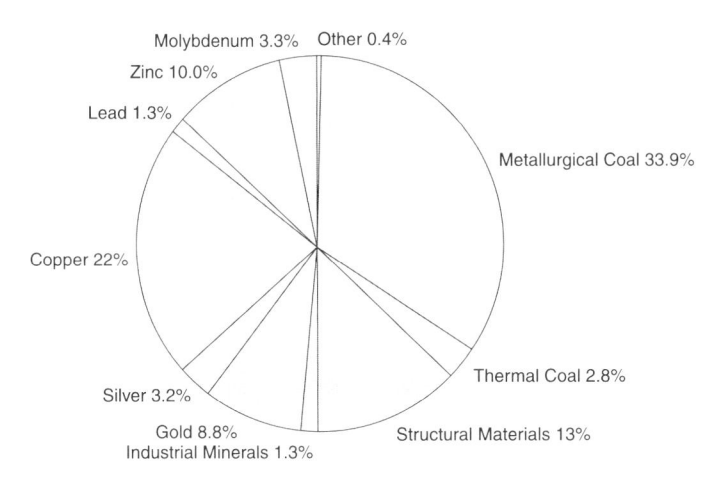

Figure 14.1 Types and share of mineral production by value, late 1990s (BC Stats)

Molybdenum 3.3% Other 0.4%
Zinc 10.0%
Lead 1.3%
Metallurgical Coal 33.9%
Copper 22%
Thermal Coal 2.8%
Silver 3.2%
Gold 8.8%
Industrial Minerals 1.3%
Structural Materials 13%

The 13 metal mines operating in BC in 1997 are indicated in Figure 14.2. In 1997 there were three new metal mine openings (Mount Polley, Golden Bear, and Huckleberry) and one significant mill expansion (Eskay Creek). The production losses of copper associated with the previous closures of the Ajax, Similco, and Goldstream mines were balanced by production from the new mines at Mount Polley and Huckleberry. The number of direct mining employees in BC in 1997 is estimated at about 9,700, including 3,600 at metal mines, with wages totalling $550 million. The multiplier for jobs which exist as a result of the mining industry, such as catering and road clearing contractors, dry-cleaning, restaurant workers, and other jobs, ranges from 1.5 to 3 dependent on the community. Mining therefore remains a major employer in the province at this time.

THE PHYSICAL SETTING

The great diversity of geological environments in BC is reflected in a wide variety of mineral and energy deposits. Most of the mineral production in the world comes from two types of geological terrain—cordilleran belts and precambrian shields. Over 85% of BC is underlain by cordilleran belts of various metamorphic, faulted, and folded rocks that range in age from Precambrian to recent.

The province can be divided geologically into six distinct regions (Figure 14.3). The Insular Belt, the westernmost region, consists of heavily faulted, unmetamorphosed volcanic and sedimentary rocks that range in age from Tertiary to Paleozoic. The area is known for coal deposits and minerals, such as copper and iron ore. The mountainous Coast Plutonic Belt is a crystalline region comprised of coarse intrusives of the late Cretaceous to early Tertiary age. It consists of granitic rocks and crystalline gneisses. A fairly wide range of metal ores is associated with these rock formations. In the Intermontane Volcanic Belt, the formations consist mainly of unmetamorphosed sedimentary and volcanic rocks. Extrusive lava flows of late Tertiary age dominate in the southern and northern extremities. Streams have deeply eroded parts of this region and exposed intrusive complexes, such as copper porphyries. The area includes many fault and contact zones where copper and molybdenum are commonly found. The Omineca Metamorphic Belt consists of very old

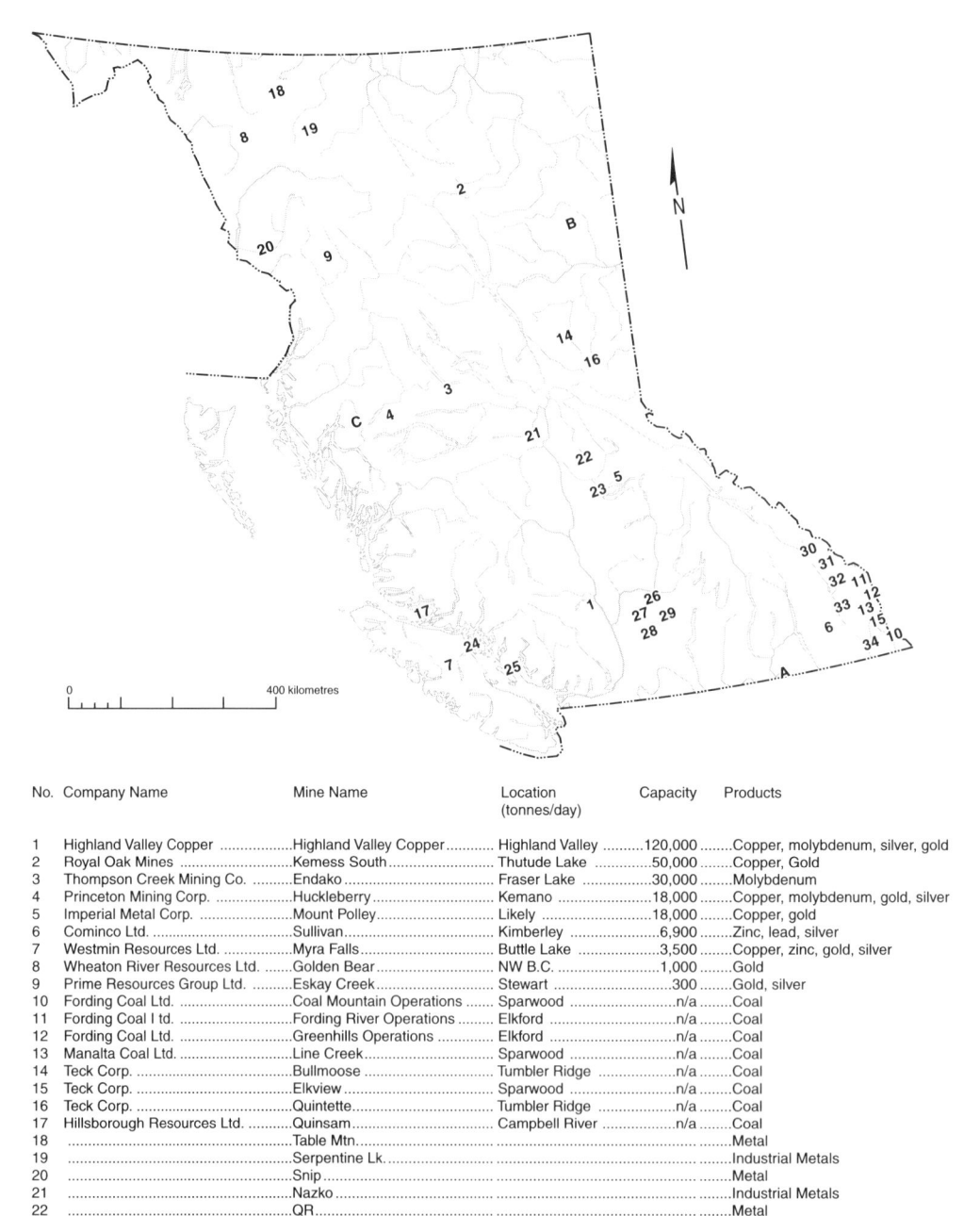

No.	Company Name	Mine Name	Location	Capacity (tonnes/day)	Products
1	Highland Valley Copper	Highland Valley Copper	Highland Valley	120,000	Copper, molybdenum, silver, gold
2	Royal Oak Mines	Kemess South	Thutude Lake	50,000	Copper, Gold
3	Thompson Creek Mining Co.	Endako	Fraser Lake	30,000	Molybdenum
4	Princeton Mining Corp.	Huckleberry	Kemano	18,000	Copper, molybdenum, gold, silver
5	Imperial Metal Corp.	Mount Polley	Likely	18,000	Copper, gold
6	Cominco Ltd.	Sullivan	Kimberley	6,900	Zinc, lead, silver
7	Westmin Resources Ltd.	Myra Falls	Buttle Lake	3,500	Copper, zinc, gold, silver
8	Wheaton River Resources Ltd.	Golden Bear	NW B.C.	1,000	Gold
9	Prime Resources Group Ltd.	Eskay Creek	Stewart	300	Gold, silver
10	Fording Coal Ltd.	Coal Mountain Operations	Sparwood	n/a	Coal
11	Fording Coal Ltd.	Fording River Operations	Elkford	n/a	Coal
12	Fording Coal Ltd.	Greenhills Operations	Elkford	n/a	Coal
13	Manalta Coal Ltd.	Line Creek	Sparwood	n/a	Coal
14	Teck Corp.	Bullmoose	Tumbler Ridge	n/a	Coal
15	Teck Corp.	Elkview	Sparwood	n/a	Coal
16	Teck Corp.	Quintette	Tumbler Ridge	n/a	Coal
17	Hillsborough Resources Ltd.	Quinsam	Campbell River	n/a	Coal
18		Table Mtn.			Metal
19		Serpentine Lk.			Industrial Metals
20		Snip			Metal
21		Nazko			Industrial Metals
22		QR			Metal
23		Gibraltar			Metal
24		Quinsam			Coal
25		Texada			Industrial Metals
26		Ajax (closed)			Metal
27		Pavilion			Industrial Metals
28		Craigmont			Tailings
29		Kamloops			Industrial Metals
30		Mt. Moberly/Nicholson			Industrial Metals
31		Mt. Brussilot			Industrial Metals
32		Parson			Industrial Metals
33		Elkhorn			Industrial Metals
34		Canal Flats			Industrial Metals

Note: The Quesnel River gold-silver mine and the Gibraltar copper-molybdenum-silver mine shut down in May and December, 1998, respectively. Blackdome gold mine reopened in June 1998. Kemess South copper-gold mine opened in June 1998.

Figure 14.2 Mines and products (BC Financial and Economic Review, 1999)

Mineral Development

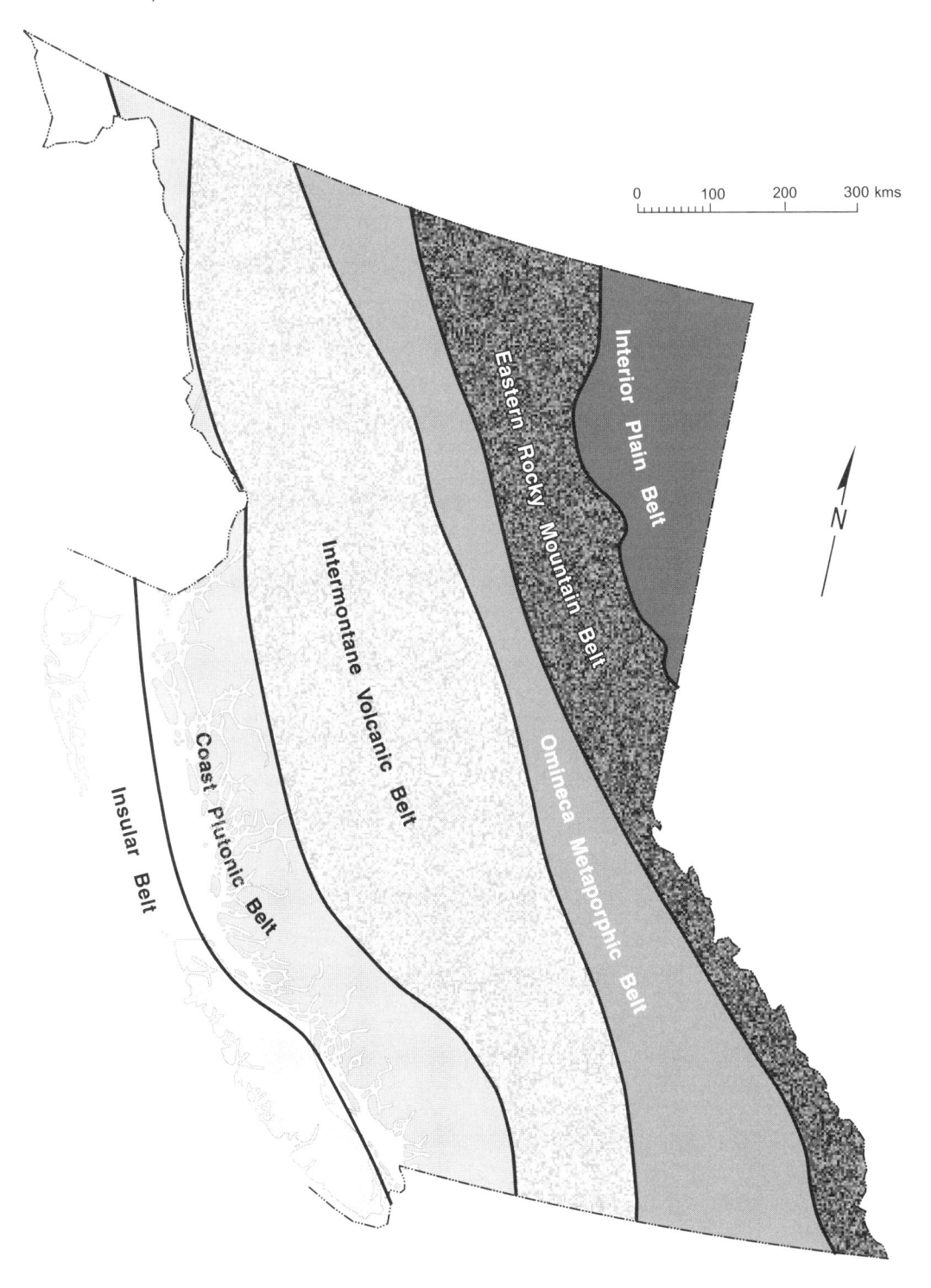

Figure 14.3 Geologic regions

sedimentary rocks, primarily schists and granitic intrusions. The major lode metal industries in the province are found in this belt, notably the historic Boundary area in the south, well known for copper, lead, silver, and zinc deposits. The Rocky Mountain Belt consists mostly of sedimentary carbonate rock. Thrust faulting is evident throughout the region and, unlike the situation in the Omineca Belt, there is very little volcanic rock. The best known mineralization in this region is in the southern and central areas where metallurgical quality coal deposits are found. The sedimentary rocks seen in the Interior Plain Belt lie horizontally and have not been folded as in the Rocky Mountain Belt. The sandstones and shales are of Cretaceous and Early Tertiary ages and it is here that natural gas and petroleum are to be found.

THE MINING INDUSTRY IN PERSPECTIVE

The early history of BC's mining industry was dominated by coal and placer gold, but ever since the CPR was completed in the 1880s, lode minerals and fossil fuels have constituted the majority of provincial mining revenues. The earliest mining in the province took place along the coast. Coal was mined at Saquash on the northeast coast of Vancouver Island as early as 1836, and later at Nanaimo in 1852. There are also records that show gold being found in a small quartz vein on Moresby Island in the early 1850s, but all of these early developments were overshadowed by the placer gold mining in the lower Fraser River in 1858 and upriver in the Cariboo in 1861 and 1862. Coal was an important resource, because it attracted shipping and gave promise of industrial development, but the discovery of gold was more important to the early rapid growth of the region and to the creation of BC as a province within the Canadian Confederation.

By the early 1880s, most of the rich deposits of gold had been mined and prospectors began to turn their attention elsewhere. They moved up from the south through the Columbia and Kootenay valleys, concentrating their attention on the areas along and south of the CPR route.

Many significant discoveries were made, including silver and copper at Nelson in 1886, gold and copper at Rossland in 1889, copper at Boundary Camp and Greenwood in 1891, and silver, lead, and zinc at Slocan in 1891 and at Kimberley in 1892. Some silver and lead ore was shipped south to San Francisco for smelting, but between 1896 and 1901 a number of smelters were brought into production at Nelson, Trail, Grand Forks, and Greenwood. In addition to the lode minerals noted above, coal production in this period increased significantly. The coastal areas, particularly Vancouver Island, dominated production and new coal mines were opened in the East Kootenay. The product from these mines was used by the railroads for fuel and by the newly built smelters for coking coal.

Between 1900 and 1935, the production of gold continued to decline, while copper production increased substantially. Zinc and silver emerged as important minerals during the period and the volume of lead production was stable. The spatial pattern did not change significantly from the previous period. Coal was important on Vancouver Island and in East Kootenay. Some gold was taken from the northern part of the province in the Cassiar Mining District in the early part of this period and later copper was mined at Anyox, on Observatory Inlet. Silver, lead, and zinc production was dominated by the Sullivan Mine at Kimberley.

By the late 1950s, there were profound changes in the mining industry. Demand for industrial minerals increased after World War II, and substantial amounts of capital became available. Technological improvements in mining led to the large-scale production of lower grade ores and the appearance of open-pit mines in the province, where previously most mining was underground. Production from these open-pit mines was often sold to overseas buyers in large quantities under long-term contracts. Mines that were opened during this period include the iron ore mine at Tasu, the asbestos mine at Cassiar, and the Craigmont copper mine in the Highland Valley.

The earliest commercial natural gas in BC was discovered at Pouce Coupe in 1948 and oil at Boundary Lake in 1955. These discoveries ushered in an era of unprecedented growth in the oil and gas industry. Most of the oil and gas production is concentrated in the Peace River area. The gas reserves have always exceeded those of oil. BC produces sufficient gas for its own needs and exports large quantities to the US. The oil production, on the other hand, has seldom met more than 50% of the province's needs.

The trends that emerged during the 1950s intensified during the 1960s and 1970s. More and more large low grade open-pit operations replaced the small high grade mines of the past. The Sullivan Mine at Kimberley declined in importance as open-pit mining intensified in the Highland Valley. New mines were opened in the Omineca area of northern BC. Coal re-emerged as a significant mineral with large-scale operations in southeast BC. Unit trains were used to transport this coal from the mines to Roberts Bank near Vancouver from which the coal was shipped to Japan (Ross, 1973).

By the late 1970s, coal, copper, iron ore, oil, and natural gas dominated the export oriented mineral production, while sand, gravel, and cement were produced in large quantities to serve the domestic construction industry which grew rapidly between 1950 and 1960.

The primary use for metallurgical coal is for steel in the manufacture of cars. By the 1980s, Japan had become a major producer and exporter of automobiles. To keep pace with demand, Japan required vast, secure sources of coal to service its smelters, and actively facilitated development of new metallurgical coal mines in the US, Australia, and Canada. In BC, Canada's major exporter of metallurgical coal, a consortium of Japanese steel companies assisted with the financing, joint management, and long-term contracts for the development of the Quintette and Bullmoose coal mines in the northeast of the province. The Northeast Coal "megaproject" saw the development of the new town of Tumbler Ridge, hundreds of kilometres of railway line across the province, and a new coal port at Ridley Island, near Prince Rupert. Although the price of metallurgical coal has decreased in the ensuing decade, it is still the most valuable mineral commodity exported from the province. This operation is now winding down due to low coal prices (currently $36.9/tonne compared with $42 in 1980) (Mertl, 2000).

As much of the reserves come close to exhaustion, trends in gold and silver production in the southeast of the province are for smaller mines based on exploration at existing operations. Major discoveries in the lesser-explored northwest, however, enabled the development of larger mines, such as Eskay Creek, Golden Bear, Huckleberry, and Kemess South, where gold is either the prime target or a valuable by-product of copper extraction.

Structural materials have become of increasing economic significance in the past decade, and provide some stability for the value of mineral production. Prices for building materials are not subject to the vagaries of international commodity markets, and increasing populations contribute to growing demand.

PATTERNS OF MINERAL DEVELOPMENT

Patterns associated with mineral production in BC vary considerably. Much of the variation can be attributed to basic physiography, changes in ore prices, qualities of ore bodies, and operating costs.

A number of points about the spatial pattern of mines operating in the province are noteworthy, as seen in Figure 14.2. First, the mines in the northeast and southeast of the province produce mainly coal, with the exception of the Sullivan Mine at Kimberly that produces lead, silver, zinc, and iron. These coal mines have vast reserves, and could continue for many decades given increased demand and value. Secondly, many of the large copper mines in south and central BC (Highmont, Craigmont, Brenda, Gibraltar, Afton, Similco) have closed due to economic resource depletion. The exception is the largest mine, Highland Valley Copper near Kamloops, which is expected to close in the year 2006. Shutdown of Highland Valley would signal an end to a concentration of copper production in the south central area dating back to the turn of the century. Development of new copper mines now trends northwest along the centre of the province, to include Mount Polley (near Williams Lake), Huckleberry (near Smithers), and Kemess South under construction to the northwest of Williston Reservoir. Thirdly, the new gold mines are located in the northwest of the province (Golden Bear, Snip, Premier, Eskay Creek), with the exception of the QR Gold mine, near Quesnel. Importantly, in May of 1998, Royal Oak Mines Ltd. commenced production at its Kemess South open pit gold/copper mine, 200 kilometres north of Smithers. Production, at a rate of 50,000 tonnes per day, is expected to produce 250,000 ounces of gold and 60 million pounds of copper per year for 16 to 20 years. The downturn in the price of gold, however, has seen these new mines struggle for economic survival.[3]

An anomaly in the trend towards development in the northwest was the closure of the Cassiar Asbestos mine, about 120 kilometres north of Dease Lake, in 1992. Health concerns regarding asbestos, combined with difficult conditions at the mine (a labour strike, oversize ore, water inflows, difficult ground conditions, and depletion of reserves) saw closure of the property, after 40 years of production. Cassiar employed over 350 people and was the sole support for the community of Cassiar, which is now on a caretaker basis.

Smelters

In 1998, the BC government released a consultant's report supporting the development of three new aluminium plants in BC, representing $3.6 billion in investment, about 48,000 person-years of employment during construction, and more than 6,000 permanent new jobs. At this time, some major US producers with potential interests in locating in the province are conducting similar feasibility studies.

From time to time, interest is shown in the construction of a leading technology copper smelter in the province, and such investigations are ongoing. Presently, there are only two major smelters operating in the province: a zinc/lead smelter at Trail and an aluminium smelter at Kitimat. Their contribution to employment, and the economy generally, is significant.

Trail Lead/Zinc Smelter

The Trail Smelter, in southeastern BC, is the world's largest zinc and lead smelting complex. In operation for over 100 years, the smelter has evolved from crude to sophisticated modern technology and provides the province with an economic mainstay.

Approximately 51% of the zinc concentrate treated at Trail during 1996 came from the Red Dog mine in the Northwest Territories, 41% was from the Sullivan mine, and the remainder was purchased from other sources. Of the lead concentrate treated, 58% was from the Sullivan Mine, with the rest purchased mainly from sources in North and South America.

An extensive modernization program at Trail included:

- A zinc expansion project, with the addition of 20 new electrolytic cells for zinc refining. Project completion will see annual zinc capacity reach 290,000 tonnes, an 18,000-tonne increase over existing capacity.

- A new $6 million zinc pressure leaching autoclave to replace the original unit built in 1979.

- Construction of a new Kivcet lead smelter and slag fuming plant. At a cost of $152 million, the new lead smelter will lower lead emissions by 75%, particulate emissions by 90%, and sulphur dioxide emissions by 75%. Once it reaches normal operation, the new smelter will also reduce operating costs and provide additional revenue from increased production.

During 1996, Cominco concluded an agreement with the Columbia Power Corporation, a BC government Crown corporation, for the sale of the Brilliant hydroelectric generating dam and related transmission lines for a total price of $130 million. Cominco owns the Waneta Dam near Trail, which, together with its coordination agreements with BC Hydro and West Kootenay Power, provides more than enough electricity for Cominco's industrial needs at Trail and Kimberley.[4]

Kitimat Aluminium Smelter

In the 1940s, the BC government determined to develop the considerable resources of the sparsely populated northwest and north central areas of the province, and to establish new population centres. Alcan was invited by the BC government to investigate the establishment of an aluminium industry in the northwest, and subsequently began the huge Kitimat-Kemano project, located in the Nechako watershed, a vast river and lake system draining 14,000 km^2 of north central BC. At the time, Kitimat-Kemano was the largest privately-funded construction project ever undertaken in Canada, costing $500 million in 1950 dollars—or more than $3.3 billion today.

The project included construction of several major components including:

- the Kenney Dam in the Nechako River Canyon, which reversed the river's eastward flow and created the Nechako Reservoir, including a mechanism for controlling reservoir water levels, commonly referred to as a spillway, at Skins Lake;
- a 16-km tunnel, as wide as a two-lane highway, through the coastal mountains to carry water to the twin penstocks of the Kemano powerhouse. Through these penstocks, the water descends 800 m—nearly 16 times the height of Niagara Falls—to drive the generator turbines;
- a powerhouse, also drilled and blasted 427 m inside the granite base of Mount DuBose, to house eight 112-megawatt generators;
- an 82-km power transmission line from Kemano to Kitimat across some of the most rugged mountain territory in BC, through the Kildala Pass, 1,500 m above sea-level;
- construction of a smelter and wharf at tidewater in the previously undeveloped Kitimat Valley; and
- creation of two townsites from wilderness territory in Kitimat and Kemano.

Since the mid-1970s, Alcan has invested approximately $300 million in an extensive modernization program of the Kitimat smelter to improve working conditions, further protect the environment, and upgrade equipment and technology. Today, the Alcan smelter produces aluminium at a rate of 272,000 tonnes per year, which is shipped on ocean-going vessels to Pacific Rim markets.

Oil and Gas Development

Oil exploration began in BC at the turn of the century, but it was not until the 1950s that development of natural gas in the northeast region of the province began in earnest. When the first gas pipeline was completed from the Peace River District to Vancouver in 1957, gas began to flow south for both domestic and export consumption. This added stimulus to exploration of BC's northeastern gas resources. Subsequent development of additional delivery and regulatory infrastructure has greatly enhanced the province's petroleum markets (Figure 14.4).

Approximately 19,000 km of gas gathering and transmission lines are now in use in the province, including the Vancouver Island pipeline which began delivering natural gas to Island customers in 1991. Gas is processed at 23 plants located in northeast BC, many of which recover sulphur and liquid by-products. Processing was approved in 1997 at new plants, Cariboo, Highway, Jedney II, and Ring/Border Gas Sweetening. The major plants are located at Taylor, Fort Nelson, and Pine River.

Three main gathering systems deliver crude oil and natural gas liquids to facilities at Taylor. Four other lines deliver oil and liquids from the northeast fields to provincial and Alberta systems. Although some of the oil is processed at a refinery in Prince George, most is transported by pipeline to Kamloops and then to Vancouver and Washington area refineries via the Trans Mountain pipeline. There are about 5,100 km of oil gathering and transmission lines in the province (Figure 14.4).

The oil and gas industry has emerged in recent years as a major sector in the provincial economy, enjoying a record year in 1997. During the year, the oil and gas sector invested more than $1.8 billion in the province; BC set an all-time high of $217 million for sales of oil and gas rights; 583 wells were drilled—25% more than 1996 and the highest number drilled in a year in the province's history. Gas production was 24.7 billion m^3—also BC's highest ever. Overall, in 1997, the value of annual production was estimated at $1.5 billion, which provided a direct revenue to the province of about $510 million. The oil and gas sector provides more than 14,500 direct and 23,000 indirect jobs.

The northeast is the only area of the province producing commercial quantities of oil and gas, and has been a focus of petroleum exploration and development since 1952. Its 142,000 km^2 include the northern foothills of the Rocky Mountains and the southwest part of the Western Canada Sedimentary Basin. Approximately 2,500 oil and gas pools have been identified in this region and about 9,700 wells were drilled to the end of 1997. At the end of that year, 553 billion m^3 of natural gas had been established as initial marketable reserves, and up to 1,400 billion remain to be discovered. The BC foothills, in particular, hold potential for significant additional gas reserves. At the end of 1997 there were up to 48 million m^3 of potential recoverable oil in addition to the estimated 112 million m^3 of initial established reserves (Figure 14.4).

Other regions with extensive areas of sedimentary rocks may some day prove productive. Exploration in the Fernie-Flathead area in the southeast has focused on both conventional oil and gas resources and carbon dioxide. Although significant amounts of natural gas have been indicated in this area, no commercial discoveries have yet been made. The Fernie-Flathead area has also been the focus of interest in coalbed methane development. The central Interior of the province contains significant quantities of sedimentary rock; however, due to geological factors, hydrocarbon potential is problematical. Recent studies in the central Interior indicate potential for dry gas reserves. Limited drilling, without commercial success, has been conducted on Vancouver Island and in the Fraser Valley; recent resource assessments however do indicate potential for natural gas in the Georgia Basin. Although recent studies and previous drilling programs indicate potential for large accumulations of both oil and gas in the Queen Charlotte Basin, the BC offshore region has been closed to exploration since 1968.

High technology has caused fundamental changes in the way companies search for oil and gas deposits. About 80% of the world's offshore oil exploration now utilizes satellite pictures beamed from 800 km above the surface of the ocean which show and monitor oil slicks caused by natural oil seeping to the ocean's surface. The satellite images show both colour differences and the wave-calming effect oil has on waters. Repeated passes showing a consistent pattern of surface slicks indicate where to drill. It is estimated that the use of this new technology has saved the oil industry about $500 million worth of "dry holes." Forefront in the development of the concept is BC's Radarsat International who teamed up with Earth Satellite Corporation of Maryland, US to win the 1998 Award for Canadian-American Business Achievement given by a Washington, DC foundation to innovative business partnerships that straddle the border.

Radarsat also uses the technology extensively in the handling of oil spills, where satellite images can be delivered within hours of the satellite acquiring the data. Further uses for the images include onshore oil and gas exploration, flood evaluation, iceberg detection, monitoring of shipping lanes, spotting illegal fishing vessels, and identifying large fields of cocoa plants. More potential users are examining the technology to determine ways of adapting it to their needs.

In tandem with increasing sophistication in the mining and oil and gas industries has been the development of a more comprehensive environmental review system which sets out the procedures required for any development proposal on Crown Land.

The Environmental Assessment Process

Prior to 1995, proposed new mine developments were reviewed under the *Mine Development Assessment Act*. In June 1995, following public consultation, the provincial government

Mineral Development 271

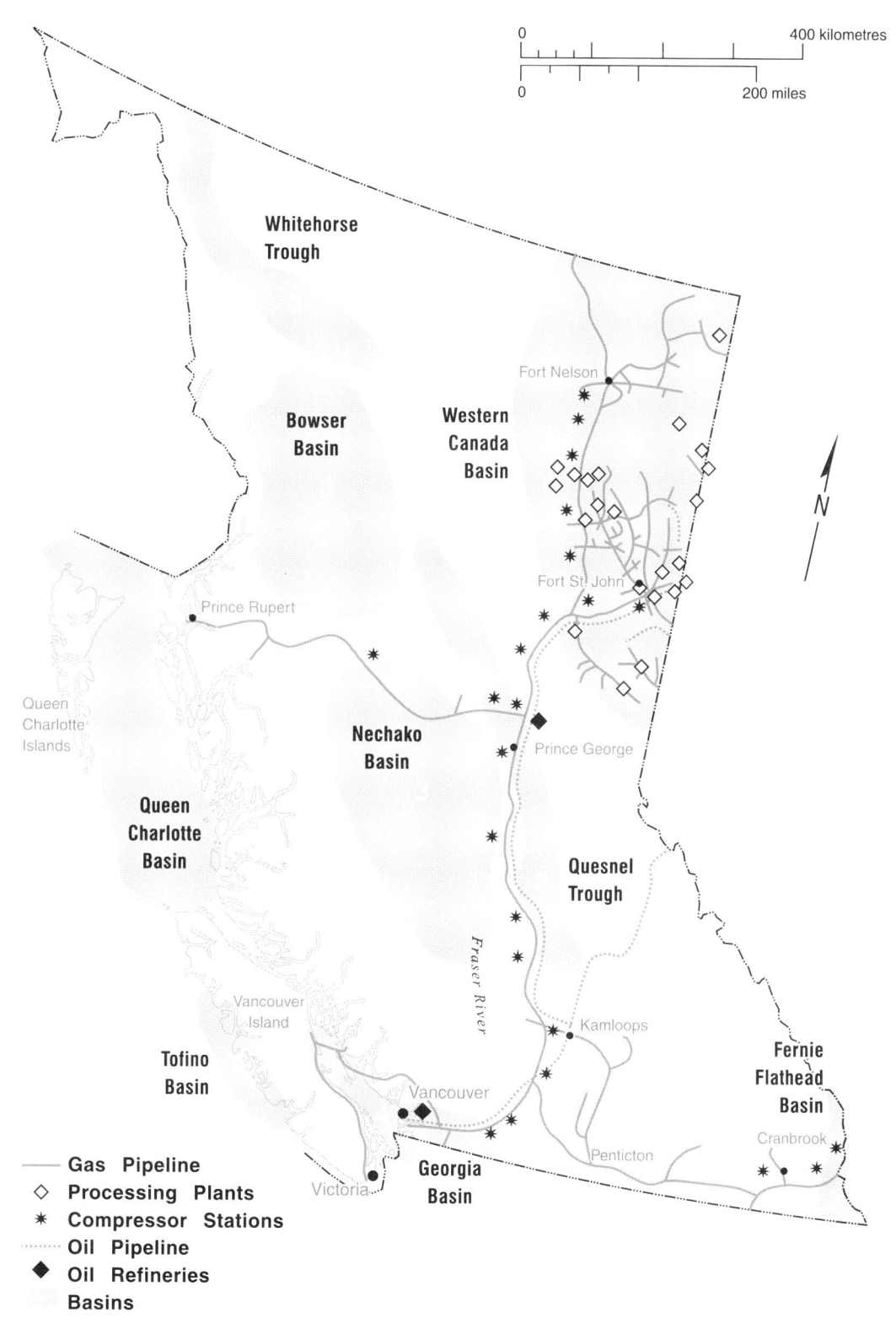

Figure 14.4 Sedimentary basins, hydrocarbon production and transportation

introduced the *Environmental Assessment Act*, bringing the review of all major projects, with the exception of forestry, under one standardized process. Based on the approach previously used for mine reviews, the new assessment process is designed to provide consistency and neutrality of review, and has introduced legislated project review timelines.

The Act sets out a "one-window" process to assess a range of major industrial, energy, mining, water management, waste disposal, food processing, transportation, and tourism projects. The process provides for assessment of the environmental, economic, social, cultural, heritage, and health effects of all reviewable projects. Depending on the complexity of the project and issues that may arise, the review may entail one, two, or three stages. The project review may be completed after the first, second, or third stage of review.

Specific purposes of the *Environmental Assessment Act* are to:

- promote sustainability by protecting the environment and fostering a sound economy and social well-being;
- provide for the thorough, timely, and integrated assessment of the environmental, economic, social, cultural, heritage, and health effects of reviewable projects;
- prevent or mitigate adverse effects throughout the lifecycle (i.e., design, construction, operation, modification, and closure) of reviewable projects;
- provide an open, accountable, and neutrally administered process for the assessment of reviewable projects and activities; and
- provide participation in assessments under the Act by the proponents, the public, First Nations, municipalities and regional districts, federal and provincial governments and their agencies, and BC's neighbouring jurisdictions.

Proposed projects and activities automatically subject to the *Environmental Assessment Act* are specified in regulation by both category and minimum size threshold. Under the Reviewable Projects Regulation, the review process typically applies to the construction, operation, dismantling, and abandonment of new facilities and the modification, dismantling, or abandonment of existing facilities.

The Act requires joint decision making by the Minister of Environment, Lands and Parks and the minister responsible for the project or activity. Should the Environmental Assessment Board conduct public hearings, Cabinet makes the final decision. In project reviews, and in formulating recommendations to the ministers, a balanced approach is strived for with the involvement of provincial and federal agencies, local governments, First Nations, and neighbouring jurisdictions.

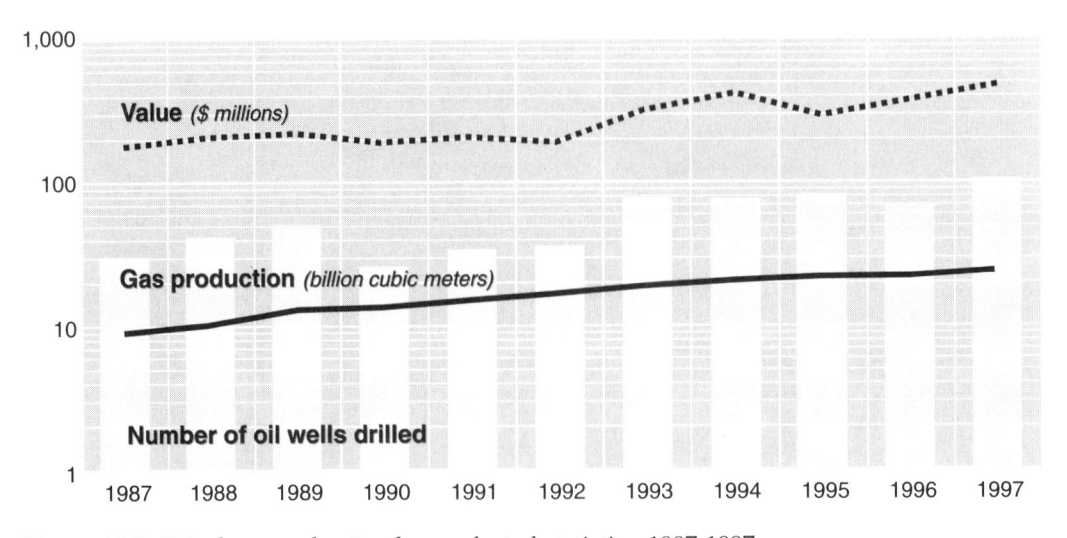

Figure 14.5 Petroleum and natural gas selected statistics, 1987-1997

Mineral Development

Time frames to be followed throughout the process are specified in the Prescribed Time Limits Regulation, including timelines for receiving review comments and for decisions by ministers or Cabinet. Timelines are specified so that proponents and participants can estimate the duration of the review process with reasonable confidence (Figure 14.6).

The Environmental Assessment Office is a neutral agency within the provincial government which acts as a central, one-window contact for applicants, government agencies, First Nations, and the public on matters related to the review of proposed major projects.[5]

CONCLUSIONS

The quest for mineral riches, especially gold, was a main attraction for Europeans and Americans to develop BC in the mid 19th century. As the mineral potential of the province became apparent, more hard rock mines were opened in the southeast region. The mineral potential and growth of mining were key factors in the expansion of the railroad system and connection with eastern Canada and the US. Coal mines on Vancouver Island and in the Rocky Mountain region provided fuel for steamships, trains, and the expanding industries of the west.

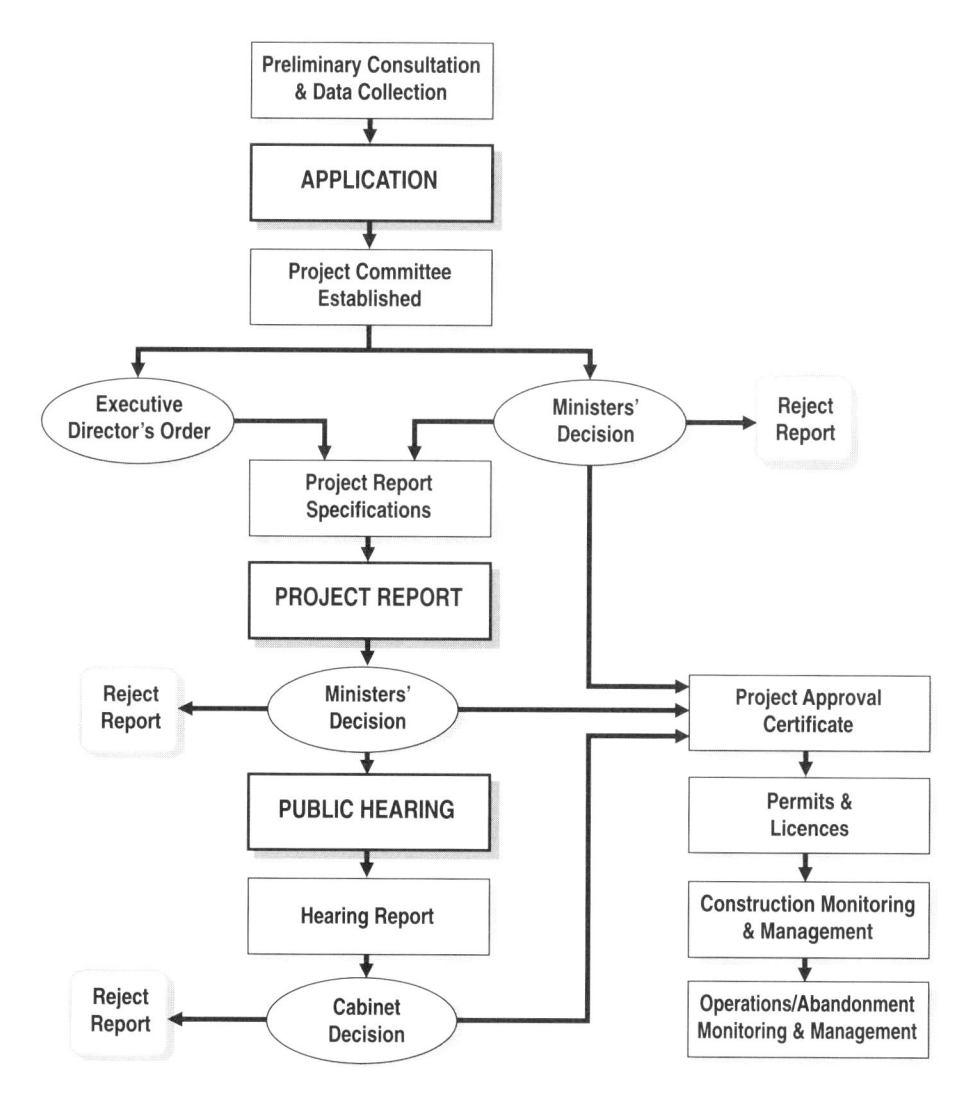

Figure 14.6 The environmental assessment review process

As the deposits and veins were worked out in the south, the focus of mining activity shifted to the northern region of BC. Many hard rock mines produced several different metals which helped buffer the effects of the fluctuations in the world price for a particular metal. Mine deposits are rarely completely exhausted. A mine usually closes because the grade of ore becomes so low that the operation is no longer profitable at current prices. Gold, for example, has varied between $708 (1980) and $270 (2001) per ounce. Prices can tumble if a leading holder of gold decides to sell off relatively large amounts, as the UK government did recently, causing repercussions in the industry. The mining industry in BC has survived and competed with other regions that have richer deposits through substantial capital investment to enable high output levels per worker. However, this strategy may not be sufficient to continue operations when prices decline. Stockpiling can be a short-term strategy.

In the early days of mining, little thought was given to the environmental side effects of mining activities. Now it is necessary to have a well researched environmental impact proposal before operations can commence, monitoring during operations, and a bond to ensure proper post-operations clean up. For its part, the provincial government has to manage a balancing act between encouraging investment and the need to protect the environment in the long term.

While most of the richer deposits of metals have been exploited, there are still ample reserves of hydrocarbons. These undoubtedly will become attractive at some future date when the price once again makes a profit possible.

Mining remains one of the major forms of economic activity in BC with metals, hydrocarbons, and construction aggregates contributing about $3 billion in annual output value to the provincial economy (late 1990s). The fortunes of the industry have fluctuated as new discoveries are developed, exploited, and then decline as the mineral deposit is extracted to its point of lowest economic feasibility. With the exception of construction aggregates, which enjoy a price/weight locational advantage, the industry functions in relation to the world demand/supply and hence market price for minerals. Lower cost producers in other countries force companies in BC to maximize efforts to control costs and stay competitive. For example, BC has generally accounted for about 60% by value (about 30% by tonnage) of Canadian coal output, all of which is exported; but it would appear that coal exports will decline in the foreseeable future as world prices decline.

The province still has substantial reserves of minerals, particularly hydrocarbons, which are not feasible to exploit given current world prices, but which have value in the long run. The availability of relatively cheap energy in large amounts also has the potential for metal reduction and smelting. Another prospective area for development lies in the offshore sedimentary basins; however, their exploitation in the immediate future is unlikely, for a number of environmental and political reasons. Even so, as demand for natural gas continues to increase even these reserves may eventually be exploited, as in the case of the east coast offshore areas and Arctic Canada.

The BC government's decision to strengthen the industry with the *Mining Rights Amendment Act* of 1998 is intended to give greater security to several aspects of mining leases with compensation for expropriations and tax credits to encourage exploration. Also, the environmental impact assessment procedure has been streamlined in order to speed up the approval process for exploration. The land use planning processes that were developed in the 1990s and applied throughout much of the province (see **Chapter 13**) should also reduce the conflicts that arise over the extractive industries. The message is that the BC government welcomes mining activities.

REFERENCES

BC Financial and Economic Review (1999). Victoria Crown Publications.

Daniels, A. (2001). Millions of tonnes from our quarries are destined for US. *Vancouver Sun*, March 23, 2001, Business Section.

Mertl, S. (2000). Northeast coal winding down. *Times-Colonist*, February 19, 2000, p. D3.

Ross, W.M. (1973). Mining. In C.N. Forward (Ed.), *British Columbia: Its resources and people* (pp. 162-176). Victoria, BC: University of Victoria, Department of Geography, Western Geographical Press, Vol. 22.

BC Ministry of Energy and Mines. *http://www.em.gov.bc.ca/mining/*.

ENDNOTES

[1] Prices for metals which are set by global levels of supply and demand can fluctuate rapidly. They may drop when a newer, richer source comes on stream. Conversely, if the supply is affected by civil war, for example, prices may rise rapidly. It may take several years of planning and construction, involving millions of dollars of investment before an operation becomes productive. Demand for minerals tends to swing in concert (with some lags) with the general level of economic activity in the developed world. Producers may attempt to offset these effects by cartels and/or buffer stocks.

[2] Construction and infrastructure development in BC provide a steady market for aggregate and fill material. BC producers are also responding to fill and aggregate demand in coastal areas of California. This has required new rock loading systems in BC and specially designed self-unloading ships (Daniels, 2001).

[3] Moves to develop a new road to the Kemess mine from Stewart, using existing logging roads and constructing 125 km of new road, have been proposed.

[4] In response to recent power shortages in California, it has been more profitable for the company to close the smelter for extended maintenance and sell their unused electrical power to the US.

[5] Amendments to the Act were made in 1998 to speed up the application/review process in the oil and gas industry.

Plate 12 The Jordan River hydroelectric dam near Victoria ▸

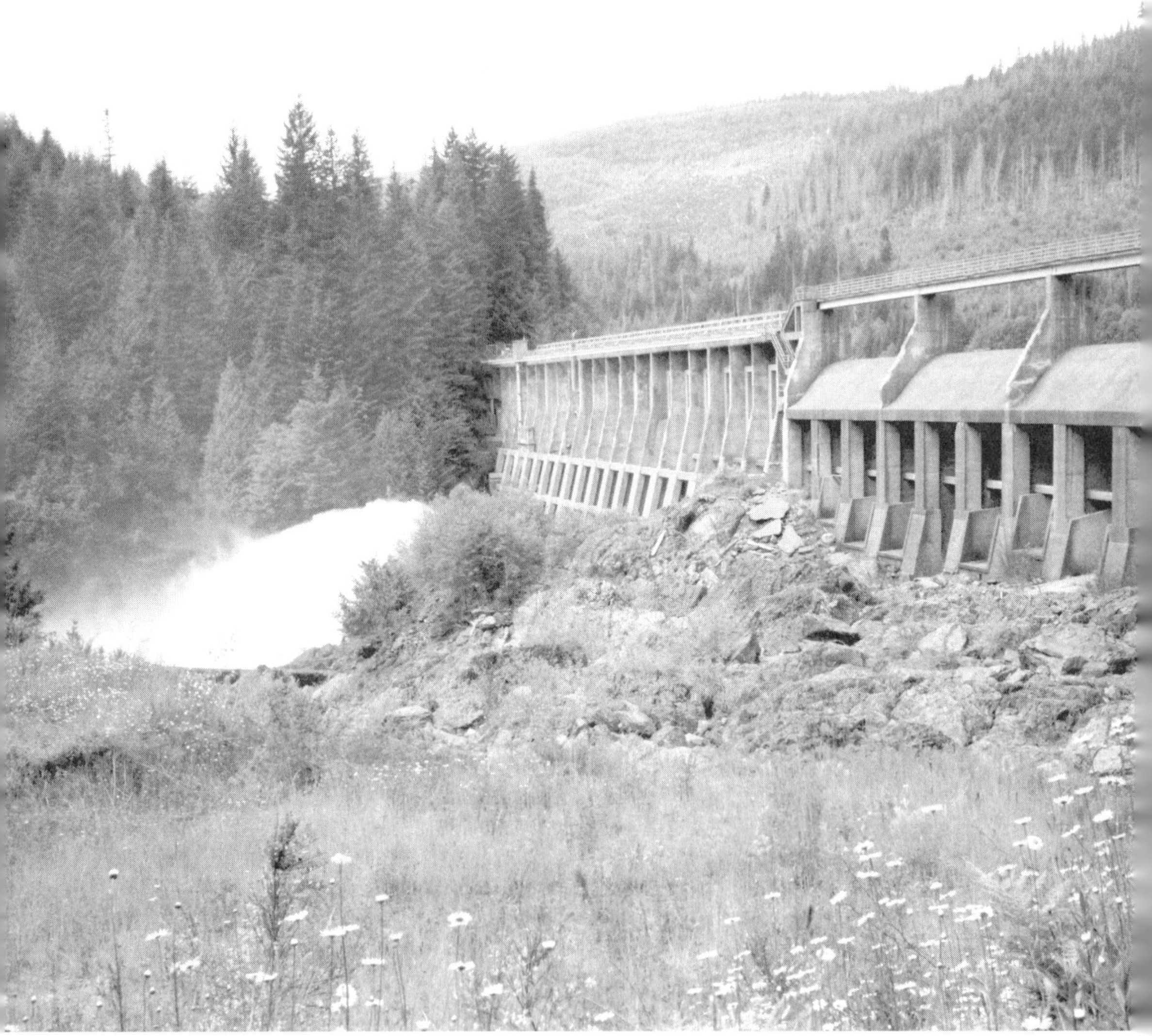

Energy

John Newcomb

Department of Geography, University of Victoria

Introduction

The economic development of BC has been closely tied to success in searching for and exploiting energy resources, but the pace has often been set by the continuing integration of the province into both North American and international economic developments. Most recently, environmental concerns and new paradigms of natural resources studies at both provincial and international levels have resulted in a view of energy extraction and development as a central environmental issue. This was already apparent to the late Derrick Sewell by the time his chapter on Energy appeared in the first edition, *British Columbia: Its Resources and People* (Forward, 1987). However, what was only on the horizon 15 years ago is now much closer, with deregulation of energy markets and the challenge of meeting "Kyoto" agreements on climate change.

Sewell summarized the nature of the energy resources situation in BC into the mid-1980s as being in a state of "flux" (Sewell, 1987). By 2000, it was again possible to say that there has been a significant change in the situation for energy. The energy resource situation is "in flux," but there has been an evolution of the context for how British Columbians perceive the role of energy as both a resource and for its environmental impacts. Energy prospects in BC are still being challenged by highly-variable oil prices, and energy projects (both old and new) remain a lightning rod for environmental concerns.

What is evolving in the province's social and political environment is a growing population mainly concentrated in the southwest, a maturing of energy projects that were being initiated in the mid-1980s, and a realization by political leaders that energy "mega-projects" will present political difficulties for some time to come. Perhaps most important is the increased integration of our regional energy exploitation in continental markets and in global environmental terms. The impacts of free trade on energy and global warming have entered the political arena in BC and are beginning to impact energy policy decisions in the province.

This chapter reviews the present energy supply, outlines the geography of supply and demand, including "demand management." Brief attention is given to current issues of natural gas and electricity exports.

The Present Energy Situation in BC

Coal

In the context of the Canadian energy picture, BC is in an enviable situation, as the province has a continuing supply of hydrocarbons and hydro-power, except for petroleum. Twenty years ago, the energy picture for the province was focused on the development of coal, whose reserves were estimated to be about 2,740 million tonnes, or about 60% of Canada's metallurgical coal and 10% of the country's thermal coal (Sewell, 1987). While much of this coal was not destined for thermal energy requirements, being of metallurgical quality, coal's overall impact on the regional development of the province has been significant. Coal deposits lie mainly in four BC regions, including the southwest, the Interior, the northeast, and the northwest (Figure 15.1). Expensive transportation and related infrastructure improvements during the early 1980s provided the necessary means for exporting the coal from the farthest

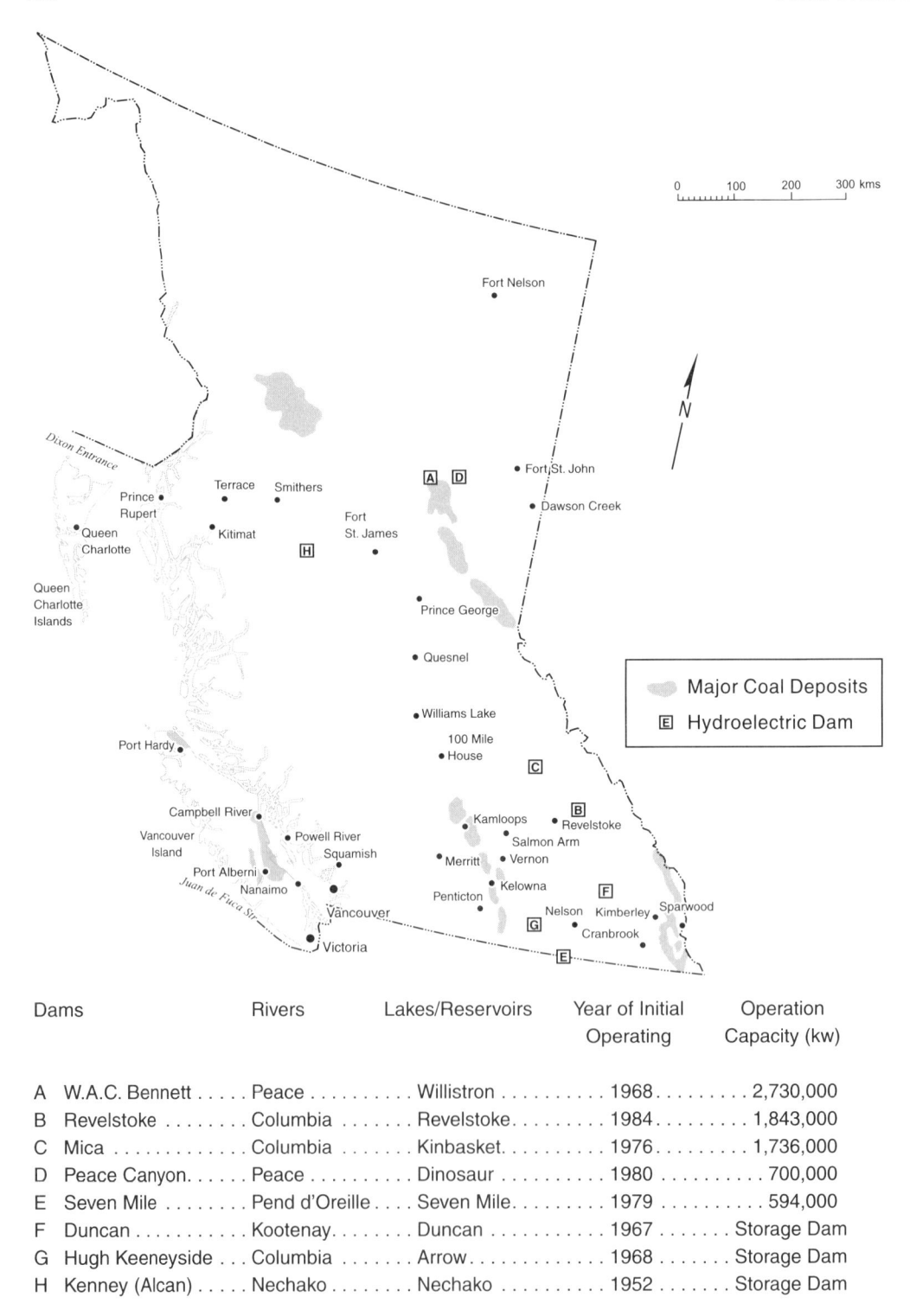

Dams		Rivers	Lakes/Reservoirs	Year of Initial Operating	Operation Capacity (kw)
A	W.A.C. Bennett	Peace	Willistron	1968	2,730,000
B	Revelstoke	Columbia	Revelstoke	1984	1,843,000
C	Mica	Columbia	Kinbasket	1976	1,736,000
D	Peace Canyon	Peace	Dinosaur	1980	700,000
E	Seven Mile	Pend d'Oreille	Seven Mile	1979	594,000
F	Duncan	Kootenay	Duncan	1967	Storage Dam
G	Hugh Keeneyside	Columbia	Arrow	1968	Storage Dam
H	Kenney (Alcan)	Nechako	Nechako	1952	Storage Dam

Figure 15.1 Major coal deposits and hydroelectric dams; see previous chapter for pipelines and other hydrocarbons—**Figure 14.4** (from 2000 BC Financial and Economic Review, 60th edition, Ministry of Finance and Corporate Relations, page 20)

regions, but the economics of coal profitability over the last 20 years in a competitive global market has not always made for stable development of the resource. Since 1980, the production of coal in BC has risen dramatically, from 24% of the provincial total, to 39% (Figure 15.2). However, the export focus of coal is apparent when we see that the current energy consumption of coal rests at a very low 1% of provincial energy consumption.

Wood

Wood has been an important source of energy historically in BC, including in the aboriginal period. However, apart from a brief resurgence as an opportunistic way to reduce waste heaps outside of sawmills, wood has been in a steady decline as an energy source. "Hog-fuel" was a by-product of the forest industry's mill industry, together with pulp mill waste and pulp mill liquor. While wood residue energy consumption in BC has declined only slightly since 1980, from 17% down to 16%, the production of wood residue as an energy source has fallen more drastically, from 15% down to 9% (Figure 15.2).

Petroleum and Natural Gas

Weathering the oil price shocks of the 1980s and early 1990s, BC has, until 2000, enjoyed some stability in a diversified energy sector. Most recently, both oil and natural gas prices have risen significantly.

As suggested by Figure 15.2, the production and consumption of energy remains out of balance. In BC, oil consumption still far exceeds production, and most imported oil comes from Alberta (BC Ministry of Finance, 1998). By 1999/2000, there were about 650 oil and gas wells drilled—a record number (BC Ministry of Finance, 2000).

As indicated in Table 15.1, the historical value of petroleum and natural gas production in BC experienced extremely variable growth in the period 1988 to 1999.

BC government revenue from the petroleum and natural gas sector increased significantly between 1998/99 and 1999/00 (up 85%, from $362 million to $670 million). The revenue from water charges grew by 23.1%, from $322 million to $396 million (BC Ministry of Finance, 2000). In the period from 1992 to 1996, electrical power production in BC maintained an average annual production of 62,500 gigawatt-hours (GWh) (BC Ministry of Finance, 1998); within that 5-year period, production varied by as much as 22%, and 1995 saw domestic consumption exceed production. Such variability in electrical production can be accounted for by both the physical and economic geography of the province. The climate and economy have interacted to produce surpluses or deficits. For example, reasons for a higher-than-expected surplus energy volume in 1998 (up 108% from the previous year), include higher inflows to reservoirs and reduced domestic sales (BC Ministry of Finance, 1999).

Petroleum and natural gas appeared to be the most vibrant elements of BC's mining sector in 1997, with steeply rising natural gas production value (19% increase), in part because of higher volumes (5% increase). Crude oil had increased 13% in the same period (BC Ministry of Finance, 1999).

Production Oil 4%, Hydroelectricity 14%, Natural Gas 36%, Wood Residue 15%, Coal 24%

Consumption 45%, 15%, 22%, 17%, 1%

Type of Use Commercial 12%, Residential 15%, Transportation 24%, Industrial 39%

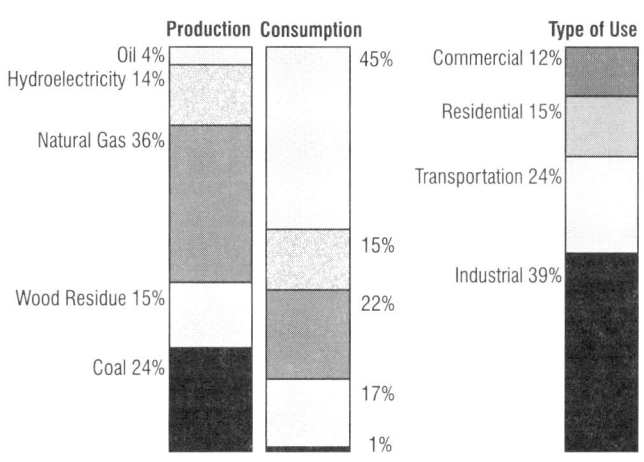

Figure 15.2 Production, consumption, and type of use of energy in BC, 1997

Table 15.1 Petroleum and natural gas industry production in BC

	1988	1989	1990	1991	1992	1993	1994	1995	1996	1997	1998	1999
$(millions)	736	783	899	858	890	1,089	1,270	1,040	1,333	1,588	1,561	2,109
%	—	6.4	14.8	-4.6	3.7	22.4	16.6	-18.1	28.1	19.1	-1.7	35.1

Source: BC Ministry of Finance and Corporate Relations (2000), extracted from Table A1.20, page 134.

Exploration for oil and gas in BC increased from 461 wells drilled in 1996 to 650 in 1998, and by the end of 1998 oil reserves had grown 12% to more than 26 million m^3 and natural gas reserves had increased to more than 283 billion m^3. There were 884 producing oil wells and 1,601 producing gas wells at year end. Natural gas production stood at greater than 23 billion m^3 in 1998, the highest in BC's history (BC Ministry of Energy and Mines and Ministry Responsible for Northern Development, 1999, *http://www.em.gov.bc.ca/publicinfo/ newsreleases/memnrs99/mem034nr99.htm*).

The northeast remains the only area of the province currently producing oil and gas (Figure 15.1). The gas is processed at several plants, then sent by transmission pipelines to Vancouver. The main line was built in the 1950s and later extensions brought pipelines to Fort Nelson, Prince Rupert, and southern BC. Petroleum pipelines extend from the northeast to the Lower Mainland and Alberta systems. The pipeline network for natural gas now joins Vancouver Island, the Interior, and the Vancouver region. As of December 1, 2000, a 'lateral' extension connects the Fort St. John area to the Alliance Pipeline in Alberta (Figure 15.1)

A recently completed project to augment BC's oil and gas transmission system with more Alberta gas includes BC Gas Inc's "Southern Crossing," a $350 million, 312 km pipeline that carries 8.5 million m^3 of Alberta gas through the southeastern part of the province to link with a main pipeline transporting gas to the Lower Mainland in BC and to the northern US (Chase, 1999). The proposal had been challenged by competing gas producers who said that the transmission project would increase gas costs to consumers. BC Gas defended its project by pointing to a "huge increase" in demand, as new Lower Mainland gas-fired electrical power plants are planned for construction.

A much more controversial energy supply proposal is the resurrected North Coast Oil and Gas project off the Queen Charlotte Islands. Project backers estimate the reserves would bring in provincial royalties of more than $12 billion (MacQueen, 1998). However, there are still many unanswered environmental questions about offshore drilling in a hazardous area of the province. The provincial government's Northern Development Commissioner, John Backhouse, has hired a consultant to study the present moratoriums (both provincial and federal) on offshore oil projects in the area (*Victoria Times-Colonist*, 1999b).

BC has only two oil refineries at present, with one at Prince George and one in Burnaby. Together, the two plants refine slightly more than half the provincial crude oil production, with the balance being exported. The spatial arrangement of energy sources and distribution in BC suggests that energy—whether it is hydroelectricity or petroleum/natural gas—moves from north to south, from hinterland to heartland (**Figure 14.4**).

Hydro Electric Power

Hydroelectric power in BC has passed its first century of development, starting from the first plant in Nelson in 1896, and followed soon by a plant near Victoria in 1898. However, it was only in the aftermath of World War II that the provincial government created the BC Power Commission in order to consolidate several small, private power companies and to promote public hydropower (see **Chapter 7**). BC Hydro is not the sole producer of electricity in the province, as several other companies produce much smaller amounts of power. However, BC Hydro alone currently delivers electricity to in excess of 1.5 million customer accounts, in a geographic area containing more than 94% of the province's population, utilizing a network of 74,000 km of transmission and distribution lines.

While operating a total of 61 dams in 43 locations, more than 80% of the electricity produced by BC Hydro still comes from just two rivers—the Peace River in the northeast and the Columbia River in the southeast corner of the province.

Electrical energy can be exported and imported because BC Hydro's distribution system is connected to systems in Alberta and the US. Besides producing revenue for the utility, this "electricity trade" is seen by BC Hydro as providing a means of reducing environmental risk factors, such as dry conditions in the province, by importing electricity. Conversely, wet conditions in the province can be exploited by exporting surplus electricity (BC Hydro, 2000, *http://eww.bchydro.bc.ca/powersupply/power_generation/electrade.html*).

GEOGRAPHY OF SUPPLY AND DEMAND

Understanding the structure of *specific* consumption on energy supply and demand and on BC's location within North America and the world is essential for analysing our provincial energy geography. Apart from a few exceptions, energy forms, including electricity, natural gas, petroleum, coal, and wood, have been historically closely tied to either static or motive power uses.

The main consumptive demand in BC for hydroelectricity is in residential and commercial power plants, while petroleum demand is for both residential heating and transportation. Wood residue energy has been tied closely to mills. Until recently, the growth in natural gas consumption has been in residential and commercial heating applications. However, the development of natural gas electrical generation facilities is promoting much of the current demand for this resource.

Specific consumption is a liability and a constraint on the most flexible and profitable development of energy resources. Concerns about environmental impacts of energy consumption have prompted an exploration of ways to reduce this specificity, such as using natural gas and electricity for transportation applications.

Public versus Private Energy Development

The history of the development of energy in BC, following the general pattern of development in the province, has been that the first energy projects had been privately held (such as early gas and electric lighting in Victoria), however over the past century—and especially since the end of World War II and again after the oil crisis of 1972—there had been a growing demand for public review and control of energy.

At present, the mainstay of direct provincial public involvement in energy is focused through energy policy legislation, including the *Utilities Commission Act*, the *Hydro and Power Authority Act*, and the *Petroleum and Natural Gas Act*. Public organizations such as the BC Utilities Commission (BCUC), BC Hydro, and the Ministry of Energy and Mining direct much of the provincial involvement in energy policy and development. Major private sector actors include corporations such as BC Gas Inc. and Westcoast Transmission Inc.

However, while there may be an increasing trend to further deregulate energy as provincial governments change, there is already a trend toward recognition of market principles and issues around provision of public energy. For example, one might ask exactly who the shareholder is for BC Hydro, if it is not the public:

Anticipating and preparing for the future is essential if BC Hydro is to provide superior value to our customers, our employees, our shareholder and, ultimately, the public.

Michael Costello President and CEO, BC Hydro (BC Hydro, 1998)
http://eww.bchydro.bc.ca/about/ar/1997/bch97.pdf

West Kootenay Power Ltd. (WKP) is an interesting example of one of six existing investor-owned private hydroelectric utilities in BC. Now more than 100 years old, and owned by an American company since 1987 (West Kootenay Power, 1998), WKP purchases about half of the power that it then re-sells. WKP applied to make much of its electrical load "contestable"—meaning more open market access for competition—which led the BCUC to defer the hearing and initiate the BC Task Force on Electricity Market Reform.

BC Task Force on Electricity Market Reform

The Task Force Final Report, authored by Dr. Mark Jaccard in 1998, emphasizes the impact that technology has had on prompting market openness and competition between energy forms in BC (Jaccard, 1998). The decrease in the price of natural gas and the cost of natural gas energy production technology has created a viable competitor for hydroelectricity. Since the Task Force could not find a consensus on reforms, Jaccard's views became the context for the Final Report. His position was that the BC electricity market would need both "vertical deintegration" (both BC Hydro and WKP are vertically integrated) and customer market access. Among other recommendations, Jaccard suggested that a new "power exchange" be created to become a "market-making" agency for energy buyers and sellers in the province (Jaccard, 1998).

Linking Energy Internationally

Figure 15.2 also illustrates roughly the nature of energy imports and exports for BC. The province imports petroleum, however it exports hydroelectric power and natural gas to the US, and coal to Japan. The pricing of BC petroleum imports remains dependent on international markets. Even hydroelectricity has become increasingly integrated into continental markets. While hydroelectric exports may be thought of as "surplus" to consumption requirements in BC, the modern coal industry has been more clearly established for export sales. Coal now accounts for 6% of the province's total commodity exports, but coal prices remain dependent on the health of Japanese industries (BC Ministry of Energy, Mines and Petroleum Resources, 1996).

FORECASTING FUTURE ENERGY DEMANDS FOR BC

The Ministry of Energy, Mines and Petroleum Resources undertakes annual forecasts of energy demands and occasional broader policy reviews (BC Ministry of Energy, Mines and Petroleum Resources, 1990). In their *Supply and Requirements Forecast 1993-2015*, the Ministry sees the relation of overall energy supply and production remaining in balance for the forecast period. Total end-use energy requirements are forecast to grow at an average of 1.3% per year, from 979 petajoules in 1992 to 1,317 petajoules in 2015. Natural gas and hydroelectricity will increase their share, while oil and others will decrease (BC Ministry of Energy, Mines and Petroleum Resources, 1993). However, assumptions that would see oil prices increasing from US $20.50 in 1992 to US $30 per barrel by 2011 (BC Ministry of Energy, Mines and Petroleum Resources, 1993) were already met in the early months of 2000 (US $34 in March, 2000).

The particular form of energy mix (hydro, fossil, solar, nuclear) does pose fundamental concerns about attitudes and energy type and its environmental implications.

For example, the National Media Archive research on the *Vancouver Sun* coverage in 1997 of reports discussing environmental impact of specific energy sources, and fossil fuels, accounted for 75% of the coverage (National Media Archive, 1998, *http://www.fraserinstitute.ca/publications/onbalance/1998/april*). Of a total 408 statements in the *Sun*, references to oil were 10 times more negative than positive, and 5 times more negative for fossil fuels in general. Hydroelectric power had 3 times more negative than positive references. Coverage of natural gas was more evenly balanced, with only slightly more negative than positive comment (a 1.2:1 ratio). For alternative energy sources, positive comments outweighed negative ones by 2.8:1. Researcher Jim Bruce commented sarcastically that if workers in the BC coal towns of Sparwood, Tumbler Ridge, or Elkford suffer massive job loss, "Maybe they could make solar panels or wind-powered systems or develop bio-mass" (National Media Archive, 1998).

"Power for Jobs" Program Introduced

The widely-held belief that energy sources are a fundamental input for creating economic development was made explicit in 1998 as the provincial government initiated the "Power For Jobs" program, where less expensive energy might compensate for lower resource product prices and maintain a steady economic development climate in the province. Such initiatives are not new—New York State, for example, has introduced similar programs. Intrawest Corporation has received an unspecified reduction in electric rates for the Whistler-Blackcomb resort, with the promise of creating an additional 140 jobs at the resort (Gibbon, 1999). By 2000, there had been six "Power for Jobs" agreements approved, and the total number of new or maintained jobs should exceed 1,500 over the next decade (BC Ministry of Finance, 2000).

DEMAND SIDE MANAGEMENT: A NEW TOOL FOR ENERGY CONSERVATION

There is no indication that most public or private policy makers in BC have left behind the classical natural resources "super-abundance" paradigm that sees the "stock" of energy in a way that brooks little interference with its extraction:

BC has a diverse and abundant energy-resource base, with significant exports of coal and natural gas (BC Ministry of Finance, 1998).

Traditional resource managers looking only at expanding energy supply have been viewed critically by geographers for many years (cf. Kuhn, 1992). The role of energy conservation in the total array of energy options has been building for more than a quarter of a century, mostly since the "crisis" of supply caused by the Middle-East war in 1972. Also during this period, one of increasing resistance to new energy mega-projects such as the Site C Dam proposals (O'Riordan and O'Riordan, 1993), the perception of the role of conservation of natural resources has become so well-entrenched that it is considered a unique source of energy "supply" itself. In recent testimony before the House Committee on Energy and Commerce, Hearing on Energy Efficiency and National Energy Policy, David Nemtzow, President of the Alliance to Save Energy, said that energy-efficiency must be seen as an energy source *itself*:

...for 1999...energy efficiency was the second leading source of energy for U.S. consumption, and if we consider only domestic energy sources, it's number one. Mr. Chairman, it would have been number one if we declined to count oil imports, now more than half of this nation's oil consumption. Our analysis of 1999 energy consumption shows that energy efficiency provided the nation with 27 quadrillion Btus (quads), approximately 22 percent of U.S. energy consumption. While energy efficiency trails our mammoth oil consumption (38 quads), it significantly outstrips the contribution of natural gas (22 quads), coal (22.0 quads), nuclear (8 quads) and hydro (4 quads) (Nemtzow, 2001, http://www.ase.org/policy/testimony/nemtest060122.htm).

The conservation of natural resources has been defined in many ways. Baumann and colleagues, in seeking a comprehensive definition of water conservation, arrived at it being "any beneficial reduction in water use or in water losses" (Baumann, Boland, and Sims, 1980), but a new paradigm of Integrated Resource Planning (IRP) seeks, in part, to "equally compare options that involve changes in both supply and demand" (BCUC, 1996), with conservation complementing efforts to supply the resource product.

Supply Management defines the problem as 'not enough of' and the solution as 'more of.' Demand management offers a different perspective on the same problem. It is a perspective that defines the problem as having too much demand for a service or resource" (King, 1988).

A broad perspective on energy conservation must take into account the impact of energy generation on other resources of the environment. For example, much of the discussion in the 1980s was around the negative impacts of further hydroelectric dam building on BC river systems and fisheries. BC Hydro's response to this resource conflict has been to attempt to meet the demands for full recognition of the value of these competing resources. However, resource conflicts have remained to haunt other power producers, such as Alcan's demands for increased Nechako River water.

The Ministry of Energy, Mines and Petroleum Resources' *Supply and Requirements Forecast 1993-2015* reviewed contributions of energy efficiency and energy intensity, and included them in their energy supply forecast (1993). Energy savings due to rising energy prices, improved construction techniques, and government programs would need to be balanced against economic growth demands, the increasing population of BC, and increased "saturation" of energy using devices. According to the Ministry, there are two types of conservation: "natural" conservation promoted by rising energy prices and technological change, and "strategic" conservation initiated by government programs (Ministry of Energy, Mines and Petroleum Resources, 1993). "Natural" energy conservation would appear to be no different from market-based programs, but labelling them "natural" may give some insight as to the perceptions of the Ministry's policymakers. The Ministry's energy demand forecast for 2015 would see about 9% shaved off the total energy demand at that time by energy conservation, or "demand side management" (Ministry of Energy, Mines and Petroleum Resources, 1993).

The BCUC saw demand side management (DSM) as a "...deliberate effort to decrease, shift, or increase energy demand" (BCUC, 1996), similar to the view of DSM by the BC Energy Council as "increasing or reducing energy use or to shift it from peak to off-peak times," with most DSM programs focusing on reducing or shifting energy use. The BC Energy Council saw DSM programs as having five thrusts, including rate design, information programs, efficiency standards, customer incentives, and manufacturer/distributor/retailer incentives (BC Energy Council, 1994).

DSM has also been defined by BC Hydro as,

...broader utility activities designed to influence customer use of energy in a way that will produce desired changes in the utilities load... [DSM] encompasses both load building and load reduction, [whereas] strategic energy conservation...is intended to reduce utility load [with] the reduction from increased efficiency of energy use on the part of the customer that has been induced by the utility" (BC Hydro, 1987).

DSM for energy in BC may be traced to a decision of the BCUC in 1986, where their recommendation was that BC Hydro begin a "purchased conservation" program immediately (BC Hydro, 1987). The first DSM programs were to be focused on residential users, commercial lighting, and encouraging use of efficient motors. Residential users would be targeted to reduce their electrical heating, but instead, gas heating would be promoted. In hindsight, the move to gas heating could be seen to be problematic, in light of the growing concern about global warming and carbon dioxide emissions.

This first "Progress Report" on the impact of DSM on the BC Hydro systems plan was charted from 1987/88 to 2006/07, and suggested strongly that the growing benefits of DSM would become apparent during the second decade of the program (Table 15.2, 1987).

The major costs for DSM would be incurred in the first 5 years of the projections, with relatively small reduction in revenue requirements. After this initial 5 year period, the DSM costs diminish and the revenue requirements quickly increase, ending with a final 5 year period savings of an average of $160 million per year.

The "BC21 Power Smart" program was created in 1995 as a cooperative move by BC Hydro, BC Gas, Pacific Northern Gas, West Kootenay Power, Centra Gas, and BC Credit

Table 15.2 DSM load reduction, costs and impacts

Year	GWh	Cost ($'000)	Change in revenue requirements ($'000)
1987/88	0	670	700
1988/89	0	1,040	1,110
1989/90	24	1,640	1,200
1990/91	108	1,850	(370)
1991/92	179	2,340	(1,680)
1992/93	297	2,180	(4,750)
1993/94	408	2,190	(7,750)
1994/95	498	440	(12,300)
1995/96	576	450	(15,500)
1996/97	652	460	(26,600)
1997/98	732	400	(37,000)
1998/99	812	340	(32,000)
1999/00	912	320	(27,300)
2000/01	1003	290	(32,700)
2001/02	1084	50	(41,200)
2002/03	1146	50	(117,800)
2003/04	1233	50	(229,400)
2004/05	1306	50	(146,200)
2005/06	1365	50	(128,400)
2006/07	1420	50	(184,400)

Source: BC Hydro Project 8607, Demand Side Management, A Progress Report, 1987.

Unions, with goals to reduce water consumption by 3.8 million m^3, to achieve a 21.7 GWh reduction in electrical energy consumption, to reduce natural gas consumption by 145,000 gigajoules, and to create 488 person-years of employment (Kassirer, 1998). This was accomplished by home energy efficiency audits, 81,000 of which were completed by June, 1996. Total funding for the program was $20 million, and by the end of 1996, $15 million had been spent (Kassirer, 1998). The 10th anniversary of BC Hydro's "Power Smart" energy conservation program was marked in 1999 with "The Power Smart Generation: 10 Years Young." Approximately 700,000 BC Hydro customers have participated in Power Smart from its inception in 1989. Since that time, more than 16,000 homes have become more energy efficient with upgraded insulation and draft proofing, ventilation, thermostats, windows, and doors through the Power Smart Home Improvements program. Close to 20,000 commercial buildings have benefited from Power Smart energy efficiency improvements, saving almost 600 million kilowatt hours (kWh) of electricity per year, enough to meet the needs of about 60,000 homes (BC Hydro, 1999, *http://eww.bchydro.bc.ca/powersmart*).

Demand management has become a major consideration of energy production policy issues, and each component in the provincial energy production mix has been faced with its own economic or environmental issues that have led it to embrace some form of demand management. On a positive note, the increasing costs of energy supply have generated a growing market for technology that can help the energy producers meet new demands for energy conservation.

A GEOGRAPHIC PERSPECTIVE ON EMERGING ENERGY ISSUES OF BC

BC's highly-variable development pattern with energy suggests that the energy sector has been the focus of political debate over economic development of the hinterland for several years.

The role of geographers in natural resources management has often focused on behavioural research. As noted by Mitchell (1989), geographers have been active in illuminating the role of public participation in natural resources management. Energy geography in Canada has been approached by Foster and Sewell (1976), who examined various options for federal energy policies, and by Chapman's (1989) foundation work on geography and energy.

In 1990, BC's Minister of Energy, Mines and Petroleum Resources, Jack Davis, released a new energy policy. This was the first major energy policy update since *An Energy Secure BC* (1980). *New Directions for the 1990s* signalled the beginning of several energy policy examinations over the next 9 years (Ministry of Energy, Mines and Petroleum Resources, 1990). A decade earlier, the focus for provincial energy policy had been to assure secure supplies of energy in the face of major geopolitical threats arising from tensions in the Middle East. After a decade of steadily declining fossil fuel prices, however, the issue of energy security had been joined by (and to a great extent, replaced by) new concerns about the environmental impacts of energy.

New Directions for the 1990s was intended to illustrate that the provincial government could respond to emerging priorities of energy efficiency and environmental protection by structuring its review in major parts, including Efficient Energy, Clean Energy, Secure Energy, and Energy for the Economy.

In 1994, the Ministry of Energy, Mines and Petroleum Resources released a report, *Cleaner Fuels for Cleaner Air: The Role of Alternative Transportation Fuels in BC*. The Alternative Transportation Fuels Task Force (ATFTF) had been formed in 1992 as an inter-agency committee "with the mandate to review ATFTF policies, programs and regulatory initiatives, and to recommend policy options and strategies for BC." It is interesting to note that the provincial government would still be phasing out financial support for ATFs through the tax system, because the government would need to weigh this financial support, "against other provincial priorities."

Choosing the most appropriate scale for a geographical perspective on energy resources in BC is a vital step in assessing how to reach conservation and resource management goals. For example, the provincial goal of reducing provincial-level greenhouse gas emissions from energy production is a "macro scale" attribute and depends heavily on the cooperation of individual consumers—a "micro scale" response. This is then reflected in retail energy sector meso-scale environments such as municipal transit and highway construction.

Technology also prompts shifting in scale of energy production, as meso scale natural gas cycle turbines become cost-competitive with macro scale hydroelectricity, and transmission grids integrate provincial energy markets (macro scale) into international markets (macro-macro scale).

FIRST NATIONS PEOPLES OF BC AND ENERGY RESOURCES

The influence of First Nations peoples (including aboriginal and metis) as stakeholders in the province's natural resources has strengthened as courts have issued a series of decisions defining their rights (Calder, Sparrow, Ryan, Gladstone, Metecheah, Adams, Cote, Delgamuukw). Much First Nations' involvement in energy decisions has centred either on the impacts of energy projects on other resources, such as fish (Kennedy, 1998), or on appropriating more of the resource rent from energy projects (Howes, 1999). However, there are initiatives that are taking First Nations peoples much closer to controlling the production of energy resources itself. While it has thus far not been successful, the Huey Lakes hydro project would have been the first aboriginal-owned and operated hydroelectric development in BC (*Victoria Times-Colonist*, 1999a). In March 1998, the government of BC signed an agreement in order to "provide greater operating certainty" for the oil and gas industry in northeast BC (BC Ministry of Employment and Investment, 1998, *http://www.em.gov.bc.ca/Publicinfo/newsreleases/memnrs98/MEM006nr98.htm*).

INTEGRATING INTO CONTINENTAL ENERGY MARKETS FOR NATURAL GAS AND ELECTRICITY

BC's electrical energy exports may have begun in earnest with the Columbia River Treaty, but only recently has a regulatory, economic and political infrastructure been established that more systematically integrates BC into a continental energy market structure.

Early elements leading to this new structure included dismantlement of Canada's National Energy Program by the mid-1980s, followed closely by the move to "Market Based Procedures," natural gas deregulation in the National Energy Board, and the initiation of the Canada-US Free Trade Agreement in 1989 (Ryan, 1991). In the early 1990s, the BC Utilities Commission had moved toward wholesale competition. However, in 1988, BC Hydro had already created its energy marketing subsidiary, Powerex. By 1996, BC Hydro was providing access to its transmission system for wholesale electricity "wheeling," whereby other Canadian and American power producers are sold reciprocal transmission privileges on BC's electrical transmission grid (International Energy Agency, 1996).

Powerex is not only able to trade electricity for BC, but in 1997 was authorized by the American government to buy electricity in one US location for sale in another US location, and "became the first Canadian entity to sell electricity from Canada to Mexico" (Powerex, 2000). Accessing American electricity markets has meant that Powerex, BC Hydro, BCUC, and BC's ministries of Employment and Investment and Energy, Mines and Petroleum have become integrated as members of (and/or doing business with) several US-based regional electricity "regional transmission" organizations, including the Electric Reliability Council of Texas, Committee on Regional Electric Power Cooperation, Mid-Continent Area Power Pool, Northwest Power Pool, Northwest Regional Transmission Association, Southeastern Power Pool, Southwest Power Pool, Western Interconnection Coordination Forum, Western Regional Transmission Association, Western Systems Coordinating Council (Powerex, 2000).

The convergence of energy-related policies (birth of FTA/NAFTA, NEB deregulation of provincial power marketing, market-based), rising market prices for electricity and natural gas, and new technologies in power generation, such as natural gas electrical generation, have combined to signal a revolution in BC's energy sector. John Reid, president of BC Gas, expressed his concern in early December, 2000 that BC's natural gas resources are becoming too expensive for home heating now that US power generators can bid up the price significantly and still be profitable (Reid, 2000).

CONCLUSIONS:
THE FUTURE OF ENERGY IN BC

While BC residents are in the fortunate position of having several sources of renewable and fossil energy, the near-term horizon for predicting energy resource management in BC should include both supply-side and demand-side perspectives. Furthermore, the introduction of new actors—such as First Nations peoples—in the process of decision making, together with concerns about the environmental impacts of energy projects and energy use and deepening of continental integration systems, are additional variables in the energy planning framework.

For the past 40 years, BC's energy resources have been open to the increasing globalization of our provincial economic development, but it is only from the mid-1990s that provincial environmental policy makers have started weighing energy resources and development in BC against their impact on the global environment. Energy conservation in the province is an ongoing issue that enters into a variety of policy initiatives and programs, notably home insulation, transit development, and urban containment. This environment promises to bring significant changes to our way of understanding how energy resources in the province will be seen in the near future.

REFERENCES

Baumann, D., Boland, J., and Sims, J. (1980). The problem of defining water conservation. In W.R.D. Sewell and M. Barker (Eds.), *Water problems and policies* (pp. 127-134). Cornett Occasional Papers No. 1. Victoria: Geography Department, University of Victoria.

BC Energy Council (1994). *Planning today for tomorrow's energy: An energy strategy for British Columbia*. Vancouver: BCEC.

BC Hydro (1987). *Project 8607 - Demand side management: A progress report*. Vancouver.

BC Hydro (1998). *1997 Annual Report*. Vancouver.

BC Hydro (1999). *Power Smart fact sheet. http://eww.bchydro.bc.ca* (accessed 20 May 1999—no longer available).

BC Hydro (2000). Electricity trade, in *About BC Hydro*.

BC Ministry of Employment and Investment (1998). *Agreement between government and Treaty 8 Tribal Association provides greater certainty for oil and gas industry in northeast*. News Release: 24 March.

BC Ministry of Energy, Mines and Petroleum Resources (1990). *New directions for the 1990s*. Victoria, BC.

BC Ministry of Energy, Mines and Petroleum Resources (1993). *Energy: Supply and requirements forecast 1993-2015*. Victoria, BC.

BC Ministry of Energy, Mines and Petroleum Resources (1996). *Mining and energy activity in British Columbia 1995 regional analysis*. Victoria, BC.

BC Ministry of Energy and Mines and Ministry Responsible for Northern Development (1999). Report shows increased oil and gas reserves in BC. News release, 18 August.

BC Ministry of Finance (1998). *1997 BC financial and economic review, 57th edition*. Victoria, BC.

BC Ministry of Finance (1999). *1998 BC financial and economic review, 58th edition*. Victoria, B.C.

BC Ministry of Finance (2000). *2000 BC financial and economic review, 60th edition*. Victoria, B.C.

BCUC (1996). *Understanding utility regulation—A participant's guide to the BC Utilities Commission*. Vancouver: BCUC.

Chapman, J. (1989). *Geography and energy: Commercial energy systems and national policies*. Essex: Longman Group.

Chase, S. (1999). Pipeline proposal riles oil, gas lobby. *Globe and Mail*, 3 February: B11.

Forward, C.N. (Ed.) (1987). *British Columbia: Its resources and people*. Victoria, BC: University of Victoria, Department of Geography, Western Geographical Series, Vol. 22.

Foster, H.D., and Sewell, W.R.D. (1976). *Images of Canadian futures: The role of conservation and renewable energy*. Ottawa: Environment Canada.

Gibbon, A. (1999). Intrawest to get discount on BC Power. *Globe and Mail*, 6 February: B3.

Howes, C. (1999). BC royalty regime getting makeover. *Financial Post*, 31 May: C3.

International Energy Agency (1996). *Canada 1996 Review—Energy policies of IEA countries*. Paris: OECD.

Jaccard, M. (1998). *Reforming British Columbia's electricity market: A way forward*. Vancouver: Ministry of Employment and Investment.

Kassirer, J. (1998). *Tools of change: Proven methods for promoting environmental citizenship*. Ottawa: National Round Table on the Environment and the Economy.

Kennedy, P. (1998). Cheslatta band sues over '50s Alcan deal. *Financial Post*. 15 April: 9.

King, N. (1988). Managing the demand for government services. In A.C. Paul (Ed.), *Managing for tomorrow*. International City Management Association.

Kuhn, R. (1992). Canadian energy futures: Policy scenarios and public preferences. *The Canadian Geographer*, 36(4), 350-365.

MacQueen, K. (1998). Oil sought to refuel recovery. *Vancouver Sun*. 19 December: B.1.

Mitchell, B. (1989). *Geography and resource analysis*. 2nd edition. Essex: Longman Group.

National Media Archive (1998). *On Balance*, 11(4).

Nemtzow, D. (2001). *Nemtzow to Congress: Efficiency was 2nd greatest energy source in 1999*. Testimony before the House Committee on Energy and Commerce, Hearing on Energy Efficiency and National Energy Policy, June 22, 2001.

O'Riordan, T., and O'Riordan, J. (1993). On evaluating public examination of controversial projects. In H.D. Foster (Ed), *Advances in resource management* (pp. 19-52). London: Belhaven Press.

Powerex (2000). Power-History. *http://www.powerex.com/commit/commit_histor.html* (accessed 1 January 2001—no longer available).

Reid, J. (2000). Notes for a news conference, 6 December. Vancouver: BC Gas.

Ryan, J. (1991). The effect of the Free Trade Agreement on Canada's energy resources. *The Canadian Geographer*, 35(1), 70-82.

Sewell, W.R.D. (1987). Energy resources. In C.N. Forward (Ed.), *British Columbia: Its resources and people* (pp. 227-257). Victoria: University of Victoria, Department of Geography, Western Geographical Press, Vol. 22.

Victoria Times-Colonist (1999a). Native hydro project collapses. 28 May: E8.

Victoria Times-Colonist (1999b). Oil exploration studied. 5 June: A.6.

West Kootenay Power (1998). *1997 Annual Report*.

Western Interconnection Coordination Forum (2000). *Biennial Transmission Plan*.

Forestry

Alan Vyse
Department of Natural Resource Sciences, University College of the Cariboo

Introduction

British Columbia is a society built in part on "green gold," not the yellow metal that fuelled the gold rush fever of the 19th century, but the products and services that flow from the forest (Marchak, 1983). Consequently, the forests of BC have had, and continue to have, a powerful influence on the lives and imaginations of its people. Barely a day passes without the media detailing a news item about BC's forests and its associated industries. Most British Columbians live surrounded by forests. Their houses are largely built of wood, and their employment often is dependent upon some aspect of the wood industry whether they live in a logging town or the metropolis of Vancouver. Young and old recreate in the forest in large numbers on ski runs or by lake shores. The water supplies for communities of every size flow directly from forested mountain slopes. Images of the forest, in full splendour or felled in chaotic disarray, have resonated in the public mind, from Emily Carr's swirling paintings of the West Coast forest to the images of poets celebrating the forest and bemoaning its loss. Children learn that many provincial emblems are derived from the forest, including the dogwood flower, the western red cedar, and a noisy, blue-black, forest dwelling bird—the Steller's Jay.

British Columbians share this forest heritage with other parts of Canada and northern European nations, but in three respects BC stands out. First, the experience with the primeval forest is very recent. Large portions of the forests of BC are still largely untouched by visible human impacts. Second, BC contains within its boundaries a substantial proportion of the earth's remaining giant conifer forests. Many of them will be cut at some point in the future. Third, the forests remain in public ownership (Crown Land) (Table 16.1).

These three facts have drawn increasing international attention to the region. In particular, the protection of the coastal temperate rain forest has become a global conservation issue. Well-publicized protests have been organized by environmental groups for 30 years and are continuing despite substantial, recent changes in the management of public forests. Consumer boycotts of forest products from the province are being used as a new tool in the environmental battle against logging. This has created further concerns for an industry suffering through production costs increases, a significant downturn in Asian markets and tariff disputes with the major wood buyer, the US. The green gold that once offered so much promise now seems a little tarnished.

This chapter sets out to explain, in brief, the extent of the forests, and how they have been exploited and managed over the last 150 years. It continues with an assessment of the economic and social power of green gold in BC and the struggles to balance the power of competing interests in the management of the public forests. It ends with a speculative look at the future of the forestry industry. Of course, there are many important issues pertinent to the exploitation of the forest resource base that are beyond the scope of the chapter—such as biodiversity, CO^2 and global warming, BC's importance as one of the last great refuges for large wild mammals, and the impact of forest harvesting on stream water quality for fish populations.[1]

Table 16.1 Ownership of commercial forest land base (%) in five temperate latitude countries which produce coniferous forest products

Country	Public land	Private forest industry	Other private forest land
British Columbia	94	5	1
Finland	28	72	-
Sweden	25	24	51
New Zealand	50	28	22
United States	28	15	57

Source: Council of Forest Industries, 1999, http://www.cofi.org.

THE FORESTS OF BC

There are 52 million hectares (ha) of forest in BC[2] which represents about 55% of the total area; the remainder is either grassland, semi-desert or alpine tundra/icefield. The variety of forest ecosystems is greater in BC than any other part of Canada. Forests cloak the mountains of the coast and spread out over the giant river basins of the North and the plateaux of the central Interior. In the dry, southern Interior valleys, lower moisture excludes forests from the valley bottoms, but they soon regain their prominence further up the slope until the alpine climate reduces the forest to *krummholz*. Throughout BC, the forests are dominated by coniferous species, with the exception of the north east region where conifers and broadleaves form the boreal mixed-wood forest that stretches across Canada, and the small area of garry oak/arbutus along the southwest inner coast (see **Chapter 6**).

Eleven of the 14 biogeoclimatic or ecological zones in the province are forested (**Figure 6.3**). The largest is the Boreal White and Black Spruce zone which dominates the north eastern quadrant of BC. The Engelmann Spruce-Subalpine Fir zone that skirts the mountain tops well above the valley floor throughout the Interior cordillera is next in size. The third largest and most productive zone is the Coastal Western Hemlock zone. This area also contains the forests of old and awe-inspiring giant conifers whose valley by valley demise stimulated the environmental protest movement in BC. The area and the common tree species in each zone and an estimate of potential forest productivity are shown in Table 16.2.

If the area of forest in BC is staggering, then the volume of wood is almost beyond belief. Inventory estimates are almost 9 billion m³, despite 150 years of logging. Like all inventories, the precise amounts are hard to capture because trees and forests are never static, even without human intervention. They grow each year, and are also depleted by a variety of natural disturbances. During the 20th century, however, knowledge of the forests grew from very rough guesstimates to the reasonably accurate picture of today.

Whole forests may die, usually as a result of forest fires. In BC, they destroy or damage about 400,000 ha of forest every decade (1984-94), with most of them occurring in 1 or 2 years when moisture is below average and/or lightning strikes are more prevalent. For example, in 1998 there were 2,663 forest fires causing destruction to 78,000 ha. The effects of insects and diseases are less dramatic, but far more widespread. Like the effects of fire, the extent of their impact varies from year to year, but over the same period the damage covered about 8 million ha. Examples of insect damage include bark beetles, which usually kill trees, and defoliating insects, which reduce their growth. Root diseases are widespread and result in considerable mortality. Dwarf mistletoe and needle casts reduce growth. By

Forestry

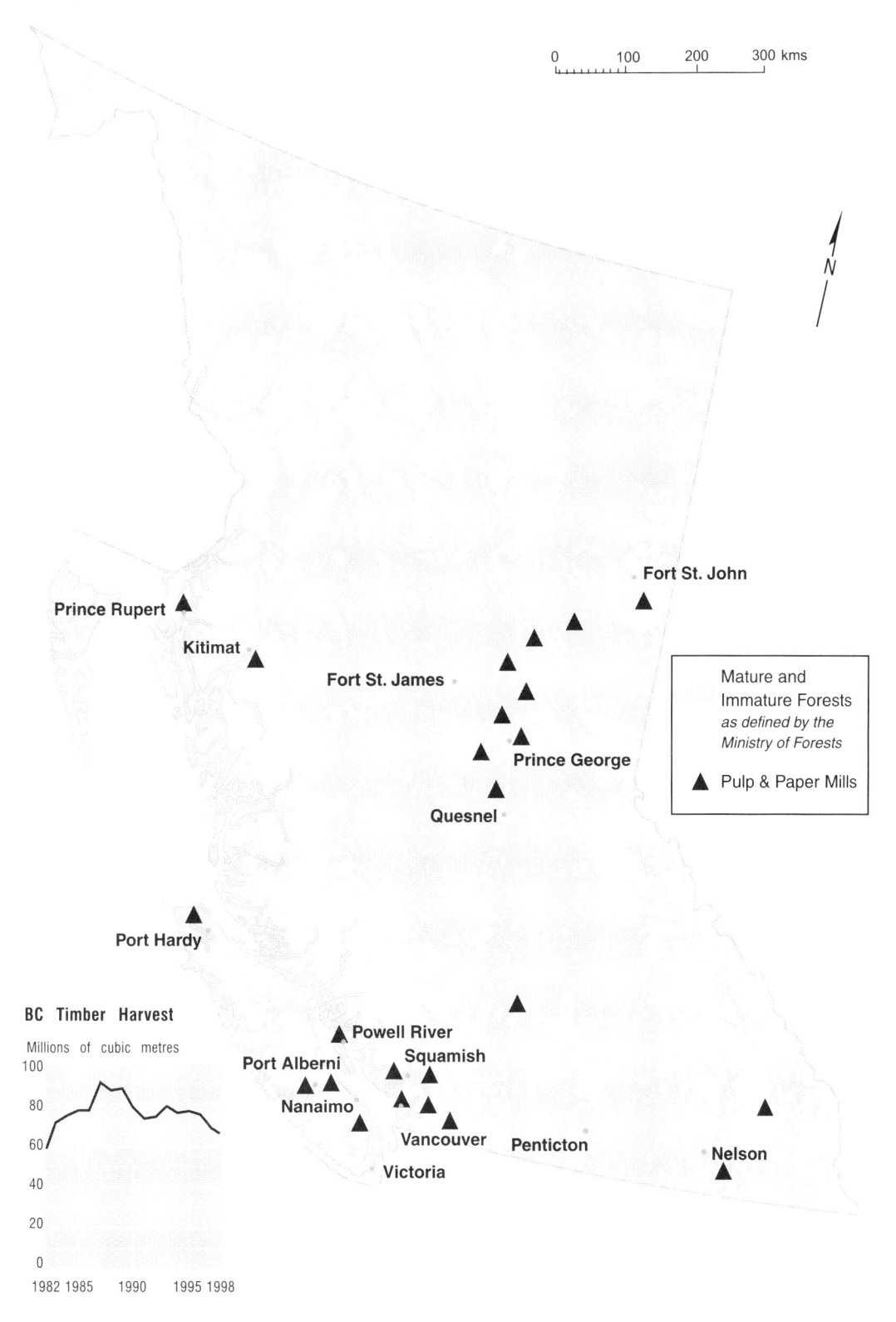

Figure 16.1 The forests of BC; harvest and pulp/paper mills (BCFER, 1996-2000)

Table 16.2 Area and potential productivity of forested ecological zones in BC

Forested ecological zone	Area (million ha.)	Productivity (site index)	Common tree species
Coastal Douglas-fir arbutus	0.2	16-32	Douglas-fir, grand fir Garry oak,
Coastal Western hemlock	10.6	8-40	Western hemlock, amabilis fir, western red cedar, sitka spruce, red alder
Mountain hemlock	4.1	8-16	Mountain hemlock, western hemlock, yellow cedar, western red cedar, amabilis fir
Ponderosa pine	0.5	6-20	Ponderosa pine, Douglas-fir
Interior Douglas-fir	4.0	8-24 (36 in wet subzone)	Douglas-fir, ponderosa pine, lodgepole pine, interior spruce, aspen, birch
Montane spruce	2.6	12-21	Interior spruce, lodgepole pine, aspen
Interior cedar-hemlock	5.0	15-27	Douglas-fir, lodgepole pine, white pine, western larch, interior spruce, western hemlock, western red cedar, cottonwood, birch, aspen
Engelmann spruce subalpine fir	13.3	6-21	Engelmann spruce, subalpine fir, lodgepole pine, white-bark pine
Sub-boreal pine spruce	2.4	6-21	Interior spruce, lodgepole pine, aspen
Sub-boreal spruce	9.9	9-24	Interior spruce, lodgepole pine, subalpine fir, birch, aspen
Boreal white and black spruce	15.1	6-18	White spruce, black spruce, lodgepole pine, aspen, balsam poplar

Note: Site index gauges forest productivity by indicating the height of dominant tree species measured at 50 years after the tree reaches 1.3 metres in height.

comparison, logging of mature forests is estimated at 2 million ha over the same period (3.8% of the total). The forests are also subjected to a multitude of other minor disturbances—wind, snow, drought, and landslides all cause damage throughout the province.

The response of the forest to disturbance is varied. Sometimes recovery is swift when a fire burns through stands of lodgepole pine and releases the vast store of seed held in cones high in the trees. In other cases, shrubs and herbs occupy the former forest site for many decades. Logged lands also vary considerably in the rate of seedling ingress, and their regeneration to forest is often speeded by replanting. Agricultural fields in some parts of the province require constant cultivation to exclude trees regenerating from seed drifting in from the surrounding forest. In general, the capability of the forest to regenerate itself is little short of phenomenal.

EARLY EXPLORATION AND MANAGEMENT: GREEN GOLD IS DISCOVERED

Forestry has been defined as "the art and science and practice of managing forested landscapes to provide a sustained production of a variety of goods and services for society"

(Kimmins, 1999). In pursuit of this objective Kimmins suggests that forestry generally goes through four stages.

- The initial stage is unregulated exploitation, negative effects of which lead to stage two.
- At this point, legal and political mechanisms are put in place to regulate the rate and location of exploitation and to determine who reaps the benefits and who pays the costs, usually in very uneven fashion.
- Stage three involves modification of these mechanisms to improve their ecological, economic, and social sensitivity, but the focus of management is on marketable products such as timber.
- The final stage sees the development of a forestry that is responsive to a much wider range of demands from society, including values and goods that have no obvious market and price. The benefits and costs of forestry activities are more evenly distributed among communities local and distant, land owners, owners of capital, and providers of labour.

According to Kimmins, provincial forestry policies in Canada, including BC, have passed through the first two stages and are now struggling to move to the fourth.

After millennia of extensive aboriginal use of the forest, the systematic exploitation of BC's forests began with the European settlement and the migration of gold seekers in 1860. Wood was the primary construction material and fuel of the day; it was needed for all manner of local purposes from houses to boats, to powering early machines and mining props, and heating homes, offices, and stores. Thus the need to regulate the cutting of timber was recognized early. In 1865, a Land Ordinance was passed that permitted the colonial governors of the day to make timber available in the form of leases, but left the land in government hands. This began a regulatory mechanism that continues to this day and deeply affects the way in which forestry is conducted in the province.

Until the early 1900s, the cutting of timber was licensed without much thought to economic or social development; leases were given no set time frame. Wood was needed to build the sternwheelers to carry gold seekers or to ferry settlers and their products along the lake chains of the southern Interior. It was needed for irrigation flumes and barns and apple boxes as agricultural land was carved out of the wilderness. In addition, large tracts of land were handed over to the new government of Canada in return for the promise of a transcontinental railway; smaller tracts were awarded to privately owned railway companies, most notably the owners of the Esquimalt to Nanaimo railway. Vast quantities of timber were used to build the bridges, to lay the track, and to fuel the engines that made the railways a reality (Seager, 1996).

At the beginning of the 20th century many people realized that the large resource base of North America—soils, wildlife, forests, waters, and minerals—was being seriously and recklessly depleted.[3] Many of these issues were discussed at the White House Conference (1908) initiated by President Theodore Roosevelt. It dealt with the significant problems of resource use and conservation occurring in many parts of the continent. A direct result of this considerable public and political interest in conservation issues led to federal, state, and provincial forest (and other) conservation regulations in both the US and Canada. A leading figure in these initiatives was a forester, Gifford Pinchot. He brought to North America many European ideas concerning long-term forest production and conservation, especially the practice of *sustained yield* in forestry (Cutter and Renwick, 1999). It quickly became apparent to people in BC that as the forests of North America were being depleted, BC's forest assets would be in demand and that improved regulations were in order to protect them and ensure that they were used wisely. The *Fulton Commission of Inquiry* (1910) recommended a series of measures to improve the protection of BC's forests and to foster their development as an economic engine for the growth of the province as a whole. The value of green gold had been recognized. These recommendations were adopted and the *Forest Act* (1912) was passed with the aim of using the forest resource for the maximum benefit to society. The legislation led to the creation of the Forest Branch, later the Ministry of Forests (MoF), with a mandate to:

- administer timber leases, value timber, and collect royalties;
- protect forests against damage, especially fire; and
- undertake reforestation.

With this, BC passed into Kimmins' second stage, from exploitation to management.

A fledgling forest industry started up on the coast, close to tidewater and low cost transportation, aimed at supplying export markets that rose with World War I and then fell precipitously with the worldwide economic depression in the 1930s. Interior mills supplied local needs such as the demand for fruit boxes, and construction requirements in the Prairie provinces, easily accessible by rail. Management of the forest amounted to little more than passing out licences for cutting timber and fighting forest fires, although the first seedling nurseries were started, which heralded the beginning of scientifically based production techniques. An important development was the foundation of a school of forestry at the University of BC. It marked the start of science-based forestry practices and more research into forest biosystems.

More Commissions of Inquiry were held in 1945 and 1955, each time under the guidance of W.G. Sloan. The *Sloan Commissions* built on the earlier principles of public ownership and conservation of the forest resource, but went much further to develop the notion of sustained yield as required policy. Sloan was pressed to favour substantial private ownership of forest lands, but he recommended and the government adopted measures to create a licensing system that created long-term leasing rights for large companies and short-term rights for small operators. He also recommended a regulatory framework for a continuous and steady yield of timber products from regional areas, in perpetuity. He favoured substantial public investments to improve the protection of the resource from fire, insects, and disease, to measure the extent of the forest, to restore the forest on logged lands, and to explore innovative means of managing and utilizing the forest.

THE MODERN PERIOD: FORESTS TURNED TO GOLD

While the Sloan Commissions in 1945 and 1956 provided the basis for a revised regulatory framework, aggressive government resource development policies (see **Chapters 7** and **10**) set in motion a rapid expansion in timber processing throughout the province over the next 20 years. Various forms of timber licences were made available to provide security of wood supply and encourage capital investment in modern sawmills and pulpmills. One of the most secure timber tenures, and also one of the most controversial, was the *Forest Management Licence*. This licence sought to entice owners of large tracts of private land, primarily on the coast, to practice sustained yield by adding substantial areas of public land to their control for lengthy terms before renewal. No up-front payments were required and the fight for control was fierce to the point that bribery of public officials was attempted and proved in court. The name of the licence was changed to *Tree Farm Licence* (TFL) shortly after this event, but media and public suspicion of the concentration of control of public lands has persisted to the present day. To deal with the problem of many small operators demanding access to the forest, primarily in the Interior, shorter-term timber licences were granted within newly created *Public Sustained Yield Units* (PSYUs). Once again the aim was to control the rate of exploiting the forest and again it was carried without cost to the beneficiaries. The variation in licensing arrangements are shown in Table 16.3.

Following the establishment of TFLs and PSYUs, the rate of harvest in the province increased from 22 million m^3 in 1950 to 55 million m^3 in 1970 and to 70 million m^3 10 years later. Expansion was extremely rapid, reflecting the advances in logging, yarding, and transportation techniques—many of which were developed in BC—but so was consolidation of corporate control. For example, in the Prince George area there were 401 sawmills processing 1.5 million m^3 of timber in 1960, and many of these sawmills were semi-portable operations in forest locations at some distance from

Table 16.3 Forest tenures in BC

Tenure	Rights	Responsibilities	Term/size/ replacement provisions
Tree Farm Licence (TFL)	– to carry out forest management on a specific area of Crown Land and almost exclusive rights to harvest an AAC from the licence area, under cutting permits	– licencee responsible for resource inventories, strategic and operation, planning, road building, and reforestation; licencee must maintain a manufacturing facility if required in original licence	– 25 year term; typically very large-scale operations; replaceable every 5 years
Forest Licence (FL)	– to harvest an annual volume of timber within a TSA, under cutting permits	– licencee responsible for operational planning, road building, and reforestation; licencee must maintain a manufacturing facility if required in original licence	– typically 15 year term; typically medium- to large-scale operations; replaceable every 5 years
Timber Sale Licence (TSL)	– to harvest timber from a specified area of Crown Land within a TSA or TFL area	– MoF is responsible for operational planning, road building, and reforestation on TSLs sold under the SBFEP* – licencee must maintain a manufacturing facility if required in original licence	– typically 6 months to 5-10 years; typically small- to medium-sized operations; most not replaceable
Wood Lot Licence (WL)	– to carry out forest management on a specific area of Crown Land (maximum 400 ha on Coast, maximum 600 ha in Interior) every 5 years and exclusive rights to harvest an annual volume of timber from the licence area, under cutting permits	– licencee responsible for strategic and operational planning, road building, and reforestation; licencee must not own or operate a manufacturing facility	– 15 year term; small (family-focused) operations; replaceable
Pulpwood Agreement (PA)	– to harvest up to a maximum annual volume within the TSA or TSLs, in the event that its holder cannot meet its fibre requirements privately	– licence requires management plan; if harvest occurs, responsibilities are similar to FL; licencee must maintain a manufacturing facility	– up to 25 years; potentially very large-scale operations; new contracts may or may not be replaceable
Timber Licence (TL)	– exclusive rights to harvest merchantable timber from a defined area of Crown Land, under cutting permits	– operating plan required; licencee responsible for operational planning, road building, and reforestation; once forest is re-established, area reverts to Crown and becomes part of the TSA or TFL	– variable; individual licences are relatively small; not replaceable

Source: BC Ministry of Forests, 1997

*SBFEP = Small Business Forest Enterprise Program

rail connections. A decade later, the bush mill era was gone; by 1977 there were only 110 mills but they processed *four times* as much timber. Part of this change also came from the introduction of regulations to harvest smaller trees (close-utilization policy) and requirements for chip contracts with pulp mills.

The economies of scale and new high speed, capital intensive sawing techniques were partly responsible for consolidation of sawmilling operations, but another powerful influence was the establishment of pulp mills at key locations throughout BC. They were an integral part of W.A.C. Bennett's grand scheme for development of the province. Pulp mills were established on main stem river systems to take advantage of ample water supplies, on electrical power grids to operate machinery, and on rail lines, especially BC Rail, to ensure cheap transportation of pulp and supplies. However, they also needed raw materials in the form of wood chips from sawmill residues. Chips became a profitable by-product of sawmills, and new mills were built close to pulp mills or beside cheap transportation. New construction and resulting economic activity led to a late 1960s boom in small communities. New workers flooded into towns like Prince George where three pulp mills were built, and Williams Lake where five sawmills were constructed or expanded. At Mackenzie, south of the Peace River pondage created to supply electrical power to the northern expansion, an entirely new town was built to provide accommodation for workers at the pulp and sawmill (Figure 16.1).

In 1975, a new Royal Commission on forest resources—the *Pearse Commission*—urged a rethinking of forest policy. Dr. Peter Pearse recognized the dangers of short-term thinking about economic development and urged that protection of the long-term productivity of the forest should be given higher priority. Much greater thought and planning were needed to ensure that the flow of timber over time, or *allowable cut*, was evaluated for short- and long-term impacts and reviewed by the public. He also urged that protection of non-timber resources and values in the forest be given greater recognition than in the past (Pearse, 1976).

Based largely on this advice, the BC government passed a greatly revised *Forest Act* (1978) that streamlined the old tenure system. It also refined the allowable cut planning process by combining Sustained Yield Units (SYUs) and creating new *Timber Supply Areas* (TSAs), and by instituting new review procedures. A *multiple use planning process* was also established. Under the revised *Ministry of Forests Act*, more precise goals for forest management were established. These two pieces of legislation continued and strengthened the long standing public policy to grant forest tenures to large companies, and continued the expansion of economic activity in the forest, albeit with some reforms to increase public participation in planning processes. The partnership of forest industry companies, workers, and government that arose in the 1960s as a way of creating the forestry economic powerhouse was continued. Another objective of the revised act was the more detailed regional inventories of forests, operations, allowable cut, and projected deficits (falldowns). The reports also took into account the needs of recreation and cattle grazing (BC Ministry of Forests, 1980).

The success of the partnership between government and industry is reflected in statistics. By 1988, the forest industry generated about $5 billion of shipments, which accounted for close to 50% of the value of shipments from all manufacturing industries in the province (BCFER, 1989). Approximately 75% of shipments were exported, generating significant amounts of foreign exchange for the Canadian economy. Government revenues from the forest also climbed substantially over the same period, but government expenditures also rose as a result of the reform in administration and increased government efforts in all realms of forest management. Net revenue from the forest was low, however, reflecting the pervasive problems of low commodity prices.

At the end of the 1980s, direct employment in the forest industry had risen to over 100,000 people a year, leading to population growth and economic prosperity throughout much of BC. Direct revenues (royalties) from the industry were important for the BC government, together with the indirect revenue (personal taxes) from those employed in the industry (see **Chapter 10**). Although employment was cyclical, following the markets for pulp and sawn timber, many of the workers were represented by strong labour unions and wages were high relative to the average rates in the Canadian industrial sector as a whole. As illustrated in Table 16.4, BC also led the national production table in forest products.

Satisfaction with the economic success of the forest sector was not universal. Strong public concerns over air and water pollution from industrial processes and over the clearcutting of coastal forests were expressed, but the criticisms appeared to have limited, short-term impact. First Nations groups were also pressing for redress for the licences and harvesting which they thought had seriously impinged on their traditional lands. The support for environmental issues in the forest came from the main metropolitan areas, whereas people in single enterprise towns would generally brook little criticism of the forest industry. Environmental concerns began to expand from these specific issues to include a more general concern about loss of the pristine coastal rain forest. Campaigns to protect the southern half of the Queen Charlotte Islands and the West Coast Trail as national parks received a sympathetic hearing in Ottawa and were ultimately successful (Dearden and Rollins, 1993). The pressure for native control of their traditional territories and the resource base was also gathering momentum (see **Chapter 8**).

The slow regeneration of logged-over areas also raised fears about the long-term production of timber. A federal-provincial agreement was negotiated in the mid 1980s specifically to investigate the causes of slow regeneration and boost the production of seedlings in provincial tree nurseries, with considerable success. However, the balloon of self-satisfaction was about to burst. Demands for changes in the administration and management of the public forest lands was coming from all sides to the extent that the forest sector in BC appeared to be in a state of crisis. Developing a forest management strategy that was sensitive to the environment *and* satisfied the demands from a host of interest groups was proving to be a difficult task.

CONTEMPORARY ISSUES: WHO OWNS THE GREEN GOLD?

In the 1980s and 1990s, a succession of BC provincial governments initiated and responded to demands for change in forest policy in a number of ways; however, the initiatives were not always connected coherently. Competing interests were strong, and determining who should benefit from exploiting the forests and what they should be used for became more difficult. Several authors and much media commentary addressed these issues, providing

Table 16.4 Canadian forestry production by leading provinces in the late 1990s

	Productive forest (million ha)	Annual allowable cut (million m^3)	Lumber (million m^3)	Value sawmill shipments ($ billion)	Pulp (000 tonnes)
British Columbia	46	75	31	6.5	7,000
Quebec	54	55	15	2.3	7,800
Ontario	42	45	5	.8	4,600
Alberta	25	27	<1	.8	
Canada	**245**		60		26,000

NB Figures are rounded; Canadian totals do not include numbers from provinces not listed here.

a considerable range of interpretations and offering several solutions and advice to the government (Marchak, 1983; Marchak, Aycock, and Herbert, 1999; Drushka, Nixon, and Travers, 1993; Binkley, 1997; Barnes and Hayter, 1997; Kimmins, 1999; M'Gonigle and Parfitt, 1994). Government actions, interest group responses, and the subsequent reactions by all parties became increasingly tangled. Issues were further complicated by insufficient data, disputes over interpretation of the same information, misinterpretation, and misrepresentation of information. There were, for example, major differences over value systems and the long-term projection of harvest rates.

The fundamental elements of the forest resource use system as it functions today are shown in Figure 16.2. It depicts the main sectors, the major actors, and some of the linkages. The system hinges on certain key components, notably:

- external demand, the global market, corporate lobbies in the US;
- the AAC and the amount of revenue that the government decides to appropriate;
- form and effectiveness of forestry legislation;
- corporate organization: labour organization; and
- public interest in environmental/forestry issues.

Clearly, there are several complex issues involved with the organization, operation, and perpetuation of the forest resource system that are beyond the scope of this review. The remainder of this section focuses on eight key issues that are fundamental to both the long-term vitality and sustainability of the forest industry and the protection and conservation of the forest resource base.

Who Really Owns the Forest?

Although the public owns the land and the timber, a complex system of tenures provides for the legal granting of rights to timber cutting. Since timber cutting requires occupancy for a substantial time period and disturbance of the forest on a large scale, the timber rights create a strong appearance of ownership. The present system of granting rights to public timber was established by the Royal Commissions of 1945 and 1955 and changed little until 1987. At the same time as stumpage rates were increased, the costs of forest management such as road building and reforestation were transferred to licence holders thereby reducing direct government responsibility for regional/local planning and forestry activities. The government then moved this concept one step further by proposing to convert many short-term licences into longer term TFLs. Public fears were voiced loudly at special hearings around the province. The principal concern was that the long-term renewable licences would further transfer effective forest ownership to large corporations, which could not be expected to act in the public interest. The proposal to increase TFLs was dropped but some additional licences were granted later with little debate.

General public distrust of large forest corporations peaks every time a major mill closure is announced, or industry experts propose that the government sell or lease forest land. These issues resound throughout BC and generate responses from many interest groups. The government has tried to reduce these concerns in a number of ways. Small woodlot licences are available for rural landowners as a means of supplementing farm incomes or seeking innovative small-scale forestry ideas. On a larger scale, special community forest licences, modelled on those granted to corporations, have been issued to build on successful earlier examples in Mission, Cowichan, and Revelstoke.

Much of the effective political criticism of the timber tenure system had come from small business operators who saw themselves as being squeezed out of business by the "majors." The government responded to this criticism by creating the *Small Business Forest Enterprise Program* with the objective of providing logging contractors and small timber processing plants an opportunity to gain access to public timber outside the mainstream tenure system. Timber sales are mostly awarded on a sealed bid system. The program has expanded from its start in 1987 to about 18% of the timber sold

Forestry

FOREST RESOURCES BASE

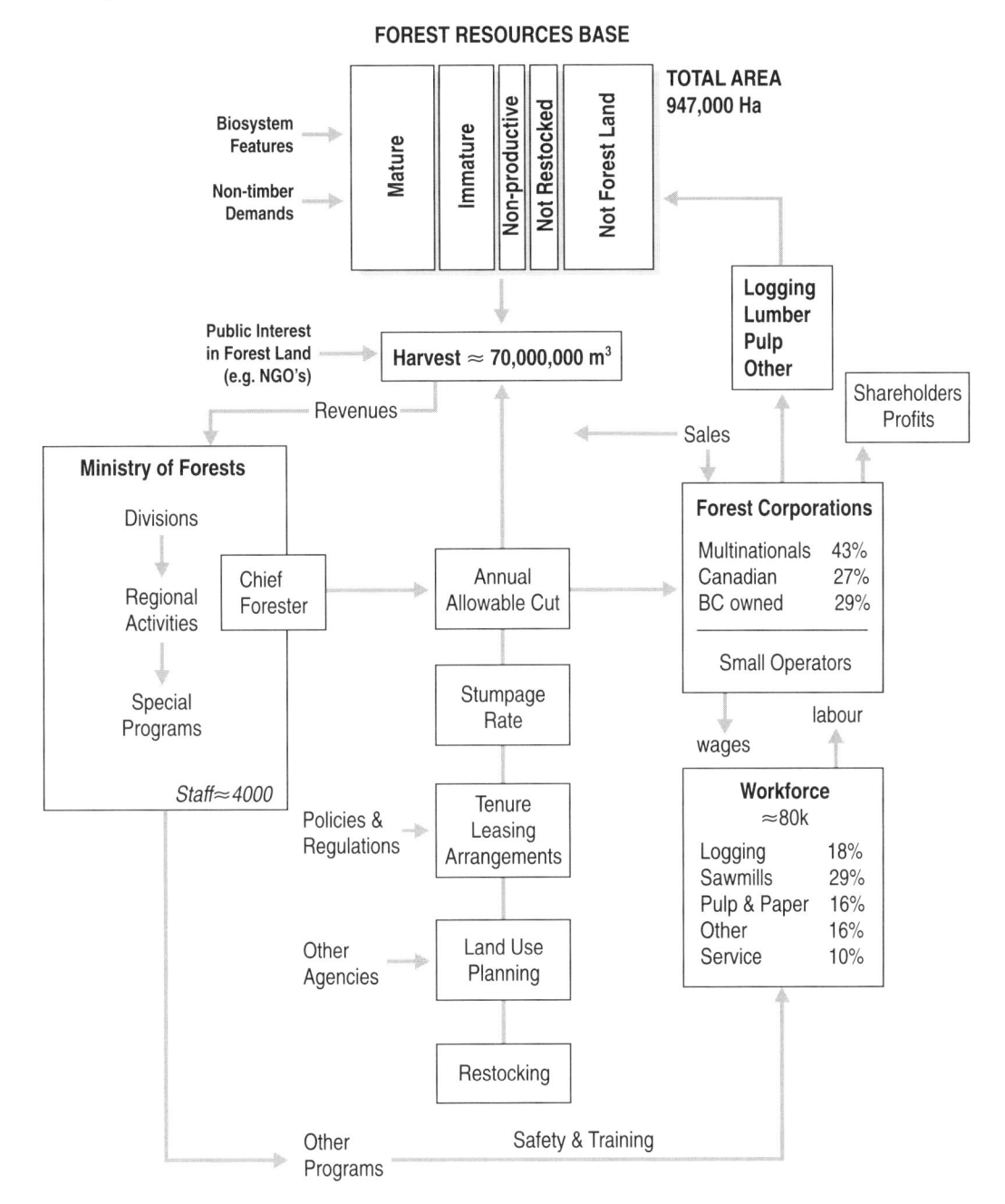

Figure 16.2 The forest resource system and its major components (BC Ministry of Forests Annual Reports: BC Financial and Economic Reviews 1985-2000)

each year and produces substantial revenues for the provincial treasury. A large part of the initial concern of the large timber processors has been alleviated over the years as partnerships between small and large operators have developed. Increasing amounts of timber are made available for the Small Business program by a clause in the Forest Act requiring major licence holders to relinquish 5% of their timber rights with each change in ownership.

Despite these effective changes, critics continue to argue for a dismantling of the forest tenure system. Some argue on social and ecological grounds that the current system fails to protect the forest, the interests of communities, and the interests of forest workers. Others argue that the system is neither efficient nor effective in social and economic terms. The government, historically, has tried to take a middle course (Marchak et al., 1999).

The Price of Timber

The price that forest companies paid for timber had long been a secondary issue in government policy. Developing the timber processing industry was given first priority and early efforts to develop market pricing of timber through auctions or similar mechanisms were dropped in favour of a tightly administered system of awarding timber rights to licensees who owned processing plants. *Stumpage*, originally the price paid for timber based on counting stumps, was calculated by using a system of standard costs and subtracting those costs from end product prices, and applying the resultant value to the amount of timber cut. Complex procedures were put in place for use by trained government employees to measure or scale the timber in order to maximize revenues and to keep timber theft to a minimum.

Substantial change began in 1987 when the price for Crown timber of stumpage was raised substantially as a way of appeasing American lumber companies competing with Canadian imports. These companies were putting pressure on the US government to impose import tariffs on Canadian lumber on the grounds that provincial governments in Canada subsidized lumber production by failing to charge competitive prices for wood. Canadian economists had criticized these low cost wood policies for many years and the American argument was seen as having considerable force.[4] Accordingly, in 1986 the Canadian government instituted an export tax on lumber shipments to the US as a way of avoiding unpredictable political actions in that country. The government in BC responded shortly thereafter by increasing the stumpage prices, thus avoiding the export tax. Industry representatives were dismayed, but the government had the advantage of arguing that their action would head off another depression in timber processing, save jobs, and boost government revenues. The success of this initiative was short lived as American criticisms continued and eventually resulted in a Canadian-imposed system of lumber export quotas as a way of further appeasing the influential American lumber lobby. The development of a market pricing system for collecting stumpage will pose a major challenge for the government now that agreements have expired (early 2001).

What is an Allowable Cut of Timber?

The amount of timber cut in the forest is set by the Chief Forester and controlled by limits placed on individual licensees, under the authority of the *Forest Act* (Utzig and Macdonald, 2000). The amount of timber that is allowed to be cut has risen steadily over the years to its current level of approximately 70 million m^3. The actual amount of timber cut depends on market conditions as the many individual licensees have some flexibility over the amount they may cut in any given year and this accounts for the difference between published allowable cut and actual cut figures.

The level of the *Allowable Annual Cut* (AAC) is a matter of great controversy (Utzig and Macdonald, 2000). For some, the allowable amount is clearly too high and cite government reports to support their view. Others argue that the cut is too low and similarly cite government reports to back their position. Clearly, the Chief Forester has an unenviable balancing act to perform (Marchak et al., 1999).

The allowable cut decision is made easier by the division of the province into *Timber Supply Areas* (TSAs). A separate cut is established for each of the 36 TSAs. Allowable cuts are also established for 35 TFLs and for the many small woodlot licences. The cut calculation is based on many highly technical issues. These include inventory information on the actual amount of land available, taking account of the creation of new parks or the building of transmission lines, the many types of timber and their volume and growth rates, the depletion of timber by agents such as fire, insects, and disease, the timber utilization rate (or the amount of a tree that can be used), and the accessibility of timber using current technology.[5] Just as the ability to use wood chips in pulp mills changed ideas about the volume of wood available 40 years ago, recent advances in helicopter logging have changed ideas about what timber is economically accessible. The data and assumptions on these technical matters are reviewed and made available to the public for any given TSA on a 5 year basis. The inventory and projected growth rates are the key components for forecasting potential yields and harvests. Inventory knowledge improved significantly in the last 3 decades with better access, field techniques, and cruising. The MoF uses GIS techniques and a range of computer assisted techniques and a simulation program (FSSIM) to estimate potential yields and harvest rates.

The first 5-year review was completed for all areas in 1996 and the second 5-year review will be complete by 2002. In each review the data and assumptions used in arriving at AACs for every TSA and TFL are made available to the public for comment before a final decision is made. The primary source of controversy over allowable cuts lies in how the Chief Forester handles one indisputable fact. Many of the province's forests have never been cut and their age and accumulated volume is high. When these forests are cut they are replaced with faster growing stands that are scheduled to be cut long before they reach the former high volumes of the original stands. Thus, if current assumptions continue to hold, the cut from future forests will be less than the current cut. Figure 16.3 shows the forecast change in age classes within a sample TSA. The attempt to achieve a balanced distribution of age classes over the next 100 years is quite evident. The example is extreme; some timber supply areas already have a balanced age class distribution and their harvest level is not expected to decline. The timing of this decline varies. On the coast, the AAC of some areas has already been reduced. For many interior areas, the decline is not scheduled for many decades.

The calculated decline in cut is referred to as the *fall down effect*. Critics who want the cut level to be lower than it is at present argue that the fall down effect demonstrates that the current cut is unsustainable, and the social and economic pain of a reduced cut is better suffered now than later. Others hold the opinion that technology will change many of the factors used in cut calculations, and that any decline is unnecessary. The Chief Forester has stated that the Province will follow a policy of gradual decline in AAC. The general parameters of harvesting are shown in Figure 16.4.

Clearcutting Old Growth Forests and Environmental Activism

Much of BC's forest area is old forest, even after one and a half centuries of exploitation. These areas are the result of growth conditions and natural disturbances that took place hundreds, and perhaps thousands of years ago. Individual trees in the forest are often large, and on the coast, on sites with good moisture and nutrient supply, the trees can reach exceptional sizes. In addition, the old forests have special structural features, including deep, multi-layered canopies, standing dead trees, and centuries of accumulated deadfall on the forest floor. These features provide a rich habitat for a wide range of organisms, some of which are thought to be completely reliant on old growth forest conditions (Harding and McCullum, 1994).

When the old forests are logged, the usual practice is to clearcut, or remove all the usable trees at one time. The resulting scene is one of devastation. Environmental groups have focused on such scenes as a means of protecting coastal old growth forest from logging, saving the habitat for forest creatures, and generally expressing dissatisfaction with the way forests are managed in BC. Campaigns to save the forest have usually focused on particular areas of coastal forest (such as the Nitinat Triangle, South Moresby, Carmanah, Walbran, Clayoquot Sound), and have succeeded in raising support

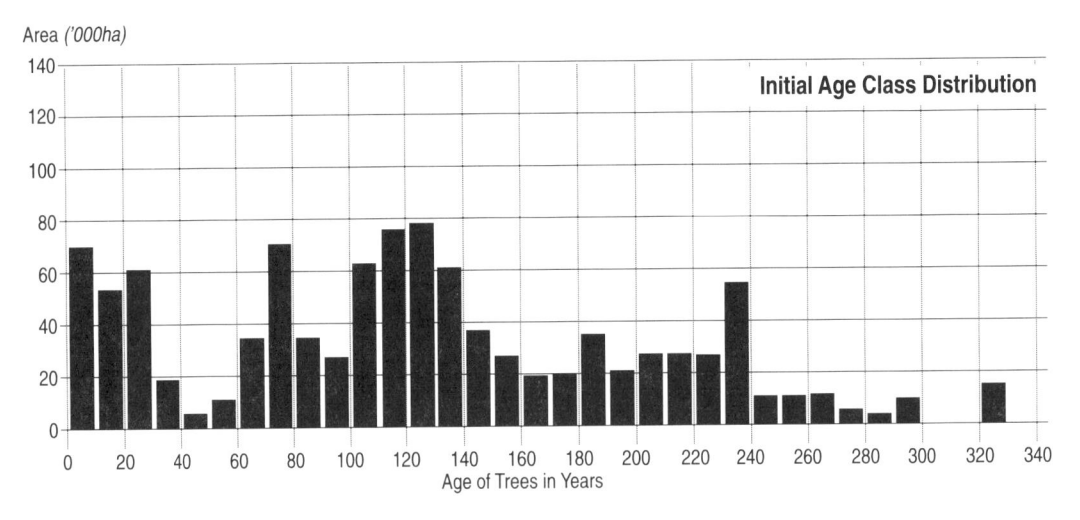

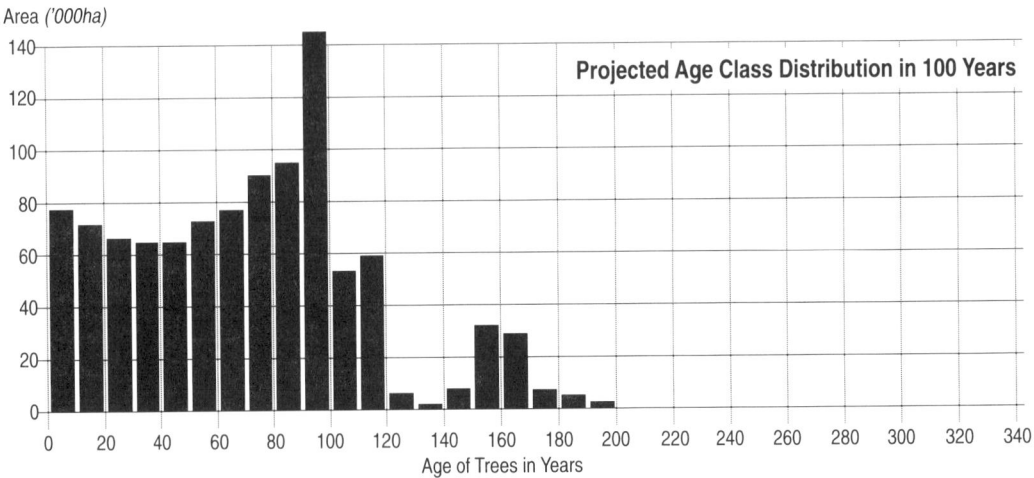

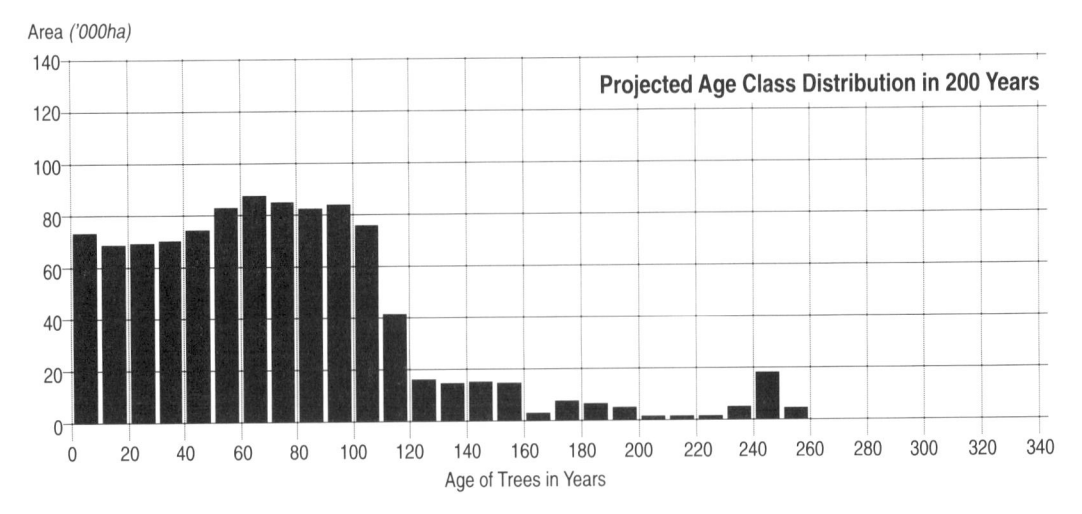

Figure 16.3 Projected changes in the age class distribution for the Okanagan TSA over time (BC Ministry of Forests, Okanagan Timber Supply Area)

Harvest Area

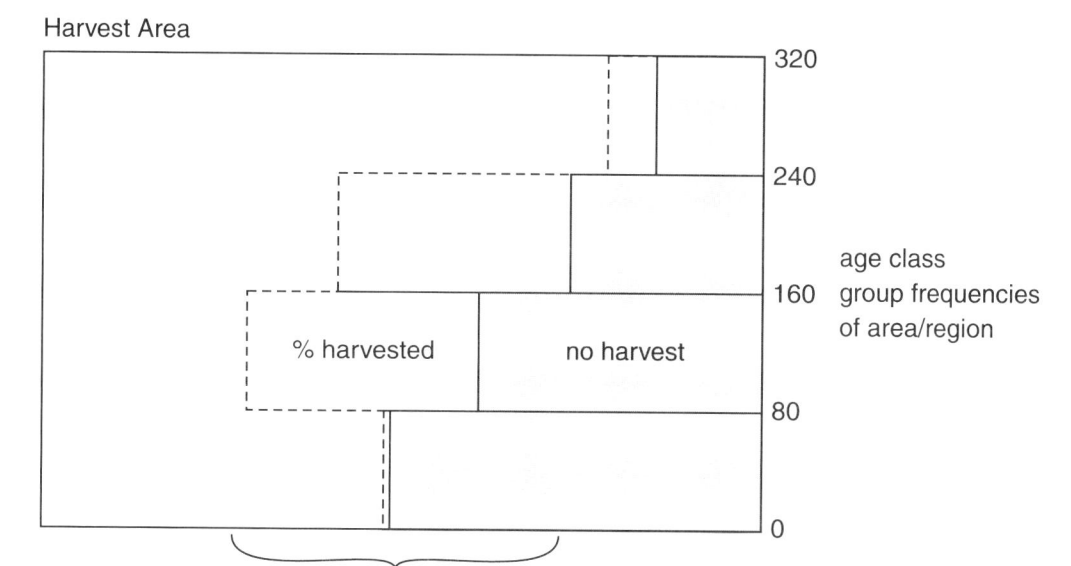

Figure 16.4 General parameters associated with harvesting

[Diagram shows stepped bars with age class group frequencies of area/region at levels 0, 80, 160, 240, 320, with "% harvested" and "no harvest" regions indicated.]

determination of harvest/unharvested proportion to balance age class and maintain a proportion of natural conditions such as old growth or scenic values, according to age/class growth increments

and, more importantly, substantial funds locally, nationally, and internationally. The funds have allowed organizations to make use of a wide range of public relations materials and effectively counter pro-logging campaigns by the forest industry, labour organizations, and communities dependent on logging activity. In some cases, the campaigns were accompanied by remarkable displays of public disobedience. Hundreds of people were arrested in 1993 over the effort to save parts of Clayoquot Sound. All of the campaigns have been successful so far. Not only were the specific areas of protest largely protected from logging, but a system of old growth reserves was also established throughout the province. In addition, the protests played a significant role in prompting the government to announce in 1991 that 12% of the province would be placed in permanent reserves or parks.

The current disputes over protection of the "Great Bear Rain Forest" on the central and northern coasts and the Elaho Valley north of Vancouver have seen a new development. A few purchasers of BC forest products have announced that they will no longer purchase wood from endangered temperate rain forests, apparently as a result of environmental groups threatening consumer boycotts.

Public dismay with clearcutting in general has also prompted several changes in forestry practices in the province as a whole. Limits on the size of cutting areas, and requirements to protect streamside forests and wildlife tree reserves were put into place. A major forest company—Macmillan Bloedel (now part of Weyerhaeuser)—went further and in 1998 announced an end to clearcutting in its operations (Matas and Lush, 1998). The cutting method was replaced with one that preserved much more of the original forest structure; similar efforts are being made in many other parts of the province and the rest of North America (Kohm and Franklin, 1997).

Environmental activism has proven to be remarkably successful in a sector of economic activity that was conservative and relatively immune to criticism for many years, but the cost has been high and could climb much higher. At some point a balance has to be reached between the desire to protect "green gold" and the desire to use "green gold." There has to be recognition that old trees do not live forever (Kimmins, 1999), that the scenes of devastation that evoke so much sympathy are short lived, and that forests regenerate and grow rapidly to cover logging scars (Robson, Butch, and Walker, 1995).

How Should Forestry Be Practised?

For many years the BC Forest Service, formed in 1912, managed the forest. At first it did so independently, often with few funds and little support, except for fire-fighting activities. As the industry grew and regulation and management costs began to rise, government sought to reduce the direct costs by forming management partnerships with the forest industry, first on TFLs and then on all major licences. Public involvement in these arrangements was virtually non-existent.

In 1947, the *Foresters Act* was passed. This legislation permits only professional foresters who have the specialized training, knowledge, and experience, as judged by their professional association, to practise forestry in the province. There are now about 3,000 practising professional foresters in BC. Much responsibility is placed in their hands as they are required to write prescriptions and formulate plans for forest management on a site by site basis and are accountable for their actions to both their peers and the public, according to the Act. Considerable criticism for its apparent acquiescence has been directed at the profession by environmental organizations who point out that many foresters are directly or indirectly employed by the forest industry. Robson and colleagues (1995) in the Working Forest Project have mounted a vigorous defence of the profession.

When complaints over forest practices began, efforts were made to reduce the worst cases of environmental abuse, especially those associated with forest streams that supported fish. Significant efforts were also made to protect scenic views and recreational assets. However, public discontent was unabated in 1990 when the Forest Resources or *Peel Commission* recommended that the government regulate forest practices more closely by introducing a Forest Practices Code, a system based on similar codes used in Washington and Oregon. A made-in-BC code was put into force in 1994.

According to the published preamble, the *Forest Practices Code Act* (1994) was enacted to ensure sustainable use of the forests held in trust for future generations, and defined sustainable use as:

- managing forests to meet present needs without compromising the needs of future generations;
- providing stewardship of forests based on an ethic of respect for the land;
- balancing economic, productive, spiritual, ecological, and recreational values of forests to meet the economic, social, and cultural needs of people and communities, including First Nations;
- conserving biological diversity, soil, water, fish, wildlife, scenic diversity and other forest resources; and
- restoring damaged ecologies.

Many of the ideas incorporated in the Code had been in use for several years, but often in piecemeal fashion. However, it did break ground by giving considerable legislative force to an integrated set of management ideas about planning and implementation of forestry activities. The Code created one new body, the Forest Practices Board, which was given independent powers to investigate public complaints and audit licence holders of every size. This body has found that companies, with few exceptions, are conducting business in accordance with the Code regulations. They have also commented that the parts of the Forest Practices Code relating to the protection of biodiversity have not been implemented in the spirit of the Code.

At about the same time the Code was put into practice, another means of regulating forest practices was emerging—Forest Management Certification (FMC). The concept of certifying consumer products "safe" had been in the market place for many years, but certifying forests was another matter. The Forest Stewardship Council was set up, with headquarters in Oaxaca, Mexico, in response to the belief among environmental organizations that governments worldwide were incapable of policing regulations to control forestry practices and their negative effects on the environment (see, for example, *http://www.fscoax.org*). Their idea was that consumer choice would drive a system of private certification based on voluntary implementation of sustainable forest practices. Millions of hectares of forest land on several continents have now been certified by the Stewardship Council. Most of this land is privately owned as intended. Governments, not surprisingly, have preferred to pursue their own certification initiatives, either alone or in partnership with other nations. Canada's sustainable forest management scheme, in common with several others, proposes to use a series of criteria and indicators to measure progress toward sustainability (Canadian Council of Forest Industries, 1997). The impact of either public or private certification schemes on the market place for timber products is not yet clear.

Codes of practice, like regulations of any kind, have a cost—often a significant cost. The Council of Forest Industries in BC has argued that the Forest Practices Code has increased operating costs substantially since its introduction, and that industry and shareholders have borne the brunt of this cost. International competitiveness has been hindered, according to industry spokespeople. Considerable efforts have been made by the government to streamline and otherwise revise the Code. Third party certification also incurs significant costs which are borne by the companies. Tangible benefits of certification in the form of better sales have yet to be experienced. Intangible public relations benefits are more apparent. The search for an effective and low cost system of ensuring influential interest groups that public land management is environmentally sound and in capable hands will take many years.

Planning Future Forest Use

The public forests of BC are a source of many values and services other than timber. Ideally, land use planning is a systematic process that balances decisions about areas according to fundamental environmental parameters such as biodiversity, biosystem integrity, and bioregional systems with socioeconomic requirements such as employment, community and profit levels for industry sustainability, equity, and efficiency (see **Chapter 13**). When BC's population was small and the industrial use of the forests dominated government policy, public input was absent and forest harvesting was the main (i.e., single) use. Planning, as such, consisted of cut plans for specified licence areas and little else. However, from the 1930s onward, as highways improved and automobile use increased, more people were using forest land (i.e., areas not designated as parks) for recreation. Originally, a parks division (created 1939) within the MoF managed recreation on Crown Land; it was later transferred to the Ministry of Recreation and Conservation (1956). In the early 1970s, the MoF began to develop more comprehensive plans with overlays indicating values other than timber harvesting. These procedures were formalized by the requirements of the revised Forest Act of 1978, which required a multiple use planning process. Eventually, with improved technical capabilities through the gradual emergence of Geographic Information Systems (GIS), it was possible to accomplish regional plan systems, more realistic forecasting, and the development of alternative scenarios (BC Ministry of Forests, 1994). The enactment of CORE and LUCO in the early 1990s (see **Chapter 13**) saw the first real attempts at comprehensive planning with substantial stakeholder/public input and a clearer articulation of planning goals, objectives, and procedures.

The BC government now has a comprehensive land use planning system in place with the main focus being directed at the LRMP level (see **Chapter 13**). It would be naive to assume that a decade of comprehensive land use planning could rectify the problems created by a century of aggressive logging, a highly competitive industry, and at times poorly coordinated regulatory management. However, this seems to be the only solution in the long run if the conflicts in the woods are going to be resolved.

Investing in the Forest and Jobs

A long-standing complaint is that government has failed to invest enough in forest management, whether for timber production or any other valuable forest asset. There is a history of successive governments establishing special funds for protecting and renewing the forest, and then raiding the funds for other purposes.

The most recent and largest government initiative is Forest Renewal BC (FRBC), established in 1994. It sets out to renew BC's forests by investing in practices that increase forest growth, by repairing environmental damage, particularly in streams, enhancing community stability in areas dependent on forest industry, and increasing employment in the forest sector. FRBC is funded by a complex formula in which the corporation receives stumpage revenues in excess of certain base line levels. FRBC has spent over a billion dollars in the last 5 years pursuing these goals. Concern about the program was voiced by the Auditor General in a 1999 report.

Moving From Primary Processing

Another issue is that the provincial government, in partnership with large corporations, in pursuing a course of timber development focusing on exporting primary products has ignored the options of developing secondary processing industries in the province (see **Chapter 10**; Barnes and Hayter, 1997). This direction of policy, along with technological advancement in the processing industries, resulted in a constant decline in employment per cubic metre of timber cut. BC does not fare favourably concerning job generation when compared with other countries (Marchak et al., 1999). The reality is that the economic factors responsible for this development are not clear and it is improbable that the situation can be changed by government actions alone. The economy and the forest industry of the province are undergoing reorganization.[6] For example, technological change has had a profound effect on the market for sheathing products in the construction industry. Plywood has been largely replaced by composite wood products, notably by oriented strand board. This change has rendered obsolete much of the formerly large coastal plywood industry and resulted in substantial unemployment. However, the construction of new mills to produce oriented strand board from cheap fibre in the Interior of the province has created employment. In the pulp sector, technological change has resulted in stiff competition from other countries in markets that were formerly the exclusive domain of long-fibred pulp from BC and other Canadian mills. The aging of the industrial plant has also played a major role in closures. FRBC has invested in a number of long-term training initiatives to increase the capability of workers and entrepreneurs to develop new ways to use, process, and market forest products, but the success of these ventures is not yet known. On an even broader front, governments and industry have failed to invest in research and development to fill the vacuum left by multinationals who tend to maintain their research centres at their headquarters.

CONCLUSIONS: FOREST MANAGEMENT FOR A NEW MILLENNIUM

Forest management in BC has gone through numerous changes since the Forest Act of 1912 was put into place to control corruption, speculation in leases, reckless exploitation, and loss of revenue. During the modern (Fordist) era, a corporate, industrial forestry system evolved and expanded as the demand for lumber and newsprint increased. In addition, forest policy, regulations, and management evolved and increased in complexity as a result of numerous government commissions. It is clear that management of the forests—whether measured in terms of conservation, revenue maximization, or benefit spreading—improved enormously during the last century. There is now more accurate and scientific knowledge of the forests and their characteristics—from individual species to biosystems—on which to build sound, sustainable policies. This is a primary requirement for formulating an effective forest policy and management practices. There is, however, a need for more research, whether concerning disease infestations, harvesting, restocking techniques, future wood products, or interconnections between the life forms of the forest system (Binkley and Watt, 1999).

The issues outlined in the previous section suggest also that there is a palpable urgency to resolving them. How they might be mitigated or even solved depends ultimately on the government in power, its ideological orientation, and how the electorate understands forest management issues. The last decade has seen the BC government using a more sophisticated land use planning process that will go a long way in helping to resolve the "war in the woods." Alternatively, a change in government might see a more pronounced "market solution" to many of the problems. The actors on the forest policy stage are now struggling to write their own play, while the industry generates enormous economic benefits for the people of the province.

Forestry policies and activities in BC (and in the rest of Canada) have passed through Kimmins' first two stages into the third stage, and are now struggling to move to the fourth, where forestry activities are sanctioned by a broad population base. Within the province this struggle seems likely to be dominated by several themes, notably:

- Aboriginal concerns and rights;
- options for the future and satisfying the plurality of interests;
- water catchment and water quality;
- wildlife protection and recreation access;
- certification according to use of ecological/ sustainable management practices; and
- the threat of a softwood lumber tariff war.

Aboriginal rights to the forest and treaty negotiations, for example, have the potential to change the long-standing partnership between government and industry in a few short years. The forest industry in the province is already attempting to mitigate the possible effects of ownership changes and the economic dislocation that such changes might bring. Several business partnerships with Aboriginal groups have been formed in recent years with some success, but considerable and costly uncertainty remains.

Water catchment is significant in terms of quality and quantity of supplies. Post Walkerton Canada is increasingly sensitive to the likelihood of any pathogens or toxic chemicals in drinking supplies. This issue is relevant in terms of mill effluents and spraying programs. A more determined effort has been made to control the impact of logging on salmon streams and to restore those water bodies damaged by earlier forest operations.

Wildlife protection and recreation access are complex topics which reflect the range of demands on the forest environment. The expansion of reserved land from 6 to 12% of the area of BC has reduced the pressure on forest areas. Further, the LRMP process is attempting a more balanced allocation of land uses.

In the background, and showing no signs of going away, are two global issues that will eventually have a profound impact. Firstly, global warming and its effects on forests, linked with the role of forests in fixing carbon, is undoubtedly a major issue. Secondly, where do we get the wood to meet the increasing worldwide demand? It is difficult to stop harvesting certain forest types without considering the consequences to other areas of forest. If BC saves substantially more of its forests from logging and reduces its allowable cut as many propose, what will be the effect on South American forests, where biodiversity values may be much higher than in BC?

One direction for the future may be more intensive management of a smaller area of cultivated forest as opposed to the current exploitation seen in the extensive harvesting of wild forest systems. The rising price of fuel may eventually force this kind of geographic efficiency on the industry and thereby make it possible, as a spin off, to reserve more land for natural reserves. While the efforts of individuals to log selectively are instructive,[7] the industry as a whole is still oriented to capital intensive, labour-replacing methods (driven by stiff competition and profit levels) and an industrial system based on economies of scale.

To some extent there is a parallel between forestry and trends in agriculture. Small scale organic farming rejects the industrial system of large scale corporate produced food; however, organic foods invariably tend to be more expensive. Similarly, careful, selective logging would lead to forest products that the consumer would perhaps find very expensive.

It is apparent that there are many unresolved and complex issues in the exploitation of BC's forests. Economic dislocation is already occurring as a result of the high cost of wood in BC brought about by efforts to make forestry more socially acceptable. Further economic losses are inevitable. Fears about trading sanctions placed upon BC wood products by wood producers in the US and environmental campaigns that seek to influence major US buyers of the same wood products are reducing investor confidence even further. Yet confidence is needed if the industry is to continue to make investments that reduce operating costs.

There are also major scientific problems to be resolved. In the background, beyond the borders of the province, the almost certain prospect of global climate change with its alarming environmental consequences and unpredictable political responses could conceivably produce big changes in the way forests are managed around the world. In addition to this, the growing world population and increasing demands for wood may also bring difficult questions in its wake. If the province restricts logging in more of its forests, and reduces the allowable cut for non-timber values, what will be the effect on forests elsewhere, where those values may be much higher than in BC?

Somehow a route must be found between the rocks that can wreck the ship of public forest policy if forest management is going to reach Kimmins' fourth stage. No shortage of solutions have been proffered, from illusions of a sylvan paradise for a few to thoughtful proposals promoting intensive timber production, thus allowing reservation of more forest for natural reserves. Efforts to encourage innovative forest management via small scale private and community forests are already being investigated. Further, more radical ideas, such as selling off the public land base, may take hold if economic problems deepen. However, the route chosen depends ultimately on the government in power, its ideological orientation, and how the electorate understands forest management issues.

While the industry can no longer ignore public opinion and the impacts of certification, recycling, and enhanced environmental quality standards, so too environmentalists must be realistic about the way in which the BC economy functions. Changes to forest policy affect the direct and indirect revenues that derive from exploitation of the forest resource base, and must therefore be carefully considered. It is also apparent that green gold no longer lies in timber values alone.[8]

Despite the problems of the present and challenges of the future, the influence of the forest on life in BC is unlikely to wane, no matter which routes are chosen. The economic power of green gold may have lost its allure, but forests continue to be part of the unique sense of place held by those who live in BC. While yellow gold drew people to BC and disappointed most if not all of its seekers, the green gold has proved to be different. Green gold means so many things to so many people that it reflects the wishes of the beholder and it endures. The forests remain.

Acknowledgements:

The author wishes to thank Colin J.B. Wood for his assistance in preparing this chapter. M.E. Edgell and Ms. Judith O. Stoute provided information and data.

References

Anderson, F.J. (1991). *Natural resources in Canada: Economic theory and policy.* Toronto: Nelson Canada.

Barnes, T., and Hayter, R. (Eds.) (1997). *Troubles in the rainforest: British Columbia's forest economy in transition.* Victoria, BC: University of Victoria, Department of Geography, Western Geographical Series, Vol. 33.

BC Ministry of Forests (1980). *Forest and range resource analysis* (2 vols). Victoria, BC: Government of BC.

BC Ministry of Forests (1994). Forest, range and recreation resource analysis. Victoria, BC: Government of BC.

BC Ministry of Forests (1997). Timber Tenure System. Table 1.

BCFER (1996). *British Columbia Financial and Economic Review*. Victoria, BC: Government of BC.

BCFER (1997). *British Columbia Financial and Economic Review*. Victoria, BC: Government of BC.

Binkley, C.S. (1997). A crossroad in the forest: The path to sustainable forestry in BC. *BC Studies*, 113, 39-61.

Binkley, C.S., and Watt, S. (1999). The status of and recent trends in forest sector research in British Columbia. *Forestry Chronicle*, 75, 607-614.

Canadian Council of Forest Ministers (1997). *Criteria and indicators of sustainable forest management in Canada*. Ottawa: CCFM.

Council of Forest Industries (1999). A blueprint for competitiveness (*www.cofi.org*).

Cutter, S., and Renwick, W. (1999). *Exploitation, conservation, preservation: A geographic perspective on natural resource use* (3rd Ed.). New York: Wiley.

Dearden, P., and Rollins, R. (1993). *Parks and protected areas in Canada*. Toronto: Oxford University Press.

Drushka, K., Nixon, R., and Travers, R. (1993). *Touch wood: BC forests at the crossroads*. Madeira Park, BC: Harbour Publishing.

Dufour, J. (1995). Towards a sustainable development of Canada's forests. In B. Mitchell (Ed.), *Resource and environmental management in Canada* (pp. 183-206). Toronto: Oxford University Press.

Harding, L., and McCullum, D. (Eds.) (1994). *Biodiversity in BC: Our changing environment*. Vancouver: UBC Press/Environment Canada, Canadian Wildlife Service.

Kimmins, H. (1999). *Balancing act: Environmental issues in forestry* (2nd Ed.). Vancouver: UBC Press.

Kohm, K., and Franklin, J. (1997). *Creating a forestry for the 21st century: The science of ecosystem management*. Washington, DC: Island Press.

Lavender, D. (Ed.) (1990). *Regenerating British Columbia's forests*. Vancouver: UBC Press.

Marchak, P. (1983). *Green gold: The forest industry in British Columbia*. Vancouver: UBC Press.

Marchak, P., Aycock, S., and Herbert, D. (1999). *Falldown: Forest policy in BC*. Vancouver: Ecotrust Canada.

Matas, R., and Lush, P. (1998) How a forestry giant went green. *Globe and Mail*, 18th June.

M'Gonigle, M., and Parfitt, B. (1994). *Forestopia: A practical guide to the new forest economy*. Madeira Park, BC: Harbour Publishing.

Pearse, P. (1976). *Timber rights and forest policy in BC: Report of the Royal Commission on Forest Resources*. Victoria: Government of BC.

Robson, P., Butch, G., and Walker, A. (1995). *The working forest of BC*. Madeira Park, BC: Harbour Publishing.

Seager, A. (1996). The resource economy, 1871-1921. In H. Johnston (Ed.), *The Pacific province* (pp. 205-252). Vancouver: Douglas and McIntyre.

Utzig, G., and Macdonald, D. (2000). *Citizen's guide to annual allowable cut determinations: How to make a difference*. Vancouver: BC Environmental Network.

ENDNOTES

[1] The nature of globalization also means that regional issues can quickly assume international attention. For a recent overview of Canada's forests and sustainable practices see Dufour, 1995.

[2] Inventories of BC's forests improved dramatically in the 1950s with the growth of aerial photography and better ground sampling techniques. In 1964, the area capable of supporting forest (includes land cleared for agriculture) was estimated at 58.2% (Inventory of the Natural Resources of BC, 1964). In 1999 the total productive forests were estimated to be 46.5 million ha; of this total, 22.8 million ha is currently commercially accessible. An average size telephone pole uses a cubic metre of wood.

[3] Many early American writers (Emerson, Thoreau) advocated greater care in resource exploitation, environmental harmony, and preservation of areas of wilderness. George Perkins Marsh's *Man and Nature, or Physical Geography as Modified by Human Action* (1864) was the first real attempt to document the changes in the landscape and became very influential in developing conservation attitudes.

[4] Resource economists have played an interesting role in developing theories of resource rents, royalties, and taxation rates in relation to resource depletion; they have also contributed to the various royal commissions on forest tenures (see Anderson, 1991).

[5] Determining the AAC is the pivot at the centre of the whole forest resource use system; criticism of the government's forest policy focuses on this calculation (see, for example, Utzig and Macdonald, 2000). Despite the improved data collection and analysis, uncertainties still persist in setting harvest rates. Harvest levels are adjusted according to sensitivity analysis.

[6] Various authors (see **Chapter 10**) have determined from economic data that the service sector of metro BC is now the key dynamo of the economy and that the commodity sector is of secondary importance. However, the forest products industry is a crucial component of the overall economy, especially in the *periphery* of the province.

[7] The best known practitioner of selective logging in BC is Mr. Merv Wilkinson of Ladysmith (Vancouver Island) who until recently managed 56 ha and pro-

duces a selectively logged harvest—with a rotation age of 125 years—worth about $12,000 to $15,000 per year (see D. Todd, *Vancouver Sun*, 28th September, 1999). This traditional, labour intensive approach, reminiscent of Schumacher's *Small is Beautiful* (1973), should be compared with Lavender's *Regenerating British Columbia's Forests* (1990), which gives insight into the technical complexities of the problem. See also the BC-based journal *Ecoforestry* for research on alternative forestry.

[8] The newly elected Provincial government has announced that it will make substantial changes to forest policy and regulations (June 2001).

Agriculture in Perspective

Colin J.B. Wood

Department of Geography, University of Victoria

INTRODUCTION

In a province dominated by mountain ranges, valleys filled with swift flowing rivers, and a deep indented fiord coastline, good farmland is a scarce resource; indeed, land suitable for agriculture accounts for only 5% of the total area. Yet, despite these constraints, farming plays an important part in the economy and way of life in BC. Although resource-linked activities in the province have traditionally been dominated by forestry, mining, fisheries, and tourism, by the mid-1990s agricultural activities generated cash receipts of more than $1.8 billion, a doubling in value since the 1980s. Agriculture now produces 45 to 55% of the province's food needs—an increase over a decade earlier, but an indication that more growth is possible. While there are opportunities for expansion in some sectors, others such as beef cattle are experiencing the downswing phase of the produce cycle and possible long term structural change reflecting changing diet preferences. By virtue of its varied climate and terrain, BC, of all the provinces, produces the greatest range of agricultural products; they come from operations that range from extensive ranches to small specialty farms.

Generally, farmers in BC contend with high input costs, price uncertainties, a small market base, pressures from urban expansion, and the impending impacts of the North American Free Trade Agreement (NAFTA). Agriculture is one activity, however, in which both the federal and provincial governments play important roles in dealing with these and related issues, such as environmental quality. In this chapter, the resource base will be described and the evolution and current operation of the industry outlined. Attention will also be given to institutional arrangements, sectoral and regional variations in operations, and the range and complexity of issues facing the farming community.[1]

THE RESOURCE BASE

A comprehensive estimate of BC's agricultural resources, based on the Canada Land Inventory (CLI) soils-based rating system, is shown in Table 17.1. The Agricultural Land Reserves (ALR), designated in 1972 as land with some farming capability according to CLI ratings, total 470 million ha, or approximately 5% of the province.[2] About 50% of this total is actively farmed, with about 12% in cropland. Much of the most productive land is located in valleys such as the lower Fraser Valley, the southern Interior, and the southeastern coastal plain of Vancouver Island. The Peace River region, east of the Rocky Mountains, is an outlier of BC in the northern prairie growing environment (Figure 17.1). Soils in the province are mainly youthful so that quality can change quickly over small areas due to the widespread effects of glacial/glacio-fluvial processes and the varied physiography; coastal soils are frequently of marine origin, a result of post-glacial sea level fluctuations. Altitude, slope angle, and aspect also play a key role in soil capability.

Agricultural potential is also related to climate, with growing season or number of *degree days* and available moisture being important. The coasts of Vancouver Island and the extreme southwestern mainland experience mild winters, in some years permitting almost continuous forage growth. In the rest of the province, the growing season decreases north and eastward, restricting the range of

Table 17.1 Classification of soils with capability for agriculture

Land Capability Type	Characteristics	Area in Hectares	Percent of Total Land Area
1	No limits	70	.07
2	Moderate limits	398	.40
3	Moderately severe limits	1,000	1.00
4	Severe limits (e.g., stone and rocks)	2,132	2.30
5	Very severe limits	6,138	6.60
6	Perennial forage only	5,358	5.70
7	No capability	15,000	16.00
TOTAL LAND AREA		93,056	

Source: British Columbia, *Agricultural Land Capability in British Columbia*. Victoria: Environment and Land Use Committee Secretariat, 1976.

possible crops. The Coast Mountains have a rain shadow effect on the Interior, accentuating the more continental regime; as a result, the interior valleys have long, hot summers. Apart from the coastal region, cold winters with no plant growth and dry, hot summers are the norm, requiring irrigation in most regions to sustain growth and increase yields. The Peace River region in the north east is restricted by a short growing season; if cloudy conditions occur, farmers have to resort to crop drying equipment. Generally, most temperate region crops can be grown in BC. The high number of sunshine hours and mild winter climate in southwest BC have resulted in a very active greenhouse industry in the outer metropolitan areas of Vancouver and Victoria. Furthermore, kiwi fruit and figs, usually marginal crops in temperate areas, flourish on southern Vancouver Island. Adverse environmental factors include pests and the diffusion of exotic weeds, such as the European knapweed, that can affect wild and domestic grassland grazers (Figure 17.1). Losses in potential hay production are estimated at close to half a million dollars per year (Maxwell, Drinkwater, Clark, and Hall, 1992).

Location is also a key factor in agricultural production and potential. There is clearly a greater economic incentive to farm good land more intensively if it is close to the main urban centres. Indeed, this has been the pattern in both Europe and eastern North America during this century—increased productivity on the most accessible areas while isolated farm land reverts to forest. BC's mountainous terrain makes for keen competition between various land users in the valleys, putting considerable pressure on the farming community. Rapid, sprawling urbanization in the 1960s-1970s led the BC government to conserve agricultural land through the *Land Commission Act* (1973) (**see Chapter 13**). A loophole introduced in the 1980s, whereby golf courses became an allowed use of Agricultural Land Reserve (ALR) land was closed in the early 1990s. Suburbs continue to expand higher up along valley sides and through increased density of housing units in existing areas. This has exacerbated problems of trespass and odour complaints against long established farming operations, leading to "green zone" committees to pressure municipalities to recognize and protect farmers' rights. The *Farm Practices Act* (Right To Farm) was introduced in 1995 to address this significant issue.

EVOLUTION

Early European settlement was stimulated by the fur trade and the gold rush (Farley, 1979).

Agriculture

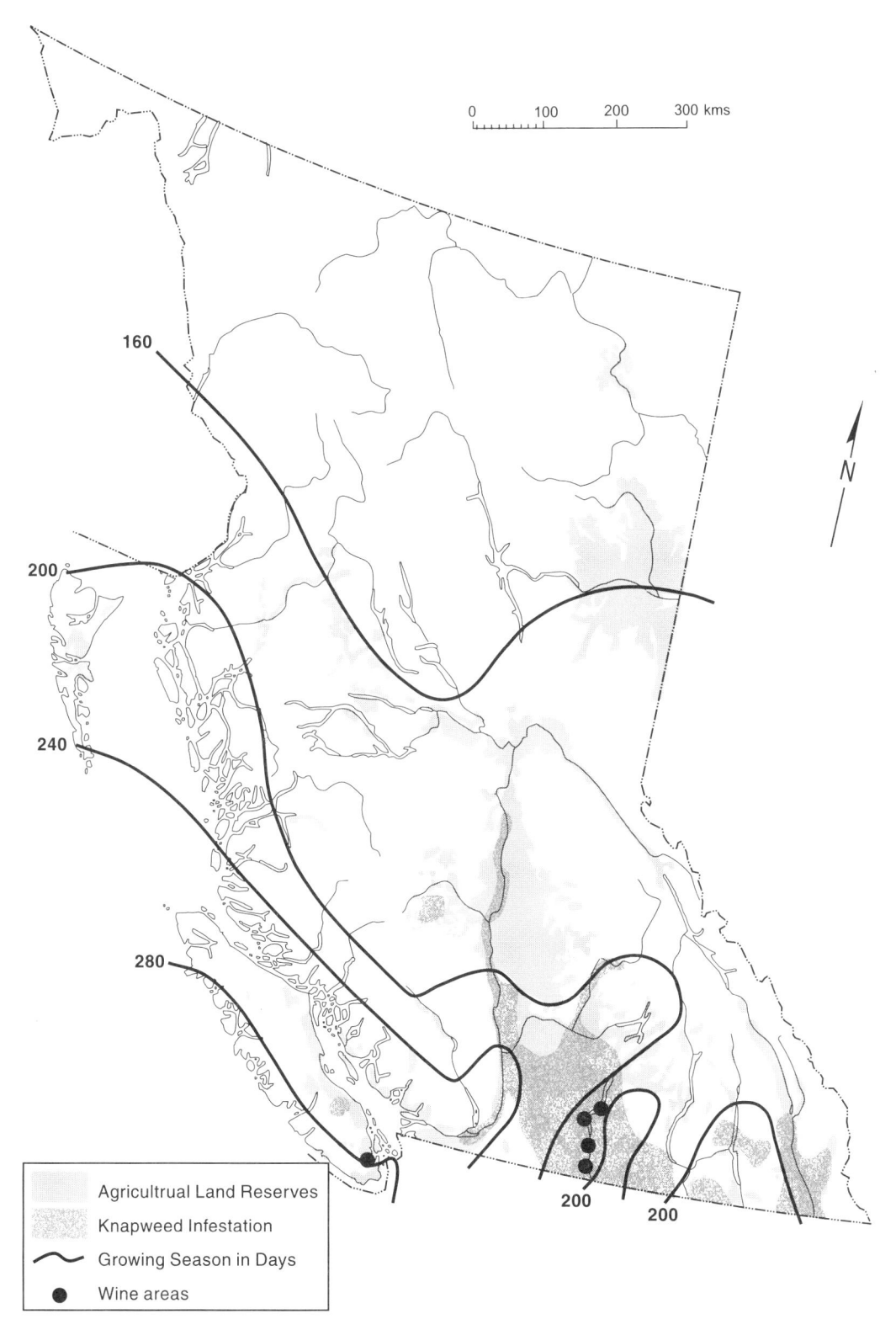

Figure 17.1 Agricultural land and factors affecting production

Farming initially evolved in order to provide food for the trading posts and later the gold and coal miners. Many prospectors stayed after the gold rush ended and settled down to ranching or subsistence farming in the interior valleys and along the coast. In the 1870s, agricultural settlers from Britain and the US began pioneering along the southeast coast of Vancouver Island, in the lower Fraser Valley, and in small pockets of level land along the mainland coast. Farming was subsistent in nature, with some produce being sent to the growing coastal towns and the coal mining communities of the Nanaimo region. The indigenous native people did not resist this settlement, mainly because they were small in number, poorly organized, and their economy revolved around the fisheries.[3]

The real surge in development came with the era of the Canadian Pacific Railway construction in the 1880s which allowed contact and trade with the east, stimulated settlement, and permitted easier movement of produce to the growing lumber towns and mining areas. As transportation improved, produce was sent eastward to the growing settlements of the Prairies, particularly in the winter months. A boom in greenhouse construction occurred in the early part of the 20th century as growers on the coast took advantage of the mild climate and cheap fuel.[4] In the lower Fraser Valley and on the Saanich Peninsula on Vancouver Island the introduction of electric railways— a transportation method that was soon to be superseded by trucks—provided a means of getting produce to market quickly. The southern Interior region was initially developed as a ranching enterprise area, but fruit growing in the valleys quickly became established where sufficient water was available for irrigation. The development of irrigation systems and fruit farms was often organized by land companies, who easily attracted immigrants drawn by the prospect of prosperity in a beautiful location. A small number of very large land holdings modelled on European estates which included ranching, farming, and fruit activities in one unit were established at Coldstream and Invermere. In the Chilcotin and Cariboo regions, a livestock economy evolved around very large ranches, such as the Gang Ranch, where stock ranged on private and Crown Land leases; at round-up time the operators drove their cattle to the railheads. The establishment of federal agricultural research stations to study and test new plant varieties, methods of cultivation, animal husbandry, pest control, soils, and irrigation practices made an important contribution to the farming community's evolving expertise in Agassiz (1906), Saanichton (1906), Kamloops (1930), and Kelowna (1920). Later, the establishment of departments of agriculture and horticulture at the University of British Columbia began training the future generations of farmers and agricultural specialists, besides developing several important research programs.

The early decades of the 20th century saw the completion of the Grand Trunk Pacific Railway to Prince George and Prince Rupert, which opened up the Bulkley Valley for settlement. The Peace River region in the northeast remained isolated until the Northern Alberta Railway reached Dawson Creek in 1931; even so, the area was cut off from the rest of the province until the British Columbia Railway (originally the Pacific Great Eastern) was extended to the region in 1958. The northeast region is in many ways still a pioneer fringe with strong ties to Alberta.

The pioneering phase in the south ended as specialization gradually developed after World War I, and improved transportation and modern marketing began to take shape. These improvements also resulted in increased competition in fruit and vegetable production from other regions, especially California. The advent of refrigerated rail cars meant that competing produce from California, where the growing season was much longer and economies of scale made better use of evolving technology, could be shipped north and east across the continent. By the late 1930s, these changes led to the formation of the first *agricultural commodity boards*—provincial regulatory bodies set up to stabilize production and sales. They were predated by cooperatives and grower associations, which had already attempted, although less successfully, to manage production and coordinate marketing in the face of strong external competition. During World War II, there was a boom in seed growing that declined as cheaper European seeds reappeared in the postwar era. From the 1950s to the 1970s, the population of BC increased significantly. It maintained the increasing demand for agricultural products, but it also began to put pressure on the land base; new suburbs were competing with farms. In 1951, the maximum number of 26,406 farms was reached; a steady decline followed, levelling off at about 20,000, and then a modest increase to 21,835 was experienced in 1996, mainly due to an increase in small farms. From 1951 to 1971, many farms succumbed to urbanization; others were consolidated and in a few instances abandoned in the more remote areas.

Recent Trends (1980s to 1990s)

The 1996 census reveals that, except for dairy, grain/oilseed, and tree fruit production, all sectors of the industry experienced growth since 1991. Farm numbers grew to 21,835 (13.6% increase), while the area in farmland expanded to 2,529,060 ha (5.7%); the capital value of farms rose 64%, to $13.8 billion. Details for the various subsectors of the livestock industry show considerable variation, reflecting the characteristic production cycles and where BC producers were positioned in that cycle in the mid-1990s. A significant increase is seen in intensive operations such as greenhouses (65% increase by area); berries and grapes (13%), poultry (22%), mushrooms (21%), horses (25%), and goats (43%). While beef cattle numbers grew by 10%, other livestock fell: pigs (–20%); sheep (–4%). Extensive operations growing field crops changed only marginally.

Although the census information for 1971 and 1996 highlights the trends that took place during that period, more complex developments not apparent in the data also occurred that reflect evolving political arrangements and economic realities. The rapid loss of high quality farmland to urbanization was halted in 1972 with the ALR (legislated in 1973), a form of zoning almost unique in North America. More recently, high interest rates and inflation have been replaced by low inflation and interest rates. Until 1998, BC experienced rapid population growth in the metropolitan areas, which helps to explain the expansion and greater intensification in table-ready production. The increase in the total number of farms is also partially attributable to expanding specialty crops, notably vineyards, ginseng, herbs, greenhouse products, specialty fruit, and hobby farms, the latter associated with the expanding pleasure horse population.

The onset of NAFTA is a major change in the operating conditions for the industry. The implications are that price controls, program support, and commodity boards will gradually be phased out as the North American market is opened to all producers. A precursor came with the federal government's policy shift in 1989 emphasizing market responsiveness and self-reliance, greater regional specialization, and environmental sustainability. In 1995, this was reinforced by the termination of the Crow's Nest transportation subsidy to Prairie grain growers. The sentiments of members of the farming community vary. The reaction to a proposed "level playing field" is not so much alarm as a need for reassurance that it *really is level*. There is anger over the hidden subsidies that most producers in California enjoy through preferred rates for irrigation water. Clearly, uncertainty will continue until the full impact of NAFTA works its way through the system. The simple geographic reality of perishability and transport costs should ensure that a certain degree of localized monopoly continues in farm production. Possible strategies to deal with large multinationals lie in cooperatives and health quality controls in food production.[5]

Institutional Arrangements

In most developed countries, resource exploitation and associated primary processing are usually undertaken by large private and public corporations; this also frequently includes agriculture. In BC, farms are still predominantly family owned, and so are important social as well as economic units. Their geographic significance is in the fact that they are production units outside of the metropolitan south west, having considerable regional economic and social value in terms of community continuity. However, due to the small size of operation, restricted financial resources, and the high commercial and weather risks, they are vulnerable. A cogent reminder of this fact nationally is that, during the period 1981 to 1996, the number of farms in Canada fell from 316,000 to 276,000, or approximately 2,600 per year—although in BC the numbers actually increased.

While not simply at the mercy of economic pressures, the success of farming also relies on the institutional support that individual operators receive, principally from cooperation with other specialty farmers, government agencies, educational institutions, a well developed farm service industry, and a public who support the continuation of the industry and farm way of life in addition to buying the products. Farm workers also need the support of unions to protect their interests.[6]

Institutional arrangements (Table 17.2) also play a role in two other ways with implications for long term sustainability of the industry and its resource base. First, the Agricultural Land Commission maintains the general public and intergenerational interes in protecting the resource through ALR zoning. Second, agencies play a role in the more difficult problem of resolving externality issues (Barichello, Porter, and Van Kooten, 1995); moreover, it is clear that their roles and the realization of sustainability may be enhanced by recoupling (financial incentives to reduce environmental degradation) and decoupling (taking away present program incentives that are environmentally harmful). It is clear that, mainly through the problems of non-point-source pollution and the ineffectual policing of the system, issues such as pollution of the aquifer in the Abbotsford area will persist (Barichello et al., 1995).

The BC Ministry of Agriculture and Food has expenditures of approximately $68 million per annum and provides a range of marketing,

Table 17.2 Agricultural groups/institutions

Specialty Groups	
Beef	9
Bees	26
Dairy	21
Horticulture	25
Other	36
Farmworkers' union	1
Breeding	19
Equipment	79
Institutional	
Farmers' institutes	59
Womens' groups	10
Agricultural fairs	56
Marketing	11
Educational	12
Services auction	16
Management	14
Supplies	51

Source: *BC Digest Directory*, 14(8), August 1995.

research, support, and development services. The federal government focuses on research, product inspection, and marketing services. The BC Agricultural Council, formed in 1997, represents common concerns among sectors, and coordinates responses and provides an important forum for communication.

Farming employs a significant number of full time and seasonal workers—wage earners gradually replacing the unpaid labour of the traditional farm family. Seasonal employees are important in the fruit picking and horticultural sectors. Between 1971 and 1996, the number of corporate farms grew from 101 to 573, underlining the trend to use employees; the number of weeks of paid labour increased from 310,000 to 712,000, and the ratio of year-round to seasonal labour grew from 1:1 to 4:3. For a variety of reasons, in the resources industries, farm workers as a whole have been the least able to extract a reasonable wage, working conditions, and benefits. Ethnicity, class, cultural and language barriers, and indifferent governments have all played a part in maintaining low wage levels and sometimes deplorable working conditions (Dutton and Cornish, 1988). The eventual formation of a farm workers' union began the slow process of reform and advancing the lot of the predominantly East Indian farm worker. The root of the problem lies in the situation of farm labour in North America as a whole. American producers frequently use cheap, often illegal, immigrants who are willing to work for very low wages, undercutting BC producers. This is very apparent, for example, in the costs of labour for fruit picking in Washington and truck farming in California.

The main components of the BC agricultural system are set out in organigram form in Figure 17.2, illustrating the linkage between them but not the degree of interdependence involved. Some relationships are formally designated, such as the Federal/Provincial interface. In contrast is the marijuana industry, which is not part of the mainstream industry; its link with the underground economy and crime are not well understood. While approximate multiplier linkages can be estimated, a complete analysis has yet to be undertaken.

REGIONAL VARIATION AND SPECIALTIES

The varied physical environment, circumstances of settlement, and economic development result in regional variations in farming (Table 17.3). With the exception of the Peace Region, all areas support a mix of types in addition to their regional specialty.

Livestock

The livestock sector is dominated by dairy and beef operations, with an approximate cattle population of 814,000 head; in addition, there are smaller scale sheep and pork enterprises. Poultry operations almost doubled from 7.8 to

Table 17.3 Farm activity by region (1996)

Region	Number of farms	Farm population ('000)	Average farm size (acres [ha])	Receipts as % of province	Greenhouses (mill. sq.ft.)	Dairy location quotient*	Specialties
Vancouver Island	2,992	7.6	47 [18]	6.5	3.0	3.3	Dairy, mixed, greenhouse, wine
Lower Mainland	6,671	20.0	41 [16]	58.0	21.6	3.7	Dairy, mixed, berries, poultry
Thompson/ Okanagan	5,933	16.0	246 [98]	20.0	2.0	.4	Tree fruit, wine, cattle, horticulture
Kootenay	1,425	3.5	267 [106]	2.3	.2	.4	Cattle, tree, fruit, Christmas trees
Cariboo	1,799	4.6	644 [257]	3.4	.4	.1	Cattle, mixed
North Coast	222	0.4	151 [60]				Game farms
Nechako	970	2.7	608 [243]	3.8	.1	.4	Cattle, some grain
Peace	1,823	5.0	1,134 [453]	6.0		.2	Grain, honey, game farms
Total	21,835	59.8	300 [120]		27.3		

* calculated by author

Source: Census of Agricultural Statistics Regional Districts M.A.F.F., Government of BC, 1997.

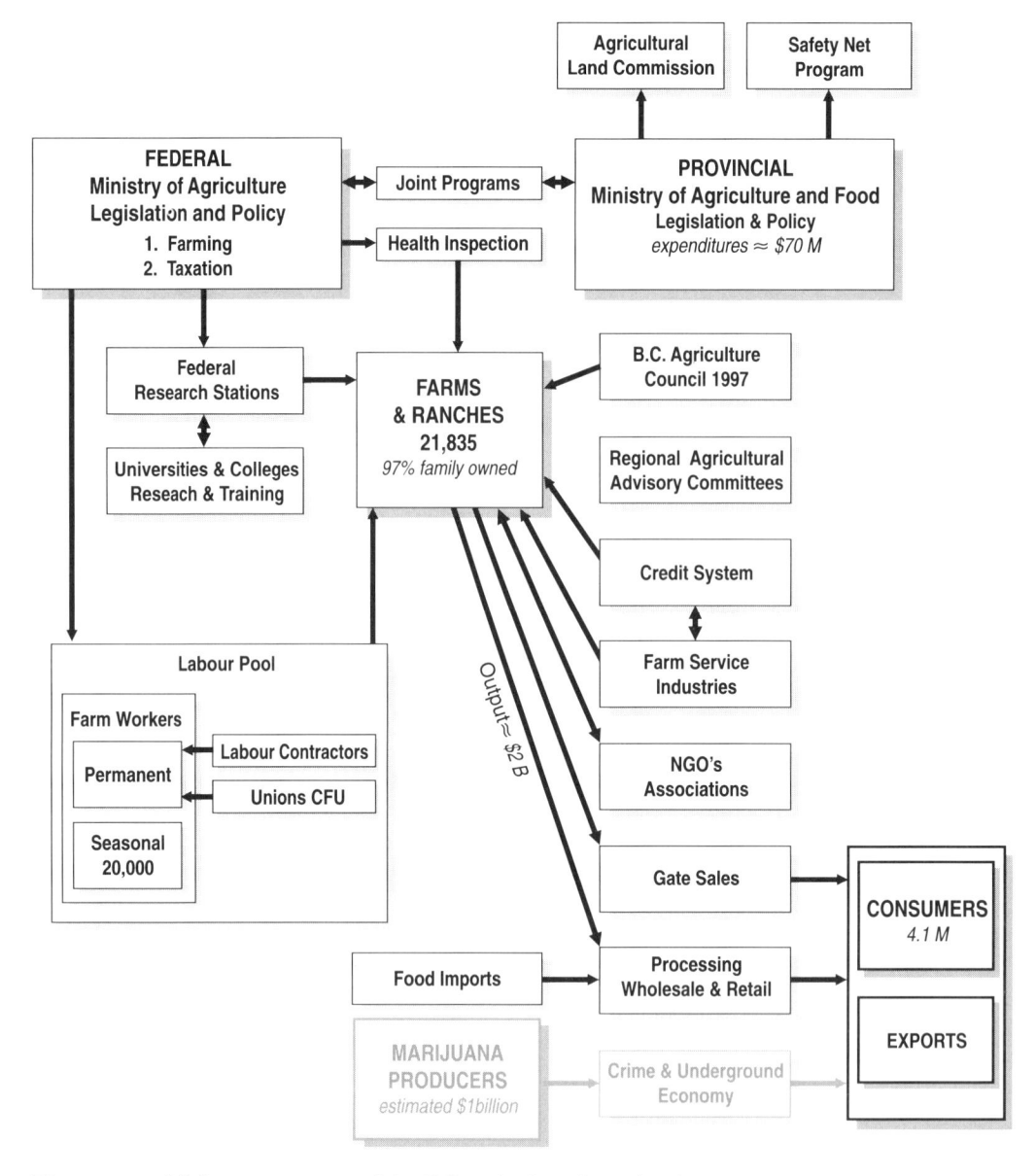

Figure 17.2 Main components of the BC agricultural production system

13.8 between 1971 and 1996, and are the one sub-sector of livestock showing a higher concentration than the national average. Total livestock numbers have changed according to market conditions over the last 30 years (Table 17.4).

Dairying

While most urban centres in the province have local dairy operations, the bulk of the industry, as shown by location quotient values in Table 17.3, is concentrated in the lower Fraser Valley and on southeast Vancouver Island, supplying the main urban centres with fresh milk and dairy products.

Dairy farmers of the coastal region are able to capitalize on the mild winters, long growing season, and rich pasture lands of the river valleys and deltas. Improvements in breeding and management methods, such as irrigation for

Table 17.4 Livestock numbers ('000) in BC and percentage of Canadian total (1996)

	1961	1971	1981	1996
Cattle	461	573	789	814 (6.5)
Milk cows	91	80	89	82 (6.8)
Hogs	41	78	254	174 (1.5)
Sheep	102	50	66	71 (8.0)
Hens	5,600	7,800	9,900	13,700 (13.0)

Source: Census of Canada 1961, 1971, 1981, 1996.

hay production, have contributed to a steady increase in output per animal from 2,725 kg (6,000 lb) in the 1920s to 6,800 (16,000) today. Outputs in many herds are among the highest in Canada, however herein lies a problem. The very efficiency and skill shown by dairy farms produces periodic gluts on the market. The difficulties of over-production along with the producers' relationships with the creameries and retailers led to significant conflict as early as the 1920s between dairy farms, independent creamery operators, and cooperatives, ultimately requiring provincial government inquiries (1927) and legislation (1929). Further commissions of inquiry and legislation (1955) and studies (1966) indicated that problems were persisting, particularly through the vertical integration of milk sales by supermarket retailing outlets and the decline of door-to-door sales. This has resulted in an industry concentrated generally into larger production units and strictly controlled by the provincial Milk Marketing Board. Entry is restricted according to possession of a quota which belongs to a specific dairy herd, while the actual production is allocated according to the quota. NAFTA agreements may see these production control arrangements phased out.

An example of a medium to large dairy operation is Pendray Farm near Sidney on Vancouver Island. Originally, the family farm was located closer to Victoria, but urban expansion made farming increasingly difficult, hence the move. The new location required substantial investment in new equipment and buildings. The terrain is generally flat, with a mixture of sandy loam and clay loam soils, enabling large-scale operations. Irrigation is practised to ensure and enhance yields. As the surrounding land is in the ALR, it is unlikely that they will have to move again through urban pressures. Their herd size has stabilized at about 200, however, through breeding improvements, yields have doubled over two decades.

The dairy industry has been experiencing deteriorating returns in the face of rising costs and relatively stable demand. Only efficient operators with large capital investment are able to survive. Over a 30 year period, the total number of dairy cows has decreased from 91,000 to 82,000 but, as noted earlier, output per animal has increased.

Ranching

Ranching was the first type of farming practised in western Canada on any scale. It grew in response to the meat requirements of both the mining industry and the fledgling coastal cities; furthermore, the product could be driven to the markets. Ranchers were attracted to the extensive natural grazing available in the Interior grasslands and open forest (Gould, 1978). Pioneer cattlemen quickly evolved a form of transhumance between the valley hay meadows, the ranges, and the open forest of higher altitudes. Railway construction in the late 19th and early 20th centuries stimulated growth. In the early years, range management was not well controlled and disputes were frequent. The establishment of cattle overseers in 1896 brought order and smoothed problems during round-up. By the 1900s, virtually all of the natural grassland had been pre-empted for settlement, with many Crown Land parcels being held as leaseholds. Herds were comprised of slaughter cattle nearly 2 years old or older, while the remainder were put out in natural pastures to fend for themselves during the winter. Generally, carrying capacities were low: 20 ha (49 acres) per animal.

The inexpensive natural grazing inevitably began to deteriorate. Gould quotes G. Dawson of the Geological Survey as noting that, as early as 1878, the native bunch grass was badly deteriorating, so operators turned to producing forage crops to over-winter their stock (Gould, 1978).[7] Natural grass meadows were tamed, seeded, and irrigated. The increased costs led, in turn, to further specialization. Animals were marketed earlier and separate finishing outfits arose. Thus, the beef industry is now generally a two-step process, with "cow-calf" operations that produce "feeder cattle," and a second stage that fattens and finishes them. In some cases, both activities may be carried out in the same unit.

Consequently, from the southern provincial boundary northward to the Chilcotin, Cariboo, and Bulkley valleys, ranching has evolved as a dominant land use activity in the Interior, being supplanted in importance only by the specialized fruit growing areas of the Interior valleys and the grain growing of the Peace River region. Input costs obviously play a key role in the industry's viability, of which forage conditions are a major component. With a reliable source of forage, ranchers are able to exert a measure of control over feed costs. However, this in turn has generated other problems. It has meant more investment in equipment. Irrigation for forage has resulted in conflict with the fishery agencies' requirements of specific stream and river levels for maintaining fish spawning environments.

Finishing feeder cattle has depended to a large extent on Prairie grain since the 1950s, and because feed lot operations are market-oriented, many are located in the Lower Mainland. There is generally a close correlation between number of livestock and grain prices which, in turn, interact with beef prices. An important variable in this equation is the freight rate for grain. The federal government abolished the preferential Crow's Nest freight rate structure (which was related to export grain). This had significant repercussions in the whole system of grain and livestock farming in western Canada and location costs.

Western beef producers face keen competition from Australia and New Zealand, where grass-fed livestock can be grazed cheaply all year round. Import controls have been instituted since the late 1970s to prevent further underselling by these exporters who tend to compete at the cheaper end of the market.

Neither the government nor the operators have sat idle in the face of such challenges. On the contrary, several measures have been undertaken to increase the viability of the livestock industry. BC is a beef deficit region, producing 40% of its consumption, so there is a rational basis for developing it, providing that input costs can be kept competitive with those of other producers. The government is improving the resource base by upgrading rangeland through reseeding and knapweed control (Figure 17.1), breeding improvement, disease eradication, and technical information diffusion. In many cases, producers have taken collective and individual actions to enhance the industry. The formation of the BC Livestock Producers Cooperative Association in the 1940s, was important in providing a reliable market and competitive pricing for operations. It was instrumental in setting up markets at Williams Lake, Okanagan Falls, Merritt, and Kamloops.

Grain

Approximately 85% of grain production (except corn) occurs in the Peace River region. A short growing season sometimes makes production precarious. As a consequence, this region has a productivity potential that is only 50% of the Red River region, Canada's best area for grain.

Arable farms do have some short run flexibility compared to livestock enterprises, being able to switch between the five main grains and oilseeds, according to price trends and rotation requirements. Since the region only accounts for 2% of Canada's total grain area, growers follow grain price trends (Table 17.5).

Tree Fruit

One of the most distinctive characteristics of BC's agriculture is fruit growing. The European pioneers invariably planted orchards as part of their farm operations, both for self-sufficiency and as cash crops to supply the infant cities,

Table 17.5 Grain area by type 1979-1996 and tame hay/forage (nearest '000 hectares)

	1971	1981	1991	1996
Wheat	44	42	44	40
Barley	79	93	43	45
Oats	52	50	29	34
Canola	8	25	40	25
Tame hay	217	304	326	347

Source: Census of Agriculture 1996 BC Summary: Victoria Ministry of Agriculture Fisheries and Food.

towns, and mining centres. More specialized orchards were planted in the late 19th century around Victoria, on the Gulf Islands, and in the lower Fraser Valley. These were comprised of varieties and types of apples that have virtually disappeared, such as Bellflower and Lemon Pippin (Upshall, 1976). Such peri-urban farms also supplied strawberries and other berries.

The coastal areas produced well into the 20th century, but disease, the storage and marketing problems of the varieties grown, and the attractions of the better growing conditions of the dry Interior valleys, led to the Okanagan Valley's domination. The recent development of dwarf varieties, better pomological practices, and "pick your own" sales has seen a small comeback for the original coastal areas, with new plantings of small orchards of 2 to 5 ha (5 to 10 acres) near the cities.

The Okanagan is synonymous with fruit production in Western Canada. Although the first fruit trees were planted by Father Pandosy at the Oblate Mission near Kelowna in 1862; extensive modern plantings date from the early 1900s. Land development schemes drew immigrants to the region, extolling the attractions of its environment and the financial benefits of fruit farming. Some areas eventually proved to be unsuccessful due to stressful growing conditions, as in parts of the Kootenays farther east, and the Wallachin area to the west. Fruit growing boomed in the Okanagan as orchards were planted on the frost-draining, lower valley slopes. Varieties included the Delicious group, whose strains now dominate the retail market, while Bartlett and Anjou have become the main pear varieties.

The viability of tree fruit production in a relatively isolated region has been possible through three factors. First, development of extensive irrigation networks based on a well organized water licence system enabled the main obstacle of summer drought to be overcome. Second, even in the early years of this century it was clear that cooperation between growers was necessary to establish quality control, manage the occurrence of fluctuating production, and coordinate marketing (Canada West, 1980). The BC Fruit Growers Association was formed in Vancouver in 1889, but as the locus of tree fruit production moved to the Okanagan, the association moved there also in 1932. Legislation to control production was introduced in 1937.[8] Third, to remain competitive, modern pomology requires extensive ongoing research in all stages of production. The industry has had substantial support from provincial, federal, and university research into the newer cultivars, harvesting and storage methods, and marketing techniques.

Producers today are faced with a variety of environmental, managerial, and marketing issues, the particular combination depending on the orchard involved. Fruit growing is prone to several problems, notably rain and hail damage on cherries, causing split and rot. Some producers use fibreglass sheeting as protection, but the costs are as high as $25,000 per ha ($10,000 per acre). Other hazards include Little Cherry disease (related to zinc deficiency and mealybug infestation), which killed off cherry growing in the Kootenays in the 1940s (*Country Life*, 1983). Such problems can only be solved by destruction. Spraying against biological hazards is an integral part of modern fruit farming.

The management of fruit production generally entails a long run investment in factors of production and careful evaluation of input costs because fruit trees take several years to mature and produce. However, development of dwarf cultivars has resulted in a shortened time span between planting and production of a profitable crop. Many producers grow a range of fruit and different varieties of the same fruit. In this way, labour can be used more evenly, as different fruits and varieties ripen at different times. Indeed, there are also environmental benefits associated with this approach.

Since the late 1980s, traditional low density orchards have been in the process of being replaced with high density plantings of dwarf varieties, at rates of 1,400 to 2,400 trees per ha (600 to 1,000 trees per acre) for medium density, to high density of more than 2,400 trees per ha (more than 1,000 trees per acre). There are several advantages to this innovation, such as fruit production within 2 years, easier maintenance and harvesting, more fruit per unit area, and lower rates of water and fertilizer demand. The disadvantages are that more care is required in training, particularly if the *espalier* system is used, and greater attention to the correct amounts of nutrients and water is necessary.

Bruce Currie at Peachland was among the earliest innovators when he planted 4 ha (10 acres) of dwarf Macintosh and Spartan at 1,200 per ha (500 per acre) in 1986. In the 1990s, his 16 ha (40 acre) orchard was entirely replanted, with densities as high as 2,400 trees per ha (1,000 per acre). Commencing in 1991, the BC government in association with the Okanagan Tree Fruit Authority began a program of encouraging high density replantings with a subsidy of $4 per replaced tree.

Wine

One of the more remarkable changes in BC's agriculture has been the development of a wine industry in one of the most northerly locations in the world for grape production. In the Okanagan and Similkameen Valleys (Figure 17.1), areas favoured with hot summers, the early emphasis was on table grapes. The construction of a winery in Kelowna in 1972 by Herb Capozzi made possible the switch to wine grapes. *Labrusca* was the main variety grown for the next 40 years, with little improvement or expansion taking place, aside from an additional winery in Victoria.

In the 1960s to 1970s, Canadians showed greater interest in quality wines and found the local products wanting. Ontario growers were the first to respond by improving their products. However, it was not until late in the 1970s that a new direction was possible in BC. The creation of the Estate Winery Licence by the BC government in 1979 meant that, on the one hand, wineries could now grow grapes according to their own specifications, while grape growers had an incentive to produce wine. The desire for quality improvement entailed a switch to European hybrid varieties which, in turn, prompted more careful evaluations of the micro-site geography of potential vineyards (Nichole, 1983; Kung, 1995).

Successful trials with Johannisberg Riesling and Gewürztraminer showed that *vinifera* varieties could be grown. These, together with Pinot Blanc, became the basis for the high quality white wines (Kung, 1995). Given BC's high latitude and pronounced topographic variation, the microclimate of vineyards is a very important factor in the growing requirements of particular varieties. In the Okanagan area, vineyards are generally located between 30 and 100 m above Lake Okanagan so that the temperature moderating influences of the water occur during winter; however, they are not too close to the lake because in summer the water would cool down the local microclimate. On Vancouver Island, growers are concentrated in the lower Cowichan Valley and the Saanich Peninsula, where they have sought out suitable microclimates. To enhance production and fruit quality, vine plantings are orientated so as to maximize sun penetration. Aside from the cold spells, one of the main hazards facing growers is flocks of birds who like to feast on the fruit at harvest time.

The revitalization and expansion of the wine industry came about through the efforts of several far-sighted, hard working families, assisted by provincial and federal horticultural researchers. This trend is significant not only for the vitality of BC's agriculture. Due to their direct-to-customer sale feature, estate wineries also

Agriculture

add an important attraction to the tourism industry and regional prosperity of southern Vancouver Island and the southern Interior regions.

Specialty Products

In addition to the dairying and mixed farming activities of southeast Vancouver Island and the lower Fraser Valley, berries, vegetables, mushrooms, filberts, honey, flowers, and ornamentals are grown, encouraged by mild winters, high sunshine hours, and proximity to markets.

Strawberries have gone through several cycles of expansion and decline, responding to changing competition from the US and Mexico and disease problems. Raspberries require the special growing conditions found in BC and account for 90% of the national production. Raspberry output has also experienced periods of prosperity and decline, with growers recently facing intense competition from Oregon and Washington. In contrast, cranberry production is very stable, reflecting the restricted area of suitable sites for production and the near monopoly of the industry in North America by Ocean Spray, a US growers' cooperative.

Vegetable production benefits from the climatic advantages of the region, but invariably is struggling against competition from the US. Mushroom producers appear to be one of the few groups that are able to make profits consistently and have expanded from 67 to 243 million m^2. Mushrooms are grown in 12-week cycles, using Californian spawn. Currently, as long as a grower can produce over 14.6 kilograms per m^2 (3 pounds per square foot), a profit will be realized. Greenhouse production of fruit, vegetables, and ornamentals has increased substantially from .5 to 2.8 million m^2 with 65% being located in Greater Vancouver. Floriculture continues to flourish as a specialty of the province. In March, daffodils are air freighted to eastern Canada to herald the arrival of Easter, and in December, holly is air freighted to the east for the Christmas season.

The intensity and high technology of farming in the southern part of BC contrasts with the experimentation and pioneering spirit of the more remote regions. In some Interior locations growers are experimenting with ginseng production (661 ha). On remote Flores Island one farmer grazes his beef stock (Brown Swiss, Durham Shorthorn, and some Welsh Black Cross), specially bred to withstand rain, on the muskeg of a former lake bed drained by missionaries in 1893.

Conclusions

Agriculture has changed considerably in the last decade (Wood, 1987). There are now approximately 235,000 farms in Canada (1999) of varying size and type of operations, from the large grain operations of the Prairies to small, specialty hobby farms. BC represents about 7.6% of this total, showing a slight growth from the 1981 figure of 6% in contrast to the national decline. The difference between BC and the Canadian average is particularly apparent in Figure 17.3. About 3.5% of the total population is directly involved in farming. Generally, capital investment in farming in the west is higher than the national average; for BC, the figure is $620,000 per unit—approximately 12% higher than the national mean (Table 17.6). Returns on investment and farm incomes are low, adversely affecting Canada's export position; a situation exacerbated by the subsidy strategies of other countries and trade areas, especially the EC.

There are various ways in which the relative productivity of farm units can be understood. The national average for the value of products sold per farm per year is approximately $117,000, with BC at $87,000 or about 75% of the national figure. These figures reflect the higher number of small farms in BC and the fact that there are a relatively small number of large commercial farms/ranches and a large number of small, semi-commercial ones. However, when the figures are calculated in terms of receipts *per hectare*, BC shows a much greater intensity of operation, with average returns of $735 as opposed to the national figure of $475 per hectare. There may of course be some under-reporting, as many small farms rely on roadside cash sales.

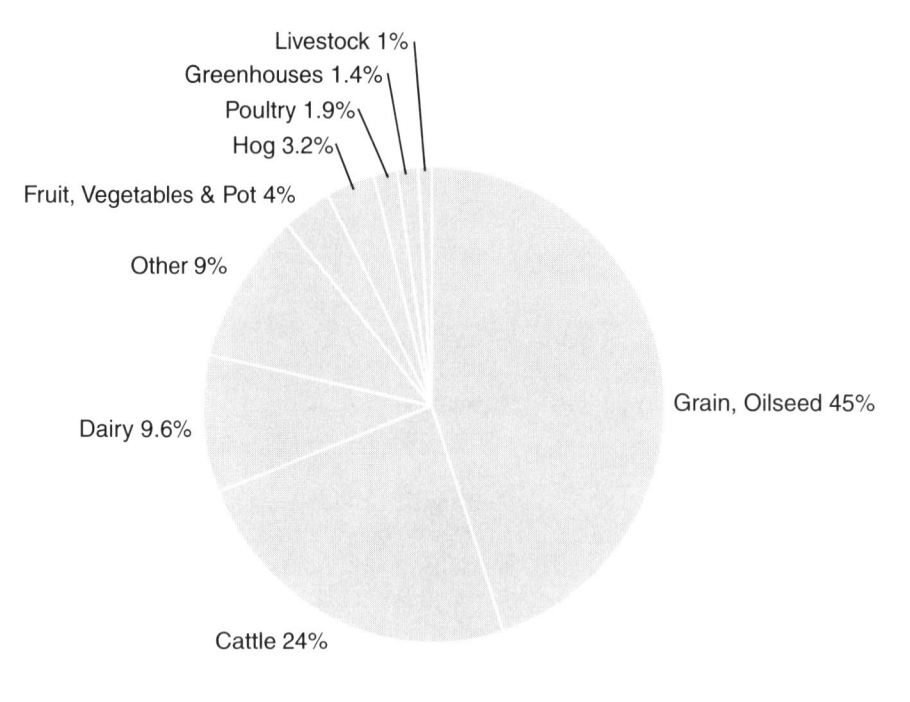

Canada 1996

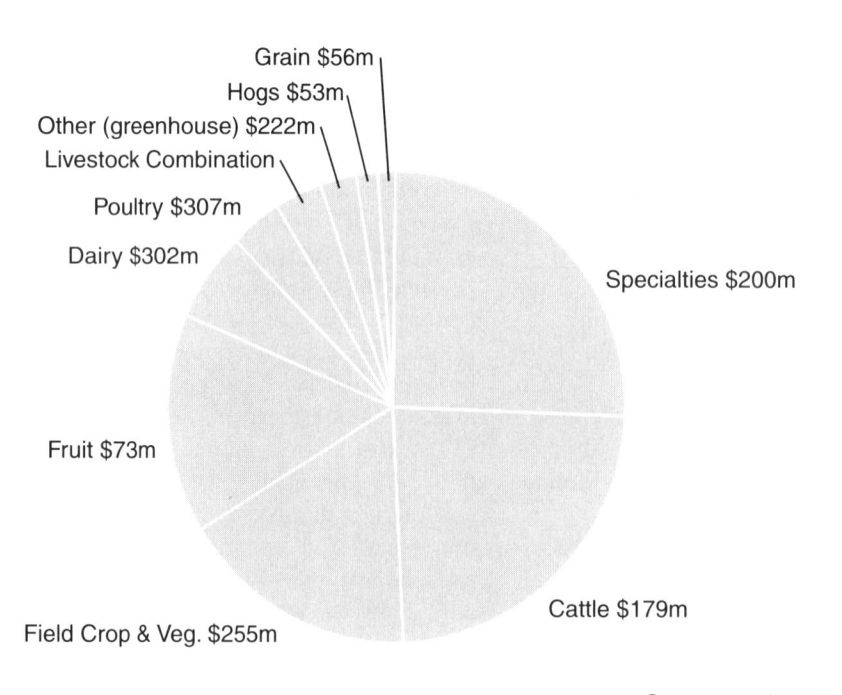

- Livestock 1%
- Greenhouses 1.4%
- Poultry 1.9%
- Hog 3.2%
- Fruit, Vegetables & Pot 4%
- Other 9%
- Dairy 9.6%
- Cattle 24%
- Grain, Oilseed 45%

British Columbia 1996

- Grain $56m
- Hogs $53m
- Other (greenhouse) $222m
- Livestock Combination
- Poultry $307m
- Dairy $302m
- Fruit $73m
- Field Crop & Veg. $255m
- Cattle $179m
- Specialties $200m

Segments show % of farmers in that sector

Figure 17.3 The Canadian and BC agricultural systems showing output by subsectors

Generally, BC is midway between the extensive, large-scale, high output farms of the Prairies and the low production of the Maritimes. Returns per hectare underline the relative intensity of the operations in BC, which, given the small amount of quality agricultural land, makes economic sense in land rent terms. As Canadian farming is facing adverse economic forces (Found, 1996; MacKinnon, 1998), it would seem that the large commercial and small niche operations are the most viable. If this is the likely scenario for the next decade, farming in BC would seem able to continue, particularly if linked with tourism and natural foods strategies. Indeed, various innovations such as hemp, llama, and ostrich indicate the enterprise of the farming community and its willingness to experiment.

Federal agricultural policies have a direct impact at the regional level; others, such as taxation and transportation, are also important. The federal promotion of a more open economy through the provisions of NAFTA has significant implications for farming, where supply management through commodity boards has been the norm. It is perhaps too early to estimate the effects of such policies and the deregulation process. If there is a truly free market, based on land rent principles (Von Thunen) and transportation factors (Weber), fluid milk production should survive, along with specialized products and ranching, while operations likely to disappear are perhaps tree fruit growing and high latitude grain producers.

Agriculture plays an important role in the way of life of the province, particularly on the rangelands, in the southern villages and towns of the interior, the lower Fraser Valley, and southern Vancouver Island. It is a productive, stable resource industry that enhances the aesthetic quality of the environment. This is not to deny that problems such as conflict with wildlife, run-off pollution, and careless biocide use occur. Agriculture is generally facing difficult times as commodity prices remain low or even decline. In the North American context, BC's agriculture is small in size, faces high input costs, and has to compete with cheap, often subsidized, imported produce (Table 17.6).

These difficulties are offset, however, by certain locational and organizational advantages. The dairy industry, in the fresh milk/products subsector, is protected by a certain degree of locational monopoly reinforced by supply management through a quota system. Even with a completely free market, it is likely that most of it will survive. The specialized wine, flowers, berry fruit, and even mixed farming groups will continue if the emphasis on quality/organic produce develops in strength and the various organizations and government agencies maintain their support. Ultimately, it is consumer awareness and support that is crucial, backed by the food retail and restaurant industries. As Canadians become more aware of higher levels of biocides in imported food and the ongoing issues associated with genetically modified foods, it is probable that they will seek uncontaminated food that is organically certified. It is likely that the tree fruit and grain producers are the most vulnerable operations at the present time, so that if they are to survive, some support is necessary, given the support that the EC and US give farmers.

The industry continues to benefit from the farsighted passing of the *Agricultural Land Commission Act* in the 1970s, which ensured protection of the land resource base (BC Agricultural Land Commission, 1995; 2001). It is also supported by committed governments, educational institutions, and NGOs. As Quayle (1998) recently recommended, while there is clearly a strong provincial, and hence public interest in the industry and the maintenance of the ALR Act to ensure viability of the system, there have to be modifications of process and procedure (e.g., more accountable, open decision making). Furthermore, in light of the increasing and varied demands on the land resource base, the promotion of integrated land management has to continue. Ultimately there will be a new generation of farmers and new initiatives have to be explored.[9] Farmers have a good record of sustaining their resource sector in BC, despite the vagaries of the marketplace. Careful planning with the support of other parties (Smith, 1998) will ensure that farming will continue and prosper.

Table 17.6 Agricultural characteristics by province

	British Columbia		Alberta		Saskatchewan		Manitoba		Ontario		Quebec		Maritimes	
	1981	1996	1981	1996	1981	1996	1981	1996	1981	1996	1981	1996	1981	1996
Total number of farms (thousands)	20	21.8	58	59	67	51	29	24	82	67	48	35	12.6	10.8
Total farm area (millions of hectares)	15	25	12	21	17	26	5	7	4	5.6	3	3	.9	1.0
Average farm size (hectares)	108	120	329		385		258		73		78		84	
Area rented (millions of hectares)	.6	.9	6.0		8.0		2.0		1.4		4		.16	
Total produce (billions of dollars)	.8	1.8	3.2		7.9		3.0		5.6		1.4		2.9	
Value of produce sold per farm (thousands of dollars)	39	85	56		45		49		57		42		36	
Average capital value (thousands of dollars)	426	619	634		466		355		381		197		183	
Total weeks of paid labour per reporting farm	61		31		20		26		50		39		55	
Equity (Networth) (Mid 1990s)	694		520		425		430		560		400		400	

Source: Census of Canada, 1981, 1996.

REFERENCES

Barichello, R., Porter, R.M., and Van Kooten, C. (1995). Institutions, economic incentives and sustainable land use in BC. In A. Scott, J. Robinson, and D. Cohen (Eds.), *Managing natural resources in British Columbia: Markets, regulations and sustainable development* (pp. 6-53). Vancouver: UBC Press.

BC Agricultural Land Commission (1995). *Strategic plan: Victoria, Agricultural Land Commission*. Victoria, BC.

BC Agricultural Land Commission (2001). *Annual Report*. Victoria, BC.

Berry, B.J., Conkling, E.C., and Ray, D.M. (1997). *The global economy in transition* (2nd ed.). New Jersey: Prentice Hall.

Canada West (1980). Western Canadian Agriculture to 1990, Calgary. Canada West Foundation.

Chan, T. (1997). *The social and regulatory relations of Metropolitan Victoria commercial greenhouse industry 1900-1996*. MA thesis, Department of Geography, University of Victoria (unpublished).

Dutton, A., and Cornish, C. (1988). Ethnicity and class in farm labour process. In R. Warburton and D. Coburn (Eds.), *Workers, capital and the state in British Columbia* (pp. 161-176). Vancouver: UBC Press.

Farley, A.J. (1979). *Resource atlas of British Columbia*. Vancouver: UBC Press.

Found, W. (1996). Agriculture in a world of subsidies. In J. Britton (Ed.), *Canada and the global economy* (pp. 155-174). Montreal & Kingston: McGill-Queens.

Garrish, C. (2000). The demise of the orderly marketing system. Okanagan History: 64th Report of the Okanagan Historical Society.

Gould, E. (1978). *Ranching*. Seattle: Hancock House.

Kung, R. (1995). *British Columbia's wines: A geographical appreciation*. Department of Geography, University of Victoria.

Maxwell, J.F., Drinkwater, R., Clark, D., and Hall, J. (1992). Effect of grazing, spraying and seeding on knapweed in British Columbia. *Journal of Range Management*, 45(2), 180-182.

MacKinnon, M. (1998). Rock bottom prices crunch profits. *Globe and Mail*, p. (B)1,3.

Nichole, A.E. (1983). *Wines and vines of BC*. Vancouver: Boltesini Press.

Pierce, J.T. (1994). Towards the reconstruction of agriculture: Paths of change and adjustment. *Professional Geographer*, 46(2), 178-190.

Quayle, M. (1998). *Stakes in the ground*. Report prepared for the (BC) Agricultural Land Commission. Victoria: Government of BC.

Smith, B.E. (1998). *Planning for agriculture*. Victoria, BC: BC Agricultural Land Commission.

Turner, N.J., and Peacock, S. (in press). Solving the perennial paradox: Ethnobotanical evidence for plant resource management on the Northwest coast. In E. Duer and N.J. Turner (Eds.), *Keeping in living: Indigenous plant management on the Northwest coast*. Seattle: University of Washington Press.

Upshall, W.K. (1976). *History of fruit growing and handling in the United States and Canada*. University Park, Pennsylvania: Pomological Association of America.

Wood, C.J.B. (1987). Agriculture. In C. Forward (Ed.), *British Columbia: Its resources and people* (pp. 139-159). Victoria: University of Victoria, Department of Geography, Western Geographical Series, Vol. 22.

ENDNOTES

[1] For an overview and general critique of the adjustments that Canadian farming is undergoing, together with a review of the alternative paths for the future see Pierce (1994).

[2] The Agricultural Land Commission Annual Report (2000) states that the overall integrity of the ALR system has been maintained and the best quality agricultural land preserved for the future. During 1999-2000, the Commission received 488 applications for exclusion from the reserves. These ranged from minor road adjustments to subdivision applications. In the previous year, 22% of applications had been refused. In April 2000, the Agricultural Land Commission was merged with the Forest Land Reserve Commission.

[3] While the Europeans are usually regarded as the first farmers in the Pacific Northwest, recent research indicates a substantial horticultural tradition (proto-agricultural) among the Northwest Coast peoples (Turner and Peacock, in press).

[4] The greenhouse industry has received little attention in the academic literature, despite the significance of BC producers in the North American picture. For a detailed recent study of the Victoria region, see Chan (1997).

[5] A review of agricultural location theory, land rent, and land values is beyond the scope of this chapter. For a useful introduction see Berry, Conkling, and Ray (1997). Genetic engineering and genetically modified foods are emerging as a major debate in agriculture and the food industry. The attitude of the food industry in North America seems quite casual compared with European concerns.

[6] A persistent and serious issue among farm workers has been the side effects of pesticide applications on workers in the Fraser Valley, especially in the berry sector. Since a Canadian Farm Workers Union study brought attention to the matter in the early 1990s, greater care in application, inspection, and reduction in overall use has occurred.

[7] A new major initiative to map, study, and develop a strategy for the grasslands of the province is underway by the Grasslands Conservation Council. The Council is a coalition between government agencies, First Nations, the Cattlemen's Association and NGOs such as the Canadian Parks and Wilderness Society.

[8] For a recent review of the growth of the Okanagan fruit industry and the marketing issue, together with some detailed family insights see Garrish (2000).

[9] In addition to the provincial and sector level initiatives to cope with the issues facing farming today, several local/regional groups, such as the Saanich Peninsula Agricultural Strategy Committee (Strategic Plan published June 1997), are actively working on these matters. For example, one problem in this area is that there is a great variation in the rates that farmers have to pay for water for irrigation (varies between $214 and $610 per acre foot according to the municipality).

Fisheries

Colin Wood and Cimarron Corpé
Department of Geography, University of Victoria

INTRODUCTION

The waters of the North Pacific Ocean abound in a great variety of life forms. Along the coast of BC, the marine ecosystems have a particular richness—from minute crustaceans to the world's largest octopus and the mighty Gray whales (Carefoot, 1977). This diversity and abundance stems from the favourable physical conditions: the cool, nutrient-rich ocean currents offshore; the mighty rivers and multitude of small streams that disgorge into the sea; the seasonal regularity of the temperate climatic regime; and the large area of relatively shallow sea zone. These are ideal environments for ecosystems to flourish. At times, the marine and terrestrial systems overlap, often far inland; when bears fish for migrating salmon; when migrating salmon seek the oxygen-rich gravel beds of their breeding stream habitats.

For thousands of years the resources of the marine and riverine zones provided an important basis for the First Nations' way of life. Salmon were especially valued, having a significance that extended beyond the basic requirements of food (Bennett, 1973; Muckle, 1998). The reliability and abundance of the migrating schools of salmon enabled one of the most advanced and culturally rich, non-agricultural societies to evolve. The traditional Native salmon fishery was

- riverine and terminal, selective, run specific, regulated by community tradition, technologically simple with low capital investment, maintained genetic diversity/sustainability.

In contrast, the commercial fishery that replaced it is generally

- offshore and estuarine, partly selective but mainly mixed catch; imperfectly regulated by state and market place, over capitalized, over harvested, eliminating genetic diversity and barely sustainable (Glavin, 1996).

This chapter reviews the main features of commercial fisheries in BC, especially those that evolved since Bill Ross' (1987) concise appraisal. Many technical and management issues discussed by Larkin and colleagues (1964) and Ellis (1977) are pertinent today and worth consulting. However, major changes have occurred in many aspects of the industry, including:

- international relations and agreements between Canada and the US;
- fishing technology and the structure of the industry;
- policies of regulation administered by the federal and provincial governments;
- evolution of aquaculture and the rearing of Atlantic salmon;
- allocation of the catch to the Native people;
- restoration of stream and river habitats; and
- the role of sports fishing and the "image" of BC.

Indeed, there has been a virtual tidal wave of information on the industry and its problems.[1] Moreover, these technical and policy changes are set against the backdrop of a changing climatic and oceanic environment that appears to be dynamically unstable and different from anything that has preceded it. Many of the current problems of low anadromous fish stocks may stem principally from the following "development chain" of causation:

changed climate–changed upwelling–less nutrient–less food–less fish–smaller harvests
(after Welch, 2000)

There is little doubt that the subject matter is complex and conflict ridden. There have been many dismal failures and some notable successes; indeed, virtually any appraisal of the situation appears to add to the controversy. Globally, the fishing industry is described as "a war on fishes" beset with "madhouse economics" (Safina, 1998). Crutchfield's (1977) economic appraisal of the Pacific salmon fishery summarized it in terms of "sadness due to depletion and extinctions and wonder at the gross economic waste involved through overcapitalization." What cannot be denied is that in BC the salmon fishery had an historic annual commercial catch of approximately 75,000 tonnes. In 1998, the wild salmon harvest was 32,000 tonnes, the lowest harvest on record (BC Ministry of Finance and Corporate Relations, 1999). Is the situation yet another example of the resource cycle characterized by Clapp (1998) as a negative sum game in its latter stages?

Ecosystems

The waters of BC teem with marine life and so provide a rich fisheries resource. However, much less is known about them than terrestrial ecosystems, ; their populations, dynamics, and inter-species relationships. What *is* known is that the North Pacific in its natural state is much richer and more diverse than the Atlantic. Each of the major groups—anadromous, demersal, pelagic, and crustaceans/molluscs—contribute in some way to this renewable resource. Many species have no real commercial value due to their properties of size, taste, and/or abundance; often, little is known about them and their place in the biomass and food chains. For many years they were categorized as "trash" or "scrapfish" or "a scientific curiosity."

The general features and hypothesized relationships of the fisheries resource "system" are set out in Figure 18.1. Its viability depends on the sustainability of the Total Allowable Catch (TAC). The TAC is the regulated harvest according to the estimated population which, in turn, ideally requires a scientifically-based estimate of each species' population, predation, breeding, and survival rate. Therefore, the TAC should at least perpetuate the population. The actual historical record varies between species.

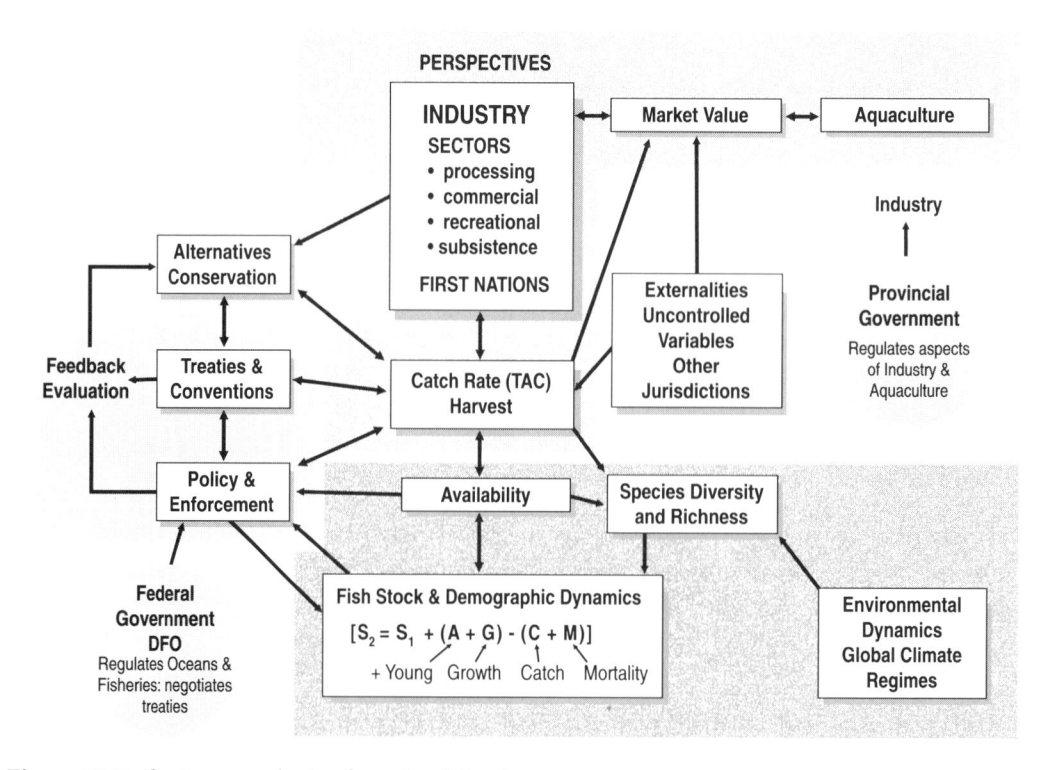

Figure 18.1 Systems analysis of marine fisheries

Recent harvests categorized by species and their value are shown in Table 18.1.

Anadromous stocks can be determined most accurately, as can the relatively immobile dwellers of the intertidal and shallow zone such as shellfish. However, in the real world more complexity is present, mainly due to:

- short run climatic perturbations, notably the impact of the Aleutian low pressure system and its ability to draw nutrient rich cooler water from great depths. Also, the impact of El Niño and increased water temperatures affecting river temperatures and survival rates, and routes taken by migratory species, which may vary according to temperatures/ feed availability;
- impact of mixed fishing and catch disruption (i.e., incidental catch of other species) on juvenile and protected stocks and rare species (e.g., sturgeon);
- illegal fishing – high seas, inshore, and riverine;
- natural predators and their impact (seals, sea lions, and whales);
- impact of human activity on spawning areas – dam construction – pollution – gravel extraction – dredging – mill effluent – highway, winter salt application; and
- impact of "legal" high seas fishing and American interception of migratory species.

Jurisdiction

The Government of Canada claims jurisdiction from the low tide line to the 200 mile limit and exerts management through the Department of Fisheries and Oceans (DFO). According to the constitution, territorial oceans and their fisheries are a federal responsibility; however, once landed, the catch and many other aspects of the industry are also a provincial concern (the BC government tried to take the State of Alaska to court over interception of salmon, but eventually dropped the lawsuit when it was clear that it had no jurisdiction—March 2000). The thrust of federal policy in the late 20th century was to effect control of the territorial zone and thereby validate claims; the territorial sea was extended from 5 km (3 mi) to 14.5 km (9 mi) in 1964, and then an exclusive economic zone (EEZ) was declared in 1977 to extend it to 321.9 km (200 mi), a declaration endorsed in 1982 by the UN Convention of the Law of the Sea. Canada briefly exercised "hot pursuit" jurisdiction beyond this zone to control illegal fishing on the east coast (1996). The motivation came from a desire to protect fish stocks from foreign fleets roaming international waters, accompanied by processing vessels and engaging in pulse fishing (indiscriminate mixed catch). Offshore hydrocarbon potential was another factor. In 1970, Hecate Strait and Queen Charlotte Sound were declared exclusive Canadian zones. An unresolved issue is the boundary line between Canada and the US at Dixon Entrance.

The migratory nature of fish, particularly salmon, has led to conflicts and conventions between Canada and other countries, especially the US. The large water power projects in the Columbia River Basin reduced the "American" Pacific salmon population by about 80%. In the late 1980s, efforts at more improvements in conservation were initiated (Lee and Kneese, 1989). However, large dams on river systems cause increased dissolved nitrogen and higher water temperatures—difficult problems for salmon populations. Canada, the US, and Japan entered into agreements on high seas fishing to protect North American salmon stocks (International Commission for High Seas Fisheries of the North Pacific, 1953). The real jurisdictional issues arise between Canada and the US, with recent increased American interception in Alaskan waters and the Straits of Juan de Fuca of salmon bound for Canadian spawning areas. As part of the general agreement that emerged, it was decided to share the Fraser River stock on an "even basis." Another problem is hake allocation: the US wants 80%; scientists believe that 37% of the stocks are in Canada's waters.

FISHERIES

Fishing activities are usually divided into three main sectors: commercial, sports, and aboriginal (Native or First Nations). The commercial sector accounts for the greater part of the TAC.

Table 18.1 Seafood production, 1993-1997

	Wholesale Value ($ millions)					Landed Value ($ millions)					Landings ('000 tonnes)				
	1993	1994	1995	1996	1997	1993	1994	1995	1996	1997	1993	1994	1995	1996	1997
Salmon															
Chinook	31.2	24.4	11.7	6.8	7.8	14.6	14.2	5.6	1.6	5.8	4.8	3.6	1.5	0.5	1.7
Sockeye	284.1	269.0	182.8	167.2	207.3	140.6	196.2	39.8	78.0	88.8	42.5	30.8	10.5	15.4	25.2
Coho	19.6	42.5	29.1	24.1	6.7	10.9	22.6	13.4	10.2	1.8	4.3	7.7	4.8	3.9	0.8
Pink	75.3	47.8	75.8	51.4	43.8	11.5	2.4	14.9	4.6	6.6	16.1	3.4	19.7	8.4	12.2
Chum	56.6	64.4	46.4	34.5	34.8	23.4	21.9	12.1	4.8	6.4	17.3	20.3	12.0	6.4	8.7
Subtotal	466.8	448.1	345.8	284.0	300.4	201.0	257.3	85.8	99.2	109.4	85.0	65.8	48.5	34.6	48.6
Herring															
Spawn-on-kelp	11.8	17.1	22.2	22.2	17.0	11.8	17.1	22.2	22.2	17.0	0.27	0.26	0.26	0.35	0.38
Roe herring	187.5	170.0	182.4	166.3	95.0	70.47	76.0	63.7	77.3	45.0	39.9	40.0	26.3	21.7	31.2
Food & bait	3.4	5.1	3.2	2.5	4.0	0.9	0.5	0.5	0.2	0.3	1.1	0.7	0.3	0.4	0.3
Subtotal	202.7	192.2	207.8	191.0	116.0	83.1	93.6	86.4	99.7	62.3	41.3	41.0	26.9	22.5	31.9
Halibut	35.8	52.4	45.6	50.9	64.0	30.3	37.4	33.0	32.7	38.2	4.8	4.4	4.1	4.1	5.1
Groundfish	111.0	119.2	121.5	108.0	140.2	73.8	89.6	86.1	71.8	89.0	134.5	166.8	132.4	131.2	136.7
Shellfish	116.8	124.2	136.6	146.9	153.0	79.6	97.1	115.0	114.2	108.8	27.2	26.9	24.7	24.4	18.1
Other	2.5	2.9	2.5	2.5	0.5	1.3	2.0	2.0	1.4	0.3	0.7	0.8	1.0	0.6	0.1
Grand Total	1083.8	1097.8	859.8	783.3	774.1	607.6	731.6	408.3	419.0	408.0	319.2	328.4	237.6	217.4	240.6

Table prepared with information from: The 1995 BC Seafood Industry Year in Review (Ministry of Agriculture, Fish and Food), and The 1997 BC Seafood Industry Year in Review (Ministry of Fisheries). *All figures are estimates.

Fisheries

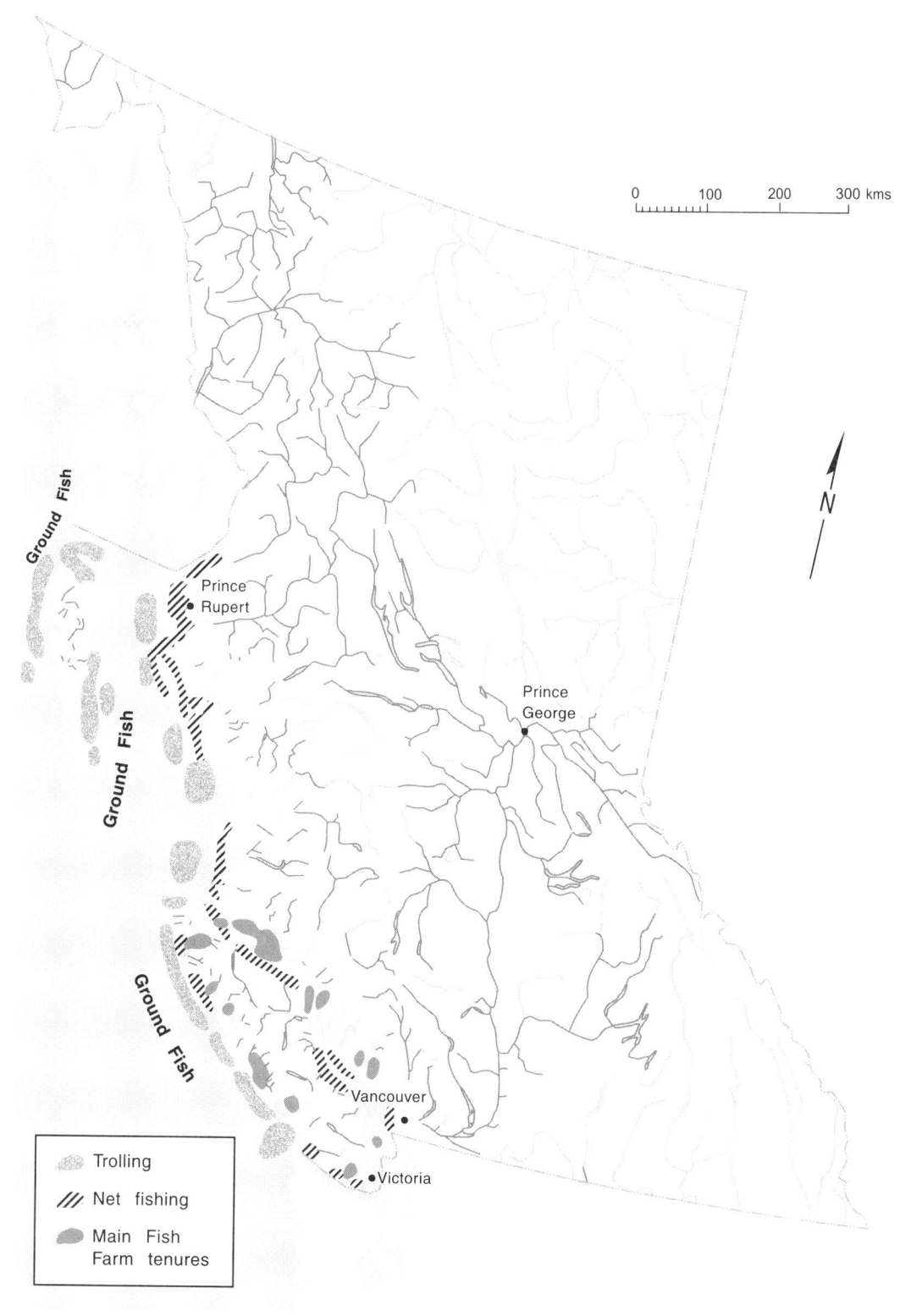

Figure 18.2 Main marine fishing areas by type of operation and main spawning rivers (bold)

The variety of fish species and historical evolution of the industry have resulted in several distinct types of commercial fishing operations (Larkin et al., 1964). It is possible for vessel owners to hold more than one licence (termed "stacking") for different fish species and different areas; in 1996, for example, 375 licences were stacked. The industry is regulated and requirements enforced by the DFO, who licence commercial and sports fishers according to area, species, open season, and many other more detailed aspects. While rivers, spawning environments, and freshwater fish are a provincial jurisdiction (a provincial Ministry of Fisheries was created in 1998), both levels of government cooperate extensively on many aspects of conservation, including habitat restoration and general research. The latter is very important because management of species is based on stock estimation according to scientific measurement/sampling, TAC, and the estimated proportion needed to survive and reproduce, designated the *escapement*. Fishing areas and aquaculture sites are shown in Figure 18.2.

Salmon

Undoubtedly the most complex, conflict ridden and contentious fishing is for salmon—an anadromous fish that generally has a 4 year life cycle ("pinks" have a 2 year cycle) of birth and initial development in fresh water, migration to the ocean and maturation and then return to its birth stream to breed and die (Figure 18.3). Conflict has occurred often over salmon because they:

- have high value (Canada Department of Fisheries and Oceans, 1995);
- are something more than food for the First Nations, being central to the traditional way of life and also of the coastal towns and villages generally;
- require a high quality environment to breed and survive;
- migrate through different jurisdictions; and
- can be caught using a variety of methods.

A further complication is that there are six species of Pacific salmon that return to North America to reproduce, and although they may exist in the same habitat, do not interbreed (Figure 18.3). Two other species return to Asia for the breeding stage. One variety of sockeye salmon, the Kokanee, lives in land-locked lakes and does not migrate. The steelhead (*salmo gairdneri*) is a sea trout, not unlike the Atlantic salmon in appearance. It is not part of the commercial catch and therefore is significant mainly for sport fishers. The salmon species vary in breeding, juvenile and adult stage development, and precisely where and when these take place. This is partly at the root of the fisheries problem of "mixed catches," which can have adults of one species and an incidental or "by-catch" of juveniles of another and other species too. It is therefore understandable that fishing is often likened to clear-cut timber harvesting. From the commercial fishers' viewpoint, specific harvesting is technologically difficult and uneconomical in the ocean environment.

The salmon fishery is also complicated by the genetic diversity that exists in the natural state, for each breeding area results in a genetically distinct variety (or stock) of that species. The estimate for BC is 9,600 different stocks of which 142 are now extinct and 600 threatened with extirpation. Hatchery programs tend to focus on a few stocks to maintain or maximize output, but the consequence is a reduction in genetic diversity.

Commercial Salmon Fishing

The commercial fleet of approximately 2,560 vessels (December 1999) accounts for 95% of the catch with three main types of operation, all of which are relatively close to the shore; an International Agreement (1992) ended Pacific high seas monofilament fishing by foreign fleets with its considerable salmon by-catch—not to mention a host of other marine life.

- *purseseiners*: a net is set and pulled around a school of salmon and the net is then pursed (closed), and hoisted on board—pinks, sockeye, and chum are the main species—accounting for 50% of total salmon catch.
- *trollers*: pull hooks with lures at varied depths mainly for chinook and coho—24% of salmon catch.

Fisheries   335

PINK *(35%) 2.25k: 5 lbs*
Migrating

Male

SOCKEYE *(40%) 3.2k: 7 lbs*
Migrating

Male

Female

CHUM *(12%) 4.5k: 10 lbs*
Male

Female

CHINOOK *(3%) up to 54k: 120 lbs*
Migrating

Male

Female

COHO *(10%) 6.5k: 15 lbs*
Migrating

Male

ATLANTIC SALMON

STEELHEAD *(sea going Rainbow Trout)*

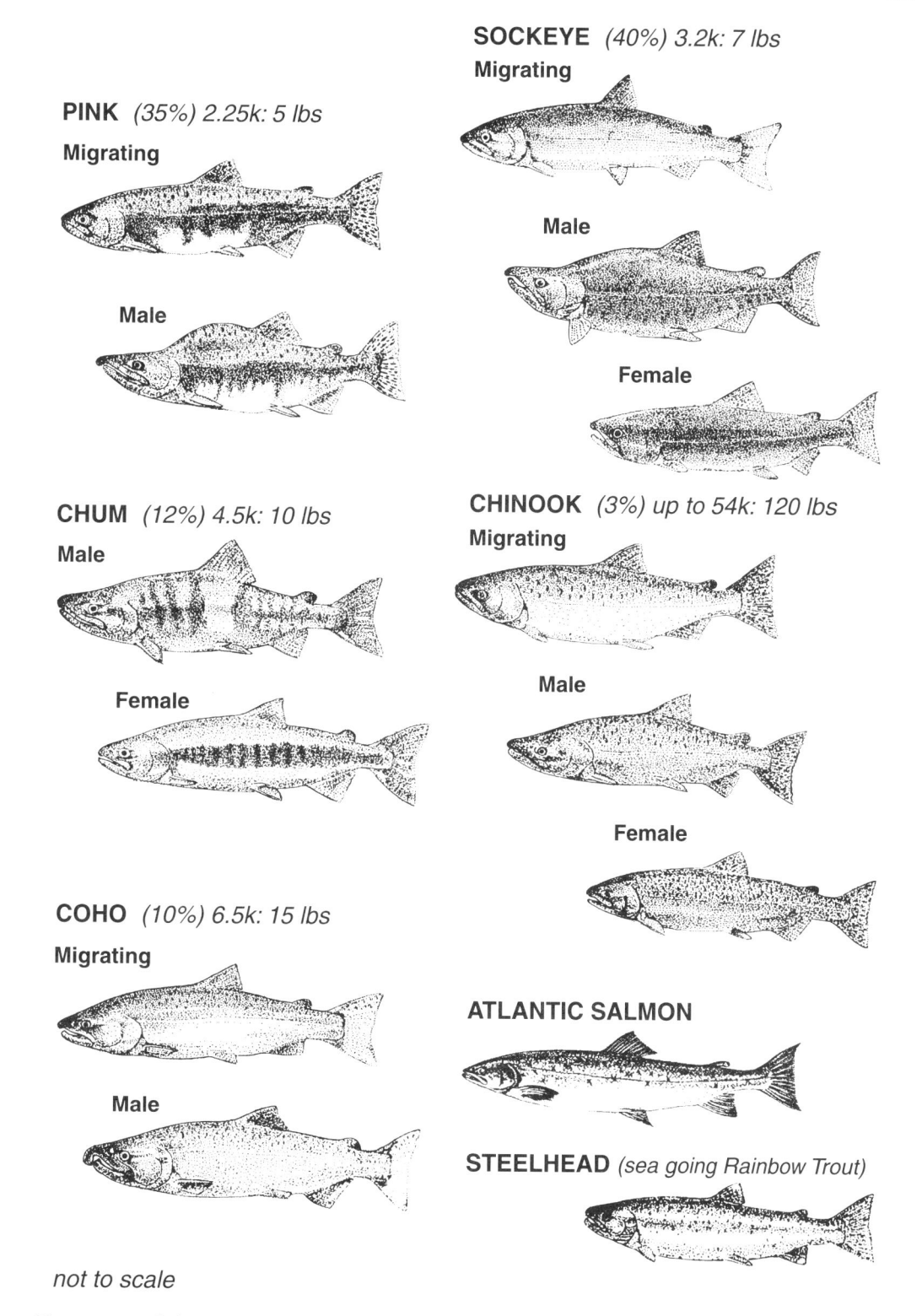

not to scale

Figure 18.3 Salmon species showing average weight at maturity and percent of wild salmon harvest

- *gillnetters*: set vertical nets near river mouths from relatively small vessels; the fish are caught by their gills—sockeye, pinks, and chum—26% of salmon harvest.

Sports Fishing

Sports fishing is very important to BC's lifestyle and coastal tourism industry. Together with First Nations fishing, it accounts for 5% of the TAC. River sports fishing is often for steelhead, but in recent years populations have been so low that fishing is now severely restricted. Coastal fishing is by trolling from small boats mainly for chinook (the large, prized sports trophy fish) and coho; the latter's stocks are especially at risk. The coho breed mainly in small coastal streams— habitats that have been damaged by coastal logging, road construction, and urbanization (Sierra Club, 1998). Data on them is meagre, and unfortunately for their sustainability, they tend to take lures easily.

It is generally recognized that sports fishing generates considerable income with significant multiplier effects from fishing lodge operations through to individual enthusiasts. A 1996 study estimated that sports fishing generated $671 per fish, while the commercial catch generated only $26 per fish. Benefits for the former were also dispersed more widely between 400,000 recreational licences. As a rule, BC residents account for about 70% of licence holders. The recreational sector accounts for a surplus in government revenues, whereas the commercial sector operates at a deficit: +$66.9 million versus –$2.4 million (BC Job Protection Commission, 1996). Sports fishing groups are usually critical of the political influence that corporate commercial activities have on federal policy. There is, however, a firm economic basis to their views. The root of the problem is the nature of the historic allocations and how to compensate for change in the portion of the TAC allocated to the three main sectors. Some argue that it is easier for the federal government to influence and deal with a few corporate organizations and their lobbyists than a diverse group with a weakly focused constituency. The present federal government has few western MPs, so many in the west view federal fisheries policies sceptically.

However, as May's study of the intersectoral issue shows, on the one hand changes in the allocation are necessary while on the other, with a diminishing resource, it is very difficult to achieve cooperation between the major stakeholders (May, 1996).

Fish Processors

A dominant sector of the industry consists of companies that process and market the fish and have a particular influence on about 60% of the seine fishery (which accounts for about 10% of all fishing vessels, but approximately 50% of commercial salmon harvest). The structure of the processing and canning companies, vessel ownership and leasing, and relations between fishers and the corporate sector has a complex history that is beyond the scope of this chapter (Carrothers, 1941; Sandberg, 1979; Marchak, 1987; Ross, 1987; Conley, 1988; Glavin, 1996; Garvey and Giammarino, 1996). The Strategic Task Force on Fish Processing's (1994) examination of the system identified many of the issues involved. Two significant points were: first, the rapid decline in the number of processing companies from 1934 (50 companies) to 1974 (12 companies) to 1996 (3 companies), resulting in concentration of corporate ownership; second, international trade agreements mean unprocessed fish can be exported to the US and processed where wage rates are lower; in effect, exporting jobs. Garvey and Giammarino (1996) suggest that capital shortages are part of the problem, together with *inflexibility* in the licencing arrangements. Redressing these issues and conferring a degree of ownership rights on communities would in theory result in better protection and exploitation of the resource. In recent times about 25% of fish plant workers have been First Nations and have suffered from the trend to offshore processing.

First Nations' Fisheries

Several authors have detailed the importance of the salmon fishery to the First Nations of BC (Bennett, 1973; Kennedy and Bouchard, 1983; Notzke, 1994; Muckle, 1998) and attribute the abundance and vitality of groups settled along the rivers of BC, especially the Fraser River, to the richness of this resource. All the salmon species are fished, with white sturgeon and eulachon being of lesser importance. Bennett (1973) determined that 91 bands from 10 main cultural groups fish the Fraser River system. Recent estimates of the population depending directly on salmon are between 25,000 and 30,000. Estimates of salmon biomass production prior to the commercial fishery were 140.4 kg per km^2, and consumption of approximately 320 kg per annum (Rostlund, 1952). This suggests an approximate harvest survival rate of 12% compared with contemporary estimates of between 2% and 5%.

To the First Nations, the central issue is that their rights did exist at the time of European colonization, and that title to lands and hence resource use was never extinguished. Few treaties that specified rights and obligations, responsibilities, compensation, and procedures for management were signed in BC. By not signing treaties the argument is that rights were not given up. However, in this century, the general federal and provincial interpretation that was actually implemented as fisheries policy was to allow native communities a portion of the salmon harvest for direct consumption only (i.e., subsistence), but none could be sold commercially. First Nations could, however, hold regular fish boat licences and participate in the commercial industry; this currently stands at about 19% of (salmon) licences.

Growth of the commercial industry, government regulations, the prohibition of fish weirs, and an erratic, seasonal wage labour system had a catastrophic impact on the Native economy and society. The bond with the resource base that held society together was replaced by seasonal employment in canneries, and fisheries' officials clamping down on the "illegal" sales of salmon. Agitation and important test cases in court have altered the situation significantly and along with a new provincial government have prompted another generation of treaty negotiations (Cassidy and Dale, 1988; Notzke, 1994). Those test cases were:

- Calder (1973) — Supreme Court of Canada affirmed the Nisga'a tribal title to lands never extinguished; governments to negotiate settlement.
- Boldt (1974)—US litigation over treaty rights; impacts on State of Washington fisheries.[2]
- Sparrow (1990) — Ronald Sparrow's conviction in BC Court for illegal fishing is overturned; aboriginal fishing rights protected.
- Delgamuukw (1997) — Gitxsan and Wet'suwet'en claim title and compensation for losses. Case starts 1984, eventually Supreme Court of Canada rules in favour of First Nations (Muckle, 1998).
- Mi'kmaq (1999) — a ruling by the Supreme Court recognizes claims to resource (fish) in the original treaty (East Coast of Canada), but also applicable to the Douglas Treaty, on Vancouver Island.

The joint initiatives of the 1970s between government and First Nations did not change the status quo significantly (Notzke, 1994). The complexities of the issue can only be alluded to here. In an effort to reduce uncertainty, the DFO introduced the Aboriginal Fisheries Strategy (1992). Individual food fish permits were replaced with communal licences administered by the tribe, and the *Fisheries Act* was therefore amended to permit "Aboriginal fishing agreements" (Glavin, 1996). After a century of denial by federal and provincial governments, the courts finally required that effective negotiations take place, a step that would have serious implications for the allocation of the fish harvest. The first of the new generation of treaties is between Canada, BC, and the Nisga'a and has among its agreements the following:

- conservation of fish stocks the primary consideration;
- allocation of 17% of the catch (TAC) of the Nass river system; can be sold; and
- federal and provincial governments retain responsibility for conservation and management (BC Ministry of Finance and Corporate Relations, 1998).

The significance of the Native fishery is that it effectively perpetuated the biosystem yet provided a major source of food—unlike the modern international, commercial fishery which, together with habitat destruction, have decimated many species of the Pacific fishery.

Other Fisheries

Halibut

Halibut is one of the oldest fisheries on the coast, although commercial harvest is mainly in northern BC. As was the case in Europe, halibut (Dutch for the "holy flounder") were almost fished out in BC by the 1920s, leading to a Canadian/US convention and management agreement (1923). It was one of Canada's first international agreements (*International Pacific Halibut Commission*). Consequently, stocks gradually improved. However, in the 1970s, a high by-catch of halibut by foreign fleets was partly responsible for declaration of the 200 mile *Exclusive Economic Zone* (EEZ). This also ended Canadian fishing in the now extended US EEZ. The current annual harvest is about 4,000 tonnes. Trawling for other species still impacts halibut as a by-catch. Alaskan trawler fishers are experimenting with varied net mesh sizes to permit escape (i.e., enhanced specific fishing and reduced halibut by-catch). Sports fishers resorted to developing more interest in halibut due to reduced availability of salmon.

Herring

Herring were once found in enormous numbers in both the North Atlantic and Pacific. Indeed, the name means an "army of fish." Overfishing and spawning habitat destruction have seriously affected their numbers in both oceans. Variations in ocean temperature and natural predators are also significant factors. Traditionally, they have been used for food in Europe, and more (after processing) for meal, oil, and bait in North America. In BC, landings in the early part of the 20th century were generally about 90,000 tonnes, but declined significantly in the 1960s, leading to closure. This measure was effective in the gradual recovery of the stock, which saw a reopening in the 1970s with the incentive of the Japanese roe market. Fishing takes place in spring, close to shore, and just prior to spawning. The herring roe fishery occurs in a crowded and very intense 3-week period; openings may last for only a few hours or even minutes. Currently, landings are between 25,000 and 40,000 tonnes. Until the DFO and Coast Guard asserted greater surveillance, overloading, capsizing, drownings, and collisions were not uncommon. Many formerly rich herring locations appear to have been fished out (Glavin, 1996).

Groundfish

A variety of other fish are taken by trawls in the inshore waters—cod varieties, sole, dogfish, and pollack. There is midwater trawling for shrimp, while hake is sought by deeper trawls off the west coast of Vancouver Island. The catch accounts for the majority of the total fish harvest—about 130,000 of 240,000 tonnes (1997 figures). The current active fleet is about 70 vessels with a large portion of the catch being made by a few large vessels and 10 to 20% being processed offshore.[3] Trawling is a highly contentious form of fishing due to concern that trawls damage the sea bed and its habitat, thus impacting on a significant sector of the biomass and food chain system. A bill to ban bottom trawling was introduced in the US Senate (Rep. Jack Hefley–Colorado). Significant support has come from ecologists such as Elliot Norse of the Marine Conservation, Biological Institute. Fishers are trying to overcome the problem by using rollers to avoid bottom scraping (Haig-Brown, Chambers, Drouin, and Warren, 1999).

Shellfish

Shellfish were a traditional, valued food of the First Nations—many midden sites along the coast of BC are usually thickly distributed with shells, proof of the antiquity of the food source and the habitation sites. First Nations continue to assert claims over traditional collecting areas. This has led to some conflicts, particularly with recent immigrants who are unfamiliar with local customs and conservation practices and have stripped some areas of shellfish.

Clams are the main 'wild' shellfish by value, and oysters (4,000 tonnes/year) are the major cultivated variety. Harvests have fallen from the usual 25,000 tonnes per year partly due to the prevalence of red tide conditions in recent years and over-harvest of wild stocks. A recent appraisal of the contribution of cultivated ocean products to the BC economy identified a range of creative options (BC Shellfish Growers Association, 1998).

Examples of Extirpation:

Pilchard (California sardine) fishing began in 1917 and expanded after WWI, but declined after WWII due to Californian harvest of 4-year-old fish, leaving few survivors to reach BC, where older, larger fish were usually caught.

Sea Otters: one of the original attractions to the coast for Europeans—extirpated in the 19th century. Otters fed on sea urchins who fed on kelp. Without this control the urchins reduced kelp areas significantly, further impacting on fish habitat (Glavin, 1996). Recently, attempts have been made to re-establish sea otter colonies.

POLICIES

A multiplicity of participants and jurisdictions, a variety of species with different behaviours, controllable and uncontrollable variables, set within a dynamic of people versus fish, leads to a complicated management situation. The following brief outline focuses on the more significant threads in the complex weave of fisheries policy, mostly as they relate to salmon. The main policy factors are:

- perpetuation of the stocks;
- allocation of TAC to participants;
- sharing arrangements, international and regional, catching method; and
- bureaucratic system for implementation.

Added to these explicit foci are: the context of the political significance of BC's communities to the federal government and the party in power; bureaucratic operation of the DFO; fisheries in the agenda of relations with a powerful neighbour and trading partner; the power and standing in cabinet of the prevailing minister of fisheries; and relations between the governments of BC and Canada. Finally, contrary to popular understanding of the situation, according to international law, also acknowledged in treaties with the US, Canada does not *own* migratory salmon outside of the zone of national jurisdiction, the EEZ (Keevil, 1999).

The Commercial Salmon Catch: A Synopsis

1835	Hudson's Bay Co. exports 4,000 barrels of (Native caught) salmon.
1835-1870s	Canneries spring up along the coast; BC joins Canada.
1880-1900s	Attempts at restricting fleet size; unsuccessful.
early 1900s	Native weirs banned; first hatcheries; strikes between fishers and canneries.
1930s	Dam construction on western US rivers; impediments result in higher river temperatures; increased dissolved nitrogen.
1940s	Advances in catching techniques; vessels move offshore; decline in Native licence numbers.
1950s	Agreements between Canada-USA-Japan to protect stocks
1958	Sinclair appointed to examine the fishery; recommends licences and levies.
1968	Davis Plan, based on Sinclair's study; fleet reduction; buy outs, but increased capitalization occurs – catching power triples; consolidation of companies.
early 1970s	UN endorses 200 mile EEZ; concerns increase over coastal logging; prosecutions.
1977	Salmonid Enhancement Program (SEP) – hatchery and (Native) community oriented: but focus on few large hatcheries
1981	Pearse reviews the industry; proposes modifications; not adopted.
1985	Pacific Salmon Treaty with US; coordination of harvest share; conservation
1992	Canada and US disagree on share and interception; Supreme Court "Sparrow" decision leads to Aboriginal Fishing strategy – apportion of catch for sale; Pearse and Larkin report on poor sockeye runs.

Recent Developments

The 1994 season saw dramatic changes in the North Pacific oceanic/weather conditions as *El Nino* induced sockeye to move towards cooler Alaska water where they were caught by US fishers. As stocks approached BC waters, it was apparent that river temperatures were abnormally high. A higher proportion of sockeye than normal went through the Johnstone Strait. It also emerged that DFO catch samples, and hence population projections and TAC, were wide of the mark. The result was a degree of chaos in the fishery to the extent that Hon. Brian Tobin, Federal Minister of the DFO, appointed John Fraser to examine the problems.

Fraser Inquiry: 1994

The 1994 Fraser Inquiry found that:

- aggressive Canadian fishing policy due to struggle with the US was poorly conceived;
- major problems existed with estimating size of fish runs; and
- dysfunction at the senior management level; understaffing at the field level; illegals unchecked.

Mifflin Plan: 1996

Continuing problems with the fishery led new minister of the DFO Hon. Fred Mifflin to propose new strategies based on fleet reduction, risk averse conservation, and community-based management. For example, on fleet reform it advocated:

- a continuation of the earlier buy-back system with $80 million available;
- single gear licences (gillnet, troll, or seine);
- area licensing, two for seine; three for gillnets; three for trollers: one licence per area; and
- stacking of licences is permitted.

The plan resulted in tremendous criticism with many arguing that communities would be devastated by all the actions it proposed. Little stakeholder input had taken place. So great was the outcry that a joint federal-provincial review panel was struck to visit fishing communities and gather input. It was the proverbial "after-the-fact tokenism" of centralized bureaucracies. The review panel found that the plan was too technical for most people; short term replacement job creation was a priority; decisions should be made in BC rather than Ottawa (Canada Department of Fisheries and Oceans, 1996).

Federal/Provincial Strategy: 1996

The BC government proposed a new direction to conserve the salmon stocks by giving more responsibilities to the local communities over management and increasing coordination between the agencies involved (BC Ministry of Agriculture, Fisheries and Food, 1999). Its principal components were:

- enhance stream habitats to protect fish;
- increase agency cooperation, resolve treaty problems with the US;
- generate diversification by greater processing, sports fishing, and tourism; and
- create sustainable communities through development programs.

Federal-Provincial Memorandum of Understanding: 1996

An attempt to resolve the jurisdictional dispute that continued to simmer contained two key elements:

- review each government's roles and responsibilities; and
- secure greater provincial government and stakeholder input into fishing policies.

In the late 1990s, the situation concerning salmon stocks was clearly becoming critical and a change in policy and management took the form of a series of severe restrictions that were imposed, for example, on coho stocks; it appeared to have some success. Another encouraging aspect appears to be the greater co-operation that is now occurring between the main fishing sectors (WCF, 1999). By mid 1999, selective fishing strategies—avoiding stocks of concern and releasing those that are encountered—had become a major priority of the DFO. It appears that, given the precarious situation for salmon stocks, aboriginal, commercial, and sports fishing sectors are embracing these new initiatives.

Were it not for the international complexity of the situation, salmon stocks may have been on the road to recovery. It was increasingly apparent that Americans were intercepting large numbers of "Canadian fish" in Alaskan waters, necessitating negotiations between the two countries and a revisitation of the Treaty. In 1998, the provincial government formed a Fisheries Ministry as part of their strategy—perhaps indicative of the poor relationship with Ottawa (1998). Unfortunately, a deterioration of relations between Ottawa and Victoria led to a renegotiation by the federal government of the Pacific Salmon Treaty with the US, with no participation by the government of BC or any stakeholders. An attempt to improve relations between Victoria and Ottawa is now occurring (early 2000) which could have implications for the fisheries.

Another major provincial initiative was the *Fish Protection Act* (1997), which focused on water levels for fish, protecting/restoring habitat, protecting riparian lands, and strengthening local environmental planning.[4]

International Context

The 1985 *Pacific Salmon Treaty* between Canada and the US was signed in order to establish conservation objectives and to share the catch fairly. The sequence of main events that followed was:

- *Treaty signed (1985)*
- a gradual increase in interception of "Canadian" fish (esp. chinook) in Alaskan waters
- *Treaty expires*
- 1996—Canada levies toll on American fishing vessels passing through BC waters: BC wants renegotiations
- 1997—Canadian fishing boats are used to block a US ferry in Prince Rupert
- June 1999—DFO Minister Honorable David Anderson renegotiates without BC input.

New Agreements - 1999 (main points)

- 10 year fisheries management agreement, 12 years for Fraser sockeye and pinks
- refined arrangements for the Commission
- provision for habitat restoration/protection
- US to provide two financial support funds
- comprehensive fishing arrangements.

AQUACULTURE

Successful, environmentally compatible cultivation of oysters has existed along the coast of BC for decades. In 1905, attempts to introduce Atlantic salmon (*Salmo salar*) to Lower Mainland and Vancouver Island rivers were unsuccessful (Larkin et al., 1964). As salmon aquaculture grew in Norway and Scotland in the 1960s—a response to greater restrictions on fishing areas in the North Atlantic—interest began to focus on the BC coast as a potential location for fish farming. It was not until 1984 that the federal government approved the introduction of *Salmo salar* eggs to BC. Immediately, a rush to start up fish farms took place, because salmon prices were high and more people were favouring more fish in their diets.

Rearing units consist of anchored floating pens or a similar arrangement attached to dock and jetty systems. Juveniles are raised in hatcheries onshore and then transferred to the pens. Generally, sheltered locations with good water circulation for natural disposal of wastes are preferred. Atlantic salmon are the favoured species because of finished size, feed conversion efficiency, rate of weight gain, being ready in 2 to 3 years, good flesh quality, and docility. Given the 1905 experiments it was thought that if any escapes occurred, survival to breed in the Pacific environment was unlikely. The industry has gradually increased output; in 1998 to 39,000 tonnes, surpassing the wild catch at 32,000 tonnes (a record low) (Table 18.2).

There has been good success in terms of production and employment in the industry, but several issues have arisen concerning its compatibility with the Pacific environment.

Currently the main issues are:

- 121 fish farm leases exist, although only about 85 are in operation. While the total is capped, five new leases are available to promote closed containment systems (of feed, anti-biotics, and wastes);

Table 18.2 Aquaculture production 1995-1997*

	Wholesale Value ($million)			Farmgate Value ($million)			Harvest ('000 tonnes)		
	1997	1996	1995	1997	1996	1995	1997	1996	1995
Salmon	195.0	172.0	172.8	175.5	158.9	170.4	40.6	27.6	27.3
Rainbow Trout	0.7	0.5	0.5	0.7	0.5	0.5	0.15	0.8	0.1
Pacific Oyster	6.2	8.3	7.7	4.9	6.3	5.4	4.7	5.4	5.3
Clams	5.4	5.3	4.9	4.5	4.5	3.9	1.0	1.0	0.9
Scallops	0.7	1.0	0.3	0.6	0.9	0.2	0.09	0.14	0.02
TOTAL	208.0	187.1	186.2	186.2	171.1	180.4	46.5	34.9	33.6

Table prepared with information from 1998 MELP statistics

*All figures are estimates.

- a substantial number of escapes have occurred; also in adjacent Washington State—at least 30 escapes from 1991 to 1997, with two recent incidents totalling 70,000 fish;[5]
- stream monitoring shows that *Salmo salar* can survive and breed in the Pacific environment; 42 juveniles were recently found in a north Vancouver Island stream (Schmidt, 1999);
- the major issue of disposal of wastes led to a review by the province's Environmental Assessment Office (1995-97) which identified poor standards of environmental management in the industry as a whole and recommended changes. The Suzuki Foundation has campaigned strongly for closed containment systems, especially to prevent release of anti-biotics and the potential development of "superbug" strains; and
- In 1999, the BC government required: a waste management regime; escape prevention rules and penalties for non-compliance; relocation of poorly sited operations; a progress review and evaluation in 2001.

The gold rush era of fish farming appears to be over, in the sense of a rapidly growing, loosely regulated and monitored activity. The challenge to improve holding systems is on, with several pen closure systems currently being developed and tested. The BC government has become more vigilant about the environmental issues involved. The Atlantic Salmon Watch Program was recently inaugurated to report on and investigate sightings of Atlantic salmon in the natural setting. The program draws on participation by the range of stakeholders in BC fisheries specifically, and environmental protection generally. There are environmentalists and resource geographers who are questioning the merits of harvesting large volumes of "low quality" wild fish, reducing them to feed for farmed salmon at a conversion ratio of approximately 2.8/3.0 to 1.0. This is part of the wider issue of human interference in biodiversity, efficiency of food chains, and inefficiency in energy conversion.

CONCLUSIONS

The pressures on the BC fishery have remained virtually unchanged for decades and are characterized by:

- excess capital investment; aggressive international competition, due in part to state subsidies;
- neighbours who have virtually destroyed their fish stocks through hydroelectric power, and are powerful and difficult to negotiate with;
- too many participants;
- habitat deterioration; and
- a low political priority in a distant government (Ottawa).

Clearly, many of these variables are at odds with the usual Canadian way of "reasonableness" in problem solving. Canadian fisheries policy has gone through a parade of ministers and strategies that often antagonized the scientists, stakeholders, and the "unaffiliated public" while trying to perpetuate and enhance the resource base. Reduction of the fleet size with compensation has been a sensible long term strategy that other countries should emulate. Aquaculture, which at first sight seemed to fill many of the gaps brought about by a deteriorating wild harvest, has generated its own set of issues, but still has some promise if we can learn from the problems encountered in Europe.

The original inhabitants, the First Nations, depend most directly on the fishery and suffered most from the decline in wild fish stocks. Recent and ongoing treaty negotiations signify a fairer allocation of the catch—but will there continue to be one of any realistic size? An expanded effort to restore breeding habitat is under way by provincial and federal governments with a greater focus on diversity, but many stocks remain in peril of extinction. Much has been learned, however, from the SEP program of the 1970s. Furthermore, there is a tremendous, widespread interest in saving the salmon —at all levels.[6] The main difficulties are in the distant locus of power, and getting a reasonable share with a powerful, aggressive neighbour. Clearly, the sustainability of fisheries requires cooperation rather than conflict. As opposed to a negative sum game, as posited by Clapp, the management of fisheries has more characteristics of a Prisoners' Dilemma Game (Wood, 1976). The whole set of complex management issues is set against a physical environment that is itself becoming less predictable.

The issues are also part of the wider problem of maintaining ecological diversity in the face of an industry driven by quantity and the most marketable species. The recent treaty with the US (Paulson, 1999) is an attempt to sort out the issues and agree on a plan of action in a cooperative and neighbourly way. However, it is truly remarkable for its lack of Canadian stakeholder input—aside from the federal government, there was none.

REFERENCES

Bennett, M.G. (1973). *Indian fishing and its cultural importance in the Fraser River system*. Ottawa: Government of Canada, Department of Environment, Fisheries Series.

BC Job Protection Commission (1996). *Fishing for answers: Coastal communities and the BC salmon fishery*. Victoria, BC.

BC Ministry of Finance and Corporate Relations (1999). *BC financial and economic review 1998*. Victoria, BC: Ministry of Finance and Corporate Relations.

BC Ministry of Agriculture, Fisheries and Food (1999). *BC fisheries strategy: Towards a made-in-BC vision to renew the Pacific salmon fishery*. Discussion Paper. Victoria, BC: Ministry of Agriculture, Fisheries and Food.

BC Shellfish Growers Association (1998). *Ocean opportunities for tomorrow*. Conference Proceedings. Prince Rupert, BC. May 1998.

Canada Department of Fisheries and Oceans (1995). *The economic value of salmon: Chinook and coho in BC*. Ottawa: DFO.

Canada Department of Fisheries and Oceans (1996). *Tangled lines: A joint federal-provincial review of the Mifflin Plan*. Ottawa: DFO.

Carefoot, T. (1977). *Pacific seashores: A guide to intertidal ecology*. Seattle, WA: University of Washington Press.

Carrothers, W.A. (1941). *The British Columbia fisheries*. Toronto: University of Toronto Press.

Cassidy, F., and Dale, N. (1988). *After Native claims? The implications of comprehensive claims settlements for natural resources in British Columbia*. Lantzville, BC: Oolichan Books and the Institute on Research on Public Policy.

Clapp, R.A. (1998). The resource cycle in forestry and fishing. *Canadian Geographer*, 42(2), 129-144.

Conley, J. (1988). Relations of production and collective action in the salmon fishery, 1900-1925. In R. Warburton and D. Coburn (Eds.), *Workers, capital and the State in British Columbia: Selected papers* (pp. 86-116). Vancouver: UBC Press.

Crutchfield, J.A. (1977). The fishery: Economic maximization. In D.V. Ellis (Ed.), *Pacific salmon: Management for people* (pp. 1-34). Victoria, BC: University of Victoria, Department of Geography, Western Geographical Series, Volume 13.

Ellis, D.V. (Ed.) (1977). *Pacific salmon: Management for people*. Victoria, BC: University of Victoria, Department of Geography, Western Geographical Series, Vol. 13.

Garvey, G.T., and Giammarino, R.M. (1996). *Corporate concentration in the Pacific salmon fishery: Draft report for Pacific revitalization plan*. Vancouver: UBC Press.

Glavin, T. (1996). *Dead reckoning: Confronting the crisis in Pacific fisheries.* Vancouver: Greystone Books.

Haig-Brown, A., Chambers, S., Drouin, M., and Warren, B. (1999). The future of trawling. *Pacific Fishing,* 20(12), 30-46.

Keevil, R. (1999). Mouse makes deal with elephant. *Westcoast Fisherman,* 14(1), 37-39.

Kennedy, D., and Bouchard, R. (1983). *Sliammon life, Sliammon lands.* Vancouver: Talon Books.

Larkin, P.A., et al. (1964). Fisheries. In *Inventory of the natural resources of British Columbia* (pp. 194-306). 15th Edition. Victoria, BC.

Lee, D.C., and Kneese, A.V. (1989). Fish and hydro power vie for Columbia River waters. *Resources for the Future,* 94, 1-4.

Marchak, P. (1987). *Uncommon property: The fishing and fish processing industry in British Columbia.* Toronto: Methuen.

May, A.W. (1996). *Altering course: A report to the Minister of Fisheries and Oceans on intersectoral allocation of salmon in BC.* St John's: Memorial University.

Muckle, R.J. (1998). *The First Nations of British Columbia.* Vancouver: UBC Press.

Notzke, C. (1994). *Aboriginal peoples and natural resources in Canada.* North York: Captus Press.

Paulson, M. (1999). Rifts threaten salmon treaty, *Seattle-Post Intelligencer*: October 29th.

Rimmer, D. (1999). Atlantic salmon (Salmo salar) in the Tsitika River. *Westcoast Fisherman,* 14(April), 34-37.

Rostlund, E. (1952). *Freshwater fish and fishing in Native North America.* Berkeley: University of California Press.

Ross, W. (1987). Fisheries. In C.N. Forward (Ed.), *British Columbia: Its resources and people* (pp. 179-198). Victoria, BC: University of Victoria, Department of Geography, Western Geographical Series, Volume 22.

Safina, C. (1998). The world's imperilled fish. *Scientific American,* 9(3), 58-63.

Sandberg, A. (1979). *A study of Canadian political economy: A critical review and the case of the BC salmon canning industry, 1870-1914.* M.A. thesis. Department of Geography. University of Victoria.

Schmidt, S. (1999). Fish and chips, *The Globe and Mail,* November 18th, pp. T3-4.

Sierra Club (1998). *Turning the tide on the salmon crisis.* Victoria, BC: Sierra Club of BC.

Welch, D. (2000). *Ocean climate change and the management of endangered Pacific salmon stock.* Colloquium, Department of Biology, University of Victoria. March 3rd, 2000.

Wood, C. (1976). Conflict in resource management and the use of threat: The Goldstream controversy. *Natural Resources Journal,* 16, 129-142.

ENDNOTES

1. The authors examined a large number of sources of information, too numerous to list in the references. Good current sources of information are DFO briefing reports; Westcoast Fisherman (monthly); Sports Fishing Institute Newsletter 'Action Update' (bimonthly).

2. Washington State Native Peoples had pressed for an equitable share of the salmon stocks based on historic rights. The US Court (Boldt) decision allocated them 50% of stocks, including rights to Fraser-bound stocks (although in any given year the salmon may not migrate through American waters of Juan de Fuca in commercial numbers.

3. Allocation of the hake fishery between the US and Canada is under review. Trawler operators argue that offshore sales are a 'safety valve' in case there are processing problems in Tofino. The hake fishery suffered a serious drop in catch size in 2000.

4. The protection of riparian land was initially aimed at non-urban regions. In 2001, the metropolitan areas (southwest BC) were also included, leading to predictable outbursts from Vancouver media.

5. In 1998, several reports confirmed the presence of Atlantic salmon (*Salmo salar*) in the Tsitika River on Vancouver Island (Rimmer, 1999).

6. Many local, small scale volunteer projects are taking place across the province with many groups working in partnership (volunteers and Pacific Salmon Foundation). See *Westcoast Fisherman,* April 1999, p. 23.

Marine Conservation

Philip Dearden
Department of Geography, University of Victoria

Introduction

The coastal zone of BC, encompassing some 41,000 km of highly indented coastline between Prince Rupert in the north and Victoria in the south, is one of the most biologically productive areas on the planet. On the land, in the temperate rainforest, the highest precipitation levels in Canada combined with a long growing season and fertile valleys give rise to the tallest trees in the nation. The oceans, with deep up-welling currents, host some 400 species of fish; 161 marine bird species; 29 marine mammal species; the world's largest octopus, barnacle, sea slug, and chiton; and more than 3,800 species of invertebrates—about 3.5% of the global total and three times that found on the Atlantic coast at similar latitudes (Mercier and Mondor, 1995). At various times of the year cetaceans such as minke, Gray, humpback, and killer whales can be seen along with harbour and Dall's porpoises and Pacific white-sided dolphins. The region also supports a substantial proportion of the global numbers of pelagic sea birds such as rhinoceros auklets (25%), Cassin's auklets (70%), ancient murrelets (40%), and 75% of Canada's tufted puffins (Mercier and Mondor, 1995).

This biological abundance provided sustenance for rich First Nations' cultures for thousands of years. The lure of sea otter pelts and later exploitation of other marine mammal and fish resources encouraged rapid colonization. Some species, such as the sea otter, were extirpated, and most others have been vastly reduced in abundance. One by one, fisheries have been closed as the stocks were fished to exhaustion—halibut, pilchards, and abalone, to name a few. However, perhaps the greatest shock arrived in 1998 when virtually the entire salmon fishery was closed for conservation reasons. Fisheries biologists estimate that some 140 genetic stocks of salmon are already extinct and many others in precarious positions.

Over-exploitation such as this has given new impetus to the need for stricter marine conservation on the West Coast, even though conservation measures have already been enacted. For example, an Act to Protect Sea Otters was promulgated in 1911, but they continued to be poached, with the last allegedly shot on the BC coast in 1914. Fisheries restrictions have been placed on all species that have been fished to exhaustion, but they did not work to prevent their demise. In other words, even the best conservation measures in the world will be ineffective if they are not based upon a sound understanding of the marine ecosystem and if they are poorly enforced. It is within this context that this chapter is cast.

The purpose of this chapter is to review current developments in two main areas of marine conservation. First is the initiative to create a coordinated federal-provincial system of marine protected areas along the BC coast. Although marine provincial parks have existed since 1957 when Montague Harbour and Rebecca Spit were established, the parks created were largely anchorages for boaters and served little purpose for conservation. In many cases, these parks became so overcrowded that conservation was inhibited, rather than served, by park designation (Dearden, 1986). Recently, new initiatives have emerged to create a co-ordinated federal-provincial system of marine protected areas along the Pacific coast, and description of these initiatives constitutes the first section of this chapter.

All protected areas must precisely establish what is being protected, why it is being protected, and whom it is being protected from. Throughout this last decade there has been an explosion of interest on the BC coast in ecotourism (see Dearden, 1990). On the one hand, ecotourism may benefit conservation by exposing people to the beauty and wonder of nature which, hopefully, will encourage them to support conservation activities. On the other hand, by increasing the exposure of nature to more people, ecotourism can also impact negatively the very organisms that provide the source for this wonder. Whale-watching is a good example of this phenomenon, and has grown by massive proportions over the last decade. The second part of this chapter will describe some of the research being undertaken to ascertain the various dimensions and impacts of this activity on the BC coast. The discussion section will then explore some of the challenges facing marine protected areas in terms of wildlife conservation.

MARINE PROTECTED AREAS

The Global Context

The United Nations declared 1998 the 'Year of the Oceans.' There was good reason to do so. As the global population continues to increase, the population is becoming increasingly littoral. Over half the world's population lives within 200 km of the coast. Only in Africa is there more population in the interior than on the coast (Hinrichsen, 1998). More people means more waste products, and more people depending on the ocean for their livelihood. The Food and Agriculture Organization (FAO) estimates that 70% of the world's marine fisheries are over-exploited, with a continuing trend to catch more fish at lower trophic levels (Pauly, Christensen, Dalsgaard, Froese, and Torres Jr., 1998). The first major international survey of coral reefs found 69% of reefs were seriously degraded (Anon., 1998), and over half the world's salt marshes, mangroves, and coastal wetlands have been destroyed.[1]

As a result of these trends and the obvious signs of increasing marine degradation, nations all over the world are seeking to improve marine conservation activities. Creation of marine protected areas is one such activity. Internationally, marine protected areas (MPAs) are defined as, "Any area of intertidal or subtidal terrain, together with its overlying waters and associated flora, fauna, historical, and cultural features, which has been reserved by legislation or other effective means to protect part or all of the enclosed environment" (Kelleher and Rechia, 1998, p. 1). The potential contributions of MPAs include:

- protection of marine biodiversity, representative ecosystems, and special natural features (Sobel, 1993);
- support rebuilding of depleted fish stocks, especially groundfish, by protecting spawning and nursery grounds (Wallace, Marliave, and Martell, 1998);
- insurance against current inadequate management of marine resources (Lauck, Clark, Mangel, and Munro, 1998);
- provision of benchmark sites against which to evaluate human impacts elsewhere and undertake scientific research;
- recognition of the cultural links between coastal communities and local marine biodiversity; and
- provision of opportunities for recreation and education.

More than 1,300 MPAs have now been established to serve these purposes in various countries throughout the world.

The Canadian Context

Canada has the longest coastline of any country in the world and the second largest area of continental shelf. For more than 30 years, Canada has sought to extend its jurisdiction over these waters gradually and was an enthusiastic and significant contributor to the UN Law of the Sea Convention between 1974 and 1982. In 1986, Parks Canada published the National Marine Parks Policy (Environment Canada, 1986), and in 1987, a core policy was published by Fisheries and Oceans Canada entitled *Ocean Policy for Canada: A Strategy to*

Meet the Challenges and Opportunities on the Ocean Frontier (Fisheries and Oceans Canada, 1987). Duffus and Dearden (1993) provide more discussion on this historical context. However, establishment of national MPAs in Canada has been slow, with only three currently covered by federal-provincial agreements (Saguenay, Fathom Five, and Gwaii Hanaas). There are several reasons for this tardiness. For example, Parks Canada has affirmed terrestrial protected areas as its priority over marine areas. In addition, there is a lack of public pressure for the creation of marine protected areas coupled with the jurisdictional complexity of federalism. For example, in offshore areas the seabed is under federal jurisdiction, but in internal waters it is a provincial area; federal agencies manage organisms in the water column, but commercial harvests of oysters and aquaculture are provincial responsibilities.

However, this complexity does not just stem from federal-provincial splits. At the federal level, three different agencies have the power to establish some form of areal marine protection; these are Fisheries and Oceans, Environment Canada, and Parks Canada. Table 19.1 gives a summary of the various agencies and the legislative tools at their disposal to designate protection. As can be seen from the tabulation, the mandate of Parks Canada differs from the other federal agencies in that there is an explicit statement regarding encouraging public understanding, appreciation, and enjoyment, whereas Fisheries and Oceans and Environment Canada are especially concerned with conservation issues. Furthermore, Parks Canada has a specific goal of establishing a system of national marine conservation areas that includes each of the 29 defined marine natural regions represented by one or more protected areas (Mercier and Mondor, 1995). In 1994, Parks Canada also produced a revised National Marine Conservation Areas Policy (Canada Ministry of Supply and Services, 1994) in which it is emphasized that, unlike their terrestrial counterparts, National Marine Conservation Areas (NMCAs) are managed for 'sustainable use' rather than strict protection of ecological integrity. They will be managed on a partnership basis with local stakeholders allowing most existing extractive uses to continue. In addition, unlike terrestrial parks, other agencies would have jurisdiction within NMCAs for managing renewable marine resources and navigation and shipping. Within these multiple-use areas it is anticipated that there will also be zones where higher levels of protection may be achieved. Only ocean disposal, seabed mining, and oil and gas extraction will be totally prohibited.

In June 1998, an Act to establish NMCAs was given its first reading in the House of Commons, but by the end of the century had still not been passed into law. Planning studies are underway to establish NMCAs in a number of locations including western Lake Superior, Bonavista and Notre Dame Bays in Newfoundland, and Gwaii Hanaas and the southern Strait of Georgia in BC. The other major player at the federal level, Fisheries and Oceans Canada, has adopted many of the same approaches as Parks Canada, in that NMCAs will be oriented towards sustainable use and established through partnerships. They have also added the complete lexicon of approaches currently fashionable in resource management, including "adaptive management, precautionary approach, integrated management, ecosystem-based and regional flexibility" (Fisheries and Oceans Canada, 1997). It remains to be seen exactly how these approaches will be implemented.

There is a similar lack of certitude regarding location of NMCAs in that, unlike Parks Canada, there is no pre-determined goal of representing different regions. Instead, areas will be established in terms of nominations that are forthcoming from regional groups, supplemented by regional overviews undertaken by technical interdisciplinary teams. An area identification list (AIL) of various candidates that will have met yet to be defined criteria will be produced. To choose between the proposed areas, these candidates will then be subject to a more intensive examination. No timetable has been set for this process.

Similar to the Parks Canada approach, once the NMCA is established, it is envisioned that there will be zoning within the protected area allowing various levels of resource extraction. The *Oceans Act* provides regulations for managing NMCAs, but does not specify exactly what these are, leaving a wide degree of interpretation and regional flexibility. The lack of national standards raises the quintessentially Canadian debate about whether the programme is national at all, or might just as well be left to provincial jurisdiction.

The third federal component, Environment Canada, will generally play a lesser role than the others in terms of areal protection (Table 19.1). A more detailed discussion of the goals of the programme is found in Zurbrigg (1996). The main focus is on wildlife and particularly on migratory bird species. Again, the approach is a cooperative and regionally flexible one that allows various uses, such as ecotourism, that are not seen to damage the target species. In BC, Boundary Bay is an example of an area currently protected as a Wildlife Management Area, and the Reifel Bird Sanctuary is an example of a Migratory Bird Sanctuary.[2]

The Provincial Context

Table 19.1 also shows the various provincial statutes that have been used for areal protection of the marine environment. Again, there are several programmes, of which the *Ecological Reserves Act* and *Parks Act* are most significant. The Ecological Reserves programme is oriented strictly toward a preservation mandate with no special orientation toward the marine environment. Nonetheless, a substantial number of the Reserves (25) have a marine-oriented component, and some also include sub-tidal components, however they are quite small. The Provincial Park System similarly has parks that include marine components (69), but no separate marine legislation exists at the provincial level for marine designations. There are, however, a number of policies that now require the provincial government to:

1. undertake marine inventories to ensure that a representative system of marine reserves will be protected, with priority given to areas that may be considered threatened;

2. create partnerships with various other stakeholders to manage the marine protected areas and develop more detailed management plans for the marine environment;

3. give highest management priority to endangered, threatened, and vulnerable species and special or unique marine features;

4. give precedence to conservation of viable, natural marine ecosystems over their use by people. This entails maintaining a range of habitats that are closed to all consumptive uses. Any use outside these no-take zones is secondary to conservation objectives. Permissible uses include recreational fishing and shellfish harvesting;

5. phase out commercial harvest of species that are attached to, and/or otherwise part of the sea bottom ecosystem within the boundaries of parks and ecological reserves;

6. not allow aquaculture within park boundaries;

7. allow sustenance and ceremonial fishing by First Nations with aboriginal or treaty rights; and

8. allow commercial fishing of transient species (e.g., salmon, herring) subject to federal fisheries regulations.

CURRENT INITIATIVES

It was due to this complexity that the need for a coordinated approach to the establishment of MPAs was finally recognized. In 1994, an inter-governmental Marine Protected Areas Working Group and a senior Steering Committee were formed to develop a more integrated approach to protected area planning on the Pacific coast. In addition to the agencies mentioned above, the BC Land Use Coordination Office (LUCO) and the BC Ministry of Agriculture, Fisheries and Food were invited to join the Working Group. The Group has proceeded by organizing a series of multi-stakeholder forums at various coastal locations to gather input and feedback regarding key questions on the nature of MPAs and the process by which they should be established. The main output of the Working Group's deliberations is a paper

Table 19.1 Federal and provincial statutory powers for protecting marine areas (Government of Canada and Government of BC, 1998)

Agency	Legislative Tools	Designations	Mandate
Fisheries and Oceans Canada (Federal)	Oceans Act	Marine Protected Areas	To protect and conserve: • fisheries resources, including marine mammals and their habitats; • endangered or threatened species and their habitats; • unique habitats; • areas of high biodiversity or biological productivity; and • areas for scientific and research purposes.
	Fisheries Act	Fisheries Closures	Conservation mandate to manage and regulate fisheries, conserve and protect fish, protect fish habitat and prevent pollution of waters frequented by fish.
Environment Canada (Federal)	Canada Wildlife Act	National Wildlife Areas Marine Wildlife Areas	To protect and conserve marine areas that are nationally or internationally significant for all wildlife but focusing on migratory birds.
	Migratory Birds Convention Act	Migratory Bird Sanctuaries	To protect coastal and marine habitats that are heavily used by birds for breeding, feeding, migration and overwintering.
Parks Canada (Federal)	National Parks Act Proposed Marine Conservation Areas Act	National Park National Marine Conservation Areas	To protect and conserve for all time marine conservation areas of Canadian significance that are representative of the five Natural Marine Regions identified on the Pacific coast of Canada, and to encourage public understanding, appreciation and enjoyment.
Ministry of Environment, Lands and Parks (Provincial)	Ecological Reserve Act	Ecological Reserves	To protect: • representative examples of BC's marine environment; • rare, endangered or sensitive species or habitats; • unique, outstanding or special features; and • areas for scientific research and marine awareness.
	Parks Act	Provincial Parks	To protect: • representative examples of marine diversity, recreational and cultural heritage; and • special natural, cultural heritage and recreational features. To serve a variety of outdoor recreation functions including: • enhancing major tourism travel routes; and • providing attractions for outdoor holiday destinations.
	Wildlife Act	Wildlife Management	To conserve and manage areas of importance to fish and wildlife and to protect endangered or threatened species and their habitats, whether resident or migratory, of regional, national or global significance.
	Environment and Land Use Act	"Protected Areas"	To protect: • representative examples of marine diversity, recreational and cultural heritage; and • special natural, cultural heritage and recreational features.

published in August 1998 entitled *Marine Protected Areas: A Strategy for Canada's Pacific Coast*, outlining the joint governmental approach to creating a system of MPAs by 2010. The paper contains little that is new, but is rather a compilation of materials from the past. Three important elements provide the corner stone:

- a joint federal-provincial approach;
- shared decision-making with the public; and
- building a comprehensive system of marine protected areas by 2010.

The marine protected areas so created would:

- be defined in law by one or more of the statutes shown in Table 19.1;
- protect some, but not necessarily all elements of the marine environment in the MPA; and
- ensure minimum protection standards prohibiting ocean dumping, dredging, and exploration for and development of non-renewable resources. Above these minimums, levels of protection would vary from area to area and also within areas.

The MPA system will be delivered as part of a comprehensive coastal planning process aimed at ensuring ecological, social, and economic sustainability. Six planning regions have been identified (Figure 19.1), and the first step in establishing MPAs would be the nomination of key areas for evaluation within each planning region by stakeholders or technical committees. Six objectives for the programme are suggested to:

- contribute to the protection of marine biodiversity, representative ecosystems, and special natural features;
- contribute to the conservation and protection of fishery resources and their habitats;
- contribute to the protection of cultural heritage resources and encourage understanding and appreciation;
- provide opportunities for recreation and tourism;
- provide scientific research opportunities and support the sharing of traditional knowledge; and
- enhance efforts for increased education and awareness.

The discussion paper solicits feedback and hopefully revisions will occur before a final strategy is implemented. For example, there needs to be greater clarification of the relative priorities of the objectives that are listed above, emphasizing that the primary reason for the creation of marine protected areas is to protect biodiversity and ecosystem processes. The minimum standards to ensure that this occurs are also not very ambitious. There is clear evidence, for example, that bottom trawling is highly disruptive of marine ecosystems, and yet it is not necessarily excluded from the MPA. The same claim can be made for other activities, such as finfish aquaculture. The process for establishment of conservation areas is also lacking clarity. At the moment, there is no coast-wide "gap analysis" that would assess the current status of protection and determine where the main gaps are for conservation purposes (see Ray and McCormick-Ray, 1995). Establishment is also tied to broader marine planning processes, which theoretically is a positive step, but in practice may lead to long delays in MPA establishment. There needs to be a separate process for the creation of MPAs that can proceed even in the absence of such a broader marine planning process, which is described below.

In addition to a coordinated strategy, there are also other initiatives that are occurring. Many countries, for example, have designated harvest refugia that prohibit the extraction of any living or non-living resource for any purpose (see Ballantine, 1995). Canada now has two such areas, both in BC (Whytecliffe Park and Porteau Cove, both in Howe Sound). Pilot projects under the Fisheries and Oceans' Marine Protected Areas initiative have also been designated at Gabriola Passage off Nanaimo and at Race Rocks off the southern tip of Vancouver Island. In addition, there are two offshore sites, at the Endeavour Hot Vents, 250 km southwest of Victoria, and the Bowie Seamount, 180 km west of the Queen Charlotte Islands (Figure 19.1). The hot vents are important sites for marine biodiversity. Of 236 species that have been collected at the vents, 223 were previously unknown to science and represent at least 22 new families and 100 new genera. The food chains around the vents do not rely on the sun for energy supply, as do most other species, but rather on bacteria that make carbon compounds from the sulphur-rich emissions. Seamounts are also important sites for marine biodiversity, rising more than 1,000 m from the surrounding ocean floor and providing feeding sites of great importance to migratory seabirds and distinctive rockfish communities. Bowie Seamount rises to within 40 m of the surface from depths of over 3300 m.

Marine protected area designations are intended to be embedded within a broader coastal zone planning process.[3] The recently completed Central Coast Land and Resources Management Plan (April 2001) attempts to reconcile competition and conflict between protected areas and economic development and between First Nations and non-Natives. Within this process, LUCO has the lead provincial role and Fisheries and Oceans Canada the lead federal role. The goal is to develop a consensus-based, coastal, near-shore planning process that will meet the present and future needs of the area. LUCO will concentrate on the land and near-shore portions, while Fisheries and Oceans has started an Integrated Coastal Zone Management programme (ICZM) that will address marine areas as well as the coastal zone. In both cases, a common planning approach involving issue and value identification, general management objective specification, determination of strategic-level zones and sub-zones, and specific management prescriptions will be followed. The MPA strategy discussed earlier will provide policy input to assist in making recommendations for coastal marine protected areas within this broader process, whereas the ICZM process will deal with the offshore component.

From this brief review it is apparent that there is, at least on the surface, considerable interest in moving forward with areal designations for marine protected areas in the near future. However, major questions remain as to how useful such reserves will be in actually aiding conservation and protecting marine biodiversity values. Some issues related to these questions are discussed in the next section.[4]

MARINE WILDLIFE

Marine wildlife encompasses some of the most high profile species in the collective human consciousness. Whales and dolphins are amongst the most beloved species of wildlife. Their mystery and beauty has caught the human imagination through television, recordings, posters, and increasingly have formed the core of the largest ecotourism industry worldwide (Hoyt, 1995). The coast of BC is one of the most popular and oldest whale-watching areas, with nodes of development in three locations around Vancouver Island. Since 1980, killer whales and gray whales have been the foundation of major ecotourism growth from the ports of Tofino, Ucluelet, Telegraph Cove, and Victoria (Figure 19.1). About 135,000 users currently go whale-watching at these sites and contribute about $20 million to the local economies.

Killer Whales

Killer whales are the largest member of the family of oceanic dolphins, the *Delphinidae*. While their distribution is cosmopolitan and generally sparse, they concentrate at certain times in a few locations in various seas. The most well known concentrations are those off the BC coast, where four populations or ecotypes have been designated, two of which are called 'Residents' and form a predictable presence that supports whale-watching between May and September. These animals forage primarily for fish and seem to concentrate on migratory salmon as they approach coastal river mouths during the summer and fall months. Occasional visits by what are known as "transient" and "offshore" animals occur, but their movement patterns are less predictable and thus only supplement the whale-watching resource base.

From a scientific viewpoint, killer whales in BC waters are among the most well studied of all cetaceans. Long term research by Bigg, Ford, and colleagues (Bigg, Ellis, Ford, and Balcomb, 1990; Olesiuk, Bigg, and Ellis, 1990; Ford, 1991) has established the social structure

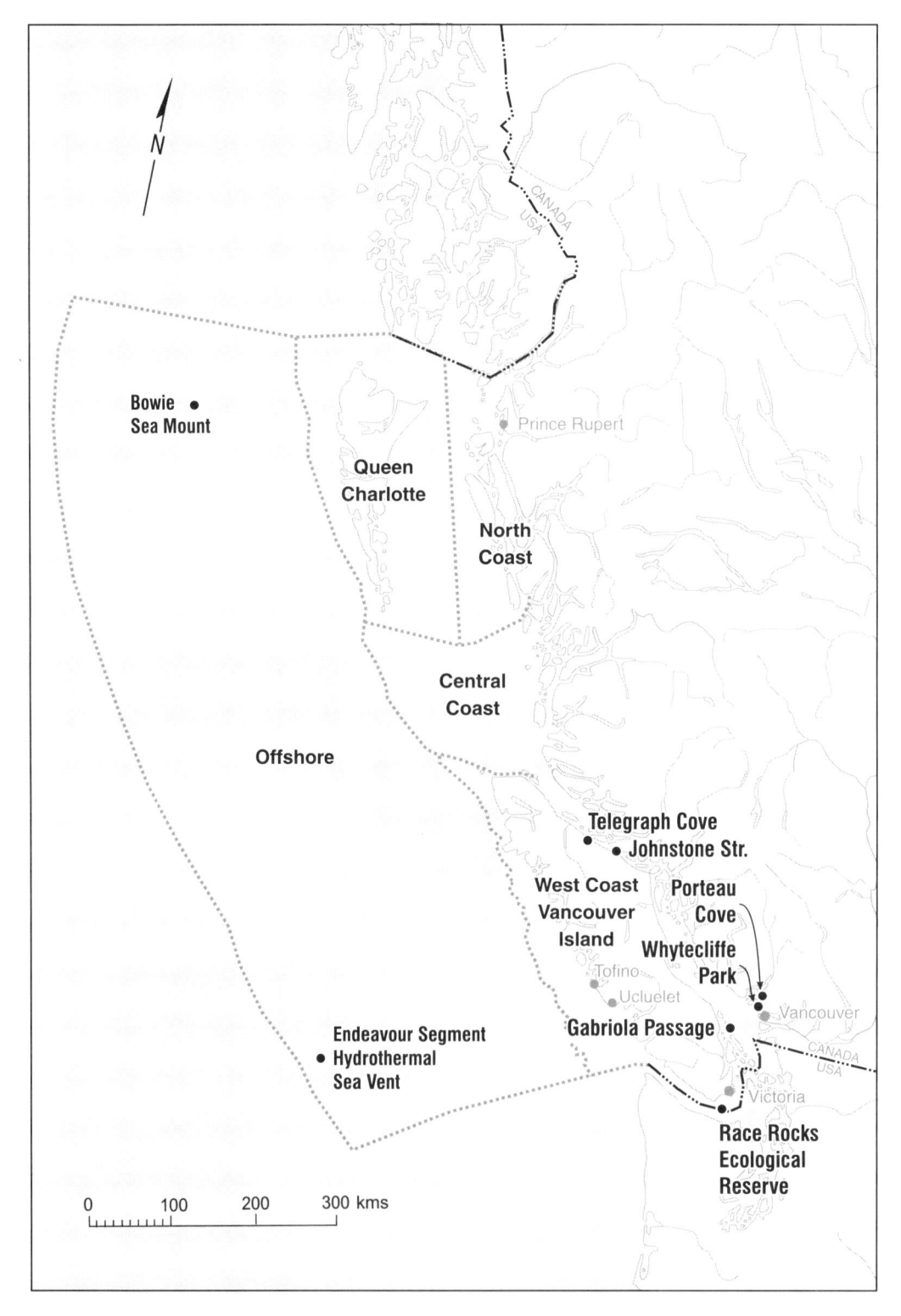

Figure 19.1 Proposed marine conservation regions (dotted lines) and existing protected areas/reserves (solid dots)

and population structure of residents, while Baird and colleagues (Baird, Abrams, and Dill, 1992; Baird and Dill, 1995, 1996) have published detailed ecological and behavioural research regarding the transient killer whales. The genetic structure of the populations has been studied by Hoelzel and Dover (1991), while Calambokidis and colleagues (1990) have looked at environmental contaminants. Collectively, this research has developed a relatively good description of many aspects of the lives of these killer whales. However, ecological research on foraging, and behavioural research on the effects of disturbances, still require finer scale study to serve the needs of managers dealing with the potential impact of whale-watching on killer whales (Duffus and Baird, 1995).

Gray Whales

Gray whales hold a distinction in that they are the only species of great whale to have recovered to what are believed to be pre-whaling population levels, at least in the case of the eastern Pacific stock. Western Pacific stocks are precariously perched near extinction, and Atlantic gray whales are believed to have gone extinct 300 years ago. As gray whale populations in the eastern Pacific have risen, they have once again become a common sight during the spring migration as they move to foraging grounds in the Bering and Chukchi Seas, and also in summer as more animals use foraging sites along the BC coast, and Vancouver Island in particular. During the summer, gray whales concentrate in foraging sites and exchange often between sites when food is exhausted or for other unknown reasons. Movements over the short term can be allocated to prey density (Duffus, 1996; Dunham and Duffus, 2000) and feeding preferences. Current research indicates that the gray whale is a much more ecologically complex organism than the earlier literature suggests and that perhaps land-ocean nutrient exchange and highly localized hydrological conditions may influence the whales' distribution during the summer on the Vancouver Island coast.

Impacts of Whale-Watching on Marine Mammals

Studies researching the impact of whale-watching activity on the whales have been largely inconclusive. This is in part due to the difficulty found in studying these types of animals, and in part due to the lack of research support and effort. There is no persuasive evidence that vessel traffic has altered the spatial patterns, behaviours, or, most importantly, the population sizes of either the killer or gray whale. Of course, that does not mean that no influence exists. Rather, it suggests that considerably more research is needed. In the face of this high uncertainty, management efforts have moved forward combining a strong community base with high levels of cooperation between the whale-watching industry and scientists.

Johnstone Strait, on the northeast coast of Vancouver Island (Figure 19.1), drew such a high level of public attention that both the federal and provincial governments joined forces to develop a multi-stakeholder planning and implementation process for the management of whale-watching. The success of this effort has not yet been measured. Although most of the management actions required were moved forward, some important issues still had not been resolved, including regulating commercial fisheries in the protected area, and the larger issue of the role of First Nations and claim settlements.

Recently, Canadian authorities (COSEWIC) have designated the resident killer whale populations as "threatened." The status report (Baird, 1998) points out that environmental contamination, vessel traffic, and fish stocks all put pressure on populations; the strength of those effects is not likely to lessen in the near future. Killer whale populations are falling, especially in the Strait of Georgia, which is likely due to the live capture fishery that operated in the late 1960s and early 1970s. Given this and the large degree of uncertainty surrounding the whales it was thought wise to provide them with threatened status. Unfortunately, in Canada, declaring threatened status has no basis in legislation, nor does it mandate any government action. Politically, it is a bold and important move. In terms of really protecting the animal it does little, if anything, except draw attention to the multiple threats to the coastal marine environment and the large amount of scientific uncertainty involved. Although these populations are among the best known of all cetaceans worldwide, it cannot be said conclusively that the populations are sufficiently robust to avoid an extinction vortex. The status report is a landmark in marine wildlife management in Canada and has caused consternation on the American side of the border where the same designation has not yet been applied, but may be under consideration. If that should happen, much stricter controls would be applied to users that would impact the whale-watching industry immensely.

In Victoria, where highly visible whale-watching industry growth has fuelled controversy over the number of vessels surrounding whales, an industry organization, the 'Whale-Watch Operators, Northwest,' has recently been developed in an effort to address some of the concerns. In 1999, a workshop was convened at the University of Victoria that brought the Department of Fisheries and Oceans (DFO), provincial authorities, researchers, and the industry together to look at ways in which the industry, and the appearance of the industry, could be managed. The result was the creation of working groups and a higher level of communication that will provide at least a foundation for management programmes of the future.

The situation is different in Tofino, where there are fewer private/recreational boaters (who often do not have the skill to avoid conflicts with whale movement patterns) than there are in Victoria. With fewer boats crowding whale sites, community self-regulation has been largely effective in maintaining high standards of vessel behaviour in this area (personal observations, 1988-1999).

In each case mentioned above, the growth has been rapid and there have been definite signs of reaching carrying capacity in terms of industry growth and visitor satisfaction (Duffus and Dearden, 1990, 1993; Duffus, 1996).

After 20 years of relatively successful self-management of this marine wildlife based industry, governments are now becoming interested in regulating the activity, although they have not yet done so. Regardless of who manages the whale-watching industry, the fundamental question still remains: on what basis are regulations to be designed? Many heads have turned toward scientists on the BC coast for answers. While several studies have been done, they have as yet offered few clues into the issue of whale disturbance. In that light, it is likely that regulators will use informed opinion and practical considerations, and will at least outwardly use a precautionary principle that dictates the spatial pattern of vessel behaviour around whales. While this is probably effective over the short term, and in line with most other jurisdictions (International Fund for Animal Welfare, 1995), it should not be promoted as a substitute for a more science-based management approach.

Other Marine Mammals

There are also issues surrounding seals and sea lions on the coast. These species also hold an elevated position in our appreciation of marine wildlife. Canada has been continually embarrassed around the world by the Atlantic seal hunt and the closely entwined issues of bad science, political pressure, and adventuring animal rights activists. Seals are not immune to the same consideration on the Pacific coast. Since gaining protection, the harbour seal has made significant increases in population and once again has been accused of resource competition with commercial and sports fisheries. Calls have been made to cull populations, especially in areas where habitat destruction and over-fishing have reduced individual runs of Pacific salmon and sea-run trout to the point where a few seals could actually wipe out the stock. Now American authorities have designated the Stellers sea lion within their powerful Endangered Species legislation. In what is a reverse of the killer whale situation, Canada has not done the same for the Stellers in our waters. This is largely due to different ecological conditions, though there are still many questions to be asked about this case, as uncertainty about these animals persists (Bigg, 1985, 1988).

DISCUSSION

What is protected in a marine protected area, or if your ideology demands, what is conserved in a marine conservation area? Presumably, wild species of plants and animals and the ecological processes in which they participate. If that is the case, then there are important ecological considerations that any human protective process must build into the programme. Fundamentally, we should address the issue of spatial domain and divisibility of the ecological processes and second, the role of mixed scale phenomena in time and space.

Few marine taxa are static; even sessile organisms and attached plants usually have some aspect of their life history when they float or swim over spaces of varying size in three dimensions. Organisms may spend periods of time in specific locales and then desert those for entirely different physical settings for adult life stages. Thus, the ideal of a protected space must be very carefully examined in light of the suite of organisms that are being proposed as 'protected.' Once more, when considering ecological process, food webs for example, the interaction of spaces required for the array of members in even a simple, short food chain of predators and prey will create a large overall spatial requirement. Similarly, consider the temporal domain in the case of some planktonic larvae that may float into BC coastal waters under certain current or water temperature conditions, where they may have been absent for decades. Yet these larvae may become ready prey for a group of predators that will forsake more common prey in favour of them for the duration of their presence.

Clearly, these kinds of ecological issues should directly inform the planning of an MPA given the mandates of both federal and provincial parks agencies. If we even take a step far back from an 'ecological protection' mandate to a 'sustainable use protected area' such as advocated by DFO, we still require volumes more ecological information than is presently available to construct a protected area that actually protects population functions to provide a harvest (Wallace et al., 1998). The suggestion here is that protection of specific areas, a cornerstone of terrestrial conservation efforts, will not suffice to protect or conserve marine ecosystems, except in the case of very small scale systems. Marine conservation demands that much closer attention be paid to *ecosystem process and linkages* than more static, component-oriented terrestrial efforts. A well thought out network of linked reserves of various sizes is required.

The possibility also exists that a programme of marine protected areas, or conservation areas, will do more harm than good. If the public is the driving force in the protection of nature, then that same public may be misled by the lofty titles of protected area programmes in the marine environment. If that happens, there may be no pressure on the resource management bureaucracies to enlarge the scope and domain of marine protection programmes. Ecologically speaking then, we will be left with a group of fragments of sea floor and water column that may encompass small and temporally disjunctive bits of marine nature.

At the broader policy level, the issue of marine-terrestrial linkages is always present. Although large rivers have well-known influences on coastal environments, small streams and localized effects are often believed to be inconsequential. However, there are definite patterns of association between marine wildlife and small embayments on the coast. Clearly, some kind of spatial subsidy occurs involving prey species for some large animals, but the potential to have nutrient flow between forests and other landscapes determining distributions has implications for protection strategies in both the terrestrial and aquatic ecosystems (see Gattuso, Frankignoulle, and Wollast, 1998).

The other side of the MPA issue is whether or not the public will gain a deeper understanding of the needs of marine nature through these conservation areas and also become a more active player in the process of protecting natural areas. This question has, as of yet, received little research attention.

Conclusions

Marine conservation is still in its infancy when it is compared with terrestrial efforts. Unfortunately, the learning curve is steep and we do not have the luxury of a long period for experimentation. A science-driven approach with a need to err on the side of conservation rather than exploitation is clearly called for. In other words, we need an adaptive approach with full adherence to the Precautionary Principle (Lauck, Clark, Mangel, and Munro, 1998). Not only is the biophysical element of marine conservation little understood, there are many existing uses demanding to be taken into account. This has led to an emphasis on consensus-based decision making in an attempt to appease all interests. This may not be the most satisfactory approach if marine conservation is actually the goal, rather than conflict resolution, as pointed out by Ray and McCormick-Ray (1995):

> *Unfortunately, there is an expedient tendency to speak to the lowest common denominator in proposing MEPAs [marine and estuarine protected areas] and their management, resulting from consensus-based participatory processes. This is self-defeating in the end...perhaps sooner rather than later* (p.37).

Other more general issues abound, some of which require species specific, coast-wide management, and some that would be amenable to MPA management tools. If the political will should develop, the jurisdictional issues can be resolved. As it now stands, some rather comical issues arise. A 'federal' gray whale can enter a provincial marine park, and while still in the federal water column, it may disturb the provincial substrate and eat a provincially protected amphipod. That amphipod may have spent a short time as a free-swimming, federally managed larva, then settled into a benthic provincial existence, subsisting on federally supplied detritus from the water column. That same gray whale can then, in subsequent years, enter a biosphere reserve in Mexico, a port authority in California, cross federal and state marine protected areas, become a target for Makah traditional fisheries, or even become a member of the International Whaling Commission sanctioned hunt in the Chukchi Sea. Or it might wash up in a municipality on southern Vancouver Island and confound authorities as to who exactly is responsible for disposing of the remains of this once great and wonderful thing.

Clearly, we can and must do a better job of mediating our behaviour towards marine wildlife. They are amongst the most highly recognized and loved creatures on the planet. In the near future we will be creating 'protected' areas for them. The success of these efforts hinges on addressing the large spaces and long times in which many of the animals exist, and in challenging ourselves to do more for them, even when it may mean taking less for ourselves. As Allison and colleagues (1998) point out as the title in their review of marine conservation, 'Marine reserves are necessary but not sufficient for marine conservation.'

References

Allison, G.W., Lubchenco, J., and Carr, M.H. (1998). Marine reserves are necessary but not sufficient for marine conservation. *Ecological Applications*, 8, S79-S92.

Anon. (1998). Reef check. *People and the Planet*, 7, 5.

Baird, R.W. (1998). *Status of killer whales in Canada*. Draft report submitted to COSEWIC, Nov. 16, 1998.

Baird, R.W., Abrams, P.A., and Dill, L.M. (1992). Possible indirect interactions between transient and resident killer whales: Implications for the evolution of foraging specializations in the genus *Orcinus*. *Oecologia*, 89, 125-132.

Baird, R.W., and Dill, L.M. (1995). Occurrence and behaviour of transient killer whales, seasonal and pod specific variability, foraging and prey handling. *Canadian Journal of Zoology*, 73, 1300-11.

Baird, R.W., and Dill, L.M. (1996). Ecological and social determinants of group size in transient killer whales. *Behavioral Ecology*, 7, 408-16.

Ballantine, W.J. (1995). Networks of 'no-take' marine reserves are practical and necessary. In N.L. Shackell and J.H.M. Willison (Eds.), *Marine protected areas and sustainable fisheries* (pp. 13-20). Wolfville: Nova Scotia.

Bigg, M.A. (1985). Status of the Steller sea lion (*Eutometopias jubatus*) and California sea lion (*Zalophus californianus*) in British Columbia. *Can. Spec. Pub. Fish. Aquati. Science*, 77, 20p.

Bigg, M.A. (1988). Status of the Steller sea lion, *Eutometopias jubatus*, in Canada. *Canadian Field Naturalist*, 102, 307-314.

Bigg, M.A., Ellis, G.M., Ford, J.K.B., and Balcomb, K.C. (1990). Feeding habits of the resident and transient forms of killer whales in British Columbia and Washington State. *Abstracts of the Third International Orca Symposium*, March 1990, Victoria.

Calambokidis, J., Langelier, K.M., Stacey, P.J., and Baird, R.W. (1990). Environmental contaminants in killer whales from Washington, British Columbia and Alaska. *Abstracts of the Third International Orca Symposium*, March 1990, Victoria.

Canada Ministry of Supply and Services (1994). *Guiding principles and operational policies*. Ottawa: Parks Canada.

Carlton, J.T., Geller, J.B., Reaka-Kudla, M.L., and Norse, E.A. (1999). Historical extinctions in the sea. *Annual Review of Ecology and Systematics*, 30, 515-38.

Dearden, P. (1986). Desolation Sound Marine Park, British Columbia. In J. Lien and R. Graham (Eds.), *Marine parks and conservation challenge and promise, Volume 2* (pp. 157-67). Toronto: National and Provincial Parks Association.

Dearden, P. (1990). Pacific coast recreational patterns and activities in Canada. In P. Fabbri (Ed.), *Recreational uses of coastal areas* (pp. 111-123). Amsterdam: Kluwer Academic Publishers.

Duffus, D.A. (1996). The recreational use of gray whales in southern Clayoquot Sound. *Applied Geography*, 16(3), 179-190.

Duffus, D.A., and Baird, R.W. (1995). Killer whales, whale-watching and management: A status report. *Whalewatcher*, Fall/Winter, 14-18.

Duffus, D.A., and Dearden, P. (1990). Non-consumptive wildlife oriented recreation: A conceptual framework. *Biological Conservation*, 53, 213-231.

Duffus D.A., and Dearden, P. (1993). Marine parks: The Canadian experience. In P. Dearden and R. Rollins (Eds.), *Parks in Canada: Planning and management* (pp. 256-272). Oxford University Press.

Dunham, J., and Duffus, D.A. (2000). Planktonic and infaunal prey threshold levels determined by feeding gray whales in Clayoquot Sound, B.C., Canada. (in press).

Environment Canada (1986). National Marine Parks Policy. Ottawa: Environment Canada.

Fisheries and Oceans Canada (1987). *Ocean policy for Canada: A strategy to meet the challenges and opportunities on the ocean frontier*. Ottawa: Department of Fisheries and Oceans.

Fisheries and Oceans Canada (1997). *An approach to the establishment and management of marine protected areas under the Oceans Act*. Ottawa: Department of Fisheries and Oceans.

Ford, J.K.B.(1991). Vocal traditions among resident killer whales (Orcinus orca) in coastal waters of British Columbia. *Canadian Journal of Zoology*, 69, 1454-83.

Gattuso, J.P., Frankignoulle, M., and Wollast, R. (1998). Arbon and carbonate metabolism in coastal aquatic ecosystems. *Annual Review of Ecological Systems*, 29, 405-34.

Government of Canada and Government of BC (1998). *Marine protected areas, a strategy for Canada's Pacific coast*.

Hinrichsen, D. (1998). *Coastal waters of the world: Trends, threats and strategies*. Washington, DC: Island Press.

Hoelzel, A.R., and Dover, G.A. (1991). Genetic differentiation between sympatric killer whale populations. *Heredity*, 66, 191-195.

Hoyt, E. (1995). *The worldwide value and extent of whale-watching 1995*. Bath: Whale and Dolphin Conservation Society.

International Fund for Animal Welfare (1995). *Scientific aspects of managing whale-watching*. Report of the Workshop, Montecastello Di Vibio, Italy, March 1995.

Kelleher, G., and Rechia, C. (1998). Lessons from marine protected areas around the world. *Parks*, 8, 1-4.

Lauck, T., Clark, C.W., Mangel, M., and Munro, G.R. (1998). Implementing the precautionary principle in fisheries management through marine reserves. *Ecological Applications*, 8, S72-S78.

Mercier, F., and Mondor, C. (1995). *Sea to sea to sea: Canada's National Marine Conservation System Plan*. Ottawa: Canada Heritage, Parks Canada.

Olesiuk, P.F, Bigg, M.A., and Ellis, G.M. (1990). Life history and population dynamics of resident killer whales (*Orcinus orca*) in the coastal waters of British Columbia and Washington State. *Reports of the International Whaling Comm*ission (Special Issue 12), 209-248.

Pauly, D., Christensen, V., Dalsgaard, J., Froese, R., and Torres, F., Jr. (1998). Fishing down marine food webs. *Science*, 279, 860-863.

Ray, C.G., and McCormick-Ray, M.G. (1995). Critical habitats and representative systems in marine environments: Concepts and procedures. In T. Agardy Gland (Ed.), *The science of conservation in the coastal zone* (pp. 23-40). IUCN.

Sobel, J. (1993). Conserving biodiversity through marine protected areas: A global challenge. *Oceanus*, 36, 19-26.

Wallace, S.S., Marliave, J.B., and Martell, S.J.M. (1998). The role of marine protected areas in the conservation of rocky reef fishes in British Columbia: The use of lingcod (*Ophiodon elongatus*) as an indicator. In N.W.P. Munro and J.H.M. Willison (Eds.), *Linking protected areas with working landscapes conserving biodiversity* (pp. 206-213). Proceedings of the 3rd International Conference on Science and Management of Protected Areas, Wolfville, Canada.

Willison, M. (2001). Endangered marine species and marine protected areas in Canada. In K. Beazley and R. Boardman (Eds.), *Politics of the wild* (pp. 94-116). Oxford: Oxford University Press.

Zurbrigg, E. (1996). *Towards an Environment Canada strategy for coastal and marine protected areas*. Hull: Canadian Wildlife Service.

ENDNOTES

[1] The World Wildlife Fund listed 328 species "at risk" in Canada. Of these, approximately 8% are (mainly) marine mammals (Carlton, Geller, Reaka-Kudla, and Norse, 1999).

[2] For a recent comprehensive review of the national situation, see Willison (2001).

[3] The complex questions concerning marine conservation and the economic viability of coastal communities in BC and the broad policy guidelines required in response are addressed in the Government of BC's Coastal Zone Position Paper (1998).

[4] Clearly, this brief review can only focus on a few key aspects of marine conservation in BC. Other current issues include fisheries conservation (**Chapter 18**), marine avian habitat protection, oil and gas exploration, gas pipeline routing, marina development, and estuary conservation. Some progress has occurred. For example, the recently completed Central Coast Land and Resource Management Plan (April 2001) has attempted to reconcile the conflict between protected areas and economic development, and between Native people and non-Natives.